Existential
and
Spiritual Issues
in Death Attitudes

Existential
and
Spiritual Issues
in Death Attitudes

Edited by

Adrian Tomer • Grafton T. Eliason • Paul T. P. Wong

LEA Lawrence Erlbaum Associates
Taylor & Francis Group

New York   London

Cover design by Tomai Maridou, based on photographs taken in Vancouver, British Columbia, by Grafton Eliason and Adrian Tomer.

Lawrence Erlbaum Associates
Taylor & Francis Group
270 Madison Avenue
New York, NY 10016

Lawrence Erlbaum Associates
Taylor & Francis Group
2 Park Square
Milton Park, Abingdon
Oxon OX14 4RN

© 2008 by Taylor & Francis Group, LLC
Lawrence Erlbaum Associates is an imprint of Taylor & Francis Group, an Informa business

Library of Congress Cataloging-in-Publication Data

Existential and spiritual issues in death attitudes/edited by Adrian Tomer, Grafton T. Eliason, Paul T. P. Wong.
    p. cm.
  Includes bibliographical references.
  ISBN-13: 978-0-8058-5271-4 (c : alk. paper)
  ISBN-13: 978-0-8058-5272-1 (c : alk. paper)
  ISBN-13: 978-1-4106-1650-0 (e)
  ISBN-10: 0-8058-5271-9 (c : alk. paper)
  [etc.]
  1. Death—Psychological aspects. 2. Death—Religious aspects—Psychology. I. Tomer, Adrian. II. Eliason, Grafton. III. Wong, Paul T. P.

BF789.D4E95 2007
155.9'37—dc22
                                        2006038481

Visit the Taylor & Francis Web site at
http://www.taylorandfrancis.com

To our wives, Daniela and Lilian, with love and thanks

—A. T. and P. P. W.

To my family and friends,
Grafton and Zoe,
Deighn and Laurie,
With much love and thanks

—G. T. E.

Contents

About the Contributors

Monika Ardelt, PhD, is Associate Professor of Sociology at the University of Florida and a Brookdale National Fellow. She is also a Founding Faculty Member and Member of the Advisory Committee of the Center for Spirituality and Health at the University of Florida. Dr. Ardelt received her Diploma (MA) in Sociology from the Johann Wolfgang Goethe-University of Frankfurt/Main in Germany and her PhD in Sociology from the Uinversity of North Carolina at Chapel Hill. Her research focuses on successful human development across the life course with particular emphasis on the relations between wisdom, religion, spirituality, aging well, and dying well.

Joyce Catlett, MA, author/lecturer, is the co-author of *Fear of Intimacy, Psychological Defenses in Everyday Life, Conquer Your Critical Inner Voice* (2002), *Creating a Life of Meaning & Compassion: The Wisdom of Psychotherapy* (2003), *and Sex and Love in Intimate Relationships* (2006). She has collaborated with Dr. Robert Firestone in writing 20 professional articles and 10 books, including: *The Fantasy Bond, Compassionate Child-Rearing* and *Voice Therapy*. She has co-produced 37 video productions for the Glendon Association in the areas of parent-child relations, suicide, couple relations, and Voice Therapy.

Victor G. Cicirelli, PhD, is Professor of Developmental and Aging Psychology in the Department of Psychological Sciences at Purdue University. His research has been in the area of end-of-life decision-making and older adults' views on death. He is the author of numerous journal articles, book chapters, and books, including the volume *Older Adults' Views on Death.*

Wendy L. Dobson, MA, earned her MA from Trinity Western University. She is currently a counselor.

Grafton T. Eliason, EdD, is currently Assistant Professor in the Department of Counselor Education and Services at California University of Pennsylvania. He has taught courses in death, dying, and spirituality and has a special interest in existential philosophy and religion. He received his Doctorate in Counselor Education and Supervision from Duquesne University. He has also earned an MDiv from Princeton

Theological Seminary and an MEd in School Counseling from Shippensburg University. He has numerous certifications including National Certified Counselor (NCC), Licensed Professional Counselor (LPC) in Pennsylvania, Certified School Counselor (K-12) in Pennsylvania, and he is an Ordained Presbyterian Minister. He has taught at the Citadel, Duquesne University, and Chatham College. Grafton and Adrian Tomer have been collaborating and publishing on the topics of death, dying, spirituality, and wisdom since 1992.

The late Victor Florian (1945–2002) completed his university studies in Israel and received a PhD degree in Psychology at Bar-Ilan University in 1979 despite a tragic accident at age 16 that made him severely physically disabled for the rest of his life. His PhD dissertation presented a multidimensional model of explicit and implicit manifestations of the fear of personal death. From 1979 and until his death in 2002, he published more than 100 articles and book chapters. His main research interests were death anxiety, terror management theory, rehabilitation psychology, family dynamics and well being, and cross-cultural differences in social attitudes and family relations. From 1995, he was a professor of Psychology at Bar-Ilan University. He was Chair of the Rehabilitation Psychology Program at Bar-Ilan University and served as a member of the educational board of *Omega.*

Donna M. Gibson, PhD, is an assistant professor of counselor education in the Department of Educational Studies at The University of South Carolina. She completed her PhD in Counseling and Counselor Education at The University of North Carolina at Greensboro and has master's and specialist's degrees in School Psychology. Her professional experiences include providing psychological and behavioral assessments for preschool-aged developmentally disabled children and their families, counseling cardiac rehabilitation clients, providing counseling services in private practice and mental health settings, as well as providing counseling services to women and their families who are experiencing assistive reproductive technology interventions for infertility.

Jamie Goldenberg, PhD, received her PhD from The George Washington University, followed by post-doctoral work at the University of Colorado at Colorado Springs. She is currently an Assistant Professor of Psychology at the University of South Florida. She conducts research on terror management theory with emphasis on the impact of existential concerns on attitudes toward the body and sex.

Joshua Hart, PhD, received his PhD from the University of California at Davis. He is now a post-doctoral Fellow at Lawrence University. His research integrates terror management theory and attachment theory by examining the common defensive aspects of attachment, self-esteem, and world view processes.

Debra A. Ivoncavich, MA, earned her MA in Counseling Psychology from Trinity Western University. She is currently a Counselor

Ann Laughlin, PhD, MSN, and RN, is an Assistant Professor of Nursing at Creighton University School of Nursing in Omaha, Nebraska. Ann has spent the last 10 years teaching at Creighton in the accelerated nursing program. Responsibilities have included course design, the instruction and supervision of beginning and senior level nursing students in the area of medical-surgical nursing, and the development and implementation of the school health nursing program. Her research efforts have focused on the impact involuntary interinstitutional relocation has on the physical, psychological, and cognitive functioning of older individuals.

Mark Lepore, EdD, currently teaches at Chatham College in Pittsburgh, Pennsylvania. His training includes a Doctorate in Counselor Education and Supervision from Duquesne University, a master's degree in Social Work and a master's in Counseling. He has obtained a Clinical Social Work License and Pennsylvania educational certifications as Home and School Visitor, Elementary School Counselor, Secondary School Counselor, and Principal (K-12). Additional training includes Critical Incident Stress Debriefing and other crisis response and management techniques. Mark's research interest includes principals and theories related to grief and trauma counseling, secondary traumatic stress, and the development of models of counselor supervision and interventions for at-risk youth in schools and communities. Extensive experience as a practitioner and professional counselor include Director and Department Head for Psychiatric Rehabilitation Department for Westmoreland Hospital, Director of Mental Health Wrap Around Services, Partial Hospital, and School Based Services for Bradley Center in Pittsburgh. In addition, Mark served as Home and School Visitor and School Counselor for Baldwin-Whitehall School District for 10 years.

Mary Beth Mannarino, PhD, earned her MA and PhD in Clinical Psychology from the University of Louisville in Louisville, Kentucky. She has worked for more than 20 years with children and families in the Pittsburgh area. In 2002, Dr. Mannarino joined the faculty of Chatham College, where she is currently the Director of the Masters of Science in Counseling Psychology program. Among Dr. Mannarino's current interests include the role of religion and spirituality in psychotherapy with clients of all ages, and the stigmatization of mental illness and mental health treatment.

Mario Mikulincer, PhD, completed his university studies in Israel and received a PhD degree in Psychology at Bar-Ilan University in 1985. His PhD dissertation presented a Coping Model of Human Learned Helplessness. From 1985, he published more than 220 articles and book chapters and one book (*Human Learned Helplessness: A Coping Perspective, Plenum Press*, 1994). His main research interests are: Attachment styles in adulthood; Terror Management Theory; Personality processes in interpersonal relationships; Evolutionary psychology; Trauma and Post-traumatic processes; Coping with stress; Qualitative research of emotional states. From 1992, he has been a Professor of Psychology at Bar-Ilan University. Between 1995–1999, he acted as the Chair of the Psychology Department at Bar-Ilan University and today he acts as the Chair of Interdisciplinary Studies of Bar-Ilan University. He currently serves as a member of the editorial boards of the following journals: *Journal of Personality and Social Psychology: IRGP; Journal of Personality; Personality and Social Psychology Bulletin; Personality and Social Psychology Review; Psychological Inquiry*. Since January 2003, he acts as an associate editor of *Personal Relationships* and *Journal of Personality and Social Psychology*. In 2004, he received the E.M.E.T. Prize in Social Science for his contribution to psychology.

Chris Morrant, MD, was qualified in medicine from London University, England in 1964 and received an English diploma in psychological medicine. Dr. Morrant came to Canada in 1969 where he worked in Psychiatric Hospitals specializing in psychogeriatrics. Dr. Morrant had a psychoanalytic training and has been in private practice for about 30 years. In the last 10 years he placed an increased emphasis upon voice therapy in his private practice.

Rick Myer, PhD, received his doctorate in Counseling Psychology from the University of Memphis, Tennessee. He is currently Associate Professor and Interim Associate Dean in the Counselor Education

Department, School of Education, Duquesne University, in Pittsburgh, Pennsylvania. He is also Director for the Center for Crisis Intervention and Prevention. Rick is a licensed psychologist and has published extensively on the topics of crisis intervention and counseling. He published *Assessment for Crisis Intervention: The Triage Assessment Model.*

Robert A. Neimeyer, PhD, is Professor in the Department of Psychology, University of Memphis, where he also maintains an active clinical practice. Since completing his doctorate at the University of Nebraska, he has conducted extensive research on the topics of death attitudes and suicide intervention. Dr. Neimeyer has published more than 20 books, including *Lessons of Loss: A Guide to Coping; The Death Anxiety Handbook: Research, Instrumentation and Application; Dying Facing the Facts (with Hannelore Wass); Meaning Reconstruction and the Experience of Loss; and Advances in Personal Construct Psychology (Vol. 5; with G. J. Neimeyer).* Dr. Neimeyer is the author of nearly 300 articles and book chapters. He is currently involved in advancing a more adequate theory of grieving as a process of meaning reconstruction. Dr. Neimeyer is the editor of the prestigious journal *Death Studies,* serves as co-editor of the *Journal of Constructivist Psychology* and is on the editorial board of six other professional journals. Dr. Neimeyer served as President of the Association for Death Education and Counseling

Gloria Nouel, PhD, is an Assistant Professor of Psychology and the director of the Master of Arts in Leadership and Organizational Transformation at Chatham College in Pittsburgh, Pennsylvania. Dr. Nouel has a PhD in clinical Psychology with an Existential-Phenomenological approach from Duquesne University. She has a Master of Arts in Psychology with a humanistic focus from West Georgia College in Carrollton, GA. In addition to grief and bereavement, Dr. Nouel's areas of expertise and interest are in the psychology of groups and organizations, the psychology of women and cultural diversity. Dr. Nouel is committed to a holistic approach to psychology, encompassing the social, spiritual, and symbolic dimensions of human life.

Israel Orbach, PhD, is a professor of psychology at Bar-Ilan University in Israel. He received his PhD in psychology from Yeshiva University in New York and was trained at Albert Einstein College of Medicine. For 30 years now he has been engaged in teaching, research, and psychotherapy. His main interest is in suicidal behavior in all ages. He has founded, with others, the Israeli Association for Suicide Prevention and has served as its first president. He is the recipient of the American Association of Suicidology Dublin award (2002) and of the International Association of Suicide Prevention (2003) both for distinguished contribution to the understanding of suicide.

Jayna Rubin, MA, earned her Bachelor's degree at Allegheny College and her master's degree in Counseling Psychology at Chatham College. Jayna is currently a Middle School Guidance Counselor, working with 7th and 8th graders, in the Upper St. Clair School District. In her free time, she volunteers at The Highmark Caring Place, working with grieving children and adolescents. She also maintains strong interest in adolescent grief and working with families in transition.

Professor Ernesto Spinelli, PhD, is a practicing existential psychotherapist and past Academic and currently senior Fellow of the School of Psychotherapy and Counseling at Regent's College, London. Professor Spinelli is Past Chair of the Society for Existential Analysis and of the British Psychological Society's Division of Counseling Psychology. He is a registered existential psychotherapist, an accredited counselor, and a Chartered Counseling Psychologist. He has gained an international reputation for his exposition of various key issues in existential-phenomenological inquiry, most notable with regard to the question of the development of the self-construct, the relational realms within the psychotherapeutic relationship and the inter-subjective factors which inform an existential theory of human sexuality. For these, and other, original contributions, Professor Spinelli was awarded a Personal Chair in Psychotherapy Counseling and Counseling Psychology in 1998. His many papers and publications include *The Interpreted World: an introduction to phenomenological psychology, Demystifying Therapy*, and *Tales of Unknowing: therapeutic encounters from an existential perspective*.

James A. Thorson, PhD, is the Jacob Isaacson Professor and Chairman of the Department of Gerontology at the University of Nebraska at Omaha. He has written 16 books, 18 book chapters, and 85 scholarly articles dealing mainly with attitudes and coping, especially in terms of aging, death, and sense of humor. His research is involved with caregivers of the older and terminally ill. He received his bachelor's degree from Northern Illinois University, his master's from the University of North Carolina at Chapel Hill, and his doctorate from the University of Georgia. Dr. Ann Laughlin was the 35th doctoral graduate he has mentored.

Adrian Tomer, PhD, is a Professor in the Department of Psychology at Shippensburg University. Since completing his doctoral training at the University of Florida in 1989, he has conducted research, has published and has organized international symposia on the topics of death, dying, and meaning. In addition, he has published in the area of cognitive aging and has conducted and published methodological work in the area of Structural Equation Modeling. His publications in the field of death and dying include the edited book *Death Attitudes and the Older Adult* (Taylor and Francis) as well as many other articles and chapters.

Paul T. P. Wong, PhD, is Professor Emeritus, Counseling Psychology at Trinity Western University, Langley, British Columbia, Canada. He received theology training at the Toronto Bible College (now Tyndall University College and Seminary) and PhD in psychology from the University of Toronto. He taught at the University of Texas in Austin, York University, Trent University, and the University of Toronto. He has been promoting the role of personal meaning in aging and health. His latest edited book is *Handbook of Multicultural Perspectives on Stress and Coping*, published by Springer, 2005. His 1998 book *The Human Quest for Meaning: A Handbook of Psychological Research and Clinical Application*, published by Lawrence Erlbaum Associates, is in its second printing. Dr. Wong is the founding President of the International Network on Personal Meaning (www.meaning.ca) and the International Society for Existential Psychology and Psychotherapy (www.existentialpsychology.org). He has spoken internationally on positive existential psychology and meaning-centered counseling.

Foreword

Ernesto Spinelli
Regent's College, London, UK

It should come as no surprise to readers of this text that existential thinking has placed great significance upon our stance toward, and preparedness for, ceasing to exist. Paul Tillich, for instance, in *The Courage to Be* asserted that "neurosis is the way of avoiding non-being by avoiding being" (Tillich, 2000, p. 26).

In several significant ways, existential thinking regarding dying coincides with a much earlier and broader set of questions posed by philosophers: How does one die well? What is a "good death"? Cicero's answer, for instance, was unequivocal: "to philosophise is to prepare for death." (Yalom, 1980, p. 30).

Cultural historians have also discerned that both pre-Christian and early Christian teachings took the preparation for death to be a very serious task. One of the most popular books of the 15th century AD was *Ars Morendi* [*The Art of Dying*]. Interesting for contemporary thanatologists, the text addresses various stages or temptations which are gone through: temptations against faith and toward despair, covetousness, impatience, and vainglory. Each movement is carefully described and illustrated. To assist themselves in this task, believers employed what have become known as *memento mori* – reminders of the transience of life – examples of which might include drawings and everyday objects that served as points of meaning for, and remembrance of, the individual life path undertaken.

In general, these traditions reveal that they were as much about "good living" as they were about "good dying." In brief, their message appears to be: live a life that is conscious of death. Perhaps, in an age and a culture that prefers to mythologize death rather than embrace its all too ordinary reality, it has fallen to existentially-informed theorists and practitioners to remind us of our temporality as human beings and of the inescapable inter-relationship between living an dying, so that we, too, like our ancestors, can attempt to live lives that include death within our awareness of living. Such attempts, however, inevitably expose us to the various uncertainties of human existence and, by doing so, provoke unavoidable unease.

Existential authors and therapists, influenced in particular by the writings of Martin Heidegger, have tended to refer to the universal human experience of death awareness and the accompanying inescapable disquiet it provokes as *death anxiety* (Heidegger, 2001). While the term might seem initially straightforward in its meaning, once examined more carefully it reveals concerns that are as much about living as they are about fears and concerns directly focused upon death itself.

From an existential standpoint, death anxiety is a fundamental universal aspect of human existence. As Hans W. Cohn has summarised it, it is an "anxiety rooted in the realization that life is inevitably moving towards death" (Cohn, 1997, p. 60). How each of us responds to and deals with this realization reveals our stance toward the various 'existential givens' of our being such as uncertainty, meaning, freedom and choice. And, through this stance, each of us derives a specific worldview through which are manifested those meanings we make of self, others, and the world in general, as well as the attitudes, values and behaviours that give expression to those meanings. As such, existential authors have suggested, our particular worldview reveals our relationship to *the* foundational inter-relation between living and dying (Spinelli, 2005).

Existentially speaking, death anxiety is a descriptive rather than a prescriptive term in that it seeks to express a core aspect of human existence rather than any form of symptomatology which can be alleviated or cured. How each of us responds to this anxiety, however, and how, in turn, our responses may overly restrict, diminish or disturb our possibilities for being and relating, becomes the appropriate arena for psychological and psychotherapeutic study and intervention.

As central to our lives as death anxiety might be, it remains the case that the various possibilities of relation arising from its avoidance or embrace and their consequent impact upon our worldview and the joys, fears, aspirations and dilemmas which emerge from it for each of us have not been sufficiently explored by existential writers. For example, many of the implications arising from Rollo May's pioneering work focused on contemporary Western culture's 'taboo' of death (May, 1969) remain neglected even though such issues as the social and psychological impact on the ways in which we relate to, and make provisions for, an increasingly elderly population take on an ever escalating significance for both inter-personal relations and social policy in the 21st century. Similarly, there exists as yet minimal exploration of the death anxiety that is evoked when contemplating a continued existence beyond that of one's family, friends and social milieu, even though it takes minimal reflection to imagine that such a state of affairs might well evoke anxieties that can be at least as intolerable, if not more so, as any that might focus upon one's own personal temporality.

Existential and Spiritual Issues in Death Attitudes, edited by Adrian Tomer, Grafton T. Eliason and Paul T. P. Wong, provides a significant and much-needed counter-balance to the dearth of studies on the human dimensions of living *with* death. Drawing together a wide variety of scholars and professionals, the various papers contained herein alert us to the plethora of issues and concerns requiring consideration and discussion. Just as significantly, Tomer, Eliason and Wong's text brings an explicitly existential focus which underpins each of the various and varied chapters and provides an overall breadth and depth of argument and analysis that, as far as I am aware, no other existing contemporary text on this topic can match. This book is both a major and a valuable achievement which I hope will gain the attention and respect it deserves.

REFERENCES

Cohn, H. W. (1997). *Existential thought and therapeutic practice.* London: Sage.

Heidegger, M. (2001). *Zollikon Seminars: Protocols-converstations-letters.* (M. Boss, Ed., F. Mayr & R. Askay, Trans.). Evanston, IL: Northwestern University Press.

May, R. (1969). *Love and will.* New York: W.W. Norton.

Spinelli, E. (2005). *The interpreted world: An introduction to phenomenological psychology* (2nd ed). London: Sage.

Tillich, P. (2000). *The courage to be* (2nd ed). New Haven: Yale University Press.

Yalom, I. (1980). *Existential psychotherapy.* New York: Basic Books.

Preface

There has been a renewed interest in issues of meaning, spirituality, and existential approaches in the psychological and counseling literature. This renewed interest is expressed in publications in the professional literature, as well as in presentations in this area at national and international conferences. Indeed, the idea for this volume on *Existential and Spiritual Issues in Death Attitudes* originated with one of the three editors of this book, Paul Wong, who organized the first international meeting on issues of meaning and spirituality, the biennial International Conference on Personal Meaning. The other two editors, Adrian Tomer and Grafton Eliason, were among the early contributors to the International Conference on Meaning, as were indeed many of the contributors to this volume. Together with the burgeoning interest in spirituality and existential psychology, we witnessed an increased realization that death attitudes and grieving are in many ways complex phenomena and that this complexity is related in a way or another to the efforts either to defend oneself against the dissolution of meaning or to transcend one's limitation and finitude, by an opening to meaning and/or by construction of meaning. This volume constitutes an attempt to integrate these two undercurrents in the psychological and counseling literature. Correspondingly, death is being treated here as both a threat to meaning, on one hand, and as an opportunity to create meaning, on the other hand.

This book is divided into three parts. The first part is theoretical and methodological in nature and serves as a base and as an introduction to the rest of this volume. Its purpose is to connect the empirical research on death anxiety and, more generally, on death attitudes, to the philosophical/psychological existential literature, as well as to the psychological literature on spirituality. Chapter 1, in this part, includes presentations and analyses of a number of influential philosophical and psychological approaches. In doing so, this chapter reveals a large variety of death attitudes and ways either to defend against them (i.e., to defend against the terror of death) or to promote them (as it is the case with different types of death acceptance). Different notions of death transcendence are also surveyed in this chapter which presents recent psychological approaches that build on the vast existential literature. These include, among other views, the Terror Management Theory developed by Greenberg, Solomon, and Pyszczynski on the basis of Becker's writings, the concept of *Microsuicide* put forward by Firestone, and a comprehensive Model of Death Anxiety formulated by Tomer and Eliason. Other theories of relevance to an examination of death attitudes, spirituality, and perception of time across the life-span such as the theory of Gero-transcendence (Tornstam) and the Socio-Emotional Selectivity Theory (Carstensen & colleagues) are also presented and discussed in this chapter. A second chapter (written by Mario Mikulincer) examines, through the eminent work of the late Victor Florian and of his colleagues in Israel, issues related to the multidimensional character of fear of death and how this multidimensional character can qualify other approaches such as Terror Management Theory. Finally, the third chapter in this part comprehensively presents an important alternative to the largely negative view of death attitudes that tend to emphasize mechanisms that are used to buffer or to protect us against the terror that comes with awareness of our own mortality. In this chapter, Paul Wong articulates a full-fledged theory of meaning management that postulates the existence of three main types of meaning related processes: processes of seeking for meaning, processes of meaning-making, and processes of reconstruction of meaning. The relationship of these three types of meaning related processes to our perception of mortality is also examined in this chapter.

The second part of the volume is empirical in nature. In chapter 4, Hart and Goldenberg apply Terror Management Theory to the problem of the physical body and incorporate a discussion of the concept of spirituality as a main mode of death transcendence that moves us away from the physicality of our existence. In chapter 5, Victor Cicirelli presents interesting data regarding end-of-life decisions. The data suggests that there is a reciprocal relationship between end-of-life decisions and spiritual growth in the last part of life. Monika Ardelt presents in chapter 6 of this part an analysis of data collected on death attitudes, religiosity and wisdom on older hospice patients, nursing home residents, and community dwelling adults. Chapter 7, by Adrian Tomer and Grafton Eliason, includes empirical evidence showing that, consistent with the Tomer–Eliason model, both past- and future-related regret are connected to fear and avoidance of death. Chapters 8 and 9 discuss the importance of existential and spiritual coping in HIV positive women (chap. 8 by Dobson & Wong) and in anticipatory grief (chap. 9 by Ivancovich & Wong) and help to show

how the meaning-management theory can be applied in counseling. A phenomenological analysis of the experience of bereavement and of the meaningful transformation that may accompany it is presented in chapter 10. In the final chapter of this part James Thorson and Ann Laughlin demonstrate the deleterious consequences of the disappearance of meaning: the increased mortality among nursing home residents transferred to a different facility.

The third and last part considers issues such as suicide (Orbach, chap. 12), infertility (Gibson, chap. 16) applications of regret therapy and the concept of regret to loss and bereavement (chaps. 13 and 17), and the use of Voice Therapy (chap. 14 by Morrant & Catlett) to eliminate destructive thoughts and to allow one to live fully, facing one's mortality rather than trying to escape it. The Tomer-Eliason model of death anxiety is used in chapters 13, by Mannarino, Eliason, and Rubin, and 17, by Eliason, Lepore, and Myer, to deal with issues of loss and grief. In chapter 14, Wong introduces the concept of meaning-centered counseling (MCC) and shows how it can be applied to grief counseling and discusses the positive transformation of grief as part of positive existential psychology. Finally, in the concluding chapter, the editors focus on common themes in this volume and on several open questions. In particular, the need for further empirical exploration of the issues of death attitudes, mainly fear and acceptance of death, and the relationship between them are emphasized in this chapter. In this context, both the Model of Death Anxiety formulated by Tomer and Eliason and the Meaning-Management Theory that unites an existential-humanistic approach with a positive psychological approach, are in need of further exploration.

This volume is unique in a number of ways. First, it includes an in-depth treatment of the topics on death and spirituality meaning and their relationships. Second, it places an emphasis on theoretical models as well as on clinical applications of these models to real life issues such as infertility, bereavement, anxiety, and suicide. Third, it places an important emphasis on issues of death acceptance by formulating a theoretical model of meaning-management.

We believe this book is relevant to a variety of professionals, including nurses, physicians, social workers, psychologists, ministers, pastors and other clergymen, as well as academics in the fields of psychology, gerontology, sociology, medicine, and nursing. To strengthen the use of the book as an educational tool we included Main Points that summarize the important ideas of each chapter. We see the book as either a primary textbook in a course on issues of death and spirituality, or as a undermining life's meaning, or alternatively, offering the very grounds for living authentically. Further layers of this tradition offer elaborations and counterpoints to these largely individualistic, and often explicitly atheistic or agnostic formulations by emphasizing the prospects for transcendence of existential isolation in the face of death through cultivation of relatedness to others (as in the work of Buber or Levinas) or to a sense of oneness with the natural world (as in the work of Brown or Wilber). Finally, admittedly optimistic voices are added to the discourse through an evocation of the work of Tillich, Frankel and Yalom, each of whom finds grounds for hope even in the face of human contingency in the experience of faith, purpose, and committed action, respectively. Thus, from the very outset, the reader is invited into a deep-going dialogue about the place of death in human life, and its relation to matters of ultimate concern. With this as a background, he or she is then well-positioned to follow the conceptual, empirical and clinical extensions of these theories into a variety of research and practice contexts in subsequent chapters.

For me, at least, these contemporary outgrowths of existential psychology were characteristically rich, and sometimes brilliant. A particularly strong example was provided by recent extensions of Terror Management Theory, a systematic network of testable hypotheses derived from Becker's influential work on the denial of death, which argues that people characteristically defend against death anxiety through conformity to mainstream values, or even "heroic" accomplishments that buffer their self-esteem and promise a kind of symbolic immortality through identification with cultural worldviews. Building on nearly two decades of research supporting this central thesis, contributors to this volume summarize recent research that suggests that spirituality, in the form of identification with an eternal soul, can be recruited as a bulwark against the anxiety aroused by a reminder of the creaturely physical self. Other contributors qualify this conclusion through research that identifies those whose specific death anxieties make them more or less prone to this defensive motivation, or alternatively situate Terror Management Theory research within potentially more inclusive frameworks in which fears of death are modulated by a broader system of beliefs about the self, the world, and death itself. Like the themes and counter-themes that characterize symphonic compositions, those that run through this volume stimulate the reader precisely because of their contribution to the complexity and multidimensionality of the resulting work.

For a volume that is admittedly philosophical in its underpinnings, *Existential and Spiritual Issues in Death Attitudes* is also surprisingly rich in its implications for practice. In these pages the reader will find thoughtful demonstrations of the role of past- and future-related regret in death anxiety, consideration of how religiosity shapes end-of-life decisions and is in turn shaped by them, and how meaning-based procedures can play a role in promoting death acceptance and the integration of grief and loss. Likewise, various chapters will caution against the "microsuicide" by which people protect themselves from fear of death by forfeiting, day by day, the uniqueness of their lives, advance novel voice therapy practices for countering this inauthentic solution to existential dread, and describe ways of working with regrets accumulated across a lifetime to promote greater integrity and acceptance as life draws to a close. Populations to whom these ideas have relevance are diverse, as studies of college students, people living with HIV/AIDS, suicidal clients, and couples struggling with infertility amply demonstrate. In sum, the reader is offered a vision of psychological science and practice that is as broad as it is deep, moving considerably beyond the preoccupation with minutiae and technologies of mood control that typify much of contemporary social and clinical psychology, respectively.

In closing, I found the book to deliver what it promised: a philosophically informed, but psychologically trenchant exploration of how we, as human beings, cope with the inevitability of death by defending against its harsh reality, and perhaps also by transcending its constraints through acts of meaning and spiritual commitment. To the extent that it helps graft the best of current psychological theory and method onto the deeper roots of existential thought, it will have achieved its purpose.

I

Theoretical
and Methodological
Positions

1

▼▼▼▼

Existentialism and Death Attitudes

Adrian Tomer
Shippensburg University of Pennsylvania

Grafton T. Eliason
California University of Pennsylvania

Let each one examine his thoughts, and he will find them all occupied with the past and the future. We scarcely ever think of the present; and if we think of it, it is only to take light from it to arrange the future. The present is never our end. The past and the present are our means; the future alone is our end. So we never live, but we hope to live; and, as we are always preparing to be happy, it is inevitable we should never be so.

—*Pascal (1670/1978), pp. 64–65*

Let us imagine a number of men in chains, and all condemned to death, where some are killed each day in the sight of others, and those who remain see their own fate in that of their fellows, and wait their turn, looking at each other sorrowfully and without hope. It is an image of the condition of men.

—*Pascal (1670/1978), p. 76*

Between us and heaven or hell there is only life, which is the frailest thing in the world.

—*Pascal (1670/1978) p. 78*

INTRODUCTION: EXISTENTIALISM AND DEATH

The connection between existentialism and "the problem of death" seems natural. Jacques Choron (1963), for example, in his *Death and Western Thought* (p. 222), mentions that one of the roots of existential thinking is the "philosophy of life." Reflection on life is impossible without reflection on the end of life. In existentialism, reflection on life frequently takes the form of reflection on human existence, in particular on human existence as limited and contingent, ungrounded, thrown in the world without justification. The interest in death is double-fold. Death illuminates the concrete existence of the individual, helps us understand what is limited, unique, problematic, or precious in this existence. On the other hand, our concepts of the nature of the individual, of concrete life, can illuminate the event of dying. Thus, meditations on life and death complement one another and may point both to strengths and to weaknesses in one another. In addition to being connected to an examination of human life and its meaning, or lack of meaning, philosophical reflection on death has engaged in an examination of Being, and the meaning of it. The concept of nothingness, as an important element of what "man" is, is central in the philosophical thinking that, starting with Hegel and Heidegger, and through the considerable impact of Kojeve, influenced a whole generation (including Sartre) in France (see Safranski, 1998, for a vivid description of this influence). In Heidegger's *Being and Time* (1927/1996), the presence of things and the presence of the individual to oneself are made possible by this nothingness. Death, in this sense, is always present at the core of human existence, is what makes this existence the clearing in which things appear (but see also Zimmerman, 1993).

We start by first examining the concept of spirituality and the connections between spirituality, meaning, and death. The concept of death in several existential philosophers is next examined in the section titled Existential Philosophers, followed by a brief discussion of several psychological or anthropological views influenced by existential thought. The goal in these sections, as throughout the whole chapter is not to be exhaustive, but rather to touch on important views and concepts. In the fourth section, we discuss connections between time, spirituality, and death attitudes. A final fifth section is dedicated to a presentation and discussion of several specific models of death attitudes that, again, were influenced by existential approaches.

SPIRITUALITY, MEANING, AND DEATH

Spirituality and Death

What is spirituality? Wong (1998) offers in his chapter on *Spirituality, Meaning, and Successful Aging,* an enlightening review of different meanings of the term spirituality and how spirituality relates to personal meaning. Similarly, Wilber (2000) describes five definitions or meanings of spirituality. The differences between the variety of approaches are related to the range of emphases placed on dimensions such as: asking questions versus providing answers, reliance on faith, developmental aspects, consideration of the relationship with God or the universe, and emphasis on feelings including, well-being, life satisfaction, self-transcendence, awe, wonder, or hope.

Our tentative approach here is to see spirituality as a type of attitude reflected in questions, feelings, and concerns, while not necessarily in answers, beliefs, faith, and so forth. From this perspective, the latter belongs more to religion or religiosity. The type of questions, feelings, and concerns that are at the core of spirituality are those dealing with the meaning of life, the human existence, and the meaning of Being. Frequently, philosophers and scientists express a sense of beauty and wonder generated by both the successes and the failures of modern science. There is a sense of mystery and awe, surprise that nature can be grasped by human reason, as well as a sense that ultimate questions, including our own success in understanding nature, might be incomprehensible. Such a feeling is common among great scientists and thinkers (see for, example, Margenau and Varghese, 1992, for the opinions expressed by over twenty Nobel Prize winners and distinguished scientists on issues such as the origins of the universe, life, science and religion, and the existence of God). An example of spirituality in the sense described here can be found in Norman Malcolm's memoir about Ludwig Wittgenstein (Malcolm, 1984, p. 59). Wittgenstein, not a person of faith, described an experience typically associated with "I wonder at the existence of the world" or "How extraordinary that anything should exist." This is, of course, a classical question that was already posed almost precisely in these terms by Leibnitz, about 300 years ago. The point here is that a pondering of these questions and the associated feelings of wonder, surprise, awe, and so on, constitutes spirituality, no matter what the answer is, indeed even in the absence of any answer. Thus, spirituality is closely connected with existential experiences that "pose the questions" or that suggest formulations such as the ones mentioned previously.

Indeed, Wittgenstein would deny not only the possibility of formulating non-nonsensical answers but even the possibility of formulating non-nonsensical questions. In the *Tractatus* he writes: "When the answer cannot be put into words, neither can the question be put in the words" (Wittgenstein, 1921/1969, proposition 6.5, p. 149). He would also acknowledge, however, referring to the "things" that cannot be put into words: "They make themselves manifest. They are what is mystical" (6.5222, p. 151).

This approach to spirituality is consistent with Tillich's definition of spirituality as "ultimate concerns" (1952, p. 47) and with the reference to some "peak experiences" as spiritual (see, e.g., Wilber, 2000, p. 134).These peak experiences should not be conceptualized, however, as including only "mystical states of consciousness," either of Eastern or Western tradition (see, e.g., James, 1902/2004, lectures 16 & 17). An important contribution of the existential tradition coming from Martin Buber, Gabriel Marcel and, more recently, Emmanuel Levinas, emphasized, for example, the I–Thou relation (Buber, 1923/1970) and the "proximity of persons," or the fact that others do not appear to me as objects (Levinas, 1987). According to this view, spirituality is expressed not only in our thoughts but is manifested daily in our numerous encounters with others.

Spirituality, Meaning, and Death

The connection of spirituality to meaning is clear. For example, to ask why there is anything is to look for a meaning behind existence, a reason. Moreover, in this broad sense, spirituality does not assume a positive experience of finding meaning. The spiritual experience may come together, in fact, with an experience of lack of meaning. For example, William James (1902/2004, p. 113) describes the loss of meaning in Tolstoy's life that preceded his recovery and the finding of God. Similarly, both Sartre and Levinas describe the feeling of nausea at the discovery of "pure being" (Levinas, 1982, p. 90), of a world for which there is no reason to exist, that is superfluous ("de trop," Sartre, *La Nausée*, 1938, p. 182) but for which it was impossible not to exist (p. 190). Such an existence is pure contingency and absolute absurdity.

If spirituality implies a quest or a question about overall meanings or, at the very least, involves feelings that imply or deny overall meanings, then one can see how death is related to spirituality. Viewed either from the perspective of the abhorrence of emptiness, or from the perspective of an insatiable "hunger for immortality" (de Unamuno, 1913/1954, p. 36), the end of life is an event that puts in question our very ability to ask questions, our spirituality. The challenge of death to the meaning of life is analyzed by Baumeister (1991) in terms of his four needs for meaning: purpose (or purposiveness), value, efficacy (control), and self-worth. Death is the event that makes future (and, in fact, present as well) unavailable, thus disallowing any possibility of undertaking a project. The meaning of our past deeds is not under our control but rather is at the mercy of others and is potentially affected by a vicissitude of unforeseeable events. Moreover, those deeds, even if they include considerable achievements, will eventually be forgotten and ignored (loss of value). Meditating on our death we realize that we'll be easily replaced. After a while, it will be like we have never lived. Baumeister's fourth need for meaning, the meaning for self-worth, is severely compromised when the upcoming death brings for us the end of time and plunges our life into utter futility. What is important to realize is that death does not only make the satisfaction of our basic needs impossible. In a sense this might not matter because we are not around any more. But death tends to dispel our "myths of higher meaning" (Baumeister, 1991, p. 58), essentially the myth that our life, considered as a totality, has special, or deep, meaning and value, is composed of elements that fit perfectly together forming an exceedingly harmonious, everlasting whole. Our awareness of mortality helps to bring home a much humbler message, that eventually, perhaps, it will not matter if we lived or not.

This bleak portrayal of death as a meaning annihilator can be mitigated to some extent by "imposing meanings on death" (Baumeister, p. 286), for example by dying while engaging in a significant project. This is the case of the soldiers who believe that they die while defending their home. Essentially, it is only by moving beyond oneself toward a broader context that one can perhaps escape the threat to life's meaning.

There is another way in which death and death awareness can have a positive effect on life. Indeed, nothing can make us stop our absorption in everydayness (Heidegger) and encourage us to ponder the meaning of our fleeting existence more than the anticipation of our own death. Thus, death and awareness of finitude may create a sense of urgency that act as an incentive to deepen our spirituality. Generally speaking, death is potentially (as awareness and meditation) an incentive to dedicate oneself to what matters, to ignore the trivial and to start living an authentic life. The transformative power of death was emphasized by novelists, philosophers, psychologists, and psychiatrists. Yalom (1980), for example, in his *Existential Psychotherapy*, documents some of the positive effects of the "close encounter with death" (p. 33). Similarly, beneficial effects following the death of a loved one were reported in the literature dealing with grief and bereavement (i.e. Schaeffer & Moos, 2001). The basis for an existential psychotherapy can be seen in the premise that death anxiety is both fundamental to human beings and hidden (Yalom, 1980; see also Spinelli, 2005, p. 154). In addition, making the individual aware of it might have salutatory effects (i.e., Yalom, 1980, p. 165).

If death, or the threat of death, has the potential of deepening spirituality, then it is also true that contact with meaning can transform the way we see ourselves and, by doing this, the way we see death. For example, according to Buber, the individual can get a glimpse of the relation with the Eternal Thou—with God, on the basis of the relation with the human Thou (see also Levinas, 1987, in *Martin Buber, Gabriel Marcel and Philosophy*). In this process, the relation to our own death is being transformed (see also the section on Buber discussed later). Another example is Heidegger's view of death articulated on the basis of his view of the Dasein. This view is discussed later.

EXISTENTIAL PHILOSOPHERS

Early Existentialists: Pascal and Kierkegaard

Although existentialism, strictly speaking, belongs to the 20th century, the idea that human beings have a special type of existence goes back at least as far as Kierkegaard. Similarly, the idea that rational philosophical systems cannot "catch" the uniqueness of human existence goes back centuries, at least to Pascal. We include here a short discussion of their views on death.

Section II in Pascal's famous *Thoughts* (1670/1978) is entitled "The misery of man without God." This section is followed by "of the necessity of the wager," in which Pascal tries to convince the skeptic of the rationality of opting to believe in the truth of Christianity and in God. The description of human condition by Pascal in these and other sections is both powerful and gloomy and his similes have become almost modern clichés. Humans are similar to prisoners, waiting in chains to be executed while in the meantime watching the executions of others. Unhappiness is the common lot of humans. Occupied to use their past as a means, unsatisfied with their present, they run toward a future and substitute the hope of living for the real thing. Unable to deal with their mortality and insignificance in face of the infinite, they try to convince themselves that they can reach real understanding in science. Moreover, humans are constantly busy in using a variety of diversions designed to prevent them from seeing the precipice into which they are headed. Pascal, anticipating Kierkegaard, talks about the lack of happiness of the "diverted" individual that flees into idle amusement, into vanity, and into busyness.

the premise was cogito, for Heidegger the premise is "moribundus" (Hoffman, p. 210).

Camus: Death Attitudes in an Absurd World

Strictly speaking, it is not the world that is absurd. "In the world everything is as it is," famously remarked Wittgenstein in his

Behind all the thoughts of Pascal's description there is a clear sense of the horror of death. If there is greatness in man, this is "in that he knows himself to be miserable" (p. 130). The only way to deal with the absolute need to achieve immortality is the Christian faith in God.

Many years later, Kierkegaard (1844/1957) had reached a conclusion that is not very different. Dread or angst is described in *The Concept of Dread* as a feeling of dizziness that alarms us (p. 55). Distinct from fear, which is a defined emotion, dread has nothingness as its object. Kierkegaard describes it as being "freedom's reality as possibility for possibility" (p. 38) and the "alarming possibility of being able" (p. 40). The individual should allow himself to be educated by dread that will open him toward infinity. Kierkegaard agrees with Hegel in relating to faith as an inward certainty anticipating infinity (p. 140). This certainty is achievable through the good services of dread. Eventually, when the dread comes, the individual is ready "…he does not recoil, still less does he attempt to hold it off with clamor and noise, but he bids it welcome, he hails it solemnly, as Socrates solemnly flourished the poisoned goblet" (p. 142). The alternative to faith is despair. Despair is described by Kierkegaard in *The Sickness Unto Death* (1849/1954) as a condition (perhaps unconscious) of the individual who attempts to escape his condition, to escape dread. On this issue Pascal and Kierkegaard achieve remarkably similar conclusions.

Heidegger and the Being-Towards-Death[1]

Heidegger (1927/1996) characterizes Angst as an "attunement" or "mood." In the language of *Being and Time* mood, prior to being a psychological phenomenon at the level of a person, is an existential that characterizes the existent individual, the Dasein. Mood is a way of relating to the world. As such, it sheds light on the Dasein, and on the world itself. Fear and Angst are examples of moods. Although fear, however, discloses a particular aspect of the world as threatening, one does not feel Angst about anything specific. Angst is "oppressive and stifles one's breath—and yet it is nowhere" (Heidegger, 1996, p. 174). For Heidegger, Angst has this character of nowhere because, in fact, is Angst about the world, which, again, means Angst about "being-in the-world-itself" (p. 175). One can see here the influence of Kierkegaard on Heidegger. It was indeed Kierkegaard who made a clear distinction between fear (as determined, precise) and Angst (undetermined, the effect of "nothing"), which is also our possible freedom. Usually, what

---

[1]On this topic see also Tomer and Eliason (2003).

future in *The Spectrum of Consciousness*, 1993, p. 116). Death is still pure violence, unacceptable but unavoidable.

Sartre's View on Death

Sartre, in *Being and Nothingness* (1943/1966), examines death as part of his general discussion of the "situation" and the "being-in-the-situation." The situation is defined as my position in the world, a position that includes components such as my neighbor, my surroundings, my past. The discussion is designed by Sartre from the beginning to be a retort to Heidegger's construction of death as a possibility that the Dasein assumes. Against this position, Sartre argues that death, as the annihilation of all my possibilities, cannot be made into a possibility, that is, cannot be assumed as a project. I cannot even await my death because my death is, essentially, an unexpected event (even in old age!). Death, indeed, would devoid such an anticipation of its meaning. Thus, according to Sartre, death, far from giving meaning to my life, deprives me from the possibility of giving meaning (by projecting myself toward the future)—and is, in this sense, absurd. I can certainly project myself toward a death. I can, for example, commit suicide. According to Sartre, however, I cannot project myself toward *my* death. I cannot be the being-toward-death that Heidegger described. Sartre's critique makes several interesting distinctions. One is the distinction between dying of old age and the abrupt death. A second distinction is between mortality and finitude. Sartre argues (contra Heidegger) that even an immortal being (in the sense of everlasting) is limited because it has to make choices, to engage oneself in one direction rather than another, and so forth. Thus, Sartre rejects the idea that death is intrinsic to the structure of the Dasein, that it reveals to Dasein its finitude and its uniqueness. We would make unique, irreversible decisions even if we were unlimited in time. A third distinction is between awaiting death and awaiting *my* death. The terrorist has made death (but not really his or her death) a part of an important existential project. The terrorist typically imagines oneself in an after world/life. Only from this illusionary perspective of an after-life does the act of suicide have meaning.

Sartre, therefore, cannot find a place for death in the "for-itself" (which constitutes Sartre's version of the Dasein). The indeterminacy of death ensures that our life itself is indeterminate, senseless, in the sense that its sense is determined from outside by the "other." On the other hand, there is an element of truth in the Epicurian dictum about death: "As long as we live it does not exist. And when it is present then we are not" (in Diogenes Laertius, 1925, Letter to Meneceus,

Dasein has no ground *but* the ground that arises through its own project. Therefore, it is a nullity (p. 263). Guilt is defined by Heidegger, in ontological terms (thus, prior to any psychological or ethical distinctions), as the character of nullity of the Dasein which is thrown and "fallen prey" (see also Hoffman, 1993, p. 195). The Dasein awakens us from this inauthentic state of falling prey through the call of conscience which is, therefore, a call to recognize its guilt, its groundlessness. Angst performs an important role in this. Hoffman compares this role of Angst to the role of the Cartesian Cogito. Although for Descartes

p. 651). Death can't be an obstacle to our projects, precisely because death cannot be present when my projects are undertaken. In this sense it is possible to take Sartre's perspective as the basis for a death attitude that is the opposite of the one described by Heidegger: My death *is not* my business.

Psychological Implications of Heidegger's Analysis

Notwithstanding Sartre's criticism, Heidegger's position on death and death anxiety presents considerable interest to the social scientist. His ontological-existential interpretation can provide the basis for a psychological model dealing with death anxiety and the mechanisms by which we defend ourselves against, as well as the mechanisms by which we move back to ourselves, regain our authenticity as human beings. We saw that the Dasein is originally entangled into the They. From a psychological viewpoint we have to talk about a movement of identification or absorption into the They of an individual threatened by his or her anxiety. The They, with the covering over and the disburdening of the self, is reminiscent of Becker's denial of death and of the terror management theory that considered identification with one's cultural system to be a protective mechanism. Certainly, Heidegger would object to a strictly psychological interpretation of his approach. In the language of *Being and Time*, the descriptions are not "ontic," empirical, but ontological, belonging to the structure of being. Nevertheless, his analysis can inform and "legitimize" psychological models. On the other hand, Heidegger moves beyond the defensive approach, beyond Becker's "best illusion," to the concept of acceptance of our mortality as essential to an understanding (and acceptance) of ourselves. He introduced the challenging concept that anxiety (Angst) is positive because it brings us to authentic living, an idea emphasized also by some contemporary writers in the field of death and dying (see Firestone, 2000).

The idea of totality of life that influenced much of Heidegger's approach to death also plays an important role in Erikson's view on wisdom and death as formulated in his psychosocial theory (i.e., Erikson, 1963, 1982).

Martin Buber: I and Thou

Buber (1923/1970) transforms the nihilistic view of meaninglessness, and as such humanities separateness, in his interpretation of the *I and Thou* experience. This is accomplished through a relational view of the experience on three levels, which in essence are one. Each of us experiences a perception of nature. Each individual experiences You, Thou, through other humans. A relationship is also possible with the spiritual Thou, or God. The experience of You on any level is impossible without an I, just as an experience of I is impossible without a You. In order to experience I, or even to speak I, one must do so with his or her whole being or essence. It is an essential deed. To speak or to experience You is to stand in relation of reciprocity. "I require a You to become, becoming I, I say You. All actual life is encounter" (Buber, 1923/1970, p. 62).

Buber also plays on the present, often showing no distinction between the present in time and the presence of being. "Only as the You becomes present does presence come into being" (Buber, 1923/1970, p. 63). In *Between Man and Man*, Buber (1947/2002) reacts to Heidegger's position on death. If we are thinking of the objective being, then death is with us in the present, as a force in the life struggle. This helps one to determine one's nature, existence, and whole being at that moment (p. 195). Buber sees Heidegger, however, as limiting human relation to a very "narrow sense, that is, to the relation of the individual to his own being" (p. 195). Buber sees this as reflecting only a "curious partial sphere of life, not a piece of the whole real life as it is actually lived" (p. 195). On one hand, Heidegger would see existential guilt as a part of life due to the inability for self-fulfillment, or the failure to reach one's full being. On the other hand, Buber maintains that guilt is a result of not being fully present to experience other, or You, and thus not able to fully experience life without reduction. For Buber, the presence of death creates an urgency to live more fully in the present, and thus to interact more fully with other.

Buber (1947/2002) sees Heidegger's fundamental-ontological question as the relationship between human existence and its *own* being. Buber's ontological question is based on relationship to *other*, to You, on all levels. "When the man who has become solitary can no longer say 'Thou' to the 'dead' known God, everything depends on whether he can still say it to the living unknown God by saying 'thou' with all his being to another living and known man" (p. 198).

Emmanuel Levinas's Analysis of Death: We Are the Being for Death and the Being Against Death

Levinas continues the existential meditation on death and his analysis contains elements of both Heidegger's and Sartre's position, although he also moves beyond them. We do bear in ourselves a fundamental knowledge of death ("savoir de la mort," *Totalité et Infini*, 1965, p. 209) as imminent. It is an instinctive knowledge that precedes any experience we might have with the death of the "other." The description of the death in *Totalité et Infini* (p. 210) is the description of the absolute violence, the murder in the middle of the night. In *Time and the Other* (1987), Levinas describes the death as a condition in which one is not able to be able, a condition characterized by a complete loss of mastery. Thus, Levinas agrees with Sartre that death is the impossibility of having a project, and, as a consequence, an event that we are not capable of assuming. For Levinas, however, death also indicates that we are in relation with an absolute other. The relationship we have with the other and the relationship with death partake the same type of mystery—a relationship with something that is not us, with a fundamental alterity or otherness. The meaning of our existence "toward death" consists in living for a time when we'll be dead, for a future that will not exist for us, in essence living for the other (*Totalité et Infini*, p. 213). In *Otherwise than Being or Beyond Essence* (1974/1981) this meaning is further elaborated. Levinas draws first the picture of the human subject trapped, absorbed into being and into "essence" (which is being conceived as the event or the process of being). From this perspective, there is no chance to give a meaning to death— "essence has no exits" (p. 176)—and, even when we think that we have "transcended it," this is an illusion of transcendence rather than the real thing. Eventually, we are brought back to reality: "to the death anxiety is added horror of fatality, of the incessant bustling of the *there is*, the horrible eternity at the bottom of essence." (p. 176). Against this backdrop Levinas struggles to define a passing over to "what is other than being," to define a real transcendence. The answer, again, is in an openness to "beyond essence" and the "otherwise than being," openness toward the other. This openness toward the "proximity of a neighbor" is described by Levinas in terms of disinterested responsibility and "substitution." These terms are incomprehensible from the point of view of the ego concerned exclusively with oneself. This ability of the subjectivity to find its way to what is beyond essence can be called spirituality or religiosity. The contact with the "beyond essence" is the contact with what Levinas calls goodness (e.g., *Otherwise Than Being*, p. 18).

To conclude, the description of the individual in relation to his or her death is complex. For Levinas, the individual is at the same time profoundly "interested" or absorbed in essence (and as such refusing death) and disinterested, forgetting oneself, moving to beyond oneself, and, as such, finding a meaning beyond time, finitude, and mortality.

PSYCHOLOGICAL VIEWS

Ken Wilber

Ken Wilber (1993) in *Spectrum of Consciousness* argues that the existential Angst is a result of the original separation between the organism and the environment—the Primary Dualism. The result of the severance is the appearance of the conscious fear of death together with the lack of possibility to accept imminent annihilation. Wilber's analysis is based, to a great extent, on Norman Brown's theses in *Life Against Death* (1959). An interesting part of it is the analysis of Time, which is presented as being a result of the refusal to accept the reality of the future-less Moment, the Eternal Now. The absolute Present is that which has no Past and no Future, which therefore combines birth and death into one timeless Moment (Wilber, 1993, p. 111). Not understanding that life and death are one, the individual tries desperately to flee death, among other things, by creating an idealized image, an ego. Thus, according to Brown/Wilber, the original unity is replaced by the duality ego (or soul, psyche) versus body (or flesh, soma). The body, being the mortal part, is also the part from which one needs to flee, or repress. Brown's own solution, "the way out," is foreshadowed throughout the text and given "in full" in the last chapter of *Life Against Death*, titled the Resurrection of the Body. Here Brown advocates the abolition of repression in a "resurrected body" that in which both the life instinct and the death instinct are satisfied and reconciled one with another in an unrepressed life (p. 308). Incidentally, for his "way out" Brown was taken to task by Becker in the latter's *Denial of Death* (1973, pp. 260–263). According to Becker repression and guilt cannot be undone, because, as part of ego development, they represent necessary adaptations to the reality in which the child finds himself or herself; they are, in this sense, existential.

Wilber's synthesis in *The Spectrum of Consciousness* (1993) suggests a somewhat different solution based on the distinction in his model between three main levels: The Ego Level, the Existential Level, and the Level of Mind. The first includes our self-image (conscious and unconscious) and our analytic powers. The second includes our total organism—both the mind and the body. Finally, the level of the Mind includes the mind, the body, and the universe, and corresponds to our feelings of being one with the Cosmos (p. 8). In the development of the organism, the Existential level and the Ego level are generated out of the mind by a process of dualistic thought that splits the unity, represses aspects of it, and projects other aspects into the environment. First, the dualism organism-environment that was mentioned previously is introduced.

The secondary dualism involves the separation between life and death and, together with the first dualism, marks the Existential level. At this level the individual is "in flight from death" (p. 116) and in chase of futile promise in the future. More positively, courageous existentialistic thinking, according to Wilber, allows us to face and to accept the primary and the secondary dualisms. The existentialist cannot completely transcend the duality that created the level in the first place. But the existentialist can face this duality courageously. For example, he or she can accept his or her anxiety as unavoidable and can conceive of death as something that "completes and makes authentic my being" (p. 246). The Ego Level is even father removed from the original Level of the Mind and is obtained when a further dualism, the Tertiary, takes place. In the Tertiary dualism, the ego is separated from the body. (The mechanism proposed by Wilber follows Freud and Freud's interpretation by N. O. Brown). Finally, a Quaternary dualism eventually generates a fourth level of the Shadow. This dualism involves the formation of the "Persona" that includes a distorted and impoverished self-image and the repression/projection of aspects of oneself into the "Shadow." The whole process of introduction of dualisms is portrayed by Wilber as one of a progressive narrowing of identity from the universe (mind), to the organism (existential), to the psyche (ego), and to parts of the psyche or Persona (p. 187). This model suggests that the therapeutic process for the adult individual should involve a healing of dualisms. It also suggests a distinction between different types of anxiety, depending on what level one is. Angst, a result of the split between oneself as an organism, and the environment, can be transcended only by following the mystics, descending to the Level of the Mind and finding immortality in "that which is always already," the timeless Mind that exists in a timeless Moment.

Paul Tillich: The Three Types of Ontological Anxiety

Paul Tillich's discussion of anxiety in *The Courage to Be* is consistent with Heidegger's (and, indeed, Kierkegaard's) analysis. He distinguishes between three types of anxiety "according to the three directions in which nonbeing threatens being" (p. 41). One is anxiety of death, the second is anxiety of meaninglessness, and the third anxiety of condemnation. The death threat is present, according to Tillich "relatively" in our every day life as an awareness of being contingent, of not having any ultimate necessity. We try to evade this anxiety by transforming it into well defined fears, but this attempt cannot be successful. The absolute threat of death is the foundation of the relative threats. The anxiety of meaninglessness is defined as a threat to spiritual life. The experience of meaninglessness (or emptiness in its more relative, everyday life manifestation) as described by Tillich is similar to the idea of the absurd in Camus. It is aroused by a loss of certitude—the certitude that existence has an ultimate, profound meaning—and by the perception of the possibility that there might be no truth. Finally, the anxiety of condemnation is related to the sense of responsibility for oneself, the responsibility "to make of himself what he is supposed to become, to fulfill his destiny" (p. 52). Again, in everyday life, this anxiety manifests itself relatively as guilt. Tillich emphasizes the interconnectedness of the three types of anxiety: "the anxiety of the one type is immanent in the anxiety of the other types" (p. 53). We are for example (more) afraid of death to the extent we feel more guilty and we tend to feel more guilty when we experience the threat of death. In the same vein, the loss of meaning and the loss of oneself (death) reinforce one another.

Tillich's "solution" to the problem of nonbeing and anxiety is based on the idea of courage. "Courage is the self-affirmation of being in spite of the fact of nonbeing. It is the act of the individual self in taking the anxiety of nonbeing upon itself by affirming itself either as part of an embracing whole or in its individual selfhood" (p. 155). Courage allows the transcendence of nonbeing. This courage for Tillich, although demonstrated by the individual, should be rooted in the power of "being-itself" (God). Nonbeing, ultimately, not only belongs to being at the individual level, but also belongs to being at the level of infinity: "Nonbeing makes God a living God" (p. 180). Tillich makes a distinction between his approach and other approaches that base transcendence on a personal encounter with the divine or on the mystic experience. One important distinction is that his approach preserves doubt and meaninglessness (similarly to Camus, which reaches quite similar conclusions coming from a completely secular direction) to the very end. Meaning is eventually affirmed in the very state of despair induced by the experience of meaninglessness. "The act of accepting meaninglessness is in itself a meaningful act" (p. 176). This state of mind is called by Tillich absolute faith. Tillich rejects the idea of "immortality of the soul" as "time and world without end" (p. 110) in which he sees elements of the courage to be, but also evasion. In final analysis, one is left with an irreducible fact: the power of saying *Yes* to meaninglessness and death.

Victor Frankl: The Search for Meaning

Frankl (1946/1984, 1955/1986) sees humans living in three dimensions: somatic, the mental, and the spiritual. In what many existentialists may view as a meaningless world, Frankl refocuses our attention to our will-to-meaning, which is tied closely with our spiritual dimension or that which makes us uniquely human. Physical and psychological survival, when one is forced to experience severe conditions (such as Frankl's experience in the Nazi concentration camps), is many times only accomplished when one's survival is perceived to have meaning. His theory of logotherapy begins here, *logos* connoting *spiritual* or *the meaning*. Logotherapy focuses on existential neurosis, or existential frustration. If existential frustration about one's life meaning results in neurotic symptomatology, Frankl refers to this as noögenic neurosis. This can be traced to a fear of responsibility and an escape from freedom (Frankl, 1955/1986, pp. xvi–xxiii).

Even in death, life can have meaning, in the way one faces his or her suffering and fate. Ultimately Frankl says that "man should not ask what he may expect from life, but should rather understand that life expects something from him." (Frankl, 1955/1986, p. xxi) It is not our place to ask "what is the meaning of my life," but rather to understand that life is asking us a question, which we must respond to responsibly by answering with our life (Frankl, 1955/1986, pp. xxi, 63; 1946/1984, p. 139).

The finiteness of our lives does not decrease the meaningfulness of life, quite the contrary, its poignancy contributes to meaning. Death limits our possibilities, but in doing so, motivates responsible action without hesitation. In an existential analysis of our life, Frankl (1955/1986) writes, "live as if you were living for the second time and had acted as wrongly the first time as you are about to act now" (p. 64). The gravity of the present, every moment, and every action, is then made clearer. Yet, time itself, or the length of life, does not determine the quality or meaning of a life.

Irvin Yalom: The Ultimate Concerns

Irvin Yalom (1980) bases his exposition of existential psychotherapy on "concerns that are rooted in the individual's existence" (p. 5). These ultimate concerns are given in the sense that they are "an inescapable part of the human being's existence" (p. 8). Yalom distinguishes between four existential concerns: death, freedom, isolation and meaninglessness. Although, by necessity, they are discussed separately, Yalom emphasizes the fact that "in vivo" these concerns are "intricately interwoven" (p. 485). Of particular importance for us here is the connection between death and meaninglessness, a topic that was mentioned repeatedly in this chapter. Death anxiety may present itself as a sense of meaninglessness, or, it may take even the form of a philosophical argument in the favor of the thesis "nothing matters." Both logically and therapeutically, the "nothing matters" is suspect, both as a logical conclusion and as genuine psychological state. Logically, as shown by Nagel (1979), if nothing matters then it does not matter that nothing matters and we can go on with our life. Psychologically, the person arguing that nothing matters still cares (e.g., to make the argument to others). In fact, it is because things matter to us and we matter to ourselves that we are concerned about our death. Moreover, a sense of meaninglessness as suggested by Bach (1973) represents just one type of experience. Many other experiences are, in fact, experiences of meaning. Why should we bestow a privileged status to the experience of meaninglessness?

More frequently death anxiety manifests itself not as philosophical argument but rather as denial. Yalom distinguishes between two main forms of denial. One form consists of one's belief in his or her "specialness," a belief that is at the root of the drive toward heroism (similar to Becker's position). The second type of mechanism consists of a belief in an "ultimate rescuer" (p. 129), either God or a godlike figure, perhaps an admired political figure or an omnipotent physician, a spouse that makes all the decisions for you, or a caring parent who takes care of you.

Although both types of defense mechanisms may be adaptive, they can also unravel and break down. What can then replace them? Yalom's advice to both the individual, and the therapist, is the "oblique" pursuit of meaning (p. 482) which can be undertaken by following our inner desire to engage life, and by facilitating its deployment. Yalom's solution, the "leap into commitment and action," as he himself points out, is a classical solution that goes back to Hume, Tolstoy, Camus and Sartre.

Ernest Becker's Approach

From his early writings, Ernest Becker was preoccupied with the idea of a "unified science of man" and the achievement of "comprehensive meaning" (Becker, 1971). Under the influence of psychoanalytic readings, particularly those of Rank, Becker changed his early views in a pessimistic direction. This view came to full expression in his last books, *Denial of Death* and *Escape From Evil*. According to this view, the challenge to meaning resides not outside but rather inside the individual that is faced with the terror of death. To defend against the terror, the individual needs "character armor," conceived as multiple layers neurotic structure (Becker, 1973, p. 57). The character armor term was borrowed by Becker from William Reich, and goes back to Kierkegaard's descriptions of the character as a flight from the truth and as a defense against dread, as something that includes a "vital lie."

In addition to the character armor, humans maintain a sense of self-esteem by the practice of either low (or safe) heroics or high heroics. The first comprise the performance of usual social roles and activities, doing what you are expected to do. The latter refer to extraordinary accomplishments that only a few can attain. Both character and the performance of heroics in the service of the society can be seen as tools of self-esteem maintenance and, as such, constitute basic defenses against the terror of death. According to Becker, they are a dishonest but necessary attempt (a vital lie) designed to ensure meaning and immortality. The risks of *not* engaging in enough denial are shown conclusively by the mentally ill, in particular by the schizophrenic patient. The schizophrenic has nothing to offer to the society, i.e. no heroics are possible. Nor can he take a refuge into the "animal pleni-tude" of his body, because his body feels foreign to him. Therefore he is exposed to terror more than the normal person and has to rely exclusively on an internal system of meanings that is completely disconnected from reality and cannot take a creative form as it happens in the case of the artist (i.e., Becker, 1973, pp. 217–221).

Although Becker devotes the *Denial of Death* to an examination of the terror and the related defenses, he also argues for an ontological structure of human beings, which is based on the duality Eros-Agape, a duality adopted by Freud in his later work. The first motive, the Eros corresponds to the tendency for life expansion via individuation and uniqueness. The second motive represents the tendency to move beyond the ego and to merge with the transcendent reality, with the All. Thus, both these motivations can be seen as contradictory ways to move beyond the present self toward more life and toward an expansion of meaning. Consistent with this ontology, Becker describes the urge to immortality as a reflection of the motivation for more life. Similarly, transference, in the sense of going beyond oneself in the direction of the other and deriving power from the other, reflects both fears (of life and death) but also the tendency for self-expansion. According to Becker the two fundamental fears, of life and death, are flip sides of the two basic ontological motives, Agape and Eros. Becker calls "natural guilt" or "badness" the feeling of being "unworthy" and "small" (p. 154). To be good, the individual can do two things: conform to the rules of others (the society, the cultural system) in order to belong, and/or perform some rather special feat as a heroic gift to the society. Becker's analysis emphasizes the contradiction between the two basic motivations, the motivation to lose one's isolation and to belong, and the motivation to stand out and to be unique or exceptional. By the practice of safe heroics, however (i.e., by doing things to please others), the individual manages to satisfy what looked like contradictory motivations. These ideas of the two basic ontological motivations and the dual nature of transference portray a complex and, potentially, positive view of human nature. For example, the individual's attempts to achieve greatness or to connect with others and with the universe do not reflect only fears. They reflect the individual's basic motivations to both belong and to stand out. In this sense, it is arguable (contra Becker) that they may constitute authentic existence rather than distortion designed to protect from terror. Paul Tillich, for example, in *The Courage to Be* talks about individuation and participation as two sides or two poles that reflect the ontological structure of being, corresponding to self and world. The self wants to be as oneself but also to be "as a part" (Tillich, 1952, chapters 4 & 5; see also Liechty, 1995). Interestingly, however, Becker, while aware of this possibility, would not make full use of it. Transference is described toward the end of *The Denial of Death* as reflecting "some universal betrayal of man's own powers" (p. 279) and Becker stipulates that "there is simply no way to transcend the limits of the human condition or to change the psychological structural conditions that make humanity possible" (p. 277). Psychotherapy can't help to transcend those limits. Eventually the individual—here Becker agrees with Tillich—has to face his or her limitations, to face or absorb the meaninglessness inherent in his or her conditions. One can see that, at this point, the absorption of meaninglessness becomes meaning and Becker's analysis can be continued in a positive direction by something similar to Camus' analysis in the *Myth of Sisyphus* and the *Revolted Man*. Becker himself is willing to open a small door of hope: "Ideally they (*men*) would wait in a condition of openness toward miracle and mystery, in the lived truth of creation, which would make it easier both to survive and to be redeemed because men would be less driven unto themselves and would be more like the image that pleases their Creator: awe-filled creatures trying to live in harmony with the rest of creation." (p. 282)

Becker has not completely ignored life-expansion forces: the tendency of human beings to transcend themselves (the Agape motive), as well as their tendency to develop beyond the present self (the Eros motive). Although life-expansion forces coexist with the fear of death, it is the latter that imbues them with urgency.

Becker's work inspired the formulation of a psychological theory of social motivation, the Terror Management Theory (see section titled Empirical Modes of Death Anxiety).

TIME, SPIRITUALITY, AND DEATH ATTITUDES

The Socioemotional Selectivity Theory

Carstensen (1991, 1992) bases the socioemotional selectivity theory on the idea that social interaction serves several important functions or goals that, however, change in salience from one point in the life cycle to another. Some of the goals, such as acquisition of knowledge for the purposes of attaining independence or finding social acceptance, or promoting one's career, are more future-related. Other goals include the pursuit of emotional regulation or the goal of "seeking meaningful emotional experiences" (Lang & Carstensen, 2002, p. 126). These goals change as a function of time perception. Specifically, older adults who perceive their future time as limited, tend to emphasize more emotion-regulatory goals that are attained in the present. Of course, one can expect a strong negative correlation between chronological age and "future time perspective." Lang and Carstensen (2002) report in their study a correlation of –70. Older adults have shorter time perspectives. Consistent with the theoretical predictions, the researchers found that a good match between priority of goals and perception of time translates into social satisfaction and less negative feelings vis-à-vis others (or less strain). Such a finding suggests that strategies directed to changing one's selection of goals (and also perhaps to changing one's future time perspective) may be beneficial. One can also speculate that the selection of goals appropriate to one's future time perspective may be beneficial in terms of reducing death anxiety. Such a result would also be consistent with Tomer and Eliason's regret model of death anxiety. Overall, Carstensen and her colleagues suggest that the focus on the present is highly effective in reducing negative effects related to the perception that life is coming to an end. For example Carstensen, Isaacowitz, and Charles (1999) cite evidence pointing to relatively low levels of anxiety disorders in older adults and to fewer negative emotions. On the positive side they also point to evidence showing relatively high life satisfaction and less loneliness in older adults than in younger adults. The existence of many "exceptions to the rule" (p. 178) is recognized by the authors who suggest that, for the clinically depressed, reframing of time, and the redirection of attention to the present and to goals that can be achieved in the present, may be of great therapeutic value. The focus on the present and on encounters with a relatively small number of close relationships does not mean that older individuals experience only positive emotions. Mixed (both positive and negative), bittersweet, complex emotions are prevalent (Carstensen Pasupathi, Mayr, & Nesselroade, 2000, Carstensen, Fung, & Charles, 2003) and are unavoidable for an individual who is approaching the end of his or her life. The positive effects that the authors mention, in spite of the existence of death awareness and time limitations, may be perceived as a triumph of meaning over meaninglessness.

Gero-Transcendence

Tornstam's (1992, 1994) theory of gero-transcendence takes, as a point of departure, theories and concepts developed by Erikson (1963), Jung (1930), and Gutmann (1976). According to his theory, living into old age is associated with a shift of perspective toward the cosmic dimension. This process is considered to be intrinsic to the developmental process, although it is modified by the specific cultural setting in which the aging person lives and by the personal circumstances of one's life, for example by life crises (Tornstam, 1997b). Based on qualitative and quantitative analyses, Tornstam (1996) distinguishes among three dimensions of gero-transcendence: the cosmic dimension, the self dimension, and the social and individual relations dimension. The cosmic type of transcendence refers to the relationship with the universe—being a part of an encompassing reality. The Self dimension focuses on the internal relationship to oneself. It incorporates, for example, ego integrity, the perception that one's life possesses coherence or meaning (Erikson, 1963, p. 268). The social and individual relations dimension refers to issues such as the meaning of social contacts and the proclivity for solitude, and includes a tendency toward unconventional behavior and toward deemphasizing the importance of material assets.

Tornstam provides qualitative and quantitative evidence indicating developmental changes in the direction of an increase in different types of transcendence (e.g., Tornstam, 1997b). It is plausible to believe that an individual, who is capable of transcendence, in particular of cosmic and self transcendence, should not be afraid of death. As Erikson put it in *Childhood and Society*, "The lack or loss of this accrued ego integration is signified by fear of death" (pp. 268–269). Surprisingly, Tornstam (1997a) was not able to confirm a significant relationship between gero-transcendence and fear of death. Notwithstanding this negative finding, it is still plausible to assume that subjects high in gero-transcendence are more capable to accept death (see also Wittkowski, 2005 on this point).

EMPIRICAL MODELS OF DEATH ANXIETY

Firestone's Approach: The Concept of Microsuicide

Robert Firestone's views are treated at large in chapter 14. It will suffice here to briefly indicate several distinctive characteristics of his approach to death anxiety. Firestone's treatment can be contrasted with the more customary view that sees in self-actualization a "solution" to death anxiety. According to Firestone (e.g., 1994, 2000), rather the opposite is true: to the extent that one tries to fulfill and to expand oneself, one is more likely to open oneself to existential anxiety. In contrast, the attempt to defend oneself against the existential threat may bring one to a state of closeness vis-à-vis the world and the life experiences. The person may avoid intimacy to escape the threat of separateness. In order to escape themselves as individuals he or she may identify with a leader or group. People try to create a simulacrum of immortality in signs of external status that "prove" their "specialness." By engaging in these types of behaviors, the individual, in fact, renounces his or her individuality or uniqueness—commits "microsuicide." The logic of microsuicide is crystal clear. Because life awakens the anxiety of annihilation, the solution is to renounce being wholly alive (see also Becker, 1973, p. 66). The price, however, of engaging in this defensive behavior is high. The individual gives up authentic life and real meaning (see also Tomer & Eliason, 2000). Firestone complements this general approach to the topic of anxiety with a developmental mechanism that generates the core defenses against death anxiety. The mechanism involves the formation of a *fantasy bond* in children as a substitute for the real bond. The idea that self-actualization promotes individuation and, ipse facto, death anxiety that comes with being an individual, is consistent, according to Firestone (e.g., Firestone, 1997, p. 10), with the ideas presented by Becker (preceding) and used in the Terror Management Theory (see next section). It should be noted, in this regard, that self-actualization is close to what Becker called heroics, in fact, high heroics. It can be seen as a way to create self-esteem and to achieve symbolic immortality and, in this sense, it is a way to defend, at least for a while, against death anxiety. On the other hand, self-actualization may increase the sense of standing alone. This openness vis-à-vis reality brings the creative person in contact with the terror of disappearance. According to Becker, the individual, while, on the one hand, is overwhelmed by the creative process, is aware, on the other hand, that his or her creation is only transitory. In the language of self-actualization we may say, in the spirit of Becker: even a "fully actualized" individual is impermanent and even major accomplishments don't secure immortality. Eventually, the self-actualizer may feel the terror of death and the absurdity of the human condition more than the person who chose not to stand out, the one who, in Firestone's language, chose to "commit microsuicide."

Firestone's theory is also reminiscent of Heidegger's approach to death anxiety—as something that the authentic individual should "await" (see the section on Heidegger). Firestone, however, seems to be less optimistic regarding the ability of the individual to accept his or her anxiety. Death anxiety remains, by definition, unpleasant and terrifying.

Terror Management Theory

Terror Management Theory (TMT) was developed by Greenberg, Pyszczynski, and Solomon (1986) in a remarkable effort to transform Becker's original synthesis into a testable, empirical theory of human motivation, a theory that will provide "a broad integrative framework that illuminates how seemingly diverse social psychological phenomena relate to each other" (Pyszczynski, Greenberg, Solomon, Anndt, & Schimel, 2004a, p. 487). The gist of the theory is its concept of self-esteem as a universal need in humans that fulfills a protective buffering function against the existential anxiety created by the mortality awareness (the anxiety buffer hypothesis, see, e.g., Pyszczynski, Greenberg, Solomon, Anndt, & Schimel, 2004b). Self-esteem refers to a person's concept of self worth and is a cultural construct in the sense that it is contingent on functioning in a cultural system that has prevalent basic assumptions (worldview). Self-esteem depends, at least in part, on societal feedback to the individual as to his or her "performance" in the societal system. Eventually, however, the individual internalizes his or her own version of the worldview as well as his or her belief of living up to the standards implied by this internalized worldview. In most presentations of TMT, self-esteem is presented as one component of the buffer, the other component being the belief in the validity of the cultural worldview. Strictly speaking, however, self-esteem is based on the belief in the validity of the worldview and in measuring up to the basic standards of value (Pyszczynski et al., 2004b). The anxiety buffer hypothesis has inspired numerous studies producing a body of largely confirmatory evidence. For example, increasing self-esteem by providing bogus positive feedback on an intelligence test reduced the level of physiological arousal in anticipation of a painful electric shock in comparison with a control group of participants who received neutral feedback (Greenberg, Simon, Pyszczynski, Solomon, & Chatel, 1992).

Most of the manipulations used in TMT studies were manipulations of the salience of death produced, for example, by having respondents describe their own death (emotions, physical changes). Manipulations of the salience of death have already revealed a large number of effects, for example an increase in the inclination to respond favorably to people who bolster one's worldview and to respond negatively to people who challenge one's worldview (e.g., Greenberg et al., 1990; Rosenblatt, Greenberg, Soloman, Pyszczynski, & Lyon, 1989). More recently Ben-Ari, Florian, and Mikulincer (1999) showed, in a series of studies conducted on Israeli soldiers, that manipulations of the salience of death may increase risky driving in soldiers as an expression of self-esteem striving. The buffering properties of self-esteem are a basic postulate of the theory. But why is self-esteem a buffer against death anxiety? The closest TMT proponents come to an answer is when (following Becker) they talk about feeling valuable, or worthy, by virtue of taking part in a meaningful universe. The "logic" of self-esteem as a protective mechanism seems to be: "I am part of a meaningful whole, therefore I am (in some sense) immortal." To what extent, however, this type of logic exists as a real psychological phenomenon remains to be established. The connection between self-esteem and the fear of non-existence was provided, empirically by the studies that manipulated participants' belief in (literal) immortality (see Pyszczynski et al., 2004b, for a review). For example, participants who read an article that argued that near-death experiences indicate the existence of an after-life were less prone to endorse a self-serving personality profile of themselves (Deshesne et al., 2003), thus indicating a reduced need to "defend themselves."

Terror Management Theory has generated a very large amount of interesting hypotheses and relevant research and also produced an enviable amount of corroborating evidence. There is certainly some remaining skepticism (see for example the discussion in volume 130, issue 3 of the Psychological Bulletin). Some of the issues that still need to be resolved or dealt with in more detail belong to the dialectic of defense and growth (an issue that was left unsolved by Becker; see the previous relevant section about Becker). TMT theorists have indeed proposed a theory of growth (e.g., Greenberg, Pyszczynski, & Solomon, 1995) in which growth motivation is conceptualized as an expression of the self as agency (the "I"). The defensive motivation, on the other hand, is viewed as an expression of the self as an object created by self-awareness (the "me"). Between the two systems there is a dynamic dialectical balance. Growth is likely to engender awareness of one's limitations and, therefore, to make one more susceptible to death terror. On the other hand, growth, via creation of meaning, provides the mechanism to buffer against the terror of death. The development of a complementary growth theory is promising and might help to explain paradoxical acceptance of death in spite of relative proximity as it happens in older adults (see, for example, McCoy, Pyszczynski, Soloman, & Greenberg 2000). In this volume, Wong (2006) presents a full-fledged theory of meaning management that deals with the processes of seeking for meaning, meaning making and reconstruction of meaning, and their relationship to death attitudes in general and death anxiety, in particular.

THE TOMER–ELIASON MODEL OF DEATH ANXIETY

Tomer and Eliason (1996, 2000, 2005; see also chap. 7 in this volume) proposed a model of death anxiety that includes several components: death salience, belief systems regarding the self and world, and three main antecedents: past-related regret, future-related regret, and meaningfulness of death. The first aspect in the model, death salience, refers to the degree to which individuals contemplate their mortality and death. The intensity with which death salience is experienced is related to their exposure to death, either their own or to others' deaths in their lives. The degree of emotional closeness, or the importance of the relationship, in conjunction with the recentness of the loss, also influences the extent of death salience.

The second component involves belief systems that are moderated by coping processes. The two belief systems identified concern beliefs about the world or external assumptions, and beliefs about the self or internal assumptions. Beliefs about the world are culturally determined and involve individuals' identification with culture, religion, politics, and education. Related issues include whether or not life is fair or just. Beliefs about the self include self-esteem, locus of control, and individual's perception of virtue. Regret can be defined as a type of emotion/cognition related to one's past (errors of commission—things that the person did but should not have done; or errors of omission—things the person should have done but did not do.) This is past-related regret. Future-related regret is one that we feel when important projects or future actions are made impossible. The third antecedent, meaningfulness of death, refers to the individual's conceptualization of death as positive or negative, as making sense or as being senseless or absurd. If issues of past and future-related regret are unresolved, or death is perceived as meaningless, then the person will experience higher death anxiety. Although the model was originally proposed as a model of death anxiety, it is tempting to try to generalize it to other death attitudes, in particular to death acceptance (see Wong, Reker, & Gesser, 1994; also see Neimeyer, Moser, & Wittkowski, 2003, for an examination of methodological issues related to assessing death attitudes). However, although empirical findings provide support for the importance of regret factors in determining death anxiety, no support was found so far for the idea that acceptance of death is conditioned by lack of regret (see chapter 7 for a description of relevant empirical findings). An integrative theory of attitudes toward one's death (fear, on the one hand, and acceptance, on the other hand) based on an integration of terror management theory, the theory of personal meaning, and the theory of gero-transcendence was recently proposed, as an alternative to the Tomer–Eliason model by Wittkowski (2005). We can only hope that further empirical and theoretical work will help to reach firmer conclusions regarding the antecedents of death attitudes.

CONCLUSION

An examination of several existential positions reveals a variety of death attitudes. These range from strictly negative positions (Sartre) through more "nuanced" positions that, while rejecting death as "absurd," find meaning in the very act of facing up to it (Camus). Even further to the right side of the continuum rejection-acceptance we can locate other positions such as Tillich's "courage to be" (to face non-being) and Heidegger's "being-towards-death." Different approaches also differ as to their emphasis on a movement of transcendence beyond the individual self, for example in the direction of the other (Buber, Levinas). Psychological approaches influenced by philosophical existentialism tend to emphasize a movement toward meaning (Frankl), toward cosmic transcendence (Tornstam), or ego integrity (Erikson). Alternatively, they view death anxiety as a price to pay in the movement toward authentic living (Firestone). It is fair to say, though, that mainstream psychology tends to emphasize the necessity of defense against the terror that is associated with an awareness of mortality and to deemphasize acceptance. This is the case with Becker's approach and with the TMT. Quite similarly, the Tomer–Eliason model stipulates that death anxiety may be decreased by a reduction of life regrets but pays less attention to death acceptance. Death acceptance was therefore relatively neglected in mainstream psychology. We further pursue these lines of thought in the final chapter of this volume.

MAIN POINTS

1. The problem of death is central in the existential philosophical and psychological literature.
2. Personal death can be conceived as both a threat to the meaning of life and as an incentive to deepen its meaning, to deepen spirituality.
3. There are a variety of death attitudes, from a strictly negative fear of death constructed as the embodiment or epitome of our absurd condition (Sartre) to an acceptance of death conceived as the crowning of our existence (Heidegger).
4. Much of the philosophical, and, to a lesser extent the psychological literature, can be seen as an attempt to define a real type of transcendence (in the sense of moving beyond my everyday self) that recapture and deepens meaning "in spite of death".
5. Transcendence can take the form of a type of self-understanding and liberation from illusions of immortality, as it is the case with Heidegger. It can also take the form of a movement toward the other (Buber, Levinas) and, perhaps, toward God.
6. Still, current psychology has emphasized until recently fear of death, death anxiety as a negative phenomenon, and the notion of defense mechanisms that protect us from our fear and anxiety. This is the case with Terror Management Theory. Recent developments, as illustrated by the work of Firestone, Wittkowski and Wong, started paying increased attention to the development of models that emphasize death acceptance through a process of meaning making and/or openness to meaning.

REFERENCES

Bach, K. (1973). *Exit-existentialism: A philosophy of self-awareness*. Belmont, CA: Wadsworth.

Baumeister, R. F. (1991). *Meanings of life*. New York: Guilford.

Becker, E. (1971). *The birth and death of meaning*. New York: The Free Press.

Becker, E. (1973). *The denial of death*. New York: The Free Press.

Becker, E. (1975). *Escape from evil*. New York: The Free Press.

Ben-Ari, O. T., Florian, V., & Mikulincer, M. (1999). The impact of mortality salience on reckless driving: A test of terror management mechanisms. *Journal of Personality and Social Psychology, 76*, 33–45.

Brown, N. (1959). *Life against death*. Middletown, CT: Wesleyan University Press.

Buber, M. (1947/2002). *Between man and man*. New York: Routledge.

Buber, M. (1923/1970). *I and thou*. New York: Charles Scribner's Sons.

Camus, A. (1942/1955). *The myth of Sisyphus and other essays*. New York: Alfred A. Knopf.

Camus, A. (1961). *The rebel*. New York: Alfred A. Knopf. New York: Alfred A. Knopf

Carstensen, L. L. (1991). Selectivity theory: Social activity in life-span context. *Annual Review of Gerontology and Geriatrics, 11*, 195–217.

Carstensen, L. L. (1992). Social and emotional patterns in adulthood: Support for socioemotional selectivity theory. *Psychology and Aging, 7*, 331–338.

Carstensen, L. L., Isaacowitz, D. M., & Charles, S. T. (1999). Taking time seriously: A theory of socioemotional selectivity. *American Psychologist, 54,* 165–181.

Carstensen, L. L., Pasupathi, M., Mayr, U., & Nesselroade, J. (2000). Emotional experience in everyday life across the adult life span. *Journal of Personality and Social Psychology, 79,* 644–655.

Carstensen, L.. L., Fung, H. L., & Charles, S. T. (2003). Socioemotional selectivity theory and emotion regulation in the second half of life. *Motivation and Emotion, 27,* 103–123.

Choron, J. (1963). *Death and Western thought.* New York: The Macmillan Company.

Choron, J. (1964). *Death and modern man.* New York: The Macmillan Company.

Dechesne, M., Pyszczynski, T., Arndt, J., Ransom, S., Sheldon, K. M., van Knippenberg, A., & Janssen, J et al. (2003). Literal and symbolic immortality: The effect of evidence of literal immortality on self-esteem striving in response to mortality salience. *Journal of Personality and Social Psychology, 84,* 724–737.

Diogenes Laertius. (1925). *Lives of eminent philosophers* vol (Vol. 2). Cambridge, MA: Harvard University Press.

Erikson, E. H. (1963). *Childhood and society* (Rev. ed.). New York: Norton.

Erikson, E. H. (1982). *The life cycle completed.* New York: Norton.

Firestone, R. W. (1994). Psychological defenses against death anxiety. In R. A. Neimeyer (Ed.), *Death anxiety Handbook* (pp. 217–241). Washington, DC: Taylor and Francis.

Firestone, R. W. (1997). *Suicide and the inner voice: risk assessment, treatment, and case management.* Thousand Oaks, CA: Sage Publications.

Firestone, R. W. (2000). Microsuicide and the elderly: A basic defense against death anxiety. In A. Tomer (Ed.), *Death attitudes and the older adult* (pp. 65–84). Philadelphia: Taylor and Francis.

Florian, V., & Mikulincer, M. (1998). Terror management theory in childhood: Does death conceptualization moderate the effects of mortality salience on acceptance of similar and different others? *Personality and Social Psychology Bulletin, 24,* 1104–1112.

Frankl, V. E. (1946/1984). *Man's search for meaning.* New York: Washington Square Press.

Frankl, V. E. (1955/1986). *The doctor and the soul: From psychotherapy to logotherapy.* New York: Vintage Books.

Greenberg, J., Pyszczynski, T., & Solomon, S. (1986). The causes and consequences of a need for self-esteem: A terror management theory. In R. F. Baumeister (Ed.), *Public self and private self* (pp. 189–212). New York: Springer-Verlag.

Greenberg, J., Pyszczynski, T., & Solomon, S. (1995). Towards a dual motive depth psychology of self and social behavior. In M. Kernis (Ed.), *Self-efficacy and self-regulation* (pp. 73–99). New York: Plenum.

Greenberg, J., Pyszczynski, T., Solomon, S., Rosenblatt, A., Veeder, M., Kirkland, S., et al & Lyon, D. (1990). Evidence for terror management theory: Part 2. The effects of mortality salience on reactions to those who threaten or bolster the cultural worldview. *Journal of Personality and Social Psychology, 58,* 308–318.

Greenberg, J., Pyszczynski, T., Solomon, S., Rosenblatt, A., Veeder, M., Kirkland, S., Lyon, D et al. (1990). Evidence for terror management theory: Part 2. The effects of mortality salience on reactions to those who threaten or bolster the cultural worldview. *Journal of Personality and Social Psychology, 58,* 308–318.

Greenberg, J., Simon, L, Pyszczynski, T., Solomon, S., & Chatel, D. (1992). Terror management and tolerance: Does mortality salience always intensify negative reactions to others who threaten one's worldview? *Journal of Personality and Social Psychology, 63,* 212–220.

Gutmann, D. (1976). Alternatives to disengagement: The old men of the Highland Druze. In F. Gubrium (Ed.), *Time, roles and self in old age*. New York: Human Sciencess Press.

Heidegger, M. (1927/1996). *Being and time* (J. Stammbaugh, Trans.). Albany, NY: State University of New York Press. (Original work published 1927).

Hoffman, P. (1993). Death, time, history: Division II of *being and time*. In C. B. Guignon (Ed.), *The Cambridge companion to Heidegger* (p. 195–214). Cambridge, MA: Cambridge University Press.

James, W. (1902/2004). *The varieties of religious experience*. New York: Touchstone.

Jung, C. G. (1930/1982). Die Lebenswende [Life's turning point]. Lecture, *Ges. Werke, 8,* Olten: Walter-Verlag.

Kierkegaard, S. (1844/1957). *The concept of dread* (W. Lowrie, Trans.). Princeton, NJ: Princeton University Press.

Kierkegaard, S. (1849/1954). *Fear and trembling and the sickness unto death* (W. Lowric, Trans.). Princeton, NJ: Princeton University Press.

Lang, F. R., & Carstensen, L. L. (2002). Time counts: Future time perspective, goals and social relationships. *Psychology and Aging, 17,* 125–139.

Levinas, E. (1965). *Totalité et infini*. La Haye: Martinus Nijhoff.

Levinas, E. (1974/1981). *Otherwise than being or beyond essence* (Alphonso Lingis, Trans.). The Hague: Martinus Nijhoff Publishers.

Levinas, E. (1982). *De l'évasion* [on escape]. Montpellier: Fata Morgana.

Levinas, E. (1987). *Time and the other* (Richard Cohen, Trans.). Pittsburgh, PA: Duquesne University Press.

Levinas, E. (1987). *Outside the subject* (M. Smith, Trans.). Stanford, CA: Stanford University Press.

Liechty, D. (1995). *Transference and transcendence: Ernest Becker's contribution to psychotherapy*. Northvale, NJ: Jason Aronson Inc.

Lifton, R. J. (1979). *The broken connection*. New York: Simon & Schuster.

Malcolm, N. (1984). *Ludwig Witgenstein: A memoir with a biographical text by G. H. Von Wright* (2nd ed.). Oxford, UK: Oxford University Press.

Margenau, H., & Varghese, R. A. (1992). *Cosmos, bios, theos*. La Salle, IL: Open Court.

McCoy, S. K., Pyszczynski, T., Solomon, S., & Greenberg, J. (2000). Transcending the self: A terror management perspective on successful aging. In A. Tomer (Ed.), *Death attitudes and the older adult* (pp. 37–63). Philadelphia, PA: Taylor and Francis.

Nagel, T. (1979). *Mortal questions*. London: Cambridge University Press.

Neimeyer, R. A., Moser, R. P., & Wittkowski, J. (2003). Assessing attitudes toward dying and death: Psychometric considerations. *Omega, 47*(1), 45–76.

Pascal, B. (1670/1978). *The thoughts of Blaise Pascal*. Westport, CT: Greenwood Press.

Pyszczynski, T, Greenberg, J., Solomon, S., Annt, J., & Schimel, J. (2004a) Converging toward an integrated theory of self-esteem: Reply to Crocker and Nuer (2004), Ryan and Deci (2004), and Leary (2004). *Psychological Bulletin, 130,* 483–488.

Pyszczynski, T., Greenberg, J., Solomon, S., Anndt, J., & Schimel, J. (2004b). Why do people need self-esteem? A theoretical and empirical review. *Psychological Bulletin, 130,* 483–488.

Rosenblatt, A., Greenberg, J., Solomon, S., Pyszczynski, T. & Lyon, D. (1989). Evidence for terror management theory: Part 1. The effects of mortality salience on reactions to those who violate or uphold cultural values. *Journal of Personality and Social Psychology, 57,* 681–690.

Safranski, R. (1998). *Martin Heidegger—Between good and evil*. Cambridge, MA: Harvard University Press.

Sartre, J. P. (1938). *La Nausée* [The nausea]. Galimard.

Sartre, J. P. (1943/1966). *Being and nothingness: An essay on phenomenological ontology* (H. Barnes, Trans.). New York: Citadel Press. (Original work published 1943)

Schaeffer, J. A., & Moos, R. H. (2001). Bereavement experiences and personal growth. In M. S. Stroebe, R. O. Hansson, W. Stroebe, & H. Schut (Eds.), *Handbook of bereavement research*. Washington, DC: American Psychological Association.

Spinelli, E. (2005). *The interpreted world: An introduction to phenomenological psychology.* London: Sage.

Tillich, P. (1952). *The courage to be.* New Haven, CT: Yale University Press.

Tomer, A., & Eliason, G. (1996). Toward a comprehensive model of death anxiety. *Death Studies, 20,* 343–365.

Tomer, A., & Eliason, G. (2000). Attitudes about life and death. In A. Tomer (Ed.), *Death attitudes and the older adult* (pp. 3–22). Philadelphia: Taylor and Francis.

Tomer, A., & Eliason, G. (2003). Theorien zur Erklärung von Einstellungen gegenüber Sterben und Tod. In J. Wittkowski (Ed.). *Sterben, Tod und Trauer: Grundlagen-Methoden-Anwendungsfelder* (pp. 33–51). Stuttgart: Kohlhammer.

Tornstam, L. (1992). The Quo Vadis of gerontology: On the Scientific paradigm of gerontology. *The Gerontologist, 32,* 318–326.

Tornstam, L. (1994).Gerotranscendence–A theoretical and empirical exploration. In L. E. Thomas & S. A. (Eds.), *Aging and the religious dimension* (pp. 203–225). Westport, CT: Greenwood Publishing Group.

Tornstam, L. (1996). Gerotranscendence—A theory about maturing into old age. *Journal of Aging and Identity, 1,* 37–50.

Tornstam, L. (1997a). Gerotranscendence in a broad cross-sectional perspective. *Journal of Aging and Identity, 2,* 17–36.

Tornstam, L. (1997b). Life crises and gerotranscendence. *Journal of Aging and Identity, 2,* 117–131.

Unamuno, M. de (1913/1954). *Tragic sense of life.* New York: Dover Publications.

Wilber, K. (2000). *Integral psychology.* Boston, MA: Shambhala.

Wilber, K. (1993). *The spectrum of consciousness* (2nd ed.). Wheaton, IL: Quest Books.

Wittgenstein, L. (1921/1969). *Tractatus Logico-Philosophicus.* (D. F. Pears & B. F. McGuiness, Trans). London: Routledge & Kegan Paul. (First German ed. published 1921).

Wittkowski, J. (2005). Einstellungen zu Sterben und Todd im höheren und hohen lebensalter: Aspekte der grundlagenforshung [Attitudes toward dying and death in the elderly: Issues of basic research]. *Journal of Geronotological Psychology and Psychiatry, 18,* 67–79.

Wong, P. T., Reker, G. T. & Gesser, G. (1994). Death Attitude Profile-Revised. In R. A. Neimeyer (Ed.), *Death anxiety handbook* (pp. 121–148). New York: Taylor & Francis.

Wong, P. T. P. (1998). Spirituality, meaning and successful aging. In P. T. P. Wong & P. S. Fry (Eds.), *The human quest for meaning* (pp. 359–394). Mahwah, NJ: Lawrence Erlbaum Associates.

Wong, P. T. P. (2006). Meaning management theory and death acceptance. In A. Tomer, G. Eliason, & P. T. P. Wong (Eds.), *Existential and spiritual issues in death attitudes.* Mahwah, NJ: Lawrence Erlbaum Associates.

Yalom, I. D. (1980). *Existential psychotherapy,* New York: Basic Books.

Zimmerman, M. E. (1993). Heidegger, Buddhism, and deep ecology. In C. B. Guignon (Ed.), *The Cambridge companion to Heidegger* (pp. 240–269). Cambridge, MA: Cambridge University Press.

The Complex and Multifaceted Nature of The Fear of Personal Death: The Multidimensional Model of Victor Florian

Mario Mikulincer
Victor Florian
Bar-Ilan University

For in that sleep of death, what dreams may come…

—*William Shakespeare, Hamlet*

The psychological encounter with death, the overwhelming experience of death anxiety, and the cognitive and behavioral consequences of this terrifying and paralyzing experience have fascinated social scientists for many decades. In psychology, two theoretical and research trends have attempted to examine and delineate human reactions to the psychological encounter with death. One trend, which emerged from thanatos psychology, mainly focuses on the assessment of a person's fear of death and the way cultural, personal, and contextual factors affect the intensity of this fear (e.g., Kastenbaum, 2000; Neimeyer, 1988, 1994). The other trend, which emerged from social psychology, mainly focuses on the cognitive and behavioral repercussions of the encounter with death and the way people cope with death-related concerns (e.g., Solomon, Greenberg, & Pyszczynski, 1991). Although these two trends initially conceptualized death-related concerns in a unidimensional manner, the work of Victor Florian has moved the field to the recognition that fear of death is a complex, multidimensional construct and that people differ not only in the intensity of this fear but also in the meanings they attach to death and the concerns that characterize their experience and reactions to the encounter with death. In particular, Victor Florian has developed and empirically validated a multifaceted theoretical framework for assessing and analyzing the multidimensional meanings, manifestations, and psychological consequences of the fear of personal death.

In this current chapter, we present and explain Florian's multifaceted perspective on the fear of personal death, state its major theoretical propositions, and summarize empirical findings concerning three major aspects of this fear. First, we review studies conducted by Florian and his colleagues on the contribution of cultural, social, demographic, personal, and contextual factors to individual variations in the meanings and expressions of the fear of death. Second, we review findings from our laboratory that have refined Terror Management Theory (Greenberg, Pyszczynski, & Solomon, 1997) and highlighted the important role of a multidimensional conceptualization of the fear of death for understanding a person's defensive reactions against death-related concerns. Third, we present new unpublished findings from our laboratory showing that a person's death-related concerns and the meanings he or she attributes to death are a reflection of the motives, goals, and concerns that guide his or her behaviors in everyday encounter of living and in their lives overall.

A TRI-DIMENSIONAL MODEL OF
FEAR OF PERSONAL DEATH

The human encounter with death has generally been seen as a source of fear, terror, and paralyzing anxiety (Bakan, 1971, Pollack, 1979). However, the conceptualization and operationalization of the fear of death during the first 25 years of research, from the mid-1950s through the late 1970s, were often ambiguous and contradictory (Kastenbaum & Costa, 1977). For example, researchers disagreed as to whether the fear of one's own mortality is a pathological or normal human emotion (e.g., Feifel, 1959; Kastenbaum & Aisenberg, 1972; Zilboorg, 1943) and have indiscriminately assessed the fear of one's own death, the fear of death of others, and the fear of dying (e.g., Kastenbaum, 2000; Nelson & Nelson, 1975). In addition, early attempts to study the fear of personal death relied on simplistic, unidimensional conceptualizations, and were limited to unidimensional measures of fear of death (e.g., Cameron, 1968; Durlak, 1973; Lester, 1971; Templer, 1970). Although these self-report scales tapped diverse death-related worries (e.g., concern over loss of bodily integrity, fear of a painful death), a single fear of death score was computed for each participant by averaging all the scale's items. As a result, early studies could not delineate qualitative differences in death-related concerns and were not able to fully assess the complexities of a person's fear of death.

In a preliminary response to these early simplistic conceptualizations and imprecision in measurement, Collett and Lester (1969) made important qualitative distinctions that were organized in a bi-dimensional two dimensional model of death anxiety. The first dimension distinguishes between types of fear of death, such as fear of death itself and fear of the process of dying. The second dimension distinguishes between objects of the fear, such as fear of one's own death and fear of other people's deaths. Subsequent studies provided strong empirical support to this bi-dimensional model and showed that fear of one's own death can be distinguished from other categories (e.g., Durlak, 1972; Nelson & Nelson, 1975). However, although Collet and Lester (1969) considered the fear of personal death as a separate psychological entity, they still viewed this fear as a unitary concept. As a result, they failed to deal with the diverse concerns and worries that underlie one's fear of personal death and the different meanings that people can attach to their own demise.

Several scholars have greatly contributed to the passage from a unidimensional to a multidimensional conceptualization of the fear of personal death and have proposed specific personal concerns underlying this fear and specific meanings attached to it (e.g., Hoelter, 1979; Kastenbaum & Aisenberg, 1972; Minton & Spilka, 1976; Murphy, 1959). For example, Murphy (1959) suggested seven components of the fear of personal death, each one representing a specific reason explaining why a person is afraid of his or her own mortality: fear of death as the end of life, fear of losing consciousness, fear of loneliness, fear of the unknown, fear of retribution, fear of consequences of death for loved others, and fear of failure. Hoelter (1979) also proposed a similar list of meanings that a person can attach to his or her own death and represent (a) concerns about decay, dissection, and isolation of the body; (b) concerns about the failure to accomplish important life goals; (c) worries about the painful consequences of one's death to family and friends; and (d) worries about the mystery surrounding what will happen after death.

The need to investigate fear of personal death using reliable and valid multidimensional instruments led Florian and his colleagues (Florian, 1979; Florian & Har-Even, 1983; Florian & Kravetz, 1983; Florian, Kravetz, & Frankel, 1984) to use content analysis to examine the various multidimensional suggestions, to integrate them into a single theoretical model, and to construct a self-report scale that can tap the various dimensions of the fear of personal death. On this basis, they proposed a tri-dimensional model of the fear of personal death dealing with the intrapersonal, interpersonal, and transpersonal meanings that people can attach to their own death. The intrapersonal dimension includes concerns and worries related to the consequences of death for one's own mind and body, such as worries about the decay and decomposition of the body and fear of the failure to accomplish important life goals and to have meaningful personal experiences. The interpersonal dimension includes concerns and worries related to the painful effects of death on one's interpersonal interactions and close relationships, such worries about the cessation of one's intimate relationships, fear of being unable to care for one's family and friends, and fear of losing one's social identity and being forgotten. The transpersonal dimension includes personal concerns related to the hereafter, such as fear of punishment in the hereafter and worries about what will happen to one's mind after death.

Following this tri-dimensional conceptualization of the fear of personal death, Florian and Kravetz (1983) constructed a 31-item self-report questionnaire—the Fear of Personal Death (FPD) scale, tapping a person's concerns about the impact of death on intrapersonal and interpersonal areas of life and worries related to the transcendental nature of the mind. In this questionnaire, each of the 31 items present a specific reason for being afraid of death and participants rate, on a seven-point scale, the extent to which they agree with an item (see Appendix for the English version of the FPD scale).

A factor analysis of the FPD scale (Florian & Kravetz, 1983) revealed that the 31 items were organized around six main factors reflecting intrapersonal, interpersonal, and transpersonal death-related concerns. Two factors deal with the intrapersonal dimension of the fear of personal death: fear of loss of self-fulfillment (e.g., "death frightens me because my life will not have been properly used"), and fear of self-annihilation (e.g., "I am afraid of death because of the decomposition of my body"). Two other factors tap the impact of death on one's interpersonal interactions and close relationships: fear of loss of social identity (e.g., "death frightens me because my absence will not be felt") and fear of consequences of death to family and friends (e.g., "I'm afraid of my death because my family will still need me when I'm gone"). Two additional factor represent worries related to the hereafter and the transcendental nature of the mind: fear of the transcendental consequences of death (e.g., "Death frightens me because of the uncertainty of any sort of existence after death") and fear of punishment in the hereafter (e.g., "I am afraid of death because of the expected punishment in the next world"). This six-factor structure has been replicated in subsequent studies using different ethnic and religious groups (e.g., Florian & Har-Even, 1983; Florian & Mikulincer, 1992; Florian & Snowden, 1989). These studies have also shown that the FPD factors have good test-retest reliability and internal consistency.

Florian (1979) viewed the construction of the FPD scale as the first step in studying the multidimensionality of the fear of personal death. In his view, this scale reliably taps conscious reports of death-related concerns, but fails to assess more implicit manifestations of the fear of personal death. In fact, several scholars have emphasized that death-related concerns are expressed at different levels of awareness, and that these concerns can differ when they are expressed in conscious self-reports or below the threshold of awareness (e.g., Kastenbaum, 2000; Neimeyer, 1997; Tomer, 2000). Moreover, cultural, personal, and contextual factors can have different effects on conscious death concerns and unconscious expressions of these concerns. Therefore, the study of the multidimensionality of the fear of personal death should include both explicit and implicit measures of the diverse death-related concerns.

Psychodynamic explanations of the ways people defend against the awareness of their own mortality put special emphasis on the study of implicit manifestations of the fear of death (e.g., Greenberg et al., 1997; Kastenbaum, 2000). These theories propose that the paralyzing anxiety elicited by the awareness of one's finitude leads to the denial of death awareness and the repression of death-related concerns. As a result, exclusive focus on conscious death-related concerns and an excessive reliance on self-report scales can lead to faulty conclusions. Denial and repression can hold the fear of death out of awareness and one can reach the faulty conclusion that a person is not afraid of death. However, the repressed death-related concerns can still be active below the level of awareness and can unconsciously influence cognition, affect, and behavior. Therefore, one needs to assess both conscious and unconscious manifestations of death concerns, because large discrepancies can exist between these manifestations. Some death concerns that cannot be found in a person's conscious self-reports may still appear below the level of awareness.

Extending the study of the multidimensionality of the fear of death to the implicit manifestations of death-related concerns, Florian, Kravets, and Frankl (1984) developed a rating scale for analyzing a person's responses to Thematic Apperception Task (TAT) cards that are known to elicit a relatively large percentage of death responses. pecifically, participants were asked to tell stories concerning four TAT cards: (a) 3BW—a boy reclining next to a gun-like object; (b) 8GF— two women huddled on a flight of stairs; (c) 15—a person in a ceme- tery; and (d) 5—a woman entering a room. Participants' stories were then content analyzed and rated along six scales: Centrality of death (the degree to which death plays a central role throughout the stories), depression (the degree of unhappiness and helplessness expressed in response to death-related concerns), anxiety (the degree of discomfort and apprehension expressed in response to death-related concerns), aggression (the degree of hostility and aggression expressed in response to death-related concerns), guilt (the degree of remorse and anger directed expressed in the TAT stories), and denial (the degree to which the TAT stories include attempts to inhibit or limit the expres- sion of death-related concerns).

A multidimensional scale analysis revealed that the six TAT scales were organized around two general dimensions (Florian et al., 1984). One dimension deals with the type of emotional reactions expressed in the TAT stories and runs from internalization and projection of anger (guilt and aggression scales) to the implicit expression of unhap- piness and discomfort in response to death-related concerns (anxiety and depression scales). The second dimension deals with the free expression of death-related concerns at the implicit, unconscious level and runs from attempts to inhibit the expression of these concerns (denial) to their identification and magnification (death centrality). That is, implicit death concerns can be freely expressed or subjected to some degree of inhibition and they can elicit a sense of resentment and hostility or a sense of helplessness and discomfort. Subsequent studies have replicated this bi-dimensional structure (Mikulincer, Florian, & Tolmacz, 1990; Ungar, Florian, & Zernitsky-Shurka, 1990).

Having constructed the FPD scale and a multidimensional projective measure of the fear of personal death, Florian et al. (1984) examined the association between these two measures in a sample of Israeli religious undergraduates. Findings revealed the complex ways in which implicit expressions of the fear of personal death are related to conscious death concerns. Specifically, the association between conscious and uncon- scious death concerns was not straightforward and could not be entirely explained simply in terms of denial and repression. Whereas implicit expressions of fear of death (centrality of death, depression, guilt) were positively associated with higher scores in the FPD's "fear of punishment in the hereafter" factor, these implicit expressions were inversely associated with the FPD's intrapersonal and interpersonal factors. At least in this sample of religious young adults, the fear of punishment in the hereafter has congruent affective manifestations on a more unconscious level. However, conscious concerns about the intrapersonal and interpersonal consequences of death seemed to maintain a compensatory association with implicit manifestations of the fear of personal death.

CULTURAL, PERSONAL, AND CONTEXTUAL CORRELATES OF DEATH-RELATED CONCERNS

The multidimensional approach to the fear of personal death have allowed Florian and his colleagues to conduct a programmatic analysis of the cultural, personal, and contextual factors that affect a person's death-related concerns. One of the cultural factors that is theoretically expected to temper the fear of death is a person's active commitment to religious beliefs and practice, because this commitment entails a promise of symbolic immortality (e.g., Feifel & Branscomb, 1973; Schulz, 1978). In support of this theoretical proposal, early studies using unidimensional measures of fear of death found this fear to be inversely associated with religiosity (e.g., Feifel, 1977; Feifel & Nagy, 1981; Templer, 1972). In four independent studies, however, Florian and his colleagues (Florian & Har-Even, 1983; Florian & Kravetz, 1983; Florian et al., 1984; Florian & Mikulincer, 1992) revealed a more complex picture of the associations between religious beliefs and the various dimensions of the fear of personal death. Whereas religious people report less fear of death due to intrapersonal reasons than non-religious persons, they report more intense fears related to interpersonal and transpersonal consequences of death. It seems that commitment to religious beliefs and practice protects people from intrapersonal worries concerning the consequences of death to the body and the self, but magnifies worries about the consequences of one's death for family and friends as well as the fear of punishment in the hereafter.

The diverse psychological benefits and costs of commitment to religious beliefs and practices have been further delineated in Florian and Mikulincer's (1992) study of death-risk experiences. In this study, Israeli Jewish soldiers who differed in their actual exposure to death-risk experiences during the previous three months (being involved in life-threatening military activities) completed the FPD scale and a measure of commitment to religious beliefs and practices. Findings revealed that exposure to death-risk experiences by itself had no significant impact on the intrapersonal, interpersonal, and transpersonal dimensions of the fear of personal death. However, among non-religious people, such exposure was associated with higher levels of worries about the intrapersonal consequences of death for one's body and self and higher fear of loss of social identity after death. Religious individuals' death-related concerns were not significantly associated with the exposure to death-risk experiences. That is, religiosity seems to act as a symbolic shield that protects people from the intrapersonal and interpersonal consequences of death particularly during the encounter with undeniably dangerous and life-threatening events.

The tri-dimensional model of fear of personal death was also useful to delineate the particular death-related concerns that characterize different religious denominations. In a study conducted among American college students that came from diverse religious backgrounds (Catholics, Protestants, Jews, Buddhists), Florian and Snowden (1989) found that these religious groups attached different meanings to death and became afraid of death due to different reasons. Specifically, whereas the Buddhist-affiliated group reported higher fear of the consequences of death to their family and friends than the other groups, the Protestant-affiliated group scored higher on the fear of punishment in the hereafter. In our view, these differences are a reflection of the value orientations and socialization practice that characterize each religious denomination. Buddhism put strong emphasis on compassionate love and genuine concern for the welfare of other persons (Dalai Lama, 2001), which, in turn, can be manifested in relatively strong worries about the consequences of one's death for the welfare of family members and friends. Protestant practices seem to emphasize personal responsibility as well as the positive and negative consequences of one's good decisions, bad decisions, and actions; making salient the fear of punishment in the hereafter.

Beyond differences in the profile of death-related concerns, Florian and Kravetz (1985) claimed that religious beliefs and practices could even affect a child's mental representation of death as an irreversible outcome of natural processes. In their view, religions that emphasize ideas of divine purpose and reincarnation can inhibit the recognition that death is an inevitable, universal, and irreversible phenomenon. In support of this view, Florian and Kravetz (1985) assessed beliefs about irreversibility, finality, causality, and inevitability of death in a sample of 10-year-old Israeli children and found that Moslem and Druze children received lower scores on scales measuring these beliefs than their Jewish and Christian counterparts. This finding implies that religion and other related cultural factors are also highly relevant for understanding the mental representation of the death concept.

Using the tri-dimensional model of fear of death, Florian and Har-Even (1983) also delineated the particular death-related concerns that characterize women and men. Furthermore, their finding clarified why early studies using unidimensional measures of fear of death consistently failed to reveal significant gender differences (e.g., Dickstein, 1972; Pollack, 1979; Templer, 1970). Specifically, Florian and Har-Even (1983) found that women reported more intense fears of death related to loss of social identity and self-annihilation than men. However, men were found to report more intense fears related to the consequences of death to family and punishment in the hereafter than women. At first sight, the finding that men reported more worries about the consequences of death to family and friends than women does not fit with the frequently reported finding than women have a stronger nurturing and caring orientation than men. However, this interpersonal dimension of the fear of death entails worries about the inability to provide material resources and a sense of security for one's family after death, which seems to be more consistent with a masculine gender role. Therefore, it seems that men particularly worry about the negative consequences that death has on the accomplishment of their gender-related tasks.

Gender differences have also been found in a person's metaphoric representation of death as a creature or person ("death personification," Kastenbaum & Aisenberg, 1972). For example, Weller, Florian, and Tenenbaum (1988) asked Israeli undergraduates to complete the Bem Sex-Role Inventory (Bem, 1974) and to rate the extent to which they use each of the feminine and masculine traits appearing in the inventory to describe death. Findings revealed that participants were more likely to use masculine than feminine traits for describing their own death and that this pattern of response was stronger in women than men. Specifically, the following masculine traits have been most frequently attached to death: forceful, dominant, independent, decisive, and authoritative. The least salient attributes of death were feminine: cheerful, likable, and smiling. This pattern of findings fits the masculine personification of death characteristic of modern Western societies (e.g., the Grim Reaper; Kastenbaum, 2000).

In his programmatic research of the fear of personal death, Florian also delineated the contribution of life circumstances (stressful life events, personal losses) to a person's profile of death-related concerns. Specifically, two independent studies (Florian, Mikulincer, & Green, 1993; Mikulincer & Florian, 1995) have shown that the experience of recent stressful life events or personal losses among middle-aged men

was associated with more intense concerns related to the consequences of death to self-fulfillment. In addition, Florian and
Mikulincer (1997b) found differential patterns of associations between
early and recent losses and young adults' profiles of death-related
concerns. Whereas the recent loss of a romantic partner or friend was
associated with more intense concerns related to the intrapersonal and
transpersonal consequences of death, loss of a parent during childhood was associated with more intense death-related fears of loss of
social identity in adulthood. According to Florian and Mikulincer
(1997b), early loss of a parent is a major source of attachment insecurity, which may become a core life motif, generalize to a wide variety
of situations throughout the lifespan, and then lead people to experience fear of death for the same reasons that they were distressed in the
original attachment situation—concerns about being unloved and
abandoned.

Having examined the contribution of life circumstances, Florian
and his colleagues also attempted to delineate the contribution of personality traits to the three dimensions of the fear of personal death. In
this context, Florian et al. (1993) asked middle-aged men to complete
the MMPI and the FPD scale and found complex associations between
personality dimension and death-related concerns. Specifically, the
MMPI subscales of paranoia, psychasthenia, and schizophrenia were
associated with higher scores on all the three dimensions of the fear of
personal death, implying that signs of maladjustment in the MMPI
tend to have a non-specific contribution to death-related concerns. In
addition, Florian et al. (1993) found that the MMPI masculinity-femi-
ninity subscale was associated with higher fear of the consequences of
death for family and friends, and the MMPI subscales of defensiveness and social introversion were associated with higher concerns of
the consequences of death to one's social identity.

In another series of studies, Mikulincer et al. (1990), and Florian
and Mikulincer (1998b) found that attachment style—the systematic
pattern of relational expectations, emotions, and behaviors that
results from a particular history of interactions with close relationship partners (Hazan & Shaver, 1987)—can also shape a person's profile of death-related concerns. Specifically, the two basic attachment
dimensions of anxiety and avoidance have been found to be associated with the interpersonal and transpersonal dimensions of the fear
of personal death. Whereas attachment anxiety—chronic worries
about rejection and abandonment and negative representations of the
self as unloved and rejected—was associated with more intense concerns about the consequences of death to one's social identity, attachment avoidance—preference for emotional distance from relationship

partners, negative mental representations of others, and emphasis on self-reliance—was associated with more intense transcendental fears of the unknown nature of the hereafter.

According to Mikulincer et al. (1990), these findings reflect the underlying action of the attachment-related strategies of affect regulation that characterize persons scoring high on attachment anxiety or attachment avoidance. On the one hand, people scoring high on attachment anxiety tend to magnify worries about rejection, separation, and others' availability (Mikulincer & Shaver, 2003), and hence tend to exaggerate concerns about being unloved, abandoned, and forgotten after death. On the other hand, people scoring high on attachment avoidance habitually attempt to cope with life adversities in a self-reliant manner in order to avoid emotional proximity, reliance, and dependence on potential frustrating partners (Mikulincer & Shaver, 2003). As a result, this defensive emphasis on self-reliance can intensify concerns about the uncertain and unknown aspects of death, because they threaten an avoidant person's sense of control and mastery. This line of thinking fits Florian and Mikulincer's (1997b) conclusion that people tend to be afraid of death for the same reasons they are distressed in attachment contexts (e.g., rejection, loss of self-reliance).

The underlying action of attachment-related strategies of affect regulation was also observed in the ways people differing in attachment style differ in the unconscious expression of death-related concerns. Mikulincer et al. (1990) asked participants, who completed a brief attachment style scale and the FPD scale, to write stories in response to death-eliciting TAT cards, and content analyzed these stories in order to uncover unconscious expressions of death concerns. Findings revealed that persons scoring high on either attachment anxiety or attachment avoidance also scored relatively high on the centrality of death and anxiety TAT scales. However, the findings also revealed that anxiously attached persons and avoidant persons differed in the observed association between self-reports of death concerns in the FPD scale and unconscious expressions of these concerns in the TAT. On the one hand, persons scoring high on attachment anxiety, who tend to hyperactivate their fears and have free access to them at different levels of awareness (Mikulincer & Shaver, 2003), showed a positive association between unconscious expressions of fear of death and conscious reports of death-related concerns. On the other hand, persons scoring high on attachment avoidance, who tend to repress their fears and prevent their intrusion into consciousness (Mikulincer & Shaver, 2003), showed an inverse association between the FPD scale and TAT scores.

A MULTIDIMENSIONAL CONCEPTUALIZATION
OF DEATH-ANXIETY MANAGEMENT

The tri-dimensional model of fear of personal death also helps us understand the ways in which people cope with death-related concerns. In 1991, a group of eminent social psychologists (Solomon, Greenberg, & Pyszczynski, 1991), inspired by the writings of psychoanalyst Otto Rank (e.g., 1941) and cultural anthropologist Ernest Becker (e.g., 1973), formulated a theory (Terror Management Theory, TMT) delineating the crucial effects that death awareness has on the daily lives of humans and the cognitive and behavioral maneuvers people activate in order to manage the terror associated with it. According to Solomon et al. (1991), humans, as other living beings, are driven by a self-preservation instinct. However, unlike other living beings, humans possess the cognitive capacity to understand that they are alive and that ultimately they must die. In their view, this unique combination of an instinct for life, coupled with the realization that death is inevitable, generates paralyzing terror and anxiety, which, in turn, demand the mobilization of symbolic defense mechanisms aimed at removing the awareness of death from conscious thought and the restoration of emotional equanimity.

Terror management theory conceptualized these symbolic defenses as a dual-process model consisting of proximal and distal mechanisms (Pyszczynski, Greenberg, & Solomon, 1999). Proximal defenses are aimed at suppressing death-related thoughts and concerns or biasing inferential processes (e.g., moving death-related concerns into the distant future). Distal defenses are aimed at modifying one's appraisals of the self or the world in such a way that they can create a solace of symbolic immortality and provide a sense of transcendence that counteract the terror of one's biological finitude. These distal defenses seem to include adherence to a cultural worldview and self-esteem enhancement (Greenberg et al., 1997).

Cultural worldviews are symbolic constructions that provide a shared conception of reality and imbue the world with meaning, order, and value (Solomon et al., 1991). According to terror management theory, these worldviews assist people in mitigating death-related concerns by turning an otherwise chaotic world into a meaningful belief system that provides answers to basic existential issues and offers a sense of symbolic transcendence and immorality. Individuals who adhere to a cultural worldview enjoy the solace of understanding how the world was created, what is the meaning and purpose of life, and what happens after death. Furthermore, they enjoy a sense of symbolic immortality (Lifton, 1973), which entails the belief that they are connected to a larger symbolic system that transcends their biological boundaries and that important facets of their own life (e.g., values, achievements, beliefs) will endure within their culture even after they will die. In this way, a cultural worldview provides a sense that one is a member of something meaningful and longer lasting than one's life, and then living by the culture's prescribed standards of behavior may offer symbolic protection against the terror of death (Greenberg et al., 1997).

One basic psychological derivate of the death-anxiety buffering function of cultural worldview is that reminders of one's own vulnerability and finitude and the consequent emergence of paralyzing death-related concerns would exacerbate one's tendency to invest cognitive and behavioral efforts in embracing the cultural worldview and behaving according to the culture's prescribed standards of behavior death-related concerns (Solomon et al., 1991). Moreover, because the encounter with a different worldview may present a threat to the validity of one's belief system, death reminders would also strengthen one's tendency to reject the alternative worldview and affirm one's beliefs (Solomon et al, 1991). As a result, when exposed to thoughts of death, people tend be particularly motivated to reject others who hold a different worldview because they threaten the validity of one's cultural worldviews and the protection from death awareness that they offer.

The second distal defense is the maintenance and enhancement of one's self-esteem, which can inoculate individuals from the anxiety associated with exposure to death reminders (Greenberg et al., 1997). According to terror management theory, positive self-esteem can be maintained or even enhanced when people believe that they are living up to cultural expectations or behaving in a way that is culturally cherished. As a result, people who believe they possess high self-esteem feel that they are good exemplars of their culture and enjoy the protection from mortality concerns that the culture offers. In contrast, people who harbor serious doubts about their own value and esteem (low self-esteem) feel that they do not fit well with societal norms or are not really loved and appreciated within their own culture, and then they feel less protected by their culture against the terror of their own mortality.

A large number of laboratory studies have provided strong support to terror management theory and show that experimentally-induced death reminders (mortality salience induction) lead people to react more favorably to other persons who adhere to their cultural values and more negatively to others who violate them. Specifically, mortality salience inductions by open-ended questions, fear of death scales, subliminal death primes, exposure to a film of fatal accidents, or proximity to a funeral home have led to more positive evaluations of in-group members and those who praise one's cultural worldview (e.g., Greenberg et al., 1990), more negative evaluation of out-group members and those who threaten one's cultural worldview (e.g., Dechesne, Janssen, & van Knippenberg, 2000; Greenberg et al., 1990), harsher punishment for moral transgressors (e.g., Rosenblatt, Greenberg, Solomon, Pyszczynski, & Lyon, 1989), increased aggression against those who criticize one's cultural worldviews (McGregor et al., 1998), increased conformity to cultural standards (e.g., Greenberg et al., 1992), and more reluctance to violate cultural standards (e.g., Greenberg et al., 1995). Florian and Mikulincer (1998a) reported that this heightened adherence to a cultural worldview following a mortality salience induction has been found among children as young as eleven (Florian & Mikulincer, 1998a). Moreover, these effects appear to be unique to death-related concerns, because other anxiety-inducing conditions (e.g., thinking about giving a speech or intense physical pain) fail to heighten adherence to one's cultural worldviews and rejection of other alternative beliefs (e.g., Greenberg, Pyszczynski, Solomon, Simon, & Breus, 1994; Greenberg et al., 1995).

There is also extensive evidence that both dispositionally high and experimentally enhanced self-esteem causes people to respond less defensively to mortality salience inductions (e.g., Greenberg et al., 1992; Harmon-Jones et al., 1997). Accordingly, studies have also shown that mortality salience inductions increase participants' strivings to enhance self-esteem and then to mitigate their death-related concerns (e.g., Goldenberg et al., McCoy, Pyszczynski, Greenberg, & Solomon, 2000).

In a series of experimental studies, Florian and Mikulincer (1997a) attempted to integrate the multidimensional model of fear of personal death with the causal pathway proposed by Terror Management Theory (Greenberg et al., 1997) going from death reminder to adherence of a cultural worldview. Specifically, Florian and Mikulincer (1997a) claimed that (a) the effects of mortality salience depend on the extent to which death reminders increase awareness to a person's predominant death concerns, and (b) the anxiety-buffering effects of cultural worldviews also depend on the extent to which worldviews touch upon a person's predominant death concerns.

Following this line of reasoning, Florian and Mikulincer (1997a) hypothesized that the activation of worldview defenses following a mortality salience induction depend on (a) a person's predominant death-related concerns (intrapersonal, interpersonal, transpersonal),

(b) the specific concerns elicited by a death reminder, and (c) the specific death-related concerns that are buffered by the validation of a cultural worldview. In their view, mortality salience should heighten a person's efforts to validate a cultural worldview when this induction increases awareness of a person's predominant death-related concern and defense of this worldview buffers the predominant fear of death. When death reminders increase death-related concerns that do not characterize a person, or the endorsed cultural worldview does not buffer the predominant death-related concern, death reminders should not heighten efforts to validate this worldview.

Florian and Mikulincer (1997a) designed a complex experimental design in which they examined a previously observed cultural world-view defense—negative reactions to social transgressors (Rosenblatt et al., 1989). In the first stage, Florian and Mikulincer (1997a) assessed participants' predominant death-related concern (intrapersonal, inter-personal) in the FPD scale. Then, participants were randomly divided into three conditions in which (a) intrapersonal death-related concerns, (b) interpersonal death-related concerns, or (c) a neutral theme (control condition) were made salient. Following a distracting task, participants received a series of 20 transgressions and they rated the severity of each of these transgressions and the severity of the punishment that the transgressors should receive. Ten of the social transgressions were described as having either intrapersonal consequences on the body and self of the victim, and the remaining ten transgressions were described as having interpersonal consequences on the social identity and family of the victims.

The findings indicated that mortality salience led to higher severity ratings of social transgressions and more severe punishments to the transgressors than a control condition only (a) when people who were predominantly afraid of the intrapersonal consequences of death were exposed to a reminder of this specific fear and were asked to judge transgressions that have direct personal effects on the body and self of the victim; and (b) when people who were predominantly afraid of the interpersonal consequences of death were exposed to a reminder of this specific fear and were asked to judge transgressions that have direct interpersonal repercussions on the social identity and family of the victim. That is, cultural worldview defenses seem to be mainly activated when there was a fit between the particular death-related concern that was made salient, the aspect of death that people most feared, and the type of judged transgression.

Overall, the reviewed findings emphasize the importance of a multidimensional approach to the fear of personal death and the need to assess the diverse meanings a person attaches to death in order to understand how he or she copes with the terror of death awareness. On this basis, Florian and Mikulincer (1997a) offered an integrative model describing the activation of distal symbolic defenses against death awareness. In their view, the activation of these defenses following the encounter with death reminders depends on the extent to which a person-environment transaction touches on the specific meanings that an individual attributes to his or /her own death. Thus, people activate terror management mechanisms particularly when those issues about which they are afraid to lose in the encounter with death are made salient and are threatened in a transaction. In other words, each person has his/or her own unique death-related concerns, and then when environmental transactions make salient and threaten these concerns (e.g., priming thoughts about interpersonal or interpersonal aspects of death), he or she would activate distal defenses in order to manage the threat.

FEAR OF PERSONAL DEATH AND THE
CONSTRUAL AND ORGANIZATION OF GOALS

In Florian's multidimensional model of the fear of personal death, the subjective construal of one's own mortality and the meanings people attach to death are an inherent part of the meanings they attach to their own life and a reflection of the motives, goals, concerns, and values that guide their behaviors in everyday life encounters. Specifically, people who put strong emphasis on the pursuit of intrapersonal goals related to achievement, power, personal success, and career development throughout life would be particularly afraid of death due to its intrapersonal consequences to self-realization and the accomplishment of one's projects. Similarly, people who put strong emphasis on the pursuit of interpersonal goals related to connectedness, belongingness, attachment, intimacy, and caregiving throughout life would be particularly afraid of death due to its interpersonal consequences to their social identity and the welfare of family and friends. On this basis, we want to propose that ways people cognitively construe and organize intrapersonal and interpersonal goals throughout life would be directly manifested in the intensity of intrapersonal and interpersonal fears of personal death.

In a review of research on *personal strivings* - the goals a person regularly tries to attain—Emmons (1992, 1997) indicated that people differ in the cognitive ways that they appraise and organize their goals. Specifically, he delineated four dimensions that organize the subjective construal of personal strivings. The first dimension is *degree of commitment*—the importance placed on personal goals and the time and energy invested in pursuing them. The second dimension is *anticipated outcome of goal pursuit* - the expectations of efficacy, control, and success in attaining one's goals. The third dimension is *appraisal of threats/demands in goal pursuit* - the difficulties, obstacles, and problems people anticipate encountering while pursuing their goals. The fourth dimension is *level of abstraction* - the extent to which people frame their goals in broad and abstract terms (being a physician) versus narrow and concrete terms (getting an A in the anatomy course).

Emmons (1997) also mapped three other dimensions that reflect different ways of organizing personal strivings within a superordinate goal system. The first dimension is *level of inter-goal conflict* - the extent to which people believe that the pursuit or attainment of one goal interferes with the pursuit or attainment of another. The second dimension is *goal differentiation*—the extent to which people perceive their goals as dissimilar and unrelated to each other. The third dimension, *goal integration*, concerns the extent to which people connect different goals within a superordinate goal system while maintaining distinctions and dissimilarities between them.

According to Emmons (1992, 1997), individual variations along the different construal and organization dimensions are important for understanding goal pursuit, goal-oriented plans and behaviors, and the affective states that follow successes and failures in goal attainment. On the one hand, goal commitment and positive expectations of anticipated outcomes can facilitate goal pursuit. On the other hand, high levels of threat appraisal and inter-goal conflict can interfere with goal pursuit and strengthen negative affect following failure to attain the goal. Furthermore, research has shown that these variations have important implications for psychological and physical well-being (e.g., Emmons, 1992; Emmons & King, 1988), with inter-goal conflict being associated with depression and distress and the tendency to frame personal goals in concrete and narrow terms being associated with physical disorders.

This research led us to propose that variations in the way people construe and organize their goals would be manifested in the intensity of the intrapersonal and interpersonal components of fear of personal death. Specifically, we made the following three hypotheses. Our first hypothesis is that the higher the value and importance placed on a specific type of goal (intrapersonal, interpersonal), the stronger the congruent fear of personal death (intrapersonal, interpersonal). Whereas people who show a high degree of commitment to intrapersonal goals (e.g., achievement, career) would report stronger concerns related to the intrapersonal consequences of death, people who show high commitment to interpersonal goals (e.g., connectedness, intimacy)

would report stronger concerns related to the interpersonal consequences of death. In other words, we view intrapersonal and interpersonal fears of death as direct expressions of the concerns people
harbor about the negative consequences of death to the attainment of
intrapersonal and interpersonal goals. As such, the intensity of these
concerns should be a direct function of the value or importance people attach to the congruent goal.

The second hypothesis is that the higher a person's doubts and worries concerning the attainment of a specific type of goal, due to either
low self-efficacy expectations, high appraisal of threats/demands in
goal pursuit, or high levels of inter-goal conflict, the stronger the congruent fear of personal death. Whereas people who have serious
doubts about the attainment of intrapersonal goals would report
stronger concerns related to the intrapersonal consequences of death,
people who express serious doubts about the attainment of interpersonal goals would report stronger concerns related to the interpersonal consequences of death. In our view, death can be viewed as the
ultimate obstacle to goal attainment and fear of death as the extension
of the major doubts and worries that one harbors throughout life. As
such, doubts about goal attainment would exacerbate the appraisal of
death as the symbolic realization of these doubts and worries, and
then intensify the concerns people harbor about the negative consequences of death to the attainment of intrapersonal or interpersonal
goals.

Our third hypothesis concerns the dimension of goal integration
and its implication for the fear of personal death. According to
Emmons (1992, 1997), highly integrated people can compare different
goals, appraise the interactions among the goals, evaluate tradeoffs,
and view specific goals as alternative means for attaining similar
superordinate goals or supporting global meaning structures. In contrast, less integrated people fail to link different goals to an overarching, unifying goal or set of goals, and this fragmentation interferes
with the formation of integrated and coherent global meaning structures. Furthermore, Sheldon and Emmons (1995) found that people
who show a low degree of goal integration feel less successful in
attaining them than more integrated people. On this basis, we hypothesized that the lower the integration of different goals within a superordinate goal category (intrapersonal, interpersonal), the stronger the
concerns people harbor about the negative consequences of death to
the attainment of that superordinate goal category. Whereas people
who fail to integrate specific intrapersonal goals within a coherent
structure would report stronger concerns related to the intrapersonal
consequences of death, people who fail to link specific interpersonal

goal to a superordinate goal category would report stronger concerns related to the interpersonal consequences of death.

We recently conducted a correlational study examining the hypothesized associations between the construal and organization of personal goals and the fear of personal death. In the first session of the study, 60 Israeli undergraduates (37 women, 23 men) completed the intrapersonal and interpersonal subscales of the FPD scale, along with measures of trait anxiety and self-esteem. In the second session, conducted 3–4 weeks later, each participant was asked to generate two lists of personal strivings. In one list, they were asked to provide six intrapersonal goals that they are typically trying to accomplish or attain in their academic career, profession, or personal life. In the other list, they provided six interpersonal goals that they are typically trying to accomplish or attain in their close relationships with family members, friends, and romantic partners.

After writing the two lists of goals, participants made a series ratings for each of the twelve generated goals. Specifically, participants rated (a) how committed they felt to each goal, (b) the degree to which they had succeeded with each form of striving in the past, and (c) the difficulty each form of striving had caused them. All three dimensions were assessed using 6-point scales. These ratings were adapted from the Striving Assessment Scale (Emmons, 1992). For each participant, we then computed six total scores by averaging his or her ratings in a specific dimension across the six goals he or she generated in a specific list. These scores represent participant's commitment, anticipated success, and difficulty of intrapersonal and/or interpersonal goals.

For each of the two lists of goals, participants were also asked to make three additional ratings. First, they provided ratings of inter-goal conflict in accordance with Emmons and King's (1988) procedure. For each list, they received a 6 × 6 matrix, the rows and columns of which were labeled with the six goals they generated, compared each goal with every other goal (30 comparisons), and rated, using a 6-point scale, "how much being successful in one striving has a harmful effect on the other striving." For each participant, we computed two inter-goal conflict scores: (a) average of the 30 conflict ratings of intrapersonal goals, and (b) average of the 30 conflict ratings of interpersonal goals.

Second, participants provided ratings of goal differentiation using Sheldon and Emmons's (1995) procedure. For each list of goals, they received a 6 × 6 triangular grid on which they rated, using a 6-point scale, every possible pair of goals as to how dissimilar the two strivings were. For each participant, we computed two goal differentiation scores: (a) average of the 15 differentiation ratings of intrapersonal goals, and (b) average of the 15 differentiation ratings of interpersonal goals. Third, participants provided ratings of goal integration. For each list of goals, they received another 6 × 6 triangular grid, identical to the one described previously, and rated, using a 6-point scale, every possible pair of goals as to "how much you perceive the two strivings as being part of a single broader purpose in life." For each participant, we then computed two goal integration scores: (a) average of the 15 integration ratings of intrapersonal goals, and (b) average of the 15 integration ratings of interpersonal goals.

The findings were consistent with our reasoning and hypotheses. First, ratings of intrapersonal goals were significantly associated with participants' scores in the intrapersonal fear of death subscale: The higher the ratings of commitment, difficulty, and conflict, and the lower the ratings of anticipated success, differentiation, and integration of intrapersonal goals, the stronger the intrapersonal fear of death (rs ranging from .32 to .45, all ps < .05). Second, ratings of interpersonal goals were significantly associated with participants' scores in the interpersonal fear of death subscale: The higher the ratings of commitment and conflict, and the lower the ratings of anticipated success and integration of interpersonal goals, the stronger the interpersonal fear of death (rs ranging from .35 to .41, all ps < .05). Importantly, ratings of intrapersonal goals were not significantly associated with the interpersonal component of fear of death, and ratings of interpersonal goals were not significantly linked to intrapersonal fears of death (rs < .20, all ps > .10). Overall, the findings highlight the relevance of the construal and organization of personal goals for understanding the meanings people attach to death and the concerns that characterize their fear of personal death.

CONCLUSION

The theoretical and empirical work by Victor Florian has greatly contributed to the formalization of the multidimensional conceptualization of the fear of personal death and the integration of terror management theory, Thanatos psychology, and social psychology. In this chapter, we reviewed the multifaceted theoretical framework Victor Florian developed for assessing and analyzing the multidimensional meanings, manifestations, and psychological consequences of the fear of personal death. This framework delineates the existential meanings people attach to their own mortality, with death being conceptualized as having intrapersonal, interpersonal, and transpersonal consequences, as well as the unconscious manifestations of the fear of death. On this basis, we reviewed extensive empirical evidence mapping the cultural, personal, and contextual factors that shape a person's unique profile of death-related concerns, clarifying the way these death-related concerns are involved in the activation of symbolic defenses against death awareness, and showing that these concerns are a reflection of the motives, goals, and concerns that guide one's life. Overall, the work by Victor Florian provides solid theoretical and empirical foundations for the assessment and understanding of the diverse facets of the fear of personal death and at the same time reveals the roles played by these facets in regulating the activation of terror management mechanisms.

MAIN POINTS

1. Victor Florian has developed and empirically validated the Fear of Personal Death (FPD) scale that is based on the assumption that fear of death is a complex, multidimensional concept.
2. Factor analysis of FPD revealed the existence of six factors dealing with either intrapersonal, interpersonal or transpersonal death-related concerns. The first include fear of loss of self-fulfillment and fear of self-annihilation. The second include fear of loss of social identity and fear of consequences of death to family and friends. Finally, the third include worries related to the hereafter and fear of punishment in an afterlife.
3. Florian's work includes the development of a measure of implicit fear of death based on the use of TAT cards. This measure allowed examination of relationships between explicit (FPD) and implicit measures of fear of personal death.
4. Studies by Florian and colleagues have been instrumental in clarifying relationship between fear of death and a number of cultural, personal and contextual factors. Those include religious commitment, gender, life events and personality traits.
5. In particular work by Mikulincer and Florian discovered interesting relationships between attachment style (anxiety versus avoidance) and type of death concern (social identity versus fear of the nature of the hereafter).
6. Florian and Mikulincer used the multidimensional model of fear of personal death to qualify Terror Management Theory. According to their approach, effects of mortality salience depend on the match between the nature of the death reminder and the person's main death concerns. Moreover, worldviews that are directly related to the predominant death concern are more likely to perform an anxiety buffer function. A series of experimental studies conducted by Florian and Mikulincer supported this integration of the two approaches.
7. Florian's multidimensional model was also found to be consistent with Emmons's conceptualization of life goals. Specifically, goals of high value, goals that are associated with doubts regarding their attainment, and goals that are poorly integrated, are associated with an intensified fear of death in the relevant domain.

LIST OF RECOMMENDED READINGS

Becker, E. (1973). *The denial of death.* New York: The Free Press.

Florian, V., & Kravetz, S. (1983). Fear of personal death: attribution, structure, and relation to religious belief. *Journal of Personality and Social Psychology, 44,* 600–607.

Florian, V., Kravetz, S., & Frankel, J. (1984). Aspects of fear of personal death, levels of awareness, and religious commitment. *Journal of Research in Personality, 18,* 289–304.

Lifton, R. J. (1973). The sense of immortality: On death and the continuity of life. *American Journal of Psychoanalysis, 33,* 3–15.

Mikulincer, M., Florian, V., & Tolmacz, R. (1990). Attachment styles and fear of personal death: A case study of affect regulation. *Journal of Personality and Social Psychology, 58,* 273–280.

Neimeyer, R. A. (1997). Death anxiety research: The state of the art. *Omega, 36,* 97–120.

Pyszczynski, T., Greenberg, J., & Solomon, S. (1999). A dual process model of defense against conscious and unconscious death-related thoughts: An extension of terror management theory. *Psychological Review, 106,* 835–845.

REFERENCES

Bakan, D. (1971). *Disease, pain, and sacrifice: Toward a psychology of suffering.* Boston, MA: Beacon.

Becker, E. (1973). *The denial of death.* New York: The Free Press.

Bem, S. L. (1974). The measurement of psychological androgyny. *Journal of Consulting and Clinical Psychology, 47,* 155–162.

Cameron, P. (1968). The imminence of death. *Journal of Consulting and Clinical Psychology, 32,* 479–481.

Collett, L. J., & Lester, D. (1969). The fear of death and the fear of dying. *Journal of Psychology, 72,* 179–181.

Dalai Lama. (2001). *An open heart: Practicing compassion in everyday life.* (In N. Vreeland (Ed.), Boston, MA: Little Brown.

Dechesne, M., Janssen, J., & van Knippenberg, A. (2000). Derogation and distancing as terror management strategies: The moderating role of need for closure and permeability of group boundaries. *Journal of Personality and Social Psychology, 79,* 923–932.

Dickstein, L. (1972). Death concern: Measurement and correlates. *Psychological Reports, 30,* 563–571.

Durlak, J. A. (1972). Measurement of the fear of death: An examination of some existing scales. *Journal of Clinical Psychology, 28,* 545–547.

Durlak, J. A. (1973). Relationship between various measures of death concern and fear of death. *Journal of Consulting and Clinical Psychology, 41,* 162–168.

Emmons, R. A. (1992). Abstract versus concrete concrete goals: Personal striving level, physical illness, and psychological well-being. *Journal of Personality and Social Psychology, 62,* 292–300.

Emmons, R. A. (1997). Motives and goals. In R. Hogan, J. Johnson, & S. Briggs (Eds.), *Handbook of personality psychology* (pp. 485–512). New York: Academic Press.

Emmons, R. A., & King, L. (1988). Conflict among personal strivings: Immediate and long-term implications for psychological and physical well-being. *Journal of Personality and Social Psychology, 54,* 1040–1048.

Feifel, H. (1959). *The meaning of death.* New York: McGraw-Hill.

Feifel, H. (1977). *New meanings of death.* New York: McGraw-Hill.

Feifel, H., & Branscomb, A. B. (1973). Who's afraid of death? *Journal of Abnormal Psychology, 81,* 282–288.

Feifel, H., & Nagy, V. T. (1981). Another look at fear of death. *Journal of Consulting and Clinical Psychology, 54,* 479–481.

Florian, V. (1979). *Personal fear of death as expressed among religious and non-religious Jewish groups.* Unpublished doctoral dissertation, Bar-Ilan University, Israel.

Florian, V., & Har-Even, D. (1983). Fear of personal death: The effects of sex and religious beliefs. *Omega, 14,* 83–91.

Florian, V., & Kravetz, S. (1983). Fear of personal death: attribution, structure, and relation to religious belief. *Journal of Personality and Social Psychology, 44,* 600–607.

Florian, V., & Kravetz, S. (1985). Children's concept of death. *Journal of Cross-Cultural Psychology, 16,* 174–189.

Florian, V., Kravetz, S., & Frankel, J. (1984). Aspects of fear of personal death, levels of awareness, and religious commitment. *Journal of Research in Personality, 18,* 289–304.

Florian, V., & Mikulincer, M. (1992). The impact of death-risk experiences and religiosity on the fear of personal death: The case of Israeli soldiers in Lebanon. *Omega, 26,* 101–111.

Florian, V., & Mikulincer, M. (1997a). Fear of death and the judgment of social transgressions: A multidimensional test of terror management theory. *Journal of Personality and Social Psychology, 73,* 369–380.

Florian, V., & Mikulincer, M. (1997b). Fear of personal death in adulthood: The impact of early and recent losses. *Death Studies, 21,* 1–24.

Florian, V., & Mikulincer, M. (1998a). Symbolic immortality and the management of the terror of death—The moderating role of attachment style. *Journal of Personality and Social Psychology, 74,* 725–734.

Florian, V., & Mikulincer, M. (1998b). Terror management in childhood: Does death conceptualization moderate the effects of mortality salience on acceptance of similar and different others? *Personality and Social Psychology Bulletin, 24,* 1104–1112.

Florian, V., Mikulincer, M., & Green, E. (1993). Fear of personal death and the MMPI profile of middle-age men: The moderating impact of personal losses. *Omega, 28,* 151–164.

Florian, V., & Snowden, L. (1989). Fear of personal death and positive life regard: A study of different ethnic and religious-affiliated American college students. *Journal of Cross-Cultural Psychology, 20,* 64–79.

Goldenberg, J. L., McCoy, S. K., Pyszczynski, T., Greenberg, J., & Solomon, S. (2000). The body as a source of self-esteem: The effects of mortality salience on identification with one's body, interest in sex, and appearance monitoring. *Journal of Personality and Social Psychology, 79,* 118–130.

Greenberg, J., Pyszczynski, T., & Solomon, S. (1997). Terror management theory of self-esteem and cultural worldviews: Empirical assessments and conceptual refinements. In P. M. Zanna (Ed.), *Advances in experimental social psychology,* (Vol. 29, pp. 61–141). San Diego, CA: Academic Press.

Greenberg, J., Pyszczynski, T., Solomon, S., Rosenblatt, A., Veeder, M., Kirkland, S., & Lyon, D. (1990). Evidence for terror management theory: Part 2. The effects of mortality salience on reactions to those who threaten or bolster the cultural worldview. *Journal of Personality and Social Psychology, 58,* 308–318.

Greenberg, J., Pyszczynski, T., Solomon, S., Simon, L., & Breus, M. (1994). The role of consciousness and accessibility of death related thoughts in mortality salience effects. *Journal of Personality and Social Psychology, 67,* 627–637.

Greenberg, J., Simon, L., Harmon-Jones, E., Solomon, S., Pyszczynski, T., & Lyon, D. (1995). Testing alternative explanations for mortality salience effects: Terror management, value accessibility, or worrisome thoughts? *European Journal of Social Psychology, 25,* 417–433.

Greenberg, J., Solomon, S., Pyszczynski, T., Rosenblatt, A., Burling, J., Lyon, D., & Simon, L. (1992). Assessing the terror management analysis of self-esteem: Converging evidence of an anxiety-buffering function. *Journal of Personality and Social Psychology, 63*, 913–922.

Harmon-Jones, E., Simon, L., Greenberg, J., Pyszczynski, T., Solomon, S., & McGregor, H. A. (1997). Terror management theory and self-esteem: Evidence that increased self-esteem reduces mortality salience effects. *Journal of Personality and Social Psychology, 72*, 24–36.

Hazan, C., & Shaver, P. R. (1987). Romantic love conceptualized as an attachment process. *Journal of Personality and Social Psychology, 52*, 511–524.

Hoelter, J. (1979). Multidimensional treatment of fear of death. *Journal of Consulting and Clinical Psychology, 47*, 996–999.

Kastenbaum, R. (2000). *The psychology of death* (3rd ed.). New York: Springer.

Kastenbaum, R., & Aisenberg, I. (1972). *The psychology of death*. New York: Springer.

Kastenbaum, R., & Costa, P. T. (1977). Psychological perspectives on death. *Annual Review of Psychology, 28*, 225–249.

Lester, D. (1971). Attitudes towards death today and thirty-five years ago. *Omega, 2*, 168–174.

Lifton, R. J. (1973). The sense of immortality: On death and the continuity of life. *American Journal of Psychoanalysis, 33*, 3–15.

McGregor, H. A., Lieberman, J. D., Greenberg, J., Solomon, S., Arndt, J., Simon, L., & Pyszczynski, T. (1998). Terror management and aggression: Evidence that mortality salience promotes aggression against worldview threatening others. *Journal of Personality and Social Psychology, 74*, 590–605.

Mikulincer, M., & Florian, V. (1995). Stress, coping, and fear of personal death: The case of middle-aged men facing early job retirement. *Death Studies, 19*, 413–431.

Mikulincer, M., Florian, V., & Tolmacz, R. (1990). Attachment styles and fear of personal death: A case study of affect regulation. *Journal of Personality and Social Psychology, 58*, 273–280.

Mikulincer, M., & Shaver, P. R. (2003). The attachment behavioral system in adulthood: Activation, psychodynamics, and interpersonal processes. In M. P. Zanna (Ed.), *Advances in experimental social psychology* (Vol. 35). San Diego: Academic Press.

Minton, R., & Spilka, B. (1976). Perspectives on death in relation to powerlessness and form of personal religion. *Omega, 7*, 261–268.

Murphy, C. (1959). Discussion. In H. Feifel (Ed.), *The meaning of death*. New York: Mc-Graw-Hill.

Neimeyer, R. A. (1988). Death anxiety. In H. Wass, F. M. Berardo, & R. A. Neimeyer (Eds.), *Dying: Facing the facts* (pp. 97–136). New York: Hemisphere Publishing Corporation.

Neimeyer, R. A. (1994). (Ed.). *Death anxiety handbook: Research, instrumentation, and application*. New York: Taylor & Francis.

Neimeyer, R. A. (1997). Death anxiety research: The state of the art. *Omega, 36*, 97–120.

Nelson, L. D., & Nelson, C. C. (1975). A factor analytic inquiry into the multidimensionality of death anxiety. *Omega, 6*, 171–178.

Pyszczynski, T., Greenberg, J., & Solomon, S. (1999). A dual process model of defense against conscious and unconscious death-related thoughts: An extension of terror management theory. *Psychological Review, 106*, 835–845.

Pollack, J. M. (1979). Correlates of death anxiety: A review of empirical studies. *Omega, 10*, 97–121.

Rank, O. (1941). *Beyond psychology*. New York: Dover.

Rosenblatt, A., Greenberg, J., Solomon, S., Pyszczynski, T., & Lyon, D. (1989). Evidence for terror management theory: Part 1. The effects of mortality salience on reactions to those who violate or uphold cultural values. *Journal of Personality and Social Psychology, 57,* 681–690.

Schulz, R. (1978). *The psychology of death, dying, and bereavement.* Reading, MA: Addison-Wesley.

Sheldon, K. M., & Emmons, R. A. (1995). Comparing differentiation and integration within personal goal systems. *Personality and Individual Differences, 18,* 39–46.

Solomon, S., Greenberg, J., & Pyszczynski, T. (1991). A terror management theory of social behavior: The psychological functions of self-esteem and cultural worldviews. In Berkowitz, L. (Ed.), *Advances in experimental social psychology* (Vol. 24, pp. 93–159). New York: Academic Press.

Taubman-Ben-Ari, O., Findler, L., & Mikulincer, M. (2002). The effects of mortality salience on relationship strivings and beliefs—The moderating role of attachment style. *British Journal of Social Psychology, 41,* 419–441.

Templer, D. I. (1970). The construction and validation of a death anxiety scale. *Journal of General Psychology, 82,* 165–174.

Templer, D. I. (1972). Death anxiety in religiously very involved persons. *Psychological Reports, 31,* 361–362.

Tomer, A. (2000). *Death attitudes and the older adult: Theories, concepts, and applications.* New York: Brunner-Routledge.

Ungar, L., Florian, V., & Zernitsky-Shurka, E. (1990). Aspects of fear of personal death, levels of awareness, and professional affiliation among dialysis unit staff members. *Omega, 21,* 51–67.

Weller, A., Florian, V., & Tenenbaum, R. (1988). The concept of death—"masculine" and "feminine" attributes. *Omega, 19,* 253–263.

Zilboorg, G. (1943). Fear of death. *Psychoanalytic Quarterly, 21,* 465–475.

APPENDIX

The Fear of Personal Death scale
Items (all the items are completions of the statement "Death frightens me because_____"):

1. Cessation of creative activities
2. Cessation of all plans and activities
3. Cessation of all spiritual activities
4. Cessation of the ability to think
5. My life will not have been exploited
6. Severance from life itself
7. Missing future events
8. Necessity of realizing life goals
9. Severance of ties with loved ones
10. Loss of life's pleasures
11. Absence will not be felt
12. Events will take place without me
13. I will be forgotten
14. My loss will not hurt close others
15. Burial deep in the earth
16. Life will go on without me
17. Loss of human resemblance
18. Fate of the body
19. My family will still need me
20. Relatives will not overcome sorrow
21. Sorrow to relatives and friends
22. Inability to provide for family
23. Uncertainty of what to expect
24. Uncertainty of existence after death
25. Its mysteriousness
26. Unknown associated with it
27. Decomposition of the body
28. Loss and destruction of the self
29. State of everlasting sleep
30. Destruction of personality
31. Punishment in the hereafter

3

Meaning Management Theory and Death Acceptance

Paul T. P. Wong
Trinity Western University

Imagine yourself on board a train, which is out of control and doomed to end in a fatal crash. Nothing can be done to slow it down or to change the track. Worse still, there is no exit—no one can get out of the train. As a passenger, how would you cope? What would ease your death anxiety? Would denial help? How about illusion? How would you live a vital and meaningful life in spite of the anticipated terror of death? These are the challenging questions confronting all mortals.

Death is the only certainty in life. All living organisms die; there is no exception. However, human beings alone are burdened with the cognitive capacity to be aware of their own inevitable mortality and to fear what may come afterwards. Furthermore, their capacity to reflect on the meaning of life and death creates additional existential anxiety.

There is a tacit understanding that sooner or later, we all have to come to terms with our own mortality. As surely as night follows day, so death awaits us all. The certainty and inevitability of death make its presence felt in every arena of human existence. There is no escape from its shadow, no refuge from its power. How we react to the prospect of personal death would have impact on how we live.

Biologically, death can be defined as the permanent cessation of all vital functions. However, because of the human capacities for meaning-construction and awareness of our own demise, the concept of death becomes very complex and broad—a wide variety of psychological, spiritual, societal, and cultural meanings have been attached to death. The meanings we attached to death have important implications for our well-being. This chapter is about meaning-management—how we manage the meanings of death and life in such a way that our meaning systems not only protect us against the terror of death but also propel us toward the path of accepting the reality of death and living a vital and productive life.

Elisabeth Kübler-Ross (1969) was largely responsible for making death a popular and respectable topic for research. Her five stages of coping with death (denial, anger, bargaining, depression, and acceptance) have had a powerful and lasting impact on our understanding and study of death. Although the sequential stage concept has been widely criticized, she has at least identified some of the defense mechanisms (denial and bargaining) and emotional reactions (anger and depression) involved in facing and accepting the reality of death. This chapter focuses on the meaning-based processes involved in death acceptance. The importance of the role of meaning and death acceptance in dealing with the end-of-life issues has received increasing recognition in recent years (Neimeyer, 2005; Wong, 2000; Wong & Stiller, 1999).

THE DIFFERENT MEANINGS OF DEATH ACCEPTANCE

In the past 40 years, the psychology of death has been dominated by how to measure death anxiety and what factors influence it (Kastenbaum, 2000; Neimeyer, 1994a, 1994b); there was only some recognition of death acceptance in the early literature. Ray and Najman (1974) developed a new scale to measure death acceptance, and found that it was not the opposite of death anxiety. In fact, it was even positively correlated with two measures of death anxiety. Wong and his associates (Gesser, Wong, & Reker, 1987–1988; Wong, Reker, & Gesser, 1994) developed the Death Attitude Profile (DAP), which identifies three distinct types of death acceptance: (a) neutral death acceptance—facing death rationally as an inevitable end of every life; (b) approach acceptance—accepting death as a gateway to a better afterlife, and (c) escape acceptance—choosing death as a better alternative to a painful existence. Evidence is accumulating regarding the validity and reliability of DAP (Gesser et al., 1987–1988) and DAP-R (Wong et al., 1994). Neimeyer, Moser, and Wittkowski (2003) confirm that DAP-R remains the main instrument to assess death acceptance.

Approach acceptance is rooted in transpersonal religious/spiritual beliefs in a desirable afterlife. To those who embrace such beliefs, afterlife is more than symbolic immortality, because there is a spiritual or transcendental reality. More specifically, Harding, Flannelly, Weaver, and Costa (2005) reported that scales that measure Belief in God's Existence and Belief in the Afterlife were both negatively correlated with death anxiety but positively correlated with death acceptance. Escape Acceptance is primarily based on the perception that life is so painful and miserable that it's not worth the trouble of living. Suicide and assisted suicide are expressions of Escape Acceptance. Cicirelli's (2001) observed that when individuals experience intractable pain or loss of function, they want to end their own lives. In such cases, the terror of death seems less fearful than the terror of living.

The construct of neutral acceptance needs closer examination. Clements and Rooda (1999–2000) examined the factor structure, reliability, and validity of DAP-R using a sample of 403 hospital and hospice nurses. They were able to replicate the first four factors reported by Wong et al. (1994): Fear of Death, Death Avoidance, Approach Acceptance, and Escape Acceptance. However, the items which loaded on the Neutral Acceptance subscale were split across two factors. It seems reasonable to suggest that this subscale may not be measuring a unitary construct, because conceptually, Neutral Acceptance encompasses the whole spectrum, from the mere recognition that death is no more than the extinction of a candle, to a most positive variation, such as identifying oneself with culture, completing one's mission in life, and leaving a legacy. In fact, Cicirelli (2001) identified four different Personal Meanings of Death: Extinction, Afterlife, Motivator, and Legacy. Belief in Afterlife is similar to Approach Acceptance; however, Extinction, Motivator, and Legacy can all come under the umbrella of Neutral Acceptance.

THE DIFFERENT MEANINGS OF DEATH FEAR

What are your fears of death? Likely they are rooted in the bases of death anxiety:

1. The finality of death—There is no reversal, no remedy, no more tomorrow. Therefore, death signifies the cessation of all hope with respect to this world.
2. The uncertainty of what follows—Socrates has made the case that, because we really don't know what will happen, we should not fear. But uncertainty coupled with finality can create a potential for terror.
3. Annihilation anxiety or fear of non-existence—The concept of non-being can be very threatening, because it seems to go against a strong and innate conviction that life should not be reduced to non-being.

4. The ultimate loss—When death occurs, we are forced to lose everything we have ever valued. Those with the strongest attachments toward things of this world are likely to fear death most. Loss of control over affairs in the world and loss of the ability to care for dependents also contribute to death anxiety.
5. The disruption of the flow of life—Death can be very disruptive of existing relationships and ongoing projects.
6. Fear of leaving the loved ones behind—The closer the relationships, the greater the fear of separation; this fear is often compounded by future regrets of not being able to care for them any more.
7. Fear of the pain and loneliness in dying—Many are afraid that they will die alone or die in pain, without any family or friends around them.
8. Fear of an untimely and violent death—Sooner or later people learn to accept their own mortality, but most people are afraid of dying prematurely and violently.
9. Fear of failing to complete life work—According to Goodman's (1981) interviews with eminent artists and scientists, many people are more afraid of a meaningless existence than death itself; their fear of death stems from fear of not being able to complete their mission or calling in life.
10. Fear of judgment and retributions—Western religions teach that there is judgment after death, while Eastern religions teach karma or retributions. In either case, individuals may worry about facing the negative consequences of all their bad deeds throughout their lifetime.

Mikulincer and Florian (2006) identify three dimensions of death fear: intrapersonal, interpersonal, and transpersonal death-related concerns. Intrapersonal death fear seems to be primarily concerned with whether one is able to accomplish major life goals and fulfill one's meaning of life. In fact, the Fear of Personal Death scale developed by Florian and Kravetz (1983) reveals two subscales in the intrapersonal domain: Fear of loss of self-fulfillment (e.g., fear that my life has not been properly used) and Fear of self-annihilation (e.g., fear of the decomposition of my body). Thus, living a full life can at least reduce the fear of failure in self-fulfillment. Interpersonal death fear is based on worries about leaving the loved ones, being unable to care for them, or being forgotten by them. Having made ample provisions to take care of one's family members will help reduce interpersonal death fear. Transpersonal death fear is concerned with what happens after death, such as fear of punishment. Thus, efforts in seeking redemption and forgiveness may diminish transpersonal fear.

MANAGING THE MEANINGS OF LIFE AND DEATH

The preceding analysis clearly shows that various meanings of death are intricately and irrevocably related to meanings of life (Mikulincer & Florian, 2006; Wong, 2000). If we have lived a meaningful life and achieved ego-integrity (Erikson, 1982), we are able to face death without fear. However, when we have too many regrets and a profound sense of failure and despair, then death is feared, because of the fear that we have never really lived when death beckons us (Tomer & Eliason, chap. 7, this volume; Wong, 2000).

By accepting our mortality, we declare our intention to invest our energy and time in living the good life rather than defending ourselves against the inevitable death. Ideally, death acceptance should set us free from anxiety and energize us to live with vitality and purpose. By the same token, when we have lived a wonderful life and completed our life's mission, we would be prepared to face death. Ultimately, death acceptance is one of the cornerstones for the good life.

However, we can never be completely free from death anxiety. As we grow older, we brace ourselves for the bad news with every annual physical checkup. With aging parents, we are always prepared for their death and burial. Somehow, the specter of death is always hovering over us, reminding us of our mortality. No matter how we rationalize or think about death, our instinctive reaction is rarely one of unalloyed joy.

The relationships between death acceptance and death fear are complex and dynamic. They may co-exist under some circumstances like a rain cloud in an otherwise blue and sunny sky. Furthermore, for most people different kinds of death attitudes may dominate, depending on their stage of development (Erikson, chap. 7, 1963, 1964, 1982) and life experiences and regrets (Tomer & Eliason, chap. 7, this volume). That is why death acceptance and death anxiety are not simply opposites (Ray & Najman; 1974; Tomer & Eliason, Chap 7, this volume; Wong et al., 1994).

In sum, we are all confronted with two fundamental psychological tasks: to protect ourselves against the terrors of loss and death (e.g., managing death anxiety) and to pursue the good life of living meaningfully and abundantly (e.g., managing death acceptance). These twin tasks of living well and dying well are interconnected in important ways because of the intimate relationships between the meanings of life and the meanings of death. This chapter makes the case that the most promising way to achieve these two major psychological tasks is through managing the meanings of life and death.

MEANING-MANAGEMENT THEORY

What Is Meaning Management?

In the business world, management simply means to manage various resources, such as people, finances, and technology to achieve company goals. Management is needed to ensure that resources are developed and utilized strategically and efficiently in order to achieve short-term and long-term goals. In the business of living, management means how to manage one's internal and external resources to achieve one's life goals. Because we only have one life to live, and life is short, we really need to manage our time investment and choose our life goals wisely. Meaning management refers to managing our life through meaning. More specifically, it refers to the need to manage meaning-related processes, such as meaning-seeking and meaning-making, in order to understand who we are (identity), what really matters (values), where we are headed (purpose), and how to live the good life in spite of suffering and death (happiness).

Therefore, meaning management is to manage our inner life, which is the sum total of all our feelings, desires, perceptions, thoughts, our inner voices and secret yearnings, and all the ebbs and flows of our consciousness. The objective of meaning management is to manage all our fears and hopes, memories and dreams, hates and loves, regrets and celebrations, doubts and beliefs, and the various meanings we attach to events and people, in such a way as to facilitate the discovery of happiness, hope, meaning, fulfillment, and equanimity in the midst of setbacks, sufferings, and deaths.

Meaning management becomes increasingly important, because we live in the midst of ambiguity, uncertainty, and rapid social change, with the unraveling of values and traditions which used to provide reliable guides for living. That is why we need to develop our own inner life, which defines who we are, even when the world is falling apart all around us. At the core of this inner life are our assumptions, beliefs, and values. According to O'Neil and O'Neil (1967):

> By managing ourselves we come to know more completely what we want for ourselves, we come to know our priorities, our needs, our wants far more clearly, and this knowledge inevitably brings a greater sense not only of freedom but of security. The person who knows himself or herself, and manages his or her life, can tolerate a higher level of ambiguity than before, can deal more successfully with anxiety and conflict because he is sure of his own capabilities. (p. 243)

Meaning management capitalizes on the human capacities for awareness, reflection, imagination, symbolization, self-transcendence, creativity, narrative construction, and all sorts of meaning-based processes. However, it does not mean that it ignores behavior or environment. At the behavioral level, we act and react, and we are engaged in a variety of activities. People see us—our expressions, articulations, and behaviors. The outward manifestations are just a small part of what our true being is, the inner life which is hidden from public view. We can act out different roles, but we cannot escape from ourselves— our inner being. That is why what is lived on the inside is more important than what is lived on the outside. We can live the life of a rich man and give the appearance of being a very happy person, but our inner life may be starved, impoverished, and troubled. By the same token, our inner life may be abundant, rich, vibrant and peaceful, even when we live below the poverty line.

Meaning management recognizes the importance of actions, because when our actions and activities are consistent with our core values and meaning-systems, they strengthen and enrich our inner life and at the same time contribute to the overall quality of life. Therefore, meaning management of our inner life involves making sure that our actions service our deepest psychological and spiritual needs. When people are centered in who they are and what they really want in life, they are able to focus their actions on life goals that really matter to them. Meaning-making in daily living is primarily based on purposeful and growth-oriented actions. O'Neil and O'Neil (1967):

> It is the feedback between focusing and centering that gives meaning to our actions. And when our actions have meaning, we feel a sense of security. When the feedback mechanism breaks down, so does meaning, and without meaning, we feel lost and afraid. (p. 150)

Meaning management also recognizes the importance of communication, because language plays a crucial role in how we construe reality and how we interact with each other. According to the theory of coordinated management of meaning (Cronen & Pearce, 1982; Pearce & Cronen, 1980), communication enables us to makes sense of the world and manage social reality. We interpret images and sounds, engage in speech acts, enter into social contracts, and follow cultural patterns through the process of communication. A major aspect of meaning-management has to do with how we manage the communication process in order to facilitate understanding of ourselves, other people, and the social reality.

Different from cognitive reframing, meaning-management is capable of transforming our assumptive world and core values. It also has the motivational function of empowering us to embrace and engage life regardless of physical condition and life circumstances. Furthermore, meaning management is relevant to a wide variety of psychological phenomena and life situations. However, this chapter will only focus on death, specifically death anxiety and grieving. It will show how meaning management can facilitate death acceptance in both personal mortality and bereavement.

What Is Meaning-Management Theory (MMT)?

MMT is rooted in existential-humanistic theory (Wong, 2005a) and constructivist perspectives (Neimeyer, 2001b), but it also incorporates cognitive-behavioral processes. It is a comprehensive psychological theory about how to manage various meaning-related processes to meet our basic needs for survival and happiness. It can be subjected to empirical testing as well as applied to clinical situations. Here are several basic propositions or tenets of MMT:

1. Humans are bio-psychosocial-spiritual beings. The increasing recognition of spirituality as an important area of research reflects the widespread acceptance of this holistic perspective. We are wired for community and transcendence and we cannot be fully human by ignoring the social and spiritual aspects of our being. MMT predicts that all things being equal, the incorporation of spiritual values and beliefs can facilitate and protect against death fear and facilitate death acceptance better than without recognizing the spiritual dimension.

2. Human beings are meaning-seeking and meaning-making creatures, living in a world of shared, socially constructed meanings. They react to perceived meanings rather than actual events, and they actively and constantly engaged in meaning-construction in order to make sense of life. In spite of the often contradictory and fragmented nature of life experience, their capacities for symbolic meanings and story-telling help achieve a sense of unity and coherence. MMT predicts that a sense of meaning and purpose not only offers the best protection against the terrors of life and death, but also contributes the most to healing and well-being as compared to other psychological variables such as internal control and self-efficacy.

3. Humans have two primary motivations: (a) to survive, and (b) to find the meaning and reason for survival. The quest for meaning is necessary, because of our capacity to become aware of our eventual demise and the fear of extinction. Such awareness awakens in us not only the defense mechanisms against the terror of death, but also the quest for meaning and purpose for living in the face of death. Suffering has a similar effect on us. MMT predicts that when the business of mere survival is fraught with struggle and suffering, it will trigger a quest for reasons for living in spite of the pain.

4. Meaning can be found in all situations, including the most hopeless and horrific situations such as Nazi concentration camps. Individuals are capable of growth and transformation in spite of mounting problems, because of their capacity for self-transcendence and their freedom to choose their own destiny. MMT predicts that meaning is essential for maintaining hope and happiness in the face of suffering and death.

5. The motivational tendencies of avoidance and approach may complement each other to maximize positive motivation. For example, fear of failure and the desire to succeed can work together to maximize goal striving to

achieve success. Similarly, the tendency to avoid death and seek a happy life can work together to maximize our motivation to live and die well.

These two complementary tendencies in us represent two different paradigms of research on death and life attitudes. The defensive tendency to avoid pain, suffering, dangers, anxieties, and death serves a protective function. It is the tendency to seek security and self-preservation in a chaotic and dangerous world. It involves various defense mechanisms, both unconscious and conscious ones, to safeguard our psychological and physical integrity. Those who prefer a defensive stance would be very cautious and timid, afraid of making changes or taking risk.

The positive and proactive tendency to create a happy and meaningful life serves a growth-oriented function. The positive individuals would be willing to confront the crisis and create opportunities for personal development. Their tendency is to take on the difficult tasks and risk even death in order to achieve some significant life goals, such as competencies, self-efficacy, creativity, or a higher purpose. When individuals are primarily propelled by an irresistible urge toward self-actualization and fulfillment, then less energy is invested in defensive mechanisms, even though death anxiety may still be present. Therefore, meaning-management theory predicts that if one wants to live a vital and meaningful life, it is better to focus on the positive tendency of personal growth rather than on defensive mechanisms against death fear. MMT also predicts that the best way to reduce death anxiety is to facilitate death acceptance and positive tendencies.

These five basic propositions form the foundation for both research and applications of various meaning-based processes. This chapter will briefly discuss three basic processes and how they can facilitate death acceptance. The literature often uses meaning-seeking, meaning-making and meaning-reconstruction interchangeably (Neimeyer, 2001a, 2004). This chapter differentiates these three processes to facilitate research, communication, and counseling.

Managing Meaning-Seeking

Meaning seeking is probably the most primitive-based process. We are born into a world full of sensory data—a continuous flood of confusing, meaningless information that needs to be processed. In order to survive, we need to at least predict and control some of the significant events. Both Pavlovian conditioning and operant condition teach us the significance of various stimuli. In addition, we also actively engage in attribution processes to discover not only cause-and-effect relationships but also the reasons and purpose for certain events (Wong, 1991; Wong & Weiner, 1981). The existential search for meaning and purpose has not received nearly as much research attention as causal attribution, but it is more important for meaning-seeking in the face of unavoidable suffering and death. In such cases, causal understanding is less helpful than existential understanding. Existential attribution also includes the proverbial search for the silver lining, a process similar to benefit-seeking. Both causal and existential attributional processes enable us to make sense of the world.

We are able to adapt to the ever-changing world through the previously mentioned processes almost without any conscious effort. However, a variety of situations may trigger an urgent quest for meaning; these situations include life transitions, major stressful events, trauma, natural disaster, life-threatening illness, and untimely death of a loved one. Whenever an event shatters our assumptive world or challenges our very identity (Janoff-Bulman, 1989; Janoff-Bulman & Frantz, 1997), meaning-seeking is activated. In some individuals, even becoming aware of death and suffering is sufficient to trigger a persistent quest for meaning as in the case of the Buddha.

MMT differentiates between causal attribution and existential attribution (Wong, 1991), and between situational meaning and ultimate meaning (Wong, 1998). Managing meaning-seeking involves empowering and guiding these different search processes until one is satisfied with the finding. MMT predicts that we can adjust well to the transitions and disruptions to the extent that we are are able to (a) discover attributions and meanings that enhance our sense of hope, or (b) discover some benefits for our sufferings. Therefore, finding meaning and benefits makes it easier for us to accept death and face life with hope.

Frankl (1984) has consistently insisted that meaning is to be discovered rather than created. I suspect that meaning is not something that can be arbitrarily created based on one's ambition and bias, such as Hitler's mad ambition for domination of Europe and the destruction of the Jews. True meaning of life has to be based on some long-lasting time-tested values. Another reason for his position is that one's life is accountable to a Task Master, a Higher Power. Frankl reports that the following three values are the royal roads to discovering meaning.

1. Creative value—What I give to life through making a difference in the world.
2. Experiential value—What I take from life through experiencing the joy and pain of living.

3. Attitudinal value—How I view life—accepting what cannot be changed and taking a defiant attitude toward suffering.

Creative value emphasizes the giving of ourselves or dedicating our lives to something larger than ourselves. Creative value seems similar to the idea of creating meaning through personal projects and I would classify it as an example of meaning-making because it involves active, creative work. However, Frankl considers it a pathway of discovering meaning, because (a) it involves an awareness or realization that one's creative work is meaningful, and (b) it needs to be consistent with some proven cultural values. Experiential value emphasizes the joy of simply receiving what life has to offer, this includes listening to music, taking in the sunset, or enjoying the view from a mountain top. It also includes the joy and peace one experiences in mindful meditation, especially the experience of oneness with the universe at a higher level of consciousness. This pathway to meaning frees us from cognition and thinking and enables us to soak in the beauty of life without the mediation of language.

Attitudinal value is essential in situations of unavoidable and inescapable suffering. The only way to find meaning in such situation is the recognition that one is chosen and given the privilege to suffer with courage, equanimity, and joy. This positive stance in the face of suffering serves as an encouragement to fellow sufferers, a testimony to the defiant human spirit or the all sufficient grace of God. Most people do not realize that attitudinal value is similar to existential coping, which involves two coping strategies, namely, accepting what cannot be changed, and affirming that there is something valuable and meaningful in suffering (Wong, 1993; Wong, Reker, & Peacock, 2005). Frankl's three pathways to meaning are very helpful. They provide insights and guidelines on how to discover meaning when life is full of uncertainty and troubles. Frankl has described many clinical examples illustrating how these three avenues can help people who are overwhelmed by a sense of hopelessness and meaninglessness.

Managing Meaning-Making

Although meaning-seeking emphasizes the processes of questing and finding meaning, meaning-making focuses on the processes of actively construing, constructing, and creating meanings. There are four major avenues for meaning-making: Social construction, storytelling, goal-striving, and personal development. Social construction of meaning through language and culture plays a major part. It involves the socialization and acculturation processes. As cultural beings, we collectively construct patterns of meaning and values to imbue life with coherence and significance. We learn to identify with enduring cultural norms and icons and derive meaning by behaving accordingly. Story-telling encompasses a wide range of narrative devices and processes, such as letter-writing, journaling, life review and reminiscence, and myth making. It involves the ability to weave a story by connecting different fragments, filling in the gaps, and reconciling the contradictions. Story-telling is essential to develop self-identity and holistic self-understanding. All the studies of attribution processes, defense mechanisms, and belief systems only reveal some aspects of us. Only the creative process of story telling is capable of revealing the whole, full-bodied person actively engaged in the dynamic business of living.

Goal-striving involves the pursuit of long-term life goals as well as short-term specific projects. Meaningfulness depends on both the significance and success in goal-striving. I have identified several major coping strategies (Wong, 1993, 1995) and spelled out that persistence and flexibility are important in meaning-making (Wong, 2006). Emmons (1992, 1997) has found that differential orientations in goal striving may have different effects on people's physical and psychological well-being.

Personal development is also fundamental to meaning-making. It typically involves the development of one's worldviews, philosophy of life, values and beliefs systems. Education, religion, culture, and personal and family experiences all contribute to personal development. It is possible that this development may be arrested or facilitated, depending on person-environment interactions. The stage of development we may be in, and who we are profoundly influence how well we cope with the challenges of life and death. All other processes of meaning-seeking and meaning-making are shaped by the lenses we wear.

Wong (1998) has identified seven sources of personal meanings. Further research with samples from other cultures, such as Japan (Takano & Wong, 2004), Korea (Kim, Lee, & Wong, 2005) and China (Lin & Wong, 2006) has shown that these sources appear to be universal. Therefore, managing meaning-making will likely yield positive results, if it is concentrated in any one of the following areas:

1. Achievement and goal striving (agency).
2. Intimacy and family (love).
3. Relationships (community).
4. Self-transcendence (larger cause).
5. Religion (spirituality).
6. Self-acceptance (maturity).
7. Fair treatment (justice and morality).

Managing Meaning-Reconstruction

Meaning-reconstruction occurs whenever one cannot assimilate events that shatter one's assumptive world and question one's cherished life goals. The reconstruction process often involves intense meaning-seeking and meaning-making aimed to restore a sense of order and coherence. The biggest challenge is how to transform very negative events and integrate them with positive events and future planning. The transformative process can be both narrative and personal. Personal transformation entails revamping one's worldviews and core values. Narrative transformation entails re-authoring and re-storying. Other processes involved in meaning-reconstruction include confronting and re-experiencing the past, reviewing and reconstructing the past, collecting relevant information from various sources, re-examining one's assumptions, and exploring alternative assumptions and meanings.

MMT and Death Acceptance

All three processes are intentional, conscious efforts to imbue life and death with meaning, thus facilitating death acceptance. They are often interrelated and interact with each other in the service of finding and creating positive and adaptive meaning for living. There is heuristic value in disentangling these processes and studying them separately.

The main message of MMT is that the best defense is offense. Although recognizing the value of defensive mechanisms, MMT maintains that the most effective way to protect oneself against death anxiety is to focus on how to live a vibrant, meaningful life.

Dennis Yoshikawa, a Shin Buddhist, explained that according to Shin Buddhist teaching, "to solve the problem of death, one must first solve the problem of life, living life. If one is able to do that, to live a truly human life, then there's nothing to be feared by the experience of death, because the experience of death is a natural part of life" (Palmer, 1993, p. 279).

Awareness of personal death may actually energize rather than paralyze individuals. According to Konosuke Matsushita, "What we should fear is not so much death itself as being unprepared for the eventuality…. To be prepared for death is to be prepared for living; to die well is to live well" (as cited by Yamaguchi, 1994). Matsushita also believes that one has to find out the mission God has given to fulfill in this world. Archbishop Desmond Tutu, winner of the 1984 Nobel Prize for his role in the antiapartheid movement in South Africa, said, "When you have a potentially terminal disease, it concentrates the mind wonderfully. It gives a new intensity to life. You discover how many things you have taken for granted—the love of your spouse, the Beethoven symphony, the dew on the rose, the laughter on the face of your grandchild" (as cited by Kuhl, 2002, pp. 17–18).

Living and Dying Well Through Meaning Management

MMT provides a conceptual framework and guidelines on how to facilitate death acceptance and meaningful living as an indirect but effective way to combat death anxiety. Meaning management helps deepen our faith and spirituality. It also enables us to achieve a better understanding of the meaning and purpose of life. More importantly, it motivates us to embrace life—to engage in the business of living, regardless of our physical condition and present circumstances.

From the perspective of MMT, we can either face death with fear or with hope, and we can either be concerned with death or with life. The choice is entirely ours. We need to ask, what matters most? What is worth living and dying for? Life is too short and too valuable to waste on things that don't really matter.

"Do I embrace life, or do I prepare to die? And for all of us, the answers are ultimately similar. Living fully and dying well involve enhancing one's sense of self, one's relationships with others, and one's understanding of the transcendent, the spiritual, the supernatural. And only in confronting the inevitability of death does one truly embrace life" (Kuhl, 2002, p. 291). MMT suggests that we should view death as our master teacher rather than monster terror. By accepting death and understanding its full meaning, we acquire wisdom. By accepting death through faith, we find courage and an undying hope.

In his presentation on Claire Philip's journal and poems in her dying days, Thomas Cole (1994) concluded with this powerful statement:

> Her journal and poetry showed me that it is possible to live out the paradox contained in the old proverb: "Live every day as if you will be able to do good for a hundred years and live every day as if it were your last." In reading Claire Phillip, I met a friend whose courageous growth will reassure me in times of doubt that the human spirit can continue to evolve until the very end of life.

Meaning-Management Theory Versus Terror-Management Theory

At present, terror-management theory (TMT; Greenberg , Pyszczynski, & Solomon, 1986; Pyszczynski, Greenberg, & Solomon, 2002; Solomon,

Greenberg, & Pyszczynski, 1991;) remains the most dominant theoretical account on how we cope with the terror of death. Simply put, TMT posits that humans have an inclination for self-preservation, and their capacity for self-awareness makes them terrified of their own mortality. Therefore, humans defend their sense of significance against death anxiety through the defensive mechanisms of participating in cultural worldviews and deriving their sense of self-esteem from these worldviews.

Terror-Management Theory of Death Anxiety. Greenberg, Arndt, Simon, Pyszcznski, and Solomon (2000) showed that people engaged in denial of their vulnerability to death (proximal defenses) in order to block out the terror of death, when their mortality was made salient and death-related thoughts were in their immediate conscious aware-ness. However, they engage in affirming their cultural worldview and self-esteem (distal defenses) when mortality was made salient but death-relevant thoughts were not in immediate conscious awareness. The mechanism of cultural defense manifests itself in cognitive and behavioral efforts to defend or validate one's cultural worldview. The mechanism of self-esteem manifests itself in cognitive and behavioral efforts to bolster self-esteem according to the standards prescribed by one's culture.

There is plenty of empirical support of the cultural defense hypoth-esis. However, the results supporting the self-esteem hypothesis remain equivocal and subject to alternative interpretations (Crocker & Nuer, 2004; Greenberg, Koole, & Pysczynski, 2004; Ryan & Deci, 2004). Overall, TMT is a powerful theory and difficult to refute logically or empirically. Elsewhere, I have expressed some of my reservations about TMT (Wong, 2005b). In this chapter, I want to emphasize that in spite of believability and truthfulness of TMT, it cannot be the whole story about how humans cope with the reality of death. For example, we already know that some people may have already developed the attitudes of death acceptance (Wong et al., 1994). In the case of "escape acceptance," where death is more desirable to living hell, death salience manipulation would increase suicide ideation rather than cul-tural defense or pursuit of self-esteem. In the case of "approach accep-tance," death salience would not result in defensive cognitive and behavioral efforts, if one feels that one has lived a meaningful life and is ready to meet the Master in Heaven. Finally, when one adopts "neu-tral acceptance," death salience manipulation would only serve an energizing function; in other words, those who believe that death is only a natural part of the life cycle, and life is meant to be lived fully— to fulfill one's potential and complete one's mission.

One of the problems with TMT is that when mortality salience energizes one to pursue whatever dreams one has, it would be interpreted as an unconscious defensive mechanism rather than an intrinsically motivated conscious choice to accomplish one's major life goals. Crocker and Nuer (2004) have expressed a similar concern and pointed out that the studies cited as supporting TMT cannot unequivocally prove that the main reason for activating the self-esteem system is a defense mechanism against death anxiety. They suggest that a different paradigm is needed to emphasize the human capacity and motivation to seek meaning and purpose in order to enhance their well-being. In this paradigm, reminder of death would not be a source of terror that calls for defense mechanisms but a source of inspiration that energizes people. Similarly, Ryan and Deci (2004) also question whether the pursuit of self-esteem in the face of death salience is an evidence of avoiding death or engaging life. Ryan and Deci argue that people's search for self-esteem and personal significance cannot be simply reduced to defensive mechanisms. They offer an alternative but complementary perspective based on their self-determination theory (STD). According to STD, such pursuit of self-esteem may reflect an authentic kind of psychological needs for competence, significance, meaning and intrinsic satisfaction.

MMT as a Complementary and Comprehensive Theory

MMT represents this alternative but complementary paradigm. Although recognizing the validity of TMT, in contrast MMT emphasizes for some people the motivation to live a meaningful and happy life is more dominant than the motivation to avoid the terror of death. "Since we only go through this life once, we have reasons to make the most of it. The worse fear is not death, but the discovery that we have never really lived when the time comes for us to die. We all have the urge, the desire to live fully, to do something significant, to make a difference, so that we don't have to dread the death-bed realization that we have squandered away our precious life" (Wong, 2005c).

Frankl (1984) emphasizes the quest for meaning is the universal, primary motive, which not only makes humans different from other animals, but also enables humans to survive unimaginable horrors with dignity. Many studies support the imperative of the quest for meaning (Batthyany & Guttman, 2006; Wong & Fry, 1998). According to MMT, meaning offers the best protection against the terror of death not only through unconscious defense mechanisms as proposed by TMT, but also through conscious transformation of the negatives about death into positive thoughts. For example, people may view death as a passage to a better afterlife or an appropriate conclusion and celebration of a life well lived. More importantly, MMT focuses on the human tendency toward leading happy, significant, and productive life.

In his research on creative people, Goodman (1981) discovered that they feared an incomplete and meaningless life more than death itself. He also reported that defensive mechanisms are not really very effective in protecting us against death anxiety: "The existential fear of death, the fear of not existing, is the hardest to conquer. Most defensive structures, such as the denial of reality, rationalization, insulation erected to ward off religiously conditioned separation-abandonment fears, do not lend themselves readily as protective barriers against the existential fear of death" (p. 5). Therefore, those interviewed by him preferred the alternative approach of focusing on living a significant and fulfilling life.

Another source of support for MMT is research on near death experiences (NDEs). I cannot think of any mortality salience exposure as compelling as NDE. Yet, there is no evidence of denial or defense mechanisms against death anxiety. In fact, many who report NDEs typically show a major positive transformation to what they call "a more loving life." NDEs tend to increase individuals' sense of purpose in life, appreciation of life, interest in spirtualtiy and empathy, coupled with a decrease in death anxiety (Greyson, 2003; van Lommel, van Wees, Meyers, & Elfferich, 2001). Many who experienced NDE felt that they have found evidence of an afterlife (Kelly, 2001).

FROM DEATH ANXIETY TO DEATH ACCEPTANCE AND SELF-ACTUALIZATION

When people are exposed to mortality salience, both TMT and MMT predict an increase in pro-culture and pro-esteem activities, but for very different reasons. The former is for minimizing terror of death, but for the latter, it is for maximizing death acceptance and self-actualization. The main difference is between a fear-based defensive posture toward life and a meaning-based positive posture. This difference can have real consequences in how people live their lives and make critical choices.

We need defensive responses to protect our ego against anxieties, uncertainties, and threats, but we also need the authentic, creative responses to pursue our dreams and what life has to offer. *Life cannot be lived in the defensive mode; it needs to be lived in the proactive creative mode.* Martin, Campbell, and Henry (2004) point out the paradox that in order to live authentically, we need to confront what we try to avoid—death, uncertainty, and anxiety. This is a conscious choice to create meaning in the face of death. Paradoxically, we need to choose to embrace the unknown, the uncertainty and the threats in order to feel really alive; we need to embrace death in order to live meaningfully and fully (Frankl, 1984; Wong, 2005a, 2005b, 2005c; Yalom, 1980). In terms of motivations, the defensive mode is mostly related to anxiety and despair, while the creative mode is mostly related to positive emotions such as optimism and life satisfaction.

According to Morrant and Catlett (chap. 14, this volume), Robert Firestone sees the basic human conflict as between self-affirming and defensive aspects of personality. The core conflict is between avoiding painful existential givens and embracing life without denying death. Firestone (1997) considers defenses as maladaptive as they may lead to self-denial, self-accusation, substance abuse, bodily harm, and even suicide. He challenges people to make each day count by pursuing goals that transcend self-interests and infusing life with spirituality and compassion. "We must mourn our own end to fully accept and value our lives" (Firestone, 1997, p. 298).

Self-actualization becomes dominant when one comes to value it more than self-preservation. Thus, life without love is not worth living; life without freedom is not worth living; and one can fill in the blanks for many similar statements. For these self-actualizers, their greatest fear is not death, but not being able to do what is dearest to their hearts. When self-actualization focuses on something larger than oneself, one reaches the state of self-transcendence. This "something larger" may be religion, ideology, community, or a social cause. A truly transcendental view of life lifts the person above self-centered concerns about self-preservation or self-esteem, because self is spent or lost in something larger and more long-lasting than oneself. For example, the psalmist prays: "The Lord will fulfill his purpose for me; your love, O Lord, endures forever—do not abandon the works of your hands" (Psalm 138:8, NIV). A sense of purpose and calling imbues the psalmist's life with meaning, but here the responsibility for success no longer rests entirely with the individual. There is a strong sense of partnership between God and the psalmist. To live or die is to fulfill God's purpose in his life.

From the perspective of MMT, we do not need to over-rate the terror of death, nor do we need to deny its existence. MMT recognizes that death anxiety can have a negative or positive effect, depending on how to react to it. To invest a lifetime to defend ourselves against death anxiety can be very costly, because the defensive modes of denial and self-preservation may deprive us of many opportunities to expand ourselves and to live exciting, fulfilling lives. However, if we view death simply as a reminder of our own mortality and the need to live authentically, death anxiety will not only facilitate death acceptance, but also encourage self-actualization and self-transcendence.

Life and death are two sides of the same coin. There is no life without death and there is no death without life. Traditional existentialism focuses on how people make sense of life in the shadow of death (Tomer & Eliason, this volume). According to this view, people consciously and unconsciously defend themselves against the terror of death. Their defense mechanisms include denial, avoidance, cultural defense, and self-esteem. In contrast, positive existential psychology as initiated by Frankl and expanded by Wong (2005a, 2005b) focuses on the potential of fulfilling life's meaning. For those with a growth orientation, they are so preoccupied with the business of living a purposeful, authentic and vibrant life that death is no longer a major concern. Mortality salience would trigger defensive mechanisms in death-oriented individuals, but has little effect on individuals who are already totally engrossed with pursuing what really matters in life. I would also predict that longevity salience (e.g., extending life indefinitely) would reduce defensive mechanisms in death-oriented individuals, but may increase the quest for meaning in life-oriented individuals, because it becomes a bigger challenge to sustain meaning and passion for living for all eternity.

CONCLUSION

In sum, MMT represents a new development in positive existential psychology and existential psychotherapy (Wong, 2005a, 2005b). It provides a more positive and hopeful perspective than TMT, and can be very useful in working with people struggling with end-of-life issues. Jane Thibault (2000) recommends that the practitioner's task is to help the patient find or create meaning in the last stage of life, however long that may be. For example, individuals diagnosed as terminal cancer patients do not need to spend their remaining days waiting for death. Ten years ago, my own older brother was told that he had only three months to live, but he is still very much alive, still dreaming about getting some money to get married. He may be suffering from illusion or delusion, but he is still pursuing his dreams that are meaningful to him. Meaning-centered counseling (Wong, 1997, 1998, 1999, 2000, 2002), which is based on MMT, provides many helpful skills and strategies to facilitate meaning-seeking, meaning-making, and meaning-reconstruction. We can never escape from the reality of death, but we can always use our capacity for meaning and narrative construction to transform death anxiety into a source of inspiration for authentic living.

MAIN POINTS

1. Human reactions to death are complex, multifaceted, and dynamic. The Death Attitudes Profile, as developed by Wong and his associates, contributes to death studies and thanatos psychology by recognizing three types of death acceptance in addition to death fear and death avoidance. This chapter focuses on death acceptance as it is related to the meanings of life and death.
2. This chapter introduces the concept of meaning management and describes the scope of meaning-management theory.
3. This chapter compares and contrasts terror-management theory with meaning-management theory. It highlights the differences between the defensive and proactive ways of coping with death anxiety.
4. Finally, this chapter points out the usefulness of meaning-management theory not only in transforming death anxiety but also in facilitating death acceptance and self-actualization.

REFERENCES

Batthyany, A., & Guttman, D. (2006). *Empirical research on logotherapy and meaning-oriented psychotherapy: An annotated bibliography.* Phoenix, AZ: Zeig, Tucker & Theisen.

Cicirelli, V. G. (2001). Personal meanings of death in older adults and young adults in relation to their fears of death. *Death Studies, 25*(8), 663–683.

Clements, R., & Rooda, L. A. (1999–2000). Factor structure, reliability, and validity of the death attitude profile-revised. *The Journal of Death and Dying, 40*(3), 453–463.

Cole, T. R. (1994, November 19). *Gaining and losing a friend I never knew: Reading Claire Philip's journal and poetry.* Presented at the symposium on "Personal Narrative in the face of death: Claire Philip's journal and poem" at the Gerontological Society Meeting, Atlanta, November 19.

Crocker, J., & Nuer, N. (2004). Do people need self-esteem? Comments on Pyszczynsk, et al. (2004). *Psychological Bulletin, 130*(3). Washington, DC: American Psychological Association.

Cronen, V., & Pearce, W. B. (1982). The coordinated management of meaning: A theory of communication. In F. E. X. Dance (Ed.), *Human communication theory* (pp. 61–89). New York: Harper & Row.

Emmons, R. A. (1992). Abstract versus concrete goals: Personal striving level, physical illness, and psychological well-being. *Journal of Personality and Social Psychology, 62,* 292–300.

Emmons, R. A. (1997). Motives and goals. In R. Hogan, J. Johnson, & S. Briggs (Eds.), *Handbook of personality psychology* (pp. 485–512). New York: Academic Press.

Erikson, E. H. (1963). *Childhood and society* (2nd ed.). New York: W. W. Norton.

Erikson, E. H. (1964). *Insight and responsibility.* New York: W. W. Norton.

Erikson, E. H. (1982). *The life cycle completed.* New York: W. W. Norton.

Firestone, R. W. (1997a). *Combating destructive thought processes: Voice therapy and separation theory.* Thousand Oaks, CA: Sage Publications.

Florian, V., & Kravetz, S. (1983). Fear of personal death: Attribution, structure, and relation to religious belief. *Journal of Personality and Social Psychology, 44,* 600–607.

Frankl, V. (1984). *Man's search for meaning: An introduction to Logotherapy.* Riverside, NJ: Simon and Schuster Adult Publishing Group.

Gesser, G., Wong, P. T. P., & Reker, G. T. (1987–1988). Death attitudes across the life-span: The development and validation of the Death Attitude Profile (DAP). *Omega, 18*, 113–128.

Goodman, L. M. (1981). *Death and the creative life: Conversations with eminent artists and scientists as they reflect on life and death.* New York: Springer Publishing Company.

Greenberg, J., Arndt, J., Simon, L., Pyszczynski, T., & Solomon, S. (2000). Proximal and distal defenses in response to reminders of one's mortality: Evidence of a temporal sequence. *Personality Social Psychological Bulletin, 26*, 91–99.

Greenberg, J., Pyszczynski, T., & Solomon, S. (1986). The causes and consequences of the need for self-esteem: A terror management theory. In R. F. Baumeister (Ed.), *Public and private self* (pp. 189–212). New York: Springer-Verlag.

Greenberg, J., Koole, S. L., & Pyszczynski, T. (Eds.). (2004). *Handbook of experimental existential psychology.* New York: Guilford Press.

Greyson, B. (2003). Near-death experiences in a Psychiatric Outpatient Clinic population. *Psychiatric Services, December, 54*(12).

Harding, S. R., Flannelly, K. J., Weaver, A. J., & Costa, K. G. (2005). The influence of religion on death anxiety and death acceptance. *Mental Health, Religion & Culture, 2005, 8*, 253–261.

Janoff-Bulman, R. (1989). Assumptive worlds and the stress of traumatic events. *Social Cognition, 7*, 113–116.

Janoff-Bulman, R., & Frantz, C. M. (1997). The impact of trauma on meaning: From meaningless world to meaningful life. In M. Power & C. R. Brewin (Eds.), *The transformation of meaning in psychological therapies* (pp. 91–106). New York: Wiley.

Kastenbaum, R. (2000). *The psychology of death* (3rd ed.). New York: Springer.

Kelly, E. W. (2001). Near-death experiences with reports of meeting deceased people. *Death Studies, Apr-May, 25*(3), 229–249 .

Kim, M., Lee, H-S., & Wong, P. T. P. (2005, August). *Meaning of life according to Koreans: The Korean personal meaning profile.* Poster presented at the Annual Convention of the American Psychological Association, Washington, DC.

Kübler-Ross, E. (1969). *On death and dying.* New York: Macmillan.

Kuhl, D. (2002). *What dying people want: Practical wisdom for the end of life.* Toronto: Doubleday Canada.

Lin, A., & Wong, P. T. P. (2006, August). *The meaning of life: According to a Chinese sample.* Paper presented at the Annual Convention of American Psychological Association, New Orleans, August 2006.

Martin, L. L., Campbell, W. K., & Henry, C. D. (2004). The roar of awakening: Mortality acknowledgment as a call to authentic living. In J. Greenberg, S. L. Koole, & T. Pyszczynski (Eds.), *Handbook of experimental existential psychology* (pp. 431–448). New York: The Guilford Press.

Mikulincher, M., & Florian, V. (in press). The complex and multifaceted nature of the fear of personal death: The multidimensional model of Victor Florian. In A. Tomer, P. T. P. Wong, & E. Grafton (Eds.). *Death attitudes: Existential & spiritual issues.* Mahwah, NJ: Lawrence Erlbaum Associates.

Neimeyer, R. A. (Ed.). (1994a). *Death anxiety handbook: Research, instrumentation, and application.* New York: Taylor & Francis.

Neimeyer, R. A. (1994b). The threat index and related methods. In R. A. Neimeyer (Ed.), *Death anxiety handbook* (pp. 61–101). New York: Taylor & Francis.

Neimeyer, R. A. (2001a). The language of loss. In R. A. Neimeyer (Ed.), *Meaning reconstruction and the experience of loss.* Washington, DC: American Psychological Association.

Neimeyer, R. A. (2001b). *Lessons of loss: A guide to coping.* Philadelphia & London: Brunner Routledge.

Neimeyer, R. A. (2004). Personal construction, theory, and practice. *Constructions of death and loss: Evolution of a research program, 1.* Retrieved November 1, 2006, from http://www.pcp-net.org/journal/pctp04/neimeyer04.html.

Neimeyer, R. A. (2005). From death anxiety to meaning making at the end of life: Recommendations for psychological. *Clinical Psychology: Science and Practice, 12*(3), 354–357.

Neimeyer, R. A., Moser, R., & Wittkowski, J. (2003). Assessing attitudes toward death: Psychometric considerations. *Omega, 47*, 45–76.

O'Neil, N., & O'Neil, G. (1967). *Shifting gears: Finding security in a changing world.* New York: McGraw-Hill.

Palmer, G. (1993). *Death: The trip of a lifetime.* San Francisco, CA: Harper San Francisco.

Pearce, W. B., & Cronen, V. (1980). *Communication, action, and meaning: The creation of social realities.* New York: Praeger.

Pyszczynski, T., Greenberg, J., & Solomon, S. (2002). *In the wake of 9/11: The psychology of terror.* Washington, DC: American Psychological Association.

Ray, J. J., & Najman, J. (1974). Death anxiety and death acceptance: A preliminary approach. *Omega, 5*(4), pp. 311–315.

Ryan, R. M., & Deci, E. L. (2004). Avoiding death or engaging life as accounts of meaning and culture: Comment on Pyszczynski et al. (2004). *Psychological Bulletin, 130*(3), 473–477. Washington, DC: American Psychological Association.

Solomon, S., Greenberg, J., & Pyszczynski, T. A. (1991). Terror management theory of social behavior: The psychological functions of self-esteem and cultural worldviews. In M. E. P. Zanna (Ed.), *Advances in experimental social psychology, 24*, 93–159. San Diego, CA: Academic Press.

Takano, Y., & Wong, P. T. P. (2004, July/August). *Meaning of life according to a Japanese sample.* Paper presented at the Annual Convention of the American Psychological Association, Honolulu, Hawaii.

Thibault, J. (2000, November/December). How can health care professionals meet the spiritual needs of dying older patients? *Geriatric Times, (10), Vol. 1, Issue 4. Retrieved January 25, 2007, from* www.genatrictimes.com/goo1227.htm.

van Lommel, P., van Wees, R., Meyers, V., & Elfferich, I. (2001, December 15). Near-death Experience in survivors of cardiac arrest: A prospective study in the Netherlands. *Lancet, 358*(9298), 2039–2045.

Wong, P. T. P. (1991). Existential vs. causal attributions. In S. Zelen (Ed.), *Extensions and new models of attribution theory* (pp. 84–125). New York: Springer-Verlag Publishers.

Wong, P. T. P. (1993). Effective management of life stress: The resource-congruence model. *Stress Medicine, 9*, 51–60.

Wong, P. T. P. (1995). Coping with frustrative stress: A behavioral and cognitive analysis. In R. Wong (Ed.), *Biological perspective on motivated and cognitive activities.* (pp. 339–378). New York: Ablex Publishing.

Wong, P. T. P. (1997). Meaning-centered counseling: A cognitive-behavioral approach to logotherapy. *The International Forum for Logotherapy, 20*, 85–94.

Wong, P. T. P. (1998). Meaning-centered counseling. In P. T. P. Wong & P. S. Fry (Eds.), *The human quest for meaning: A handbook of psychological research and clinical applications* (pp. 395–435). Mahwah, NJ: Lawrence Erlbaum Associates.

Wong, P. T. P. (1999). Towards an integrative model of meaning-centered counselling and therapy. *The International Forum for Logotherapy, 22*, 47–55.

Wong, P. T. P. (2000). Meaning in life and meaning in death in successful aging. In A. Tomer (Ed.), *Death attitudes and the older adults: Theories, concepts and applications* (pp. 23–35). Philadelphia, PA: Bruner-Routledge.

Wong, P. T. P. (2002). Logotherapy. In G. Zimmer (Ed.) *Encyclopedia of Psychotherapy psychotherapy* (pp. 107–113). New York: Academic Press.

Wong, P. T. P. (2005a). Existential and humanistic theories. In J.C. Thomas & D. L. Segal (Eds.), *Comprehensive handbook of personality and psychopathology*. Hoboken, NJ: Wiley.

Wong, P. T. P. (2005b). The challenges of experimental existential psychology: Terror management or meaning management. A book review of *Handbook of experimental existential psychology. PsycCritiques (Contemporary Psychology: APA Review of Books)*. Available online at http://www.psycinfo.com/psyccritiques.

Wong, P. T. P. (2005c). *A course on the meaning of life. Part.1*. Retrieved January 25, 2007, from http://www.meaning.ca/articles05/mol/course-mol-12sept05.htm

Wong, P. T. P. (2006). *The positive psychology of persistence and flexibility*. Retrieved January 25, 2007, from http://www.meaning.ca/articles06/president/persistenceandflexibility feb06.htm

Wong, P. T. P., & Fry, P. S. (Eds.) (1998). *The human quest for meaning: A handbook of psychological research and clinical applications*. Mahwah, NJ: Lawrence Erlbaum Associates.

Wong, P. T. P., Reker, G. T., & Gesser, G. (1994). Death Attitude Profile–Revised: A multidimensional measure of attitudes toward death. In R. A. Neimeyer (Ed.), *Death anxiety handbook: Research instrumentation and application* (pp. 121–148). Washington, DC: Taylor and Francis.

Wong, P. T. P., Reker, G. T., & Peacock, E. J. (2005). A resource-congruence model of coping and the development of the coping schema inventory. In P. T. P. Wong & L. C. J. Wong (Eds.), *Handbook of multicultural perspectives on stress and coping* (pp. 223–283). New York: Springer

Wong, P. T., & Stiller, C. (1999). Living with dignity and palliative care. In B. de Vries (Ed.), *End of life issues: Interdisciplinary and multidimensional perspectives* (pp. 77–94). New York: Springer.

Wong, P. T. P., & Weiner, B. (1981). When people ask "Why" questions and the heuristic of attributional search. *Journal of Personality and Social Psychology, 40*, 650–663.

Yalom, I. D. (1980). *Existential psychotherapy*. New York: Basic Books.

Yamaguchi, T. (1994, December). Fear of dying. *Intersect*, p. 48.

II

Research

A Terror Management Perspective on Spirituality and the Problem of the Body

Joshua Hart
Lawrence University

Jamie L. Goldenberg
University of South Florida

Man has a symbolic identity that brings him sharply out of nature... Yet, at the same time, as the eastern sages also knew, man is a worm and food for worms. This is the paradox.

—*Becker, 1973 (p. 26)*

Cogito, ergo sum.

—*Descartes*

Descartes was not the first human being to recognize the apparent distinction between the body and its immaterial counterpart, the mind, but he made the point most famously, articulating an important and intuitive aspect of human existence. Although a solution to the mind/body problem has eluded scientists and philosophers alike, and modern neuropsychologists consensually defend the sober notion that the mind is reducible to cerebral (and thus biological) activity—the fact remains that the distinction between mind and body is phenomenologically and psychologically undeniable. We do not experience our thoughts as synonymous with the activity of our bodies, but strongly feel as if there is something, some aspect of our self, that extends beyond our physical bodies. Indeed, the phenomenology of mind/body distinctiveness is so basic and powerful that it led to Descartes' famous assertion that the existence of mind is the one thing a sentient being can know beyond any doubt—if anything, it is the material world that might be illusory.

Here we have a great irony: the faculty of consciousness is the source of an existential problem because it engenders awareness of one's mortality, which could potentially lead to debilitating anxiety. However, in consciousness there is also a solution to the existential problem, because the phenomenology of consciousness lends itself quite easily to the creation of spiritual worldviews in which mind or spirit is viewed as supreme and eternal, and the body is of lesser importance and mortal. Therefore, humans can create elaborate meaning-systems involving invisible, infinite realms in which the mind, soul, or spirit can enjoy unfettered immortality while roundly denying the significance of creaturely existence. Our bodies are confined by mortality, but our minds are seemingly limitless.

Following Descartes' original treatise and more contemporary existential thought (e.g., Fromm, 1955; Kierkegaard, 1849; and Rank, 1930), Ernest Becker (1973) articulated this paradox of existence:

> Man has a symbolic identity that brings him sharply out of nature. He is a symbolic self, a creature with a name, a life, a history. He is a creator with a mind that soars out to speculate about atoms and infinity, who can place himself imaginatively at a point in space and contemplate bemusedly his own planet. This immense expansion, this dexterity, this ethereality, this self-consciousness gives to man literally the status of a small god in nature, as the renaissance thinkers knew (p. 26).

But humans know that they are not gods, the body reminds them of that. Gods can accomplish great feats of creation and destruction on a scale that humans can imagine, but hardly aspire to. And most importantly, gods do not die. Becker continues:

> Yet, at the same time, as the eastern sages also knew, man is a worm and food for worms. This is the paradox: he is out of nature and hopelessly in it; he is dual, up in the stars and yet housed in a heart-pumping, breath-gasping body that once belonged to a fish and still carries the gill-marks to prove it. His body is a material fleshy casing that is alien to him in many ways— the strangest and most repugnant way being that it aches and bleeds and will decay and die (p. 26).

In this chapter, we introduce terror management theory (TMT; see Pyszczynski, Greenberg, & Solomon, 1997, for a review), an empirically oriented framework based on Becker's ideas, as a fruitful source of hypotheses related to the fear of death, discomfort with the body, and the use of spirituality as a defense against mortality concerns. We will review recent empirical evidence demonstrating that the body can serve as an existential threat and that spirituality can provide a psychological buffer against mortality concerns. We then discuss how this dual framework is applicable to the most influential religious meaning-systems that humans have constructed in the recorded past and continue to cultivate and follow. Finally, we discuss the viability of the dual solution to mortality concerns. We highlight some destructive consequences arising from the denial of the natural body and defense of one's spiritual beliefs, and we speculate about more benign approaches to spirituality.

We hope that from this analysis, a picture will emerge of the human condition as inspired toward flights of spiritual imagination in an essential reaction to our ultimate creaturely finitude. In this view, spirituality is an inevitable solution to the paradox of conscious mortal existence—inevitable because human consciousness is phenomenologically dualistic, a mind in a body; a solution because the experience of dualism can allow us to deny the fate of our physical bodies by capitalizing on our ability to think of ourselves and our universe in symbolic, meaningful terms.

TERROR MANAGEMENT THEORY

Terror management theory was developed by Jeff Greenberg, Tom Pyszczynski, and Sheldon Solomon (e.g., Greenberg, Pyszczynski, & Solomon, 1986; Solomon, Greenberg, & Pyszczynski, 1991) to provide an empirical framework for the ideas of the late anthropologist Ernest Becker (e.g., 1971, 1973). In line with the insights of other existential thinkers, Becker articulated what he considered to be the fundamental problem inherent in human corporeal existence: the body dies, and we know it. Becker suggested that for an animal that wants most of all to survive, the awareness of death is a serious affront to a tenuous psychological equilibrium that must be maintained for effective functioning. No organism with a functional survival instinct could be expected to bear the knowledge of its own mortality in a world fraught with hazards, and simultaneously carry on with the ordinary tasks of life. And yet, how is it possible to deny or make light of the inevitable cessation of being that so obviously happens to every plant and animal that lives? Because death is inescapable, Becker proposed that the problem of mortality must be dealt with psychologically, rather than directly.

Becker posited that initially, young children instinctively cope with their anxieties by forming attachments to older, wiser, more capable parents and caregivers (although Becker did not refer specifically to attachment theory, John Bowlby's work, 1969, 1973, 1980, dovetails nicely with Becker's), whose support and protection help children to feel secure. Naturally, socialization processes ensue from child/caregiver relations, which results in a sense of self-worth and lovability when one engages in parent-approved behavior, or in feelings of doubt and anxiety when one misbehaves. Thus, self-esteem is initially built up as a reflection of attachment dynamics, and the resulting learned associations are such that positive feelings about the self can provide similar comfort and security as active praise, love, or protection from a caregiver.

Eventually, as children become aware of their own mortality and their parents' limited ability to protect them, self-esteem becomes a very important defense against existential anxieties. But like secure attachment, a general sense of self-worth is not sufficient to provide full protection against the psychological threat that death imposes. Therefore, at the same time that the standards and values by which one can attain high self-esteem becomes more culturally (as opposed to parentally) derived, meaning (belief) systems, including societal norms, and personalized views of the universe and humans' role therein become the bases for self-esteem. More importantly, these worldviews confront the problem of death in a more sweeping and self-transcendent (and thus more durable) way. Spirituality has historically been a crucial example of an equanimity-providing worldview, in that it provides a meaningful framework with which to understand existence, as well as explicit guidelines of personal behavior that can qualify a person for immortality-either literally (as in an afterlife) or symbolically (e.g., living on through accomplishments and contributions to society). In sum, Becker thought that humans are able to face the psychological problem of death by creating satisfying systems of meaning that allow one to feel significant.

Terror management theory has given methodological expression to Becker's theory by empirically demonstrating that people symbolically defuse the threat of mortality by clinging to their cultural worldviews and striving to attain cultural standards of value. To test this hypothesis, terror management researchers usually begin by subtly reminding people of their own death (*mortality salience*) and then measuring how people react. Mortality salience has been operationalized with a number of experimental procedures. One of the most common includes having participants respond to two open-ended questions about the feelings associated with one's own death and what they think will happen after they physically die. This priming is followed by a delay and distraction task (e.g., completing a neutral word puzzle) so that thoughts of death are no longer in focal awareness at the time of the collection of the dependent measure (research has shown that these symbolic defenses against mortality concerns operate when thoughts of death are unconscious, see Pyszczynski, Greenberg, & Solomon, 1999). Alternatively, unconscious mortality concerns have been made salient with subliminal death primes (e.g., Arndt, Greenberg, Pyszczynski, & Solomon, 1997), and also with more naturalistic primes, such as walking by a funeral parlor (Pyszczynski et al., 1996). Research has also demonstrated that the effects of mortality salience are specific to thoughts of one's death. Thoughts of dental pain, public speaking, paralysis, meaninglessness, failing an exam, worry about the future, social exclusion, or death of a loved one do not elicit the same defensive response produced by mortality salience (e.g., Goldenberg & Hart, 2004; Greenberg, Simon, Harmon-Jones, et al., 1995).

It follows that if meaning and value serve as anxiety buffers against mortality concerns, then when mortality is salient, people should cling to their cultural worldviews and strive to maintain self-esteem. Accordingly, over 200 experiments conducted in a dozen different countries demonstrate support for this hypothesis (see Greenberg, Solomon, & Pyszczynski, 1997, or Pyszczynski, Solomon, & Greenberg, 2003, for a review). One of the most common findings is that people respond to mortality salience by clinging more rigidly to their own cultural worldviews, which has often been operationalized by how much people like others who support their beliefs and how much they dislike those who threaten their beliefs (e.g., Greenberg et al., 1990). People have also been found to exhibit more discomfort when they personally violate a cultural norm (Greenberg, Simon, Porteus, Pyszczynski, & Solomon, 1995) and recommend harsher penalties against others who transgress against cultural standards (Florian & Mikulincer, 1997) after a mortality salience induction. In addition, reminders of mortality lead people to strive harder to live up to cultural standards, by engaging in behaviors that bring value to the self and clinging to aspects of the self that are valued (Goldenberg, McCoy, Pyszczynski, Greenberg, & Solomon, 2000; Taubman Ben-Ari, Florian, & Mikulincer, 1999).

Therefore, TMT research supports Becker's idea that belief systems relating to the self and the world provide a code of values that minimize concern and preoccupation with death by focusing the individual's attention on a personalized cultural drama, in which security and self-esteem can be attained by adhering to beliefs and behaviors that contribute to a sense of personal value and lastingness, and of being part of a larger, meaningful whole.

A BODY OF TERROR

Building on the groundwork laid by Becker and terror management theory, Goldenberg, Pyszczynski, Greenberg, and Solomon (2000; see also Goldenberg & Shackelford, 2005) recently initiated a program of research based on the premise that human beings are not only strongly motivated to avoid the frightening realization that they, like other animals, are material beings vulnerable to death, but also that such a threat engenders specific anxieties related to that which reminds us of our physical, animal nature. As Becker and others understood (e.g., Brown, 1959), the body presents an existential problem for human beings. For the body, which aches, bleeds, and grows old, makes evident a trajectory toward which death can be the only end. Moreover, bodies exude all sorts of scents and substances, which reinforce the reality of one's physical, and therefore mortal, nature. If, as terror management theory suggests, human beings cope with the existential threat associated with the awareness of impending death through symbolic constructions of meaning (worldview) and value (self-esteem), then reminders of the physicality of human beings threatens the efficacy of these symbolic defenses against existential anxiety.

Demonstrating support for these ideas, Goldenberg and her colleagues have conducted a handful of experiments showing that mortality concerns underlie the pervasive human need to distance ourselves from our physical and animal nature. For example, after a mortality salience prime, Goldenberg Pyszczynski, McCoy, Greenberg, and Solomon, (2001) exposed participants to one of two essays: either describing the biological similarities between humans and animals (*creatureliness*) or emphasizing culture as distinguishing humans from animals (*cultural distinction*). The results showed that death reminders caused people to like the cultural distinction essay to a greater extent than a control prime, and also to prefer it to an essay that discussed humans' creaturely nature. In a second study, mortality salience led to greater manifestations of disgust, which has been described as an emotional reaction to that which blurs the human-animal boundary (e.g., Haidt, Rozin, McCauley, & Imada, 1997), in response to bodily products and functions.

Sex provides a particularly compelling illustration of the human tendency to experience psychological conflict, and distance from, the physical aspects of the body. For although sex is clearly a source of pleasure, it is also evident that cultures highly regulate sexual behavior and people often experience much anxiety about sex. Following Becker, Goldenberg and colleagues (e.g., Goldenberg, Pyszcynski, et al., 2000) posited that, in sharp contrast to its obvious redeeming qualities, sex poses a psychological threat due to its potential to make evident our core animal (and thus mortal) nature. In one series of studies, Goldenberg, Cox, Pyszczynski, Greenberg, and Solomon (2002) manipulated how likely participants were to perceive sex as an animalistic act by randomly assigning individuals to read one of the two aforementioned essays, highlighting either human creatureliness or the cultural distinction of human beings. In a first study, the essay prime was followed by a mortality salience manipulation and then participants were asked to rate the appeal of physical and romantic aspects of sex. Results showed that when the similarities between humans and animals were made salient via the creaturely nature essay, reminders of death decreased the appeal of physical, but not romantic (and hence uniquely human), aspects of sex. In the cultural distinction essay condition, mortality salience had no effect on the appeal of sex.

A second study tested the hypothesis that thinking about sex as an animal act would lead to heightened accessibility of death-related thought. Therefore, after reading one of the two essays, thoughts about either physical or romantic aspects of sex were primed and then *death-thought accessibility* was measured (by counting up the number of word fragments participants completed with death-related words, e.g., COFF_ _ could be "coffee" or "coffin"). Findings revealed that when participants had been reminded of their creaturely nature (but not when cultural distinction was primed) thinking about physical, but not romantic, aspects of sex increased the accessibility of death-related thoughts. These findings support the proposed association of sex with death and suggest that the connection is mediated by thinking about sex as an animalistic behavior.

Goldenberg, Pyszczynski, McCoy, Greenberg, and Solomon (1999) also examined individual differences in how apt one is to be threatened by the physicality of sex, focusing initially on neuroticism because of associated characteristics (e.g., emotional reactivity and pessimistic explanatory style) that should make the cultural defenses against mortality concerns more difficult. Goldenberg et al. (1999) hypothesized that neurotic individuals would be prone to associate the physicality of sex with death (in the absence of any explicit creatureliness prime). Indeed, the authors found that mortality salience led individuals scoring high in neuroticism to express decreased attraction to physical, but not romantic, aspects of sex. In another study, Goldenberg et al. demonstrated that although high neurotics responded to contemplations of physical sex with increased death-thought accessibility, when they were asked to think about love after thinking about sex, thoughts about death were no longer heightened.

This supports the proposition that people cope with the threat inherent in pleasures of physical sexuality by attaching symbolic meaning to it, which under ordinary circumstance may be more difficult for highly neurotic individuals.

More recently, Goldenberg (2006) demonstrated that neurotics even distance from basic, non-sexual, physical sensations after being primed with thoughts about their mortality. In response to mortality salience, individuals high in neuroticism reduced the amount of time they spent using an electric foot massager and submerging their arm in icy cold water but not how long they partook in a non-physical activity, listening to music. These experiments, demonstrating an inhibition of physical activities for which there are no cultural taboos, support the assertion that there is an inherent threat associated with the physicality of the body, rather than the alternative explanation that people are merely restricting their bodily experiences due to an effect of the mortality salience on the desire to conform to arbitrary cultural norms.

In summary, a significant body of empirical research supports two of the primary claims that we make in this chapter: one, that the body poses a threat to human beings and existential concerns underlie a pervasive tendency to distance humanity from our physical, animal nature, and two, that attaching symbolic meaning to one's bodily existence is an effective and perhaps necessary defensive outlet that can neutralize this corporeal threat.

A SPIRITUAL SOLUTION

Although we have argued that distancing from the physical body helps human beings find some security in the face of inevitable death,[1] another major proposition that we would like to make is that the denial of human creatureliness on its own is not sufficient to guard against existential terror. It is here we require an additional leap of imagination: the detailed conception of the "other" realm, the transcendent invisible dimension to which the mind naturally belongs.

---

[1]On the surface, it may seem like all of secular mainstream Western culture directly contradicts our position by embracing the physicality of the body. However, as we have argued elsewhere (e.g., Goldenberg & Roberts, 2004), this obsession with the (appearance of) the body is also a means of distancing from the natural body, by transforming the body into a cultural symbol through which one can acquire self-worth and thereby ward off fears of death. We maintain that on closer examination of secular culture, we see that the "natural" body is by no means embraced, but repelled. However, in this work our primary interest is on spiritual solution; we accordingly direct the interested reader to alternative sources (e.g., Goldenberg & Roberts, 2004; Goldenberg et al., 2000).

Becker and TMT go so far as to say that culture itself (at least immaterial culture) is elementally a denial of creatureliness. Religions, or spiritual meaning-systems, as chief pillars of culture, are charged with the task of providing a coherent framework of thought to delineate a spiritual realm that surpasses physical (bodily) existence. These systems also address, in a secure way, the relation between the two modes of being. By tying our mental or spiritual selves to the infinite supernatural realm, we create the possibility of symbolic or literal immortality. If we can view our corporeal existence in the context of a transcendent, immaterial, and eternal reality, in which we play jointly and individually significant roles, then we are in a better position to deny, at least superficially, the significance of our frail, ephemeral nature.

Although this hypothesis seems fairly intuitive, to date there have been only a handful of studies demonstrating spiritual or religious strivings as a function of mortality concerns. In one Dechesne et al. (2003) demonstrated that belief in immortality reduces defensiveness in response to mortality concerns. Specifically, the authors found that when participants were primed with mortality salience prior to receiving information arguing against the existence of an afterlife, subjects defended their cultural worldviews more strongly than in control groups without death-related priming. However, when the existence of an afterlife was supported (in a fallacious article written by the experimenters) after being reminded of death, participants did not defend their cultural beliefs. This study demonstrates that the belief in the continuation of life through immortality is important in reducing the anxiety surrounding death. Additionally, a couple of studies have provided direct evidence that contemplations of one's mortality can increase the need for literal immortality (i.e., an afterlife; Conn, Schrader, Wann, & Mruz, 1996) and the belief in the existence of an afterlife among those who are already believers (Osarchuk & Tatz, 1973). These studies provide additional empirical support for the premise that beliefs in immortality can function to assuage mortality concerns.

In a recently conducted experiment, Goldenberg and Hart (2004) further demonstrated that individuals who identify as being spiritual are particularly likely to cope with mortality concerns by distancing from the body. After a mortality salience prime, participants were asked to consider the relationship between their body and their self. Specifically, they were asked to indicate which of seven pairs of circles (in which one circle in each pair represented the self and the other represented the body; see Aron, Aron, & Smollan, 1992, for similar methodology), best represents the relationship between their body and

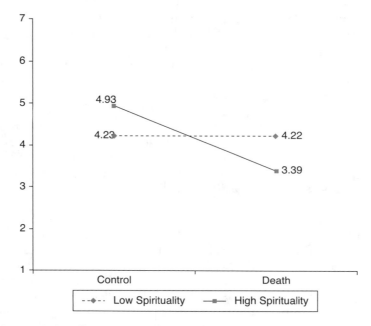

FIG. 4.1. Body-self integration as a function of mortality salience and spirituality. *Note:* Lower numbers signify the body as more distinct from the self.

their self (i.e., *body-self integration*, see Goldenberg & Shackelford, 2005). The first two circles on the scale were touching but not overlapping, with each successive pair becoming slightly more connected and over-lapped until the final two circles nearly became one. The results, as can be seen in Figure 4.1, showed that participants who were high in self-proclaimed spirituality responded to mortality salience by conceptual-izing their bodies as a less integral aspect of their self.

Thus, on an empirical level we have now shown that not only do people defend against existential anxiety by distancing from the phys-ical self, but also, the nonmaterial, or spiritual, self is embraced. Further, individuals who are especially committed to a spiritual life are especially likely to forego the body in response to contemplations of their mortality. These kinds of results provide evidence for our propositions in controlled laboratory settings. However, further confi-dence in our position could be ascertained from an examination of how these principles play out in the culture at large. We focus our analysis on religion, because we are interested in spirituality as a mode of death denial and religion has historically been the central manifestation of spiritual strivings.

RELIGION: AN ILLUSTRATION OF A DUAL SOLUTION

We have outlined our theoretical model and provided evidence of empirical support for a position in which we argue that the fear of death motivates people to drive a wedge between the body and the "soul." We next embark on a discussion of the great religious traditions of the past 4,000 or so years, to provide converging evidence for our model (see Armstrong, 1993, for an excellent overview of Jewish, Christian, and Muslim traditions). Amongst all major religions we see evidence for this psychological imperative in which the mind, soul, or spirit is deemed superior to the body, often through relations with an all-powerful God who can bring His omnipotence to the aid of helpless humanity, or through recognition of people's natural oneness with a transcendent ultimate reality.

In the Judeo-Christian tradition, the whole problem is poetically highlighted from the beginning in the book of Genesis. God alerts Adam and Eve that eating from the tree of knowledge of good and evil will result in death. The primordial couple nevertheless eats the appealing fruit, which propels them immediately into a state of shame over their nakedness. God casts them from the utopian Garden of Eden and curses them to an existence full of earthly pain, toil, and death.

Either a literal or symbolic rendering of this myth of the fall harkens back to Becker's existential paradox and parallels the psychological thesis of this chapter: upon eating from the tree of knowledge, Adam and Eve become aware of their nakedness (i.e., self-conscious), which sets them apart from the animals (i.e., gives them a spiritual dimension in addition to the physical one, bringing them "sharply out of nature"), and are horrified by their own physicality (i.e., concerned about mortality); they are ejected from utopia to live an animal-like existence, replete with suffering and death. The message to these first humans and their descendants, therefore, is that they owe their mortality to having disobeyed God, and that if they wish to benefit from God's powers and avoid the woes of corporeal existence, then they had better submit their spiritual aspects to the will of the all-powerful creator. If people remain on good terms with God, then they will be favored and protected from harm. In this way, human fate is no longer limited to the relatively impotent capacities of the body thanks to the linkage of the mind, soul, or spirit to God. Thus in the Jewish tradition, yearly atonement to God (Yom Kippur) and faithful observance of His will are paramount.

Christianity builds on the extensive mythology of Judaism and refines it to provide for the salvation of humanity and the attainment of literal spiritual immortality. In the New Testament, Jesus acknowl-edges the plight of humans in an unpredictable and cruel world, a theme that is ubiquitous in the Old Testament, and which Becker and countless others have echoed since: "I have given them thy word; and the world hath hated them, because they are not of the world, even as I am not of the world" (John 17:14, KJV). The alienation and power-lessness that seems to be inherent to the human condition, that Jews and Christians trace back to Adam's expulsion from Eden, and that we view as a natural reaction to the juxtaposition of a life instinct and the awareness of creatureliness and mortality, inspires the idea that there is something more for humans than suffering and death here on earth. For believers in the New Testament, the dream for literal immortality can finally come true thanks to Christ's sacrifice, which atoned for Adam's original sin: "Wherefore, as by one man sin entered into the world, and death by sin; and so death passed upon all men, for that all have sinned.... That as sin hath reigned unto death, even so might grace reign through righteousness unto eternal life by Jesus Christ our Lord" (Romans 5:12 & 5:21, KJV).

Therefore, according to Christian doctrine, the fall of humanity, which resulted in the curse of self-consciousness and mortality, can be overcome through the belief that God came to earth in the form of Jesus Christ to wipe the slate clean and give humans a new opportu-nity for continued spiritual existence after the body has passed on. From a Beckerian perspective, Christ's resurrection is the ultimate pro-jection of immortality strivings, and in Christianity, belief in literal immortality is among the boldest found in any faith, which may partly account for the extreme popularity of Christian religion.

The spiritual tradition of Islam, first outlined in the Koran, embod-ies many of the same themes observed in Judaism and Christianity. Muslims believe that they worship the same God as Jews and Christians, and the major emphases of Islam would be familiar to denizens of the West: the worship of one God, omniscient and omnipo-tent creator of the universe, whose moral will must be followed by humans who seek paradise after death. As in Christianity, the literal afterlife imagined by Muslims seems to be a very important aspect of the system, the culmination of a lifetime of devotion to God.

In Islam, the theme of the necessity of following God's will, obey-ing His commandments, and avoiding wrong behavior seems espe-cially important, but the same theme is common to monotheism in general. The question is begged as to why religious obedience and doctrines of sin and goodness are so ubiquitous, at least in the West. One answer is that it is useful from the standpoint of keeping civiliza-tion civil—assuming God is in favor of a good and just society (which, according to Jews, Christians, and Muslims, God is), then doing God's bidding on earth should have positive consequences at the level of community and society. Although this argument no doubt has some merit, it seems unlikely to be the whole story, especially since because historically and presently, many atrocities both large and small have been committed in the name of God, especially between but also within religious communities.

We propose that the element of following God's will in monotheism is useful from a psychological standpoint because it provides for individual salvation. In other words, from the view of each individual, the tangibility of eternal existence is enhanced when one behaves in meaningful and culturally valued ways; one is more easily convinced of spiritual immortality when one has performed small acts of heroism in order to secure it. Or as Becker put it, "If one is a servant of divine powers everything one does is heroic, if it is done as part of the consecration of one's life to those powers" (1971, pp. 124–125). Indeed, when life's actions are performed specifically in the spirit of an otherworldly, eternal value system, one is continually reminded of the supremacy of one's own spiritual nature in relation to the other, including the potential powers and immortality that come with it. In our view, this mechanism serves to amplify the existential comfort provided by spiritual meaning-systems (which might otherwise only be drawn on in times of stress), thereby conferring an increased adaptive advantage. Unencumbered by existential insecurity, devout humans are freed to apply their creative minds to the matters of earthly existence, which may be the prime evolutionary benefit of the creation and cultivation of spiritual and religious culture. Indeed, in addition to a host of psychological benefits, religious participation may be associated with longevity—that is, individuals who immerse themselves in religious or spiritual activities on a regular basis exhibit lower mortality rates than stringent secularists (Powell, Shahabi, & Thoresen, 2003).

As our brief review shows, in the three major monotheistic religions, there is a clear belief in the supremacy of the spiritual world and the spiritual aspect of individual human existence, which we view to be an essential component in the project of denying the body and emphasizing the mind, soul, or spirit. So far, we have ignored the substantial religious and spiritual traditions of the East because, in relation to our argument, Eastern and Western traditions are not easily discussed together. Whereas the major religions of the West rely on an omnipotent personality as the source of earthly and heavenly salvation (i.e., rescue from the perils and mortality of the material world), Eastern traditions are largely pantheistic and/or monistic, and the mode of spirituality is cultivated more directly through contemplative practices as opposed to a focus on good and evil action according to some arbitrary deity.

In Hinduism and Taoism, god is viewed as an impersonal source of all existence. "Salvation," according to this doctrine, can be attained through focused spiritual practices aimed at the realization of one's spiritual nature, and the merging of the spiritual self with the ultimate pantheistic reality. Although this view is clearly at odds with monotheistic interpretations of the supernatural, it is also clearly in synch with the denial of the body and the exaltation of mental/spiritual substances. Indeed, Hindus view the body as a transient shell, like an item of clothing that one casts off at the moment of death.

One Eastern tradition that offers a unique solution to the problem of self-conscious mortal corporeality is Buddhism. Instead of capitalizing on the phenomenology of dualism to deal with the problem of death by denying the body, Buddhists go a step further with the doctrine of no-self, *anatta*. By arguing that both physical and mental aspects of the self are transient illusions with no permanent existence, Buddhism makes a goal of surrendering attachment to the self and the objects of life through meditative practice. As Becker suggested, "Buddha turned against the cultural fiction and gave the value of zero to everything that people were frantically attracted to in the real world" (1971, p. 181). Thus, for accomplished Buddhists, death is nearly irrelevant:

"Do not be terrified! Do not panic! You have what is called an 'instinctual mental body' not a material, flesh and blood body. Thus whatever sounds, lights, and rays may come at you, they cannot hurt you. You cannot die" (Thurman, 1993, pp. 132–133).

For as long as history has been well-recorded, it is apparent that societies in the East and West have made sense of humans' self-conscious nature in ways that trivialize the body and glorify the spiritual self. All spiritual systems of belief focus on a nonmaterial realm that is essentially infinite and eternal. Even modern systems, such as new age spirituality, turn on the same premise, culling bits and pieces from various epistemic traditions but rarely adding anything that could be considered new. Of course, our review has necessarily neglected many spiritual traditions, but we think that an examination of ancient Egyptian, Greek, Aboriginal, and North and South American spiritual systems will reveal very similar findings. Even Neanderthals seem to have believed in an afterlife, burying their dead in the fetal position, facing east (Eliade & Couliano, 1991).

THE DARK SIDE OF THE SPIRITUAL SOLUTION

We hope that our analysis of the major religions has added to the empirical case made earlier, and in so doing, provided converging support for our model in which distancing from the natural body and clinging to the supernatural provide dual mechanisms which work hand-in-hand to help humans cope with their precarious existential position. In this section we consider, however, that although such defenses serve the adaptive function of warding off existential terror, our proposed dual solution comes with some of its own uniquely human problems.

One potential pitfall associated with the spiritual solution is that forsaking our bodies in preference for the spiritual is a feat that may not be realistic and may come with a certain psychological cost. For although we have a "symbolic identity that brings (us) sharply out of nature" (Becker, 1973), the reality of our bodies does in fact tie us to nature, and as such, we have natural inclinations, physical needs, and desires. Of course there is a long history of asceticism associated with religion, and in extreme cases the most dedicated have caused themselves bodily and psychological harm, for example, by starving or castrating oneself. Even in less extreme forms, the spiritual solution often comes with negative feelings associated with the body's natural function and desires. People who are highly religious may experience a large amount of guilt associated with sexual desire (e.g., Runkel, 1998). For instance, churchgoers are more likely to view masturbation as a sinful and unhealthy practice (Davidson, Darling, & Norton, 1995). Similarly, religious individuals are more likely to report feelings of guilt (Luyten, Corveleyn, & Fontaine, 1998), and in turn, religious guilt and fear are associated with greater risk of suicide (Exline, Yali, & Sanderson, 2000).

There is a second potential flaw in the solution. If spirituality is an essential buffer against death anxiety, then threats to one's beliefs have the potential to unleash a flood of unmanageable terror. As Pyszcynski et al. (2003) put it in their recent book on TMT and terrorism,

> Over the time our species has inhabited this planet, many wildly divergent cultural worldviews have come and gone. Our propensity to think and explore has been an ongoing challenge to existing worldviews, and there has been a perpetual tension between the security provided by existing systems of belief and the implications of both new scientific knowledge (e.g., Darwin's theory of evolution and the evidence for it) and new knowledge of alternative worldviews. These types of knowledge push our worldviews in new directions, sometimes undermine their anxiety-buffering value, and occasionally lead to their downfall (p. 149).

Just as children object to the weaknesses of their parents, human beings react poorly when they are unsure of whether their beliefs can be counted on. Unfortunately, when dealing with the invisible spiritual realm, one can't really be certain that one's beliefs are accurate, especially when they are taken on faith from authority figures. No matter how well spiritual beliefs cohere with our intuitive sense of the world, we are still equipped with reasoning skills that seem bound to poke holes in the fabric of belief. Even within religious traditions, disagreements frequently arise concerning the plausibility of certain conceptions, especially when people hold views that are mutually exclusive. Historically, reason reenters the equation in the form of rationalism and science, challenging religious systems whenever a new advance is made.

Such challenges and debates are reflected in the splintering of religions into many sects, to the point that we can barely speak about any religion without making qualifications to account for the idiosyncratic styles of different branches. Because the details of the spiritual world cannot be discerned rationally, disagreements have turned the business of spirituality into one of life and death when two or more cultures clash. Herein lies the dark side: in their efforts to defend their beliefs against contrary systems, peoples from nearly all religious backgrounds and ages have persecuted their neighbors in order to prove the righteousness of their own system:

> Because no belief system can be verified in any absolute sense, we rely heavily on social consensus to maintain faith that our conception of reality is in fact correct...those who disagree with out conceptions of reality undercut our faith in these beliefs and threaten to release the anxiety from which our conceptions shield us, thus undermining the promise of literal or symbolic immortality afforded by them. This anxiety drives the hostility we often feel toward those who view the world differently than we do...humankind has developed a variety of ways of reducing the threat posed by those who are different—from simple derogation to attempts at converting them to the "truth" of our conception to the all too common response of trying to annihilate them, thereby removing the threat posed by their divergent beliefs once and for all (Pyszczynski et al., 2003, p. 149).

In the laboratory, research on terror management theory has provided support for our position that existential concerns underlie such threats. When mortality is salient, there is evidence that people of one religion respond with increased negativity to members of different religions, even when such individuals do not make any visible demonstration of their religious beliefs (Greenberg et al., 1990). More striking, some recent terror management research (Pyszczynski, et al., 2006) conducted in an Islamic country demonstrated that participants expressed more favorable attitudes toward martyrdom (i.e., suicide bombings) against the United States and indicated they were more likely to consider such activities themselves subsequent to being reminded of their death.

In the present day, some groups have reacted to the march of modern progress, including its secular rationalism and apparent lack of use for religion, by cultivating fundamentalism. The idea behind fundamentalism seems to be a return to the basics, to old values, and a literal rendering of religious texts. It is unfortunate that many Americans and other Westerners have come to know the religion of Islam through extremists like Osama bin Laden and the violent acts of September 11, 2001. Such zealots seem to be obsessed with destruction, which in itself may be a reaction against personal impotence, made all the more salient thanks to large nations such as the United States, whose military, economic, and social tentacles wrap firmly around the world. Fundamentalism appears to represent a desperate, fervent attempt to defend one's faith in a time when scientific rationalism has led many to abandon any hope of a supernatural realm, let alone an afterlife. Perhaps it is a last-ditch effort to preserve, at all cost, spiritual beliefs that have been rendered ineffective by the psychological challenges of the information age and materialism. In *The Battle for God: A History of Fundamentalism*, religious historian Karen Armstrong (2000) captures the current and prospective fundamentalist dynamic eloquently:

> There have always been people, in every age and in each tradition, who have fought the modernity of their day. But [fundamentalism] is an essentially twentieth-century movement. It is a reaction against the scientific and secular culture that first appeared in the West.... Western civilization has changed the world. Nothing— - including religion— - can ever be the same again. All over the globe, people have been struggling with these new conditions and have been forced to reassess their religious traditions, which were designed for an entirely different type of society (pp. xiii–xiv).

THE VIABILITY OF A SPIRITUAL SOLUTION

Though the cacophonous clash between the modern pluralistic worldviews and more parochial, aggressive religious groups remains as one of the most troubling forces and conflicts of our time, it does not mean that the spiritual solution to humankind's bodily problem is itself doomed. It may be that a viable, fresh spirituality has not yet emerged. At least for now it seems clear that there are spiritual alternatives available that are less susceptible to the criticisms of other widespread views.

One of these alternatives in the West has been the spirituality of love. As Becker suggested, the modern era seems to have ushered in a spirituality of romantic love, an explicitly human-attachment-related solution to merge with others. Popular culture abounds with examples of this emphasis on romance: novels, films, songs, and music videos frequently depict people zealously pursuing ecstasy through love. Modern psychodynamic research shows that people use romantic relations to protect themselves from the fear of death (e.g., Florian, Mikulincer, & Hirschberger, 2002). It is as if, by merging symbolically (and, in the act of sex, physically) with a romantic love object, the individual can obtain a kind of freedom from the restrictions of selfhood; one can transcend the emotional perils (e.g., anxiety, loneliness) inherent in an individual existence by maintaining an exclusive attachment bond reminiscent of the relative peace and safety that young children enjoy in their parents' arms. However, with a divorce rate hovering around 50% in the United States, the romantic solution does not appear to be a foolproof one.

Science also represents a modern solution, an attempt to find order and meaning in this complex universe of ours. However, science is limited in its inability (so far) to answer the *whys* of existence—to imbue life with meaning or purpose aside from the scientific enterprise itself. In a related way, secular heroism in the form of creative contributions to the world is an avenue many travel with the apparent goal of escaping from mortal selfhood. If we can leave our mark on the world in some lasting way, then it is as if we can achieve symbolic immortality. But then again, most strongly prefer the real thing.

The individual has many choices, and with the apparently inexorable progress of information-sharing and globalization, it seems likely that at some point on the horizon, there will be a new form of integrative spirituality which will accept and assimilate various forms of ultimate truth that have been discerned through the filter of the human imagination over the millennia. Whatever the future brings, we suspect that solutions based on romance, science, and secular heroism, are too earthly to provide an effective refuge from corporeal mortality. The new spirituality will have to address the basic problem of death with some sort of immaterial meaning. Again, we follow Becker, expanding on Otto Rank, reminds us in *The Denial of Death* that "the orientation of men has to be always beyond their bodies, has to be grounded in healthy repressions, and toward explicit immortality-ideologies, myths of heroic transcendence" (1973, p. 285).

The advancements of science have only served to underscore the mystery of existence. Becker, again, articulates this point:

> We have learned that in the invisible world of the atom immense powers are locked…There seems to be empirically an invisible inside of nature from which powers erupt into the visible world from an unknown source. And since because our bodies are all composed of elements which break down

into atoms which break down into energy, it truly appears that we are constantly generated out of a void, that our physical form emanates from an unknown dimension which sustains it (1971, p. 121).

This view, which agrees with the knowledge of modern physicists that the majority of the universe is made up of *dark matter* and energy that can't be seen and is not understood, means that we are justified by science to find meaning in the mystery. It follows that a proper place to look may be the spiritual realm, which has the psychological advantage of distracting us from our most present concerns:

> ...to root one's own life in the supreme power banishes fear and weakness: what is there really to be afraid of in only one, passing dimension of the myriad miracles of creation? And to draw one's power from the source of creation itself can't fail to give one more self-reliance in the world of men...(Becker, 1971, pp. 192–193).

If our analysis is correct, then our best hope for a modern spirituality is a mode of being that perceives existence in a meaningful but rationally defensible way, and that helps us make sense of and accept our corporeal limitations. The fear of death—and discomfort with the body—won't go away, but if our existential dilemma is viewed in the appropriate light, neither does our fear need to control us or drive us to fits of hostility.

CONCLUSION

In conclusion, we would like to acknowledge that religion and spirituality serve many purposes, including, but not limited to, answering existential questions related to the origins and nature of the world, oneself, and the purpose of being. However, we would like to emphasize the theoretical utility and explanatory power of the perspective, derived from TMT, Becker, and historical observation, that distancing from the physical and striving toward the spiritual are particularly urgent because they help resolve human beings' most pressing concern: the awareness of the fact of ongoing vulnerability and inevitable mortality. We hope we have adequately presented that idea.

MAIN POINTS

1. The ubiquitous and pressing human awareness of mortality leads to a reactive disgust with the creaturely aspects of the human body, which in turn creates ambivalence about physical existence—we are happy to live, but unhappy to live in a vessel that dies.

2. Humans deal with their existential burden by creating systems of meaning that allow them to suppress the problem of mortality by adhering to belief systems and behaving in ways that affirm the belief systems.

3. Spirituality is probably the main mode of death-transcendence. Spiritual thoughts and actions are effective at attenuating the problem of mortality chiefly because they focus one's attention away from finite, corporeal matters and toward infinite, immaterial reality where one's spiritual essence can adhere to one's belief system and, in turn be, immortal.

4. There are numerous problems that have arisen throughout the history of spiritual and religious cultures, possibly because cultures can become defensive, rigid, and life-repressing in an attempt to deny the fact that humans are mortal animals.

5. A healthy, effective form of spirituality would probably entail an attitude of acceptance of the body and mortality, at the same time that it focuses one's attention on the mysterious and immaterial aspects of existence.

RECOMMENDED READINGS

Armstrong, K. (1993). *A history of God: The 4,000-year quest of Judaism, Christianity, and Islam.* New York: Ballantine Books.

Becker, E. (1973). *The denial of death.* New York: The Free Press.

Goldenberg, J. L., Pyszczynski, T. Greenberg, J., & Solomon, S. (2000). Fleeing the body: A terror management perspective on the problem of human corporeality. *Personality and Social Psychology Review, 4,* 200–218.

Greenberg, J., Solomon, S., & Pyszczynski, T. (1997). Terror management theory of self-esteem and social behavior: Empirical assessments and conceptual refinements. In M. P. Zanna (Ed.), *Advances in experimental social psychology, 29* ((Vol. 29, pp. 61–139). New York: Academic Press.

Pyszczynski, T., Solomon, S., & Greenberg, J. (2003). *In the wake of 9/11: The psychology of terror.* Washington, DC: American Psychological Association.

REFERENCES

Armstrong, K. (1993). *A history of God: The 4,000-year quest of Judaism, Christianity, and Islam.* New York: Ballantine Books.

Armstrong, K. (2000). *The battle for God: A history of fundamentalism.* New York: Ballantine Books.

Arndt, J., Greenberg, J., Pyszczynski, T., & Solomon, S. (1997). Subliminal exposure to death-related stimuli increases defense of the cultural worldview. *Psychological Science, 8,* 379–385.

Aron, A., Aron, E. N., & Smollan, D. (1992). Inclusion of Other in the Self Scale and the structure of interpersonal closeness. *Journal of Personality and Social Psychology, 63,* 596–612.

Becker, E. (1971). *The birth and death of meaning: An interdisciplinary perspective on the problem of man.* New York: The Free Press.

Becker, E. (1973). *The denial of death.* New York: The Free Press.

Bowlby, J. (1969). *Attachment and loss: Volume Vol. 1. Attachment.* New York: Basic Books.

Bowlby, J. (1973). *Attachment and loss: Volume Vol. 2. Separation: Anxiety and angerr.* New York: Basic Books.

Bowlby, J. (1980). *Attachment and loss: Volume Vol. 3. Loss.* New York: Basic Books.

Brown, N. O. (1959). *Life against death: The psychoanalytical meaning of history.* Middletown, CT: Wesleyan University Press.

Conn, R., Schrader, M. P., Wann, D. L., & Mruz, B. (1996). Reduction of anxiety about death: Need for beliefs in immortality. *Psychological Reports, 79,* 1315–1328.

Davidson, J. K., Darling, C. A., & Norton, L. (1995). Religiosity and the sexuality of women: Sexual behavior and sexual satisfaction revisited. *Journal of Sex Research, 32,* 235–243.

Dechesne, M., Pyszczynski, T., Arndt, J., Ransom, S., Sheldon, K. M., van knippenberg, & Janseen. (2003). Literal and symbolic immortality; The effect of evidence of literal immortality on self-esteem striving in reponse to mortality salience. *Journal of Personality and Social Psychology, 84,* 722–737.

Eliade, M., & Couliano, I. P. (1991). *The HarperCollins concise guide to world religions.* San Francisco: HarperSanFrancisco.

Exline, J. J., Yali, A. M., & Sanderson, W. C. (2000). Guilt, discord, and alienation: The role of religious strain in depression and suicidality. *Journal of Clinical Psychology, 56,* 1481–1496.

Florian, V., & Mikulincer, M. (1997). Fear of death and the judgment of social transgressions: A multidimensional test of terror management theory. *Journal of Personality and Social Psychology, 73,* 369–380.

Florian, V., Mikulincer, M., & Hirschberger, G. (2002). The anxiety-buffering function of close relationships: Evidence that relationship commitment acts as a terror management mechanism. *Journal of Personality and Social Psychology, 82,* 527–542.

Fromm, E. (1955). *The sane society.* New York: Fawcett Books.

Goldenberg, J. L., Cox, C. R., Pyszczynski, T., Greenberg, J., & Solomon, S. (2002). Understanding human ambivalence about sex: The effects of stripping sex of meaning. *Journal of Sex Research, 39,* 310–320.

Goldenberg, J. L., & Hart, J. (2004). *Distancing from the body as a reaction to death reminders among spiritual people.* Manuscript in preparation.

Goldenberg, J. L., Hart, J., Pyszczynksi, T., Warnica, G. M., Landau, M., & Thomas, L. (2006). Ambivalence toward the body: Death, neuroticism, and the flight from physical sensation. *Manuscript under review.Personality and Social Psychology Bulletin, 32,* 1264–1277.

Goldenberg, J. L., McCoy, S. K., Pyszczynksi, T., Greenberg, J., & Solomon, S. (2000). The body as a source of self-esteem: The effects of mortality salience on identification with one's body, interest in sex, and appearance monitoring. *Journal of Personality and Social Psychology, 79,* 118–130.

Goldenberg, J. L., Pyszczynski, T. Greenberg, J., & Solomon, S. (2000). Fleeing the body: A terror management perspective on the problem of human corporeality. *Personality and Social Psychology Review, 4,* 200–218.

Goldenberg, J. L., Pyszczynski, T., Greenberg, J., Solomon, S., Kluck, B., & Cornwell, R. (2001). I am not an animal: Mortality salience, disgust, and the denial of human creatureliness. *Journal of Experimental Psychology: General, 130,* 427–435.

Goldenberg, J. L., Pyszczynski, T., McCoy, S. K., Greenberg, J., & Solomon, S. (1999). Death, sex, love, and neuroticism: Why is sex such a problem? *Journal of Personality and Social Psychology, 77,* 1173–1187.

Goldenberg, J. L., & Shackelford, T. I. (2005). Is it me or is it mine? Body-self integration as a function of self-esteem, body-esteem, and mortality salience. *Self and Identity, 4,* 227–241.

Goldenberg, J. L., & Roberts, T. A. (2004). The beast within the beauty: An existential perspective on the objectification and condemnation of women. In J. Greenberg, S. L., Koole, & T. Pyszczynski (Eds.), *Handbook of experimental existential psychology* (pp. 71–85). New York: Guilford.

Greenberg, J., Pyszczynski, T., & Solomon, S. (1986). The causes and consequences of a need for self-esteem: a terror management theory. In R. F. Baumeister (Ed.), *Public self and private self* (pp. 189–212). New York: Springer-Verlag.

Greenberg, J., Pyszczynski, T., Solomon, S., Rosenblatt, A., Veeder, M., Kirkland, S., & Lyon, D. (1990). Evidence for terror management theory II: The effects of mortality salience on reactions to those who threaten or bolster the cultural worldview. *Journal of Personality and Social Psychology, 58*, 308–318.

Greenberg, J., Simon, L., Harmon-Jones, E., Solomon, S., Pyszczynski, T., & Chatel, D. (1995). Testing alternative explanations for mortality effects: Terror management, value accessibility, or worrisome thoughts? *European Journal of Social Psychology, 12*, 417–433.

Greenberg, J., Simon, L., Porteus, J., Pyszczynski, T., & Solomon, S. (1995). Evidence of a terror management function of cultural icons: The effects of mortality salience on the inappropriate use of cherished cultural symbols. *Personality and Social Psychology Bulletin, 21*, 1221–1228.

Greenberg, J., Solomon, S., & Pyszczynski, T. (1997). Terror management theory of self-esteem and social behavior: Empirical assessments and conceptual refinements. In M. P. Zanna (Ed.), *Advances in experimental social psychology, 29* (pp. 61–139). New York: Academic Press.

Haidt, J., Rozin, P., McCauley, C., & Imada, S. (1997). Body, psyche, and culture: The relationship between disgust and morality. *Psychology and Developing Societies, 9*, 107–131.

Kierkegaard, S. (1849/1954). *The sickness unto death.* (W. Lowrie, Trans.). New York: Princeton University Press.

Luyten, P., Corveleyn, J., & Fontaine, J. R. J. (1998). The relationship between religiosity and mental health: Distinguishing between shame and guilt. *Mental Health, Religion, and Culture, 1*, 165–184.

Osarchuk, M., & Tatz, S. (1973). The effects of fear of death on beliefs in afterlife. *Journal of Personality and Social Psychology, 27*, 256–260.

Powell, L. H., Shahabi, L., & Thoresen, C. E. (2003). Religion and spirituality: Linkages to physical health. *American Psychologist, 58*, 36–52.

Pyszczynski, T., Abdollahi, A., Greenberg, J., Solomon, S., Cohen, F., & Weise, D. (2006). Mortality salience, martyrdom, and military might: The great Satan versus the axis of evil. *Personality and Social Psychology Bulletin, 32*, 525–537.

Pyszczynski, T., Greenberg, J., & Solomon, S. (1997). Why do we need what we need? A terror management perspective on the roots of human social motivation. *Psychological Inquiry, 8*, 1–21.

Pyszczynski, T., Greenberg, J., & Solomon, S. (1999). A dual-process model of defense against conscious and unconscious death-related thoughts: An extension of terror management theory. *Psychological Review, 106*, 835–845.

Pyszczynski, T., Solomon, S., & Greenberg, J. (2003). *In the wake of 9/11: The psychology of terror.* Washington, DC: American Psychological Association.

Pyszczynski, T., Wicklund, R. A., Floresky, S., Gauch, G., Koch, S., Solomon, S., & Greenberg, J. (1996). Whistling in the dark: Exaggerated estimates of social consensus in response to incidental reminders of mortality. *Psychological Science, 7*, 332–336.

Solomon, S., Greenberg, J., & Pyszczynski, T. (1991). A terror management theory of social behavior: The psychological functions of self-esteem and cultural worldviews. In M. P. Zanna (Ed.), *Advances in Experimental Social Psychology: Vol. 24.* (pp. 93–159) New York: Academic Press.

Rank, O. (1930/1998). *Psychology and the soul.* (G. C. Richter & E. J. Lieberman Trans.) Baltimore, MD: John Hopkins University Press.

Runkel, G. (1998). Sexual morality of Christianity. *Journal of Sex and Marital Therapy, 24,* 103–122.

Taubman Ben-Ari, O., Florian, V., & Mikulincer, M. (1999). The impact of mortality salience on reckless driving: A test of terror management mechanisms. *Journal of Personality and Social Psychology, 76,* 35–45.

Thurman, R. (1993). *Tibetan book of the dead.* New York: Bantam.

End-of-Life Decisions: Research Findings and Implications

Victor G. Cicirelli
Purdue University

When death is near, then, it seems that many in our society struggle with two sides of this existential dilemma, that is, whether to fight on strenuously...or to attempt to bow out gracefully with the acknowledgment that meaningful life is essentially over.

—*Kleespies, 2004 (p. 11)*

END-OF-LIFE DECISIONS

End of life decisions are those that are made for the individual's last period of life, and such decisions may apply to all aspects of an individual's living and dying during that period.

Over the past two decades, well over a thousand empirical and conceptual articles have been published concerning end-of-life decisions and advance directives, in addition to numerous books. Clearly, a thorough review of this material is beyond the scope of this chapter; the reader is referred to reviews by Cicirelli (2001) and Kleespies (2004), and to George's (2002) methodological critique. The approach here is to give the reader some appreciation of existing research on the various types of end-of-life decisions and the use of advance directives. Also, end-of-life decisions, as influenced by religious, spiritual, and existential beliefs, will be considered as a general coping strategy for dealing with death anxiety, preparing oneself for death, and attaining a good death.

Who Makes End-of-Life Decisions?

The emphasis on individual autonomy in recent years has led to the view that dying individuals should be the ones to make end-of-life decisions for themselves in a way that is authentic and consistent with their beliefs and lifestyles. Yet, whether this is realistic or desirable is open to question, particularly if the dying person's decisions commit all others to carry them out without question. Some dying individuals prefer to leave end-of-life decisions up to family members or physicians. In other cases, paternalistic family members may feel that they know best and should make decisions for the dying family member. This is an area where conflict in the decision making process can occur. Callahan (2002) has cautioned that the needs of terminal patients must be considered in relation to the needs of their family and friends, of their physicians and caregivers, and to the needs and operating habits of institutions concerned with their care. Only by taking all of these influences into consideration can the most appropriate end-of-life care be achieved for all concerned. In any event, many dying patients may be incapable of communicating or making decisions, so that responsibility for end-of-life decisions falls on close family members and physicians.

How Are End-of-Life Decisions Made?

Relatively little is known about the process by which end-of-life decisions are made. It may involve a rational-analytic procedure to compare the possible outcomes of various decision alternatives and choose the course that will be most effective. It may involve some kind of heuristic procedure that combines some reasoning with emotions, values, and cultural norms to make decisions in a practical way. Or, decisions may be based on habit, simple conformance with religious or cultural norms, imitation of others, impulse, random choice, or total ignorance. Decisions may be effective regardless of how they are made, depending on the motivation of the individual involved and the context of the situation.

What Kinds of End-of-Life Decisions Are Made?

End-of-life decisions are those decisions about what happens to an individual before death and after death. Decisions about the period before death include what kinds of medical treatments will be undertaken (aggressive treatment to prolong life or palliative care), how, and perhaps when one will die (hastening death through suicide or assisted suicide), where one will die (home, hospital, nursing home, etc.), and who will make decisions in one's behalf should the individual become decisionally incompetent. Decisions about the period after death include possible autopsy and organ donation, the manner of disposition of the body after death (burial, cremation, giving the body to science, etc.), the nature of any funeral services, and disposition of possessions. One might also classify the content of decisions into formal decisions (those involving a contractual or legal arrangement of some sort, such as an advance directive, an arrangement to enter a nursing home or hospice, a will to distribute possessions, etc.), informal decisions (between family members and/or friends without any binding contract), and personal decisions (to change views in order to cope with dying). Some decisions can be made well in advance, while the individual is relatively healthy, whereas other decisions can be made or revised up to the end of life.

According to Drought and Koenig (2002), the essential end-of-life decision in regard to medical treatment in actual practice involves a choice between doing something in order to continue living and simply giving up and dying, that is, a choice between a wish to die and a wish to prolong life. Kleespies (2004) similarly categorizes end-of-life decisions into a wish to prolong life and a wish to die, but distinguishes between decisions that bring about quick death (assisted suicide and euthanasia) and decisions that do not prolong or may hasten the dying process (e.g., withholding or withdrawing treatment). Once these central decisions are made, other secondary decisions fall into place. Making end-of-life decisions is one means by which the individual is able to gain some measure of perceived control over an otherwise inevitable fate. Primary control is achieved through decisions made directly by the individual or secondary control is achieved by allowing someone (a more powerful other) to decide in one's behalf (Shroepfer, 1999).

Decisions to Prolong Life

The desire to survive is strong in most people, and many wish to do everything possible to remain alive, even if the quality of continued life is low. When the patient's cognitive faculties are adequate, and when both patient and physician agree on treatments to sustain life, there is no problem. Problems arise when there is disagreement. In cases where the physician regards further treatment as medically futile, wasteful of resources, and needlessly prolonging the patient's suffering, but the patient wishes to pursue all possible treatments to prolong life in the hope of some kind of miracle cure, there can be problems in the doctor-patient relationship. More commonly, a patient is in a comatose or vegetative state and family members wish to prolong the patient's life at any cost, either hoping for a cure or feeling that their loved one's life is of value, no matter how low the quality of that life (Rubin, 1998). Hospitals, physicians, and ethicists have struggled to establish guidelines as to when further treatment is futile, and when an institution is justified in declining to treat a patient further, yet there have been no clear-cut decisions (Kleespies, 2004). Rather, decisions are made on a case-by-case basis. Another complication arises when a patient or family might wish to continue treatments to prolong life, but are constrained by financial costs and other burdens on the family to choose other end-of-life alternatives (Emanuel, Fairclough, Slutsman, & Emanuel, 2000).

One national survey estimating the extent to which older adults want aggressive treatments to prolong life (Eleazer et al., 1996) found that 10% of Whites, 19% of Blacks, 4% of Hispanics, and 10% of Asians favored such interventions. Cicirelli (1998), using scenarios depicting terminal illness and low quality of life, found that some 52% of senior-center participants wanted to strive to live for as long as possible, although specific interventions were not examined. In studies of time-trade-offs (the amount of their remaining time seriously ill patients would be willing to exchange for a shorter life in better health), most patients were unwilling to trade much time; those who would trade the least time were more likely to want various measures to extend life (Tsevat et al., 1998).

Decisions to Refuse Life-Sustaining Treatments

Many terminally ill patients have no wish to undergo life-prolonging interventions that do not restore health, that diminish the quality of life, and are futile in the long run. Rather, they prefer that any treatments other than comfort care (e.g., relief of pain, aid in breathing, etc.) be withdrawn or withheld, and they be allowed to die more naturally as the underlying disease takes its course. Such decisions may actually hasten the dying process and thus, in effect, be a form of passive euthanasia (Kleespies, 2004). This may constitute an ethical problem for the ethicist or health care provider, but not necessarily for the patient. For example, withdrawing treatments already in place may have the effect of ending life more quickly, as when hemodialysis is discontinued. Additionally, the use of increasing doses of analgesics to control pain in an effort to provide comfort care may have the unintended effect of ending life more quickly. The principle of double effect is used to provide justification in the latter case, arguing that the intention is to relieve pain and not to cause death. Such decisions are generally approved by ethicists and religious bodies.

A large body of empirical research has investigated the preferences of patients and their surrogates for various treatment interventions and the factors influencing these preferences. Among the various interventions that are regarded as life-prolonging are respirators, intubation, intravenous feeding, hemodialysis, chemotherapy, radiation, cardiac resuscitation, defibrillation, and use of antibiotics. The degree to which treatment interventions were refused depended on the type of treatment. The more aggressive and intrusive the treatment intervention and the more serious the patient's state of health, the more likely that the treatment would be refused. For example, 92% of elderly adults would refuse a respirator, 89% tube feeding, 75% intravenous fluids, 41% antibiotics, and 21% oxygen (Henderson, 1990). Cohen-Mansfield, Droge, and Billig (1992), among others, reported similar results. With regard to CPR, 34% of elders would refuse treatment under current health conditions, 67% if acutely ill, and 92% if terminally ill (Schonwetter, Walker, Solomon, Indurkhya, & Robinson, 1996). However, stated preferences also depend on the way the questions are asked, the kinds and degree of information available to the patient, expected effectiveness of treatments in influencing likelihood of survival, and so on (e.g., Coppola, Bookwala, Ditto, Lockhart, Danks, & Smucker, 1999; Shonwetter et al., 1996). Such studies have made it clear that many patients have gross misconceptions about the effectiveness of certain treatments. Also, treatment preferences have been shown to be only moderately stable over time, and only moderately correlated with the treatment preferences of surrogate decision makers who would act if the patient became incapable of deciding (Cicirelli, 2001).

Decisions to End Life: Suicide, Assisted Suicide, and Euthanasia

When dying individuals experience a very low quality of life including intractable pain and suffering, psychological distress, loss of function, and/or loss of dignity, some seek to gain control over their situation by making a decision to end life by active means. Within the context of terminal illness, suicide is an action to end one's own life, assisted suicide is the provision of the means to end one's own life, and voluntary active euthanasia is the ending of an individual's life by another at the individual's request. Suicide, although not illegal, is condemned by many in society; assisted suicide is legal (with many qualifications) only in Oregon and the Netherlands, and voluntary active euthanasia is legal only in some countries, for example, the Netherlands and (briefly) in Australia (Leigh & Kelly, 2001).

It is difficult to know the actual incidence of these means of actively ending life, because social disapproval or illegality keeps large numbers of such cases from being reported. Suicide rates among older adults have been increasing (e.g., "Suicide rate," 1996), but one doesn't know how many of these suicides take place among the terminally ill. Although some authors (e.g., Jamison, 1996) suggest that most assisted suicides are reported as deaths from natural causes, the experience with legalized assisted suicide in Oregon indicates that relatively few terminal patients (only 91 over a four-year period) actively chose to end their lives in this way (Hedberg, Hopkins, & Southwick, 2002).

In various survey studies reviewed by Cicirelli (2001), support for legalization of assisted suicide ranged from 40% to 67% of adult respondents. However, in studies attempting to ascertain the degree to which respondents would favor assisted suicide for themselves if terminally ill, only 12% to 21% reported that they would do so (Blendon, Szalay, & Knox, 1992; Cicirelli, 1997). Results of several surveys (Cicirelli, 2001) indicated that a clear majority of adults support the legalization of voluntary active euthanasia. In general, support for euthanasia has risen over time, for older as well as younger individuals (Leinbach, 1993). In a study comparing preferences for assisted suicide and voluntary active euthanasia, potential patients preferred that a physician administer a lethal dose whereas physicians preferred that patients take the responsibility for administering lethal medications themselves (MacDonald, 1998).

Advance Directives

Advance directives are means for expressing one's wishes regarding end-of-life treatment and care before such time as one becomes incapable of making decisions for oneself. Now legal in all 50 states, advance directives in the form of a living will or a durable power of attorney for health care presumably guarantee a patient's right to refuse unwanted medical treatment, thus recognizing the autonomy of the individual to make treatment decisions. The 1990 Patient Self-Determination Act, which required federally funded facilities to ask incoming patients for advance directives, gave further support to their use.

However, both forms of advance directive have their advantages and disadvantages. Although the typical living will allows the individual to specify which of a number of life-prolonging treatments should be refused in the event of a terminal illness, thus allowing a measure of control over the dying process, critics charge that living wills are deficient in many aspects. Living wills may not apply to overall goals for the patient's treatment, may prematurely stop treatments when a patient could be saved, may not apply to the patient's actual situation, and may provide instructions that are not easily interpreted or are too vague to guide treatment in specific instances (Emanuel, 1995; Fagerlin, Ditto, Hawkins, Schneider, & Smucker, 2002). Living wills that contain a statement of the patient's basic values and goals for end-of-life care, rather than specific treatment preferences, may help to remedy some of these objections. Further, some critics question whether a document prepared at an earlier point in time can adequately represent a patient's views at some later point in time, when thinking and feelings (indeed, a person's actual identity) may have changed (Kleespies, 2004).

The second type of advance directive is the durable power of attorney for health care, which empowers a proxy to make treatment decisions in one's behalf, should one become incapacitated. This type of document offers a proxy the flexibility to make decisions in relation to specific treatment situations that might not be foreseen at the time of making a living will. However, the patient must have trust in the wisdom and integrity of the person selected as a proxy decision maker to act in a way consistent with the dying individual's basic values and goals. Existing evidence (Cicirelli, 2001; Fagerlin et al., 2002) indicates substantial lack of agreement between the treatment wishes of individuals and surrogate decision makers, with surrogates' decisions more closely reflecting their own preferences than those of patients. At the very least, effective communication between the patient and the surrogate decision maker is required.

On the positive side, however, the advance directive constitutes a legal document expressing the patient's intentions, which can be invoked when the situation requires it. Even if imperfect, it can provide evidence of the patient's wishes to discontinue life-prolonging treatment. More important, preparation of an advance directive provides an opportunity for individuals to confront and examine their feelings about the dying process and the end of life in advance of serious illness or catastrophic events. Having full and frank discussions with loved ones about end-of-life care in advance, of the actual need for such care, can result in less stress and greater satisfaction with decisions (Fagerlin et al.; 2002; Haley, Allen, Reynolds, Chen, Burton, & Thompson, 2002).

On the practical level, questions exist about the degree to which advance directives are completed and their usefulness. In their review, Fagerlin et al. (2002) estimate that only about 18% of all adults have drafted any type of advance directive, although the percentage is somewhat higher among those with chronic and terminal illnesses. The comprehensive national Study to Understand Prognosis and Preferences for Outcomes and Risks of Treatment (SUPPORT) intervention carried out with 4804 patients in acute care hospitals (Teno, Licks, et al., 1997; Teno, Lynn, et al., 1997) found that the intervention following the Patient Self-Determination Act did not influence elders' enactment of advance directives, although it did increase the recording of existing directives in patients' charts. More important, among patients who had advance directives, only 12% had discussed their advance directive with their doctor, only 35% of physicians were aware of the directive by the second week of hospitalization, and fewer than 10% of patients received treatments in accordance with the directive. The clear implication of these findings is that, when a patient is decisionally incapacitated, it is important to have someone to serve as a strong advocate (perhaps a proxy decision maker) to consult with physicians and other hospital staff so that end-of-life treatments are those that the patient desired.

Despite the somewhat pessimistic SUPPORT findings regarding the efficacy of advance directives and the equally pessimistic conclusion of Drought and Koenig (2002) that, on the practical level, no real choice in end-of-life care exists, a few studies offer more positive conclusions. In Oregon, a state which has concern for careful end-of-life planning, advance decision documents had been completed by about two thirds of deceased patients, with 90% of families well satisfied with the end-of-life care received (Wyden, 2000). Other programs, which focused on discussions of values and preferences between patients, their significant others, and clinicians (Hammes & Rooney, 1998; Molloy et al., 2000), found both a high incidence of advance directives and treatment consistent with these preferences. Clearly more extensive exploration and communication about end-of-life issues appears to achieve more satisfying end-of-life care.

RELIGIOSITY, SPIRITUALITY, EXISTENTIALISM, AND END-OF-LIFE DECISIONS

Although religiosity, spirituality, and existentialism are relatively distinct, many modern scholars have used them in combined, overlapping, or integrated form. In any event, they are reviewed here as distinct.

Religiosity

Commonly, it is characterized as a multidimensional concept (Cicirelli, 2002): (a) organizational religiosity (religious affiliation and attendance at religious activities), (b) non-organizational religiosity (practices independent of a particular religion or denomination, such as reading religious books), (c) subjective or intrinsic religiosity (feelings of intensity and commitment to one's religion, (d) religious coping (using religious faith to deal with life's problems), (e) religious beliefs (including specific beliefs about God, prayer, and an afterlife), and (f) ethical standards of right and wrong (as derived from the religion and to be followed in daily living).

The content of the beliefs may vary relative to particular religions (e.g., Christianity, Judaism, Islam, Hinduism, Buddhism, etc.), including the nature of God, the type and purpose of prayer, and the idea of immortality or an afterlife. Religion can be used as a coping mechanism for dealing with death anxieties and preparing for death. However, religious beliefs may have a negative effect for some individuals (Franks, Templer, Cappelletty, & Kauffman, 1990–1991; Fry, 1990; Koenig, 2002; Pargament, Koenig, Tarakeshwar, & Hahn, 2001), with fears of punishment, or eternal damnation by God, creating anxiety which exacerbates the dying process. Whatever the religious beliefs, they are likely to influence the nature of the end-of-life decisions that are made.

Spirituality

A somewhat elusive concept, spirituality can be viewed as an emotional reaction to experiencing a relationship, or identification with someone or something more powerful or superior to oneself, and that can provide a sense of protection and comfort (Cicirelli, 2001). It is a broader concept than religion *per se*. Walsh (1999, 2004) defines spirituality as an overarching construct that refers more generally to transcendent beliefs and practices (experienced either within or outside formal religious structures) and is both broader and more personal. In the same vein, Sulmasy (2002) defines spirituality as the individual's relationship with the transcendent; it is about the search for some kind of transcendent meaning. Spirituality may be expressed in a particular religious practice, a philosophical belief, in relationships with nature, the arts, and so on.

Koenig (2002) states that religious needs involve making peace in one's relationships with God and others and preparing oneself for a life to come, whereas spiritual needs may include religion but are not restricted to it. Spiritual needs also involve finding purpose and meaning to life, forgiving others and receiving forgiveness, accepting what one has accomplished and become during life, and saying goodbye. Following Koenig, one can view spirituality as a more encompassing term, with religious and non-religious spirituality as subcategories. The religious place their faith in God to satisfy their spiritual needs. The spiritual, but non-religious, for example, atheists, agnostics, and apathists (those indifferent to the existence of a personal God), may satisfy their spiritual needs by identifying with an impersonal God (e.g. one with no interest in individuals), the universe, science, mankind, nature, a philosophical worldview, and so on. For such people, decisions regarding immortality may mean continuation of earthly life through cloning, cryonics, and the like, or through symbolic immortality (leaving a legacy behind). Others may be indifferent to immortality of any kind and have no concern with satisfying spiritual needs. Fulfillment of spiritual needs is important for many dying patients (Fitchett, Burton, & Sivan, 1997; Koenig, 2002); others are content simply to accept death when it comes.

Existentialism

Although existentialism represents a broad domain in philosophy, the social sciences, and the literary world, the focus here will be on certain aspects related to psychology and the end of life. An existential approach to behavior emphasizes conflicts arising from an individual's confrontation with basic issues of existence with which everyone has to deal in some fashion (Cherny, Coyle, & Foley, 1994; Greenberg, Koole, & Pyszczynski, 2004; Yalom, 1980). These given issues, discovered by deep reflection, are four ultimate concerns fundamental to an individual's existence in the world: death, isolation, freedom, and meaninglessness.

The first, and perhaps the most ultimate concern, is death, with a basic existential conflict between the inevitability of death and the desire to continue to live. The second concern is existential isolation, with an individual able to share feelings, experiences, and thoughts with others only to a limited degree, never able to completely bridge the gap. The conflict is between our awareness of absolute isolation from others and our desire to fuse our inner experiences with those of others. The third concern is existential freedom, that is the absence of any external structure or basic rules by which one can organize one's life. The individual has complete autonomy. The conflict is between one's awareness of this freedom and one's desire for some external structure, or design, to channel one's choices in a constructive manner. The fourth concern is existential meaninglessness. As posed by Yalom (1980), if one must die, if one must be alone in the world, if one must live in a void with no external design for living, then what meaning does life or death really have? Is there any real value or purpose to life? The conflict is that humans are creatures who need to seek and create meaning in a universe without meaning. Some regard existentialism as pessimistic in that these basic concerns and needs cannot be met, leading to defense mechanisms to alleviate the resulting anxiety in order to survive in an absurd world. Yet others (e.g., Ryan & Deci, 2004) see existentialism as a more optimistic philosophy of liberation, personal search for meaning, and engagement.

Given the need and abilities to create subjective meanings, one can find ways of transcending this finite existence through some kind of literal or symbolic immortality, or by simply accepting the end of existence at death. People can create their own purpose in living, their own values, beliefs, meaning of death, and means of dealing with dying. Whether one considers religious, spiritual, and existential beliefs as separate, overlapping, or integrated, these beliefs influence end of life decisions in dealing with death anxiety, preparing for death, and attaining a good death.

Influence of Spirituality on Decision Making

Examples of spiritual beliefs influencing end-of-life decisions are limited. An individual may make use of spiritual beliefs and needs as guides to end-of-life decisions. Individuals may also make end-of-life decisions to satisfy spiritual needs as part of a general coping strategy to help deal with death anxiety and preparation for death.

As an example of the influence of spiritual needs on end-of-life decisions, one can mention that decisions to prolong life by aggressive treatment appear to be related to certain values and attitudes related to death. According to Cicirelli (1997), decisions in relation to end-of-life scenarios were related to greater intrinsic religiosity, less value for quality of life, less fear of the dying process, and greater fear of destruction of the body. Underlying such decisions are feelings that life is sacred and should be preserved at all costs.

Refusal of life-prolonging treatments has been related to less fear of the dying process, to greater value placed on quality of life, and to less religiosity (Cicirelli, 1997; Cohen-Mansfield et al., 1992; Mutran, Danis, Bratton, Sudha, & Hanson, 1997). Ethnicity also plays a role, with African Americans less likely to refuse treatment, compared to Caucasians, Hispanics, and Asians (Cicirelli, 2000; Eleazer et al., 1996).

Not surprisingly, existing studies indicate that greater religiousness is associated with less favorable attitudes toward suicide, assisted suicide, and euthanasia (Cicirelli, 1997; Leinbach, 1993). In addition, those who placed greater value on quality of life and less value on the preservation of life, and who had less fear of the destruction of the body, but greater fear of the dying process, were more likely to favor some active means of ending their life if terminally ill (Cicirelli, 1997; Cicirelli, MacLean, & Cox, 2000).

Cross-Cultural Variations

In a multicultural society, such as the United States, considerable variability in views about end-of-life decisions is to be expected. Braun, Pietsch, and Blanchette (2000) have presented a model of end-of-life decision making in which individual values, beliefs, and behaviors regarding end-of-life decisions are influenced by the ethnic, religious culture, regional cultures, all acting within the dominant world view. Thus, one might expect considerable variation regarding end-of-life decisions among adherents to a particular religious denomination, modified further by their ethnic culture. Furthermore, many members of a particular religious group do not accept all the aspects of religious dogma, idiosyncratically shaping the content of their religious faith. For example, some Christians have serious doubts about the existence of an afterlife (Cicirelli, 2002).

The Christian values of the dignity and sanctity of human life, the sovereignty of God over human life, the commitment to care for those who suffer, and an acceptance of suffering as witness to their faith, help shape Protestant views on end-of-life decision making, although there are wide denominational variations (Rowell, 2000). Most Protestant faiths now support the withholding and withdrawal of futile treatment, with palliative care for the terminally ill. Assisted suicide and euthanasia are typically condemned. Yet the notion that God has given humans the capacity to make free choices offers some support for the right to terminate one's own life through suicide. Indeed, many Protestants use the Christian value of compassion for the suffering as an argument for assisted suicide and euthanasia.

On the other hand, typical African American Protestant religious views are that pain and suffering in the dying process is a test of spiritual commitment, and thus adherents are less likely to subscribe to palliative care (Crawley, Payne, Bolden, Payne, Washington, & Williams, 2000). At the same time, they are more likely to want medical treatments to extend life for as long as possible (Cicirelli, 2000, 2001, 2002; Eleazer et al., 1996).

Catholic religious views about the sanctity of human life, the sovereignty of God over life, the meaning of suffering, and the importance of love and mercy lead to the endorsement of compassionate palliative care (such as hospice) during the dying process (Alexander, 2000). Assisted suicide and euthanasia are strongly opposed.

Although great diversity of religious views exists among the various branches of American Judaism (Kavesh, 2000), certain shared beliefs and values underlie typical Jewish end-of-life decisions. Saving life whenever possible is important, yet it is acknowledged that God alone determines how and when death will come. Organ transplants are viewed as consistent with the value placed on saving life. The relief of pain is regarded as a virtue, with the withholding or withdrawal of futile treatment at the end of life sanctioned. Euthanasia is universally condemned, but some branches of Judaism see the principle of autonomy as justification for suicide and assisted suicide.

Muslim beliefs (Hai & Husain, 2000) are similar in many ways to those of Judaism, with God (Allah) as the creator and master who determines when and how illness and death will come. Prolonging life on artificial life supports is discouraged and refusal of treatment is considered to be a valid choice. However, suicide, assisted suicide, and euthanasia are not acceptable. Organ donation for helping another person or saving a life is allowed.

Beliefs among the many branches of Buddhism are diverse. In general, however, because a person passes from the present life into the next, Buddhists see no meaning in treatments to extend life (Nakasone, 2000). They support palliative care to relieve suffering. Because they believe that a person should be buried with all parts of the body in order to make the transition to the next life, organ donations are considered unacceptable. Any needed end-of-life decisions are made by family consensus, not as an autonomous decision of the individual.

Hindu beliefs (Fry, 1999) similarly stress that the body and soul should be intact at the time of death so that the person will be reincarnated whole in the next life. Thus, use of artificial life supports, autopsy, and organ donations are seen as objectionable.

Non-religious individuals, while lacking specific beliefs to inform their end-of-life decisions, nevertheless are guided by their own philosophical and spiritual beliefs. Individual autonomy is important, although the content of decisions must be in accord with overall views.

Age as a Factor in End-of-Life Decisions

One might expect that age of the individual would be a factor influencing end-of-life decisions, if only because normal expectancies for additional years of life vary with the age of the individual. Older adults experience numerous reminders that death is no longer in the remote future, such as the preponderance of their peers in obituary columns, marketing of funeral plans, increase in chronic conditions, mobility limitations, and declining cognitive abilities (Cicirelli, 2003). Various authors have noted that older adults undergo a kind of psychological reorganization to cope with death fears and reach an acceptance of death (McCoy, Pyszczynski, Solomon, & Greenberg, 2000; Wong, 2000). An increasing acceptance of death is particularly noticeable among the very old, and many feel ready to go whenever death comes (Cicirelli, 2002).

In their qualitative study of terminally ill patients, Staton, Shuy, and Byock (2001) noted sharp differences between adults in their forties and those in their seventies and eighties. The older adults were more accepting and resigned to their approaching death, refusing aggressive treatments, whereas younger adults viewed their illness as an enemy to be aggressively treated. Paradoxically, spiritual growth was observed only among the younger group, once it became clear that death was unavoidable. Staton et al. concluded that the older adults had dealt with many spiritual and other death-related concerns over a long period of time.

Although terminally ill children and adolescents do not have a legal right to be involved in end-of-life decisions, Stillion and Papadatou (2002) maintain that decisions regarding treatment should be discussed with them. In most cases, parents opt for aggressive treatment hoping for a cure until the futility of further treatment becomes undeniable. Many parents and cultural groups attempt to protect children and adolescents from learning that they have a terminal condition, but the increasing severity of their symptoms, in spite of the aggressiveness of treatment, leads these young patients to suspect their true condition. Although young children's understanding of death gradually increases with age, children with a terminal illness appear to gain an unusual understanding of death and their own mortality. Adolescents who are terminally ill typically begin an active search for meaning in their dying experience.

INFLUENCE OF DYING ON SPIRITUAL GROWTH

An earlier discussion was concerned with the influence of spiritual beliefs on end-of-life decisions. Influence in the reverse direction is also a possibility, that is, appropriate end-of-life decisions will allow for spiritual growth while dying. This is an important consideration, although the degree of spiritual growth may partially depend on the extent to which the individual has already been able to satisfy spiritual needs before the end-of-life period begins.

Certainly, one of the stated goals of hospice care for those who refuse life-extending treatments in favor of palliative care is to deal with spiritual needs. However, Battin (2001) argues that terminal patients choosing assisted suicide shorten their lives by an average of only 3.3 weeks, thus avoiding the agonal phase of dying (a period when more than 50% of patients report moderate to severe pain). Unless one feels that some special aspect of spiritual growth depends on enduring pain and discomfort until the bitter end, it would seem that any spiritual needs could be met and spiritual growth achieved before the chosen time for the assisted suicide act is reached.

End-of-Life Period in Relation to Spiritual Needs

The end-of-life period is that time period when end-of-life decisions are made. It is discussed here rather than earlier in the chapter to lend more focus to the issue of whether end-of-life decisions can be made to satisfy spiritual needs.

The end-of-life period for an individual can be defined as the period from the beginning of dying until the actual occurrence of death. The duration of such a period may vary from just a few minutes or hours (as in sudden death) to a few years (as in some illnesses). Similarly, great variations as well as inaccuracies in the trajectory of dying exist, depending on the type of illness and characteristics of the individual (Bradley, Fried, Kasl, & Idler, 2000). In some cases there is continuous decline in health until death, in other cases there are intermittent acute periods separated by periods of remission of symptoms.

Typically, an illness is considered terminal when it has a predictably fatal outcome and no known cure exists (Kleespies, 2004). It is exceedingly difficult to determine just when the terminal phase of the end of life begins and to estimate the amount of time left to live. Operationally, the onset of the terminal phase is usually considered to be that time when the physician indicates that the person has only a limited time left to live. Yet physician prognosis of life expectancy is highly inaccurate (Christakis & Lamont, 2000; Drought & Koenig, 2002; George, 2002). Such estimations are rendered more problematic by the fact that Medicare regulations stipulate that payment for hospice care can be made for no more than a six month period. Because estimation of time left to live is so uncertain, most physicians typically wait to pronounce a patient "terminal" until very late in the trajectory of dying, with the result that the majority of patients who enter hospice care do so only a few weeks before death. According to Kaufman (2002), a dying trajectory cannot be identified for more than half of patients at the end of life (e.g., sudden deaths, extreme frailty and dementias, COPD, and congestive heart failure). Certainly much research is needed in this area (George, 2002).

If one had a better idea of the length of time one would live before dying, one could then make end-of-life decisions and plan more effectively for care. Travis, Loving, McClanahan, and Bernard (2001) expanded Pattison's concept of living while dying to include awareness of dying, living-dying interval, dying, and death. Extending this idea still further, one can conceive of living (prior to awareness), living while dying, dying while living, active dying, and death. During living while dying, end-of-life decisions may include decisions about relationships on a job, about relationships with a partner, about further curative attempts (or about palliative care), about maintaining control during the dying process, and so on. During dying while living, decisions may involve dealing with increased pain and other symptoms, anxiety about death, and so on.

Regardless of whether an individual may be considered terminally ill by medical personnel, many patients do not appear to be aware that death is approaching or do not seem to be willing to accept it. Hinton (1999) conducted weekly interviews with hospice cancer patients and found that, in the final eight weeks of life, only 42% were fully certain that they were going to die, although the great majority considered death to be a possibility. Acceptance of death was reported for only 51% of patients. It is of interest that both the degree of awareness and acceptance of death were not constant but appeared to fluctuate over time, with as many as 18% showing falling acceptance as death grew nearer. If lack of awareness and acceptance of approaching death is indeed typical of the majority of patients who are dying on a known slow trajectory, then one might ask whether such patients experience end-of-life spiritual needs or show spiritual growth during the dying process. The search for the spiritual dimension of the dying patient presupposes that persons near death are "sentient, responsive, expressive, and able to converse" (Kaufman, 2002). One might also wonder whether end-of-life spiritual needs and spiritual growth are at all applicable to the large number of individuals who die unexpectedly and quickly, or who are dementing, comatose, or otherwise incapable of realizing that death is close at hand. Even among those who are cognitively competent and aware of approaching death, one wonders how many have spiritual needs. One recent study (McGrath, 2003) suggests that the majority of hospice patients do not seek comfort in religious or spiritual perspectives. Certainly there appears to be little or no concern for spiritual needs among dying patients receiving substandard nursing home care when merely maintaining existence is a struggle (Kayser-Jones, 2002). However, such questions do not invalidate the importance of end-of-life spiritual concerns for those dying patients who experience them.

In the context of approaching death, individuals have three areas of concern. The first involves dealing with symptoms. The second concerns the practical need for various end-of-life decisions. The third area of concern involves the psychological need for existential and spiritual meaning. Questions about the meaning and purpose of life, about the meaning of one's illness, about the future, and about what happens after death are all part of the search for meaning. Patient's existential distress near the end of life has been viewed (Cherny et al., 1994) as, at least partially, due to such concerns as disrupted or distorted personal integrity (changes in body and intellectual functioning, changes in social and professional functioning), negative retrospection (unfulfilled aspirations, remorse and guilt, questions of the worth of achievements in life), future-related concerns (separation, hopelessness, futility, meaninglessness, death itself), and religious concerns (fear of divine retribution, illness as punishment, fear of a void). According to Wong (2000), individuals are motivated to search for personal meaning, whether religious or secular, that buffers them against personal anomie and offers a sense of predictability and control at the end of life.

Attaining a Good Death

The notion of a "good death" has been advanced by various scholars of death and dying as one aspect of preparation for death. Although what constitutes a good death may be unique to the individual, Block (2001) sees six goals to be achieved: optimizing physical comfort, maintaining a sense of continuity with one's self, maintaining and enhancing relationships, making meaning of one's life, achieving a sense of control, and confronting and preparing for death. Wong and

Stiller's (1999) conception of a good death is similar in many respects, "having a sense of control, discussing the practical implications of dying, exploring an afterlife, talking about religious/spiritual issues, reviewing the past, having a sense of humor, not avoiding painful truths, taking an interest in personal appearance, benefiting from the presence of significant others, and participating in physical expressions of caring (p. 81)." In a similar vein, Lester (1996) presented five criteria of an appropriate death: that the individual should have a role in his/her own death and not leave it to chance, that the body should retain its integrity, that the death be consistent with the person's life style, that the time of death should be appropriate, and that the different types of death (physical, psychological, social, & anthropological) coincide in time. To these criteria might be added that an appropriate death should be consistent with the person's spiritual beliefs and values.

It may be argued that individuals' end-of-life decisions are related to their conceptions of what is a good or appropriate death. Reaching end-of-life decisions that promote a good death cannot be achieved independently of spiritual needs especially those under the subcategory of existential needs. Clearly, not everyone can achieve a good death, but making good end-of-life decisions can be viewed as a means of achieving some measure of control over one's dying in a way that allows one to achieve other aspects of a good death.

CONCLUSION

The end-of-life period begins when the person becomes aware that his/her condition is terminal, extends through the duration of the dying process, and ends when death occurs. Various types of end-of-life decisions may be made during this period, with the goal of giving the dying individual greater control over the dying process. These decisions range from the enactment of formal and legal documents to informal and non-binding agreements regarding how, where, and when the person will die.

Unfortunately, advance directives specifying end-of-life treatments have been only partially successful in attaining this goal for various reasons. Only a minority of individuals have prepared advance directive, with others resisting their use. Among those who have used them, stability of preferences for treatment is only moderate, surrogate decision-makers for incompetent patients may not truly represent their views, treatment preferences may not apply to the actual situation, and medical personnel may be unaware of, or simply ignore, the advance directives of patients. Yet, some programs have been quite successful, not only in fostering completion of advance directives but in implementing end-of-life treatment consistent with the dying patient's wishes.

The role of end-of-life decisions in relation to alleviation of death anxiety and increasing preparation for death is two-fold. On the one hand, one's religious, spiritual, and existential needs or beliefs appear to have an influence on the nature of end-of-life decisions. On the other hand, the kinds of end-of-life decisions that are made can allow for deeper examination of spiritual concerns during the dying period, leading to increased spiritual growth and death acceptance. In this context, end-of-life decisions may be part of a good death. However these ideas are still in the exploratory stage.

The fact that only a minority of people have a trajectory of dying that includes a period where they are aware and accepting of impending death leads to the question of whether spiritual growth during the dying process is likely for many dying patients. At the other end of the spectrum are people whose end-of-life trajectory is very long, so that they may need to be more concerned with decisions to deal with living while dying than with end-of-life spiritual growth. The challenge for researchers and practitioners is to find ways to help both groups of people achieve as good a death as possible. To this end, better communication and cooperation must be developed between those involved in end-of-life decision making and in end-of-life care, that is, between patient and family, patient and medical personnel, and so on.

Thus far, research on how people make effective end-of-life decisions is limited, and has had only partial success. Successful results are not easily generalized, but seem to apply to particular kinds of individuals and circumstances. Further work is needed regarding the process by which these decisions are made, as well as regarding the kinds of decisions, both formal and informal, that are most effective in improving the quality of the end-of-life period.

However, this is too important an area to be ignored, and new approaches must be developed. Braun and Kayashima (1999) have an idea that may be of significance. They suggest that churches and temples can be good places to foster discussions about certain end-of-life issues, preferably including whole families. Topics such as the meanings of life and death, spiritual needs at the end of life, and end-of-life treatment and care could be explored in relation to the content of religious faith. The goal here would be to attain spiritual growth prior to the dying process, or certainly before active dying.

However, it is not clear where non-religious people would fit in or benefit. An additional challenge would be to improve the quality of the dying process for those who are not religious or feel no need to satisfy either spiritual or existential needs.

MAIN POINTS

1. The end-of-life period begins with dying and ends with death.
2. End-of-life decisions are made in last period of life.
3. Religious, spiritual, and existential beliefs influence end-of-life decisions to alleviate death fears and prepare for death.
4. Conversely, end-of-life decisions themselves may influence spiritual growth while dying.
5. A good death may also be a possible outcome of end-of-life decisions.

LIST OF RECOMMENDED READINGS

Braun, K. L., Pietsch, J. H., Blanchette, P. L. (Eds.). (2000). *Cultural issues in end-of-life decision making*. Thousand Oaks, CA: Sage.

Greenberg, J., Koole, S. L., & Pyszczynski, T. (Eds.). (2004). *Handbook of experimental existential psychology*. New York: Guilford Press.

de Vries, B. (Ed.). (1999). *End of life issues: Interdisciplinary and multidimensional perspectives* (pp. 359–378). New York: Springer Publishing Company.

Kleespies, P. M. (2004). *Life and death decisions: Psychological and ethical considerations in end-of-life care*. Washington, DC: American Psychological Association.

Koenig, H. G. (2002). A commentary on the role of religion and spirituality at the end of life. *The Gerontologist, 42*, Special Issue III, 20–23.

REFERENCES

Alexander, M. R. (2000). Catholic perspectives on euthanasia and assisted suicide: The human person and the quest for meaning. In K. L. Braun, J. H. Pietsch, & P. L. Blanchette (Eds.), *Cultural issues in end-of-life decision making* (pp. 165–179). Thousand Oaks, CA: Sage.

Battin, M. (2001). Safe, legal, rare? Physician-assisted suicide and cultural change in the future. In D. De Leo (Ed.), *Suicide and euthanasia in older adults: A transcultural journey* (pp. 203–213). Seattle, WA: Hogrefe & Huber.

Blendon, R. J., Szalay, U. S., & Knox, R. A. (1992). Should physicians aid their patients in dying? The patient's perspective. *Journal of the American Medical Association, 267*, 2658–2662.

Block, S. (2001). Psychological considerations, growth, and transcendence at the end of life: The art of the possible. *Journal of the American Medical Association, 285*, 2898–2905.

Bradley, E. H., Fried, T. R., Kasl, S. F., & Idler, E. (2000). Quality-of-life trajectories of elders in the end of life. In M. P. Lawton (Ed.), *Focus on the end of life: Scientific and social issue: Vol. 20. Annual Review of Gerontology and Geriatrics* (pp. 64–96). New York: Springer Publishing Company.

Braun, K. L. & Kayashima, R. (1999). Death education in churches and temples: Engaging religious leaders in the development of educational strategies. In B. de Vries (Ed.), *End of life issues: Interdisciplinary and multidimensional perspectives* (pp. 319–335). New York: Springer Publishing Company.

Braun, K. L., Pietsch, J. H., & Blanchette, P. L. (2000). An introduction to culture and its influence on end-of-life decision making. In K. L. Braun, J. H. Pietsch, & P. L. Blanchette (Eds.), *Cultural issues in end-of-life decision making* (pp. 1–9). Thousand Oaks, CA: Sage.

Callahan, D. (2002). A commentary—Putting autonomy in its place: Developing effective guidelines. *The Gerontologist, 42,* Special Issue III, 129–131.

Cherny, N. I., Coyle, N., & Foley, K. M. (1994). Suffering in the advanced cancer patient: A definition and taxonomy. *Journal of Palliative Care, 10*(2), 57–70.

Christakis, N., & Lamont, E. (2000). Extent and determinants of error in doctors' prognoses in terminally ill patients: Prospective cohort study. *British Medical Journal, 320,* 469–472.

Cicirelli, V. G. (1997). Relationship of psychosocial and background variables to older adults' end-of-life decisions. *Psychology and Aging, 12,* 72–83.

Cicirelli, V. G. (1998). Views of elderly people concerning end-of-life decisions. *Journal of Applied Gerontology, 17,* 186–203.

Cicirelli, V. G. (2000). Older adults' ethnicity, fear of death, and end-of-life decisions. In A. Tomer (Ed.), *Death attitudes and the older adult: Theories, concepts, and applications* (pp. 137–153). Washington, DC: Taylor and Francis.

Cicirelli, V. G. (2001). Healthy elders' early decisions for end-of-life living and dying. In M. P. Lawton (Ed.), *Focus on the end of life: Scientific and social issues: Vol. 20. Annual review of gerontology and geriatrics* (pp. 163–192). New York: Springer Publishing Company.

Cicirelli, V. G. (2002). *Older adults' views on death.* New York: Springer Publishing Company.

Cicirelli, V. G. (2003) Older adults' fear and acceptance of death: A transition model. *Ageing International, 28,* 66–81.

Cicirelli, V. G., MacLean, A. P., & Cox, L. S. (2000). Hastening death: A comparison of two end-of-life decisions. *Death Studies, 24,* 401–419.

Cohen-Mansfield, J., Droge, J. A., & Billig, N. (1992). Factors influencing hospital patients' preferences in the utilization of life-sustaining treatments. *The Gerontologist, 32,* 89–95.

Coppola, K. M., Bookwala, J., Ditto, P. H., Lockhart, L. K., Danks, J. H., & Smucker, W. D. (1999). Elderly adults' preferences for life-sustaining treatments: The role of impairment, prognosis, and pain. *Death Studies, 23,* 617–634.

Crawley, L. V., Payne, R., Bolden, J., Payne, T., Washington, P. and Williams, S. (2000). Palliative and end-of-life care in the African American community. *Journal of the American Medical Association, 284,* 2518–2521.

Drought, T. S., & Koenig, B. A. (2002). "Choice" in end-of-life decision making: Researching fact or fiction [Special Issue]. *The Gerontologist, 42(3),* 114–128.

Eleazer, G. P., Hornung, C. A., Egbert, C. G., Egbert, J. R., Eng, C., Hedgepeth, J., et al. (1996). The relationship between ethnicity and advance directives in a frail older population. *Journal of the American Geriatrics Society, 44,* 938–943.

Emanuel, L. L. (1995). Advance directives: Do they work? *Journal of the American College of Cardiology, 25,* 35–38.

Emanuel, E., Fairclough, D., Slutsman, J., & Emanuel, L. (2000). Understanding economic and other burdens of terminal illness: The experience of patients and their caregivers. *Annals of Internal Medicine, 132,* 451–459.

Fagerlin, A., Ditto, P., Hawkins, N. A., Schneider, C., & Smucker, W. (2002). The use of advance directives in end-of-life decision making: Problems and possibilities. *American Behavioral Scientist, 46,* 268–283.

Fitchett, G., Burton, L. A., & Sivan, A. H. (1997). The religious needs and resources of psychiatric patients. *Journal of Nervous and Mental Disorders, 185,* 320–326.

Franks, K., Templer, D. L., Cappelletty, G. G., & Kauffman, I. (1990–1991). Exploration of death anxiety as a function of religious variables in gay men with and without AIDS. *Omega, 22,* 43–50.

Fry, P. S. (1990). A factor analytic investigation of homebound elderly individuals' concerns about death and dying, and their coping responses. *Journal of Clinical Psychology, 46,* 737–748.

Fry, P. S. (1999). The sociocultural meaning of dying with dignity: An exploratory study of the perceptions of a group of Asian Indian elderly persons. In B. de Vries (Ed.), *End of life issues: Interdisciplinary and multidimensional perspectives* (pp. 297–318). New York: Springer Publishing Company.

George, L. K. (2002). Research design in end-of-life research: State of science [Special Issue]. *The Gerontologist, 42*(3), 86–98.

Greenberg. J., Koole, S. L., & Pyszczynski, T. (Eds.). (2004). *Handbook of experimental existential psychology.* New York: Guilford Press.

Hai, H. A., & Husain, A. (2000). Muslim perspectives regarding death, dying, and end-of-life decision making. In K. L. Braun, J. H. Pietsch, & P. L. Blanchette (Eds.), *Cultural issues in end-of-life decision making* (pp. 199–211). Thousand Oaks, CA: Sage.

Haley, W. E., Allen, R. S., Reynolds, S., Chen, H., Burton, A., & Thompson, D. G. (2002). Family issues in end-of-life decision making and end-of-life care. *American Behavioral Scientist, 46,* 284–298.

Hammes, B., & Rooney, B. (1998). Death and end-of-life planning in one midwestern community. *Archives of Internal Medicine, 158,* 383–390.

Hedberg, K., Hopkins, D., & Southwick, K. (2002). Legalized physician-assisted suicide in Oregon. 2001. *New England Journal of Medicine, 346,* 450–452.

Henderson, M. (1990). Beyond the living will. *The Gerontologist, 30,* 480–485.

Hinton, J. (1999). The progress of awareness and acceptance of dying assessed in cancer patients and their caring relatives. *Palliative Medicine, 13,* 19–35.

Jamison, S. (1996). When drugs fail: Assisted deaths and not-so-lethal drugs. *Journal of Pharmaceutical Care and Pain and Symptom Control, 4,* 223–243.

Kaufman, S. R. (2002). A Commentary: Hospital experience and meaning at the end of life [Special Issue]. *The Gerontologist, 42*(2), 34–39.

Kavesh, W. (2000). Jewish perspectives on end-of-life decision making. In K. L. Braun, J. H. Pietsch, & P. L. Blanchette (Eds.), *Cultural issues in end-of-life decision making* (pp. 181–197). Thousand Oaks, CA: Sage.

Kayser-Jones, J. (2002). The experience of dying: An ethnographic nursing home study [Special Issue]. *The Gerontologist, 42*(3), 11–19.

Kleespies, P. M. (2004). *Life and death decisions: Psychological and ethical considerations in end-of-life care.* Washington, DC: American Psychological Association.

Koenig, H. G. (2002). A commentary on the role of religion and spirituality at the end of life [Special Issue]. *The Gerontologist, 42*(3), 20–23.

Leigh, R., & Kelly, B. (2001). Family factors in the wish to hasten death and euthanasia. In D. De Leo (Ed.), *Suicide and euthanasia in older adults: A transcultural journey* (pp. 181–201). Kirkland, WA: Hogrefe & Huber Publishers.

Leinbach, R. M. (1993). Euthanasia attitudes of older persons: A cohort analysis. *Research on Aging, 15,* 443–445.

Lester, D. (1996). Psychological issues in euthanasia, suicide, and assisted suicide. *Journal of Social Issues, 52*(2), 51–62.

MacDonald, W. L. (1998). Situational factors and attitudes toward voluntary euthanasia. *Social Science and Medicine, 46,* 73–81.

McCoy, S. K., Pyszczynski, T., Solomon, S., & Greenberg, J. (2000). Transcending the self: A terror management perspective on successful aging. In A. Tomer (Ed.), *Death attitudes and the older adult: Theories, concepts, and applications* (pp. 37–63). Philadelphia, PA: Taylor & Francis.

McGrath, P. (2003). Religiosity and the challenge of terminal illness. *Death Studies, 27,* 881–899.

Molloy, W., Guyatt, G., Russo, R., Goeree, R., O'Brien, B., Bedard, M., et al. (2000). Systematic implementation of an advance directive program in nursing homes. *Journal of the American Medical Association, 283,* 1437–1444.

Mutran, E. J., Danis, M., Bratton, K. A., Sudha, S., & Hanson, L. (1997). Attitudes of the critically ill toward prolonging life: The role of social support. *The Gerontologist, 37,* 192–199.

Nakasone, R. Y. (2000). Buddhist issues in end-of-life decision making. In K. L. Braun, J. H. Pietsch, & P. L. Blanchette (Eds.), *Cultural issues in end-of-life decision making* (pp. 213–228). Thousand Oaks, CA: Sage.

Pargament, K. I., Koenig, H. G., Tarakeshwar, N., & Hahn, J. (2001). Religious struggle as a predictor of mortality among medically ill elderly patients: A two-year longitudinal study. *Archives of Internal Medicine, 161,* 1881–1885.

Rowell, M. (2000). Christian perspectives on end-of-life decision making: Faith in a community. In K. L. Braun, J. H. Pietsch, & P. L. Blanchette (Eds.), *Cultural issues in end-of-life decision making* (pp. 147–163). Thousand Oaks, CA: Sage.

Rubin, S. (1998). *When doctors say no: The battleground of medical futility.* Bloomington, IN: University of Indiana Press.

Ryan, M. R., & Deci, L. E. (2004). Autonomy is no illusion. In J. Greenberg, L. S. Koole, & T. Pyszczynski (Eds.), *Handbook of experimental existential psychology* (pp. 449–479). New York: Guilford Press.

Schroepfer, T. (1999). Facilitating perceived control in the dying process. In B. de Vries (Ed.), *End of life issues: Interdisciplinary and multidimensional perspectives* (pp. 57–76). New York: Springer Publishing Company.

Shonwetter, R. S., Walker, R. M., Solomon, M., Indurkhya, A., & Robinson, B. E. (1996). Life values, resuscitation preferences, and the applicability of living wells in an older population. *Journal of the American Geriatrics Society, 44,* 954–958.

Staton, J., Shuy, R., & Byock, I. (2001). *A few months to live: Different paths to life's end.* Washington, DC: Georgetown University Press.

Stillion, J. M., & Papadatou, D. (2002). Suffer the children: An examination of psychosocial issues in children and adolescents with terminal illness. *American Behavioral Scientist, 46,* 299–315.

Suicide rate among elderly climbs by 9% over 12 years. (1996, January 12). *The New York Times,* p. A11.

Sulmasy, D. P. (2002). A biopsychosocial-spiritual model for care of patients at the end of life [Special Issue]. *The Gerontologist, 42*(3), 24–33.

Teno, J., Licks, S., Lynn, J., Wenger, N., Conners, A. F., Phillips, R. S., et al. (1997). Do advance directives provide instructions that direct care? *Journal of the American Geriatrics Society, 45,* 508–512.

Teno, J., Lynn, J., Wenger, N., Phillips, R. S., Murphy, D. P., Connors, A. F., Jr., et al. (1997). Advance directives for seriously ill hospitalized patients: Effectiveness with the Patient Self-Determination Act and the SUPPORT intervention. *Journal of the American Geriatrics Society, 45,* 513–518.

Travis, S. S., Loving, G., McClanahan, L., & Bernard, M. (2001). Hospitalization patterns and palliation in the last year of life among residents in long-term care. *The Gerontologist, 41,* 153–160.

Tsevat, J., Dawson, N. V., Wu, A. W., Lynn, J., Soukup, J. R., Cook, E. G., et al. (1998). Health values of hospitalized patients 80 years or older. *Journal of the American Medical Society, 279,* 371–375.

Walsh, F. (1999). Religion and spirituality: Wellsprings for healing and resilience. In F. Walsh (Ed.), *Spiritual resources in family therapy* (pp. 3–27). New York: Guilford Press.

Walsh, F. (2004). Spirituality, death, and loss. In F. Walsh, & M. McGoldrick (Eds.), *Living beyond loss: Death in the family* (2nd ed., pp. 182–210). New York: W. W. Norton.

Wong, P. T. P. (2000). Meaning of life and meaning of death in successful aging. In A. Tomer (Ed.), *Death attitudes and the older adult* (pp. 23–35). Washington, DC: Taylor & Francis.

Wong, P. T. P., & Stiller, C. (1999). Living with dignity and palliative counseling. In B. de Vries (Ed.), *End of life issues: Interdisciplinary and multidimensional perspectives* (pp. 77–97). New York: Springer Publishing Company.

Wyden, R. (2000). Steps to improve quality of life for people who are dying. *Psychology, Public Policy, and Law, 6,* 575–581.

Yalom, D. I. (1980). *Existential psychotherapy.* New York: Basic Books.

6

▼▼▼▼

Wisdom, Religiosity, Purpose in Life, and Death Attitudes of Aging Adults

Monika Ardelt
University of Florida

It's very simple. As you grow, you learn more. If you stayed at twenty-two, you'd always be as ignorant as you were at twenty-two. Aging is not just decay, you know. It's growth. It's more than the negative that you're going to die, it's also the positive that you understand you're going to die, and that you live a better life because of it.

—Morrie Schwartz (Mitch Albom, 1997, p. 118)

One of the major psychological tasks in life and particularly in old age is to make sense of death and dying (Moody, 1986). Erikson (1963) proposed that a person's life can be subdivided into eight different stages or developmental tasks. In old age, people have to come to terms with their life and the "inalterability of the past" (Erikson, Erikson, & Kivnick, 1986, p. 56). If they are able to look back without any major regrets and are satisfied with the way they have lived and what they have accomplished, integrity can be achieved. The successful resolution of that last crisis, integrity versus despair, supposedly results in wisdom which, according to Erikson (1964), "is detached concern with life itself in the face of death itself" (p. 133). Wise elders are able to maintain the integrity of experience while at the same time acknowl-edging the physical deterioration of the body and the nearing of death.

Using a sample of 164 older hospice patients, nursing home resi-dents, and community dwelling adults (58+) from North Central Florida, this study examines three personality qualities that are often assumed to alleviate death anxiety and negative attitudes toward death: wisdom, religiosity, and a feeling of purpose in life (Tomer & Eliason, 2000a). Attitudes toward death are assessed by the Death Attitude Profile-Revised (Wong, Reker, & Gesser, 1994), a multidi-mensional construct that measures fear of death, death avoidance, and death acceptance. Death acceptance, in turn, is assessed by three com-ponents: neutral acceptance of death (death is accepted as a fact of life), approach acceptance of death (death is perceived as a gateway to a blissful afterlife), and escape acceptance of death (death is consid-ered an escape from a dreadful existence).

Wisdom is defined as a combination of cognitive, reflective, and affective personality characteristics (Ardelt, 1997, 2000, 2003; Clayton & Birren, 1980). This basic and parsimonious definition of wisdom is compatible with most intrinsic theories of wisdom (e.g., Clayton & Birren, 1980; Holliday & Chandler, 1986; Sternberg, 1990) and also with extrinsic theoretical approaches that follow the wisdom tradi-tions of the East (Takahashi, 2000). Wise people tend to look at phe-nomena and events from many different perspectives to overcome subjectivity and projections *(reflective dimension)* and to discover the true and deeper meaning of phenomena and events *(cognitive dimen-sion)*. This process tends to result in a reduction of self-centeredness, which is likely to lead to a better understanding of life, oneself, and others and, ultimately, to an increase in sympathy and compassion for others *(affective dimension)*. Although the attainment of wisdom does not protect people from the vicissitudes of life and the ravages of old age, it allows them to view personal suffering from a broader per-spective and to discover a deeper meaning in it (Moody, 1986). Hence, a wise person comprehends that physical deterioration and death are only another part of life, facts that can neither be ignored nor denied. Wise people are expected to be unafraid of death because they under-stand the true nature of existence, have lived a meaningful life, and, therefore, are able to accept life as well as death (Tomer & Eliason, 2000a). However, so far, the relation between wisdom and death atti-tudes has not been empirically tested yet (Kastenbaum, 1999).

Similarly, the main task of religion is to make sense of life and death (Hall, Koenig, & Meador, 2004; McFadden, 2000; Thomas, 1999; Wong, 1998). Carl Jung (1969) observed that most religions could be consid-ered "complicated systems of preparation for death" (p. 408). Similarly,

McFadden (1996) suggested that "for many older adults, religion provides meaning that transcends suffering, loss, and the sure knowledge that death looms somewhere on the horizon" (p. 163). Moreover, religious people are presumed to be less afraid of death, because they often believe that they will be rewarded for their religious behavior in the afterlife (Templer, 1972). Yet, there are important differences between an *intrinsic* and an *extrinsic* religious orientation. According to Allport and Ross (1967, p. 434), "the extrinsically motivated person *uses* his religion, whereas the intrinsically motivated *lives* his religion" (emphasis in the original).

An intrinsic religious orientation could be described as spiritual maturity (Thomas, 1994). It can be defined as a way of life and a commitment of one's life to God or a higher power. Every event is viewed through the religious lens, which provides meaning (Donahue, 1985) and establishes what Berger (1969) called "an all-embracing sacred order" (p. 51). Extrinsic religiosity, by contrast, can be defined as a "religion of comfort and social convention, a self-serving, instrumental approach shaped to suit oneself" (Donahue, 1985, p. 400).

Studies generally indicate a negative association between intrinsic religiosity and death anxiety, whereas the association between extrinsic religiosity and death anxiety is not necessarily significant (e.g., Alvarado, Templer, Bresler, & Thomas-Dobson, 1995; Falkenhain & Handal, 2003; Fortner, Neimeyer, & Rybarczyk, 2000; Hood & Morris, 1983; Rasmussen & Johnson, 1994; Templer, 1972; Thorson & Powell, 1990; Tomer & Eliason, 2000b). In fact, Donahue (1985) reports a positive relation between extrinsic religiosity and fear of death based on a meta-analysis of the literature. Similarly, subjective religiosity (importance of religion, God, and private prayer) was negatively, but weakly, related to fear of death in a study of 123 African American and 265 White older adults between the ages of 60 and 100 (Cicirelli, 1999, 2002). In addition, Falkenhain and Handal (2003) report a strong positive correlation between intrinsic religiosity and belief in the afterlife and a positive correlation between intrinsic religiosity and death acceptance in a sample of 71 older adults (ages 65 to 87).

Finally, one might suspect that older people whose lives do not appear to be worth living due to physical and/or emotional strain would welcome death the most (Wong, 2000). However, past evidence suggests that, paradoxically, those elders who have found meaning and purpose in life tend to be less afraid of death and also more ready to let go (Fortner, Neimeyer, & Rybarczyk, 2000; Nicholson, 1980; Quinn & Reznikoff, 1985; Rappaport, Fossler, Bross, & Gilden, 1993; Tomer & Eliason, 2000b; Wong, 2000). Tomer and Eliason (2000b) speculate that "... having a strong sense of one's life as meaningful may encourage an appraisal of death as an unavoidable price that one has to pay for a meaningful life and may encourage one to focus on one's life and important life goals" (p. 147).

Based on the previously mentioned literature review, the following five hypotheses are tested in this study:

> Hypothesis 1: Wisdom is negatively related to fear of death and death avoidance, but positively related to neutral acceptance of death. No predictions are made regarding the association between wisdom and approach and escape acceptance of death.
>
> Because wise older people are assumed to understand the true and deeper meaning of life and, hence, to accept life as it is, including physical deterioration and the existence of death, they are unlikely to be afraid of death or to avoid any thoughts about death and expected to accept death as a fact of life. However, not all wise elders might believe in a blissful existence after death, and they also might not conceive death as a relief from a dreadful existence.
>
> Hypothesis 2: An intrinsic religious orientation has a negative effect on fear of death and death avoidance and a positive effect on neutral, approach, and escape acceptance of death.
>
> Older adults who have devoted their lives to God or a higher power and who believe in a blissful life after death should neither be afraid of death nor try to avoid thinking about death. On the contrary, those adults should look forward to a life after death that promises to be much better than their current existence, and they should not hesitate to accept death as a fact of life.
>
> Hypothesis 3: An extrinsic religious orientation is unrelated to death attitudes or might even be positively related to fear of death.
>
> A religious orientation that is primarily based on self-interest rather than religious devotion to a higher cause is not expected to reduce fear of death or death avoidance or to increase neutral, approach, or escape acceptance of death.
>
> Hypothesis 4: A sense of purpose in life has a negative effect on fear of death, death avoidance, and escape acceptance of death and a positive effect on neutral acceptance of death. No prediction is made with regard to the association between purpose in life and approach acceptance of death.
>
> Older people who perceive life as meaningful might also perceive death as meaningful, which is likely to reduce their fear of death and death avoidance and to increase their neutral acceptance of death. Furthermore, elders who still feel a sense of meaning and purpose in life should be less likely to view death as an escape from a terrible world. However, a sense of purpose in life might or might not be related to the belief in a blissful afterlife.
>
> Hypothesis 5: Death attitudes of hospice patients and nursing home residents are not significantly different from those of community-dwelling older residents after the effects of wisdom, religiosity, and purpose in life are taken into account.

Previous studies indicate that a terminal illness by itself is not necessarily correlated with greater death anxiety (Devins, 1979; Neimeyer & Van Brunt, 1995), although a physical illness or disability that is not life-threatening might be associated with increased fear of death in older people (Cicirelli, 2002; Fortner, Neimeyer, & Rybarczyk, 2000; Mullins & Lopez, 1982). However, past research also has shown that religiosity and spirituality are negatively related to death anxiety and positively related to death acceptance in terminally ill patients and older adults (Hinton, 1999; Ita, 1995; Koenig, 1988).

Additional control variables are socioeconomic status (SES), gender, and race, although no predictions are made regarding the direction of the associations.[1] Some studies find a positive correlation between SES and fear of death (Pollak, 1979–1980), whereas other researchers report a negative relation between SES and death anxiety (Nelson, 1979–1980; Richardson & Sands, 1986–1987) or no association between SES and fear of death (Cicirelli, 1999). Similarly, the direction of the association between death attitudes and gender or death attitudes and race is not clear. Many studies indicate that women tend to report significantly higher levels of death anxiety than do men (Cicirelli, 1999; Davis, Martin, Wilee, & Voorhees, 1980; Rasmussen & Johnson, 1994; Rigdon & Epting, 1985; Sanders, Poole, & Rivero, 1980; Suhail & Akram, 2002; Young & Daniels, 1980), yet Fortner, Neimeyer, and Rybarczyk (2000) failed to discover a significant association between death anxiety and gender in a meta-analysis of 49 studies of older adults. Correspondingly, some studies find that African Americans report greater fear of death than do Whites (Cole, 1979; Sanders, Poole, & Rivero, 1980; Young & Daniels, 1980), whereas other studies indicate a greater fear of death for Whites than for African Americans (Cicirelli, 1999; Thorson & Powell, 1994) or no significant difference between African Americans and Whites with regard to death anxiety (Florian & Snowden, 1989; Marks, 1986–1987; Pandey & Templer, 1972).

In this study, SES, gender, and race are included as control variables in the analyses and their associations with attitudes toward death are treated as exploratory rather than confirmatory due to the inconclusive and contradictory results of the literature review.

---

[1]The effects of other control variables (age and marital status) were also tested, but results showed that they were not statistically significant. Those additional control variables were excluded from the analyses because they reduced the overall size of the sample in a listwise selection of cases.

METHODS

Procedure

Independent Community-Dwelling Residents. Data collection for community-dwelling older residents initially took place between December 1997 and June 1998. Respondents were recruited from 18 close-knit social groups of older adults located in North Central Florida. Group members who volunteered for a "Personality and Aging Well Study" were visited at home by a member of the research team who delivered and explained the self-administered question-naire. The research team member also offered to conduct the interview if the respondent needed assistance in completing the survey. Ten respondents accepted this offer. All other 170 questionnaires were returned by mail in stamped, pre-addressed envelopes.

Ten months after the initial interview, all respondents with known addresses were contacted by mail for a follow-up survey that also contained questions on religiosity and death attitudes. Participants who did not return the second questionnaire within two to three weeks were called by phone to remind them of the survey and to ask whether they needed assistance in filling out the questionnaire. Ultimately, 123 respondents or about 70% of the initial sample with known addresses returned the follow-up survey. For this study, two community-dwelling respondents below the age of 58 at the time of the follow-up survey were excluded from the analyses to make the sample compatible with the age range of hospice patients and nurs-ing home residents. All data for community-dwelling adults were taken from the follow-up survey with the exception of the demo-graphic variables.

Hospice Patients and Nursing Home Residents. Older hospice patients and nursing home residents were recruited through the local Hospice organization and local nursing homes, respectively, between August 1999 and September 2001. Thirty hospice patients and 27 nurs-ing home residents participated in a study that consisted of qualitative and quantitative face-to-face interviews on "Aging and Dying Well." However, some of the hospice patients and nursing home residents were unable or unwilling to take part in the quantitative interview. Hence, the study sample contains only the 20 hospice patients and 23 nursing home residents with completed quantitative questionnaires. Ten of those 20 hospice patients resided in the community, 7 lived at a hospice care center (a residential facility operated by hospice), and 3 stayed in an assisted-living residence.

Sample

The sample consists of 164 White and African American older adults, ranging in age from 58 to 98 years with a mean and a median age of 74 years. Sixty-seven percent of the respondents were women, 77% were White, and 50% were married. Eighty-five percent of the respondents had a high school diploma. Fifty-six percent had at least some college education, while 26% possessed a graduate degree. Eighty-six percent of the adults in the sample were affiliated with a religious group.

There were no significant differences in age, gender, race, marital status, educational degree, and religious affiliation between hospice patients and nursing home residents at the .05 significance level. However, community-dwelling respondents were significantly more likely than were hospice patients to be younger and female. In addition, community respondents were more likely to be married and tended to possess higher educational degrees than did nursing home residents.

Measures

To construct the scales, the mean of all scale items with valid values was calculated. Given the relatively small sample, this procedure was considered the most appropriate method. A list wise deletion of cases, by contrast, would have reduced the sample size even further.

Attitudes Toward Death. The Death Attitude Profile–Revised (Wong, Reker, & Gesser, 1994) was used to assess five attitudes toward death: fear of death, death avoidance, neutral acceptance of death, approach acceptance of death, and escape acceptance of death. *Fear of death* is the mean of seven items (e.g., "I have an intense fear of death. Death is no doubt a grim experience.") with an alpha-value of .85; *death avoidance* is the average of five items (e.g., "I avoid death thoughts at all costs. I always try not to think about death.") with an alpha of .87; *neutral acceptance of death* is the average of five items (e.g., "Death is a natural aspect of life. Death is neither good nor bad.") with an alpha of .49; *approach acceptance of death* is the mean of 10 items (e.g., "I believe that I will be in heaven after I die. I look forward to life after death.") with an alpha of .97; and *escape acceptance of death* is the average of five items (e.g., "Death will bring an end to all my troubles. Death provides an escape from this terrible world.") with an alpha of .76. The scale of all the items ranges from 1 (*strongly agree*) to 5 (*strongly disagree*), which was reversed for all items before the average was computed.

Wisdom. The Three-Dimensional Wisdom Scale (3D-WS) was administered to measure the cognitive, reflective, and affective effect indicators of the latent variable wisdom (Ardelt, 2003). The 3D-WS consists of items from already existing scales as well as newly developed items. The *cognitive dimension* of wisdom assesses an understanding of life or the desire to know the truth. It is the mean of 14 items (e.g., "I often do not understand people's behavior. Ignorance is bliss.") with an alpha-value of .87. The *reflective dimension* measures a person's ability to look at phenomena and events from different perspectives and to avoid subjectivity and projections, that is, to avoid blaming other people or circumstances for one's own situation or feelings. It is computed as the average of 12 items (e.g., "I always try to look at all sides of a problem. When I'm upset at someone, I usually try to 'put myself in his or her shoes' for a while.") with an alpha of .70. Finally, the *affective dimension* of wisdom captures the presence of positive emotions and behavior toward other beings, such as feelings and acts of sympathy and compassion, and the absence of indifferent or negative emotions and behavior toward others. It is measured as the average of 13 items (e.g., Sometimes I feel a real compassion for everyone. If I see people in need, I try to help them one way or another.) with an alpha of .69. All items were assessed using one of two 5-point scales, ranging either from 1 (*strongly agree*) to 5 (*strongly disagree*) or from 1 (*definitely true of myself*) to 5 (*not true of myself*). The scale of the positively worded items was reversed before the average of the items was taken.

Religious Orientation. Religious orientation was assessed by Allport and Ross' (1967) Intrinsic and Extrinsic Religious Orientation Scale. *Intrinsic religious orientation* is the mean of 9 items (e.g., "I try hard to carry my religion over into all my other dealings in life.") with an alpha of .89, and *extrinsic religious orientation* is the average of 11 items (e.g., "A primary reason for my interest in religion is that my church is a congenial social activity.") with an alpha of .84. All items are measured on a scale ranging from 1 (*strongly agree*) through 5 (*strongly disagree*), which was reversed for all items.

Purpose in Life. A sense of purpose and meaning in life was measured by Crumbaugh and Maholick's (1964) Purpose in Life Test (King & Hunt, 1975). The scale is the mean of 9 items (e.g., "I have discovered satisfying goals and a clear purpose in life. My personal existence often seems meaningless and without purpose."), ranging from 1 (*definitely true of myself*) to 5 (*not true of myself*). The scale of the positively worded items was reversed before the average was computed. The alpha-value for that scale is .81.

Control Variables. *Socioeconomic Status (SES)* is the average of longest held occupation and educational degree. *Longest held occupation* was coded by three raters using Hollingshead's Index of Occupations (O'Rand, 1982). At least two raters discussed and jointly decided all ratings for occupations whose code designation was not clear. The scale ranges from 1 (*farm laborers, mental service workers*) to 9 (*higher executive, large business owner, major professional*). *Educational degree* ranges from 0 (*no high school*) to 4 (*graduate degree*). It was first transformed into a 9-point scale before it was averaged with occupation. For respondents without an occupation, SES reflects their educational degree.

Gender, race, and being a *hospice patient* or *nursing home resident* were coded as dichotomous variables.

Analysis

The factor score estimates of the latent variable wisdom were computed before the variable was included in the bivariate correlation and multiple regression analyses. They are calculated by regressing the estimate of the latent variable on a weighted function of its indicators (Bollen, 1989; Jöreskog, Sörbom, du Toit, & du Toit, 1999). The resulting variable has a variance and standard deviation equal to one.

The latent variable wisdom was created through a confirmatory factor analysis procedure, using the cognitive, reflective, and affective indicators of the 3D-WS and LISREL 8.30 (Jöreskog & Sörbom, 1996). The reflective dimension of wisdom had the highest factor loading with an unstandarized factor loading of .44 and a standardized loading of .87. This result is compatible with theoretical considerations that reflective thinking should promote both a deeper understanding of life and human nature and the development of sympathy and compassion for others. The unstandardized factor loadings of the cognitive and affective dimensions of wisdom were .43 and .33, respectively, and their standardized loadings were .60 and .64, respectively.

RESULTS

Bivariate Correlation Analyses

Results of bivariate correlation analyses in Table 6.1 show that a positive correlation exists between fear of death and death avoidance, and between approach and escape acceptance of death. Escape acceptance of death is positively related to death avoidance and neutral acceptance of death as well. Wisdom and purpose in life are negatively correlated with fear of death, death avoidance, and escape acceptance of death. An intrinsic religious orientation is positively related to approach and escape acceptance of death, and an extrinsic religious orientation is positively associated with fear of death, death avoidance, and escape acceptance of death.

In addition, hospice enrollment is positively related to escape acceptance of death, and residing in a nursing home is positively correlated with fear of death, death avoidance, and escape acceptance of death and negatively associated with neutral death acceptance. SES is negatively related to fear of death, death avoidance, and approach and escape acceptance of death. Women are more likely to score higher on approach acceptance of death than do men, and African American elders tend to report greater fear of death, death avoidance, and escape acceptance of death than do White older adults.

Multivariate Regression Analyses

Multivariate regression analyses were performed to test the effects of the independent variables on death attitudes after controlling for the effects of the other independent variables in the model (see Table 6.2). As predicted in Hypothesis 1, wisdom is negatively related to fear of death ($\beta = -.38$; $p < .001$) but contrary to expectations, it is unrelated to death avoidance and neutral acceptance of death. Moreover, wisdom is negatively related to escape acceptance of death ($\beta = -.24$; $p = .014$). In accordance with Hypothesis 2, an intrinsic religious orientation has a positive effect on approach and escape acceptance of death ($\beta = .69$; $p < .001$ and $\beta = .27$; $p = .001$, respectively), but contrary to Hypothesis 2, it is unrelated to fear of death, death avoidance, and neutral death acceptance. By contrast, an extrinsic religious orientation is related to greater fear of death ($\beta = .22$; $p = .007$) and death avoidance ($\beta = .31$; $p < .001$), but also to neutral and escape acceptance of death ($\beta = .30$; $p = .002$ and $\beta = .17$; $p = .060$, respectively), thereby partly confirming and partly rejecting Hypothesis 3. As expected, extrinsic religiosity is not associated with approach acceptance of death. As predicted in Hypothesis 4, purpose in life is related to less fear of death ($\beta = -.15$; $p = .082$) and death avoidance ($\beta = -.19$; $p = .031$) but contrary to Hypothesis 4, it is unrelated to neutral and escape acceptance of death. As stated in Hypothesis 5, death attitudes of hospice patients and nursing home residents are not significantly different from those of community dwelling respondents after the effects of wisdom, religiosity, and purpose in life have been controlled. The only exception is a relatively weak negative effect of residing in a nursing home on neutral death acceptance ($\beta = -.16$; $p = .069$).

TABLE 6.1
Correlation Matrix of Attitudes toward Toward Death and Predictor Variables; Pairwise Selection of Cases

	(1)	(2)	(3)	(4)	(5)	(6)	(7)	(8)	(9)	(10)	(11)	(12)	(13)	Mean	Std. Dev.	n
(1) Fear of death	–													2.45	.84	162
(2) Death avoidance	.48**	–												2.46	.91	161
(3) Neutral acceptance of death	-.08	-.03	–											4.13	.43	163
(4) Approach acceptance of death	-.04	.10	-.00	–										3.98	.94	162
(5) Escape acceptance of death	.11	.21**	.16*	.42**	–									3.69	.74	163
(6) Wisdom (factor score estimates)	-.54**	-.36**	.01	.00	-.32**	–								7.86	1.00	164
(7) Intrinsic religious orientation	-.09	.04	.04	.74**	.26**	.08	–							3.95	.81	164
(8) Extrinsic religious orientation	.43**	.46**	.14	-.08	.31**	-.45**	-.10	–						2.96	.80	164
(9) Purpose in life	-.43**	-.36**	.07	.09	-.16*	.63**	.18*	-.30**	–					4.22	.60	164
(10) Hospice patient (1 = yes)	.05	.10	.03	-.05	.16*	-.20**	-.06	.29**	-.14	–				.12	.33	164
(11) Nursing home resident (1=yes)	.17*	.23**	-.17*	.09	.17*	-.25**	.00	.18*	-.35**	-.15	–			.14	.35	164
(12) SES	-.19*	-.39**	.13	-.31**	-.21**	.33**	-.10	-.22**	.31**	-.08	-.29**	–		5.36	2.46	164
(13) Gender (1 = female)	.06	-.06	-.10	.27**	.03	.12	.25**	-.19*	.06	-.21**	-.01	-.15	–	.66	.47	164
(14) Race (1 = White)	-.19*	-.26**	.14	-.15	-.21**	.03	-.19*	-.32**	-.02	.06	-.17*	.13	-.01	.78	.42	163

$** p < 0.01; * p < 0.05$

TABLE 6.2
Effects of Wisdom, Religiosity, and Purpose in Life on Death Attitudes; Multiple OLS Regression Analyses with Selected Controls[a]

Dependent Variables Independent Variables	Fear of Death		Death Avoidance		Neutral Acceptance of Death		Approach Acceptance of Death		Escape Acceptance of Death	
	b	beta	b	beta	b	beta	b	beta	b	beta
Wisdom (factor scores)	-.33	-.38***	-.02	-.02	.02	.05	-.02	-.02	-.18	-.24**
Intrinsic religious orientation	-.08	-.07	.09	.08	.07	.14	.80	.69***	.25	.27***
Extrinsic religious orientation	.23	.22***	.36	.31***	.16	.30***	-.07	-.06	.16	.17*
Purpose in Life	-.21	-.15*	-.30	-.19**	.00	.01	.07	.04	.04	.03
Controls										
Hospice (1 = yes)	-.17	-.07	-.08	-.03	-.11	-.08	.05	.02	.27	.12
Nursing home (1= yes)	-.08	-.04	-.01	-.00	-.20	-.16*	.12	.04	.17	.08
SES	.01	.04	-.10	-.26***	.02	.09	-.10	-.25***	-.01	-.04
Gender (1 = female)	.27	.15**	-.11	-.06	-.08	-.09	.09	.05	.06	.04
Race (1 = White)	-.25	-.13*	-.24	-.11	.23	.23***	.01	.01	-.15	-.08
Adjusted R²	.35		.32		.07		.59		.21	
n	161		160		162		161		162	

*** $p < 0.01$; ** $p < 0.05$; * $p < .10$

[a] The effects of other control variables (age and marital status) were not statistically significant.

SES is negatively related to death avoidance ($\beta = -.26$; $p = .001$) and approach acceptance of death ($\beta = -.25$; $p < .001$), female and African American older adults tend to fear death slightly more than do male and White elders ($\beta = .15$; $p = .031$ and $\beta = -.13$; $p = .079$, respectively), and White older adults are more likely than are African American elders to accept death as a fact of life ($\beta = .23$; $p = .009$). Wisdom, religiosity, purpose in life, and the control variables explain 35% of the variation in fear of death, 32% of the variation in death avoidance, 7% of the variation in neutral death acceptance, 59% of the variation in approach acceptance of death, and 21% of the variation in escape acceptance of death.

CONCLUSION

For the older adults in this study, fear of death and death avoidance are independent of their acceptance of death (Feifel, 1990; Wong, Reker, & Gesser, 1994) with the exception of a relatively weak positive correlation between death avoidance and escape acceptance of death. By contrast, the associations between fear of death and death avoidance and between approach and escape acceptance of death are positive and moderately strong ($r = .48$ and $r = .42$, respectively). Older adults tend to encounter death more frequently and on a more personal level than do younger adults, and they often have already accepted the fact that their own death is more than a theoretical possibility (Thorson & Powell, 2000). Hence, some older adults might have come to terms with the finitude of their life and might even look forward to a life after death and a reunion with their loved ones, while still being afraid of the unknown that death represents. Other older adults might neither be afraid of death nor avoid thinking about it, but they also might not be convinced that there is indeed a life after death. In fact, the relation between belief in an afterlife and death anxiety is not clear. A negative association is reported in some studies (Alvarado, Templer, Bresler, & Thomas-Dobson, 1995; Rasmussen & Johnson, 1994; Rigdon & Epting, 1985), whereas in other studies the two variables are not related (Krieger, Epting, & Leitner, 1974).

Furthermore, in this study neutral death acceptance is unrelated to the other death attitudes with the exception of a relatively weak positive association with escape acceptance of death. As shown in Table 6.1, the mean of this scale is relatively high and the standard deviation is lower than for the other death attitude scales. This indicates that most of the older adults in this study accept death as a fact of life regardless of their fear of death, death avoidance, or their belief in a blissful afterlife.

After controlling for socioeconomic status, gender, race, and the other variables in the model, multivariate regression analyses show that both wisdom and purpose in life have a negative effect on fear of death as predicted. Hence, both wisdom and a sense of purpose in life seem to be important factors in decreasing older people's death anxiety, and purpose in life also tends to reduce death avoidance. According to Van Ranst and Marcoen (2000), "from an existential point of view, attitudes toward death cannot be separated from the search for meaning. The manner in which individuals look at life affects their attitudes toward death. But the converse is also true: the manner in which people look at death affects how they see life" (pp. 67–68). Hence, older adults' degree of wisdom, their sense of purpose in life, and their death anxiety and death avoidance might be reciprocally related. Indeed, in addition to the positive association between fear of death and death avoidance, Table 6.1 shows that wisdom is positively and relatively highly correlated with purpose in life ($r = .63$) and that wisdom and purpose in life are both moderately related to less fear of death and death avoidance. However, contrary to Wong's (2000) findings, both wisdom and purpose in life are unrelated to neutral and approach acceptance of death. For the older adults in this study, neither wisdom nor a sense of purpose and meaning in life appears to be required to accept death as a fact of life or to anticipate a blissful life after death.

Only an intrinsic religious orientation is highly related to greater approach acceptance of death. Apparently, intrinsically religious older adults tend to believe in a blissful afterlife, which allows them to look forward to a life after death. Intrinsic religiosity is also significantly related to greater escape acceptance of death, although this association is much weaker than the previous one. Intrinsically religious older people, whose life is filled with physical and emotional suffering, might welcome the prospect of a blissful afterlife. Interestingly, wisdom (but not purpose in life as predicted) has a negative effect on escape acceptance of death. Wise elders might be less inclined to feel that their existence is bleak, or they might be less likely to see death as the solution to their problems than are the other respondents in the study.

Surprisingly and contrary to expectations, an intrinsic religious orientation is unrelated to fear of death, death avoidance, and neutral acceptance of death in this study of older adults, whereas an extrinsic religious orientation has a positive effect on those death attitudes.

The latter is consistent with an earlier meta-analysis of the literature by Donahue (1985) who also found a positive correlation between extrinsic religiosity and fear of death. Extrinsically religious people might be exposed to religious doctrine in church, but because they do not necessarily live a religiously devoted life they might be afraid of the unknown and an uncertain future after death. Due to their fear of death, they might also try to avoid thinking about death. However, an extrinsic religious orientation also has a positive effect on neutral and escape acceptance of death. In fact, for extrinsically religious older adults neutral and escape acceptance of death might be their way of dealing with the prospect of death. Although they might fear death and might try not to think about it, they nevertheless tend to accept the fact that death is an integral part of life that cannot be avoided and that might promise a better existence than the present life in the afterlife.

As predicted, death attitudes of hospice patients and nursing home residents in the sample did not differ significantly from those of community-dwelling older adults after controlling for the effects of wisdom, religiosity, purpose in life, and the other control variables. The only exception was a negative effect of nursing home residency on neutral acceptance of death. Apparently, the nursing home residents in the sample tended to find it slightly more difficult to accept death as a fact of life than did the community-dwelling older adults.

However, the bivariate correlation analyses in Table 6.1 show that the nursing home residents tended to fear and avoid death more than did the other respondents in the study. By contrast, hospice patients did not differ from community-dwelling respondents with regard to those death attitudes. The results confirm previous findings that a terminal or severe illness is not necessarily associated with higher death anxiety (Devins, 1979; Neimeyer & Van Brunt, 1995) but that a physical illness or physical disability, which is not life-threatening, might increase fear of death. For example, Fortner, Neimeyer, and Rybarczyk (2000) demonstrate in a meta-analysis of 49 studies that a positive correlation exists between greater physical problems and death anxiety in samples of older adults. Similarly, Mullins and Lopez (1982) report that physical illness and functional disability are related to greater death anxiety among older nursing home residents. Yet, after controlling for wisdom, religiosity, purpose in life, SES, gender, and race, those associations might disappear.

Future studies are required to replicate these analyses with a larger and more representative data set of older adults. It should also be mentioned that death attitudes in the current study were assessed through survey questionnaire items. People might not always be consciously aware of their fear of death until they are confronted with the prospect of their own death. Hence, it might be easier to profess less death anxiety and death avoidance when one is relatively healthy (Cicirelli, 2002). This might explain the greater death anxiety and avoidance of death that was expressed by the nursing home residents in the study. Hospice patients, by contrast, might have already accepted the finitude of their life, particularly because they chose to enroll in a program that administers to the dying and is available only to those whose life expectancy is less than six months. Future analyses of the respondents' qualitative interviews on their attitudes about death and dying might reveal unconscious fears that are not assessed by survey items.

ACKNOWLEDGMENTS

The research was supported by a Brookdale National Fellowship, a grant from NIH/NIA (R03 AG14855-01), and a Research Initiation Project Award from the College of Liberal Arts and Sciences at the University of Florida. Special thanks go to Carla Edwards, Cynthia Koenig, Dacia Caglin, Anna Campbell, Cathy Campbell, Mark Cohan, Heather Spring, Elizabeth Brown, Jen Crick, Rosina Everitte, Dana Federici, Nicolette Fertakis, Stephen Mayer, Amy Monk, Leah M. Polkowski, Brad Tripp, and Adeen Woolverton for their help at various stages of the research project, to the research participants for their time and commitment to the study, and to staff members of various institutions who made access to the participants possible. A previous version of this chapter was presented at the 2003 Annual Meeting of the American Sociological Association in Atlanta, GA.

MAIN POINTS

1. Analyses of survey data of 164 older hospice patients, nursing home residents, and community dwelling adults (58+) revealed that it is important to distinguish between intrinsic and extrinsic religiosity when studying the effects of religiosity on attitudes toward death in old age.
2. An intrinsic religious orientation had a positive effect on approach and escape acceptance of death but was unrelated to fear of death, death avoidance, and neutral acceptance of death.
3. By contrast, an extrinsic religious orientation was related to greater fear of death and death avoidance but also had positive effects on neutral and escape acceptance of death.
4. Only wisdom and a sense of purpose and meaning in life appeared to reduce older adults' fear and avoidance of death even if they were terminally ill or physically disabled.

RECOMMENDED READINGS

Albom, M. (1997). *Tuesdays with Morrie. An old man, a young man, and life's great lesson.* New York: Broadway Books.

Cicirelli, V. G. (2002). *Older adults' views on death.* New York: Springer.

Eisenhandler, S. A. (2003). *Keeping the faith in late life.* New York: Springer.

Ramsey, J. L., & Blieszner, R. (1999). *Spiritual resiliency in older women: Models of strength for challenges through the life span.* Thousand Oaks: Sage.

Vaillant, G. E. (2002). *Aging well: Surprising guideposts to a happier life from the landmark Harvard study of adult development.* Boston, MA: Little, Brown.

REFERENCES

Allport, G. W., & Ross, J. M. (1967). Personal religious orientation and prejudice. *Journal of Personality and Social Psychology, 5,* 432–443.

Alvarado, K. A., Templer, D. I., Bresler, C., & Thomas-Dobson, S. (1995). The relationship of religious variables to death depression and death anxiety. *Journal of Clinical Psychology, 51,* 202–204.

Ardelt, M. (1997). Wisdom and life satisfaction in old age. *Journal of Gerontology: Psychological Sciences, 52B,* P15–P27.

Ardelt, M. (2000). Antecedents and effects of wisdom in old age: A longitudinal perspective on aging well. *Research on Aging, 22,* 360–394.

Ardelt, M. (2003). Development and empirical assessment of a three-dimensional wisdom scale. *Research on Aging, 25,* 275–324.

Berger, P. (1969). *The sacred canopy: Elements of a sociological theory of religion.* New York: Doubleday.

Bollen, K. A. (1989). *Structural equations with latent variables.* New York: John Wiley & Sons.

Cicirelli, V. G. (1999). Personality and demographic factors in older adults' fear of death. *The Gerontologist, 39,* 569–579.

Cicirelli, V. G. (2002). Fear of death in older adults: Predictions from terror management theory. *Journals of Gerontology: Psychological Sciences & Social Sciences, 57B,* P358–P366.

Clayton, V. P., & Birren, J. E. (1980). The development of wisdom across the life-span: A reexamination of an ancient topic. In P. B. Baltes & O. G. Brim, Jr. (Eds.), *Life-span development and behavior* (Vol. 3, pp. 103–135). New York: Academic Press.

Cole, M. A. (1979). Sex and marital status differences in death anxiety. *Omega—The Journal of Death and Dying, 9,* 139–147.

Crumbaugh, J. C., & Maholick, L. T. (1964). An experimental study in existentialism: The psychometric approach to Frankl's concept of noogenic neurosis. *Journal of Clinical Psychology, 20,* 200–207.

Davis, S. F., Martin, D. A., Wilee, C. T., & Voorhees, J. W. (1980). Relationship of fear of death and level of self-esteem in college students. *Psychological Reports, 42,* 419–422.

Devins, G. M. (1979). Death anxiety and voluntary passive euthanasia: Influences of proximity to death and experiences with death in important other persons. *Journal of Consulting and Clinical Psychology, 47,* 301–309.

Donahue, M. J. (1985). Intrinsic and extrinsic religiousness: Review and meta-analysis. *Journal of Personality and Social Psychology, 48,* 400–419.

Erikson, E. H. (1963). *Childhood and society.* New York: Norton.

Erikson, E. H. (1964). *Insight and responsibility: Lectures on the ethical implications of psychoanalytic insight.* New York: Norton.

Erikson, E. H., Erikson, J. M., & Kivnick, H. Q. (1986). *Vital involvement in old age: The experience of old age in our time.* New York: Norton.

Falkenhain, M., & Handal, P. J. (2003). Religion, death attitudes, and belief in afterlife in the elderly: Untangling the relationships. *Journal of Religion and Health, 42,* 67–76.

Feifel, H. (1990). Psychology and death: Meaningful rediscovery. *American Psychologist, 45,* 537–543.

Florian, V., & Snowden, L. R. (1989). Fear of personal death and positive life regard: A study of different ethnic and religious-affiliated American college students. *Journal of Cross-Cultural Psychology, 20,* 64–79.

Fortner, B. V., Neimeyer, R. A., & Rybarczyk, B. (2000). Correlates of death anxiety in older adults: A comprehensive review. In A. Tomer (Ed.), *Death attitudes and the older adult: Theories, concepts, and applications* (pp. 95–108). Philadelphia, PA: Brunner-Routledge.

Hall, D. E., Koenig, H. G., & Meador, K. G. (2004). Conceptualizing "religion": How language shapes and constrains knowledge in the study of religion and health. *Perspectives in Biology and Medicine, 47,* 386–401.

Hinton, J. (1999). The progress of awareness and acceptance of dying assessed in cancer patients and their caring relatives. *Palliative Medicine, 13,* 19–35.

Holliday, S. G., & Chandler, M. J. (1986). *Wisdom: Explorations in adult competence.* Basel, NY: Karger.

Hood, R. W., & Morris, R. J. (1983). Toward a theory of death transcendence. *Journal for the Scientific Study of Religion, 22,* 353–365.

Ita, D. J. (1995). Testing of a causal model: Acceptance of death in hospice patients. *Omega—The Journal of Death and Dying, 32,* 81–92.

Jöreskog, K. G., & Sörbom, D. (1996). *LISREL 8: User's reference guide* (2nd ed.). Chicago, IL: Scientific Software International.

Jöreskog, K. G., Sörbom, D., du Toit, S., & du Toit, M. (1999). *LISREL 8: New statistical features.* Chicago, IL: Scientific Software International.

Jung, C. J. (1969). The soul and death. In *The collected works of C.G. Jung* (2nd ed., Vol. 8). Princeton, NJ: Princeton University Press.

Kastenbaum, R. C. (1999). Afterword. In L. E. Thomas & S. A. Eisenhandler (Eds.), *Religion, belief, and spirituality in late life* (pp. 203–214). New York: Springer.

King, M. B., & Hunt, R. A. (1975). Measuring the religious variable: National replication. *Journal for the Scientific Study of Religion, 14,* 13–22.

Koenig, H. G. (1988). Religious behaviors and death anxiety in later life. *Hospice Journal, 4,* 3–24.

Krieger, S. R., Epting, F. R., & Leitner, L. M. (1974). Personal constructs, threat and attitudes toward death. *Omega—The Journal of Death and Dying, 5,* 299–310.

Marks, A. (1986–1987). Race and sex differences and fear of dying: A test of two hypotheses: High risk or social loss? *Omega—The Journal of Death and Dying, 17,* 229–236.

McFadden, S. H. (1996). Religion, spirituality, and aging. In J. E. Birren & K. W. Schaie (Eds.), *Handbook of the psychology of aging* (4th ed., pp. 162–177). New York: Academic Press.

McFadden, S. H. (2000). Religion and meaning in late life. In G. T. Reker & K. Chamberlain (Eds.), *Exploring existential meaning. Optimizing human development across the life span* (pp. 171–183). Thousand Oaks, CA: Sage.

Moody, H. R. (1986). Meaning of life and the meaning of old age. In T. R. Cole & S. A. Gadow (Eds.), *What does it mean to grow old? Reflections from the humanities* (pp. 9–40). Durham, NC: Duke University Press.

Mullins, L. C., & Lopez, M. A. (1982). Death anxiety among nursing home residents: A comparison of the young-old and the old-old. *Death Education, 6,* 75–86.

Neimeyer, R. A., & Van Brunt, D. (1995). Death anxiety. In H. Wass & R. A. Neimeyer (Eds.), *Dying: Facing the facts* (3rd ed., pp. 49–88). Washington, DC: Taylor & Francis.

Nelson, L. D. (1979–1980). Structural conductiveness, personality characteristics and death anxiety. *Omega—The Journal of Death and Dying, 10*, 123–133.

Nicholson, J. (1980). *Seven ages: The truth about life crises —Does your age really matter?* Glasgow: William Collins Sons & Co.

O'Rand, A. M. (1982). Socioeconomic status and poverty. In D. J. Mangen & W. A. Peterson (Eds.), *Research instruments in social gerontology: Vol. 2: Social Roles and Social Participation* (pp. 281–341). Minneapolis: University of Minnesota Press.

Pandey, R. E., & Templer, D. I. (1972). Use of the death anxiety scale in an inter-racial setting. *Omega—The Journal of Death and Dying, 3*, 127–130.

Pollak, J. M. (1979–1980). Correlates of death anxiety: A review of empirical studies. *Omega—The Journal of Death and Dying, 10*, 97–121.

Quinn, P. K., & Reznikoff, M. (1985). The relationship between death anxiety and the subjective experience of time in the elderly. *International Journal of Aging and Human Development, 21*, 197–210.

Rappaport, H., Fossler, R. J., Bross, L. S., & Gilden, D. (1993). Future time, death anxiety, and life purpose among older adults. *Death Studies, 17*, 369–379.

Rasmussen, C. H., & Johnson, M. E. (1994). Spirituality and religiosity: Relative relationships to death anxiety. *Omega—The Journal of Death and Dying, 29*, 313–318.

Richardson, V., & Sands, R. (1986–1987). Death attitudes among mid-life women. *Omega—The Journal of Death and Dying, 17*, 327–341.

Rigdon, M. A., & Epting, F. R. (1985). Reduction in death threat as a basis for optimal functioning. *Death Studies, 9*, 427–448.

Sanders, J. F., Poole, T. E., & Rivero, W. T. (1980). Death anxiety among the elderly. *Psychological Reports, 46*, 53–54.

Sternberg, R. J. (Ed.). (1990). *Wisdom: Its nature, origins, and development.* Cambridge, UK: Cambridge University Press.

Suhail, K., & Akram, S. (2002). Correlates of death anxiety in Pakistan. *Death Studies, 26*, 39–50.

Takahashi, M. (2000). Toward a culturally inclusive understanding of wisdom: Historical roots in the East and West. *International Journal of Aging and Human Development, 51*, 217–230.

Templer, D. I. (1972). Death anxiety in religiously very involved persons. *Psychological Reports, 31*, 361–362.

Thomas, L. E. (1994). Reflections on death by spiritually mature elders. *Omega—The Journal of Death and Dying, 29*, 177–185.

Thomas, L. E. (1999). Quarreling with God: Belief and disbelief among elderly Jewish immigrants from the former USSR. In L. E. Thomas & S. A. Eisenhandler (Eds.), *Religion, belief, and spirituality in late life* (pp. 73–92). New York: Springer.

Thorson, J. A., & Powell, F. C. (1990). Meanings of death and intrinsic religiosity. *Journal of Clinical Psychology, 46*, 379–391.

Thorson, J. A., & Powell, F. C. (1994). A revised death anxiety scale. In R. A. Neimeyer (Ed.), *Death anxiety handbook: Research, instrumentation, and application.* (Series in death education, aging, and health care, pp. 31–43). Philadelphia, PA: Taylor and Francis.

Thorson, J. A., & Powell, F. C. (2000). Death anxiety in younger and older adults. In A. Tomer (Ed.), *Death attitudes and the older adult. Theories, concepts, and applications* (pp. 123–136). Philadelphia, PA: Brunner-Routledge.

Tomer, A., & Eliason, G. (2000a). Attitudes about life and death: Toward a comprehensive model of death anxiety. In A. Tomer (Ed.), *Death attitudes and the older adult: Theories, concepts, and applications* (pp. 3–22). Philadelphia, PA: Brunner-Routledge.

Tomer, A., & Eliason, G. (2000b). Beliefs about self, life, and death: Testing aspects of a comprehensive model of death anxiety and death attitudes. In A. Tomer (Ed.), *Death attitudes and the older adult: Theories, concepts, and applications* (pp. 137–153). Philadelphia, PA: Brunner-Routledge.

Van Ranst, N., & Marcoen, A. (2000). Structural components of personal meaning in life and their relationship with death attitudes and coping mechanisms in late adulthood. In G. T. Reker & K. Chamberlain (Eds.), *Exploring existential meanin:. Optimizing human development across the life span* (pp. 59–74). Thousand Oaks, CA: Sage.

Wong, P. T. P. (1998). Spirituality, meaning, and successful aging. In P. T. P. Wong & P. S. Fry (Eds.), *The human quest for meaning: A handbook of psychological research and clinical applications* (pp. 359–394). Mahwah, NJ: Lawrence Erlbaum.

Wong, P. T. P. (2000). Meaning of life and meaning of death in successful aging. In A. Tomer (Ed.), *Death attitudes and the older adul: Theories, concepts, and applications* (pp. 23–35). Philadelphia, PA: Brunner-Routledge.

Wong, P. T. P., Reker, G. T., & Gesser, G. (1994). Death Attitude Profile–Revised: A multidimensional measure of attitudes toward death. In R. A. Neimeyer (Ed.), *Death anxiety handbook: Research, instrumentation, and application* (pp. 121–148). Washington, DC: Taylor & Francis.

Young, M., & Daniels, S. (1980). Born again status as a factor in death anxiety. *Psychological Reports, 47,* 367–370.

7

vvvvv

Regret and Death Attitudes

Adrian Tomer
Shippensburg University of Pennsylvania

Grafton T. Eliason
California University of Pennsylvania

For all sad words of tongue or pen

The saddest are these: "It might have been."

— J. G. Whittier (1897)

THE CONCEPT OF REGRET

Regret is both emotional and cognitive. This double character of regret was emphasized by Landman (1987). As an emotional phenomenon it includes, at the very least, an element of displeasure or dissatisfaction. As a cognitive phenomenon, it implies counterfactual thinking, that is, the consideration of alternative actions. In conformity with this duality, Landman (1993) defines regret as a "painful cognitive/emotional state of feeling sorry for misfortunes, limitations, losses, transgressions, shortcomings, or mistakes" (p. 36). As such, it may include "features of disappointment, sadness, remorse, and guilt, but... can also be distinguished from these" (p. 56). Generally speaking, regret is a broader concept than remorse or guilt. In addition, although frequently felt in relation to actions or inactions belonging to the past and for whom the

159

person bears responsibility, regret can also involve "uncontrollable and accidental" events (p. 36). The psychological importance of regret is suggested by studies that found a relationship between the existence of regret (when no actions were taken to make changes) and well being (i.e., Stewart & Vandewater, 1999).

REGRET AND DECISION MAKING

Because regret involves negative emotions and, in addition, can be anticipated, one would expect it to play a role in decision making in conditions of risk or uncertainty. Consider the following example. I am going on a short trip and I have to choose between taking with me a big and heavy suitcase or a much smaller carry-on bag. The uncertainty in this case relates to some possible formal meetings that might or might not take place. There are gains and losses associated with each one of those two alternatives, for example the gain involved in being able to use appropriate attire for the formal meetings versus the loss involved in carrying heavy luggage, and so forth. Besides the obvious gains and losses, one should also consider the regrets involved in making the wrong decision, that is, deciding to take a heavy suitcase when there are no official meetings, and so forth. Also, in addition to regret, one can experience the positive emotion that derives from having chosen correctly. Loomes and Sugden's (1982) regret theory (also independently formulated by Bell, 1982) calls this "rejoicing." According to this regret theory one maximizes a modified utility that takes into considerations possible regrets and rejoicing. The regret theory was originally proposed as an alternative to the prospect theory (Kahneman and Tversky, 1979) that suggested radical modifications in the conventional expected utility theory, modifications designed to deal with real, every-day life decision making. Although its success as an alternative to prospect theory is questionable (e.g., Tversky & Kahneman, 1992), there can be little doubt about the reality of regret considerations in decision making, particularly when the person sees oneself as responsible for an outcome and when he or she is likely to know the results of an alternative choice.

A distinction can also be made between regret and disappointment. In the latter case, one compares outcomes rather than actions. For example, I may be disappointed that the meetings did not take place so that I do not have the opportunity to benefit from the effort involved in carrying the heavy luggage. Loomes and Sugden, in a subsequent (1986) article, as well as Bell (1985), developed a theory of disappointment (the opposite of which is elation), as a supplement to the regret theory.

ACTIONS, INACTIONS, AND TEMPTATION

Counterfactual thinking, the ability of humans to imagine alternative outcomes, is at the basis of the phenomenon of regret (i.e., Gilovich & Medvec, 1995). As observed by Kahneman and Miller (1986), it is usually easier to imagine abstaining from an action that was performed in the past than to imagine performing an action that has never been carried out. Correspondingly, regrets related to specific actions performed in the past tend to exceed those related to inactions in studies dealing with counterfactual thinking. This finding was, however, further qualified by Gilovich and Medvec (1994, 1995) who make a distinction between short term and long term regret. In the long term, as indicated by studies in which participants were asked to reflect on their life (e.g., Gilovich & Medvec, 1994; Hattiangadi, Medvec, & Gilovich, 1995), inactions or omissions tend to produce more regret.

A particular type of regret related to actions involves cases in which one succumbs to temptation. In such a situation the person typically prefers his or her short term or momentary gain over long term gains. According to Ainslie (1975; see also Nozick, 1993) there is in those cases a discounting of the future's reward value. Moreover, assuming a particular type of representation of reward values available at different times by hyperbolic discount curves, it is possible for a smaller reward that is immediately available to be valued more than a larger reward that is available later. It is plausible that different people have different discount functions, some steeper than others. It is possible to modify Ainslie's model to incorporate discount functions for regret. Steep functions for regret may exacerbate the tendency for impulsive behavior while more mild functions may allow more self-control (see also Monterosso & Ainslie, 1999, on the topic of self-control).

COPING WITH REGRETS

A consideration of possible future regrets may play a positive role in minimizing those regrets and in resisting temptation. Moreover, regrets of actions or inactions of the past may direct us in our future endeavors. In this sense, regrets are useful. On the other hand, regrets, via their emotional component, may express themselves in a variety of depressive emotions (e.g. Lecci, Okun, & Karoly, 1994). In this context, Wrosch and Heckhausen (2002) introduced the important idea of managing life regrets. They apply the distinction between primary and secondary control strategies (Heckhausen & Schullz, 1995) to the topic of regret considered from a developmental point of view. With increased age, the feasibility of implementing external changes (primary control) that may reduce past related regrets decreases. The older individual may be better off by deemphasizing internally his or her responsibility (thus using low levels of internal control attributions). In this way, the older individual can deactivate the regret (Wrosh & Heckhausen, 2002). A different prediction can be formulated for young adults. In this case, high levels of control attributions (i.e., perceiving themselves as capable of influencing the situation) may be instrumental in motivating actions that will eliminate the regret. Consistent with these predictions Wrosh and Heckhausen found an interaction between age and attributions of internal control. In older people low control attributions were associated with low levels of regret, while the opposite was true for young subjects.

REGRET AND DESPAIR IN ERIKSON'S PSYCHOSOCIAL THEORY

In a number of publications, including *Childhood and Society* (1963), *Insight and Responsibility* (1964), and *The Life Cycle Completed* (1982), Erikson made a sustained effort to delineate and describe the eighth stage of his life cycle, Ego Integrity versus Despair, that maintains the dignity of human life in the presence of declining physical and/or mental powers in the face of impending death. The eighth stage is based on the preceding seven, in particular on the seventh stage of generativity versus stagnation during which comes to fruition man's love for his works and ideas. Only a person who already "has taken care of things" (Erikson, 1963, p. 268) can attain ego integrity—"ego's accrued assurance of its proclivity for order and meaning" (1963, p. 268). Living meaningfully (i.e., coherently), human beings come in touch with the universal meaning of human existence. This awareness is achieved most clearly in older age. Accordingly, Erikson talks about "a post-narcissistic love of the human ego—not of the self—as an experience which conveys some world order and spiritual sense" (Erikson, 1963, p. 268). This awareness makes possible the strength of wisdom as "detached concern with life itself, in the face of death itself" (1964, p. 133). Regret, or, in Erikson's language, despair, is the "dystonic" element of the eighth stage, opposed to the syntonic element—integrity. Specific "disgusts" (1963, p. 269) in Erikson's description, are a manifestation of a big remorse—the remorse that comes with the realization that life is over and ego integrity is out of reach.

REGRET IN THE TOMER–ELIASON MODEL
OF DEATH ANXIETY

According to Tomer and Eliason (1996, 2000), thoughts of death are likely to activate two types of regrets. One type is similar to the dystonic element in Erikson. I would like to have the sense that I lived a coherent life, that my life has unity or wholeness, but I can't. There are too many stunted beginnings, too many undeveloped thoughts, too many aborted relationships, in general too many things I should have done and I did not do (regrets of omission). There are also miserable mistakes, things I did that I should not have done (regrets of commission). My death makes the mistakes final, uncorrectable. These thoughts are likely to exacerbate the general feeling of despair associated with the perspective of an impending death. In addition to the past-related regrets, a close death means the interruption of present projects. I would like to finish this chapter or book. I would like to see my kids get married. I would like to have grandchildren. All this will be interrupted or made impossible…. These thoughts are the source of what we called future-related regret. It is arguable that future-related regret is not regret at all. After all, my impending death is not likely to be my decision. I am not responsible for it. Notwithstanding this argument, and even if we restrict the use of the term regret to exclude cases in which the agent bears no responsibility, we can still justify the use of the term when we anticipate the end of important existential projects. First, in many cases, one is not completely innocent with respect with one's death. I might have disobeyed my physician, I might have indulged in an unhealthy lifestyle, or I might have ignored some warning signals. Second, the unfinished projects create doubts in my mind regarding my previous life decision. Perhaps I should not have postponed the writing of this chapter, perhaps I should have had children earlier, perhaps I should have encouraged them to get married earlier, and so forth. Thus, future-related regret may be after all, at least in part, reducible to past-related regret. In any case, it seems useful to continue using the regret terminology when one focuses on future projects. At the same time, we recognize the possibility that, in addition to regret proper, one can also talk about the pure disappointment involved in the fact that things turned out the wrong way and that I have to finish my life before I had a chance to complete important projects. It is also possible that disappointment may play an important role in other death attitudes, in particular in the ability to accept death.

It is worth mentioning that Lecci, Olkun, and Karoly (1994) consider regrets, defined in their article as unfulfilled or unattainable goals, together with ongoing goals, in relation to psychological well-being. Both regrets and current goals were evaluated by participants in their study on a number of dimensions (such as distress, disappointment, investment, etc.) A hierarchical regression analysis indicated that regrets accounted for significant variability in both life satisfaction and depression, after removing the variance attributed to current goals.

THE TOMER–ELIASON MODEL—OTHER VARIABLES

The Tomer-Eliason model includes, in addition to the two types of regrets, meaningfulness of death as one of the immediate antecedents of death anxiety (see Figure 7.1). Meaningfulness of death refers to the individual's conceptualization of death as positive or negative, as making sense or being senseless. According to the model, if issues of past and future-related regret are unresolved, or if an individual perceives death as meaningless, a person will experience higher death anxiety.

The model specifies other components that are connected to death anxiety, mainly by influencing the three antecedents previously mentioned. The other components of the model are death salience and belief systems regarding the self and world, as well as, coping mechanisms or processes that may affect one's beliefs.

Death salience refers to the extent to which individuals contemplate their own mortality and death. The extent of death salience is related, in part, to the degree (intensity and duration) of people's exposure to death. Thus, if individuals experience numerous losses through death, salience may increase. The amount of emotional closeness or the importance of the relationship, in conjunction with the recentness of the loss, also influences the extent of death salience. Death salience can be connected to the three antecedents directly, for example, by activating feelings of regret, or indirectly by activating a variety of coping mechanisms (such as life review, life planning, identification with one's culture, etc.). It is also possible for death salience to be directly related to death anxiety.

Two belief systems are identified. One includes beliefs about the world or external assumptions, while the other includes beliefs about the self or internal assumptions. Beliefs about the world are culturally determined and involve individuals' identification with culture, religion, politics, and education. Beliefs about the self include self-esteem and locus of control. These beliefs impact one's concept of the ideal self and the actual self. Tomer and Eliason (1996, 2000) speculate that the greater the difference between these two constructs, the more likely individuals will experience higher death anxiety. The two types of beliefs may be influenced by death salience, as well as, by a variety of coping mechanisms, for example by identification with one's culture or by transcending processes (Tomer & Eliason, 2000).

Empirical Studies

The death anxiety model was partially examined in a preliminary study of younger and older adults (Tomer & Eliason, 2000). No measures of regret were included in this study which included indicators for beliefs about the world as well as intrinsic religiosity (or religious devotion) and death anxiety as indicated by the non-being factor in the Revised Death Anxiety Scale (Thorson & Powell, 1990). Death meaningfulness was not estimated directly, but instead we used Wong, Reker, and Gesser's (1994) different types of death acceptance— neutral, approach, and escape—measured using the Death Attitudes Profile-Revised Questionnaire (Wong et al., 1994). Interestingly, it was found that, in older adults, intrinsic religiosity decreased the fear of non-being through its effects on neutral acceptance and also by increasing meaningfulness of life. Death salience was found to be connected to fear of non-being in both young and older adults directly, and also by affecting dimensions of the sense of coherence (Antonovski, 1987). The study, although not serving as a complete investigation of the Tomer-Eliason model, indicated the relevance of some of the variables in the model, in particular death salience, intrinsic religiosity, the extent to which death is accepted as a natural phenomenon, and meaningfulness of life (extent to which life is worth living). At the same time, increased manageability, that is, an increase in the belief in living the life one wants, was found to increase the fear of non-being, rather than to decrease it. This finding, which was found in both younger and older participants, suggests the possibility that manageability may be related to increased future related regret which, in turn, may translate into increased fear of non-being. This topic is addressed in the next section.

The possible influence of the two types of regret on death anxiety was examined in a further study (Tomer & Eliason, 2005). The study included 117 undergraduate students and examined both types of regret in relation to several death attitudes, including fear and avoidance on the one hand and different types of acceptance, on the other

TABLE 7.1
Types of Frequent Past-Related Regrets

Regret about	Frequency (%)
Time with good friends	57.3
Time with family	51.3
Being more open about my feelings	47.9
Expanding circle of relationships	44.4
"I wish I were a child again"	47.0
Doing things differently	51.3
Saving more money	62.4
Devoting more time to spiritual life	43.6
Being better looking	60.7
Working to improving my health/fitness	41.0

Note. Only regrets expressed by 40% or more of the participants (N = 117) were included.

hand (Wong et al., 1994). In this study, past-related regret was measured using a questionnaire that was based in part on Ruuska's (1993) regret scale, which itself was based on the Minnesota Multiphasic Personality Inventory-2 (MMPI-2). The concept of regret used by Ruuska is the one defined by Landman (1993) and it includes both regrets of omission and of commission. The scale we used contains 38 items. Examples are:

I wish my relationship with my parents was better.
I wish I would have spent more quality time with friends.
I wish I had taken more risks in the past.

The main areas of possible regret included: relationships (with family members and friends), accomplishments, life experiences, personality characteristics (such as not being assertive enough), life goals such as money, education, and health. The participant expressed how she or he felt about each one of the 38 statements on a 4 point scale going from "this is not at all how I feel" to "this very much reflects how I feel." The Cronbach alpha for the questionnaire was .86 (see also Tomer & Eliason, 2005) indicating moderately high internal consistency. Most of the types of regret included were regrets related to inactions in the past (e.g., not spending quality time with friends), having certain undesired characteristics, or lacking desired characteristics (e.g., not being independent). A few responses dealt with actions: attempting to please others, being impulsive in one's actions, following others' values, and wasting time on unimportant things (which,

TABLE 7.2
The Degree to Which Participants Would Be Upset If Something
Occurred That Prevented Them From Attaining a Goal

Goal	Mean and s.d.in Males (N = 41)	Mean and s.d in Females (N = 76)	F
Maintaining and enjoying friendships	4.70 (1.65)	5.51 (1.51)	8.238**
Taking care of family and enjoying time with family members	5.78 (1.50)	5.88 (1.57)	.127
Working in or developing new areas of interest or expertise	3.83 (1.375)	4.68 (1.41)	9.926**
Improving knowledge in various domains	3.63 (1.63)	4.36 (1.31)	6.844**
Maintaining and improving health and fitness	4.63 (1.44)	5.16 (1.39)	3.763
Maintaining and developing a sense of meaningfulness/spirituality	3.83 (1.71)	4.92 (1.89)	9.368**
Striving to be a better person	4.60 (1.74)	5.59 (1.40)	11.141***
Striving to achieve a deep understanding of life	3.60 (1.72)	4.13 (1.63)	2.685
Striving to achieve financial stability	5.10 (1.68)	5.38 (1.36)	.920
Striving to attain recognition from the society	3.18 (1.39)	3.13 (1.40)	.023
Enjoying new experiences	4.70 (1.52)	5.24 (1.31)	3.942*
Continuing formal education	4.83 (1.91)	5.64 (1.58)	5.987*

$*p < .05.$ $**p < .01.$ $***p < .001.$

however, implies the inaction of spending time on more important things). Future-related regret was measured in this study by specifying 12 life goals and asking participants to indicate on a 7 point scale how upset they would be if they could not achieve the goal as a result of some events in their life (death was not specifically indicated). This measure was based on The Goal and Mode Values Inventories developed by Braithwaite and Law (1985). Examples of goals are: enjoying time with family members and friends, developing new areas of expertise, improving health or fitness, and developing a sense of meaningfulness or spirituality. A principal component analysis indicated three main components: Cultivating Relationships and Being a Better Person, Pursuing Spirituality and Knowledge, and Pursuing or Enjoying Status or New Experiences (Tomer & Eliason, 2005). The coefficient alpha for those scales was found in our study to be .80, indicating reasonably high internal consistency.

To measure death attitudes we used the Death Attitude Profile, Revised (Wong, Reker, & Gesser, 1994). Principal component analyses revealed the existence of five components. These included three forms of acceptance of death labeled Approach Acceptance, Escape Acceptance, and Neutral Acceptance. The other two components were Fear of Death and Death Avoidance. The intercorrelation between the negative attitudes—Fear and Avoidance—was rather high (around .7) and, for this reason we decided to conduct most of the analyses on a combined index of Fear-Avoidance.

In addition to the regret measures and to the death attitudes, the study included measures of intrinsic religiosity that focus on the centrality of God in one's life and extrinsic religiosity that focuses on external behaviors, such as worship attendance. Other variables were included, in conformity with the Tomer–Eliason model, such as a self-esteem measure (Rosenberg, 1965) and three measures of Locus of Control: Internality, Powerful Others, and Chance, based on Levenson's (1981) instrument.

What Do College Students Regret?   At a purely descriptive level there is interest in knowing the types of regret that are emphasized by participants. The most prevalent regrets are presented in Table 7.1. There were almost no significant differences by gender and, for this reason, the results are presented aggregatively for both genders. The reader can see that many of the most common regrets deal with relationships: not cultivating them enough, not spending enough time with family or friends, and so forth. A few common regrets are connected to money (saving more), to health and fitness (not working hard enough to improve themselves), but also to spirituality. No regret of action reached the 40% threshold. Only about 23% of the respondents felt that they have been too impulsive in their decisions or actions. The prevalence of regrets of omission (inaction) or commission (action) is consistent with Gilovich and Medvec's (1995) hypothesis and findings according to which regrets of inaction ultimately persist longer and are more pronounced. It is also possible that the emphasis placed in the questionnaire on the omission type of regret biased the results in this direction.

Future-related regret was investigated by having participants indicate to what extent they would be upset if particular goals were not accomplished (see Table 7.2). High levels of future-related regret in both genders were related to the goals: taking care of family, enjoying time with family members, and striving to achieve financial stability. In addition, especially women, emphasized striving to be a better person, to improve health/fitness, and to continue formal education. All the means for women were higher than the comparative means for men except for one, and in seven cases the difference attains significance at least at a .05 level. The level of future-related regret appears to be higher in females than in males.

Regret and Death Anxiety. The two measures of regret, past-related and future-related, correlated with both fear (.31 and .26, respectively), and avoidance (.28 and .24, respectively), as well as, with a composite index of fear-avoidance (.35 and .26) (Tomer & Eliason, 2005). Moreover, the examination of the two types of regret, together with other variables in a path model, also produced results consistent with the Tomer–Eliason model. The variables included the ones mentioned previously—the two types of religiosity, intrinsic and extrinsic, as well as self-esteem, locus of control, and background variables. Past-related regret and future-related regret were found to be significantly related to fear-avoidance, indicating an independent influence of each type of regret on negative attitudes. This influence is preserved even when other variables are kept constant. Since the analysis of future-related regret generated the three types described earlier, we have also run and evaluated path models for each type separately. We obtained significant paths leading from each one of the three types, Being a Better Person, Pursuing Spirituality or Knowledge, and Enjoying Life/Status to Fear-Avoidance (Tomer & Eliason, 2005).

Generalizing the Model to Other Death Attitudes. It was tempting to try to generalize the original model designed to predict death anxiety to other death attitudes, in particular to death acceptance. To do this we evaluated a model similar to the one used for Fear-Avoidance but having acceptance variables (approach, neutral, and escape) as their final dependent variables. To our surprise we found that there was a significant path from past-related regret to approach acceptance, but the path coefficient was positive, indicating that people who reported more regret also tended to report more (rather than less) acceptance of death. The interpretation of this finding remains doubtful. It is possible to consider regret a consequence of acceptance, rather than an antecedent or cause. A person who is more acceptant of death may allow himself or herself to consider critically his or her life and, indeed to regret actions or inactions. Moreover, such a person may look forward to an after-life in which he or she can undo, in a sense, the regrettable actions or inactions (in case those are not undoable in this life). In retrospect, the finding that fear and avoidance of death, on the one hand, and approach acceptance of death, on the other hand, have different determinants seem plausible in the light of the rather modest intercorrelations between them. In the original study by Wong et al. (1994), the correlation of death acceptance with fear and avoidance were rather low, −.40 and −.20, respectively. In our own 2005 study, the intercorrelations were even lower: −.01 with fear and .10 with avoidance. Almost identical intercorrelations are reported by Monika Ardelt in her study (see chapter 6 in this book): −.04 and .10 with fear of death and with death avoidance. Thus, the evidence showing that acceptance and fear are not just two poles of one dimension, but rather two dimensions that are weakly intercorrelated, is pretty conclusive. Correspondingly, the explanatory models used for these different dimensions should differ. Regret might play a completely different role in a model of acceptance (or perhaps no role). On the other hand, intrinsic religiosity that was found to be crucial for acceptance is probably much less important for lack of fear or lack of avoidance. In this latter case, analyses showed (Tomer & Eliason, 2005) that neutral acceptance of death is a possible antecedent. In other words, adults who consider death an integral part of the biological-cosmological order tend to fear it less than others who don't see it in this light.

It is important to keep the limitations of the 2005 study in mind. The most stringent limitation is the sample. This is rather small and composed exclusively of college students. Thus, only young ages are represented. An examination of the model in older adults is of paramount importance. Notwithstanding this limitation, we can cautiously conclude that the concept of regret appears to play an important role in the context of death attitudes, in particular as a possible antecedent of negative attitudes—fear and avoidance. It is possible that such a role may become even more prominent in older adults. A consideration of mechanisms of regret management, perhaps in the way advocated by Wrosch and Heckhausen (2002), seems promising as a way to transform the general model formulated by Tomer and Eliason (1996) into a more specific model of fear and avoidance of death.

CONCLUSION

In conclusion, the concept of regret appears to be a promising theoretical concept in the context of a model of death attitudes. Different types of regret, related to past and future, predict independently fear and/or avoidance of death. This finding raises important questions regarding the possibility for older adults to manage life regrets (Wrosh & Heckhausen, 2002) and to minimize fear of death by doing so. The possibility of generalizing a regret model to other death attitudes, in particular to death acceptance, should be further examined and investigated empirically.

MAIN POINTS

1. Regrets play a role in decision making processes. Managing life regrets constitutes an important developmental task.
2. Regrets related to actions or inactions are related to death anxiety: according to the Tomer–Eliason model, more intense regrets translate into higher death anxiety.
3. Similarly, death anxiety is exacerbated by future-related regret—regrets felt when considering the possibility of not being able to fulfill important current life goals.
4. The empirical evidence is consistent with the Tomer-Eliason model: both types of regret are connected to fear and avoidance of death.
5. On the other hand, death acceptance seems to be mainly connected to intrinsic religiosity, not to regret.

REFERENCES

Ainslie, G. (1975). Specious reward: A behavioral theory of impulsiveness and impulse control. *Psychological Bulletin, 82*, 463–496.

Antonovski, A. (1979). *Unraveling the mystery of health.* San Francisco, CA: Jossey-Bass.

Bell, D. E. (1982). Regret in decision making under uncertainty. *Operations Research, 30*, 961–981.

Bell, D. E. (1985). Disappointment in decision making under uncertainty. *Operations Research, 33(1)*, 1–27.

Braithwaite, V. A., & Law, H. G. (1985). Structure of human values: Testing the adequacy of Rokeach Value Survey. *Journal of Personality and Social Psychology, 21*, 203–211.

Erikson, E. H. (1963). *Childhood and society* (2nd ed.). New York: W. W. Norton.

Erikson, E. H. (1964). *Insight and responsibility.* New York, W.W. Norton.

Erikson, E. H. (1982). *The life cycle completed.* New York, W.W. Norton.

Gilovich, T., & Medvec, V. H. (1994). The temporal pattern to the experience of regret. *Journal of Personality and Social Psychology, 67*, 357–365.

Gilovich, T., & Medvec, V. H. (1995). The experience of regret: What, when, and why. *Psychological Review, 102(2)*, 379–395.

Hattiangadi, N., Medvec, V. H., & Gilovich, T. (1995). Failing to act: Regrets of Terman's geniuses. *International Journal of Aging and Human Development, 40*, 175–185.

Heckhausen, J., & Schultz, R. (1995). A life-span theory of control. *Psychological Review, 102*, 284–304.

Kahneman, D., & Miller, D. T. (1986). Norm theory: Comparing reality to its alternatives. *Psychological Review, 93*, 136–153.

Kahneman, D., & Tversky, A. (1979). Prospect theory: An analysis of decision under risk. *Econometrika, 47*, 263–291.

Landman, J. (1987). Regret: A theoretical and conceptual analysis. *Journal for the Theory of Social Behaviour, 17*, 135–160.

Landman, J. (1993). *Regret.* New York: Oxford University Press.

Lecci, L., Okun, M. A., & Karoly, P. (1994). Life regrets and current goals as predictors of psychological adjustment. *Journal of Personality and Social Psychology, 66*, 731–741.

Levenson, H. (1981). Differentiating among internality, powerful others, and chance locus of control orientation. In H. M. Lefcourt (Ed.), *Research with the locus of control construct* (Vol. 1, pp. 15–63). New York: Academic Press.

Loomes, G., & Sugden, R. (1982). Regret theory: An alternative theory of rational choice under uncertainty. *Economic Journal, 92*, 805–824.

Loomes, G., & Sugden, R. (1986). Disappointment and dynamic consistency in choice under uncertainty. *Review of Economic Studies, 53*, 271–282.

Monterosso, J., & Ainslie, G. (1999). Beyond discounting: Possible experimental models of impulse control. *Psychopharmacology, 146*, 339–347.

Nozick, R. (1993). *The nature of rationality.* Princeton, NJ: Princeton University Press.

Rosenberg, M. (1965). *Society and adolescent self-image.* Princeton, NJ: Princeton University Press.

Ruuska, L. L. (1993). *Development of a regret scale based on the MMPI-2.* Dissertation submitted to the Graduate School of the University of Wisconsin-Madison.

Stewart, A.J., & Vandewater, E. A. (1999). "If I had it to do over again..." : Midlife review, midcourse corrections, and women's well-being in midlife. *Journal of Personality and Social Psychology, 76(2)*, 270–283.

Thorson, J. A., & Powell, F. C. (1990). Meanings of death and intrinsic religiosity. *Journal of Clinical Psychology, 46*, 379–391.

Tomer, A. & Eliason, G. (1996). Toward a comprehensive model of death anxiety. *Death Studies, 20*, 343–365.

Tomer, A., & Eliason, G. (2000). Attitudes about life and death: Toward a comprehensive model of death anxiety. In A. Tomer (Ed.), *Death attitudes and the older adult: Theories, concepts, and applications* (pp. 3–22). Philadelphia, PA: Brunner-Routledge.

Tomer, A., & Eliason, G. (2005). Life regrets and death attitudes in college students. *Omega, 51*, 173–195.

Tversky, A., & Kahneman, D. (1992). Advances in prospect theory: Cumulative representation of uncertainty. *Journal of Risk and Uncertainty, 5*, 297–323.

Whittier, J. G. (1897). Maud Muller. In P. Garrett (Ed.), *One hundred choice selections.* Philadelphia, PA: Penn.

Wong, P. T. P., Reker, G. T., & Gesser, G. (1994). Death Attitude Profile–Revised: A multidimensional measure of attitudes toward death. In R. A. Neimeyer (Ed.), *Death anxiety handbook: Research instrumentation and application* (pp. 121–148). Washington, DC: Taylor and Francis.

Wrosch, C., & Heckhausen, J. (2002). Perceived control of life regrets: Good for young and bad for old adults. *Psychology and Aging, 17(2)*, 340–350.

Women Living With HIV: The Role of Meaning and Spirituality

Wendy L. Dobson
Paul T. P. Wong
Trinity Western University

INTRODUCTION

The epidemic of HIV/AIDS poses a serious challenge to both the medical community and psychologists. HIV has been spreading quickly in recent years, and the resulting disease, Acquired Immune Deficiency Syndrome (AIDS), currently ranks as the fourth leading global killer (UNAIDS & WHO, 2004). It is estimated that 14,000 people are infected with HIV every day and nearly 40 million men, women, and children currently have HIV (UNAIDS & WHO, 2004). The global total is the highest since the beginning of the epidemic, despite new antiretroviral therapies.

Women are becoming increasingly affected, with global rates rising from 41% in 1997 to about 50% in 2004 (UNAIDS & WHO, 2004).

Women are more likely to become infected as a result of violence and victimization and multiple heterosexual relationships (Logan, Cole, & Leukefeld, 2002). HIV may also impact women differently than men due to their role as a caregiver (Metcalfe, Langstaff, Evans, Paterson, & Reid, 1998; Hackl & Somlai, 1997). Women often experience feelings of guilt and concern for their children's future (Hackl & Somlai, 1997). Metcalfe et al. (1998) found that the needs of HIV-positive women are not being met well due to a lack of services. More research is needed to understand women's special needs after diagnosis with HIV.

Medical research has provided new drugs which have changed AIDS from a terminal to a chronic illness. AIDS patients are now being described as "living with AIDS" (Beaudin & Chambre, 1996). The new drugs have slowed down the progression of the illness and have decreased AIDS related deaths in the last few years. The focus has changed from helping patients die comfortably to enhancing their quality of life and effective disease management. This will change the role of psychology in caring for people with HIV/AIDS. Treatment adherence has emerged as an area of contemporary concern warranting further research (Kelly & Kalichman, 2002). Although drug treatment is often available, people with AIDS may have difficulty adhering to a regular treatment regimen. Motivation is clearly a factor. Individuals with a sense of meaning and purpose are more likely to adhere to the treatment regimen, because they have a reason for living.

Negative Impact

People with AIDS have many obstacles to overcome, both physical and emotional. Coping with the burdens of daily living can be overwhelming. People with AIDS not only have to cope with physical limitations that AIDS will bring, but also have to cope with stigma and social isolation. People with AIDS have to take complicated treatment regimens, which often have many side effects, including: fatigue, nerve damage, nausea, headache, anemia, and weight loss. People with AIDS have to battle many opportunistic infections, such as pneumonia, sarcoma, and some types of cancers.

People with AIDS are often described as facing multiple losses encompassing many areas of functioning. For example, a person with AIDS may have to deal with loss of health, isolation, loss of employment, loss of identity, and death of friends. Experience of such multiple losses can lead to depression and suicide (Cantrell, 1998). Research suggests that cognitive behavioral coping and group interventions can improve mental health and coping efficacy (Heckman et al., 2001). This chapter proposes that existential and spiritual/religious copings can be effective psychological tools for women living with HIV/AIDS because of their need to address existential and spiritual issues.

Existential Crisis

Diagnosis with a life threatening illness can cause people to ask questions about the meaning of life and death, triggering an existential or spiritual crisis (Breitbart, Gibson, Poppito, & Berg, 2004). As people grapple with the realities of the illness, they can become overwhelmed with the unavoidable givens, such as suffering and death. However, Viktor Frankl (1984) believes that people are also motivated to find positive meaning in the face of adversities. By tapping into the defiant power of the human spirit, clinicians can help people create meaning and purpose to transcend their circumstances and make positive life changes. By creating meaning, they will be able to maintain hope and dignity in the face of suffering.

Existential Coping

According to Wong, Reker, and Peacock (2006) there are two basic types of existential coping: *acceptance* and *existential meaning*. Acceptance coping includes such items as "Accept what has happened." Accepting the diagnosis of a life-threatening illness is necessary for taking appropriate medical measures. Existential meaning coping includes such items as "Believe that there is meaning and purpose to the things that happen to me." Affirmation of meaning helps offset the negative impact by accepting the bad news and by restoring a sense of hope. According to Wong's (2006a) meaning-management theory (MMT), the prospect of personal death triggers an existential crisis and the quest for meaning. MMT further posits that positive meanings, which can be discovered or created in any situation, are capable of improving adjustment outcomes.

There is some empirical support for meaning-management theory. For example, Schwartzberg (1993) reported that HIV-positive gay men saw their diagnosis as a catalyst for personal and spiritual growth and a sense of belonging and community. Somlai, Heckman, Hackl, Morgan, and Welsh (2001) found that AIDS diagnosis provided new direction in the women's lives, and the diagnosis was perceived as part of a larger purpose or quest. With Aboriginal women, meaning-making plays a role in adjustment to AIDS. In Susan Gabori's (2002) book, *A Good Enough Life: The Dying Speak*, two people with AIDS reported that AIDS had renewed their love of life and they would not want a cure if one was found.

Spiritual/Religious Crisis

Existential crisis is often linked to spiritual crisis, when people's assumptions and beliefs about God are shattered. Often, people will ask questions like: *Where is God? Why did God allow such a terrible thing happen to me?* Such questions necessarily lead to meaning-seeking, meaning-making, and meaning-reconstruction in order to restore the assumptive world. A spiritual crisis may also lead to spiritual transformation through a deepening of faith, a renewal of one's core beliefs and the discovery of one's authentic self (Wong, 2005a). Different from instrumentally oriented religious coping, spiritual transformation empowers individuals to transcend suffering and the immediate situation by opening new vistas of the transcendental reality.

Religious/Spiritual Coping

There has been an increasing interest in the positive role of spirituality and religion in health (Miller & Thoresen, 2003; Seybold & Hill, 2001). Religious and spiritual beliefs may improve health through a number of mechanisms, such as positive emotions, healthy lifestyle, social support, inner resources, and religious/spiritual coping. Wong, Reker, and Peacock (2006) recognized that religious coping has two components: religious beliefs and religious practices. Wong (1998b) recognized that there was considerable overlay between religiosity and spirituality. In this chapter, we use these two terms interchangeably.

Religious/spiritual coping is a topic that is gaining attention in recent years. For HIV-positive individuals, spiritual/religious coping is employed most frequently by African Americans and women (Jenkins, 1995; Somlai & Heckman, 2000). Many HIV-positive people retain ties to churches, and employ a "spiritual outlook." However, distrust of organized religion is a commonality (Jenkins, 1995). Most of the quantitative literature has indicated that religious/spiritual coping is associated with positive mental health variables, such as decreased drug use, increased social support, a greater sense of control, increased self-esteem, lower depression, and a greater satisfaction with life (Simoni, Martone, & Kerwin, 2002; Simoni & Ortiz, 2003; Somlai & Heckman, 2000). Some qualitative studies have shown that spiritual coping is perceived to have emotional benefits, social support benefits, and existential benefits (Siegel & Schrimshaw, 2002).

Spirituality for First Nations people is a relevant topic in coping with HIV, as the "Aboriginal worldview doesn't separate spirituality from healing as it is seen as an integral part of the process" (McCormick & Wong, 2006). Often physical illnesses are understood as stemming from spiritual illnesses, therefore, spirituality takes on a central role in healing. Many traditional Aboriginal people believe that healing ceremonies have a spiritual component. For example, in the Vision Quest ceremony, the individual connects with his or her spiritual identity. Interconnectedness is a prevalent theme in aboriginal worldview. For many, there is a direct spiritual connection between people and the natural world.

Prevention

We also propose that spirituality and meaning can make a unique and significant contribution to the prevention of the spread of HIV/AIDS. Present methods of prevention focus primarily on risk behaviors that contribute to the spread of HIV (McKay, 2000; Sheeran, Abraham, & Orbell, 1999). Despite both medical and prevention efforts, the virus continues to spread faster than originally anticipated (UNAIDS & WHO, 2004).

The steady rise in HIV transmission suggests that existing prevention programs need to consider larger psychosocial factors contributing to HIV risk behavior. At the community level, discrimination, stigma, and isolation often prevent people from accessing the help they need or from disclosing their diagnosis. Prevention at the political/economical level aims to deal with issues of poverty, prostitution, and treatment access, especially in developing countries. At the individual level, prevention needs to address the existential and spiritual issues. For example, when individuals feel that there is no meaning and purpose in life and there is no point to struggle and live longer, they are likely to engage in self-destructive behaviors such as unsafe needle use, or unprotected sex. Faith in God and a strong sense of mission may empower individuals who are HIV-positive to participate in AIDS prevention campaigns.

We propose that by incorporating existential and spiritual elements in prevention efforts, we can improve the success rates. There is already some evidence supporting our existential hypothesis. In a recent study on inner-city injection drug users, Avants, Marcotte, Arnold, and Margolin (2003) reported that HIV risk behavior was inversely associated with strength of spiritual and religious beliefs. Because spirituality was conceptualized as a set of beliefs concerning the meaningfulness of life, the findings of this study suggest that spirituality and meaning can play a role in prevention efforts.

Rationale for the Present Phenomenological Study

In this chapter, we report the result of a phenomenological study designed to give voice to the lived experience of women with HIV/ AIDS. Our research question was: What is the role of meaning and spirituality for women coping with HIV/AIDS? The phenomenological method seems most appropriate for studying existential/spiritual issues, because it allows participants to share their experiences, views, and feelings without interference from the experimenter. Many studies have shown that spirituality and meaning can provide hope and strength in the face of illness, but most of these studies focus on cancer (Jenkins & Pargament, 1995).

LITERATURE REVIEW

Existential Perspectives

The existential perspective focuses on individuals' subjective experience of the world as being the primary concern (May, 1983). The meanings they attribute to events influence how they respond to the environment. One basic tenet of existential psychology is that human existence is inherently plagued by anxiety. According to Yalom (1980), humans experience four primary existential anxieties: meaninglessness, death, isolation, and freedom. If the anxiety is too strong, then people will resort to defense mechanisms. Another major theme of existential psychology is individual freedom. Frankl (1967) and Wong (2005b) are more optimistic than other existential philosophers and psychologists about the human condition. According to Frankl (1967), "man is not free from conditions, be they biological or psychological, or sociological in nature. But he is, and always retains the freedom to choose his attitude toward them. Man is free to rise above the plane of somatic and psychic determinants of his existence" (p. 3). Frankl (1967) also believed that meaning could be found in any situation. He proposed three avenues to find meaning: (a) creative value—through what we give to life, (b) experiential value—through what we take from life, and (c) attitudinal value—through the stand we take toward unavoidable and unchangeable problems (Frankl, 1967). The defiant human spirit of taking a heroic stance is very relevant to coping with incurable diseases.

Frankl (1967) depicted humanity as being a totality of three dimensions: physical, psychological, and spiritual (noetic). The noetic dimension is the core self, the self which searches for meaning. Problems arise when this dimension becomes blocked by other dimensions (physical or psychological). Logotherapy seeks to remove this blockage. Guttman (1996) listed several inner resources which can counteract the block: will to meaning, purpose, creativity, love, sense of humor, ideas and ideals, imagination, self-awareness, compassion and forgiveness, and morality.

Logotherapists do not ask for the reason for suffering, but guide their clients toward the realization of concrete meanings, and choose the right attitudes. Often, logotherapists appeal to their clients to take a heroic stand toward suffering, but suggesting that unavoidable suffering gives them the opportunity to bear witness to the human potential and dignity. According to Frankl (1986), "Whenever one is confronted with an inescapable, unavoidable situation, whenever one has to face a fate that cannot be changed, for example, an incurable disease, just then is one given a last chance to actualize the highest value, to fulfill the deepest meaning, the true meaning of suffering" (p. 178).

Wong (2005b) advocates an integration of positive existential psychology and psychotherapy. He takes the position that we need to pay more attention to the positive givens of human existence, namely, the primary motivations for staying alive, meaningful living, belonging, freedom, love, and actualization. To the extent that we intentionally pursue these positive motivations and live life to the full, existential anxieties will become less important. We can truly live only when we have the courage to confront and accept our worst fears. However, there are individual differences: some live defensively, trying to protect themselves against the terror of death and other anxieties, while others live positively and optimistically, trying to live an authentic and fulfilling life without worrying too much about existential anxieties (Wong, chap. 3, this volume). To live authentically means to be truthful to one's core values and beliefs; it means to value what really matters and become what one is meant to be. One objective of positive existential psychotherapy is to help and empower people to switch from a defensive way of life to an authentic way of life.

Meaning-Centered Counseling

Wong's (1998c) meaning-centered counseling (MCC) is an extension of logotherapy. It is integrative and empirically based. In its simplest terms, the meaning-centered approach emphasizes the human capacity for narrative construction and the healing and transforming power of meaning. It incorporates cognitive behavior theory and narrative psychology as important devices for transforming negative events and thoughts into coherent, positive stories. Wong (1998a) has identified

seven major sources of meaning: achievement, self-acceptance, transcendence, intimacy, relationship, religion, and fair treatment. Any
combination of these sources can help overcome existential anxieties.
MCC is designed to empower individuals to pursue authentic living
and discover both specific meaning in the immediate situation and
ultimate or global meaning for human existence.

Park and Folkman (1997) suggest that meaning has two levels:
global meaning and situational meaning. Global meaning is one's
beliefs, assumptions, and expectations about their world. It is widely
suggested that global meaning develops across an accumulation of life
experiences and can be shaped through extraordinary experiences,
such as traumatic events. People who have experienced repeated
trauma tend to believe less in the meaningfulness and benevolence of
the world (Overcash & Calhoun, 1996). MCC aims to transform both
specific meaning and global meanings so that they can have a positive
rather than negative effect on health and well-being.

Wong's (2006a) meaning-management theory provides a conceptual
framework for MCC. Meaning-management is concerned with how to
best manage the three basic processes: meaning-seeking, meaning-
making, and meaning-reconstruction. Effective meaning-management
enables one to discover, create or reconstruct positive meanings in
adverse circumstances. In meaning-seeking, people aim to make sense
of or find benefits in the midst of troubles or in the face of death.
People with HIV may look for both causal and existential attributions
(Wong, 1991). In making causal attributions, women with HIV will
search for the causes of their infection, such as unprotected sex, or
unsafe needle sharing. In existential attributions, women with HIV
may wonder about the reason and purpose of getting HIV—Is this a
wake-up call? Is this a warning that they need to make the necessary
changes in their lives? What can they learn from being infected with
HIV/AIDS?

Meaning-seeking is also related to finding various meanings that
may be associated with an event. For example, a study with HIV-positive gay men, Schwartzberg (1993) found that the men discovered different meanings of AIDS: as catalyst for personal growth, as
belonging, as irreparable loss, as punishment, as contamination of
one's self, as strategy, as catalyst for spiritual growth, as isolation, as
confirmation of one's powerlessness, and as relief. The type of meaning ascribed to their illness can affect their psychological well-being.
Although all the men emphasized aspects of loss, most found some
positive meaning in the situation (Schwartzberg, 1993).

Successful meaning-seeking leads to discovery of positive meaning and purpose and can have a positive effect on one's health and

well-being. In a study with HIV-positive men who recently lost a close friend or partner to AIDS, Bower, Kemeny, Taylor, and Fahey (1998) found that the discovery of meaning was associated with positive changes in CD4 T lymphocyte, a key immunological marker of HIV progression. Participants who both engaged in cognitive processing and finding meaning in their eventual death showed no decline in CD4 T cells over a two to three year follow-up period. Participants who engaged in cognitive processing but did not find meaning, and those who did not engage in cognitive processing experienced a decline in CD4 T cells at a rate that could be characterized as moderate to fast. More importantly, the discovery of meaning was associated with a lower rate of AIDS related mortality over a four to nine year follow-up period. These results clearly demonstrate the health benefits of finding meaning.

Meaning-making primarily consists of creating meaning through actions. Thus, women with HIV may commit themselves to helping those who are less fortunate or devote their lives to serve someone or some cause greater than themselves. Meaning-making also involves making life more meaningful through doing creative work, such as writing, painting, or music. Meaning-reconstruction is primarily concerned with repairing one's shattered assumptive world and reconstructing one's life story. Through successful meaning-reconstruction, one may redefine one's identity, rearrange one's priorities, and change one's life directions. For a brief review of the literature regarding the healing power of meaning-making and meaning-construction, please read Wong (chaps. 3 and 15, this volume).

Spirituality and Religion

Spiritual experience is most often defined as a multidimensional construct, consisting of the following elements: searching for meaning, an encounter with transcendence, searching for ultimate truth, respect for creation, a sense of community, and personal transformation (LaPierre, 1994). Definitions of spirituality often involve some aspect of the sacred. The sacred is something that transcends the self, thereby deserving of reverence and devotion. People will strive to hold values that are in alignment with that which is sacred. Thus, Hill et al. (2000) defined spirituality as,

> The feelings, thoughts, experiences, and behaviors that arise from a search for the sacred. The term search refers to attempts to identify, articulate, maintain, or transform. The term sacred refers to a divine being, divine object, ultimate reality or ultimate truth as perceived by the individual. (p. 66)

Spirituality overlaps with religion (Wong, 1998b), but is a broader and more inclusive construct. Spirituality can be humanistically oriented, without making any reference to God, beliefs, and rituals of institutions. Some individuals may define their spirituality simply in terms of being appreciative of nature and compassionate toward others. However, both religion and spirituality can provide an overarching framework through which people orient themselves to the world, and endow people with a sense of ultimate meaning and purpose (Hill & Pargament, 2003). As sources of meaning, religious and spiritual systems are more comprehensive, experientially ubiquitous, and oriented toward transcendence than other meaning systems (Hill et al., 2000). According to Park and Folkman (1997), religion typifies global meaning: (a) religion is central in life meaning and purpose, (b) explanatory value of religion for understanding occurrences, (c) use of a variety of religious coping strategies in response to stressful situations by many people, and (d) traumatic experience can cause long-term changes in religious beliefs. Situational meaning, on the other hand, is formed in the interaction between a person's global meaning and a particular person–environment transaction. Spiritual and religious strivings provide stability, support, direction, and offer a unifying philosophy of life.

Existential and Religious/Spiritual Coping

Wong's resource-congruence model of coping (Wong et al., 2006) also serves as a helpful framework with regards to adaptation to HIV/AIDS. The model emphasizes the importance of developing coping resources, such as social support, education, religion, physical exercise, and so forth. It also posits that one is able to cope well when one has sufficient coping resources and employs appropriate coping strategies. With regard to unchangeable and uncontrollable conditions, such as terminal illnesses and eventual death, one needs inner resources as well as congruent coping responses, such as existential and religious/spiritual coping. For example, Wong and Stiller (1999) found that some individuals with chronic illness identify faith in God as an important source of meaning and strength in coping.

According to Pargament, Koenig, and Perez (2000), religion and spirituality serve five main functions. The first function is identified as the process of finding meaning amidst suffering. In the second function, religion helps people feel a greater degree of control over their situation through spiritual practices, such as prayer, or through a belief in divine intervention. The third function includes methods aimed at gaining comfort and closeness to God. In this function, people may report that their spiritual or religious beliefs provide them with a sense of peace or hope. In the fourth dimension, religion helps people feel close to others and to God. For example, religious communities are often a major source of social support when facing an illness or difficult situation. The fifth function focuses on life transformation. In this function, one's spiritual or religious beliefs can produce long lasting behavior or changes in worldview. These five functions were used as a theoretical basis for the RCOPE, a comprehensive measure of religious/spiritual coping. The RCOPE has been used with various populations and cultures and has demonstrated good validity and reliability.

Most research examining spirituality and coping has been quantitative in nature. Quantitative studies have traditionally investigated the relationship between spirituality/religiosity, and mental health/ coping variables. It has been proposed (Simoni et al., 2002) that spirituality and spiritual-based coping may be associated with increased social support and decreased drug use. Simoni et al. (2002) hypothesized that spiritual beliefs helped HIV-positive women to reappraise the situation and gain a greater sense of control. A follow-up study (Simoni & Ortiz, 2003) demonstrated that mastery and self-esteem mediated the relationship between spirituality and depression. Similarly, Somlai and Heckman (2000) found that people with AIDS who scored higher on spirituality are more likely to develop problem-solving strategies and report greater satisfaction with life.

Some recent research has utilized qualitative methods to understand spirituality and coping from the perspective of the person with HIV. Siegel and Schrimshaw (2002) report that spiritual coping is perceived to have emotional benefits (e.g., evokes comforting feelings, offers strength and empowerment, eases the emotional burden, facilitates self-acceptance), social support benefits, and existential benefits (e.g., facilitates meaning and acceptance, relieves fear of death). There is some consistency between these results and Pargament's (1997) notion that religion offers ways of increasing control. Somlai et al. (2001) found that HIV diagnosis resulted in a spiritual awakening, causing spiritual issues to resurface. Diagnosis with HIV was found to provide new direction in the lives of the women. Many women perceived their diagnosis as being part of a larger quest or greater purpose. Developmentally, the women had moved from a primarily external religiousness to an internal personal spirituality.

Coping with stigma may be unique to people with HIV-positive. The stigma will affect their social relationships and their sense of identity. The majority of research has focused on stigma in HIV-positive gay men. Stanley (1999) asserts that the integration of HIV is an ongoing process which involves deciding between what is "self" and what is outside of "self." People with AIDS must re-establish boundaries between what is self and what is not. Spiritual meanings which promote identification with what is "good" or moral are linked to empowerment. Women tended to categorize HIV as a calling, redemption, or a blessing/gift. Experiencing HIV as a calling serves to empower them by transforming tragedy into triumph (Stanley, 1999). Some women saw AIDS as redemption, stating that it helped to save them from a life of sin, and give them a second chance. The women who described HIV as a blessing or gift explained that HIV gave them a new appreciation for life or led them to a path of self-discovery. Stanley (1999) notes that one of the most difficult problems faced by HIV-positive women is to maintain an identity as "good" when social constructions are primarily "bad," and how to resolve the inconsistency of bad things happening to good people. Attributing HIV to a higher cause provides the opportunity to transcend societal constructions which are primarily condemning. Also, constructions which provide a sense of control may help to instill hope in an illness for which there is no known cure. Stanley (1999) asserts, "whereas the social and biomedical constructions depersonalize and impersonalize meaning and support a mind/body dualism, sacred discourse emphasizes the interrelatedness of self, society, and the numinous" (p. 117).

METHOD

The phenomenological method is interested in how something is experienced, rather than just what is experienced. The object of interest in the phenomenological investigation is the totality of the relationship of the individual and his/her world (life–world). Experience does not exist inside the individual, but exists out of relationship between the individual and his/her world (Colaizzi, 1978). The individual is responsible for determining the meaning of his/her subjective world. The life–world is pre-reflective, meaning that it exists prior to objective reflection or interpretation. The starting point of the phenomenological investigation should be at the pre-reflective state.

Rationale for Phenomenological Research

The purpose of the study was to understand the lived experience of women with HIV as co-researchers. The phenomenological method "seeks to understand the human condition as it manifests itself in our concrete, lived situations" (Valle & King, 1978). Therefore, this method seems most suited to capturing the HIV experience in its complexity and totality. Co-researchers were asked to describe as fully as possible their experience of living with HIV. They were asked about how they cope with HIV. They were also asked to describe their own religious or spiritual beliefs and the role these beliefs had in their lives.

Recruitment of Co-Researchers

Eight co-researchers were interviewed in the current study. Co-researchers were screened according to selection criteria. Selection criteria are as follows. The co-researcher must be: (a) HIV-positive, (b) female, (c) able to articulate and describe their experience in a coherent manner, (d) diagnosed for 1 year or more, and (e) have some spiritual or religious experience. Recruitment of co-researchers was conducted through a networking system with a local AIDS organization. An employee at the organization was informed on the purpose of the study, and the selection criteria, and chose participants on that basis. Interviews were arranged with willing participants. The purpose of the study and confidentiality was discussed. Each co-researcher was paid $30 at the completion of the interview.

The co-researchers were HIV-positive women, ages ranging from 24–44. Seven were of First Nations descent, and one was White. This ethnic imbalance might be due to the fact that most of the clients of the participating local agency were Aboriginal. Length of time since HIV diagnosis was between 6 and 18 years, with an average of approximately 10 years. One co-researcher had been diagnosed with AIDS for about 2 years.

Data Analysis

The interviews were transcribed verbatim. Meaning units were then extracted from the narratives. A meaning unit was defined as a paragraph or a segment with a clear meaning which was relevant to the phenomenon of living with AIDS and the subject matter of religion or spirituality. Each meaning unit was described by a phrase or a sentence to capture the essence of the meaning. Finally, 25 themes were derived by combining and refining these descriptors of meaning units. To test the reliability of the themes, a graduate student was recruited as judge and given 10% of the meaning units. The judge was asked to classify these meaning units according to the themes we had identified. High inter-subjective reliability (89% agreement) between the judge and the experimenter was obtained.

TABLE 8.1
Themes and Participation and Frequency Rates

Themes	Participation rate	Frequency rate
1. Social support	8 / 8	43
2. Experiences of stigma and discrimination	8 / 8	24
3. Experience of alcohol and drug addiction	8 / 8	17
4. Negative emotional reaction following HIV diagnosis	8 / 8	12
5. Positive effects of spirituality and prayer	7 / 8	30
6. Personal responsibility for health and choices	7 / 8	25
7. Negative experience of family	7 / 8	17
8. Desire to live and overcome difficulties and suffering	7 / 8	13
9. Relational issues	7 / 8	10
10. Acceptance of HIV and death	6 / 8	15
11. Desire to help others	6 / 8	14
12. Grieving the death of friends/loved ones	6 / 8	13
13. A personal approach to believing in a transcendental, spiritual reality	5 / 8	16
14. First Nations culture and spirituality	5 / 8	16
15. Having a sense of meaning, purpose, and goals	5 / 8	15
16. Loving self and others	5 / 8	13
17. Fear of death and dying	5 / 8	11
18. Difficulty disclosing HIV	5 / 8	10
19. Issues related to medication and treatment	5 / 8	7
20. Learning through HIV and suffering	4 / 8	20
21. Health problems related to HIV	4 / 8	8
22. Positive effects of nature	3 / 8	5
23. Negative experiences of spirituality/religion	3 / 8	4
24. Questioning the meaning of suffering	3 / 8	4
25. Living in the present	3 / 8	3

RESULTS

The themes are presented in table 8.1 in descending order of participation and frequency rates. Participation rate refers to the number of co-researchers (out of a total of eight) that mentioned the theme. Frequency rate refers to the total number of times that each theme was mentioned.

Detailed Description of Themes

1. *Social support.* This theme includes experience of emotional support from family, friends, and the community. Six women agreed that family provided an important support system to cope with HIV. Six women described the importance of community organizations for people with HIV to help fill their time and provide supportive relationships.

   "But just having people say the same things all over again allowed me to realize that I wasn't any different than anybody else. We all have a common ground. And if we talk to each other and be there for each other that makes it a lot easier."

2. *Experiences of stigma and discrimination.* All eight women discussed experiences of stigma or discrimination related to having HIV. This included experiences of rejection or avoidance by others, derogatory statements about HIV or poor treatment because of HIV. Two women reported encountering cultural discrimination as a result of being First Nations.

   "Because I was a First Nations, like a Metis and I got pushed around in White homes. I was called a dirty little squaw. I learned what shame was."

3. *Experience of drug or alcohol addiction.* All eight women reported either current or past struggles with addictions. Many of the women reported using drugs and alcohol as a way to cope with emotional pain. Four women discussed the struggles and benefits of overcoming addiction.

   "A year after I found out I started using more drugs and alcohol and I came down here. Drinking and doing drugs until it got to the point where I didn't care about anything or anybody, not even me."

4. *Negative emotional reaction following HIV diagnosis.* This theme includes a range of negative feelings that were experienced after being diagnosed with HIV. The most common feelings were shock, fear, and depression. This theme is important in that all eight women reported negative feelings following HIV diagnosis, and two reported thoughts of suicide.

   "Well for a long time it was, I was just devastated. It [HIV] devastated my whole life."

5. *Positive effects of spirituality and prayer.* This theme includes positive effects of spirituality and prayer on emotions, behavior, and health. Common emotional benefits include feelings of peace, comfort, strength, less fear of death, a sense of protection and hope; behavioral benefits include a sense of compassion, less violence, and overcoming addiction; and health benefits include a belief that prayer can lessen the effect of HIV or preserve health.

   "Without spirituality there's nothing. You just die. And I think that if you have the spirituality to hang on to you'll never be alone. There will always be something, having a creator that you know is always there. You can't see it, you can't touch it, but you know it's always there."

6. *Personal responsibility for health and choices.* This theme includes beliefs that in order to live longer and healthier, one must care for her own health by taking medication regularly, seeing the doctor, eating healthy, sleeping well, and not drinking or taking drugs. It also includes beliefs that each

person is responsible to make their own choices and create their own future, and that people should take responsibility for how their actions affect others.

"Not to accuse society or my parents or my bad childhood of making my life messed up today. And just to make other people aware that no matter what kind of life you've had, once you become an adult and you become aware that you have your own freedom, you're responsible for your own life."

7. *Negative experience of family.* This theme includes experiences of childhood abuse or neglect, as well as current conflicts, lack of support or abandonment from family. This theme is important in that seven women reported experiences of abuse or neglect in childhood.

"I lost my mom when I was young and my father used to beat me all the time. I had four brothers and I was pretty much all alone. They didn't say I care for you and all that stuff like that."

8. *Desire to overcome difficulties and suffering.* This theme includes feelings of being able to cope with HIV or other challenges, overcoming fear, and a will to live despite suffering. One woman discussed her desire to overcome challenges related to being blind, and other women discussed their desire to overcome challenges of addiction.

"I'm at a point in my life where I kind of haven't like given up, but it's hard. I'm struggling with different things. It's hard. But I still have faith."

9. *Relational issues.* This theme includes various kinds of relationship difficulties in intimate or non-intimate relationships, including trust issues, issues with men, communication, boundaries, and the impact of HIV on relationships.

"At times I've felt like I've stayed with my boyfriends because he's not as well with me and he's on medication. I'd be worried about him. And also, would I find anyone else? Just that we've been together a long time. Just that we both have it. We have to stick together. So it's affected my relationship in that way, and that's probably not the healthiest way to go."

10. *Acceptance of HIV and death.* Six women discussed the need to come to terms with and accept the realities of HIV, illness, and death. Two women indicated that it is only after they came to accept having HIV that they could find ways to cope with it.

"You have to learn to embrace your disease, this disease, and come to terms with it so you can get on with living."

11. *Desire to help others.* Six women shared a common desire to reach out and help others who are struggling with HIV or addictions. Helping others provided them with a sense of meaning, purpose, and self-esteem. Two women talked about the importance of helping the general public understand HIV/AIDS through public speaking. Two women indicated a strong desire to help others live a better life than they are. One woman talked about the benefits of running a support group for women with HIV.

"It's helps me to help other people. As long as I know I'm doing something, I feel okay."

12. *Grieving the death of friends or loved ones.* This theme includes loss of family and friends from AIDS or from other causes and the impact of such losses. One woman discussed the pain of losing both her husband and infant daughter to

AIDS. Four women discussed the difficulties of constantly losing friends to AIDS.

"You're going to have more friends that pass away, going to support places and stuff. You're, there's always someone passing away."

13. *A personal approach to believing in a transcendental, spiritual reality.* This theme encapsulates approaches to spirituality which includes integrating different religious beliefs, beliefs that there is something beyond human awareness and understanding, and beliefs in a higher power of one's own understanding.

"Over a period of time I guess, and over many years it just developed on its own. I would hear something about a certain religion and I would go hey that sound kind of cool. And I would take little pieces of each religion that I kind of learned about. I did a lot of reading in fact."

14. *First Nations culture and spirituality.* This theme includes statements about the importance of First Nations cultural and spiritual practices, and experiences of them, both currently and in childhood. Common cultural and spiritual practices mentioned were: sweat lodges, drumming, carving, tobacco, and healing from elders. Many of the women expressed a desire to reconnect with their First Nations heritage.

"When I was a kid I used to go to pow-wows and dances and stuff. And my brother dances. But my parents were divorced when I was 2, and my mom was White and my dad was Native, so after that I pretty much had no culture. And right now I'm not really involved in my culture. I identify myself as Native and I definitely have a connection with it. It definitely affects me. I want to get more involved in my culture."

15. *Having a sense of meaning, purpose, and goals.* One woman talked about HIV as changing long-term goals and helping her to look for a deeper meaning in life. Three women all felt that they are being kept alive for a larger purpose, often related to helping others with HIV or helping the world understand HIV. Two women believed that everything happens for a reason, although we may not always understand the reason.

"I believe that I was kept on this earth for a reason. It may sound funny but I don't know what I'm supposed to do but I'll know when I'm ready for it. You know there's got to be some reason."

16. *Loving self and others.* These themes includes a belief that in order to love others, one must first love and accept themselves. It also encapsulates statements about seeing the good in others, and forgiving others.

"Loving yourself, loving other people as best as you can. Treating other people good too you know. And treating yourself good most of all. Because if you treat yourself good then you can be a little bit more happy and be there for other people."

17. *Fear of death and dying.* This theme encapsulates statements made by co-researchers regarding uncertainty about how long they will live, difficulty thinking about death or fear of getting sick with AIDS.

"When you wake up every day and face your own mortality it's very hard."

18. *Difficulties disclosing HIV.* This theme encapsulates statements regarding the experience of telling family or friends about having HIV. Five women

reported finding it difficult or painful to tell friends and loved ones about having HIV. Two women agreed that it was important to have full disclosure with everyone. One woman has chosen not to disclose HIV, although she fears transmitting it to others.

"Took me a long time before I told my sister though, hard. Just like it was hard for me to tell my foster mom. I cried when I told her."

19. *Experiences of medication and treatment.* This theme includes the benefits and drawbacks of taking medication and the difficulties of taking medication regularly. Two women discussed the difficulties of side effects and managing an extensive treatment regimen. Two women described the positive benefits of taking medication on their health.

"Since I've been taking the medications, it's helped me a lot. I haven't been getting sick as much. I've put on about twelve pounds since I've been taking the medication steadily everyday."

20. *Learning through HIV and suffering.* This theme describes feelings that getting HIV has helped them make positive changes, such as overcoming addiction and quitting prostitution. Two women agreed that getting HIV has helped them to be more compassionate and accepting of others.

"I believe that this is a learning thing. This is a disease to teach people how to love each other, to have compassion for anyone."

21. *Health problems related to HIV.* Four women discussed experiencing health problems from HIV/AIDS, including: muscle soreness, contracting viruses easily, and blindness. Common emotional reactions to health problems include frustration and anxiety.

"I could feel the HIV in my hands. My sister always reminds me to fix my hair nicely, but now it's a lot harder and you can't do it on your own. My hands, I can't do a lot with them sometimes. They don't look as normal as other people's hands. I couldn't hold a baseball."

22. *Positive effects of nature.* Three co-researchers felt that being outside in nature provided them with a sense of hope, peace, and connection.

"You got to be connected to all the good things we have that exist, all the good things that are alive, like sunlight, and earth and water. Because it's all good. Even though everything is messed up we still have new life and there's still hope."

23. *Negative experiences with spirituality and religion.* Three women discussed negative experiences of religion in childhood, such as being forced to go to church, feelings of guilt and shame, and abuse in the church. One co-researcher struggled with understanding the bad deeds of believers and currently avoids churches as a result of a traumatic experience in a church.

"I don't go to churches at all because I got molested in a church. I was forced as a kid to go to church. I don't do it. That is why, not a lot of pain. Just a lot of anger. There would be pain."

24. *Questioning the meaning of suffering.* Two women struggled with the question of why they had to experience HIV or other types of suffering. One woman questioned why her daughter had to die from AIDS when she felt that she was to blame.

"I just figured like what did my daughter ever do? She was just a 6-month-old baby right? Like what, why should she have to suffer because of my lifestyle, because of the mistakes that I made when I was younger?"

25. *Living in the present.* This theme includes statements about living one day at a time, letting go of the past and not worrying about the future.
"But most of all I just try not to get too wrapped up in the future. I just try to stay in the day to day thing. I wake up, I get my methadone, I get my coffee, I pop in downstairs and see if they got any good little munchies, and say hi to my friends and finish my coffee and maybe watch a movie and just getting back into regular routine."

DISCUSSION

The 25 themes that emerged from phenomenological interviews with eight HIV-positive women can be organized into six broad categories: negative impact, death concerns, health issues, social support, existential coping, and spiritual coping. The themes will be discussed according to these broad categories with an emphasis on death attitudes, existential coping, and religious/spiritual coping.

Negative Impact

The categories include the following themes: negative emotions, difficulty with disclosure, stigma, addictions, and family issues which appear to be common experiences of HIV-positive women. There is a wealth of support in the literature for the negative impact of HIV. For example, in a qualitative study with HIV-positive women, Goggin et al. (2001) explored the positive and negative consequences of HIV. Sixteen percent of the women reported death of family and friends due to AIDS, 22% reported loss of potential love relationships, 11% reported loss of the ability to have children, 11% reported the loss of the ability to work, and 22% reported the loss of their future. They also talked about experiences of rejection (7%) and the difficulties and fears surrounding having to disclose HIV status to family and friends (16%). Nine percent of the women talked about feelings of depression, anxiety, and anger related to having HIV. Nine percent of women reported struggling with fears of death, pain, and suffering.

It is not surprising that all eight women reported experiences with drug and alcohol addiction in this study. Intravenous drug use either directly or indirectly accounts for approximately 36% of cases of HIV in the US (CDC, 2004). In a review of the literature, Klinkenberg and Sacks (2004) found that intravenous drug use accounts for nearly twice as many cases of HIV in women than in men. Substance use in general is associated with greater sexual risk taking (Knight, Purcell, Dawson-Rose, Halkitis, & Gomez, 2005) and therefore has an indirect effect on the transmission of HIV. Alcohol use has also been associated with greater sexual risk taking and drug users who are also heavy drinkers reported more unsafe needle use (Stein et al., 2000). Kral, Bluthenthal, Booth, and Watters (1998) found that about 13% of IV drug users in sixteen different US municipalities had HIV, while approximately 8% of crack smokers were HIV-positive. These numbers are significantly higher than in the average population. Persons with severe alcohol abuse also have higher rates of HIV than do the general public (Klinkenberg & Sacks, 2004). Prevalence of current substance abuse disorders is about twice as high in HIV-positive people than compared to the national average (Klinkenberg & Sacks, 2004).

Although the majority of people are likely addicts before contracting HIV, addiction can also serve as a way of coping. Some women stated that they used drinking or drugs as a way to cope with the emotional pain of having HIV. One woman stated that, "A year after I found out [about HIV] I started using more drugs and alcohol and I came down here. Drinking and doing drugs and it got to the point where I didn't really care about anything or anybody, not even me." Although HIV can perpetuate addictions, some women were able to overcome addictions and described the positive impact from overcoming addiction: "I can deal with me being HIV better now than when I was drinking. I would just drink it away and everybody would forget about me but nobody did. I'm glad I did quit." These statements suggest that existential and spiritual coping mechanisms would be more adaptive than drinking and substance abuse as means of dealing with inner pain.

People with HIV often have difficulty disclosing their diagnosis to friends and loved ones due to fear of rejection, discrimination, or causing others pain. There is a wealth of literature on disclosure of HIV. In a study by Simoni et al. (1995) with 65 HIV-positive women, a survey revealed low rates of disclosure to extended family members, higher rates to immediate family members, and highest rates to lovers and friends. Reasons for disclosure differed according to target. For lovers, ethical responsibility was the biggest concern and concern for lover's health. For parents and friends, HIV was disclosed as a way to obtain support. Reasons for not disclosing to lovers and friends were mainly attributed to a desire to avoid rejection or maintain secrecy. Disclosure was withheld from parents as a way to protect them (i.e., not worry them), and avoid stigma or ignorance about HIV. With regard to reaction to disclosure, parents and friends frequently reacted by being supportive, whereas lovers were more likely to become angry and withdraw, thereby validating the fear of being rejected. In a study with HIV-positive men (Holt & Court, 1998), qualitative interviews revealed that immediately following diagnosis, men were more likely to withhold HIV status, and disclosure was used increasingly as a coping mechanism throughout the illness. From an existential perspective, failure of disclosure is ultimately related to fear to confront the full reality of HIV/AIDS, which include social stigma and rejection. Therefore, existential coping of acceptance should pave the way for self-disclosure.

In this study, all eight participants reported some experience of stigma and discrimination. However, some of the women stated that HIV stigma had decreased over the past few years. For example, one woman stated that, "it's only the ignorant and the scared and the fearful and the uneducated that are still wary of HIV and AIDS and stuff you know. But most people for the most part are wanting to help some way, wanting to get involved and they just don't know what to do." This shows that public education and awareness may have served to improve people's attitudes toward people with HIV.

Death Concerns

In this study, two themes were related to death: grieving the death of friends and loved ones (theme twelve), and fear of death and dying (theme seventeen). These two themes indicate that death anxiety may be magnified by both the loss of friends and loved ones as well as the diagnosis with a life-threatening disease. One woman stated that, "People started dying. But they seemed healthier than me, they weren't drinking, they were on the pills and they would die. I thought holy cow, I'm not even on the pills and I'm drinking so why am I still here? I'm at the point where I don't want to die and I'm not ready to die. I don't want to die just yet."

There was also the emotional reaction to the loss of a loved one. One participant expressed her anger: "You know when I lost my husband and my daughter I was just I was mad at God. I was I knew I never stopped believing in him but boy I was pissed at him and I didn't talk to him for a long time. I didn't say nothing to him for a while."

Facing one's own mortality could be difficult enough. Death anxiety can be compounded by the fear that one can get very sick anytime and die as a result. Such feelings can be prominent in some of the participants of this study. Here are two examples:

"When you wake up every day and face your own mortality it's very hard. When you have what I have. You wonder; are your days numbered? You do a lot of things that I'm supposed to do. I don't know if I'll get them done because I can't know how many days are left."

However, death concerns may also have a positive effect. For example, one woman in the study described how a life threatening disease changed her life around, "That really changed my life. I let go of a lot of stuff, especially the violence." Another woman witnessed the change in her friend:

"You know like a good friend just lost her daughter. And it's making her examine her own life now after she's getting to deal with the grief and stuff. So she's thinking about making changes in her life. And her daughter and her sister died of heroin overdose."

According to meaning-management theory (Wong, chap. 3, this volume), to move from death anxiety to death acceptance, one needs to involve a process of meaning-seeking and meaning-making. This point will become clear in the next section on existential coping. Here is one woman's account of how she overcame fear of death and dying:

"You know I used to be really afraid of dying because I didn't know what to expect. Wow what's gonna happen? Holy shit what if it's just, what if there's nothing? Shit that would suck. But now I've come to terms that there's gonna be something and I know it's gonna be even better than here because I believe that hell is down here sometimes.

"My CD4 counts are 160 right now and that's the lowest they've ever been so I'm a little I'm a little nervous about it. I'm a little bit you know but not off the chart because I know that there's a reason. There's a reason for it. There's a reason for everything that happens. I believe that also. For some reason everything happens for a reason. I don't know what the hell that reason is and that's beyond my understanding again you know but I know that it's all."

Existential Coping

Numerous themes in this study reflect different aspects of existential coping. These themes include: acceptance of HIV and death, having a sense of meaning, purpose and goals, questioning the meaning of suffering, learning through HIV and suffering, living in the present, taking personal responsibility for health and choices, loving self and others, and wanting to help others. According to Wong, Reker, and Peacock (2006) existential coping is important in coping with conditions beyond one's control, such as terminal illness and death. Existential coping consists of four functions: affective, motivational, spiritual, and existential. In the affective function, affirmation of meaning helps create positive emotions, such as happiness or hope. The motivational function provides the motivation to go on living and pursuing one's life goals. The existential function includes an acceptance of harsh realities and an affirmation of positive meaning. The spiritual function primarily deals with issues of ultimate meaning and purpose.

In this study most participants reported seeing everything as having meaning or happening for a reason. For many women, having a sense of purpose and meaning was closely tied to helping others. The theme of helping others is also related to the affective function, because altruistic or self-transcendental acts have been shown to be a source of personal meaning and subjective well-being (Wong, 1998a).

The motivational function is consistent with the theme of desiring to overcome difficulties and suffering. The will to live was often related to meaning-making and having sense of purpose. Taking a positive, heroic stand can lead to a new appreciation for life: "I feel better and happier to wake up. Even if I don't have money, just being here and being alive makes me feel happier now."

The existential function is evident in the theme of acceptance of HIV and death. In this theme women reported a need to come to terms with and accept the realities of having HIV in order to be able to cope with it. This suggests that acceptance is an essential part of the coping process. One woman talked about how accepting HIV helped her begin to cope: "To love yourself is to love your disease. You don't do anything about something that you hate, but you can come to terms with it and tell yourself there's something more here for me to learn." Learning something through suffering is also related to existential function, because it makes suffering more meaningful and beneficial. Several women talked about how getting HIV helped them change their life around in ways such as overcoming addiction, becoming more compassionate or developing self-awareness. One woman talked about the impact of HIV on her life: "I believe today that if I wouldn't have caught HIV, I would still be out there prostituting, leading the dysfunctional lifestyle that I had been leading for so long, and I'd probably be still sitting in jail for murder or something. That's why I say it was a gift because it actually has prevented me from doing a lot of the things that I was leading up to doing." Acceptance is a big part of existential coping with situations which cannot be changed. By accepting the reality, at least one can live with it one day at a time and make the necessary adjustments.

Another major component of existential coping is to learn from suffering and find some spiritual benefit from adversity.

"To learn from what I can and maybe even for things that were painful and difficult to teach me to be compassionate to other people. Or at least to be more open minded and patient and understanding. And not to be judgmental of people and to not let things make me resentful and angry."

These results are also supported by work done in the area of positive affect and coping. Folkman and Moskowitz (2000) identify three types of coping related to the maintenance of positive affect: positive reappraisal, goal directed problem focused coping, and the infusion of ordinary events with positive meaning. Positive reappraisal includes cognitive strategies that help an individual see a negative situation in a positive light. Problem focused coping includes efforts aimed to solve or manage the situation that is causing distress. According to Folkman and Moskowitz (2000), problem focused coping can be related to meaning in that it helps individuals feel competent and effective. Infusing events with positive meaning is defined as attempts to buffer negative events by either creating positive events or infusing ordinary events with positive meaning. All three types of coping are supported by longitudinal research with AIDS caregivers (Folkman, Moskowitz, Ozer, & Park, 1997; Moskowitz, Folkman, Collette, & Vittinghoff, 1996).

Similar to the current research, Schwartzberg's (1993) study with HIV-positive gay men found that some men were able to find spiritual value (high meaning) in their condition. Dunbar, Mueller, Medina, and Wolf (1998), who interviewed HIV-positive women, also found that one emerging theme was HIV as a source of self-affirmation. This is similar to the theme of loving self and others, where participants underscored the need to accept oneself in order to accept others.

Spiritual/Religious Coping

Closely related to existential coping is spiritual/religious coping. According to Pargament et al. (2000), religion serves five main functions: finding meaning amidst suffering, feeling a greater degree of control, gaining comfort and closeness to God, feeling close to others and to God and facilitating life transformation. In this study, the following themes may be considered as reflecting spiritual/religious coping: positive effects of spirituality and prayer, a personal approach to believing in a transcendental, spiritual reality, and a First Nations approach to culture, spirituality and nature.

An increasing number of studies have demonstrated the beneficial effects of spirituality and religion on health and coping (Koenig, George, & Titus, 2004; Larson & Larson, 2003; Miller & Thoresen, 2003;

Powell, Shehabi, & Thoresen, 2003). Religion in cancer patients has been linked to life satisfaction and lower pain levels (Yates, Chalmer, St. James, Follansbee, & McKegney, 1981). Women with breast cancer describe their religious and spiritual faith as giving them emotional support, social support, and meaning in everyday life (Feher & Maly, 1999).

A smaller number of studies have examined the relationship between HIV/AIDS and spirituality and religion (Siegel & Schrimshaw, 2002; Simoni, Martone, & Kerwin, 2002; Somlai & Heckman, 2000). A study with 65 HIV-positive people by Somlai et al. (1996) found a strong relationship between spiritual dimensions and indices of mental health, psychological adjustment, and coping. Extrinsically orientated religious practices were found to decrease loneliness, depression, and anxiety. In a correlational study with 230 HIV-positive women (Simoni et al., 2002), both spirituality and spiritual-based coping were positively related to psychological adaptation. A study by Somlai and Heckman (2000) assessed a sample of 275 people living with HIV to examine relationships between spirituality, quality of life, perceptions of social support, and coping and adjustment. Spirituality was measured based on a survey containing five subscales: prayer practices, alternative practices, formal religions, spiritual beliefs, and punishment. Prayer, formal religion, and spirituality were all related to being non-White, engaging in adaptive coping, and having support from family. The belief that AIDS is not a punishment was related to being White, more education, being male, and older age. These results clearly indicate that for people with HIV, spirituality is a multidimensional construct and is related to quality of life.

Qualitative studies have sought to understand the perceived benefits of spiritual and religious coping, transformation of identity, and the structure of spiritual meaning in people with HIV. In one study (Siegel & Schrimshaw, 2002), 63 HIV-infected middle aged and older adults were interviewed to understand the perceived benefits of spiritual and religious coping. Nine themes emerged: evokes comforting emotions and feelings, offers strength, empowerment and control, eases the emotional burden of the illness, offers social support and a sense of belonging, offers spiritual support through a personal relationship with God, facilitates meaning and acceptance of the illness, helps preserve health, relieves the fear and uncertainty of death, and facilitates self-acceptance and reduces self-blame. This research builds on some of the quantitative research by illuminating what it is about the experience of religion or spirituality that facilitates coping and adjustment. The current research gives support to these findings in regards to the emotional and physical benefits of spirituality for people with HIV.

Stanley (1999) found that White, middle class women with HIV/ AIDS often incorporate spiritualized and transformation rhetoric to deflect stigma and reconstruct self. For example, some women saw HIV as a calling, believing that God gave it to them to teach other people about it. Some women saw HIV as redemption—a spiritual rescue from the consequences of sin, in that getting HIV helped them make positive changes or that in some cases HIV was a punishment sent from God. A similar theme was that HIV was a blessing or gift from God which gave them a new appreciation of life or an opportunity for self discovery.

A study by Hall (1998) sought to understand how spiritual meaning is structured in advanced stages of HIV disease. Three major themes emerged: purpose in life emerges from stigmatization, opportunities for meaning arise from a disease without a cure, and after suffering, spirituality frames the life. The first theme, purpose in life emerges from stigmatization, includes experiences of social rejection, anger at God, negative experiences of religion, purpose for HIV, and reconnecting with family. It appears that people in this theme were able to transform their victimization with new spiritual meanings. The second theme, opportunities for meaning arise from a disease without a cure, describes how people incorporated illness and symptoms into their understanding of their spiritual being. The third theme, after suffering, spirituality frames the life, includes experiences of accepting self, clarification of beliefs, spiritual rituals, and acceptance. This theme suggests that after a health crisis, people question and become open to discover their unique spiritual meaning.

Co-researchers in this study reported positive effects on emotions, behavior, and health. Common emotional effects included a sense of peace, comfort, and strength. For example, one woman stated, "I just get my Bible and lay down and say a prayer. It seems to help me relax. I get my gospel tape my cousin gave me. I play that and it helps me." One woman talked about how her spirituality helps deal with feelings of isolation: "I think that if you have the spirituality to hang on to you'll never be alone. There will always be something, having a creator that you know is always there. You can't see it, you can't touch it, but you know it's always there." Some women stated that rediscovering their spirituality changed their behavior and relationships. For example, "Mostly it [spirituality] tamed the violence, the need to push people away. It changed a lot. For people that I have hurt the most with my anger it was my mission to befriend them and turn that around."

The majority of co-researchers talked about believing in a personal, transcendental reality. The predominant thought was a belief in a god of one's own understanding, which sometimes included an acceptance of and integration of various religious beliefs. This theme was touched in the study by Hall (1998) in that some participants gained spiritual insights and understanding after testing positive for HIV. Co-researchers in this study are unique in that most (seven of eight) are of First Nations background and were raised in White foster homes. This may pose a bigger challenge for them to integrate various spiritual beliefs with their identity as an HIV-positive woman. One woman who had accomplished this stated, "I don't know if you can call it God or the creator or Krishna or whatever. It's the God of my understanding. You make it your own personal relationship with God, the God of your understanding, and so it's yours. No one can take it away from you. It belongs to you. That's between you and your God."

The majority of the women described experiences of First Nations culture and spirituality. These results are unique, because little research has been done with HIV-positive women of First Nations descent. Most of the research to date, being from the USA has focused primarily on African American, White, or Hispanic cultural groups. Women of First Nations descent face unique struggles due to severe trauma histories as a result of residential schools. Many of the women, while facing stigma related to HIV, have also faced cultural discrimination. Many of the women stated a desire to reconnect with their First Nations heritage. For example, one woman stated, "I identify myself as Native and I definitely have a connection with it. It definitely affects me. I want to get more involved in my culture." Common First Native cultural/spiritual practices that were mentioned included: sweat lodge, healing ceremony, drumming, and healing ceremonies. One woman stated, "Spirituality for me is my Native culture. Like with my drumming that I do, with my talking circles that I do. I have wanted to go to sweat lodges for a while."

The theme of positive effects of nature is closely tied to First Nations spirituality and culture. For First Nations people, a spiritual connection exists between nature and humans, in that humans are seen as part of nature (McCormick & Wong, 2006). Nature may also be a source of guidance and assistance. Humans and nature are not separated, as all are equal in the eyes of the creator. In the current research, participants felt a sense of peace and comfort from nature. One participant talked about nature as providing hope and connection to something greater: "You have to be connected to all the good things we have that exist; all the good things that are alive, like sunlight and earth and water, because it's all good."

Spirituality or religion may be defined differently by different people, and people have different experiences in their spiritual journey, but the consensus is that spirituality helps people make sense of suffering and empowers them to live fully.

"Because you're more aware of your mortality so you're more thinking about death sometimes. You're more thinking about living this life more fully or being more spiritually aware or being more spiritually connected to whatever higher power."

A small number of co-researchers talked about negative experiences with religion in childhood. However, these participants managed to develop a bigger and more positive understanding of spirituality and religious faith in adulthood.

Health Issues

Only 50% of the women in this study reported health problems related to HIV. Although most of the women have had their diagnosis for 7 years or more, advances in treatment have slowed down the progression from HIV to AIDS. Only one woman in this study has been diagnosed with AIDS. In a study with 107 HIV-positive adults (Johnson & Folkman, 2004), the most common reported symptoms of HIV were fatigue, neuropathy, night sweats, and weight loss. Side effect symptoms and disease related symptoms were found to have an equal impact on quality of life, thus stressing the need to take the impact of side effects seriously.

Although a cure for HIV has yet to be found, recent medical advances have greatly extended life, changing it into a chronic illness. The women in this study reflect the challenges and benefits of antiretroviral treatment. In a study aimed to understand the barriers to antiretroviral adherence among HIV infected adults, Murphy, Roberts, Martin, Marelich, and Hoffman (2000) found that the most difficult barriers for patients were sleeping through dose times, problems following special instructions, and changes in daily routines. Some of the barriers were also emotional and included feeling depressed, hopeless, overwhelmed, and wanting to forget about HIV. Strategies that assisted with adherence fell into three categories: practical (schedules, reminders, and special containers), social support (explanation about medication, support group, support from health care provider, and disclosure with family/friends), and medical (changing medications, minimizing side effects, adjusting daily routine). We propose that having a strong sense of meaning and purpose for living would improve antiretroviral adherence.

Social Support

Social support from family, friends, and the community (theme one) was the most frequently reported theme in this study. This theme is well supported by the literature about the positive effects of social support in HIV and other diseases. A study with 161 HIV-positive IV drug users (Mizuno, Purcell, Dawson-Rose, & Parsons, 2003) found that perceived social support was significantly associated with lower levels of depression symptoms, and appeared to buffer the effects of drug use. Similarly, a longitudinal study by Siegel, Raveis, and Kraus (1997) found that HIV-positive gay men who reported higher levels of perceived social support had lower levels of depression. The buffet effect of social support has been documented by Cohen and Wills (1985). Our present finding is consistent with the notion that social support decreases stress and enhances well-being. Our participants talked about having a variety of support resources, such as family, friends, and professionals; however, support from the community was reported more frequently. Describing the importance of community support, one woman stated that, "Most of us got thrown away by our families, so we make our own little families here. It was just a nightmare before that." Social support from the community included organizations specifically for people with HIV, such as drop-in centers or support groups. One woman stated that, "We've got arts and crafts music therapy. There are all kinds of little programs that we have downstairs that help fill your day, because I think that's really important. Idle hands, it gets you into too much thinking and if you don't have things to do you get into trouble." Therefore, social support is important not only on an emotional or practical level, but also on an existential and spiritual level. Belonging to a caring group can endow individuals with a sense of purpose, as being involved with people or activities will often provide a sense of meaning and purpose.

CONCLUSION

This study suggests that existential and spiritual coping mechanisms can contribute to coping and prevention efforts with respect to HIV/AIDS. Most women in this study stated that finding meaning, purpose, and spirituality helped transform their lives and stop the risk behaviors that they were previously engaged in. Secondly, women with HIV can also be part of the solution to stopping HIV. A few co-researchers in the study mentioned that they found purpose and happiness by taking part in public education to promote HIV awareness. Thus, they become part of the solution in the battle against the spread of HIV/AIDS. Spiritual coping, in particular, is a powerful way to facilitate transformation, as demonstrated by some of the women in the study. By developing a spiritual understanding of the world, and a relationship with a higher power, they were able to overcome a dysfunctional lifestyle of drugs and prostitution.

Research in the area of prevention can focus on how existential—spiritual coping can decrease risk behaviors in people at risk for contracting HIV. Existential theory, which focuses on freedom and responsibility, can be incorporated into prevention efforts to promote responsible behavior toward others and the community. Currently, HIV education focuses on personal responsibility (clean needles, safe sex); however, promoting responsibility toward others and the community may be able to decrease secondary transmission. Research can examine how to empower people to take responsibility. Furthermore, more research can be done to understand how to engage women with HIV in the fight against AIDS.

The current findings also provide empirical support to Wong's meaning-management theory (Wong 2006a). Confrontation with a terminal illness and the prospect of personal mortality led to meaning-seeking and meaning-making. Spirituality plays a major role in death acceptance and the transformation of terminal illness into positive meanings for living. Although AIDS-related death anxiety was investigated extensively (see Neimeyer & Stewart, 1998), future research needs to focus more on death acceptance and personal growth as a result of HIV/AIDS.

ACKNOWLEDGMENT

This chapter is based on a master's thesis supervised by Prof. Paul Wong and submitted to the Graduate Program in Counselling Psychology, Trinity Western University, BC, Canada in 2005.

MAIN POINTS

1. The pandemic of HIV/AIDS poses a challenge to psychologists in efforts directed to treatment and prevention.
2. This is a phenomenological study to better understand the lived experiences of women with HIV, with a focus on the role of meaning and spirituality.
3. Themes extracted from the narratives confirm that spirituality and meaning play an important role in coping with HIV/AIDS.
4. The results demonstrated the importance of acceptance of HIV, suffering, and death.
5. Women with HIV affirmed the benefits of having a sense of meaning and purpose in life and the positive effects of spirituality and prayer.
6. Some women also talked about negative experiences of spirituality and religion, often related to religious upbringing in childhood.
7. The findings demonstrated the importance of existential and spiritual coping in HIV-positive women and the relevance of meaning-management theory.

RECOMMENDED READINGS

Bivens, A. J., Neimeyer, R. A., Kirchberg, T. M., & Moore, M. K. (1994). Death concern and religious belief among gays and bisexuals of variable proximity to AIDS. *Omega, 30,* 105–120.

Bower, J., Kemeny, M., Taylor, S., & Fahey, J. (1998). Cognitive processing, discovery of meaning, CD4 decline, and AIDS-related mortality among bereaved HIV-seropositive men. *Journal of Consulting and Clinical Psychology, 66*(6), 979–986.

Dunbar, H., Mueller, C., Medina, C., & Wolf, T. (1998). Psychological and spiritual growth in women living with HIV. *Social Work, 43*(2), 144–154.

Neimeyer, R. A., & Stewart, A. E. (1998). AIDS-related death anxiety: A review of the literature. In H. E. Gendelman, S. Lipton, L. Epstein, & S. Swindells (Eds.), *Neurological and neuropsychiatric manifestations of HIV-1 infection* (pp. 582–595). New York: Chapman & Hall.

Emmons, R.A., & Paloutzian, R.F. (2003). The psychology of religion. *Annual Review of Psychology, 54,* 377–402.

Schwartzberg, S. (1993). Struggling for meaning: How HIV positive gay men make sense of AIDS. *Professional Psychology: Research and Practice, 24*(4), 483–490.

Simoni, J., Martone, M., & Kerwin, J. (2002). Spirituality and psychological adaptation among women with HIV/AIDS: Implications for counseling. *Journal of Counseling Psychology, 49*(2), 139–147.

Wong, P. T. P., Reker, G. & Peacock, E. (2005). A resource congruence model of coping and the development of the coping schemas inventory. In P. T. P. Wong, & L. C. J. Wong (Eds.), *Handbook of multicultural perspectives on stress and coping* (pp. 223–283). New York: Springer.

Wong, P. T. P., & Stiller, C. (1999). Living with dignity and palliative care. In B. de Vries (Ed.), *End of life issues: Interdisciplinary and multidimensional perspective,* (pp. 77–94). New York: Springer.

REFERENCES

Avants, S., Marcotte, D., Arnold, R., & Margolin, A. (2003). Spiritual beliefs, world assumptions, and HIV risk behavior among heroin and cocaine users. *Psychology of Addictive Behaviors, 17*(2), 159–162.

Beaudin, C., & Chambre, S. (1996). HIV/AIDS as a chronic disease: Emergence from the plague model. *The American Behavioral Scientist, 39*(6), 684–706.

Bower, J., Kemeny, M., Taylor, S., & Fahey, J. (1998). Cognitive processing, discovery of meaning, CD4 decline, and AIDS-related mortality among bereaved HIV-seropositive men. *Journal of Consulting and Clinical Psychology, 66*(6), 979–986.

Breitbart, W., Gibson, C., Poppito, S., & Berg, A. (2004). Psychotherapeutic interventions at the end of life: A focus on meaning and spirituality. *Canadian Journal of Psychiatry, 49*(6), 366–373.

Cantrell, C. (1998). Living with HIV/AIDS and multiple losses: Paradoxes and polarities. A phenomenological exploration. *Dissertation Abstracts International: Section B: The Sciences & Engineering, (58),* 11-B.

Centers for Disease Control and Prevention (CDC). (2004). *HIV/AIDS Surveillance Report,* 2003. Atlanta, GA: US Department of Health and Human Services, Centers for Disease Control and Prevention.

Cohen, S., & Wills, T. (1985). Stress, social support, and the buffering hypothesis. *Psychological Bulletin, 98*(2), 310–357.

Colaizzi, P. (1978). Psychological research as the phenomenologist views it. In R. S. Valle, & M. King (Eds.), *Existential-phenomenological alternatives for psychology* (pp. 48–71). New York: Oxford University Press.

Dunbar, H., Mueller, C., Medina, C., & Wolf, T. (1998). Psychological and spiritual growth in women living with HIV. *Social Work, 43*(2), 144–154.

Feher, S., & Maly, R. (1999). Coping with breast cancer in later life: The role of religious faith. *Psycho-Oncology, 8*(5), 408–416.

Folkman, S., & Moskowitz, J. (2000). Positive affect and the other side of coping. *American Psychologist, 55*(6), 647–654.

Folkman, S., Moskowitz, J., Ozer, E., & Park, C. (1997). Positive meaningful events and coping in the context of HIV/AIDS. In B.H. Gottlieb (Ed.), *Coping with chronic stress* (pp. 293–314). New York: Plenum.

Frankl, V. (1967). *Psychotherapy and existentialism: Selected papers on logotherapy.* New York: Washington Square Press.

Frankl, V. (1984). *Man's search for meaning.* New York: Washington Square Press.

Frankl, V. E. (1986). *The doctor and the soul: From psychotherapy to logotherapy* (Revised and expanded). New York: Vintage Books.

Gabori, S. (2002). *A good enough life: The dying speak.* Fredericton, New Brunswick, Canada: Goose Lane.

Goggin, K., Catley, D., Brisco, S., Engelson, E., Rabkin, J., & Cotler, D. (2001). A female perspective on living with HIV disease. *Health and Social Work, 26*(2), 80–89.

Guttman, D. (1996). *Logotherapy for the helping professional.* New York: Springer.

Hackl, K., & Somlai, A. (1997). Women living with HIV/AIDS: The dual challenge of being a patient and caregiver. *Health and Social Work, 22*(1), 53–63.

Hall, B. (1998). Patterns of spirituality in persons with advanced HIV disease. *Research in Nursing and Health, 21,* 143–153.

Heckman, T., Kochman, A., Sikkema, K., Kalichman, S., Masten, J., Bergholte, J., et al. (2001). A pilot coping improvement intervention for late middle-aged and older adults living with HIV/AIDS in the USA. *AIDS Care, 13*(1), 129–139.

Hill, P., & Pargament, K. (2003). Advances in the conceptualization and measurement of religion and spirituality: Implications for physical and mental health research. *American Psychologist, 58*(1), 64–74.

Hill, P., Pargament, K., Hood, R., McCullough, M., Swyers, J., Larson, D., et al. (2000). Conceptualizing religion and spirituality: Points of commonality, points of departure. *Journal for the Theory of Social Behavior, 30*(1), 51–77.

Holt, R., & Court, P. (1998). The role of disclosure in coping with HIV infection. *AIDS Care, 10*(1), 49–60.

Jenkins, R. (1995). Religion and HIV: implications for research and intervention. *Journal of Social Issues, 51*(2), 131–144.

Jenkins, R., & Pargament, K. (1995). Religion and spirituality as resources for coping with cancer. *Journal of Psychosocial Oncology, 13*(1–2), 51–74.

Johnson, M., & Folkman, S. (2004). Side effect and disease related symptom representations among HIV+ adults on antiretroviral therapy. *Psychology, Health and Medicine, 9*(2), 139–148.

Joint United Nations Program on HIV/AIDS (UNAIDS) & World Health Organization (WHO). (2004). *AIDS Epidemic Update: December 2004.* Retrieved January 25, 2007, from www.who.int/hiv/pub/epidemiology/epi2004/en/.

Kelly, J., & Kalichman, S. (2002). Behavioral research in HIV/AIDS primary and secondary prevention: Recent advances and future directions. *Journal of Consulting & Clinical Psychology, 70*(3), 626–639.

Klinkenberg, W., & Sacks, S. (2004). Mental disorders and drug abuse in persons living with HIV/AIDS. *AIDS Care, 16*(Supplement 1), 22–42.

Knight, K., Purcell, D., Dawson-Rose, C., Halkitis, P., & Gomez, C. (2005). Sexual risk taking among HIV-positive injection drug users: Contexts, characteristics, and implications for prevention. *AIDS Education and Prevention, 17*(Supplement 1A), 76–88.

Koenig, H., George, L., & Titus, P. (2004). Religion, spirituality, and health in medically ill hospitalized older patients. *Journal of the American Geriatrics Society, 52*(4), 554–562.

Kral, A., Bluthenthal, R., Booth, R., & Watters, J. K. (1998). HIV seroprevalence among street-recruited injection drug and crack cocaine users in 16 US municipalities. *American Journal of Public Health, 88*(1), 108–113.

LaPierre, L. (1994). A model for describing spirituality. *Journal for the Theory of Social Behavior, 30*(1), 153–161.

Larson, D., & Larson, S. (2003). Spirituality's potential relevance to physical and emotional health: A brief review of quantitative research. *Journal of Psychology and Theology, 31*(1), 37–51.

Logan, T., Cole, J., & Leukefeld, C. (2002). Women, sex, and HIV: Social and contextual factors, meta-analysis of published interventions, and implications for practice and research. *Psychological Bulletin, 128* (6), 851–885.

May, R. (1983). *Discovery of being: Writings in existential psychology.* New York: W. W. Norton.

McCormick, R. & Wong, P. (2006). Adjustment and coping in Aboriginal people. In P. T. P. Wong & L. C. J. Wong (Eds.), *Handbook of multicultural perspectives on stress and copying* (pp. 515–531). New York: Springer.

McKay, A. (2000). Prevention of sexually transmitted infections in different populations: A review of behaviorally effective and cost-effective interventions. *Canadian Journal of Human Sexuality, 9*(2), 95–120.

Metcalfe, K., Langstaff, J., Evans, S., Paterson, H., & Reid, J. (1998). Meeting the needs of women living with HIV. *Public Health Nursing, 15*(1), 30–35.

Miller, W., & Thoresen, C. (2003). Spirituality, religion, and health: An emerging research field. *American Psychologist, 58*(1), 24–35.

Mizuno, Y., Purcell, D., Dawson-Rose, C., & Parsons, J. (2003). Correlates of depressive symptoms among HIV-positive injection drug users: The role of social support. *AIDS Care, 15*(5), 689–698.

Moskowitz, J., Folkman, S., Collette, L., & Vittinghoff, E. (1996). Coping and mood during AIDS-related caregiving and bereavement. *Annals of Behavioral Medicine, 18,* 49–57.

Murphy, D., Roberts, K., Martin, D., Marelich, W., & Hoffman, D. (2000). Barriers to antiretroviral adherence among HIV-infected adults. *AIDS Patient Care and STDs, 14*(1), 47–58.

Neimeyer, R. A., & Stewart, A. E. (1998). AIDS-related death anxiety: A review of the literature. In H. E. Gendelman, S. Lipton, L. Epstein, & S. Swindells (Eds.), *Neurological and neuropsychiatric manifestations of HIV-1 infection* (pp. 582–595). New York: Chapman & Hall.

Overcash, W., & Calhoun, L. (1996). Coping with crises: An examination of the impact of traumatic events on religious beliefs. *Journal of Genetic Psychology, 157*(4), 455–464.

Pargament, K. (1997). *The psychology of religion and coping: Theory, research, practice.* New York: Guilford Press.

Pargament, K., Koenig, H., & Perez, L. (2000). The many methods of religious coping: Development and initial validation of the RCOPE. *Journal of Clinical Psychology, 56*(4), 519–543.

Park, C., & Folkman, S. (1997). Meaning in the context of stress and coping. *Review of General Psychology, 1*(2), 115–144.

Powell, L., Shehabi, L., & Thoresen, C. (2003). Religion and spirituality: Linkages to physical health. *American Psychologist, 58*(1), 36–52.

Schwartzberg, S. (1993). Struggling for meaning: how HIV positive gay men make sense of AIDS. *Professional Psychology: Research and Practice, 24*(4), 483–490.

Seybold, K., & Hill, P. (2001). The role of religion and spirituality in mental and physical health. *Current Directions in Psychological Science, 10*(1), 21–24.

Sheeran, P., Abraham, C., & Orbell, S. (1999). Psychosocial correlates of heterosexual condom use: A meta-analysis. *Psychological Bulletin, 125*(1), 90–132.

Siegel, K., Raveis, V., & Karus, D. (1997). Illness-related support and negative network interactions: Effects of HIV-infected men's symptomatology. *American Journal of Community Psychology, 25*(3), 395–420.

Siegel, K., & Schrimshaw, E. (2002). The perceived benefits of religious and spiritual coping among older adults living with HIV/AIDS. *Journal for the Scientific Study of Religion, 41*(1), 91–103.

Simoni, J., & Ortiz, M. (2003). Mediational models of spirituality and depressive symptomatology among HIV-positive Puerto Rican women. *Cultural Diversity and Ethnic Minority Psychology, 9*(1), 3–15.

Simoni, J., Martone, M., & Kerwin, J. (2002). Spirituality and psychological adaptation among women with HIV/AIDS: implications for counseling. *Journal of Counseling Psychology, 49*(2), 139–147.

Simoni, J., Mason, H., Marks, G., Ruiz, M., Reed, D., & Richardson, J. (1995). Women's self-disclosure of HIV infection: Rates, reasons, and reactions. *Journal of Consulting and Clinical Psychology, 63*(3), 474–478.

Somlai, A., & Heckman, T. (2000). Correlates of spirituality and well-being in a community sample of people living with HIV disease. *Mental Health, Religion, and Culture, 3*(1), 57–70.

Somlai, A., Heckman, T., Hackl, K., Morgan, M., & Welsh, D. (2001). Developmental stages and spiritual coping responses among economically impoverished women living with HIV disease. *Journal of Pastoral Care, 52,* 227–240.

Somlai, A., Kelly, J., Kalichman, S., Mulry, G., Sikkema, K., McAuliffe, T., et al. (1996). An empirical investigation of the relationship between spirituality, coping, and emotional distress in people living with HIV infection and AIDS. *Journal of Pastoral Care, 50*(2), 181–195.

Stanley, L. (1999). Transforming AIDS: the moral management of stigmatized identity. *Anthropology and Medicine, 6*(1), 103–120.

Stein, M., Hanna, L., Natarajan, R., Clarke, J., Marisi, M., Sabota, M., et al. (2000). Alcohol use patterns predict high-risk HIV behaviors among active injection drug users. *Journal of Substance Abuse Treatment, 18*(4), 359–363.

Valle, R., & King, M. (1978). *Existential-phenomenological alternatives for psychology.* New York: Oxford University Press.

Wong, P. T. P. (1991). Existential vs. causal attributions. In S. Zelen (Ed.), *Extensions and new models of attribution theory* (pp. 84–125). New York: Springer-Verlag Publishers.

Wong, P. T. P. (1998a). Implicit theories of meaningful life and the development of the Personal Meaning Profile (PMP). In P. T. P. Wong & P. Fry (Eds.), *The human quest for meaning: A handbook of psychological research and clinical applications* (pp. 111–140). Mahwah, NJ: Lawrence Erlbaum Associates.

Wong, P. T. P. (1998b). Spirituality, meaning, and successful aging. In P. T. P. Wong & P. Fry (Eds.), *The human quest for meaning: A handbook of psychological research and clinical applications* (pp. 359–394). Mahwah, NJ: Lawrence Erlbaum Associates.

Wong, P. T. P. (1998c). Meaning-centered counseling. In P. T. P. Wong & P. Fry (Eds.), *The human quest for meaning: A handbook of psychological research and clinical applications* (pp. 395–435). Mahwah, NJ: Lawrence Erlbaum Associates.

Wong, P. T. P. (2005a). Compassionate and spiritual care: A vision of positive holistic medicine. In S. Kwan (Ed.), *The consultation on holistic health care for the medical, religious, and academic professionals in Hong Kong*. Hong Kong: Commercial Press.

Wong, P. T. P. (2005b). Existential and humanistic theories. In J. C. Thomas & D. L. Segal (Eds.), *Comprehensive handbook of personality and psychopathology* (pp. 192–211). Hoboken, NJ: John Wiley & Sons, Inc.

Wong, P. T. P., & Stiller, C. (1999). Living with dignity and palliative care. In B. de Vries (Ed.), *End of life issues: Interdisciplinary and multidimensional perspectives* (pp. 77–94). New York: Springer.

Wong, P. T. P., Reker, G., & Peacock, E. (2005). A Resource-Congruence model of coping and the development of the Coping Schemas Inventory. In P. T. P. Wong, & L. C. J. Wong (Eds.), *Handbook of multicultural perspectives on stress and coping* (pp. 223–283). New York: Springer.

Yalom, I. (1980). *Existential psychotherapy*. New York: Basic Books.

Yates, J., Chalmer, B., St. James, P., Follansbee, M., & McKegney, F. (1981). Religion in patients with advanced cancer. *Medical Pediatric Oncology, 9*(2), 121–128.

9

▼▼▼▼

The Role of Existential and Spiritual Coping in Anticipatory Grief

Debra A. Ivancovich
Paul T. P. Wong
Trinity Western University

We experience losses at every stage of life. We grieve over losses of friendships, marriages, careers, health, safety, status, and hope (Cowles & Rodgers, 1991; Moules, 1998; Pine, 1990; Rosenblatt, 1988). Sometimes grieving is experienced in anticipation of the loss. Through these losses, we learn that nothing is permanent in life; change is ever present. Preparation for death occurs throughout our lives in a myriad of less antagonistic ways than death itself. We need to be prepared psychologically for both our personal demise and the death of loved ones. For many people, their belief systems and a sense of meaningfulness enable them to live out their lives fully in spite of suffering and death (Frankl, 1984; Yalom & Lieberman, 1991). Wong (2002a) wrote, "How we live foreshadows how we die." We need to learn how to live well in order to die well. Wong (2000) has made the case that the meaning of death is inherently related to the meaning of life. Anticipatory grief of our own death as well as the death of a loved one may trigger the quest for meaning and spirituality.

Anticipatory grief is more common than bereavement grief. We may "die" and "grieve" a thousand times before death finally knocks on our doors. With so many soldiers sent to Iraq and other dangerous areas, their families know what it is like to fear the worst and anticipate the bad news. They not only grieve the temporary absence of a loved one but also feel the pain of the anticipatory grief of a losing a loved one. In fact, the first study of anticipatory grief by Lindemann (1944) was about women separated from their husbands by war.

Baby boomers are both confronted with their own mortality and burdened by anticipatory grief of their aging parents. Individuals with loved ones suffering from terminal illnesses may also wrestle with anticipatory grief. As we advance in age and spend much time seeing doctors and going through medical tests, we are constantly bracing for the bad news of being diagnosed with a terminal illness. Our capacity to become aware of eventual death makes anticipatory grief commonplace and universal. This chapter focuses on existential and spiritual copings in anticipatory grief of the prospect of losing a loved one through terminal illness.

The Concept of Anticipatory Grief

The concept of anticipatory grief was first introduced by Lindemann (1944). Bereavement grief is different from anticipatory grief because in the case of bereavement, death has already occurred; but there are similarities, because both involve elements of stage theory, identified tasks, and processes (Kübler-Ross, 1969; Westberg, 1971; Worden, 1991). Somatic distress, loss of appetite, sleep disturbance, and tightness in the chest are some of the common physiological symptoms of grief. As well, there is a similar need to ascribe some kind of meaning to death, whether anticipated or experienced. There is also death anxiety either before or after the event of death itself.

When Lindemann (1944) first introduced the term, he suggested that individuals would experience most of the symptoms associated with bereavement grief. However, Parkes and Weiss (1983) suggested that anticipatory grief could not exist because of increased attachment between husbands and wives when one of them was terminally ill. Anticipatory grief had the appearance of wishing the loved one to die. Although most researchers do affirm the phenomenon of anticipatory grief, there are still controversies regarding the definitions of the construct of anticipatory grief and its adaptive value.

Anticipatory Grief Versus Anticipatory Mourning

Therese A. Rando's (2000a) book is an edited volume on anticipatory mourning. It is noteworthy that Rando has substituted *anticipatory grief* with *anticipatory mourning*. Rando prefers a narrower definition of grief as the initial reaction to the perception of loss. Her definition of anticipatory mourning includes a broader set of processes: (a) coping and interaction, (b) psychosocial reorganization, (c) planning, (d) balancing conflicting demands, and (e) facilitating an appropriate death. These processes have historically been part of the overall "grief work." There is some justification for her position, but it is debatable whether such reversal of definitions contributes to research and communication.

In the literature, *mourning* typically refers to the public and ritualistic expressions of grief. For example, Kastenbaum and Kastenbaum (1989) defined mourning as "the culturally patterned expressions or rituals that accompany loss and allow others to recognize that one has become bereaved" (p. 128). As well, Stroebe, Hansson, Stroebe, and Schut (2001) defined mourning as "the social expressions or acts expressive of grief that are shaped by the practices of a given society or cultural group" (p. 6). Stroebe et al. (2001) defined grief as "a primarily emotional (affective) reaction to the loss of a loved one through death. It incorporates diverse psychological (cognitive, social-behavioral) and physical (physiological-somatic) manifestations" (p. 6). It is interesting to note that Fulton, the very person to whom Rando gave credit for first proposing the term *anticipatory mourning*, now concluded that this term "violates a principle of logic that informs us that a term being defined cannot be used in its own definition as Rando has promulgated" (Fulton, 2003, p. 343).

John Rolland (1990) proposed his own terminology change when he defined "anticipatory loss" as opposed to anticipatory grief. He framed his discussion around various kinds of losses—physical, psychological, and relational. It also included the loss of accustomed roles in family systems. He suggested that family systems must create meaning that enabled individual to preserve a sense of competency. Although Rolland frames his discussion around the term *loss*, his discussion is in many ways similar to other researchers regarding anticipatory grief. We prefer the historical broader definition of anticipatory grief, which includes a range of emotional, cognitive, and behavioral responses in anticipation of loss of a loved one.

Is Anticipatory Grief Beneficial?

In addition to the controversy over terminology, there is also debate regarding whether anticipatory grief reduces bereavement grief. If one believes that there is only so much grief to be experienced in total, then it makes sense that any grief work done prior to the death of a loved one will reduce bereavement grief. However, research on the beneficial effect of anticipatory grief has not yielded definitive answers. Perhaps, whether anticipatory grief is beneficial may depend on whether it has resulted in death acceptance and preparations to move forward. Kutscher (1973) suggested that the period of time after diagnosis of a terminal illness created an opportunity for experiencing a catharsis, which allowed one to face death without the fear of being abandoned or ostracized. Kutscher referred to the need to settle "troubling personal affairs" and stressed the potential of achieving some measure of acceptance about the future death. Weisman (1974) noted that although anticipatory grief did not nullify bereavement grief, it did begin a process of releasing a loved one and learning how to fill the emptiness. Welch (1982) proposed anticipatory grief to be an opportunity to engage in an emotional rehearsal with the hopes of mitigating the emotionally laden period of bereavement grief.

Hill, Thompson, and Gallagher (1988) hypothesized that older women who had forewarning about the impending death of their loved ones would adjust better to the bereavement grief than those who had no forewarning. Adjustment to widowhood was operationalized as measurable psychological well-being, physical well-being, and the intensity of grief reaction. Their hypothesis was supported by the findings. Huber and Gibson (1990) hypothesized that anticipatory grief was a mediating process affecting subsequent bereavement. Results of this study reveal that female caregivers were more positively impacted by pre-death grief work. As this study does suggest that pre-death grief work benefits those facing a transition in life due to the death of their loved one, it further bolsters the idea that anticipatory grief is a mediating influence in bereavement.

Glenda Gilliland and Stephen Fleming (1998) administered several instruments both prior to and after the death of a spouse. Perceived stress levels and coping abilities prior to death, were found to positively correlate with post-death reactions. However, it was also found that acceptance and preparation for death were associated with greater anger post-death possibly due to greater attachment to the spouse. Whereas an increased sense of loss of control was noted, there were also fewer atypical grief responses post-death when anticipatory grief work had occurred. Another study (Clayton, Halikas, Maurice, & Robins, 1973) attempted to discover whether grief reactions prior to death did, in fact, alter bereavement grief reactions. Their findings suggest that those who experienced grief symptoms prior to the death of a loved one fared no better than those who did not. Robert Weiss (1988) took the position that anticipated loss may lead to planning and preparation for the death, but may not reduce the grief experienced in the subsequent bereavement. Recovery from bereavement grief may involve the following processes: (a) cognitive acceptance, (b) emotional acceptance, (c) identity change, and (d) new social linkages. Weiss contended that anticipatory grief may be a misleading term, as it implies a recovery from a loss that has not yet occurred.

Levy (1991) conducted a study to determine if engaging in anticipatory grief work could be a risk to subsequent bereavement grief. His finding suggested that anticipatory grief might be reflective of the individual's personal coping abilities and emotional adjustment. Levy also suggested that the concept of anticipatory grief had been stretched by many to a point where it had less scientific merit. In another study exploring the lived experiences of individuals when their spouses were diagnosed terminally ill, Duke (1998) identified four themes that demonstrated a change in their relationships with their loved ones. The themes include: (a) their relationship with the spouse and with others, (b) their role as caregiver, (c) the way they integrated memories, and (d) how they felt throughout the process. The lived experience of the spouse prior to the loved one's death was characterized by the need to be with their spouse, the adoption of the caregiver role, finding themselves in limbo between the present and the future, and the awareness of the memories being made throughout the lived experience. Duke suggested the potential for psychological ill-health might result from the continued role changes during anticipatory grief.

Anticipatory grief is necessarily compounded by stress caused by caring for a dying loved person. Walker and Pomeroy (1996) stressed the opportunity to address "unfinished business," resolve old issues, and say good-byes during anticipatory grief, but it might be difficult to take care of this concern, because of the presence of significant stressors. Research findings by Cleiren (1993) in the Leiden Bereavement Study suggested that anticipatory grief incorporated significant elements of traumatic stress. He suggested that accidents and long-term illness involving a loved one might elicit similar intense stress reactions and trigger a quest for meaning. Generally, traumatic grief is viewed as related to circumstances surrounding a violent or sudden death that may result in Post Traumatic Stress Disorder. Traumatic death may also include the death of a child and deaths that appear unnecessary and arbitrary in nature. Rando (2000b) emphasized the need to address traumatic stress within the context of anticipatory mourning, because elements of trauma could impede grief work. She also posited that intimates of terminally ill loved ones might experience trauma along with their losses: (a) the loss of the loved one, (b) death of the family unit as it existed in the past, and (c) loss of the role within the family system.

Caring for the Dying

Closely related to anticipatory grief is the issue of how to care for the dying. This is a matter of concern to both family members and professionals. To encourage effective caring and helping, Larson (2000) recognizes that caregivers might experience loss or "disenfranchised grief" because professionals and volunteers are not supposed to grieve the loss of a patient. Larsen encouraged caregivers to consider carefully how to assist a dying person without become too attached. For family members, attachment with the terminally ill loved one already exists. The strength or intensity of attachment will have some impact on anticipatory grief as well as caring for the dying. Within the context of anticipatory grief, more research is needed on how to best cope with the impending loss of loved ones and how to care for the dying.

One issue that needs to be addressed is how to break the silence of conspiracy that is pervasive within families as well as within the medical profession. When a person is diagnosed terminally, ill the need for support and encouragement from the family is great. Unfortunately, this is often the time that a self-protective mechanism of distancing begins to kick in. According to Rolland (1990), "Premature distancing can occur when family members are torn between their wishes to sustain intimacy and their need to 'let go' emotionally of a member they expect to die" (p. 233). If we can encourage a willingness to share feelings and discuss the reality of the impending death, then it may facilitate caring as well as anticipatory grieving.

COPING WITH THE DYING OF A LOVED ONE

The impending death of a loved one represents a major source of stress to family members. The stress is both internal and external. A great deal of resources are needed to cope for the extra situational demands—medical expenses, disruptions of daily routines, disruption of family systems, and the burden of caring. However, there is also enormous emotional stress involved in coping with the dying of a loved one—anxiety about the deteriorating condition, anticipatory grieving, uncertainty of a future without the loved one, and existential crisis.

Existential Crisis

The impending death of a loved one is a potent reminder of one's own mortality. Denial or avoidance is no longer an adequate coping mechanism in situations where the presence of death is looming larger and larger with every passing day. There is no escape from its darkening shadow. One must confront the reality of death. One needs to wrestle with a wide variety of existential issues such as: What is the point of living if I lose my husband (or wife)? What is life all about? What is the purpose of living, when I have to carry so much worry and pain?

When the impending death of a loved one is untimely or unnatural, the existential crisis may be even more severe. There would be a lot of questioning and soul searching. One would want to find out what caused it and whether one is to blame: "Perhaps, it would not have happened, if I had come home a little bit earlier." "If I had stopped him from joining the army, he would not have been killed in Iraq." There are also the more general existential questions such as: Why me? Why this? Why did God allow this horrible thing to happen? According to Wong's (2006a) meaning-management theory (MMT), these questions invariably trigger meaning-seeking and meaning-making. Individuals engage in meaning-management not only to reconstruct the terror of death into something positive, but also to rediscover the meaning and purpose for living in spite of the anticipated loss.

Resolving Regrets

Self-blames and regrets often contribute to one's psychological distress and death anxiety in the context of anticipatory grief, according to Tomer and Eliason (1996). In reviewing one's relationship with the dying person, memories of past conflicts, unkind words and wrong deeds will likely resurface. Because one cannot undo past regrets, one can only resort to forgiveness. Anticipatory grief provides the opportunity to make amends and reconcile with the dying person. Concerns about future regrets provide added motivation to make things right. For example, one may realize: "If I don't apologize and express my love to him now, I may never have the opportunity to bare my soul when he dies." Thus, both past and future regrets can facilitate healing and grieving.

Coping With Anticipatory Grief

Coping has been defined as "constantly changing cognitive or behavioral efforts to manage specific external and/or internal demands that are appraised as taxing or exceeding the resources of the person" (Lazarus & Folkman, 1984, pp. 141–142). In further evaluating the coping concept, Tunks and Bellissimo (1988) identified three domains that may become focal points: (a) an appraisal focus that seeks to find some meaning in a crisis situation, (b) a problem-focused coping solution that attempts to confront and control the crises, and (c) an emotion-focused coping solution which attempts to gain homeostasis by dealing with the feelings associated with the crisis. The coping literature has primarily emphasized problem-focused coping and emotion-focused coping. Wong, Reker, and Peacock (2005) have expanded the construct of coping to include existential coping as well as religious/spiritual coping as the main mechanisms to cope with unavoidable problems that threaten our very existence or shatter our assumptive world.

For those who receive a terminal diagnosis, particularly those who are younger than the age of senescence, there can be a huge sense of loss and of bitterness over a life cut too short and at an unexpected time. Problem-focused and emotional-focuses by themselves are no longer sufficient, as they and their loved ones struggle to make sense of this tragic news. They need to find some way to live with this reality without being overwhelmed by the enormity of the impending loss.

Attig (1991b) stressed that even though terminal illness was something that happened to us, we could approach it as an opportunity to actively participate in the coping process and make choices of a transformational nature. Although Attig focused on the experience of bereavement, his insights are also relevant to anticipatory grief. We can choose either to be "paralyzed" by grief or to be transformed by the discovery of meaning. Attig (2000) also emphasized the transformative process of relearning relationships. He reinforced the need to attend to unfinished business in relationships in order to enjoy and interact with loved ones fully. From the perspective of Wong's (2006a) MMT, these transformative choices are examples of meaning-seeking and meaning-making. In a similar vein, Betty Davies (2000) focused on the transitional processes, such as redefining life and integrating the experience of living and dying. However, prior to making these transformational responses, most terminally diagnosed individuals would be engaged in defense mechanisms to protect them from pain. Faith and stoicism play a part in the adaptational process.

Existential Coping

Tunks and Bellissimo (1988) proposed that coping had the potential of "transforming calamities into opportunities for growth" (p. 171). Wong, Reker, and Peacock (2006) have identified several transformative coping strategies, such as Existential coping (Affirmation of meaning and Acceptance), Religious/spiritual coping, and Self-restructuring. These transformative coping mechanisms refer to the strategy of changing one's personal meaning-value systems, beliefs, worldviews, lifestyle, and some aspects of one's personality as a result of enlightenment or spiritual transformation (Wong, Wong, & Scott, 2006). Transformative coping is clearly congruent with problems that are chronic, uncontrollable, or unavoidable, such as terminal, incurable diseases and eventual death. In this chapter, we focus on the transformatory potential of existential and spiritual coping.

In a bereavement study, Yalom and Lieberman (1991) found that those who had a heightened awareness of their meaning and purpose in life demonstrated greater evidence of personal growth. Attig (1989) suggests "grieving is primarily a process of finding an appropriate meaning" (p. 366). He cites Edwin Shneidman (1980) as saying the terminally ill are faced with and bewail their pending non-existence. Existentialists refer to this as an existential plight or uncertainty about the future as well as eventual death (Thompson & Pitts, 1993). Wong (2006a) has pointed out that our capacity for symbolism, meaning, and faith offers us not only the best protection against the terror of death but also the best opportunity to live meaningfully and hopefully in the face of death. Existential and spiritual copings can fundamentally transform our lives by first transforming our attitudes and worldviews toward life and death.

Kierkegaard (1944) theorized that individuals could become aware of their own responsibility to determine how they will choose to decide and act on that decision. Soll (2001) postulated that authenticity included a need to be open to new and unknown experiences, including anxiety, and changing interpretations while taking full responsibility for those experiences and interpretations. Heidegger was more concerned with a focus on the "miracle" of human existence rather than the nothingness suggested by other existential philosophers (Owen, 1994a). Wong, Wong, and Scott (2006) emphasized the positive psychology of transformation through meaning and spirituality. Wong (2006a) pointed out that death paled in significance once we discovered how to live authentically and vitally in spite of our own mortality. An orientation toward the "miracles" of life empowers us to transcend death anxiety.

Victor Frankl (1984), who had been confined to Nazi concentration camps from 1942–1945 in both Auschwitz and Dachau, developed *logotherapy* which capitalized on the universal human quest for meaning even when conditions were horrendous and dehumanizing. In his later writings, Frankl (1986) became more explicit about the transformatory power of meaning; he said, "Suffering ceases to be suffering, the moment it takes on meaning" (p. 25). Shantall (1999) wrote, "Suffering calls us to task ... suffering challenges us with choice" (p. 111). Basic concepts of logotherapy have been adopted in counseling (Das, 1998; Graber, 2004; Wong, 1998b).

Maddi (1998) emphasized the importance of existential courage in hardiness. He identified two major assumptions of existential psychology: (a) A sense of meaning is a major determinant of an individual's action," and (b) Personal meaning derives from the day-to-day decisions an individual makes. Personal meaning makes it possible for the individual to transcend the limitations of current circumstances, whatever they might be. In sum, there is a venerable history in existential philosophy and psychology of focus on the central role of personal meaning in the ever-enfolding human drama of coping with adversities and suffering. Wong's Meaning Management Theory (MMT; chap. 3, this volume) represents a comprehensive and systematic framework to understand the transformative power of meaning in coping with suffering.

Religious/Spiritual Coping

Religious/spiritual coping tends to go hand in hand with existential coping for those whose worldviews include beliefs in a higher power or transcendental reality. According to Wong, Reker, and Peacock's (2006) resource-congruence model, both spiritual and existential copings are likely to be activated when one is confronted with problems beyond human control, such as one's own mortality and the death of a loved one. Wong (2002b) suggested that grief "awakens one's spiritual and existential yearnings to rise above the painful experiences of mourning" (p. 4).

Marrone (1999) described a "psychospiritual transformation" (p. 497) that occurs when loss shatters our assumptions about life and death. This psychospiritual transformation is a process that requires us to set aside pre-existing needs for order and control and replace them with faith in a higher order, structure, and meaning. He proposed that through whatever religious belief one has about God, one can discover meaning and purpose in life. No longer was death a wall but rather a doorway (Feifel, 1990) through which one could pass. Loss provides an opportunity to discover how awareness of death and faith can transform life and endow it with meaning. Harrison, Koenig, Hays, Eme-Akwari, and Pargament (2001) also suggested that "religious coping may be involved in the conservation or transformation of ends" (p. 86).

Both affirmation of meaning and faith in some form of immortality are important in coping with the reality of death. Doka (1993) proposed three essential tasks for those who are dying which may be applied to those who are anticipating the loss of a loved one: (a) to recognize an ultimate source of meaning in one's life, (b) to be allowed to accept death within their own construct of ultimate meaning, and (c) to know there is a future for them either in an afterlife or within a legacy left to others. Oates (1982) would contend that these tasks were part of what he referred to as *staging operations* or preparation for death. He reminded us that "death confronts us with the end of a life that demands a comprehensive faith-courage" (p. 233). Quoting Paul Tournier's statement that "we live in a rhythm between finding a place and quitting a place," Oates pointed out that there was a need to live and die within the context of discovering meaning, experiencing hope, and walking alongside others toward an anticipated future. Belief in God and an afterlife could be very comforting for those in mourning. Isaiah 61: 2–3 (New International Version) speaks of God as the One who comforts all those who mourn. He bestows beauty for ashes, the oil of joy for mourning, and a garment of praise instead of a spirit of despair. Thus, religious or spiritual coping can be a powerful source of transformation.

METHOD

This study employed both qualitative and quantitative methods to study how individuals cope with anticipated grief when a loved one was diagnosed with terminal illness. We wanted to find out whether they employed existential and religious copings and in what ways these coping mechanisms were helpful to them.

Sample

Eight individuals (five women and three men) participated in the study. They ranged in age from 29 to 70 years (median age = 57 years). The composite of the relationships included one sister, two husbands, two daughters, and three mothers. Criteria for inclusion were: (a) at least 25 years old, (b) in a familial relationship with someone who had was terminally ill, and (c) the diagnosis must have been made within the past 2 years at the point of our first contact. The respondents were recruited either by word of mouth or by personal invitation of the researcher.

Four of the eight respondents were within a middle-class socioeconomic level ($40,000–$60,000 per year) but three respondents fell within lower-middle-class socioeconomic level of $20,000–$40,000 per year. One respondent reported no income since the time of diagnosis. Of the eight respondents, seven were of Anglo-Saxon descent and the eighth respondent was of Chinese descent. Seven of the participants were Protestants and one was Catholic.

Procedure

Each respondent signed an "Informed Consent" form and was interviewed twice. The first meeting was approximately 1 hour with the subsequent meeting, about 1 month later, lasting about 90 minutes. The first meeting included filling out four pen-and-paper research instruments. This was followed by a semi-structured and audio-taped interview including four basic questions; yet, there was an opportunity for the respondent to ask questions or debrief with the researcher. There were several respondents who requested the opportunity to fill out the pen-and-paper research instruments prior to the meeting, allowing for us to meet for a shorter length of time. The first meeting also allowed for the researcher to ascertain background information about the diagnosis and the progression of events leading up to the terminal diagnosis in some cases. The second meeting included the same four research instruments as well as the same four questions with the corresponding subquestions. There were an additional four questions to allow the respondents to comment on participation in the study as well as providing an opportunity for the respondent to debrief. Although there was the use of quantitative pen-and-paper research instruments, the emphasis of the research was the qualitative experience of the eight respondents.

The meetings with the respondents were conducted either in their homes, in the researcher's office, or in his or her personal office at their request. All eight respondents completed the research project. At the conclusion of the final meeting, the respondent was left with a research evaluation form and a thank you note as a token of appreciation for their participation in the study.

Semi-Structured Interview

The semi-structured interview included a list of questions for the respondents to address. The questions were left open-ended, allowing for respondents to have greater freedom in answering them. There were initially four main questions:

1. How did you initially react to the diagnosis of your loved one's illness?
2. How are you feeling now?
3. How are you coping with the prospect of losing your loved one due to this illness?

4. What has been the impact of your loved one's diagnosis on your relationship?

At the time of the last interview, four additional questions were asked allowing for a time of debriefing as well as determining the perceived merit of the discussion for the respondent. The questions included:

1. How were you after our last interview?
2. Do you believe talking about this topic has helped you or hindered you?
3. Have you openly talked about death?
4. What has prevented it?

Instruments

Four psychometric research instruments were included within this study. Because the study addresses death and how people cope from both an existential perspective and a spiritual point of view, there were instruments focusing on each area. The Death Attitude Profile-Revised (DAP–R; Wong, Reker, & Gesser, 1994) is a 32-item, Likert-style instrument that measures a wide variety of death attitudes including Fear of Death, Death Avoidance, Neutral Acceptance, Approach Acceptance, and Escape Acceptance.

The Revised Death Anxiety Scale (RDAS; Thorson & Powell, 1994) is a 25-item Likert response format instrument that measures on a scale of 1 to 100 a person's death anxiety. This scale appears to be age-sensitive and has acceptable levels of reliability.

The third instrument is the Personal Meaning Profile (PMP; Wong, 1993) with a 57-item Likert format. Finally, this study includes use of the Coping Schemas Inventory (CSI; Wong, Reker, & Peacock, 2006). The CSI is a 76-item inventory that evaluates a wide range of coping strategies, including: (a) Religious, (b) Passive Emotional, (c) Active Emotional, (d) Situational, (e) Self-restructuring, (f) Social Support, (g) Meaning, (h) Tension Reduction, and (i) Acceptance. The Coping Schemas Inventory was chosen particularly as it is the only coping scale that provides existential and religious coping measures within the same scale.

RESULTS

Themes

Content analysis of the semi-structured interview yielded in total 704 meaning-units, which were statements made by the respondents that contained a complete idea relevant to the study. The researcher was

TABLE 9.1
Participating Rates and Frequencies of Themes

Themes	Participating rates	Frequency
Emotional responses	8/8	128
Resolution of concerns	8/8	30
Initial response/recollection	8/8	37
Relational changes	7/8	57
Relational difficulties	7/8	45
Trusting God	7/8	43
Emotionally detached/avoidant	6/8	31
Positive thoughts	6/8	27
Practical needs	6/8	23
Needs outside support	6/8	24
Denial/escape	6/8	16
Participation in study	6/8	13
Fear of future	5/8	23
Recognition of problem/ Gathering information	5/8	19
Acceptance	5/8	15
Needs family support	4/8	9
Anticipating the future	3/8	18
Focus on loved one	2/8	13
Negative medical intervention	2/8	12
Normalizing behaviors	2/8	8
Meaning making	2/8	5
Self-transcendence	2/8	5

able to consolidate the 704 meaning-units into 22 themes, which are shown in Table 9.1. To establish reliability, the researcher engaged a professional counselor who worked with individuals struggling with bereavement or expecting to lose someone to death to classify 10% of the meaning-units into appropriate themes. There was 85% agreement with the researcher.

The literature (Aldrich, 1974; Bourke, 1984; Pine, 1974, 1986; Rando, 1988; Reed, 1974; Weisman, 1974) recognizes emotional reactions as the key component of grief. For example, empirical research shows grief typically involves emotional responses such as anger and loss of emotional control (Gilliland & Fleming, 1998). All eight participants frequently talked about their negative emotional reactions. Respondent 2 expressed pent-up anger at the tobacco companies who he held partly responsible for his mother's emphysema. Respondent 5 also expressed anger that medical doctors failed to detect her daughter's cancer earlier. Respondent 8 was concerned about unresolved issues with her mother. All of the respondents reported a great need for emotional, physical, and spiritual support, both from within the family and from outside connections. They wished that people would openly ask about the condition of their terminally ill loved ones. They felt that the people around them, particularly family members and close friends, were afraid to say anything. As a result, Respondents 1, 2, and 5 felt resentful and isolated in their grieving.

Each respondent commented on the benefit of participating in this study because of the opportunity to share their feelings and understand their own coping efforts. It was interesting to note that at the beginning of the first interview there was tentativeness about speaking of their sorrows that morphed into a more comfortable conversational exchange. By the time of the second interview, it appeared that each respondent was more eager to engage in conversation. They seemed to welcome the opportunity to give voice to their concerns.

Quantitative Data

Due to the small sample, the quantitative findings of this were intended to provide some descriptive indices about the direction of changes between Time 1 and Time 2. Mean rating scores of the questionnaires can also shed some light in interpreting the themes extracted from the interviews.

The Personal Meaning Profile (PMP). The PMP provides a rough indication of the sources of meaning of our respondents during their state of anticipatory grief. The most obvious finding is that for this particular sample, religion ranked first for both Time 1 and Time 2, but in the normative study (Wong, 1998a), religion ranked last. This observation is consistent with our qualitative finding that "Trusting God" is one of the main themes. The lack of change between Time 1 and Time 2 in all the sources of meaning is not surprising, because PMP measures value-meaning systems which are rather stable over short period of time.

Death Attitude Profile–Revised. Again, there was little change in meaning scores from Time 1 to Time 2, as shown in Figure 9.1. What is noteworthy is the high scores of Approach Acceptance for both Time 1 and Time 2. These mean scores were much higher than the normative findings in Wong et al. (1994), which showed means scores of 4.7 for 30- to 59-year-olds and 5.38 for 60- to 90-year-olds. Approach Acceptance reflects the religious beliefs of our sample. According to

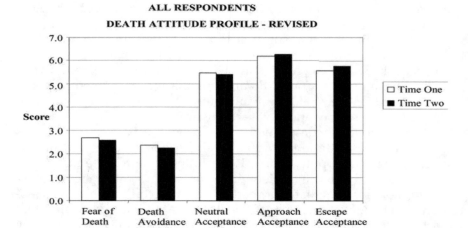

FIG. 9.1.   Mean ratings based on DAP-R.

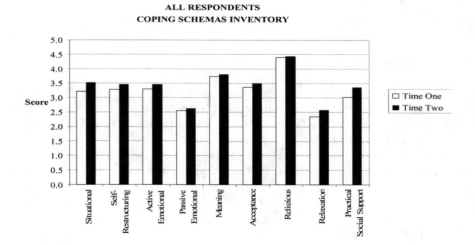

FIG. 9.2.   Mean rates based on CSI.

Klenow and Bolin (1989), greater religious involvement is the only discriminating factor in believing in an afterlife.

Escape Acceptance in this study was also higher by approximately a point than in Wong et al. (1994). This might reflect our participant's desire for relief from suffering for themselves as well as for their loved ones. In fact, the all three types of acceptance were rated much higher than Fear of Death and Death Avoidance, indicating that our participants have indeed come to accept the reality of death without much fear.

Revised Death Anxiety Scale (RDAS).   The purpose of the RDAS is to measure with reasonable ease the anxiety level of a person who is expecting death. This is a scale measuring from 1–100 an individual's level of death anxiety. The data accumulated from the respondents in this study demonstrated a mean score for all respondents of less than 39, suggesting a low level of death anxiety. This finding is consistent with the DAP-R scores on Death Fear and Fear Avoidance.

Coping Schemas Inventory (CSI).   The Coping Schemas Inventory identified the Religious and Meaning copings ranked as the two most highly endorsed coping strategies in this sample. It is noteworthy that the mean scores of all respondents in this study were nearly double the normative scores of Religious Coping and markedly higher for Meaning reported in the normative study by Wong, Reker, and Peacock (2006). This finding provides additional support for the importance of meaning and spirituality in coping with anticipatory grief.

CONCLUSION

The two key research questions of this study are: how people cope with anticipatory grief when a loved one is dying of terminal illness and whether existential and religious/spiritual coping play any significant role. Both qualitative and quantitative data confirm that existential and religious/spiritual copings play a major role in dealing with anticipatory grief and the stress of caring for the dying loved one. Up to this point little research has been done to include both qualitative information and quantitative data to study the experience and process of anticipatory grief. This study demonstrates the usefulness of using qualitative and quantitative data to triangulate the importance of meaning and spirituality/religion.

Of the 22 themes generated in this study, only 6 are specific to anticipatory grief where as the rest are relevant also to conventional or bereavement grief. First, all respondents experienced emotional responses unique to their anticipated loss of a loved one through death. Second, most of the respondents demonstrated a need to resolve old problems and issues in the time their loved one remained alive. Some were actually actively engaged in working toward resolutions. Third, most of the respondents recognized the changes in relations and roles as their loved ones physically and psychologically declined. Generally those same respondents alluded to the change in roles and recognized some fear attached to the changes. Fourth, more than half of the respondents found it necessary upon diagnosis of their loved one to search for information that may offer some hope of a cure. Fifth, there was a need to focus exclusively on the loved ones for the remainder of the loved ones' lives. Last, nearly half of the respondents anticipated or worried about what life would be like without their loved ones present.

Meaning and Religion

All respondents leaned heavily upon their faith to sustain them and attempted to find some meaning or purpose for the anticipated loss. Although these themes are not unique to anticipatory grief, they are important for us to understand why meaning and religion play a major role in coping with death anxiety and the pain of grieving. In this research, each respondent was attempting to discover some meaning in the tragic circumstances of their impending losses. Each questioned, "Why me?" "Why now?" and what purpose could or would be served when their dying loved ones succumbed to the expected death. These findings support Wong's MMT, which posits that meaning-seeking would be triggered by death concerns.

There is also evidence of meaning-making in this study, but it was unique to each individual. Terry demonstrated meaning-making as he cared for his dying sister. Norm tried to create meaning for his life by helping others. For Lily, there was a need to create positive and meaningful moments for her husband and children. All respondents gave of themselves to their dying loved ones, their families, and their communities. For most, there was a sense of serving a higher calling; this larger picture includes faith in God.

Our respondents, by and large, were able to achieve some understanding of the transformative process of meaning reconstruction. They experienced a spiritual transformation as they sought to rely on their faith to sustain them and empower their efforts to reconstruct their lives in anticipation of the death of a loved one.

Resolving Concerns and Regrets

An important aspect of coping with anticipatory grief was the attempt to resolve concerns and regrets. Every respondent in the study showed an awareness of the need to resolve old concerns and to mend their relationships. Of the eight respondents, only two did not attempt resolution with their dying loved ones. Thomas Attig (2000) reinforced the need to attend to and resolve unfinished business within relationships where a death is expected. Adrian Tomer and Grafton Eliason (2000) present a model of death anxiety including three determinants, namely, past-related regrets, future-related regrets, and meaningfulness of death. Their description of past-related regret refers to an awareness of unfulfilled aspirations, which could include unresolved issues with loved ones. They defined future-related regret as an awareness of the "inability to fulfill basic goals in the future" (p. 5). With the anticipation of death of a loved one, future regrets are very real, because if nothing is done now, there would be no more opportunity to restore the relationship when death takes away the loved one. These concerns about future regrets should propel people to make the most of the remaining time with the loved one.

Social Support

All our participants expressed the need to talk to someone who could understand the suffering they were experiencing. Therefore, there is a need for hospice service that focuses on the spiritual and psychological needs of both the patients and their loved ones. Such service will not only provide social and emotional support, but also facilitate existential and spiritual coping, which are capable of transforming their suffering into personal growth. Wong (2002c) suggested that transformative grieving was essential in moving through the recovery process. He posited that transformative grieving allows one to build the loss into his or her future in a constructive and redefining way. The transformative process could empower one to actively engage life and transcend the reality of suffering and death.

Implications for Counseling

These findings have several implications for helping professionals who work in hospice settings or provide grief counseling. As we understand more and more the transformative process of meaning and spirituality, we can be more effective in motivating individuals to embrace their life and overcome death anxiety. A meaning-centered approach (Wong, 1998c; chap. 15, this volume) would facilitate the process of making sense of the loss and creating a new life without the loved one. It could encourage individuals to create a new narrative with the dying person, allowing for (a) reconciliation, (b) forgiveness, (b) resolving regrets, and (d) preparing them to move on after the anticipated death. A new narrative could set an individual free from the burden of the past while preparing emotionally, psychologically, and spiritually for the future without the loved one present.

ACKNOWLEDGMENT

This chapter is based on a master's thesis submitted by Debra Ivancovich to the Graduate Program in Counselling Psychology of Trinity Western University in 2005 and supervised by Paul T. P. Wong.

MAIN POINTS

1. Anticipatory grief is a universal experience, involving physical, psychological, and spiritual components.
2. Existential and religious/spiritual coping play an important role in coping with anticipatory grief.
3. Resolving regrets and concerns is a major part of anticipatory grief.
4. There is need for hospice services and counseling that help individuals struggling with anticipatory grief.

RECOMMENDED READINGS

Pargament, K. I. (1997). *The psychology of religion and coping: Theory, research, practice.* New York: Guilford.
Rando, T. A. (1986). A comprehensive analysis of anticipatory grief: Perspectives, processes, promises, and problems. In T. A. Rando (Ed.), *Loss and anticipatory grief* (pp. 3–37). New York: Lexington Books.
Tomer, A., & Eliason, G. (2000). Toward a comprehensive model of death anxiety. In A. Tomer (Ed.), *Death attitudes and the older adult: Theories, concepts, and applications* (pp. 3–22). Philadelphia, PA: Brunner-Routledge.
Wong, P. T. P. (2000). Meaning in life and meaning in death in successful aging. In A. Tomer (Ed.), *Death attitudes and the older adults: Theories, concepts and applications* (pp. 23–35). Philadelphia, PA: Bruner-Routledge.

REFERENCES

Aldrich, C. K. (1974). Some dynamics of anticipatory grief. In B. Schoenberg, A. C. Carr, A. H. Kutscher, D. Peretz, & I. K. Goldberg (Eds.), *Anticipatory grief* (pp. 3–9). New York: Columbia University Press.

Attig, T. (1989). Coping with mortality: An essay on self-mourning. *Death Studies, 13* (44), 361–370.

Attig, T. (1991a). Coping with mortality: An essay on self-mourning. *Death Studies, 13* 361–370.

Attig, T. (1991b). The importance of conceiving of grief as an active process. *Death Studies, 15,* 385–393.

Attig, T. (2000). Anticipatory mourning and the transition to loving in absence. In T. A. Rando (Ed.), *Clinical dimensions of anticipatory mourning: Theory and practice in working with the dying, their loved ones, and their caregivers* (pp. 115–134). Champaign, IL: Research Press.

Battista, J. & Almond, R. (1973). The development of meaning in life. *Psychiatry, 36,* 409–427.

Bourke, M. P. (1984). The continuum of pre- and post-bereavement grieving. *British Journal of Medical Psychology, 57,* 121–125.

Bowlby, J. (1980). *Loss: Sadness and depression.* London: Basic Books.

Carlsen, M. B. (1991). *Creative aging: A meaning-making perspective.* New York: Norton.

Clayton, P. J., Halikas, J. A., Maurice, W. L., & Robins, E. (1973). Anticipatory grief and widowhood. *British Journal of Psychiatry, 122,* 47–51.

Cleiren, M. (1993). *Bereavement and adaptation: A comparative study of the aftermath of death.* Washington, DC: Hemisphere.

Corr, C. A. (1993). Coping with dying: Lessons that we should and should not learn from the work of Elisabeth Kübler-Ross. *Death Studies, 17,* 69–83.

Cowles, K. V., & Rodgers, B. L. (1991). The concept of grief: A foundation for nursing research and practice. *Research in Nursing & Health, 14,* 119–127.

Das, A. K. (1998). Frankl and the realm of meaning. *Journal of Humanistic Counseling Education and Development, 36*(4), 199–214.

Davies, B. (2000). Anticipatory mourning and the transition of fading away. In T. A. Rando (Ed.), *Clinical dimensions of anticipatory mourning: Theory and practice in working with the dying, their loved ones, and their caregivers* (pp. 135–154). Champaign, IL: Research Press.

Doka, K. J. (1993). *Living with life-threatening illness.* New York: Lexington.

Duke, S. (1998). An exploration of anticipatory grief: The lived experience of people during their spouses' terminal illness and bereavement. *Journal of Advanced Nursing, 28,* 829–840.

Erikson, E. H. (1963). *Childhood and society.* New York: W.W. Norton.

Fabry, J. B. (1968/1980/1987/1990). *The pursuit of meaning.* Berkeley, CA: Institute of Logotherapy Press.

Feifel, H. (1990). Psychology and death: Meaningful rediscovery. *American Psychologist, 45,* 537–543.

Folkman, S., & Lazarus, R. S. (1985). If it changes it must be a process: Study of emotion and coping during three stages of a college examination. *Journal of Personal Social Psychology, 48,* 150–170.

Frankl, V. E. (1959). *The doctor and the soul.* New York: Vintage.

Frankl, V. E. (1963). *Man's search for meaning: An introduction to logotherapy.* New York: Pocket Books.

Frankl, V. E. (1967). *Psychotherapy and existentialism.* Selected papers on logotherapy. New York: Simon & Schuster.

Frankl, V. E. (1984). *Man's search for meaning: An introduction to Logotherapy.* New York: Simon & Schuster.

Frankl, V. E. (1986). *The doctor and the soul: From psychotherapy to logotherapy* (Revised and expanded). New York: Vintage Books.

Fulton, R. (2003). Anticipatory mourning: A critique of the concept. *Mortality, 8,* 342–351.

Gilliland, G., & Fleming, S. (1998). A comparison of spousal anticipatory grief and conventional grief. *Death Studies, 22,* 541–562.

Graber, A. V. (2004). *Victor Frankl's logotherapy: Method of choice in ecumenical pastoral psychology* (2nd ed.). Lima, OH: Wyndham Hall Press.

Hannah, M. T., & Domino, G. (1996). The prediction of ego integrity in older persons. *Educational and Psychological Measurement, 56,* 930–951.

Harrison, M. O., Koenig, H. G., Hays, J. C., Eme-Akwari, A. G., & Pargament, K. I. (2001). The epidemiology of religious coping: A review of recent literature. *International Review of Psychiatry, 13,* 86–93.

Hill, C. D., Thompson, L. W., & Gallagher, D. (1988). The role of anticipatory bereavement in older women's adjustment to widowhood. *The Gerontologist, 28*(6), 792–796.

Hinton, J. (1999). The progress of awareness and acceptance of dying assessed in cancer patients and their caring relatives. *Palliative Medicine, 13*(1), 19–38.

Holy Bible: New International Version. (1984). Grand Rapids, MI: Zondervan.

Huber, R., & Gibson, J. W. (1990). New evidence for anticipatory grief. *The Hospice Journal, 6,* 49–66.

Jacobs, S., Kasl, S., Schaefer, C., & Ostfeld, A. (1994). Conscious and unconscious coping with loss. *Psychosomatic Medicine 56,* 557–563.

Joske, W. D. (1981). Philosophy and the meaning of life. In E. D. Klemke (Ed.), *The meaning of life* (pp. 248–261). New York: Oxford University Press. (Original work published 1974)

Kastenbaum, R., & Kastenbaum, B. (1989). *Encyclopedia of death.* Phoenix, AZ: Oryx Press.

Kierkegaard, S. (1944). *The concept of dread* (W. Lowrie, Trans.). Princeton, NJ: Princeton University Press.

Klenow, D. J., & Bolin, R. C. (1989). Belief in an afterlife: A national survey. *Omega, 20,* 63–74.

Klinger, E. (1998). The search for meaning in evolutionary perspective and its clinical implications. In P. T. P. Wong & P. S. Fry (Eds.), *The human quest for meaning: A handbook of psychological research and clinical applications* (pp. 27–50). Mahwah, NJ: Lawrence Erlbaum Associates.

Kübler-Ross, E. (1969). *On death and dying.* New York: Scribner.

Kutscher, A. H. (1973). Anticipatory grief, death, and bereavement: A continuum. In E. Wyschogrod (Ed.), *Phenomenon of death.* New York: Harper & Row.

Larson, D. G. (2000). Anticipatory mourning: Challenges for professional and volunteer caregivers. In T. A. Rando (Ed.), *Clinical dimensions of anticipatory mourning: Theory and practice in working with the dying, their loved ones, and their caregivers* (pp. 379–398). Champaign, IL: Research Press.

Lazarus, R. S. (1966). *Psychological stress and the coping process.* New York: McGraw-Hill.

Lazarus, R. S., & Folkman, S. (1984). *Stress, appraisal, and coping.* New York: Springer.

Levy, L. H. (1991). Anticipatory grief: Its measurement and proposed reconceptualization. *The Hospice Journal, 7,* 1–28.

Lindemann, E. (1944). Symptomatology and management of acute grief. *American Journal of Psychiatry, 101,* 141–148.

Maddi, S. R. (1998). Creating meaning through making decisions. In P. T. P. Wong & P. S. Fry (Eds.), *The human quest for meaning: A handbook of psychological research and clinical applications* (pp. 3–26). Mahwah, NJ: Lawrence Erlbaum Associates.

Marrone, R. (1999). Dying, mourning, and spirituality: A psychological perspective. *Death Studies, 23,* 495–520.

McHaffie, H. E. (1992). The assessment of coping. *Clinical Nursing Research, 1,* 67–80.

Moos, R. H. (1986). *Coping with life's crises: An integrated approach.* New York: Plenum Press.

Moules, N. J. (1998). Legitimizing grief: Challenging beliefs that constrain. *Journal of Family Nursing, 4,* 142–160.

Nouwen, H. (1982). *A letter of consolation.* San Francisco: Harper.

Oates, W. E. (1982). Forms of grief: Diagnosis, meaning, and treatment. In F. Dougherty (Ed.), *The meaning of human suffering* (pp. 232–265). New York: Human Sciences Press.

O'Connor, K., & Chamberlain, K. (1996). Dimensions of life meaning: A qualitative investigation at mid-life. *British Journal of Psychology, 87*(3), 461–478.

Owen, I. R. (1994a). Introducing an existential-phenomenological approach: Part 2. Theory for practice. *Counseling Psychology Quarterly, 7,* 347–359.

Owen, I. R. (1994b). On being and time: Part 1. Method and overview. *Psychotherapy Section Newsletter, 15,* 27–38.

Owen, I. R. (1994c). On being and time: Part 2. Therapeutic consequences. *Psychotherapy Section Newsletter, 16,* 21–35.

Pargament, K. I. (1997). *The psychology of religion and coping: Theory, research, practice.* New York: Guilford.

Parkes, C. M. (1986). *Bereavement: Studies of grief in adult life* (2nd ed.). Harmondsworth: Penguin.

Parkes, C. M., & Weiss, R. S. (1983). *Recovery from bereavement.* New York: Basic Books.

Pearlin, L. I., & Schooler, C. (1978). The structure of coping. *Journal of Health and Social Behavior, 19,* 2–21.

Pine, V. R. (1974). Dying, death, and social behaviour. In B. Schoenberg, A. C. Carr, A. H. Kutscher, D. Peretz, & I. K. Goldberg (Eds.), *Anticipatory grief* (pp. 31–47). New York: Columbia University Press.

Pine, V. R. (1986). An agenda for adaptive anticipation of bereavement. In T. A. Rando (Ed.), *Loss and anticipatory grief* (pp. 39–54). Lexington, MA: D.C. Heath and Company.

Pine, V. R. (Ed.). (1990). *Unrecognized and unsanctioned grief: The nature and counseling of unacknowledged loss.* Springfield, IL: Charles C. Thomas.

Rando, T. A. (1986). A comprehensive analysis of anticipatory grief: Perspectives, processes, promises, and problems. In T. A. Rando (Ed.), *Loss and anticipatory grief* (pp. 3–37). New York: Lexington Books.

Rando, T. A. (1988). Anticipatory grief: The term is a misnomer but the phenomenon exists. *Journal of Palliative Care, 4,* 70–73.

Rando, T. A. (2000a). Anticipatory mourning: A review and critique of the literature. In T. A. Rando (Ed.), *Clinical dimensions of anticipatory mourning: Theory and practice in working with the dying, their loved ones, and their caregivers* (pp. 17–50). Champaign, IL: Research Press.

Rando, T. A. (2000b). On the experience of traumatic stress in anticipatory and post-death mourning. In T. A. Rando (Ed.), *Clinical dimensions of anticipatory mourning: Theory and practice in working with the dying, their loved ones, and their caregivers* (pp. 155–222). Champaign, IL: Research Press.

Reed, A. W. (1974). Anticipatory grief work. In B. Schoenberg, A. C. Carr, A. H. Kutscher, D. Peretz, & I. K. Goldberg (Eds.), *Anticipatory grief* (pp. 346–357). New York: Columbia University Press.

Reker, G. T., & Wong, P. T. P. (1988). Aging as an individual process: Toward a theory of personal meaning. In J. E. Bitten & V. L. Bengston (Eds.), *Emergent theories of aging* (pp. 214–246). New York: Springer.

Rolland, J. S. (1990). Anticipatory loss: A family systems developmental framework. *Family Process, 29,* 229–244.

Rolland, J. S. (1991). Helping families with anticipatory loss. In F. Walsh & M. McGoldrick (Eds.), *Living beyond loss: Death in the family* (pp. 144–163). New York: W.W. Norton.

Rosenblatt, P. C. (1988). Grief: The social context of private feelings. *Journal of Social Issues, 44*, 67–78.

Sartre, J. P. (1957). *Existentialism and human emotions.* New York: Philosophical Library.

Shantall, T. (1999). The experience of meaning in suffering among holocaust survivors. *Journal of Humanistic Psychology, 39*, 96–125.

Shneidman, E. (1980). *Voices of death.* New York: Harper & Row.

Soll, I. (2001). *Existentialism.* World Book Online, Americas Edition. Retrieved October 9, 2001, from http://www.aolsvc.worldbook.aol.com.

Strobe, M. S., Hansson, R. O., Stroebe, W., & Schut, H. (Eds.). (2001). Handbook of bereavement research: Consequences, coping, and care. Washington, DC: American Psychological Association.

Thompson, S. C., & Pitts, J. (1993). Factors relating to a person's ability to find meaning after a diagnosis of cancer. *Journal of Psychosocial Oncology, 11*, 1–21.

Tomer, A., & Eliason, G. (1996). Toward a comprehensive model of death anxiety. *Death Studies, 20*, 343–365.

Tomer, A., & Eliason, G. (2000). Toward a comprehensive model of death anxiety. In A. Tomer (Ed.), *Death Attitudes and the older adult: Theories, concepts, and applications* (pp. 3–22). Philadelphia, PA: Brunner-Routledge.

Thorson, J. A., & Powell, F. C. (1990). Meanings of death and intrinsic religiosity. *Journal of Clinical Psychology, 46*, 379–391.

Thorson, J. A. & Powell, F. C. (1994). A revised death anxiety scale. In R. A. Neimeyer (Ed.), *Death anxiety handbook: Research, instrumentation, and application* (pp. 31–43). Washington, DC: Tayor & Francis.

Tunks, E., & Bellissimo, A. (1988). Coping with the coping concept: A brief comment. *Pain, 34*, 171–174.

Walker, R. J., & Pomeroy, E. C. (1996). Anticipatory grief and aids: Strategies for intervening with caregivers. *Health & Social Work, 21*, 1, 49–58.

Welch, D. (1982). Anticipatory grief reactions in family members of adult patients. *Issues in Mental Health Nursing, 4*, 149–158.

Weisman, A. D. (1974). Is mourning necessary? In B. Schoenberg, A. C. Carr, A. H. Kutscher, D. Peretz, & I. K. Goldberg (Eds.), *Anticipatory grief* (pp. 14–18). New York: Columbia University Press.

Weiss, R. S. (1988). Is it possible to prepare for trauma? *Journal of Palliative Care, 4*(1), 74–76.

Westberg, G. E. (1971). *Good grief.* Philadelphia, PA: Fortress Press.

Wong, P. T. P. (1993). Effective management of life stress: The resource-congruence model. *Stress Medicine, 9*, 51–60.

Wong, P. T P. (1998a). Implicit theories of meaningful life and the development of the personal meaning profile. In P. T. P. Wong & P. S. Fry (Eds.), *The human quest for meaning: A handbook of psychological research and clinical applications* (pp. 111–140). Mahwah, NJ: Lawrence Erlbaum Associates.

Wong, P. T. P. (1998b). Meaning-centered counseling. In P. T. P. Wong & P. S. Fry (Eds.), *The human quest for meaning: A handbook of psychological research and clinical applications* (pp. 395–436). Mahwah, NJ: Lawrence Erlbaum Associates.

Wong, P. T .P. (1998c). Spirituality, meaning, and successful aging. In P. T. P. Wong & P. S. Fry (Eds.), *The human quest for meaning: A handbook of psychological research and clinical applications* (pp. 359–394). Mahwah, NJ: Lawrence Erlbaum Associates.

Wong, P. T. P. (2000). Meaning in life and meaning in death in successful aging. In A. Tomer (Ed.), *Death attitudes and the older adults: Theories, concepts and applications* (pp. 23–35). Philadelphia, PA: Bruner-Routledge.

Wong, P. T. P. (2002a, December 14). *From death anxiety to death acceptance: A meaning-management model.* Keynote address presented at the Conference on Life and Death Education in National Changhua University of Education, Taiwan.

Wong, P. T. P., (2002b, December). *From grief to transformation.* Keynote address at National Changhua University of Education, Changhua, Taiwan.

Wong, P. T. P. (2002c, December). *Transformation of grief through meaning-management model.* Keynote address at National Changhua University of Education, Changhua, Taiwan.

Wong, P. T. P., & Stiller, C. (1999). Living with dignity and palliative care. In B. de Vries (Ed.), *End of life issues: Interdisciplinary and multidimensional perspectives* (pp. 77–94). New York: Springer.

Wong, P. T. P., Reker, G. T., & Gesser, G. (1994). Death attitude profile–revised: A multidimensional measure of attitudes toward death. In R. A. Neimeyer (Ed.), *Death anxiety handbook: Research, instrumentation, and application* (pp. 121–148). Washington, DC: Taylor & Francis.

Wong, P. T. P., Reker, G. T., & Peacock, E. J. (2005). A resource-congruence model of coping and the development of the coping schema inventory. In P. T. P. Wong & L. C. J. Wong (Eds.), *Handbook of multicultural perspectives on stress and coping* (pp. 223–283). New York: Springer.

Wong, P. T. P., Wong, L. C. J., & Scott, C. (2005). Beyond stress and coping: The positive psychology of transformation. In P. T. P. Wong & L. C. J. Wong (Eds.), *Handbook of multicultural perspectives on stress and coping* (pp. 1–26). New York: Springer.

Worden, W. (1991). *Grief counseling and grief therapy: A handbook for the mental health practitioner* (2nd ed). New York: Springer.

Yalom, I. D. (1980). *Existential therapy.* New York: Basic Books.

Yalom, I. D., & Lieberman, M. A. (1991). Bereavement and heightened existential awareness. *Psychiatry, 54,* 334–345.

10
▼▼▼▼

Construction of Meaning in the Face of Mortality

Gloria Nouel
Chatham College

In the Face of Mortality Where Do the griefs go? The breast opens out like a branch and its leafage light works in our hearts like a volley of butterflies.

—*Pablo Neruda, from "A Light From the Sea" (Ben Belitt, Trans.)*

Grief and bereavement have been studied extensively over the years. However, the primary focus of these studies has been on the difficult emotions and processes that individuals go through after experiencing a loss (Kübler-Ross, 1969/1997; Rando, 1986). There are a number of theorists looking at the experience of grief in a different manner. A number of authors within the constructivist and existential perspectives have focused on issues of transcendence and the continuation of bonds that exist after the death of a loved one (Klass, Silverman, and Nickman, 1996). This chapter falls within these perspectives by focusing on the transformative aspects of bereavement that people undergo when they become involved in community activism. Furthermore, the role of the symbolic and the development of a sense of mission in the world are looked at as an essential part of this change. In addition, the chapter posits that the process of bereavement does not necessarily require letting go of the deceased but instead changes the relationship between the deceased and the bereaved in order to continue, albeit transformed, the bonds that existed prior to the death.

The process of bereavement is one that is profoundly social and symbolic, reflecting the fundamental interpersonal and linguistic dimensions of human life. In order to illuminate this process, this chapter will look at the experience of bereaved mothers who went on to transform their world and themselves by becoming deeply engaged in changing their communities. Through symbolic representations, these women transformed their relationship to their child by finding a way to honor and give meaning to their memory.

This chapter is divided in the following way: first, it looks at the community activism engaged by bereaved mothers and the impact it had on their grieving process, reframing it within the concept of empathic activism. Second, it examines the symbolic and spiritual dimensions of this process and how it transformed their bond with the deceased child.

THE TRANSFORMATION OF MATERNAL BEREAVEMENT THROUGH EMPATHIC ACTIVISM

The process of transformation through leading and participation in support groups, advocacy activities, and/or other community work for mothers who have lost children in violent or accidental ways has seldom been investigated. Most research covering this subject has focused primarily on the role that participation in women's groups has for the empowerment of those who have been victimized (Home, 1991; Faver 1994). There have been a number of authors who have focused on maternal activism as a result of dealing with the loss of a child (Galland, 1998; Weed, 1990). However, these authors have not focused on understanding the role that altruistic actions and sustained activism by bereaved mothers has on the transformation of their grief and the effect that it has in the larger community. By applying existential-phenomenological approaches (Buber, 1996; Frankl, 1963), as well as cultural-relational theoretical approaches (Jordan, Surrey, & Kaplan, 1991; Surrey, 1991) to this experience, I will attempt to elucidate the process of transformation and transcendence for bereaved mothers who have been actively involved in helping others in similar situations. The original research was conducted as part of the researcher's dissertation study (Nouel, 2000).

EXISTENTIAL-PHENOMENOLOGICAL PERSPECTIVES ON TRANSCENDENCE

From an existential-phenomenological perspective, traucendence is understood as having three interrelated meanings: to rise above, to go beyond, and to surpass (May, 1958). This approach does not posit transcendence as overcoming or getting over a loss. Instead it looks at loss as possible transformation. This particular sense of transcendence is appropriate for bereaved mother's since research has shown that bereaved mothers do not overcome the loss of their child in the way we usually understand this process (Brice, 1989). Mothers in these situations do not leave behind their experiences or forget the deceased child. Instead, what happens is something more akin to a radical transformation in the fundamental aspects of the subjective self and worldview of the bereaved mother. In this context, transcendence also includes positive growth and a compassionate engagement with others. Let me further elaborate, Rollo May (1958) describes transcendence the following way in the book *Existence:*

> Transcendence—literally "to climb over or beyond"—describes what every human being is doing every moment when he is not seriously ill or temporarily blocked by despair or anxiety. One can of course, see this emergent evolution in all life processes…but it is much more radically true of human existence, where the capacity for self-awareness qualitatively increases the range of consciousness and therefore greatly enlarges the range of possibilities of transcending the immediate situation. (p. 70).

May speaks about transcendence in relationship to the dimension of temporality as something that is essential to human becoming and evolution. What is central to this capacity for transcendence is the awareness and reflection that individuals bring to their immediate situations. The capacity that human beings have to reflect on themselves and their worlds is an essential aspect of the transcendent nature of human existence. Among the dimensions included here are cognitive and affective aspects of existence such as remembering, structuring the world in a meaningful way, telling stories, and using symbols. Human beings are aware of their feelings and take diverse perspectives on their situations. We are often able to make choices and redefine ourselves based on these self-reflections. In this way, transcendence is tied to self-reflection, awareness, and new perspectives on life events and tragedies.

It is in this sense of transcendence that bereaved mothers move beyond their experiences. In the case of the mothers in this study, a sense of mission develops and altruistic actions become part of the process. This transformation occurs in a community of support provided by other bereaved mothers, parents, and significant others intimately involved with the bereaved. However, there are many mothers who don't take this path and instead may be blocked, unable to move forward, becoming paralyzed in their lives.

RESEARCH METHODOLOGY

Research Participants

The participants in this research consisted of four adult mothers, three who had lost a child through violence (two gang related and one unresolved murder) and one who lost a child through a drunk driving accident. The focus was on the experience of these mothers. Three of the participants were relatively advanced in the process and had spent considerable time in their own healing work. One of the participants was less advanced in the process and had many unresolved issues. I used her experience to complement the analysis of the other three. Two of the participants had been involved in therapeutic and recovery work, as well as other forms of support prior to the death of their children. Both of them were involved in these activities as a result of struggling with drug and alcohol addiction. The other two participants were involved in support groups and advocacy for the first time after the death of their children. Two of the participants were African American women in their forties living in the inner city and two were White suburban women, one in her 50s and the other in her early 60s.

The Researcher's Role

My interest in this difficult issue arose from my community work with a group of African American women who had experienced the loss of one or more of their children, most of them sons, to gang violence in the 1990s. This group of Pittsburgh's inner-city mothers had been involved in a variety of activities in order to deal with gang violence and its aftermath in the city. This included forming grassroots groups for support and advocacy in their communities. They were trying to get further support and resources for their endeavors when they came to my place of employment, the YWCA of Greater Pittsburgh. My role has been as consultant, co-leader, trainer, supportive professional, and an ally to their group. Thus, my research unfolded in an effort to illuminate a process that is often rendered invisible by the stigma of criminality, racism, and sexism in our society, as well as by the fear and anxiety related to issues of complicated parental grief. My research was also informed by my interest in how these efforts to heal one's community, and to connect private pain to the pain of the larger community is part of a larger world-wide grassroots activism (Naples, 1992; Rudick, 1990; Weed, 1990).

As a researcher, this particular experience of maternal loss was extremely difficult to deal with over time. I am not a bereaved mother, but I was the mother of an adolescent son at the time of the research and I could imagine too well this dreaded possibility. My fear of this experience and the recognition of my fear were acknowledged as part of the research. I also felt many positive emotions, such as hopefulness, when seeing what these mothers were doing for themselves and their communities.

Conceptual Framing of Empathic Activism

I developed the term *empathic activism* as I was dialoguing with the Buddhist conception of compassionate action (Chödrön, 1997). Compassionate action, refers to actions on behalf of others that come from a deep understanding of human suffering. In addition, Nancy Naples (1992) had developed the term *activist mothering*. She developed this term as a way of conceptualizing "the interacting nature of labor, politics, and mothering—three aspects of social life usually analyzed separately—from the point of view of women whose motherwork has often been ignored or pathologized" (p. 446). Although I found her term helpful, it excluded the activism of those who do not "mother" per se. Furthermore, I wanted to find a term that embodied empathic presence, as well as an action orientation across groups of people, including men. The term *empathic activism* seemed to reflect these aspects. The term empathic refers to a definite attunement to others experiences. I chose the term activism rather than action, as it refers to a sustained effort to help others and not just an isolated or static action.

Empathic activism speaks to both the psychological and social dimensions of the bereaved mothers' actions and feelings. It requires that a person move toward grasping others' experiences and be moved to act on their behalf, as well as to address the conditions from which these situations may arise. Empathic activism encompasses the interrelated dimensions of feeling, thinking, and action in the context of a relational/social world. This term was also helpful as a way of bridging a duality common in our Western thinking of action and relationship. Action and agency have usually been separated from relational concerns when equated with autonomy (Surrey, 1991). This will be examined in more depth later in relation to The Stone Center relational theorists' conceptions of mutual empowerment.

Qualitative Methodology

Existential-Phenomenological methodology was used for the research. Giorgi (1983), von Eckartsberg (1986), and others developed these methods at Duquesne University. Steps explicated by Wertz (1984) were followed while analyzing the data. In interpreting the data, I incorporated the experience that I had with the mothers in an ongoing community group. In this respect, my methodology is consistent with action research approaches (Brydon-Miller, 1997). A written protocol and interviews were used as data. This methodology integrates a contemplative/interpretive approach as well as continued involvement with the bereaved activist mothers.

A variety of themes emerged through the analysis of the data. The story of each mother was retold, staying very close to her own language. A "shared or common narrative" was written by weaving common themes from the individual narratives. At times, the narrative included how I was affected by such poignant stories. For example, one mother spoke of the excruciating physical pain that she felt when she found out her son had died. This mother described her heart as being the center of the suffering she experienced. In her words, "the pain of the reality of what happened was so overwhelming. I never felt pain like that, ever! My heart, I believed that my heart broke at that time, it actually just caved in... It was as if somebody somehow reached into my chest and grabbed my heart and ripped it out of my body, threw my heart on the ground and stepped on it." The following is my reflection on this particular segment of narrative:

> The participant's description is a powerful way of calling our attention. She wants us to hear what her anguished truth was like. You and I can no longer cover our ears and look away in fear. In other words, these vivid descriptions paint a picture of the sheer torture and excruciating pain that she experienced. ...Mary paints her agony with words...as a researcher to be present to her words is to be thrown into a place where the usual objectification that comes from the distance and perspective of researcher is extremely difficult, if not impossible. The visual images of the body being ripped apart speak to

the power of the symbolic. It truly is the word made flesh. The word "suffering" here is stripped of all its abstractions, and it lays bare the rawest of all human emotions (Nouel, 2000).

Although the research looked at both a personal transformation and a community/social movement, as a psychologist I chose to illuminate the individual process of the participants for this project, staying always mindful that the person exists in multiple contexts, historical, cultural, and political.

The analysis of the data using existential-phenomenological methods showed a number of themes common among the research participants. These themes are understood and described as being interrelated dimensions of the dialectical process of transformation and transcendence toward empathic activism. Following is a narrative encompassing the shared dimensions of the experience as recreated and re-storied by the researcher. This composite mother's story is my articulation of the many voices that were part of the research.

THE SHARED NARRATIVE

The mother's transcendence of the suffering resulting from the tragic loss of her child unfolds in a temporal and dialectical process. Moving within a prior world of complex relationships with her child, the mother had not expected that her child would die before she did. The difficulties in their relationship were experienced as part of the chaos of a complex socio-cultural world. Some examples of which are addiction, young parenthood, poverty, a child's rebellion, and a desire to be a friend rather than a responsible parent. Often others in the family have been the authority figures for the child.

The mother experiences the death of her child as an unbelievable shock, a push into an uncharted emotional territory with peaks and valleys that she is yet unable to grasp. Numbness, terror, and excruciating pain are some of the first reactions experienced when she is faced with such an incomprehensible horror. Suddenly, the world of objects, space, and others does not look the same. Its different physiognomy speaks of a new unknown space where raw emotions, constricted relationships, and hopelessness dwell together.

During the first days and months after the death of her child, she experiences multiple emotions, all so close together that it is as if they were happening simultaneously. Only in retrospect, when telling and retelling her story, can she begin to give voice to what she was feeling at the time. Her taken-for-granted world of safety is no longer there for her. Illusions of control are gone. Her ability to care for and protect her child has been shattered. Her body's regulated rhythms, marked by the occasional disruptions of everyday living, have become like a roller coaster ride followed by "dark nights of the soul." She cries, she screams, she rages, and then she stops feeling altogether. One mother lyrically speaks of leaving her body to touch the moon. She is so far from everybody else, so alone. Two mothers were angry with God, reconnecting later to their spiritual relationship with the divine. One moves closer to God and lets herself become more open and vulnerable.

The world of the grieving mother has multiple variations. Like any other grieving experience it is lived out as a unique and individual process. People often say that there are no two people that grieve alike, yet the unfolding of grief shows itself as a distinct movement in time whereby newfound meanings are usually integrated into the later narrative of the process. There is a before, a moment of knowing, the soon after, the year after, several years after, and the return to the prior world of her relationships and meanings. Having gone through a deep transformation, this return is often imbued with a new purpose, a new way of relating to others, and a changed sense of who she is.

From the beginning, she has had glimpses of transcendent moments, sparks of hope in an otherwise hopeless terrain. With the glimmer of a momentary insight, the kindness of an understanding other, she begins to reach out to others.

Moving from a feeling of isolation, the mother begins to look for others like herself. Other grieving people and other grieving mothers, in particular, make her feel that she is not alone. Sharing with those who truly understand her pain lessens her suffering. They understand her from the heart of their own experiences, a place that only other bereaved parents know. This newfound community of fellow sufferers offers her a place of hope.

She begins to have a nascent sense that she can also do the same for others. She begins to reach out in personal ways, first in the familiar ways of sharing herself, crying together, sitting over coffee. These, she feels, are particular to the relational sensibilities of being a woman and being a mother. This caring and empathic attunement is something that the bereaved mother has learned from other women in her life. These women, her grandmother, the women workers at the shelters at which she has been, other bereaved mothers, have given her inspiration. Others too have helped her, men and women who have suffered in many ways, as well as supportive and empathic professionals.

These helpful mutual relationships continue to exist within a context of a deep sorrow for the mother, a gaping hole in her heart that she knows will never close. She still experiences a visceral anger that erupts at times. She still feels her powerlessness over what happened, her guilt from not having been able to stop her child's death. She often expresses it in the form of "what if?" What if (fill in the blank) is an attempt to regain some form of power and control over what happened through a mental, imaginative exercise that throws time backwards to the moments, days, and years before the death of her child? The guilt of the mother speaks profoundly to her sense of powerlessness. If only she could have done something. She feels that she has failed in her most fundamental parenting mission, that of protecting and preserving her child's life.

The movement from being helped to being the helper is a delicate dialectic, moving back and forth as healing occurs. These are not exclusive, but interdependent parts of an evolving sense of mutuality between the bereaved mother and others who are also bereaved. By helping others, she gives back what was given to her. Helping others also helps her in return by giving her a sense that she is making a difference. She becomes aware that the knowledge and compassion gained from her experience can make a difference for others. This emerging awareness begins to give her a way out of the powerlessness that her tragic situation created in her life.

The grieving mother's empathic and compassionate understanding, rooted in her own experience of suffering, becomes the impetus for action at many different levels. Her actions can be lived in many ways. The mother often shares and supports other grieving mothers. There is also her sharing in groups, her facilitation of groups, her advocacy on behalf of other people who have been victimized, her desire and actualization of community work, her service to others, and her larger vision of being able to affect one's community and the world at large.

Often she experiences this movement to action as if she were coming around to a full circle, to the place where her life began. It is a kind of redemption for her, an example for others. At other times, she feels both that she has a sense of mission as well as a vision guided by the spiritual, unseen dimension of life, including the soul or spirit of her departed child. A newfound implicit political consciousness that includes a will to empower others in her community enlarges her vision of where change should occur.

There is a symbolic dimension to the mother's actions. She expresses these symbols in a variety of forms such as a public remembrance event or a public memorial in the place where the death occurred. Further, most of her actions (e.g., helping others, developing groups, advocating for others) are ways of both assuring that her child's death will not be in vain, and of continuing her or his life in the form of these works. She feels her dead child guides her from another realm. The continuation of her child's life has now passed to the realm of the spiritual. The mother speaks of it as an unseeing world, which she sometimes is allowed to peek into just by the power of her mind's eye and by her connections to the greater presence of God.

The symbolic dimension includes a new spiritual relationship to spiritual beings such as angels and to animals symbolizing spiritual beings, such as butterflies. This enhanced relationship to the symbolic expands the mother's world to include many levels of reality where existence can continue, and it also helps her continue to feel a connection with the dead child.

The mother's transcendence of her tragic loss is not a once and for all obliteration of her pain, and it is not a leaving behind or a forgetting of her loss. On the contrary, it is a commitment to never forget. The meaning of her life forever changed, she continues to live with an empty hole in her heart. She continues to incorporate and integrate her new articulations of what her grief means. She brings her commitment so that she can make a difference for others. She brings her care to individuals and communities that suffer. She brings forgiveness and peace to places of injury and sorrow. She wants to help others and herself out of powerlessness and to bring healing and justice to her community. She wants to make sure that her child's death was not in vain (Nouel, 2000, pp. 145–152).

RELATIONAL DIMENSIONS OF TRANSCENDENCE

Self-in-Relation Theorists

Maternal bereavement's transcending process constitutes a movement toward mutually enhanced relationships. According to the relational theorists (Jordan et al., 1991; Surrey, 1991), mutuality exists within the context of individuals' recognition of one another. For women, in particular, the ability to have mutually empathic and responsive relationships is central to their development. In this perspective, mutuality becomes the aim of development instead of the autonomous self postulated by the traditional Western developmental theories.

The transformation in the bereaved mother's sense of identity occurs within mutually empowering and responsive relationships. This is exemplified in my data by the gradual development of bereaved mothers from disconnection to responsiveness, in their supportive relationships. All three mothers whose data was analyzed found it helpful being in groups and with other bereaved individuals. In turn, they were able to be present for others, weaving a net of mutually helpful and supportive relationships in their lives. Further, these mutually empowering relationships had a synergistic quality prompting them to become involved in a variety of other actions, and to develop a larger vision of their potential impact in communities and social issues.

For example, one mother spoke of when she was working in a flower shop and heard of the death of a young man: "I walked over to the funeral home and I found the mother who was sitting there … and I told her 'you know the same thing happened to me a year ago.'… and today she is a real good friend … we did some work together and she tells me how much it helped her that I came over…" (p. 207). This exemplifies how the participant's initial supportive actions became a mutually empowering relationship, eventually considering this bereaved mother a friend.

The previously mentioned example also shows how relationships and actions are interdependent of one another. The mother said that they became friends and worked together. All the mothers that I interviewed, as well as the mothers that I worked with in the community, exhibited this inter-relationship between care and action in the world exemplifying mutually empowering relationships.

In Western society, women have historically been given the role of caretakers. They are supposed to be the holders of relationships and emotions, where as men are perceived as being movers and shakers, cared for by their wives or significant others. These examples of mutually empowering and caring actions in the greater "outside" world shift the paradigm from a duality of relationship and action toward empathic activism. The bereaved mothers exhibited empathic activist behaviors and felt that actions on behalf of others were part of their healing process. Thus, transcending their suffering involved active engagement at many levels, including an interrelationship among action, relationship, and contemplation.

In addition to these individual relationships, the mothers also took part in grassroots social movements such as AA and the women's shelter movement. Two of the women had participated in recovery groups, one had stayed and later worked at the shelter. The other two had partici-pated in bereavement groups. Many of their caring interventions were modeled after the kinds of care they had received in these environ-ments. Thus, a delicate dialectic of personal and community support existed for them, as they began to move forward to become support-ers and advocates for others.

Meaning as Self-Transcendence: A Grieving Mother's Mission. Victor Frankl (1955/1986, 1959/1963, 1969/1988) speaks of meaning as self-transcendent and as rooted in an understanding that human existence is intrinsically relational. Human subjectivity does not exist apart from its contextual world. Thus, meanings that arise from any kind of difficulties are embedded in this interdependence of self and others. The self integrates interpretations that arise from the social, cultural, and historical dimensions.

Human beings are repeatedly confronted with multiple situations. The self-transcendent characteristic of meaning points to this con-frontation between individual existences to the world beyond. In this light, the purpose of an individual life and suffering is not to actualize oneself, but to fulfill one's mission in the world. The individual has the freedom to take up an attitude that makes bearable what has been handed to her/him and transform it into a higher calling.

The grieving mother's transcending of her suffering is an example of her confrontation with the world beyond her subjectivity. All the mothers in my research at some point shifted their values in order to reframe their loss as having a particular purpose for themselves and the larger world. For example, one mother went back to the commu-nity in which her son died to help those whom she called "the lost children." She saw herself as being called by God to do this. She chose to return to a place that she dreaded in order to fulfill her mission.

This sense of mission, as exemplified by this particular grieving mother, is a poignant example of the purpose that can unfold from a tragic situation. Throughout the data, I found multiple examples of this: the grieving mother that wanted to develop self-help groups for her community and the one who wanted to volunteer in a prison min-istry represent shifts of values and a movement toward newfound purpose.

Diverging from Frankl, who emphasizes the meaning giving dimen-sion, Massey (1991) advocates that it is not enough to see human beings as giving particular meanings to the situations they confront. Individuals often take up existing meanings within the context of their communities. For example, one of the mothers found that recovery groups provided a model for empowerment and healing in community. Sharing with others proved to be a powerful tool for transformation illustrating the meaning of her phrase, "pain shared is pain lessened" (p. 178).

Martinéz Roméro (1988), on the other hand, offers a balance between individualist and collectivist perspectives. He states that each has its negative and positive sides. A collectivist perspective may deny individual meanings and experiences where as an individualist perspective may ignore important values such as solidarity. He calls for a *communal personalism* that combines individual freedom and personal responsibility with the recognition that we are "being for others." The recognition of the interdependence of society, communities, groups, and individuals, can be helpful to grassroots groups and individuals trying to help others like themselves. For example, one of the mothers often struggled with the issue of what was too much and what was appropriate help. She, often, felt the need to go beyond her personal boundaries to help the community in the light of her mission to bring healing to others. However, she also had a need to take care of herself. She needed to balance her commitment to community and commitment to herself. A fundamental recognition that she didn't need to sacrifice herself for the collective needs was an important part of her ability to continue to move on without getting burned out.

SELF-IDENTITY, DIALOGUE, AND THE SYMBOLIC IN THE EXPERIENCE OF THE BEREAVED MOTHER

According to Buber (1923/1996), an authentic dialogue ceases to exist when there is no longer the possibility of a real encounter between two people. Similarly, Brice (1989) goes on to state that the imaginary cannot substitute for this real dialogue between two flesh-and-blood human beings. It is only in the realm of the inter-human that true dialogue can exist. I would, however, like to expand on the role that the imaginary does have in the continuation of a dialogue with others.

The unfolding of a symbolic and creative relationship with her dead child through memory, evocation, and imagination is an important aspect of the mother's grieving process. This relationship takes place in the interactions that the mother has with significant others, with groups and communities, with the spiritual world, and with the symbolic expressions. These relationships with seen and unseen worlds are structured as an ongoing dialogue that symbolizes the lost "real encounter" with the dead child. Although the deceased child can not be there in flesh to provide the needed mutuality for a true I–Thou relationship, others, places, events, and good works form a symbolic relationship with the bereaved mother providing an expanding horizon of creative responses.

The symbolic relationships here are expansive and not a substitution for the lost relationship, instead they are a creation and recreation of the ability to care for and nurture the development of others, communities, and creative memorials. Let me identify a number of these relationships and elaborate them in their symbolic and imaginary aspects. I will give examples from the texts of the participants to illustrate them. They are (a) relationships with familiar others such as grandchildren, (b) relationships with others that need help, (c) relationships with communities, (d) relationships with the symbolic expressions and representations in the world of things or nature, and (e) representations with the spiritual dimensions of existence.

Relationships With Familiar Others

Relationships with familiar others, such as grandchildren, are often powerful symbols of hope for the bereaved mother. Participants one and two had surviving grandchildren with whom they continued to be involved. For example, participant one said:

> And from his death, I had two grandsons. They are both the same age. They both have my son's name ... which is another reason that I want to keep his spirit alive, because I feel like these are two sons he'll never see and they will never know their father.... I show them pictures ... and when I look at them I see my son.... I'm just trying to take the father role and do things for them my son would have done, which is real important for me ... someone told me when God closes one door he opens another one at the same time. Well, it feels that he closed one door in my life but then he opened two more doors, and those two doors are my grandsons." (Nouel, 2000, p. 182)

The statement of God opening two doors shows a symbolic dimension of hope. Her love and care can continue through her son's children. They, in turn, are a continuation of her son's life. Her love and care is also imbued with the love and care that the participant imagines her son would have given his two sons had he been alive. Two doors represent two openings into the future and a continuation of the one life that was cut so short.

Symbolic and Creative Aspects of the Relationship to Others and Communities in Need. Another aspect of the mothers transcending their loss is the continuation of their care for others and/or for the larger community. These relationships become central at some point of their grieving process. For one of the participants, going back to her community to be an outreach worker had multiple dimensions. It represented facing her fears, forgiving those who killed her child, redemption from her past life of drugs and homelessness, and saving young people and their parents in the community from similar fate such as hers. She speaks about it in the following way:

> I believe … what it meant for me is that it was a calling from God to go back, go back and work on forgiving and facing my fears…. I believe what God done for me was let me know that there are a lot of lost children out there that need some help…. They asked why I'd want to come up here and help them? … because I want to be able to help you. Just because my son is gone does not mean I don't' still have motherly instincts and I wouldn't want your mother to go through what I went through. I wouldn't want you to experience some of the things that my son experienced. (Nouel, 2000, p. 184)

This particular participant always spoke of how her helping the community was helping her to come full circle in her life. Her care, now extending to other young people, their parents, and their distressed communities, was a continuation of caring for her deceased son, as well as reparation for her own failures as a parent and redemption from her past life. She often spoke of how others in the community who had seen her at her worst, during her addiction and when she was homeless, could now see her as a helper and educator. In an implicit way, her being a role model becomes, in her perception, a representation of hope for others in the community.

Symbolic Representations Through Memorials and Sacred Places

Each of the participants I interviewed for this study had multiple ways of remembering, honoring, and representing the loss of their child. Grieving parents find ways of memorializing the lives of their children, including participation in the Day of Remembrance (a day to honor and remember the lives of the more than 300 children who have died due to urban violence in Pittsburgh since the 1990s) or a memorial place in the spot where one participant's daughter died. If not through a public display, all of my participants had special places in their homes that served this purpose. Pictures of their children pinned on their clothes, as well as butterflies and angels, were also common symbols used this way.

One mother created a memorial place for her 22-year-old daughter in the spot where she had died in a drunk driving accident in a park. It was first begun by one of her daughter's friends who placed a cross in the spot of the accident. The participant later had her brother make a permanent cross. She drove past the spot every day on her way to work, and every time it evoked images of her young daughter dying there. This spot has now become a permanent memorial for her daughter, and although she didn't intend it, it has become a symbol in the community, a sacred spot for others as well. She speaks of it the following way:

> And so that's how it came about. It just has kind of grown. First we just had the cross and then we added flowers, and we added the flagpole, and it's not a big thing but...because I think it's in such a prominent place where hundreds of people pass by there and say a prayer for her or, you know, how nice that they think it is. And every time they do, my heart skips a little because it makes me feel good...I've had parents of teenagers thanking me for putting it there to remind the children, you know, about drinking and driving and to drive safely...and I thought how odd I didn't do that for you at all. But it's been a wonderful outgrowth of that... I'm just shocked how many people are moved by that memorial. (Nouel, 2000, p. 186)

We can see that the memorial as symbolic expression has a life of its own, often unintended by those who created it. The participant and others who knew and loved this young woman began the memorial to help themselves. The memorial went beyond its initial purpose by the nature of its public life. It became part of the community, a place where others grieve, and a place where parents teach their children about the dangers of drunk driving. The grieving mother in this case hears the voices of others in the community as a response to what she created initially to remember her daughter. Symbolically, her daughter's death and life continues to have an effect on others. For her, transcending the loss of her child includes this sense of the sacredness of a place. This is not a dialogue with another human being in a literal sense, but it is a continuation of a dialogue in the symbolic world of the memorial through the interpretation by others of what her daughter's life means for them. They help her move out of powerlessness by knowing that, although unintentionally, she is positively affecting others.

The Symbolic Aspects of the Spiritual Dimension of a Mother's Loss: Angels, Butterflies, and Messages From Above. The continuation of a relationship with the dead child for the bereaved mother often shifts to a new level of existence: the realm of the spiritual. This relational dimension is often invisible to the eyes of others. Without speculating as to whether or not there is life after death, it is important to give full and faithful rendition to the symbolic and creative aspects of this experience, without reducing it to some kind of defense mechanism for survival, or even to an incomplete and imaginary substitution for the real relationship now gone.

In their popular book, *Hello From Heaven*, Bill and Judy Guggenheim (1995) have recorded thousands of stories told to them by grieving people who spoke of a connection with departed ones. They used a variety of images to describe these experiences. Among these, I found a number of symbols also used by the grieving mothers. These symbols included butterflies, angels, and messages through music. The relationship with their child continues in a symbolic way through these representations or actual encounters with butterflies, birds, or musical messages. These experiences or representations appear to be quite helpful in the grieving process. Beyond representations in objects or pictures, the mothers spoke of being guided by their children from above, or of receiving messages that they interpreted as saying that their children are doing well. These were not apparitions of ghosts, but much more subtle experiences accompanied by a different mood, a shift in consciousness, or an understanding that was intuited rather than intellectually known. Interpretation was also part of this knowing because these messages were cryptic and opaque. The language of these events was often expressed through synchronistic happenings, or meaningful coincidences. One mother speaks of her experience:

> I was riding in my car and all of the sudden, I hear myself whistling (well I don't whistle) a particular tune.... I can not carry a tune. I was thinking "Oh isn't this strange ..." over and over again, and I don't know what the name of it is.... I go home and I forget the incident.... A day later all of the sudden on the TV comes a commercial for their fall line-up and I hear this tune. It's the same tune.... I thought, "Isn't that odd...." So the next day I'm in my room ... I put a CD on and the very first song was that song I was whistling. So now this is the third time, within like three days, that this song comes to me. I thought, "Isn't that strange," I wonder what it means.... I found out it was Pachabel's Canon in D, which it turns out to be

a very famous classical musical piece … but I did not know. So I thought … "It could mean two things—I should bring more classical music into my life or learn more about the composer." The following weekend my daughter's best friend was getting married and it was a very difficult day for us because they had grown up like sisters. Her father had died five years before my daughter died. In fact, she and her father are buried side by side. She'd asked my husband to give her away … it was very emotionally packed. I thought, "How am I going to get through this day without crying?" As I went to the church I prayed for some kind of sign. We're in the second pew … waiting for my husband to come down the aisle with the bride, and the organ starts to play and guess what they played? Pachabel's Cannon in D. (Nouel, 2000, p. 189)

This is a powerful example of how the symbolic, expressed as a message from the spiritual realm, and helps the grieving mother to deal with an emotionally difficult situation. The participant interprets it as a message from above and is able to feel that her daughter has been there at her best friend's wedding. She says, "I think it was sent. It was sent from her to say, don't you see? I am here. I am here. I truly believe that it was sent to me in that sequence to say, 'It's okay and I'm fine.'"

The significant relationships in our lives always have a symbolic, imaginary aspect. They are the repositories of our hopes or dreams and may have a myriad of positive and negative meanings for us. These symbolic aspects, whether through spiritual experiences, memorials, or remembrances, are helpful for bereaved mothers in many ways. This frame helps us understand how the relationship of the mother with her dead child continues to exist and the role that symbolic expressions, such as memorial spaces, have on the continuation and transformation of the relationship. The imaginary, as we saw in the last example, is often helpful to the mother when it confirms her belief that her child's spirit has moved on to another dimension of existence. The mothers whom I interviewed often found solace in this symbolic dimension of their experiences. To say that the imaginary is deficient (Brice, 1989) is to deny the power of symbols, or even the power of faith, and these mothers spoke of a very different experience for them. Instead, the creative dimensions of these symbols expanded their horizons and acted as ripples in the water. They were an essential part of the transcending of their suffering. For those mothers who are engaged in an active process of healing through many facets, the poignancy of these events in the spirit world has as much power as anything else going on in their real lives.

The symbolic dimensions of the bereaved mothers falls within what Buber (1923/1996) calls the realm of spirit. Buber speaks of I–thou relationships as existing in different realms of existence. The difference between the objectifying attitude of the I–It and the attitude of a true encounter can be exemplified by the living relationship that the bereaved mother exhibits when speaking of the spirit world or of the actions and visions she has for herself and her community. The transcending of her suffering in this respect is a continuation of a relationship through a dialogue with others and with the symbolic dimensions of her experience. The following passage from Buber, (1923/1996) speaks to this, "Here the relation is wrapped in clouds but reveals itself, it lacks but creates language. We hear no You and yet feel addressed; we answer—creating, thinking, acting: with our being we speak the basic word, unable to say You with our mouth" (p. 57).

CULTURE AND THE CONTINUATION OF BONDS: SOME CONCLUDING THOUGHTS

Personal construction theorists have explored the roles that memory and the continuation of bonds play in the grief experience (Klass et al., 1996). Contemporary theorists question assumptions positing that the disengagement with the deceased is the ultimate goal of grieving (i.e. Wortman & Silver, 1989, 2001). Traditionally, grief has been considered pathological when difficulties arise in disconnecting from the memory of the deceased for longer than expected. Continued attachments were often considered as unresolved or complicated grief. In addition, attempting to maintain some kind of connection with the deceased was thought to be a form of denial of the reality of death. These views are not in tune with more holistic understandings that see individuals as fundamentally related and as part of a web of interdependence. In addition, symbolic and narrative aspects of diverse cultures and societies speak to the many ways in which grief can be constructed. A different paradigm based on relational, existential, ecological and constructivist models is needed to understand how the bereaved remains involved and connected to the deceased. In adopting these views we can begin to see how the construction of inner representations of the deceased, as well as memorializing, are ways that help us keep their presence alive, both personally and collectively. More research needs to be done in this area in order to elaborate the full psychological significance and cultural dimensions of the continuation of bonds as a normal part of the grieving process.

This research begins the process by articulating different aspects experienced by bereaved mothers in their path of transformation. The relational, symbolic, and spiritual dimensions explored in this chapter are understood to be part of a process of continuation of a relationship with the deceased. This relationship, no longer existing in an embodied form, continues in the lives of those left behind and it is part of the active construction of meaning engaged by individuals and groups. This work of remembrance and continuation binds our present world with the past as well as with the future.

MAIN POINTS

1. Community activism may promote meaningful transformations in the way people experience bereavement.
2. The development of a sense of mission and the symbolic are essential aspects of this transformation.
3. The process of bereavement does not necessarily require letting go of the deceased, but instead, changes the relationship between the deceased and the bereaved in order to continue, albeit transformed, the bonds that existed prior to the death.

REFERENCES

Belitt, B. (Trans.) (1961). A light from the sea. In B. Bellitt, *Selected Poems of Pablo Neruda*. New York: Grove Press.

Brice, C. W. (1989). The relational essence of maternal mourning: An existential-psychoanalytic perspective. *The Humanistic Psychologist, 17,* 22–40.

Buber, M. (1923/1996). *I and thou.* New York: Touchstone.

Brydon-Miller, M. (1997). Participatory action research: Psychology and social change, *The Society for the Psychological Study of Social Issues, 53,* 657–666.

Chödrön, P. (1997). *When things fall apart.* Boston: Shambhala.

Faver, C. A. (1994). Feminist ideology and strategies for social change: An analysis of social movements. *The Journal of Applied Social Sciences, 18(1),* 123–134.

Frankl, V. E. (1955/1986). *The doctor and the soul.* New York: Vintage Books.

Frankl, V. E. (1959/1963). *Man's search for meaning.* New York: Pocket Books.

Frankl, V. E. (1969/1988). *The will to meaning.* New York: Penguin Books.

Galland, C. (1998). *The bond between women: A journey to fierce compassion.* New York: Riverhead Books.

Giorgi, A. (1983).The importance of the phenomenological attitude for access to the psychological realm. In A. Giorgi, A. Barton, & C. Maes (Eds.), *Duquesne studies in phenomenological psychology,* (Vol. 4). Pittsburgh: Duquesne University Press.

Guggenheim, W. & Guggenheim, J.A. (1995). *Hello from heaven!* New York: Bantam Books.

Heidegger, M. (1962). *Being and time.* New York: Harper & Row.

Home, A. M. (1991). Mobilizing women's strengths for social change: The group connection. *Social Work With Groups, 14(3–4),* 153–173.

Jordan, J. V., Surrey, J. L., & Kaplan, A. G. (1991). Women and empathy: Implications for psychological development and psychotherapy. In J. V. Jordan, A. G. Kaplan, J. B. Miller, I. P. Striver, J. L. Surrey (Eds.), *Women's growth in connection: Writings from the stone center*. New York: The Guildford Press.

Klass, D., Silverman, P. R., & Nickman, S. L. (1996). *Continuing bonds: New understandings of grief*. Washington, DC: Taylor and Francis.

Kübler-Ross, E. (1969/1997). *On death and dying.* New York: Touchstone Inc.

Massey, R. F. (1991). Social conscience in logotherapy. *The International Forum for Logotherapy, 14*, 32–35.

May, R. (1958). Contributions of Existential Psychotherapy. In R. May, E. Angel, & H. F. Ellengerger (Eds.), *Existence* (pp. 37–91). New York: Simon and Shuster.

Naples, N. A. (1992). Activist mothering: Cross-generational continuity in the community work of women from low-income urban neighborhoods. *Gender & Society, 6*, 441–463.

Nouel, G. (2000). Bereaved mothers' transcending suffering by moving towards supportive actions: An existential-phenomenological study. *Dissertation Abstracts-International.* (Vol. 60, 7–B): 3574.

Rando, T. A. (Ed.). (1986). *Parental loss of a child*. Champaign, IL: Research Press Company.

Roméro, J. V. M. (1988). Group logotherapy in Latin America. *The international forum for logotherapy, 11*, 102–106.

Ruddick, S. (1989). *Maternal Thinking*. New York: Ballantine Books.

Surrey, J. L. (1991). The self-in-relation: A theory of women's development. In J. V. Jordan, A. G. Kaplan, J. B. Miller, I. P. Striver, J .L. Surrey (Eds.), *Women's growth in connection: writings from the Stone Center*. New York: Guilford Press.

von Eckartsberg, R. (1986). *Life–world experience*. Lanham, MD: Center for Advanced Research in Phenomenology & University Press of America.

Weed F. J. (1990). The victim activist role in the anti-drunk driving movement. *The Sociological Quarterly, 31*, 459–573.

Wertz, F. J. (1984). Procedures in phenomenological research. In C. Aanstoos (Ed.), *Exploring the lived world: Readings in phenomenological psychology*. Carrolton, GA: West Georgia College.

Wortman, C. B., & Silver, R. C. (1989). The myths of coping with loss. *Journal of Consulting and Clinical Psychology, 57*, 349–357.

Wortman, C. B., & Silver, R. C. (2001). The myths of coping with loss revisited. In M. S. Stroebe, R. O. Hanson, W. Stroebe, & H. Schut (Eds.), *Handbook of bereavement research.* (pp. 405–429). Washington, DC: APA.

11

▼▼▼▼

The Dark Night of the Soul

James A. Thorson
University of Nebraska at Omaha

Ann M. Laughlin
Creighton University, Omaha

I am utterly weary of life. I pray the Lord will come forthwith and carry me hence. Let him come, above all, with his last Judgment; I will stretch out my neck, the thunder will burst forth, and I shall be at rest.

—Martin Luther, as cited in James (1929, p. 135)

I recall my grandmother telling me about her relief each time the Western Union boy would pass by their house during World War II. It was the practice at that time to notify families who had a son who was killed or missing in action by telegram. It came from the Secretary of the Army and began, "We regret to inform you...."

I have a picture in my mind of Grandma the day that the telegraph delivery boy stopped at their house. I can see her now in my mind's eye: She was a big woman, bent forward at the waist, and she walked fast. She would have beaten Grandpa to the front door. Johnny was killed on October 28, 1944, but I think the telegram didn't come until December. She would be walking to the door, wiping her hands on her apron, with a worried look on her face, and then Grandpa would catch up to her as she opened the door.

It was a matter of pride in the Thorson family that the youngest son, John, who was drafted in 1942, heroically rolled over onto a Japanese hand grenade at the Battle of Leyte Gulf in the Philippines. But that pride came later, when they gave him the Medal of Honor. We'd take it out and look at it, along with the Purple Heart that had been presented to Grandpa Thorson at a ceremony at Fort Omaha after the end of the war. I saw a letter from a Pvt. Ruiz whose life had been saved, along with several other men in Johnny's squad, and the paper signed by President Truman telling what he'd done.

I can't help but reflect back to my image of that day when they first heard about the loss of their son. Grandma Thorson lived another 24 years after that, to age 84. I remember her as bright and cheerful, an optimistic person who sought to find the good in other people. But tears come to my eyes in sympathetic grief over the loss of the uncle I never knew, her 24-year-old farm boy. She was, as far as I knew, a person who exemplified spiritual well-being. At least she sure gave a good appearance of it.

I've done several articles and two books on spiritual well-being. I was part of the discussion when the definition was hammered out by the National Interfaith Coalition on Aging (Cook, 1980, p. xiii). I should know from spiritual well-being.

But I'm here to tell you that spiritual well-being is a slippery concept. Scales to measure it are psychometrically weak. It's *hard* to build a scale when you can't agree on its factors. What kind of a concept is it when the best we can say is that we can recognize it when we see it?

Well, it's a pretty good concept. We can't define beauty, either. But we can spot it when we see it. I've never seen a psychologist even try to gin up a beauty scale. However, it's clear that we live in a society that is willing to pay young women thousands of dollars to appear on the covers of magazines. And that's not for *doing* beautiful things, either, just for looking beautiful. I'll bet that Mother Theresa never made a dime posing for magazine covers.

So, what's my argument? I think that it is all well and good to identify people who have spiritual well-being, recognizing that it's a damn sight easier to have it when things are going good. Equally, though, there must be the *lack* of spiritual well-being: the terror that comes in the middle of the night, the awful loss when a spouse of 50 years becomes another person entirely because of the ravages of Alzheimer's disease, the sick feeling in the gut that won't go away when a precious granddaughter goes flying through a windshield, the emptiness when a son commits suicide, the railing against God at the unfairness of cancer striking one down before one's life's work is complete.

At the very end of his 1960 novel *Soldier in the Rain*, William Goldman has the protagonist Eustis Clay, after the death of his buddy, Maxwell Slaughter, look to the heavens and shout, "Fuck You!"

I wonder if Grandma Thorson felt the same way when she lost her baby? She wouldn't have said it, but it's only human to feel the blackness of despair when confronted with overwhelming grief.

I think that we can tolerate the slings and arrows of outrageous fortune if there aren't too many of them, but there has to be an opposite end to the continuum that features spiritual well-being at the positive side. What do we call the low point that describes the poor unfortunate who gets squashed by life, who suffers slings and arrows by the dozens, who loses all of his daughters and sons, and sits on a dung heap scratching his sores with a potsherd? What do we call it when a man indeed wants to quit trying, to curse God and die? William James took a crack at describing the sick soul:

> Not the conception or intellectual perception of evil, but the grizzly blood-freezing heart-palsying sensation of it close upon one, and no other conception or sensation is able to live for a moment in its presence. How irrelevantly remote seem all our usual refined optimisms and intellectual and moral consolations in presence of a need of help like this! Here is the real core of the religious problem: Help! Help! No prophet can claim to bring a final message unless he says things that will have a sound of reality in the ears of victims such as these. (1929, p. 159)

This comes from James's Gifford Lectures, delivered in Edinburgh in 1902, which some would call the foundation of the psychology of religion. James goes on to delineate the rotten times that afflict all of us on occasion: "The normal process of life contains moments as bad as any of those which insane (pathological) melancholy is filled with, moments in which radical evil gets its innings and takes its solid turn" (p. 160).

His point is that none of us are strangers to hell. But I submit that some of us never get out of it. Perhaps some are able to lead pretty good lives because of good fortune, luck, or being surrounded by angels. But it must be admitted too that there are those whose guardian angel was left standing behind the door when the assignments were being handed out, people who do *not* bounce back after a series of awful traumas, who descend into involutional depression, who can no longer fight the good fight, who in fact lose the will to live.

At least that's a thought I've tried to bring up for discussion in this brief introduction to a chapter in which, after a review of relevant literature, I will draw upon some current data provided by my colleague, Dr. Ann M. Laughlin. And I hope to conclude with a few suggestions. I think that the lack of spiritual well-being may be the serious psychosocial problem of our generation.

BACKGROUND

Elbert Tuttle was the Chair of Nephrology at Emory University College of Medicine. Early on in the development of the kidney dialysis machine he dealt with patients who benefited from the then-miraculous mechanical kidney. Some time early in the 1970s he told me of a curiosity.

Dialysis, early in the 21st century, is now a procedure that is pretty much available to most of the patients who need it. The machines are smaller, simpler, and less expensive than they were 30 years ago. Many of the people who go once or twice a week to a dialysis center are able to live fairly normal lives. Being tied to a machine for a certain number of hours per week has its costs—economically and psychologically—but things are generally easier now than they were then. The ultimate goal, of course, is to hang on long enough to get a transplantable kidney, but even those who never get a transplant have their lives improved and extended by hemodialysis.

Dr. Tuttle, though, told me of the early patients who sometimes balked at the prospect of further long-term dialysis. The costs of being dependent on a machine became too much for them. And the mechanism was more difficult then, leaving many of the patients feeling miserable to one degree or another. Confronted by patients who despaired of ever getting a transplantable kidney—and there were many—Tuttle naturally tried to persuade them to remain on dialysis as their only hope of remaining alive. He told me, however, that a handful decided to decline further treatment, which of course was their right. Once the decision had been made, something curious happened: most of the patients who had decided to forgo any more dialysis died pretty quickly thereafter, some even before their next treatment was scheduled to take place. Tuttle said that the nurses at Grady Hospital had a term for it: "They turned their faces to the wall and died." This is different from losing the will to live: they willed themselves to die.

Viktor E. Frankl did an in-depth memoir of his experiences in a Nazi concentration camp during World War II (1959). Frankl was one of a small percentage of the slave labor camp prisoners to survive, and he felt compelled to document his experiences, the horror perpetrated on men, women, and children, and his observations on the meaning derived from suffering.

He spoke of prisoners who died because they had lost faith in the future and lost their spiritual hold. Prisoners like these, he said, let themselves decline and become subject to decay, both mental and physical. He observed that this occurred suddenly, often because of a crisis, and that the symptoms were recognized by those inmates who had been there for a while: the individual refused one morning to get dressed or wash or appear on the parade ground. No pleas had any effect on him; he would just lay there motionless: "He simply gave up. There he remained, lying in his own excreta, and nothing bothered him any more" (1959, p. 74). Invariably, the man died shortly thereafter. Frankl also described the scramble to stay alive: At one time, particular prisoners were issued coupons for special work. These coupons could be traded for cigarettes, which could then be traded for food, "a very real respite from starvation....The only exceptions to this were those who had lost the will to live and wanted to 'enjoy' their last days. Thus, when we saw a comrade smoking his own cigarettes, we knew he had given up faith in his strength to carry on, and once lost, the will to live seldom returned" (1959, p. 6).

In his 1975 book Helplessness, Martin E. P. Seligman cites similar observations in other camps: The psychosomatic effects of exertion of will—active control over outcomes—and the will to live cannot be over-estimated. Of all psychosomatic variables, this one may be the most powerful. When a prisoner gives up, death may soon follow. Bruno Bettelheim (1960) describes those peculiar inmates, the "Muselmanner," who rapidly gave up and died without apparent physical cause in the Nazi concentration camps: Prisoners who came to believe the repeated statements of the guards—that there was no hope for them, that they would never leave the camp except as a corpse—who came to feel that their environment was one over which they could exercise no influence whatsoever; these prisoners were in a literal sense, walking corpses. Shortly after the beginning of captivity, these men stopped eating, sat mute and motionless in corners, and expired. (Bettelheim, as cited in Seligman, 1975, p. 184)

FAILURE TO THRIVE

We are not suggesting that ordinary elderly patients often confront the very depths of hell experienced by prisoners of the Holocaust. These are dramatic illustrations. However, they may be dramatic illustration of something similar that people who work with older patients are accustomed to seeing. Variously called *losing the will* to live or *failure to thrive*, it is a concept derived from pediatric literature (e.g., Bakwin, 1949) that originally sought to explain why infants in orphanages failed to develop at normal rates, had poorer rates of survival, lower intelligence, and more physical and emotional illness. Similar failure to thrive syndromes among older patients in nursing homes have been described by nurse-researchers Braun, Wykle, and Cowling (1988). Patients do unexpectedly poorly, seem to decline for no disease-related reason, and literally dwindle away. Robertson and Montagnini (2004) describe failure to thrive in elderly patients as a state of decline that may be caused by disease and functional limitation. Symptoms include weight loss, loss of appetite, poor nutrition, and inactivity. Cognitive impairment and depression combine with these syndromes and predict poor outcomes. Robertson and Montagnini take a fatalistic stance when confronted with failure to thrive: they state that this is a key decision point and that end-of-life care options should be discussed to prevent needless interventions that may prolong suffering. Those afflicted with failure to thrive have either consciously or unconsciously decided to die, and interventions are no longer useful or successful. Robertson and Montagnini (2004) state that these patients should be given the supports we have come to expect as normal and necessary for any other patients who are at the end of life. That is, hospice treatment is appropriate, as these are dying people.

TRANSFER TRAUMA

The remainder of this chapter will discuss how overwhelming social disruption may induce a syndrome, sometimes called transfer trauma, that has a great deal of similarity to geriatric failure to thrive as described in the nursing and medical literature and, indeed, similarity with the "Muselmanner" syndrome described by Bettelheim and Frankl.

The effects of relocation and institutionalization on older people have been studied for several decades. It has been known for some time that there is a greatly elevated death rate among older patients admitted to nursing homes, and that a fairly high proportion of these deaths take place shortly after admission. For example, Liu and Manton (1984) studied a national cohort of 1.1 million people admitted in one year to nursing homes in the United States. Within the first 30 days after admission 24% had died, and an additional 30% of those remaining died during the next 60 days.

Contrary to the popular stereotype, death may be a sooner rather than a later proposition for nursing home patients generally. Because of the prospective-payment and diagnostic-related group insurance plans that began to become popular in the 1980s, nursing homes now see sicker patients who are discharged from hospitals sooner than they used to be, often after only few days in the hospital. Sicker patients are more likely to die, and deaths that used to take place in the hospital now take place in nursing homes (Wachtel, Fulton, & Goldfarb, 1987).

Even prior to this development, however, an elevated mortality rate within a short time after admission was something that was commonly observed in long-term care facilities throughout the nation. Wershow, as long ago as 1976, followed the history of 460 patients who died in five different nursing homes in a major urban area. He found that 44% of these deaths took place within 30 days of admission, and of those 460 deaths, 20% of males and 10% of the females had died within a week after admission. Wershow noted that 58% of the men and 40% of the women who died were dead within a month after admission.

Tracking the history of long-term care patients is a very difficult thing to do. Many nursing home patients are hospitalized when they become acutely ill, and their beds may be assigned to other patients. Thus, going to the hospital and back to a nursing home may involve transfers between three institutions. Many patients who are institutionalized may have multiple relocations during their final year of life, from nursing home to hospital, from hospital to another nursing home, perhaps again to the same or to another hospital, perhaps home for a brief period, and then back to another institution, and so on.

Lewis, Cretin, and Kane, (1985) followed a random sample of 197 persons from 24 different nursing homes for 2 years. Only nine percent of the patients were discharged to their homes and received no further institutional care during the period of the study. A total of 37% died in the nursing home to which they had first been admitted, and 54% were transferred frequently between hospitals and other nursing homes. Over 72% (142) of the original group was dead by the end of the

2 years, and only 29 (14.7% of the original 197) were alive and living at home at the end of 2 years. The remaining 26 (13.2%) were living in a skilled care setting. In all there were only 27.8% alive at the end of 2 years (the 29 at home and the 26 in skilled nursing care), 72.2% died within 2 years after admission to a nursing home.

Unlike most studies, Lewis's research is based on a random sample and one can draw conclusions from it. One main conclusion is that the average stay in a nursing home for most people is a short one. We cannot, though, take what seems to be the next logical step and conclude from these data that the stress associated with admission to a nursing home precipitates deaths that might not otherwise have taken place. There is no way to know if these people might have died if they had remained at home or in the hospital. This problem was first discussed by Blenkner (1967) who observed it during a study of services delivered to older people. She found that older persons in a high services group had a much higher death rate relative to controls in a low-services group. The problem was that at that time high levels of service meant a high likelihood of nursing home admission. Blenkner speculated that the environmental change associated with institutionalization was the causal factor for the higher mortality rate. Again, there was no way to tell whether or not these individuals might have died during the same period had they not been relocated. Blenkner and her colleagues reviewed studies of samples of the frail older people who had been moved from one institution to another, "…in an attempt to hold constant the effects of institutionalization so as to study relocation effects *per se* on mortality rates" (Markus, Blenkner, Bloom, & Downs, 1971, p. 537).

Their review of three such studies led to the conclusion that there was a significant effect of relocation, particularly among those with what, at that time, was called "chronic brain syndrome" (today, we would identify this as Alzheimer's disease), and that the focus of services to older people should be to keep them out of institutions for as long as possible, to provide them with services that focus on maximizing independence, and to provide alternatives to relocation.

A number of studies have found significantly higher rates of mortality after populations were moved from one institution to another. Thus, Aldrich and Mendkoff (1963) found that 46 out of 121 died the year after the move of a population from a Chicago chronic disease hospital, a rate three times higher than might have been expected. Bourestom and Pastalan (1981) reported that 28 out of 87 died the year after moving among a nursing home population in Michigan.

Jasnau (1967) reported that 454 out of 1500 aged patients died within 6 months after a move to a Georgia mental hospital.

To summarize to this point, it is no surprise that there is a high death rate after nursing home admission. People are *expected* to die when they go into nursing homes: they are, after all, very sick people. Because of this, it is impossible to sort out the factor of the move from home itself and all that it implies in calculating whether or not this total life disruption contributes to deaths that might not otherwise have taken place. It would be hard to justify an experiment to an ethics committee, for example, where we could place 100 people in long-term care institutions and match them on a number of variables with similar people who are being kept home with supportive ser-vices. Although we have a pretty strong hunch that the survival rate of the at-home group will be better, there's no actual way to gather data to prove this. Not being satisfied with relying on our intuitive feeling that staying home is better, Blenkner sought to get around the transfer from home to nursing home issue by simply looking at peo-ple who had already adapted to nursing home life and how well they survived an involuntary move from one institution to another. This is easy enough when it happens: one can simply calculate the death rate among those who were scattered to other institutions after a nursing home closes for one reason or another and compare it to the original nursing home's mortality experience for several years prior to the move.

There is, however, a problem in that not all nursing home transfers are equal. For example, Aleksandrowicz (1961), in an early study of geriatric relocation, followed people evacuated from a hospital ward because of a fire. There was a 20% death rate among the survivors (no one was injured in the fire itself), a rate significantly higher than the 7.5% annual mortality rate experienced by the institution's patients prior to the fire. One might then suspect that the suddenness or the magnitude of the change could contribute a relatively higher level of stress to lives that are already vulnerable. Blenkner, after all, had pointed out in her original study that the more seriously demented, those least in touch with their environment, were the ones most likely to die after a sudden change in environment.

This was confirmed by the research of Bourestom and Tars (1974). They reported on a group of 98 patients. In addition to relocation effects, they sought to test for a more subtle concept: the involuntariness of the move that those in the sample would undergo. The 98 were matched for age, sex, length of hospitalization and primary diagnosis with a like group of controls. Physical ratings indicated that they were highly comparable. The 98 experimental participants were in two groups: one was to make a move to a new facility nearby and keep the same staff, menu, program of activities, and roommates. In contrast to this moderate-change group, the others were making a radical change from a county home to a new and much larger proprietary facility with many new adjustments to make. The respective controls made no environmental change. Data, consisting of extensive interviews, were collected one month prior to the move and 1, 4, 8, and 12 months after the relocation. "Of the radical change group, 43% died in the 6 months preceding and the year following relocation compared with a rate of 21% among their controls" (1974, p. 508). This difference was statistically significant. The moderate-change group, however, had a 37% death rate in comparison to the 26% rate among their controls, a difference that was not significant. "In terms of mortality experience, therefore, it appears that the *degree* of environmental change involved in relocation is a potent factor influencing mortality rates.... these findings confirm that the *anticipation* of relocation has effects which are nearly as lethal as the relocation itself" (1974, p. 508). The death rate went up 6 months prior to the move: anticipation evidently was stressful, just as the move itself was disrupting.

Thus a psychological variable is introduced. Anticipation of the move may be as disruptive, or nearly so, as the change in the physical environment and all that it entails in adjusting to new sights, sounds, smells, and people. Those who are having a difficult time holding onto the attachments to their surroundings seem to be particularly at risk.

Introduction of the variable of *control* might further help to explain why there are differences in the various studies of relocation. With some institutional moves, pains are taken to prepare patients, to give them choices, to get them oriented to making the move and used to the idea. Others have no control, no preparation, and no chance to participate. The decisions are all made for them. The degree of change in some of these studies must also have made a difference. If things such as staff, program, fellow patients, and menus are held constant, there are fewer stressful changes with which to cope. Thus, Schulz and Brenner (1977) suggested that the greater the choice the individual has and the more predictable the new environment is the less negative are the effects of relocation.

THE LANCASTER MANOR STUDY

We sought to apply these principles in an attempt to minimize the mortality associated with the move of a group of older individuals who were to be transferred from Lancaster Manor, a county home for the aged that was being closed in Lincoln, Nebraska, into a newly built facility (Thorson & Davis, 2000). Lancaster Manor, the 94-year-old former St. Elizabeth's Hospital, was to be demolished, and plans had been made to build a new county nursing home on property directly next door. We were approached 18 months prior to the move to consult with the administration and train the staff on how to minimize the degree of transfer trauma that might be associated with the move.

During the process we sought to emphasize openness of communication, keep staff members and residents informed of the progress of construction of the new facility, and continually to involve residents and their family members in plans for the move. Staff was advised to make frequent mention to the upcoming move in their conversations with patients so the move would take no one by surprise. Plans were made to keep roommates together in the new facility, keep the same staff attending them, and keep the same food, services, and activities of daily living. Everything was done to make even the most cognitively impaired patients aware of the anticipated move and to keep changes to a minimum after the move itself.

There were 269 patients, 204 women, and 65 men. Their average age was 79.8 years, and their length of stay ranged from one to 213 months, with a mean of 54 months. Mortality data were recorded from the facility's records for the 4 years prior to the move, as well as for 1 year after.

The relocation was accomplished with a minimum of disruption. Residents were able to keep the same roommate if they wished, have rooms on the same side of the new building as they had in the old one, and stay in the same service, thus continuing to be cared for by the same staff members. The kitchen and menus stayed the same in the new building as they had been in the old one.

For the 3 years prior to the year before the move, the institution had experienced 49, 61, and 58 deaths, respectively, an annual average of 56, which represented an annual mortality rate of about 21%. During the year immediately prior to the relocation, there were 69 deaths (a rate of 25.7%), and the year after the move there were 45 deaths (an annual mortality rate of 16.7%). Thus the number of deaths during the year *prior* to the move was significantly higher than the mean for the 3 preceding years ($t = 24.2$, $p < .0001$), and the number of deaths in the year *after* the move was significantly lower than the three-year baseline period ($t = 22.9$, $p < .0001$). There were no gender differences in rate of survival, nor were those who had been relocated within the institution prior to the move less likely to survive than those who only had been moved from the old building to the new one. Morbidity was assessed using pre- and post-move hospitalization rates; they were 13.3% and 14.4%, respectively, a difference that was not significant.

The mortality rate during the year after the move was the lowest of the 5 years for which a rate was recorded. It might be tempting to add up the deaths for the 4 years prior to the move and derive a mean (59.25). This is significantly higher than the 45 who died in the year after the move, and this might be taken as evidence that the intensive effort at preparation of the institutional population was successful at minimizing post-move mortality.

However, the apparent success for this project is moderated by the realization that the number and rate of deaths among this population were both highest during the year *prior* to the move. The 3 years' mortality experience in the institution before the year of the move yielded an annual average of 56 deaths. Taking a mean from the number of deaths for the year prior to the move (69) and the year after it (45) gives an average of 57 per year, which is pretty close to the annual average of 56 deaths found in the 3 years prior to the year before the move. Thus, about the same proportion of residents in this nursing home seemed to be bound to die. A possibility that must be considered is that the intensive preparation for the move did not minimize death in the year after the move so much as it may have hastened death during the year before it. That is, anxiety over the anticipated changes associated with an institutional relocation might, in fact, be more lethal than the move itself, a finding that is consistent with that of Aldrich and Mendkoff (1963).

About the best that can be said for the efforts in preparing the staff and patients for the institutional relocation is that, taken together, the mortality rate for the year prior to and the year following the move were about the same as the previous 3 years' experience. That is, there was no dramatic *increase* in overall mortality associated with the relocation. This might be attributed to the preparation efforts. At least, there was no dramatic increase, or in fact any increase at all, in deaths among those who were relocated.

We concluded the Lancaster Manor study by observing that it would be very difficult to follow two similar institutional relocations, one with a treatment to prepare the residents, and one with none. "Further, institutional administrators very often are reluctant to allow researchers access to patient histories, or even to provide them with a simple count of how many are alive or dead at the end of the year" (Thorson & Davis, 2000, p. 137).

We had no idea when writing those lines that they would be prophetic.

Mercy Care Center

In January of 2003, the Mercy Care Center in Omaha notified its patients that, because of a problem of mold in the building, the facility would be closed and that everyone would have to find a new place to live "by the end of the month" (about 3 weeks). Some of the patients would, it turned out, be able to transfer to another facility owned by the same corporation (Alegent Health Care), but most were pretty much on their own. Needless to say, families, patients, and staff at Mercy Care Center were upset.

As it happened, the second author of this chapter, Dr. Ann M. Laughlin, was at the dissertation stage of her doctoral program, and a colleague of hers, Dr. Mary Parsons, had just completed a study of the patients at Mercy Care Center as a part of her own dissertation (Parsons, 2004). Laughlin sought, and received, permission to track the patients moved during the relocation, using a number of measures that are described in greater detail in her dissertation (Laughlin, 2005). She received permission to study the effect this involuntary move had on the Mercy Care patients and to compare mortality and morbidity rates post-move with those of the institution for several years prior to the move. Just at the time data gathering was to begin she was notified by officials of the corporation that permission to access prior data had been withdrawn, and that there would be no further cooperation with her study.

In a town the size of Omaha, however, it is not that difficult to find out who is alive and who is dead, and Dr. Laughlin's doctoral supervisory committee urged her to not abandon the study, but to gather what data she could and to add a mixed-methods approach, interviewing persons who survived the move and family members of those who did not. The control group in another institution could still be used for a comparison of mortality rates, even if the mortality rates at Mercy Care Center for years prior to its closing could not.

Briefly, data were obtained on 83 individuals who were relocated and compared to a control group of 90 who were in another, similar institution who were not moved. Of the 83 who were involuntarily relocated, 38 died during the year after the move, a 46% mortality rate. Of the 90 who did not move, only 17 died, a 19% mortality rate. This difference was statistically significant (c^2 = 14.4, p < .001). Of the relocated people who died, the highest number of deaths occurred within the first three months after relocation: 21 of the 38 (51%). The residents who were most vulnerable were the oldest ones; of the 33 people who were aged 86 to 100, 21 died (64%); whereas of the 25 individuals aged 75 or younger, only seven (28%) died. Note that this study is different in that it has a control group for comparison purposes. In the other studies cited previously, the prior years' mortality statistics from the facilities themselves had served for comparisons.

Case Studies

Following are four case interviews, two with family members whose loved one died post-move, and two others from individuals who themselves moved and survived.

Case Study 1.

"P" was the daughter of a 93-year-old woman who died about 5 months after she was relocated from Mercy Care Center. "She was very happy at the Care Center; she looked at it like her apartment. Mom had a wonderful attitude about being in a nursing home; she was the darling of the floor. They all loved her, the nurses especially. "At the announcement that they were closing, we were in shock, very upset, hurt, disappointed because this had become home. The bad part was that my mother had spent all of her money and the last six months had been on Medicaid." The family was challenged with finding a nursing home that provided quality care and had quality professional staff as well as finding one that would accept Medicaid patients.

"In the Care Center, her care didn't change (when she went) from private pay to Medicaid. So, we narrowed it down, while the new home was probably not the nicest place to put her in Omaha, we looked at location, and we looked at the staff more than we looked at the building and the aesthetics. So we were limited, there are only so many Medicaid beds available, even at the not-so-nice places. (At this point "P" became tearful)…anyway, my one brother, who wheeled her in, he just started bawling. He's a 58-year-old, and I thought he was going to have a heart attack. He was just bawling, just a let down coming from a fairly nice place to a not-very-nice place. It was a tough day."

"Initially, she didn't like it. It took her probably, I'd say a good couple of months to accept where she was and really how long did she stay there? Six months. So probably half the time she wasn't very happy there. We just had problems along the way with things, never really got comfortable and found our niche there. It just wasn't the same, it wasn't the same level of care, wasn't the same feeling of home for us, just like day and night. Like being in a foreign country and you didn't know how to navigate. The (Mercy) Care Center was the Ritz Carlton compared to where she ended up."

Asked if she felt the move had any impact on her mother's health, "P" responded with these thoughts: "Her physical health, I don't think it had any impact, she was on the decline, and we knew that. Her mental and emotional health, I think it had a huge impact. She just wasn't as perky, as optimistic, as bright during that last six months of her life. There was a definite change."

Case Study 2.

"R" is the niece of Rita, an 82-year-old single woman who had lived at Mercy Care Center for 4 years. "She did not understand it (the move). She was 82 at the time of the move, with her dementia and everything. This was all she knew as home for 4 years. So for an elderly person to make this kind of move it was horrible, it was horrible. They go to a place where they know no one. Nobody knows how she eats her food, nobody knows how she likes it cut up. Nobody knows that before she goes to bed she likes a glass of milk. She was so freaked out that she couldn't tell them this because she was so scared of where she was. It wasn't the facility, it was just the change.

"It was not okay with the way we were told that the Center was closing because it was a phone call that said, 'Oh, by the way, you have to the end of the month to find Rita a place to live.' Granted, they claimed that mold in the walls was the reason for closing the building. There is always politics in everything. The staff was devastated. When I came the very next day, they were walking up and down the halls crying, truly crying. Everybody was numb, like a grief process. But the staff couldn't help it. The patients, like Rita who didn't quite understand, they knew something was terribly wrong. It's like kids when you try to hide something from them—they can feel it. I will say the staff bent over backwards to make this transition as easy as possible, but it all happened so fast that there was no easy way about it.

"Oh man, it was horrible! She just went downhill so bad. She went, well first I think it was a state of depression, and she never came out of her room. She only ate in her room and refused to go to the dining room. I think she was very scared. It was heartbreaking. The facility she went to doesn't have nurse call buttons in their rooms. So if anything was wrong with her or she fell out of bed and landed on the floor, she couldn't call for help. They have to lie in their beds and yell for the nurses down at the nurses' station! She always had sores on her bottom there from sitting in wet diapers or messy diapers." (Rita was relocated again, after three months, to a more satisfactory place, where she died approximately six months later.) "R" concluded: "The move was easier because I knew that everybody had to leave, and she wasn't being kicked out or she hadn't died. These workers were very sad, they were bawling, I can't tell you, to walk in there and the door opened up and it was like this cloud of sadness rolled out."

Case Study 3.

"L," a 66-year-old quadriplegic, shared the frustration he experienced with closure of Mercy Care Center and the insensitive way the news was communicated: "A lady came in, who did not have the best bedside manner, and said, 'We are closing this place and you have to get out by the end of the month.' I was shocked by the news. This lady was very blunt and matter-of-fact. Eight of us were supposed to leave by the following Friday, but instead we were shipped to the hospital. I guess we were some of the sickest ones there."

"Coming here to live from (Mercy Care Center) has been like going from the space age to the dark ages. They don't have a lot of the modern things; they still have crank beds here. It makes it tough. When I left the home, I felt like I was leaving my family behind and also my friends. People would stop in all the time just to visit. They all knew me so well. I feel so isolated. I miss my outings and the relationships that I once had at the other place. For me, that was one of the worst things about moving. Now that I have been here for almost two months it is a little easier but still hard not seeing my friends anymore. I think resigning myself to the move allowed me to cope with it. It was going to happen and nothing I could say or do was going to change the situation."

Case Study 4.

"F" is a 93-year-old female who is now a resident in an assisted living facility. She moved to a more independent living environment. She is alert and says she is in good health. "They told me I had to move and I really didn't want to do it. I called my son, and he and his friend found this place. They felt it was the best place they could find. I have help with the housekeeping here. The floor is dirty now, but today is scrub day and eventually they will get here. I haven't had any complaints about the help, it's just the food isn't splendid. I was so sick when I went in (to Mercy Care Center), and they were so nice to me and they gave me good care…you just get attached to those girls, you know. It was kind of hard to leave. Everyone was like a family there. I went in there so sick and I got well there. I had all my therapy there and it felt kind like a family. You don't have that here. It's more businesslike here. Over there my door was always open, and you know, I knew everyone on that floor and you know it was kind of hard for me; it's still hard. What helped me cope was taking it one day at a time."

CONCLUSION

Despite the limitations imposed on Dr. Laughlin's study of Mercy Care Center, a significantly elevated death rate among those involuntarily relocated from a private nursing home was found when compared to a similar group of controls in another home who were not relocated. This is consistent with most of the studies cited earlier with the exception of the one by Thorson and Davis (2000). The difference was an extensive program of preparation that began 18 months prior to the move. The number of deaths post-move at Lancaster Manor was actually lower than the institutions' mortality rate had been for several years prior to the closing of the old building and opening of the new one next door.

Mercy Care Center, on the other hand, abruptly announced that the facility would close within a matter of weeks. There was some assistance provided in relocating those who needed it, but there was no new facility built to replace the old one that was deemed to be inadequate, nor was there any attempt to provide an organized program of preparation for those forced to move. The subsequent death rate of those relocated from Mercy Care Center was over twice that of a group of controls who were not relocated.

Did the involuntary move cause more deaths? The statistics are there, and they are consistent with previous studies of transfer trauma. A more interesting question, however, is: Why did some die and others not? Why did some of these people who had grown accustomed to nursing home life experience the dark night of the soul when confronted with an unexpected move? This while others simply said, "What helped me cope was taking it one day at a time."

The same question no doubt could be asked of the deaths of prisoners described by Frankl and Bettelheim. Not everyone in the Nazi slave labor camps was selected for execution. Not everyone was starved to death, beaten to death, died of illness, or shot. Not everyone gave up the will to live and died of despair. About ten percent survived.

Why?

Frankl said that they were "...worthy of their sufferings; the way they bore their suffering was a genuine inner achievement. It is this spiritual freedom—which cannot be taken away—that makes life meaningful and purposeful" (1959, p. 66).

There are lives that are in the balance. Given no trouble, they continue to live on, perhaps close to the edge, but to live. Sometimes events conspire to push them over the edge. The death rate of civilians in war zones always goes up, usually higher than that of the combatants. Some die of starvation, others from the brutality of the war itself, but just being oppressed and on the move seems to compromise peoples' immune systems. They become prone to epidemics. Sanitation breaks down. Privation kills; there's no doubt about it. Psychosocial trauma kills. Among lives that are already frail, people who have lost a sense of purpose in life wonder why they should continue to hang on. A certain percentage is bound to die who might otherwise have continued living. Changing peoples' environments against their will, and taking away their freedom to decide, are things that might shave more than a few off the list of survivors.

Our stereotype of old age is that old people are higher in spiritual well-being. However, we have no solid evidence that religiosity in old age is anything but a cohort effect. Do people get more religious as they age? Probably not. People who were more religious in earlier years of life get old. Compared to younger cohorts, it looks like they have higher levels religion. True, older church-goers tend to be better off, physically and psychologically, than those who are not, but we can't prove that spirituality is the reason (Idler & Kasl, 1997). Our own data (Thorson & Powell, 2004), for example, indicate that religious

belief does not ameliorate depression. It seems that church attendance—socialization with others—has more of a positive effect in this
regard than intrinsic religiosity itself. Data we have presented elsewhere (Thorson & Powell, 2000) indicate that old people have less
death anxiety than young people. This is probably not because they
have a higher level of spirituality but simply because they've had
longer to adjust to the idea as they see their friends dying off.

But, back to Frankl. He says spiritual strength—having something
to hang onto—is what kept the camp survivors alive. Perhaps the
nursing home relocatees who died simply felt that life no longer had
any meaning for them, that, like the Muselmanner, there was no
reason left to fight. This should come as no surprise. We see old people throwing in the towel all the time. Why *rage* against the dying of
the light? Many older people embrace it. Suicide rates for White males
aged 85 and older have varied from 45.8 per 100,000 per year to a high
of 70.3 per hundred thousand per year over the course of the last 50
years; this is compared to an overall rate between 10.7–13.2 for the
population in general. The next highest group in numbers of suicides
is those aged 75–84 (National Center for Health Statistics, 2004). This
is not a blip in the chart; it's the experience of over half a century. The
highest rates of suicide in the population are found among the oldest
people.

Further, old men have a much worse time of it when their spouses
die. Mental health, morale, social functioning, and survivorship all
plummet (Bennett, 1998; Seeman, Kaplan, Knudsen, Cohen, &
Guralnik, 1987). This is not true for older women who are widowed;
they seem to be able to maintain a social support network that buffers
against the forces of isolation. It would seem that other people provide
a valuable source of meaning in their lives. Old women have a very
low suicide rate. Old African American women's suicide rates are so
low as to be difficult to calculate.

It's interesting that the people in American society who have historically had a host of sufferings are the least likely to take their own
lives. Frankl looks at meaning that might be found in suffering:

> The way in which a man accepts his fate and all the suffering it entails, the
> way in which he takes up his cross, gives him ample opportunity—even
> under the most difficult circumstances—to add a deeper meaning to his
> life. It may remain brave, dignified, and unselfish. Or in the bitter fight for
> self-preservation he may forget his human dignity and become no more
> than an animal. Here lies the chance for a man either to make use of or to

forgo the opportunities of attaining the moral values that a difficult situation may afford him. And this decides whether he is worthy of his sufferings or not. (1959, p. 67)

Frankl, of course, centers his entire philosophy on man's search for meaning as a primal motive in life. He suggests that we find meaning in others, in our relationships, in sharing our plans and visions. No wonder lonely old men have higher suicide rates! It is in isolation that we find the dark night of the human soul. We forget that we need other people, that solitary confinement is a torture. In an era when more and more people are deciding not to have children, where will the grandchildren come from? We are becoming rich, and alone, and stupid! Spiritual well-being means being on comfortable terms with God. How can we be on comfortable terms with God when we're not even on comfortable terms with our neighbors?

I had a conversation not long ago with a group of trust officers from some local banks. They said that one of their saddest duties is to attend the funerals of their clients, usually very old people, and some-times the only ones at the graveside are the trust officer and the under-taker. I asked one to estimate how many of these funerals without mourners he's been to. He answered, "At least two hundred." Given the decline in the birthrate over the past 50 years and the explosive current growth of the older population, we may be seeing a coming generation of urban hermits, of isolated lives lacking in meaning.

Finally, in what has become an increasingly desperate quest to get my university students to think about what really *is* meaningful in life, I ask them to choose which of these two messages they'd like to have carved on their tombstone:

"Here lies a person who owned a BMW" or,
"Beloved Grandmother"
Take your pick.

MAIN POINTS

1. Laughlin's study of Mercy Care Center showed a significantly elevated death rate among those involuntarily relocated from a private nursing home was found when compared to a similar group of controls in another home who were not relocated.
2. Perhaps the nursing home relocatees who died simply felt that life no longer had any meaning for them, that, like the Muselmanner, there was no reason left to fight.
3. It is in isolation that we find the dark night of the human soul.

REFERENCES

Aldrich, C., & Mendkoff, E. (1963). Relocation of the aged and disabled, a mortality study. *Journal of the American Geriatrics Society, 11,* 185–194.

Alexandrowicz, D. R. (1961). Fire and its aftermath on a geriatric ward. *Bulletin of the Menninger Clinic, 25,* 23–32.

Bakwin, H. (1949). Emotional deprivation in infants. *Journal of Pediatrics, 35,* 512–521.

Bennett, K. M. (1998). Longitudinal changes in mental and physical health among elderly, recently widowed men. *Mortality, 3,* 265–278.

Bettelheim, B. (1960). *The informed heart— Autonomy in a mass age.* New York: The Free Press.

Blenkner, M. (1967). Environmental change and the aging individual. *The Gerontologist, 7,* 101–105.

Bourestom, N., & Pastalan, L. (1981). The effects of relocation on the elderly: A reply to Borup, Gallego, & Heffernan. *The Gerontologist, 21,* 4–7.

Bourestom, N., & Tars, S. (1974). Alterations in life patterns following nursing home relocation. *The Gerontologist, 14,* 506–510.

Braun, J. V., Wykle, M. H., & Cowling, W. R. (1988). Failure to thrive in older persons: A concept derived. *The Gerontologist, 28,* 809–812.

Cook, T. (1980). Preface. In J. Thorson (Ed.), *Spiritual well-being of the elderly,* (pp. xii–xvii). Springfield, IL: Charles C Thomas.

Frankl, V. E. (1959). *Man's search for meaning.* New York: Simon & Schuster.

Idler, E. L., & Kasl, V. (1997). Religion among disabled and nondisabled persons I: Cross-sectional patterns in health practices, social activities, and well-being. *Journal of Gerontology: Social Sciences, 52B,* S294–305.

Goldman, W. (1960). *Soldier in the rain.* New York: Atheneum.

James, W. (1929). *The varieties of religious experience.* New York: Longmans, Green.

Jasnau, K. (1967). Individualized versus mass transfer of nonpsychotic geriatric patients from mental hospitals to nursing homes, with special reference to death rate. *Journal of the American Geriatrics Society, 15,* 280–284.

Laughlin, A. M. (2005). *The effects of involuntary interinstitutional relocation on the physical, psychosocial, and cognitive functioning of older individuals.* Unpublished doctoral dissertation, University of Nebraska.

Lewis, M., Cretin, S., & Kane, R. (1985). The natural history of nursing home patients. *The Gerontologist, 25,* 382–388.

Liu, K., & Manton, K. (1984). The characteristics and utilization pattern of an admission cohort of nursing home patients. *The Gerontologist, 24,* 70–76.

Markus, E., Blenkner, M., Bloom, M., & Downs, T. (1971). The impact of relocation upon mortality rates of institutionalized aged persons. *Journal of Gerontology, 26,* 537–541.

National Center for Health Statistics (2004). *Health U.S. 2004.* Washington, DC: National Center for Disease Control, U.S. Public Health Service.

Parsons, M. (2004). *The impact of the Eden Alternative on quality of life of nursing home residents.* Unpublished doctoral dissertation, University of Nebraska.

Robertson, R. G., & Montagnini, M. (2004). Geriatric failure to thrive. *American Family Physician, 70,* 343–350.

Schulz, R., & Brenner, G. (1977). Relocation of the aged: A review and theoretical analysis. *Journal of Gerontology, 32,* 323–333.

Seeman, T. E., Kaplan, G. A., Knudsen, L., Cohen, R., & Guralnik, J. (1987). Social network ties and mortality among the elderly in the Alameda County study. *American Journal of Epidemiology, 126,* 714–723.

Seligman, M. E. P. (1975). *Helplessness: On depression, development, and death.* San Francisco: W. H. Freeman and Company.

Thorson, J. A., & Davis, R. E. (2000). Relocation of the institutionalized aged. *Journal of Clinical Psychology, 56,* 131–138.

Thorson, J. A., & Powell, F. C. (2000). Death anxiety in younger and older adults. In A. Tomer (Ed.), *Death attitudes and the older adult* (pp. 123–136). Philadelphia: Taylor and Francis.

Thorson, J. A., & Powell, F. C. (2004). Depression and intrinsic religiosity. *Psychological Reports, 95,* 1008.

Wachtel, T., Fulton, J., & Goldfarb, J. (1987). Early prediction of discharge disposition after hospitalization. *The Gerontologist, 27,* 98–103.

Wershow, H. (1976). The four percent fallacy: Some further evidence and policy implications. *The Gerontologist, 16,* 52–55.

III

Applications

12

▼▼▼▼

Existentialism and Suicide

Israel Orbach
Bar-Ilan University

Nearing the end of my career in suicidology, I think I can now say what has been on my mind in as few as five words: Suicide is caused by psychache.

—Shniedman (1993, p. 53)

In a recent case description, Maltsberger (2000) presents what might be considered a typical example of how an existential vacuum may lead to suicidal behavior. Mansur, a 30-year-old man, came to therapy with a chronic wish to end his life. His therapist (Sabinofsky in Maltsberger, 2000) could not detect any pathology of depression or any other diagnosis beyond the high degree of hopelessness displayed by the patient. No distinct trauma, past or present, could be identified, nor could the patient's symptoms be linked to familial dysfunction. In addition, Mansur was not responding to any medication prescribed for him. In fact, the sole edifice of Mansur's suicidal inclination was the reason Mansur had voluntarily presented, that he was obsessed with his failure to find meaning, not only in his own life, but also in the entire cosmic system.

Mansur's self-description is a good illustration of existential (noögenic) neurosis (Frankl, 1967): I feel disconnected, restless...yet... lethargic, indifferent, unmotivated, an automaton....I have lost or never had the ability to feel.... As a child, I remember a sense of wonder what the world is really all about...

281

I am still preoccupied with the ultimate nature of reality ... merely existing is a burden.... I crave something else, but have no idea what I am craving for. I am unattached to any person, thing, idea, or experience. I cannot find anyone who shares my interest in exploring the meaning of life. I am an empty shell. I have yet to experience the 'essence' of life, of existence, but would prefer to remove myself.... It will make no difference whether I live out my natural life or terminate it. (Maltsberger, 2000, p. 84)

It seems that this young man in his lifestyle, as well as his self and world experiences, demonstrates and confirms the claim of the existentialists regarding the association between meaninglessness, emptiness, and suicide.

Rogers (2001) reflects on the distinction of the existential approach to suicidality—existential theory draws suicide as a less pathological and more rational act. Meaninglessness and existential isolation may lead one to choose suicide as a response to environmental stressors. Rogers also introduces a theoretical model that describes the interactions between all known risk factors of suicide, ones' construction of the meaning of life in general, and one's own life in a way that can lead to the choice of suicide as a resolution of existential dilemmas.

In this chapter I intend to critically review the theoretical claims and empirical evidence of the notion that existential issues of meaning in life, meaninglessness, and emptiness are at the heart of the suicidal drama and then suggest my own hypothesis about the relationship between existential issues and their link to suicide.

MEANING

The existential approach to meaning in life, meaninglessness, and emptiness is not comprised of a homogeneous perspective, but rather polyphony of views. In this section I present a range of these theoretical views.

Albert Camus: "Meaning Is Experiencing Life to Its Fullest"

Camus (1965) takes a very radical existential position regarding suicide. Central to Camus' theory is what he terms the *unresolvable absurdity of life*—that living necessitates both the urge to live as well as an awareness of one's own mortality. This absurdity is the driving force behind man's search for meaning in religion (belief in the hereafter), in existentialism (transcendental values), in philosophy (wisdom and reason), in science (order and truth), or in phenomenology (self-experience, experience of the world). Ultimately, seeking meaning in these arenas can not assuage, let alone resolve the absurdity, because these outlets are not authentic sources of meaning, they are forms of self-deception. In Yalom's (1980) words, Camus portrays the individual as living in state of value nihilism.

Meaning can be realized only through revolt. To be rebellious means to face life with the full awareness of mortality and, in spite of the fear and despair associated with death, to actualize one's potentials. The rebellious man chooses to attach him/herself to life and tries to live as long as possible and experience all possible diversities. The promise behind this revolt is a sense of freedom. Only when one accepts one's own mortality can one become free of the most threatening limitation of life—death. Avoiding the awareness of mortality means to be imprisoned for life. From the stance of meaninglessness and mortality one can achieve stature by living life with dignity in spite of the absurdity. Yalom (1980) summarizes Camus' position in the following way, "Camus started from a position of nihilism, but generated a system of personal meaning based on guidelines and values of courage, prideful rebellion, fraternal solidarity, love, and secular spirituality."

Binswanger and Boss: "Meaning Is Authenticity"

Binswanger (1958, 1963) and Boss (1963) are two theoreticians that attempted to generate an existential psychology from the philosophy of existentialism. Although the two differ in some respects in their interpretations of existential philosophy, they do concur on the essence of what meaning is: an effortful and concentrated focus on oneself and the world. One has to see and reflect on inner and outer experiences. The focus should be on the *what* and the *how* of these experiences. Self- and world-awareness is not like a detached and objective investigation, but rather a total subjective experience of one's being and existing in the world. Being means choosing to exist in an authentic way. Authentic being is creating and constructing one's life on the basis of what one thinks, feels, and desires and not on conventions, norms, fashions, or expectations of others. In other words, to be oneself is to realize and actualize one's subjectivity and one's own possibilities and unique potentials. Each person can become what that person aspires to be. However, being oneself is not a fact, but a task. It demands action on our part before it is made real. It requires effort, personal decision, and selection of alternatives. Decision, selection, and effort can create what one really is in one's own lifestyle. We can evaluate, embrace, discard, and affirm our own sequence of possibilities, ways of living which, when realized in our lifestyle, would make us authentic (Rychlak, 1973).

To achieve an authentic existence, one *must* make a passionate commitment to realize the possibilities and the potentials. One *must* also make choices and act on them. In other words, in order to create meaning in life by means of constructing an authentic existence, individuals have to recognize that they are free to make choices, decisions, and to act on them.

Although individuals have to recognize that they have freedom of choice according to existentialism, that freedom of choice is not put forth as an objective fact. Existentialism will not deny that there are matters beyond our reach or control. Rather, freedom of choice must be adopted as an attitude toward life. Existentialists perceive this as crucial because without the recognized freedom to choose, there can be no subjective experience of responsibility toward one's own actions, which will result in the neglect of active construction of meaning. Existential freedom has two goals. The first aim of existential freedom, or perceived freedom, is to encourage actively choosing and committing to one's self-prescribed goals. With this elicited sense of choice and commitment comes an awareness of the implications of our decisions. The second aim of existential freedom pertains to perception of one's own lack of freedom or limitations. In this regard, existential freedom is aimed at accepting that which is beyond our control. Only once a person accepts the limitations or the unpleasant consequences of their actions can they experience a sense of freedom, even where they have no control. Thus, if a person with a physical limitation can accept that this is part of their existence, then they become free of this limitation. That is, the sense of personal and subjective freedom is in part a matter of attitude and view and not always a factual given.

Meaning in life is obtained through an authentic existence. The conditions for achieving this kind of existence are commitment to actualize one's possibilities to choose and decide about the possibilities and to act on them. Another important aspect of meaning is to be future oriented and not to live in the past. Such an approach to life includes being goal-oriented, to make plans.

Yalom: "Meaning Is Responsibility and Accountability for Creative Enjoyment in Life"

Yalom (1980) fused various existential philosophies in an attempt to synthesize a psychological outlet for existentialism. Yalom has identified four ultimate existential concerns that human beings face. These concerns are a source of anxiety that each of us has to cope with during life:

Death. The fact that we are mortal constantly whirs beneath the membrane of life and influences our experiences, our actions, and our coping abilities. Our unavoidable mortality is a primordial source of anxiety and, as such, is the primary fount of psychopathology.

Isolation. Existential isolation reflects a basic phenomenological experience. No matter how close interpersonal relationships can be a gap between our own experience and the way others understand or empathize with us always remains. Existential isolation lies in the awareness of this gap.

Freedom. By freedom, Yalom refers to the absence of external or a given structure of the world—a structure that if it would exist would provide grounds and guidelines to self-definition, world definition, values, goals, and modes of conduct. Being that freedom removes structures that provide definition; the free individual is responsible to provide those structures for himself. In turn, the free individual is also held accountable for the repercussions of their freely chosen actions, freely constructed creations, and similar structures that they have erected. He or she is responsible for his or her life story.

Meaninglessness. According to Yalom, we are meaning-seeking creatures, living in a world devoid of superimposed meaning. Under these conditions, we have to create our own meaning in order to escape the anxiety and threat of nihilism.

According to Yalom (1980), certain conditions must be met in order to create meaning. First, one must recognize that it is an individual's personal responsibility to create their own meaning. This recognition of responsibility inculcates the precept that meaning must be actively sought. The second condition for the creation of meaning is the acknowledgment that preoccupation with meaning, whether it be on a cosmic scale or an individual level, is useless. Questions about why we live, what we life for, and so forth will not help us to find meaning. Rather, it is necessary to focus on one's own purpose. This leads into the third condition for meaning: The realization that meaning is the outcome of action and not only thinking. Meaning is a by-product of engaging in life. Wholehearted creative engagement in any of the infinite arrays of life's activities can enhance the possibility of creating life in some coherent fashion. "To find a home, to care about other individuals, to care about ideas or projects, to search, to create, to build—these and other forms of engagement are twice rewarding; they are intrinsically enriching and they alleviate the dysphoria that stems from being bombarded with the unassembled brute data of existence" (p. 482).

Viktor Frankl: "Meaning Is Self-Transcendence and Value"

Frankl (1959, 1963, 1973) posits that the will for meaning is the most important motivational aspect of human beings. The will for meaning, the striving for meaning, and the search for meaning have supremacy over basic needs, sexual needs, fulfillment of potentials, and self-actualization. According to Frankl, there are three types of values by which one can discover meaning: the creative, the experiential, and the attitudinal (Wong, 1998). Creative values are based on what an individual contributes to the world in terms of personal achievement and deeds. Experiential values refer to what the person receives from the world by means of experiencing or encountering someone or something. Attitude values can lead to meaning by taking a stand toward unavoidable suffering or unchangeable situations (Wong, 1998).

At the heart of the creation of meaning is self-transcendence. True meaning can be found only when an individual commits him/her self to a value outside or beyond him/herself, to a cause greater than him/herself. Finding meaning also entails being "responsible for something or to something, be it society, or humanity, or mankind, or his own conscience" (Frankl, 1973, p. 22).

Meaning, according to Frankl, also actually emphasizes the spiritual or supernatural dimension. Meaning cannot be found in the physical or narcissistic needs of the individual.

Antonovsky: "Meaning Is Self-Coherence"; Maddi: "Meaning Is Individual Decision Making"

Antonovsky (1979) defines meaning as a sense of coherence. Sense of coherence consists of three factors: comprehensibility, manageability, and emotional investment (which he terms meaningfulness)—and together these aspects provide a generalized way of viewing the world from a global, stable perspective.

Comprehensibility has to do with one's world perception, to what degree does one perceive the world as predictable, ordered, and logical. Comprehensibility allows people to anticipate and to understand events and situations. Manageability refers to the personal and social resources that one possesses while coping with predictable and unpredictable situations. The most significant factor in sense of coherence is meaningfulness, which refers to the degree to which people perceive the demands with which they are confronted as being worthy of commitment and emotional investment. The need to attain meaningfulness is the power that motivates people to search for order and to make sense of their environment. Finding meaning is an effort to restore order, predictability, and comprehension in the face of such interruptions. Some of the sources for stress are chaos and interruptions in continuity and stability. When people feel that they have some control over life events, they also evaluate the situation as worthy and are motivated to search for order. Searching for order also involves the ability to make decisions in an interrupted situation.

A closely related conception of meaning is proposed by Maddi (1998). According to Maddi, human beings are characterized by the need and ability for symbolization, imagination, and judgment. Symbolization is the mental act of going beyond the specific characteristics of experiences and events by categorizing and interpreting them. Symbolization is the mental act of going beyond the specific characteristics of experiences and events by categorizing and interpreting them. Imagination, following symbolization, mentally combines and recombines categorized experiences in a manner that transcends the way they naturally occurred. Judgment means taking an evaluative stance (either ethical or preferential) with regard to the factual or imagined experience. As human beings, we do not relate to events and experiences passively. Rather we constantly sort, reflect, integrate, resort, reconsider, and take an active stance toward them.

An inherent part of finding meaning is to make decisions about construing and interacting with the world. In a meaningful construction of the world, one has to make individualized decisions with an orientation toward the future. As decisions accumulate, an underlying direction (Sartre, 1956) emerges as a hierarchy of goals.

Baumeister: "Meaning as Four Basic Psychological Needs"

Like Antonovsky (1979) and Maddi (1998), Baumeister (1991) approaches the concept of meaning from a meta-cognitive perspective. According to Baumeister (1991) the search for meaning is evolutionarily adaptive. It involves recognizing and understanding external and internal patterns of stimulation. Discerning patterns requires an ability to make distinctions and associations between events, objects, concepts, and other entities. Ultimately, the ability to categorize likes and dislikes ascertains the gift of interpretation. The basic aspect of meaning is thus the ability to signify, to give an interpretive label (Klinger, 1998).

Assigning the world meaning grants us yet another adaptive function, the ability to control. Control pertains to two dimensions: one to external reality and the other to behavioral and emotional self-regulation. Discerning patterns out of seemingly sporadic stimuli helps us gauge our actions in a way that will allow us mastery over the world. Meaning in terms of interpretations can help us control negative emotional states. The process of attribution of meaning is achieved by comparing oneself, one's life, events, and ideas to a given standard. The essence of interpretation is the evaluation of the specific aspect of life by comparing it to a standard, to relate things to something we already know.

However, personal meaning in life is not acquired through interpretation of events in life. Personal meaning is also acquired through the fulfillment of important needs. According to Baumeister, there are four types of meaning needs. These include having a purpose, values, efficiency, and self-worth. He describes each of them as follows.

Purpose. There is a need to see one's actions as oriented toward a purpose more than the actual or full realization of the purpose. A purpose enables the person to see beyond the immediate situation and to interpret it in relation to a certain idea, need, or self-fulfillment, and fulfillment of goals makes one feel good and satisfied. Having many short-term goals does not necessarily add up to meaningful long-term goals.

Values. Refers to people's motivation to feel that their actions are right, good, and justifiable. Things are done for the sake of something (children, honor, love, God). A value base provides guidelines for making value judgments. These can be practical and self-interest values and ideological and moral values. These are positive (for certain acts) and negative (against certain acts).

Efficiency.   Feeling of control over events, that one is making a difference, that we have effective responsibilities, or changing the environment to suit the self.

Self-Worth.   People need to make sense of their lives in a way that enables them to feel they have positive value. They seek criteria according to which they can regard themselves and convince others to regard them positively—self-respect (self-worth) and respect (love) from others.

Having meaning is a necessity. Its creation is a natural process that occurs almost automatically. When meaning is endangered or lost, people are highly motivated to restore meaning or find new meaning. When purpose is lost, then people try to find new goals. When justifications and values are lost, then new justifications are sought after by means of rationalization. When people cannot control one aspect of their lives, they seek to gain control in another aspect. When self-worth is lost, then one will compare him/herself to another person lower in status.

MEANINGLESSNESS

Just as existentialists vary in their interpretation of meaning, so too they vary in their theories of meaninglessness. However, common to all existentialists is the belief that loss of meaning constitutes a negative change in life that is often accompanied by negative pathological reactions and even suicide. The following are some of the different definitions of meaninglessness and its relation to mental health and suicide.

Camus: "Meaninglessness Is Estrangement, Hopelessness, and Despair"

Camus (1965) argues that meaninglessness stems from the irresolvable absurdity of life, or the gap between the drive to live and the awareness of inevitable death. The result of this existential absurdity is estrangement, exile, and hopelessness. This is a catastrophic state from which people try to escape. Camus is often quoted as one who proposes that the absurdity of life and its ensuing sense of estrangement and desperation automatically lead to the conclusion that life is not worth living and that suicide may be a rational and logical choice. This is absolutely a misunderstanding of Camus' philosophy. Camus (1965) states very clearly that the absence of meaning does not necessarily mean that life is not worth living. Usually people commit suicide because of mental distress and not because of lack of meaning. Actually Camus does not deal, almost at all, with suicide that is related to personal distress. He states categorically that suicide is by no means a proper solution to the existential absurdity or to personal distress.

Camus deals mostly with the philosophical suicide. Philosophical suicide is a way of dealing with the existential absurdity by attributing false meaning to life by means of escape from the absurd, belief in the afterlife (religion), searching for order in life (science), or any other form that denies the absurdities of life.

Binswanger and Boss: "Meaninglessness Is Lack of Authenticity"

According to Binswanger (1958) and Boss (1963) meaning is rooted in authenticity, and meaninglessness grows from a lack of authenticity in one's being and subjective feelings. An unauthentic self-experience can result from numerous unauthentic life conditions. Conformity, for one, potentially engulfing an individual into an objective mass may chafe away at the subjective-self of an individual. Subjection to authority in general is a life condition that is corrosive to the sense of independent purpose. A state of immobility and narrowing of horizons usually characterize lack of authenticity. In addition, unauthentic personal experiences as well as unauthentic life conditions create a vicious cycle of lack of meaning. That is, leading an unauthentic life heightens an individual's vulnerability to being sucked into vulnerability or being swept under the wing of an authoritarian.

The danger in leading an unauthentic way of life lies not only in impending meaninglessness; more substantially, lack of authenticity may lead to existential neurosis. Existential neurosis usually begins with an experience of unfamiliarity or strangeness followed by a pervading uncanny feeling, due to a perception of threat imposed by the unfamiliar, eeriness yields anxiety. Gradually the loss of grasp increases until it turns into dread. Further in this sequence the sense of dread becomes fixed upon a specific object or event and turns into an affective state of fear. Thus, existential anxiety develops from an amorphous feeling into a more defined state of fear. Underlying the sequence of differentiation in the progression of existential neurosis is, beginning at the unauthentic life condition or self-experiences, a gradual fading of both the world and the self into nothingness.

Also symptomatic of existential neurosis is existential guilt. Existential guilt results from a perceived disparity between one's obligations and possibilities, and one's fulfillment of them. Thus, existential guilt is directly linked with one's subjective evaluation of their actualization.

Binswanger and Boss posit a direct link between meaninglessness and suicide. A person who leads an unauthentic life and experiences anxiety, dread, and guilt will lose the will to live and eventually will commit suicide. This assertion resonates in the documentation of Ellen West (Binswanger, 1958), a 33-year-old woman treated by Binswanger, who eventually committed suicide. Ellen West suffered from worsening depression as well as a severe/chronic eating disorder for 13 years. Her diary expresses her existential difficulties: "The world (is) a caricature and my life a hell...the torture of having each day to tilt anew against the windmill with a mass of absurd base, contemptible thoughts, this torment spoils my life" (Binswanger, 1958, p. 256). In Binswanger's reports, Ellen communicated feelings of terrible emptiness and dread, that her life was horrible, and that she had longed for death for as long as she could remember. Following Ellen's suicide, Binswanger wrote the concluding remarks of their therapy sessions. The existential analysis was sealed with the aversion that the act that Ellen had committed was an authentic, logical, and coherent development of her life-long existential state.

Yalom: "Meaninglessness Is Failure to Cope With the Basic Concerns"

According to Yalom (1980), meaninglessness results from a self-attributed failure to cope with basic existential concerns such as isolation and freedom (or lack of structure). Meaninglessness also results from a perceived inability to reduce the anxiety evoked by the awareness of mortality, or from a sense of helplessness in the face of inherent meaninglessness of the world. Essentially, Yalom contends that meaninglessness is the failure to find sufficient answers to existential concerns. When confrontation with one's own mortality reveals, instead of answers, an individual's inability to cope with this existential concern, death-related anxiety will overflow, at times to the point of madness. So too, an inability to resolve innate existential isolation will evoke a sense of painful, irreparable loneliness. Existential freedom bestows the responsibility of independently creating life-structure, a task that some individuals may find overwhelming.

Ultimately, says Yalom (1980), meaninglessness, which results from failure to cope with basic existential concerns (i.e. those discussed previously), may potentially lead to suicide, especially when there is a lack of engrossment in life.

Frankl: "Meaninglessness Is Emptiness, Boredom, and an Existential Vacuum"

Existential vacuum is Frankl's (1967) term for meaninglessness, properly illustrates the experiential facets of lack of meaning that his theory highlights—emptiness, void, boredom, numbness, apathy, and frustration. In a state of existential vacuum, one looses their inner sense of direction. The sunder created between an individual and their internal compass, by effect of existential vacuum, makes way for depression, addiction, alcoholism, obsessionalism, delinquency, the hyperinflation of sex and daredevilry, and relapses of existential (noögenic) neurosis.

Because meaning is the most essential need for living, then in the face of failure to find meaning or escape the *vacuum*, suicide may then be chosen as a viable solution to relieve this stressful state of being. Suicidal feelings may also be perpetuated by the tremendous guilt that an *empty person* may feel because of a sense of failure in taking responsibility in finding faith and meaning (Frankl, 1967, 1975).

Maddi: "Meaninglessness Is a State of Vegetative Life and Indifference"

Says Maddi (1998), the meaningless state of mind inevitably yields a vegetative state of being. This is because, meaning can only result from responsible conscious decision-making, meaninglessness is linked to an individual's negligence in making choices pertaining to their life. It follows that wallowing in meaninglessness one may sink into severe aimlessness and loose faith in the usefulness and value of initiating or sustaining life endeavors. It seems as if the person is not troubled with anything, be it guilt, esteem, identity, sex, or aggression. He or she feels indifferent to life on the emotional level—vegetativeness, in values, apathy, boredom, depression, and a low level of activity. Other forms of meaninglessness are nihilism and adventurousness as attempts to avoid negativeness and indifference. The nihilistic anti-meaning attitude is characterized by not conforming to anything that purports to have meaning and emotionally responding with anger, disgust, and cynicism. Adventurousness is a form of achieving meaning by means of risky activities, excitement, and heroic intensities (Maddi, 1988; see also Yalom, 1980). People who experience these states may withdraw from engagement with life by becoming a recluse, a chronic alcoholic, a hobo, or by adopting some other analogous form of life. Maddi considers such people as existentially ill.

Antonovsky: "Meaninglessness Is Inner Chaos"

The core of Antonovsky's (1990) contention regarding meaning is that meaning is based on the ability to perceive the world as ordered, predictable, and manageable. The ability to manage resources, to cope and adapt is contingent upon being able to understand the world. It logically follows that in a state of meaninglessness the world is perceived as a buzzing confusion, as chaotic, ambiguous, and generally incoherent. Being that comprehension is impaired; manageability is slighted, leading to a reduced ability to cope. Thus, world perception (as meaningful or meaningless) may domino into suicidality (see also Petrie & Brook, 1992).

Baumeister: "Meaninglessness Is Painful Dissatisfaction"

Baumeister (1991) has posited that meaning ensues when there is satisfaction in life, which comes when the four basic needs of life—purpose, values, control, and esteem—are satisfied. When an individual fails to satisfy these needs, life is meaningless and is accompanied by painful dissatisfaction. Failure to satisfy the needs is not judged by objective measures, but rather by a subjective judgment regarding the gap between the achievement of a desired standard (e.g., ideal self or ought self; Higgins, 1989) and actual achievement (e.g., actual self). This discrepancy produces an intense emotional stress in the form of negative self-esteem. If the responsibility for failure to achieve the desired standards regarding purpose, values, control, and esteem is attributed to the self rather than to external circumstances, the individual may lose their goals (standards), may feel guilty (no value base), may feel helpless (control), and may lose their self-esteem. Such a state may drive the individual to suicide (see Baumeister, 1991).

Empirical Evidence for the Relationship Between Meaninglessness and Suicide

From a theoretical perspective, it is clear that meaning and meaninglessness in life have an extensive association with happiness, distress, and pathology. It is proposed that meaning in life is positively related to mental and physical well-being (Ryff & Singer, 1998). At the same time, it is suggested that lack of meaning is related to pathology and suicide (Yalom, 1980; Petrie & Brook, 1992).

Based on a phenomenological study, Hazzel (1984a, b) was able to define two aspects of the search for meaning (or existential concerns;

e.g., "I think about the meaning of my life," "I try to discover my life's purpose") and sense of emptiness (e.g., "I feel a vague inner emptiness," "I feel as though a part of me is missing"). Interestingly, the personal descriptions of emptiness on the basis of which the scale was constructed were congruent with the theoretical formulations people described: emptiness as loss of control, being terrified, being unauthentic and false, feeling bored, helpless, numb, miserable, and lonely, having no desire or goals, and having no feelings (not feeling anything). In two subsequent studies (1984, 1989), Hazzel found that existential emptiness was positively and significantly correlated with depression, but no significant association was found between depression and existential concern (meaning).

Flannery, Perry, Penk, and Flannery (1994) and Korotkov (1998) found that lack of meaning in life (in terms of comprehensibility and manageability) has strong correlations with daily hassles, depression, and anxiety. Petrie and Azariah (1990) found that meaningfulness best predicted life satisfaction.

Shek (1992) found that envisioning oneself as having goals in life is crucial for deriving a sense of psychological well-being and existential fullness.

Debats, Drost, and Hensen (1995) have found that life regard was found to be strongly associated with the interpersonal dimension of well-being. Further, effective coping with stressful life events in the past was associated with a current sense of meaninglessness.

Newcomb and Harlow (1986) studied the sense of meaninglessness (having no direction or solution) in two samples of adolescents and young adults. Meaninglessness mediated the effects of perceived loss of control and uncontrollable stress. In a different study, Man, Stuchlikova, and Klinger (1998), the clinical group of alcoholic patients reported fewer goals, fewer commitments to their goals, and indicated less ability to influence the course of goal attainment.

Several studies have dealt directly with the relationships between suicidal behavior and meaning in life or meaninglessness. Lester and Badro (1992) found that purpose in life scores were associated with previous suicide attempts, previous suicidal ideation, and current suicidal ideation in undergraduate students. Edwards and Holden (2001) studied the relationship between meaning and life, on the one hand, and hopelessness, coping, suicidal ideation, past suicide attempts, and self-reported likelihood of future suicidal behavior, on the other hand. They found that coherence (along with other variables) contributed to the statistical prediction of all suicidal variables in women, but only suicidal ideation in men. Kinnier, Metha, Keim, Okey, Adler–Tabia, Berry, Mulvenon (1994) examined the relationship between depression, meaninglessness, suicidal ideation, and substance abuse in high school students and inpatients. The correlational analysis indicated that those who viewed themselves negatively were depressed or had found little meaning in their lives were more likely to consider suicide or drugs. The regression analyses indicated a strong mediational relationship between purpose in life, the precursor of depression, and the consequence of substance abuse, but not with suicidal ideation.

Petrie and Brook (1992) examined the relationship between sense of coherence, on one hand, and suicidal ideation, depression and hopelessness, on the other hand. They found that all three components of sense of coherence (comprehensibility, manageability, and meaningfulness) were associated with all depression, hopelessness, and suicidal ideation, but the meaningfulness component had consistently higher correlations across all of these latter variables.

Orbach, Mikulincer, Gilboa-Schechtman, and Sirota (2003) studied the relationship between a newly developed measure of mental pain, suicidal behavior, and life meaning. It was found that the suicidal inpatients scored higher on mental pain and lower on life meaning. Further, there were significant negative correlations between meaning in life, on one hand, and suicidal behavior measures and mental pain, on the other hand.

Finally, a deep sense of emptiness was found to characterize suicidal individuals in two separate studies. In one study, Verkes et al. (1998) found that low levels of platelet serotonin which are characteristic of suicidal individuals were associated with chronic feelings of emptiness. In another study (Schnyder, Valach, Bichsel, & Michel, 1999), it was found that suicidal individuals tended to describe themselves in interviews as suffering from a sense of emptiness.

At face value, the studies on suicide seem to confirm the notion that suicide may be viewed as individual attempts to escape from meaninglessness (Jacobson, Ritter, & Mueller, 1977). The previously reported studies indicate that there is a sound basis for the conclusion that meaning in life is strongly related to well-being and to mental pathology, as well as to suicidal behavior. People who report having meaning in life also report high levels of well-being. People who report lacking in meaning also report suffering from pathology and suicidal ideation and behavior. However, the exact nature of these relationships is not clear. Indeed, it is possible that sense of meaning in life is functional in producing a sense of well-being and the lack of it is responsible for pathology dissatisfaction and suicidal behavior. However, at the same time an opposite causative relationship can be posited. Yet, as in any other correlational study, it can be hypothesized that both meaning and well-being or suicidal behavior are products of a third factor.

I would like to posit the hypothesis that the relationship between meaning and satisfaction or, more specifically, between lack of meaning, and suicidal behavior is more complicated than what existential theory and the empirical data seem to suggest. My argument is that it is not the lack of meaning that brings about suicidal behavior, but that mental pain is the emotional state that produces both lack of meaning as well as suicidal behavior. Further, it is mental pain that resides at the heart of suicidal wishes, lack of meaning, existential concerns, and emptiness and not that lack of meaning causes suicidal urges or mental pain. I will develop this idea by using the concepts of high order meaning, low order meaning interception in producing meaning, and by focusing on the relationship of mental pain and suicide.

HIGH-ORDER MEANING AND LOW-ORDER MEANING

At first glance, Baumeister's (1991) theory on the search for meaning appears contradictory. On one hand he concurs with theoreticians in his field that assert an inexorable link between the granting of meaning and human nature, human brain structure, and the survival and evolution of man (Klinger, 1998). Correspondingly, simple means to creating meaning, namely contextualization, signification, interpretation, symbolization, and the identification of patterns is almost automatic. Acknowledging the aforementioned precept, Baumeister claims that people are capable of living happily without any coherent/explicit life philosophy (Baumeister, 1991). This is because people can have meaning in their lives, even if they are incapable of articulating it. This seeming contradiction is resolved by making a distinction between high order meaning and low order meaning.

Multiple theoreticians suggest that meaning is multi-leveled (Baumeister, 1991; Ebersole, 1998; Klinger, 1998; Yalom, 1980). According to Baumeister there are four categories of meaning or the search for meaning: goals, value base (need for justification), efficiency (control), and self-worth. Each of these four is equally vital and fulfills one's need for meaning in a different yet complimentary way. The attainment of these four is closely related to learned needs or basic psychological needs (Murray, 1938). Apparent in the search for the four levels of meaning is the natural human tendency to move toward goals. They are largely learned and involve goals and actions more concrete and close to everyday life (e.g., affiliation, achievement, power). Need is a force in the brain that organizes perception and interpretation in such a way as to transform an unsatisfying situation in a certain direction. As with any other need, important needs are frustrated, the individual feels tension and tries to seek new ways to satisfy them. Fulfillment of the basic needs is actually the attainment of low order meaning.

The four categories of meaning posited by Baumeister are closely related to satisfaction of needs. These can relate to daily short-term actions. Although low order meaning is absolutely necessary for physical survival, the absence of this type of meaning can cause great dissatisfaction. This dissatisfaction, in turn, serves as an impetus to; as Baumeister puts it, restore meaning within the four realms of meaning. Baumeister (1991) argues that desperate people do not ponder the meaning of life but search for needs fulfillment (low order meaning). Only those who are not desperate, who can count on survival, comfort, and security have the luxury of searching for high-order meaning.

In contrast to low-order meaning, high-order meaning does not pertain to specific goals and actions of everyday life, but rather they refer to complex, integrative, far-reaching implications that transcend the immediate everyday life situations and may approach morality, high values, timelessness, metaphysical systems, eternal and spiritual perspectives that encompass all aspects of life (Baumeister, 1991). This category of meaning includes concepts, such as self-transcendence, spirituality, commitment, religiosity, worldview, perceiving life as whole, existential concerns, and the like. These categories of meaning attempt to answer questions, such as: Why are we here? How should we live? What is our place in the universe? Where do we go after death? Authors such as Gange-fling (1996) and McCarthy (1966) who have elaborated upon high order meaning, define spirituality, for example, as:

> a complex, multifaceted construct that involves ultimate and personal truths that individuals hold as inviolable in their lives… (It) is broad enough to incorporate religion, existential and unstructured orientations, as well as concepts of God's higher power and spiritual source. Spiritual well-being can be conceptualized as affirmation of life in a relationship with God, self, community, and environment that nurtures and celebrates wholeness. (Moberg & Lazarus, 1990, p. 6)

Many existentialists believe that only high-order meaning can provide deep satisfaction, whereas the lack of it may lead to emptiness and suffering and even suicide. In contrast, Baumeister believes that it is possible to live quite happily or satisfactorily without a high-order meaning that encompasses all of it.

I would like to advance a different hypothesis here. In this hypothesis, I include the distinction between low-order and high-order meaning and their relationship to suffering. According to this hypothesis, lack of meaning does not cause suffering; rather suffering is the cause for lack of meaning. Suffering causes an interruption in the natural flow of the creation of meaning.

We have to start with the notion of low-order meaning. Similar to Baumeister, I recognize that there are categories of meaning. However, I believe that there are more than four meaning categories. Categories of meaning can incorporate other important life needs, such as, affiliation, and love. When the smooth fulfillment of these needs is interrupted, one experiences suffering and mental pain. The emergence of pain interrupts the flow of low order meaning and the individual may then experience a sense of lack of meaning or emptiness. Baumeister claims that, at this point, one is motivated to restore low-order meaning in life, that is, to find ways to restore the sense of having a goal, value, control, self-worth, and we may add affiliation, love. If these attempts to restore low-order meaning fail, then suffering persists and increases. At this stage, when low-order meaning fails, one might turn to find high-order meaning (self-transcendence, spirituality, religion, etc.). If this search is successful and the individual can see their lack of satisfaction and their suffering from a broad perspective, then one may even find benefits in suffering. This alleviates the suffering. If one is unsuccessful in this second attempt to find meaning, then they may turn to find meaning in death, that is, to become suicidal.

Therefore, when the natural tendency to find low-order meaning is interrupted by external or internal trauma, pain is the end result. This pain further blocks the tendency to find meaning. The search for high-order meaning is a compensatory action. It is true in my opinion that pain and suffering are invariably implanted in living. However, the source of this pain comes from the fact that the fulfillment of the basic needs, for living low-order meaning, is constantly frustrated due to the transience (not only of life itself, but also of the satisfaction of the needs), partiality (we cannot get all that we want), and responsibility (we are responsible for the satisfaction of our needs and this does not come easily).

Life events and inner tendencies are responsible for the interruption of the sense of stability and of the smooth flow of need-fulfillment, not the lack of high-order meaning. During the greater part of our lives, we may suffer much more from being rejected by a loved one than by the awareness that life is temporary or that we do not have an encompassing world perspective.

The view presented here is closely related to the one held by Janoff-Bulman and Berger (2000). Untraumatized individuals characteristically view the world as meaningful. To them the world is benevolent, imbued with justice, and personal outcome contingency. Traumatized individuals, on the other hand grant different meaning to the world, often times to the extent that they deem the world as lacking in meaning. Negative events in the form of tragedy, trauma, or loss, potentially shatter one's assumptions about the world as being benevolent, or just, as well as one's concept of self-worthiness. When the world looses its meaning it also becomes incomprehensible. However, personal trauma and its subsequent existential crisis need not necessarily leave an individual's system of meaning in shambles. Rather, breaking down the walls that were used to define one's surroundings may allow for transcendence or exploration into new realms of meaning.

According to Janoff-Bulman trauma precipitates existential crisis. What she fails to mention, however, is that not only trauma can bring about a breach in meaning, but the suffering that results from trauma can have this effect as well. In other words, I suggest that an alternate sequence of events can be discerned, whereby firstly trauma occurs, then the suffering that results from that trauma is experienced, and only then are the foundations of one's meaning shook.

There are very few of the nature of the relationships between negative life events, mental suffering, and meaning. There is one qualitative study that delineates this question to some extent. Everall (2000) studied the meaning of suicide attempts by young adults. In this study, the life narratives of suicidal youngsters were followed in order to find the sequences that lead to suicidal behavior as described in the self-reports. Participants were stressed by cognitive, affective, and social processes precipitated by the accumulation of distressing life events that required much emotional energy. This state led to the evocation of meaning in life. Similarly, Harlow, Newcomb, and Bentler (1986),using a structural equation procedure with a very large sample of young adults that depression and self-derogation lead to a lake of purpose in life which in turn lead to suicidal ideation and substance use. These findings confirm to some degree the hypothesis that I am trying to advance.

The previously mentioned theories and studies all point to the need to differentiate meaning into hierarchal levels in order to truly understand the disruption and creation of meaning as an existential mechanism. The concept of low order meaning, especially its ability to outlive, as well as to resolve an existential crisis, suggests a revision of the theoretical relationship between trauma, pain, and existential crisis.

SUFFERING, MEANING, AND SUICIDE

The hypothesis that was introduced is that suffering produces meaninglessness via the distinction of low-order and high-order meaning. This hypothesis stands in contrast to the theory that meaninglessness produces suffering. On this basis, I will now try to further develop theoretically the relationship between suffering, meaning, and suicide.

Based on my experience with suicidal individuals, especially suicidal youth, I have found that the complaints they voice in therapy, about life boring them or that life has no meaning to them, are not expressions of an experienced void. Rather, I believe, such complaints hint at an internal state of painful emotions that, when unavailable to conscious scrutiny, are reported as a lack of experienced emotions, and mistakenly deemed as an experience of emptiness. In other words, based on the contention that suffering yields meaninglessness, and not vice versa, it is a mistake to address the existential complaints of a suicidal individual by helping them to seek or create meaning in their life. Doing so would mean treating the individual on a superficial level, as well as ignoring the mental anguish that is generating the emptiness that ultimately leads to the suicidal urges. Getting entangled in philosophical issues instead of addressing the pain that is behind these issues may result in a tragedy of suicide.

Mental pain, anguish, and mental suffering are not caused only by external traumatic events. Mental pain is also produced from the inside. This is especially true for suicidal people. Elsewhere I (Orbach, 2001) have posited the existence of inner pain-producing patterns. Inner experiential patterns can be defined as an integrated cluster of beliefs and cognitions about the self and the world, emotions, and action tendencies. Pain-producing inner patterns can also be described as a web of negative representations of the world and the self, negative expectations, and extreme negative emotions, as well as self-destructive action tendencies.

The pain-producing inner patterns stem from a life-long internalization of negative experiences in the past and from abusive and rejecting behaviors by others. Throughout life, the individual construes their perception in a way that produces negative experiences and a negative orientation toward reality. The suicidal person reacts to life circumstances and self-perception with habitual, ineffective coping mechanisms that in and of themselves create mental pain. Eventually, these experiences crystallize into self-destructive forms of self-abusive behavior that erode one's well-being, self-love, interpersonal relationships, and harmony with reality, thereby making it very difficult to go on living. The suicidal individual may become entrapped in their own pain-producing inner patterns and eventually seek total self-destruction to escape the intolerable pain.

I would like to describe briefly two such basic inner patterns common in many suicidal individuals: self-hate and the sense of loss. Self-hate refers to what Shneidman (1993) has termed as *inimicality*. This is not just a reflection of a negative self-view, low self-esteem, self-anger, or lack of self-satisfaction; rather, it is a hateful offense by the self against itself. It is an offense by one's self-destructive tendency against one's mental existence and the essence of their individuality. Self-hate in some suicidal individuals takes on a form of mental and physical self-abuse. This is in line with Firestone (1997) who characterizes depressed and suicidal people as suffering from a bad and derogatory inner voice representing the internalized hating primary caretakers. The self-description of one depressed young woman who eventually killed herself may be captured in the following words: "I am disgusting, I stink, I am dirty, filthy, lazy. There is nothing good about me. I only hate, damage, and destroy everything. I am one big bad thing." This woman simply could not stand herself. Any attempt to negate this self-perception was met with aggressive resistance. As with other pain-producing experiential patterns, such self-hate can be latent much of the time, but when it awakens at a time of crisis it may become lethal.

The constant and continual sense of loss as well as expectations of future losses is yet another inner pain-producing experiential pattern that is characteristic of suicidal individuals. This pertains to the experience of repeated and accumulative losses. The life narrative is perceived as a sequence of endless losses. Social and materialistic losses are paralleled by inner losses and at times require major adjustments and compromises the individual is not capable of making or enduring. Suicidal people may not only expect future losses in life, but may assume an active role in creating losses.

Similarly, Shneidman (1993) claims that to understand suicide one must understand individual differences in thresholds for enduring mental pain. This understanding is necessary because suicide occurs when mental pain, *psychache*, is conclusively deemed unbearable by a suffering individual. Shneidman's approach to explaining suicide is very mental-centered. The decision to take one's life is born of cognitive reflection and evaluation of one's life-situation. Mental pain results, according to Shneidman, from the frustration of an individual's perceived vital needs. Unbearable pain is caused by the frustration of one's most essential needs. When there is no foreseeable future change in need satisfaction, or lack thereof, the suicidal person will seek to escape the pain by committing suicide.

One description of the experience of mental pain, and one of the most moving accounts that I have reviewed, is Styron's (1990) autobiographical documentation of his own painful episode of depression.

To utilize this firsthand personal account for the study of the experience of mental pain, I (Orbach, 2003) have conducted a content analysis of the book depicting all sentences that relate to mental pain directly or indirectly. Next, the sentences were categorized based on similarity in the main theme expressed in each sentence. Several key categories emerged in this content analysis including the following: a sense of perturbation, emotional stagnation, estrangement, surfeit of the pain, submission to a torturing inner evil force, destruction of the mind, loss of self, changes in perception, and physical pain.

Bolger (1999) performed a narrative analysis of suffering clients. According to Bolger's analysis, emotional pain can be described along several high-order categories, such as sense of brokenness, loss of control, and alarm. Pain can be further described by subcategories of experiences, such as woundedness, disconnection, loss of self, and physical pain (all part of the high-order category of brokenness), and then by more specific categories of experiences, such as damage, hurt (part of woundedness), broken bonds, loneliness (part of disconnection), and so on. According to Bolger, at the heart of mental pain are the sense of an inner rupture, being damaged and shattered, losing parts of the self, losing self-coherence, losing the ability to fully function, and losing connectedness with others. These experiences are accompanied by a sense of lack of control over the negative mental events and by feelings of alarm and panic.

In yet another attempt to understand the meaning of mental pain, Orbach and Mikulincer (2000; see also Orbach, Mikulincer, Gilboa-Shechtman 2003) studied the experience of mental pain both qualitatively and quantitatively. These studies yielded a mental pain scale consisting of nine factors: sense of the irreversibility of the pain, loss of control, flooding of emotions, narcissistic wounds, estrangement, stagnation, confusion, loneliness, and emptiness. On the basis of this study, we have defined mental pain as a sense of irrevocable loss (irreversibility), narcissistic hurt, and perception of negative changes in the self and in its functions (loss of control, flooding, estrangement, freezing, confusion, emptiness), accompanied by negative feelings and cognitions that are brought about by loss of another or by loss of self (e.g., self-disappointment, losing goals).

Orbach et al. (2003) have found that suicidal inpatients suffer more intense mental pain than nonsuicidal inpatients and normal controls, and also that pain was associated with depression, hopelessness, and meaninglessness. However, in that study, the causal relationships between mental pain and suicide were not explored.

In accordance with the basic argument that it is suffering and mental pain that lead to loss of meaning and may subsequently lead to suicide, I further suggest that suicidal individuals may seek meaning in death rather than in life. If low-order meaning due to suffering from trauma or unbearable pain from inner processes cannot be restored, then people tend to turn to high-order meaning. If this endeavor fails, then they might turn to suicide and to replace the search for meaning in life by the search for meaning in death.

Suicidal people do not turn to death as an escape to nothingness or emptiness, but rather they project meaning onto death in terms of low-order meaning and high-order meaning. They tend to endow death with achievement of specific goals, fulfillment of wishes, rebirth, revenge, atonement, love, self-punishment, control, union with a great power, union with a spiritual power, need to be saved, and so on (see, for example, Maltsberger & Goldblatt, 1996; Orbach, 1988, Shneidman, 1985). That is, suicidal people seek cessation of pain in death and, consequently, a fantasy of another state of being.

CLINICAL IMPLICATIONS FOR THERAPY

Various existential theories on suicide have produced a range of clinical approaches to the treatment of suicidal individuals (see, e.g., Yalom, 1980; and Wong, 1998). A widely accepted clinical approach based on existentialist theories is proposed by Frankl (1967). In his book, he demonstrates how providing meaning can make suffering loom through the following example:

An older doctor consulted me in Vienna because he could not get rid of a severe depression caused by the death of his wife. I asked him, 'what would have happened, doctor, if you had died first, and your wife would have had to survive you?' Whereupon he said: 'For her, this would have been terrible; how she would suffered!' I then added: 'You see, doctor, such a suffering has been spared her and it is you who have spared her this suffering; but now you have to pay for it by surviving and mourning her.' The old man suddenly saw his plight in a new light and reevaluated his suffering in the meaningful terms of a sacrifice for the sake of his wife" (p. 15).

Frankl prides himself in that, within one minute of therapy he managed to relieve the old doctor's suffering and to bring him consolation. I take issue with Frankl's conclusion. In my own experience, I have learned that suicidal patients can find little meaning in life as long as the suffering and anguish continue. Only when the pain is relieved will one accept more easily new perspectives to look at life endowed with new meaning.

In the following sections are a number of strategic and tactical therapeutic principles that I have found to be useful in working through the mental anguish experienced by suicidal individuals (see Orbach, 2001).

What Does the Therapist Know About the Patient's Suffering?

The knowledge the therapist has about the patient's pain often has a calming influence. The patient may gain relief through the sharing of this knowledge and by discovering that are going through an experience that is not unique. The patient can learn that their malady is well known, is part of a phenomenon that can be dealt with, and one that people in the past have overcome.

Therapist-to-patient empathy begins with the therapist sharing their knowledge about such painful states. This grants them their much needed sense of hope even before the actual therapeutic work begins to take effect. I have found that often patients arrive at therapy already fatigued and saturated with feelings of despair, disappointment, and confusion from their previous attempts to cope. Often they panic in the face of the disintegration and loss of control. Thus, people in such a state who also lack the ability to withstand the unbearable pain are in need of immediate help and relief just to stay alive. When such patients ask, in an emotional mixture of hope and fear, if there is any chance that their suffering will ease, I choose to answer in the affirmative without any hesitation whatsoever. I am not making a promise—I am sharing my convictions with the patient.

As therapists, we know a fair amount about such maladies. We know that there are people who feel that they have been burnt out slowly and steadily from the inside and who have traveled a long and agonizing road until arriving at the decision that life has no meaning to it. Conversely, we know of others who are suddenly overwhelmed with anger, hate, and longings for revenge, and who want to explode and destroy the entire world. This knowledge is power—the power to grant or create empathy, to prepare the patient for what may yet come, to ensure the patient that their suffering is of phenomenal proportions, and, on the steadfast basis of its very phenomenality, to advise the patient as to what may alleviate the problem and that the problem may be overcome as a result. A young man who committed suicide in his mid-twenties expressed this experience succinctly in his diary entries for the last few days of his life. His family brought the young man's diary to me when they sought help following the tragedy. On a page dated one day prior to his suicide, there was a list of self-help instructions aimed at reestablishing his intense sense of lack of control:

- (Believe more in God) Have greater faith in God.
- Pray.
- Prepare a list every evening for the next day.
- Don't think about everything I do in a negative light.
- Seek out the positive.
- Speak with confidence.
- Recognize my worth.
- Read about how to gain self-confidence.
- Speak to Karen.
- Say what I think and don't hide anything.
- Remind myself that I took the right step when I left work.
- "If I am not for myself, who is for me"?
- Straighten up my room.
- Learn meditation in order to relax.

The list provokes compassion for the young man who tried with all his might to reinstate his life, to calm his inner turmoil, and find an inner sense of control once more. The list also reflected an attempt, typical of suicidal individuals, to escape this depression. This attempt is also quite strategic. By talking with his family, I understood that this entry was written in the few moments when the young man had actually felt a change for the better in his mood. It is possible to surmise that, like others who are depressed, he subsequently felt his mood reverse direction for no apparent reason. Most likely, his despair returned with a vengeance and overwhelmed him once more. It is typical of the depressed and suicidal state of mind that good feelings that the individual holds onto are merely temporary. They are slowly eroded from within and the mood quickly returns to despair. The constant vicissitudes, commonly known as "ups" and "downs," are wearying and interfere with any attempt to regain energy and start afresh. Each new descent is more painful than its predecessor. Over a period, these extreme fluctuations and the sudden sharp deterioration in mood become increasingly severe and are highly destructive. The emotional roller coaster and lack of stability are perhaps the most consistent experiences of severely depressed and suicidal patients. The belief that nothing can help restore peace and quiet begins to gradually penetrate the individual's consciousness. Eventually, the tranquil moments become ever more elusive and difficult to cling to. Ultimately, the despair that life in general and one's self in particular can never be restored to their previous state strike the individual down with full force. It is in this state of mind that suicide is attempted.

The therapist can communicate to the patient what they know about depression, despair, anxiety, the extreme fluctuations between hope and dread, the sense of loss of the self and of inner control, the doubts that eat away at the fragile balance attained, the mental pain, and the fear of losing one's sanity. The therapist can also share what they know about the thoughts that accompany this state, about the feelings regarding death and the perception of death. Clearly, this knowledge should not be presented as a lecture, but in the context of an empathic dialog.

What Does the Patient Know About His or Her Own Pain?

Each painful experience has its own inner course. Often the encounter with one's own pain and the acquaintance with its course can have a calming effect in and of itself by gaining a measure of control over it. I am not referring here to a theoretical understanding, but rather to the encounter with the patient's subjective experience. It is easier to cope with pain when it can be defined in a concrete and detailed form than in an amorphous, all-inclusive undefined state. Being able to foresee the "behavior" of the pain can give the patient a certain sense of control over it.

By sharing the patient's suffering, the therapist can guide and accompany the patient in their difficult journey. Patient and therapist can learn what happens when the patient is depressed, anxious, in panic, and despairing, what thoughts come to mind, how the world appears to them, what sets off the depression, how it progresses, what happens afterward, what the most difficult moments are, as well as if there are relatively more tolerable moments.

Eventually, therapist and patient learn about the internal and external triggers of the pain and of its development. It may become evident that the pain has its own distinctive behavior, that it does not come and go at random, nor is it not uncontrollable. Each person's pain has its own distinctive pattern and process, and can be monitored.

In many ways, suffering in itself constitutes a trauma. Not only does the person experience the depression itself, the despair, the wish to die, but quite often, they also respond to these experiences with a secondary response somewhat akin to the response to trauma. The despair is not just painful and dispiriting, its very existence is frightening and induces alarm. Likewise, the loss of self-confidence, suicidal urges of feeling trapped with no escape, all can be experienced as traumatic.

The therapeutic significance of the careful delineation and detailing of the painful subjective experience of the patient can be seen in the following example, a case of a depressed man who began to think about suicide. A careful inquiry into the suffering he felt with his depression enabled him to see, for example, that his difficulties in the morning were different from those in the evening, not only in intensity but also in quality. In the mornings, he mainly experienced great anxiety, in the evenings he experienced sadness, fatigue, and sometimes despair. In the course of his observations, he was surprised to discover that he actually managed to forget his suffering to a certain extent when he was immersed in his work. However, in the afternoon as his return home approached, a terrible sadness would descend on him and would progressively worsen throughout the evening. He noticed that the presence of his wife and children often made things difficult for him and was even oppressive at times. In this case, the difficulty was not in his intolerance of their company per se, rather their presence revived/elicited feelings of shame, guilt, and failure he experiences in his role/relationship with them. These feelings stem from his perceptions that he was not sufficiently attuned to their needs because he was a weak person. After careful observation, he realized that occupying himself on the weekends with cooking, his favorite hobby, also helped him forget and escape his distress for a while. This inner tour of his suffering and the distinctive course it followed during the week turned the all-encompassing and overwhelmingly frightening experience of his depression into a more familiar experience with its predictably alternating more and less difficult moments. He realized that his depression was of an oscillating nature.

This man also learned to recognize and distinguish between the more familiar feelings and experiences at times of sadness and pressures of life he had had in the past and the ones unique to his present state of depression. Most importantly, the inner tour helped him recognize the shame he felt, as well as his paralyzing fear of disappointing others. This, in turn, gave a clue to the meaning and source of his depression. The inner demon of his depression had been located, defined, and classified. By doing so, it had been given clearer and therefore more manageable dimensions with which to fight it and ease it off.

Encountering the Full Intensity of Mental Pain

In time, once the therapeutic trust is formed, therapy with suicidal patients requires facing their pain in its full intensity. I hold that suicidal longings cannot be fully treated without such an experience. There can be no short cuts or compromises. Mental pain is often compared to an abscess precisely because of the agonizing pain that is an unavoidable part of recovery. Part of the process is getting to the root of the pain and facing it. In the case of one patient, Diane (see Orbach, 2001), this process took the form of confrontation with her murderous aggression and her intense feelings of guilt. The climax of this process was expressed in Diane's eventual ability to ask herself, "Maybe I really caused my husband's suicide," and in our meticulous examination of her contribution to this suicide.

The emphasis of this therapeutic method is on the descent to the bottom of the abyss, to the place that holds the most pain for each individual. It is essential that the patient's encounter with such intense pain be a gradual process and one that also relies on their tempo and strength. However, I believe that the only way up and out of the abyss is via this exhaustive examination of the pain. This process can be defined as the confrontation of the patient with that which is the most terrifying for them. One particular patient of mine almost left therapy when he began to uncover the great rage within himself that he had for his beloved parents. He was simply unable to stand and face this rage head on. The process of cognitively recognizing the fact that he might actually be angry with his beloved parents was more than he could bear and truly shook him to the core.

At times this therapeutic process may necessitate the interaction of an empathic, direct, and even provocative approach. The therapist might conjecture, "So, you believe that without your mother you simply cannot exist," "without admiration you are simply a non-person," "deep down you feel that you are a murderer," "you believe that you are worth nothing." These direct interpretations actually reflect the patients' own convictions about themselves. In therapeutic reality, of course, this direct method is a much slower and more careful process than the way it is described here. It took Diane, for example, a very long time to realize that here murderous anger was the source of her greatest pain.

At this point, the therapist can take a softer, more healing attitude by questioning the patient's negative self-convictions. "Does this really mean that you are a murderer? A non-person? A total failure"? This direct but empathic confrontation and eventual intimate acquaintance with the pain, its meanings, and roots open up possibilities for a new internal organization within the individual.

Encountering the Roots of Suicidal and Self-Destructive Inclinations

Many suicides and suicidal longings have an extensive developmental history. The wish to die is not simply the product of a present crisis, but has deep roots in the past and gradually comes into realization. The individual plays an instrumental role in weaving the suicidal urges into a self-destructive and painful lifestyle. A major part of therapy is recognizing these self-destructive mechanisms and taking personal responsibility for suicide as a choice. Clearly, this step comes at a later stage in therapy.

I was treating a 16-year-old who came to therapy after he had shot himself. He acted following an argument with his parents and was only saved by a miracle. He identified the roots of his suicidal tendency during the period that he was a star pupil in elementary school. His personal road to self-destruction began when he deliberately failed in his studies in order to "save" his brother who was two years older and a failing student. The boy excelled in school and the teachers recommended that he be skipped to a higher grade. This would have shamed some of his best friends.

An important part of the mourning process is the separation from the inner representation of the lost entity. I often ask my patients if they have something to say to the lost part of their lives, if they want to converse with it, be angry at it, protest, or express their yearnings for it. If the patient is able to conduct such a dialog, then this is often a sign of the beginning of reconciliation.

There is also place in the dialog for more direct and active work of acceptance of the loss. The mourning helps the patient explore it and how it is possible to compromise, compensate, and change. In addition, it can give direction as to what has to happen in order to enable life to continue in spite of everything. In my opinion, the climax of the process of recovery from a loss is signaled by the ability to find new meaning in life. This idea will be elaborated further later under the following heading.

Restoring the Loss

If we truly succeed in understanding the suicidal patient's experience of loss, then we also hold in our hand the clue that can lead to the restoration of that loss. To help the patient find such an anchor, as therapists we need to employ deep insight toward the meaning and essence of the loss. The most striking example of this comes, not from my own experience, but from one of Meichenbaum's case histories (personal communication). This particular case is of a woman who came to him after having lost her young son in a gun accident. The woman was in a deep depression, tormented by terrible guilt, and could find no comfort. Moreover, she related that she felt that her son was calling her, that she wanted very badly to be reunited with him and had, in fact, decided to join him. Meichenbaum pondered for a while and then turned to the woman and said, "It is true that you sorely miss your son, and that you yearn to be with him more than anything and connect him to you by killing yourself. I know that you hear him calling you. However, although you can interpret this call as a call to join him in a real and concrete manner, he probably means something else, that he wants you to join him *in spirit*." At this point, Meichenbaum presented the woman with some statistics of the number of children in the world who are killed each year in firearm accidents, explaining, "If you could do something to reduce the number of innocent children who are killed in this tragic way that took your son, maybe this could be a way to be close to him." Consequently, the woman got up from the patient's chair and went out into the world to found an organization for the prevention of firearm accidents among children. By understanding the source of the woman's despair in her failed efforts to turn back the clock and save her son, Meichenbaum was able to show her a way to restore her loss through active coping that helped in reducing her despair, anguish, and longing for her son and eventually find new meaning in her life. I find Meichenbaum's approach different from that of Frankl. Meichenbaum offers a way of coping with the pain that can lead to new meaning. He does not merely provide a new perspective on the suffering.

The Gift That Is in Suffering

When the Boltons lost their adolescent son to suicide, they turned for help that very evening to a renowned psychiatrist in their city (Bolton, 1983). Immediately in the first meeting he dared to tell them that: "There is a gift for you in your son's death. You may not believe it at this bitter moment, but it is authentic and it can be yours if you are willing to search for it" (p. 16). The Boltons were confused by this statement, which seemed so inappropriate at that moment. What did that psychiatrist mean and why did he deem it proper to give them this message precisely at that difficult hour of their lives? In a personal account, the mother, Iris Bolton, allows the reader to share her experiences in her search for that gift, which in time she indeed began to uncover. She understood that her son had left the family an important message about life and about being aware of the limitations of our ability to control or plan everything for our loved ones. The parents accepted this gift with much pain.

In general, there is an appropriate moment to talk with the suicidal patient about the gift that is in suffering, loss, and depression, but there are also times when this could be counterproductive. Contrary to the Bolton's psychiatrist, I do not believe that this can or should be done at the apex of the pain, while it is still directly stabbing at the heart. However, later on, when the storm has calmed a little, it is of utmost importance to do so.

The suicidal crisis, depression, or any period of severe suffering constitutes a break in the continuity of life. It disrupts life goals and plans and causes disarray in our beliefs, hopes, and dreams. Yet in every such fissure, a gift can also be found, the gift of new understanding that comes from such a rift in our lives. In helping to find this gift, we help prevent the experiences of suffering from being superfluous and worthless. The gift can take many forms. It can be a new outlook on life, true maturity, increased understanding of others, the satisfaction of being able to withstand the suffering and survive it, or the ability to share and teach others what one has learned. Recognizing the gift in any hardship gives meaning to the suffering. It can turn weakness into strength, inferiority into pride, and the sense of helplessness into potency.

I present here only a single example from a young patient. I asked her if she could find any benefit in the fact that she had experienced terrible depression and had almost killed herself. Without hesitation, she answered in the affirmative.

Because of my depression and intense suffering, I had the courage for the first time ever to talk to my father as I had often wanted to but had never dared. I talked to him directly and without fear. Knowing that he would not hurt me because I suffered from my depression I was able to tell him what I thought about his male chauvinism, of his discrimination between his sons and daughters, and of his inappropriate tomfoolery at times. For the first ever, he remained silent and did not answer me. This was the best answer I have ever received from him.

CONCLUSION

This chapter has dealt with the role of meaning in life and death. There are many interpretations of meaning and meaninglessness. These range from experiencing life to its fullest versus estrangement, authenticity versus nothingness, responsibility for creative enjoyment versus failure to cope with basic life concerns, self-transcendence and value versus emptiness, vacuum, and inner chaos, fulfillment of basic needs versus painful dissatisfaction.

Some existentialists believe that meaning is critical to life and living, and that its absence may lead one to lose interest in life and commit suicide. Other interpreters of existential theory do not see meaning as being vital to life itself and emphasize the importance of need-fulfillment and security as being fundamental for the preservation of life.

On the basis of Baumeister's approach and similar approaches, I have made a distinction between low-order meaning and high-order meaning. Low-order meaning actually refers to a person's most important needs and specific goals that their fulfillment provides a sense of individuality, worth, and provides a sense of order in life. High-order meaning refers to a complex, integrative system of beliefs and values that transcends immediate life situations (e.g., a spiritual perspective).

According to the hypothesis in this chapter, lack of meaning does not cause suffering; rather, suffering is the cause of lack of meaning. When the low-order meaning is interrupted by traumatic life circumstances or inner mental disturbances, the suffering and pain are the motivating forces driving one to suicide and experiencing suffering. At this point, one is motivated to restore low-order meaning and to eliminate the pain by searching for high-order meaning as compensation.

This view implies that meaning in life can be restored only when the mental pain has eased off. Therefore, in order to avoid suicide caused by despair and anguish, the therapist has to find ways to help the suicidal person work through and cope with their mental pain in order to prevent suicide. Only when this has been accomplished to some degree can one find renewed meaning in life.

Several therapeutic principles are offered to help the suicidal individual cope with their pain. These include focusing on suffering from the therapist's and the patient's perspective, encountering the full intensity of the pain and the roots of self-destruction, restoration of the loss, and finding a gift in the suffering.

MAIN POINTS

1. There is a distinction between low-order meaning and high-order meaning. Low-order meaning refers to a person's most important needs and specific goals that provide a sense worth and individuality. High-order meaning refers to a complex, integrative system of beliefs and values that transcends immediate life situations (e.g., a spiritual perspective).
2. Lack of meaning does not cause suffering; rather, suffering is the cause of lack of meaning.
3. Meaning in life can be restored only when the mental pain has eased off. Therefore, in order to avoid suicide caused by despair and anguish, the therapist has to find ways to help the suicidal person work through and cope with his or her mental pain in order to prevent suicide.

REFERENCES

Antonovsky, A. (1979). *Health, stress and coping: New perspectives on mental and physical well being*. San Francisco: Jossey-Bass.

Antonovsky, A. O., & Sagy, S. (1990). Religiosity and well-being among retirees: A question of causality. *Behavior, Health, and Aging, 1*, 85–97.

Baumeister, R. (1991). *Meanings of life*. New York: Guilford Press.

Binswanger, L. (1958). The existential analysis school of thought. Insanity as life historical phenomenon and as mental disease: The case of Ilse. The case of Ellen West: An anthropological-clinical study. In R. May, E. Angle, & H. F. Ellenberger (Eds.), *Existence: A new dimension in psychiatry and psychology* (chaps. 7, 8, and 9). New York: Basic Books.

Binswanger, L. (1963). *Being in the world*. New York: Basic Books.

Bolger, E. A. (1999). Grounded theory analysis of emotional pain. *Psychotherapy Research, 9*, 342–362.

Bolton, I. (1983). *My son, my son*. Belmore, GA: Bolton Press.

Boss, M. (1963). *Psychoanalysis and daseins analysis*. New York: Basic Books.

Camus, A. (1965). The fall and exile of the kingdom. New York: Modern library.

Debats, D. L., Drost, J., & Hansen, P. (1995). Experiences of meaning in life: A combined qualitative and quantitative approach. *British Journal of Psychology, 86*, 359–375.

Ebersole, P. (1998). Types and depth of written life meanings. In P. T. Wong (Ed.), *The human quest for meaning* (pp. 179–191). Mahwah, NJ: Lawrence Erlbaum Associates.

Edwards, M. J., & Holden, R. R. (2001). Coping, meaning in life, and suicidal manifestations; Examining gender differences. *Journal of Clinical Psychology, 57,* 1517–1535.

Everall, R. D. (2000). The meaning of suicide attempts by young adults. *Canadian Journal of Counselling, 34,* 111–125.

Firestone, R. W. (1997). *Suicide and the inter voice.* London: Sage Publications.

Flannery, R. B., Perry, J. C., Penk, W. E., & Flannery, G. J. (1994). Validating Antonovsky's sense of coherence scale. *Journal of Clinical Psychology, 50,* 575–577.

Frankl, V. E. (1959). The spiritual dimension in existential analysis and logotherapy. *Journal of Individual Psychology, 3,* 157–165.

Frankl, V. E. (1963). *Man's search for meaning: An introduction to logotherapy.* Oxford, England: Washington Square Press.

Frankl, V. E. (1967). *Psychotherapy and existentialism.* New York: Washington Square Press.

Frankl, V. E. (1973). Encounter: The concept and its vulgarization. *Journal of the American Academy of Psychoanalysis, 1,* 73–83.

Frankl, V. E. (1975). Paradoxical intention and dereflection. *Psychotherapy: Theory, Research and Practice, 12,* 226–237.

Ganje-fling, M. A. (1996). Impact of childhood sexual abuse on client spiritual development: Counseling implications. *Journal of Counseling and Development, 74,* 253–258.

Harlow, L. L., Newcomb, M. D., & Benttler, P. M. (1986). Depression, self derogation, substance abuse, and suicidal ideation: Lack of purpose in life as a mediational factor. *Journal of Clinical Psychology , 42,* 5–21.

Hazzel, C. G. (1982). An empirical study of the experience of emptiness. *Dissertation Abstracts International, 43,* 1836.

Hazzel, C. G. (1984a). A scale for measuring experienced levels of emptiness and existential concern. *Journal of Psychology, 117,* 177–182.

Hazzel, C. G. (1984b). Experienced levels of emptiness and existential concern with different levels of emotional development and profile of values. *Psychological Reports, 55,* 967–976.

Hazzel, C. G. (1989). Levels of emotional development with experienced levels of emptiness and existential concern. *Psychological Reports, 64,* p. 838.

Higgins, E. T. (1989). Self-discrepancy theory: What patterns of self-beliefs cause people to suffer? In L. Berkowitz (Ed.), *Advances in experimental social psychology* (Vol. 22, pp. 93–136). San Diego, CA: Academic Press.

Jacobson, G. R., Ritter, D. P., & Mueller, L. (1977). Purpose in life and personal values among adult alcoholics. *Journal of Clinical Psychology, 33,* 314–316.

Janoff-Bulman, R., & Berger, A. R. (2000). The other side of trauma: Towards a psychology of appreciation. In J. H. Harvey (Ed.), *Loss and trauma: General and close relationship perspectives* (pp. 29–44). New York: Brunner Routledge.

Kinner, R. T., Metha, T. K., Keim, J. S. O., Okey, J. L., Adler–Tabiz, R. L., Berry, M. A. & Mulvenon, S. W. (1994). Depression, meaninglessness, and substance abuse in "normal" and hospitalized adolescents. *Journal of Alcohol and Drug Education, 39,* 101–111.

Klinger, E. (1998). The search for meaning in evolutionary perspective and its clinical implications. In P. T. Wong (Ed.), *The human quest for meaning* (pp. 27–50). Mahwah, NJ: Lawrence Erlbaum Associates.

Korotkov, D. L. (1998). The sense of coherence: Making sense out of chaos. In P. T. P. Wong & P. S. E. (Eds) *THe human quest for meaning: A handbook of Psychological research and clinical applications* (pp. 51–70). Mahwah, NJ: Lawrence Erlbaum Associates.

Lester, D., & Badro, S. (1992). Depression, suicidal preoccupation and purpose in life in a subclinical population. *Personality and Individual Differences, 13*, 75–76.

Maddi, S. R. (1998). Creating meaning through making decisions. In P. T. Wong (Ed.), *The human quest for meaning* (pp. 3–26). Mahwah, NJ: Lawrence Erlbaum Associates.

Maltsberger, J. T. E., & Goldblatt, M. J. E. (1996). *Essential papers on suicide.* New York: New York University Press.

Maltsberger, J. T. E. (2000). Case consultation: Mansur Zaskar: A man almost bored to death. *Suicide and Life Threatening Behavior, 30*, 83–90.

Man, F., Stuchlikova, I., & Klinger, E. (1998). Motivational structure of alcoholic and nonalcoholic Czech men. *Psychological Reports, 82(3, Part 2)*, 1091–1106.

Moberg, P. J., & Lazarus, L. W. (1990). Psychotherapy of depression in the elderly. *Psychiatric Annals, 20*, 92–96.

Murray, H. A. (1938). *Explorations in personality: a clinical and experimental study of fifty men of college age.* Oxford, England: Oxford University Press.

Newcomb, M. D., & Harlow, L. L. (1986). Life events and substance use among adolescents: Mediating effects of perceived loss of control and meaninglessness in life. *Journal of Personality and Social Psychology, 51*, 564–577.

Orbach, I. (1988). *Children who don't want to live.* San Francisco: Jossey-Bass.

Orbach, I. (2001). Therapeutic empathy with the suicidal wish: Principles of therapy with suicidal individuals. *American Journal of Psychotherapy, 55*, 166–184.

Orbach, I. (2003). Mental pain and suicide. *Israel Journal of Psychiatry, 40(3)*, 91–201.

Orbach, I., Mikulincer, M., & Gilboa-Schechtman, E. (2003). Mental pain and its relationship to suicidality and life meaning. *Suicide and Life Threatening Behavior, 33(3)*, 231–241.

Orbach, I., Mikulincer, M., Gilboa-Schechtman, E., & Sirota, P. (2003). Mental pain: A multidimensional operationalization and definition. *Suicide and Life Threatening Behavior, 33(3)*, 219–230.

Petrie, K., & Azariah, R. (1990). Health-promoting variables as predictors of responses to a brief pain management program. *Clinical Journal of Pain, 6*, 43–46.

Petrie, K. & Brook, R. (1992). Sense of coherence, self-esteem, depression and hopelessness as correlates of reattempting suicide. *British Journal of Clinical Psychology, 31*, 293–300.

Rogers, J. R. (2001). Theoretical grounding: The "missing link" in suicide research. *Journal of Counseling and Development, 79*, 16–25.

Rychlak, J. F. (1973). *Introduction to personality and psychotherapy: A theory-construction approach.* Oxford, England: Houghton Mifflin.

Ryff, C. D., & Singer, B. (1998). The role of purpose in life and personal growth in positive human health. In P. T. Wong (Ed.), *The human quest for meaning* (pp. 213–235). Mahwah, NJ: Lawrence Erlbaum Associates.

Sartre, J. P. (1956). *Being and nothingness.* New York: Philosophical library.

Schnyder, U., Valach, L., Bichsel, K., & Michel, K. (1999). Attempted suicide: Do we understand the patients' reasons? *General Hospital Psychiatry, 21*, 62–69.

Shek, D. T. (1992). Meaning in life and psychological well-being: An empirical study using the Chinese version of the Purpose in Life questionnaire. *Journal of Genetic Psychology, 153*, 185–200.

Shneidman, E. S. (1993). *Suicide as psychache: A clinical approach to self-destructive behavior.* Northvale, NJ: Jason Aronson.

Shneidman, J. L. (1985). Psychohistory: Expanding the parameters of historical causality. *Journal of Psychohistory, 12(3)*, 353–361.

Styron, W. (1990). *Darkness visible.* New York: Random House.

Verkes, R. J., Van der Mast, R. C., Kerkhof, A. J. F. M., Fekkes, D., Hengeveld, M. W., Tuyl, J. P., et al. (1998). Platelet serotonin, monoamine oxidase activity, and [-sup-3H] paroxetine binding related to impulsive suicide attempts and borderline personality disorder. *Biological Psychiatry, 43,* 740–746.

Wong, P. T. P. (1998). Meaning-centered counseling. In P. T. Wong (Ed.), *The human quest for meaning: A handbook of psychological research and clinical applications* (pp. 395–435). Mahwah NJ: Lawrence Erlbaum Associates.

Yalom, I. D. (1980). *Existential psychotherapy.* New York: Basic Books.

Regret Therapy: Coping with Death and End of Life Issues

Mary Beth Mannarino
Chatham College

Grafton T. Eliason
California University of Pennsylvania

Jayna Rubin
Chatham College

Make the most of your regrets; never smother your sorrow, but tend and cherish it till it comes to have a separate and integral interest. To regret deeply is to live afresh.

—Henry David Thoreau

Death involves loss. With one's own death comes the loss of one's self, and with the death of a loved one comes the loss of other. The loss of self or other is one of the most significant trials that a human faces, and often requires one to draw upon spiritual resources in the effort to make sense of the experience. Loss of self or other is a major transition that leads many toward contemplation of life's big questions: What was the life worth? Did it have meaning for oneself or others? Was it a good and satisfying life? Was the self or person valued or valuable?

When asking these existential questions, humans must confront the fact that real lives fall short of the ideal, by a little or by a lot. Humans, with their fallibility and imperfection, make mistakes or bad choices, commit transgressions, miss opportunities, and fail to achieve dreams and goals. With the end of one's own or another's life in mind, faced with the reality that life does eventually end, a person may look back on mistakes and unrealized hopes, and experience regret. Regret occurring near the end of one's own life or upon the loss of another can present unique challenges. How the regret is managed can significantly affect the quality of one's life and one's sense of life's meaning.

In this chapter, we explore regret related to death, dying, and loss from our perspectives as psychologists and counselors. We build on Landman's (1993) seminal work on regret and on Tomer and Eliason's (1996) model of death anxiety to develop a counseling approach for clients who are experiencing regret related to loss of self or other. We propose that it is possible for individuals to move from loss-related regret toward experiences of hope, joy, and enhanced personal meaning.

Our discussion begins with an exploration of the concept of regret, then follows with a discussion of how regret may be related to death anxiety. We then move to a description of our approach to working with clients who are dealing with loss-related regret.

PORTRAIT OF REGRET

Description of Regret

We have often encountered many clients who express intense regret about some aspect of their life. What exactly is regret? In common terms, regret is the experience one has when realizing that life did not, or will not, turn out as one had hoped. From a more scholarly viewpoint, Janet Landman (1993) portrays regret as a very complex construct involving many other concepts. In her book, *Regret: The Persistence of the Possible,* she provides a comprehensive review of the concept of regret through the perspectives of philosophy, economics, religion, theology, psychology, and literature.

First, regret is both a feeling and a thought, both *felt thought* and *reasoned emotion* (Landman, 1993, p. 45). A person who regrets cognitively recognizes a discrepancy between a goal or aspiration, and the reality of what exists. For example, a person may think, "It was a bad decision to drop out of college. I am now not able to get the job that I could otherwise have." The person who regrets also feels a sorrowful emotion related to the discrepancy, wishing that the gap between dreams and reality did not exist. The same person described earlier may report feeling sad, hopeless, or even angry at herself that her decision resulted in a lack of occupational opportunities.

In addition, regret has content—the matter that is regretted. The individual described previously regrets a particular decision—the decision to drop out of college before earning a degree. The regrets of other people may involve different content. Research sheds light on the matters that most commonly cause Americans to experience regret. Much of the empirical research on regret has examined individuals' feelings about actions taken or not taken with regard to financial opportunities. For example, a question often asked is whether or not people regret having made a decision (action) that resulted in loss of money more or less than having not made a decision (inaction) that would have resulted in financial gain. Although such economic dilemmas are frequent topics of study, they do not necessarily reflect the content of the most common regrets voiced by American people. The content areas of regret most commonly reported are, in order of decreasing frequency, education, work, marriage and family, and other relationships (Landman, 1993).

Landman (1993) also notes that regret may have different agents: it can be experienced in relation to one's own actions or thoughts, to the actions or thoughts of another person or group, or to simple circumstance. Thus, while one individual regrets his own decision to marry at a young age, another person may regret how the particular actions of a family member hurt him/her. Still another may regret the life of mental and physical disability that they must lead in the aftermath of a war, a circumstance beyond his control. Regret may also be related to the past or to the future, an idea that we will return to shortly (Landman, 1993; Tomer & Eliason, 2000). In addition, regret may or may not be related to legal or moral issues.

Landman (1993) further demonstrates the complexity of regret when she describes it as "a superordinate concept that subsumes certain defining features of disappointment, sadness, remorse, and guilt, but ... can also be distinguished from these" (p. 56). Indeed, we have found that individuals who seek counseling often describe very complex and intertwined feelings and thoughts that, when finally unraveled, lead to regret. Based on such work with clients, we would, however, also add shame and anger to the list of experiences related to regret.

Landman (1993) asserts that regret is often incorrectly seen as interchangeable with one or more of the other experiences described previously. She compares regret with each of the other emotions and thoughts, concluding that regret is indeed the superordinate concept. For more detailed discussions of the relationship between these concepts, the reader is referred to chapter two of Landman's book.

Regret About the Past and Future

As noted previously, regret may be related to the past or to the future. Regret is probably most often thought of in terms of actions (commissions) or inactions (omissions) of the past. We often hear from regretting clients a litany of "If only I hadn't" and "I coulda, shoulda, woulda." Such sentiments indicate that the client wishes to undo or to have undone whatever has passed, in order to yield a better outcome. When reading the following examples of past-related regret, keep in mind the complex nature of the regret in terms of related feelings, thoughts, content, and agent:

- I did not spend enough time with my family, depriving them and myself of love. (omission)
- I never told my mother how much I loved and respected her before she died. (omission)
- I said hurtful things to my spouse and we never reconciled before he died. (commission)
- I decided to be a business person even though I was never happy with this career choice. (commission)

Regret can also be related to the future. Sometimes called anticipatory regret, future-related regret refers to the realization that, for any number of reasons, certain hopes for the future will not be fulfilled. Some examples of future-related regret follow:

- Because I am in prison, my son will never have a full-time father.
- Because of my illness, I will not live to be a grandparent.
- My husband has died and our children will grow up without him in their lives.
- Our daughter's serious illness means that she will not be able to achieve her dreams of attending college.

It should be noted that, in the examples of past- and future-related regret listed previously, each type of regret may be related to the other. That is, a person may experience future-related regret because of mistakes made in the past. It is not always simple to label an individual's regret as one type or another. According to Tomer and Eliason (1996), however, regret of either type may have a relationship to death anxiety.

Outcomes of Regret

What happens with regret experienced either during daily life or when facing death or loss? Regret can have positive or negative outcomes. In common language, phrases such as "No use crying over spilt milk" and "What's done is done" imply that regret can be nonproductive, a waste of time and energy. Regret can be viewed even more negatively than simply nonproductive. The experience of regret can be quite distressing and may lead a person to seek counseling or psychotherapy. Individuals may seek help because of regret about missed opportunities in relationships or work, about poor choices made in the past, about the loss of dreams for the future, or about betrayals of others.

We have found that regret is often accompanied by anxiety and distress. Some people become so mired in their regret that their ruminations actually interfere with growth. For many individuals, the focus on regret can become all-consuming and can impair healthy functioning in daily living. The preoccupation with past- or future-related regret limits a person's ability to experience, appreciate, and live in the present, and interferes with the process of flow, or optimal functioning (Csikszentmihalyi, 1990). Further, a person who is consumed with regret, and related feelings of guilt, shame, or anger, may experience an existential despair about one's life, a sense of purposelessness, and a loss of meaning (Erikson, 1963, 1982; Tomer & Eliason, 1996).

Some studies support the view that regret is at times a negative or nonproductive experience. For example, Lecci, Okun, and Karoly (1994) explored life regrets and current goals as predictors of psychological adjustment, asking if a gap between what happened in the past and one's current goals is related to psychological adjustment. Lecci et al. found that the discrepancy between one's past desired goal state, about which one has regret, and the person's current goals sometimes interfered with one's current level of goal functioning, or one's ability to work toward a planned future. In addition, a study of mid-life reviews made by women found that many of the middle-aged women were not able to use examination of life regrets to motivate goal setting for the future: "regret alone is insufficient to bring about actual life changes, just as external barriers are insufficient to prevent them"

(Stewart & Vandewater, 1999, p. 21). Regret may or may not be followed by psychological reorganization or planning for the future.

Several approaches to the treatment of emotional problems, such as existential, psychotherapy, logotherapy, gestalt therapy, rational emotive therapy, and cognitive behavioral therapy, recognize the negative effects of a preoccupation with regret. These treatment approaches are based in part on helping individuals learn to correct or challenge feelings or thoughts of regret that are interfering with life. The elimination of regret and its effects may also be a goal for the general public, apart from those who have been identified as having emotional or psychiatric disorders. For example, when the word *regret* was typed into the search engine of a major online bookstore, nine of the first ten books that were listed provided spiritual, religious, or psychological advice for preventing or overcoming regret and its effects.

Regret can also have positive outcomes, serving important functions for both individuals and societies by providing useful information about our behaviors and choices (Landman, 1993). Pragmatically, acknowledging and examining regret is one way in which both individuals and societies learn from their mistakes and become mobilized to make things right in the present or not to make the same mistake in the future. The process of dealing with regret may also have ethical benefits:

> Regardless of how bad are the regretted matters, genuine regret signifies that you have standards of excellence, decency, morality, or ethics you still care about—a good thing in itself. In addition, remaining in connection with your better values through regret can further the purpose of moving you to behave differently if a similar situation should present itself in the future. (Landman, 1993, p. 26)

Examining one's regrets can be extremely important for selfhood, potentially leading one toward a life of greater integrity and connecting the individual "with values that are part of what make him or her humane" (Landman, 1993, p. 28).

Regret acknowledged and dealt with can move an individual beyond guilt, shame, disappointment, and sadness. Many of our clients have delved deeply into regretful feelings and thoughts and, in encounters with themselves, other people, or a higher power, have experienced authentic remorse about the fact that things are not as they would wish. There is often a recognition and acceptance of one's own and others' humanity and fallibility, so that clients can eventually experience repentance or reconciliation. Regret can become a catalyst for personal transformation—for emotional, interpersonal, and spiritual growth.

Thus, regret can have both liabilities and benefits, depending in part on the individual's own perceptions and reactions. Viewing regret as related to a person's own experiences is important. Regret is individually and subjectively experienced, "defined not by events or choices, but by the person's experience of the choice and the desire to go back and change the decision" (Lucas, 2004, p. 65). The regret experienced by one individual may not be understood by another. In discussing the subjective nature of regret about one's own actions or inactions, Lucas states:

> Existential regret is expressed as a profound desire and aching to go back and change a past experience in which one has failed to consciously choose or made a choice which did not follow one's beliefs, values, or growth needs. It is a painful blending of existential anxiety and existential guilt … the object of regret is an experience in which one failed to make a conscious, whole-hearted choice and instead made a choice in a moment of bad faith or lack of authentic presence and subjectivity. One's sense, then, is of having abandoned and betrayed the self. (p. 59)

From this perspective, regret is related to an individual's meaning of life. For clients, regret may be associated with an individual's experience of living incongruently or inauthentically (Rogers, 1951). When such regret is present at the end of someone's life, how it is dealt with, how it is recognized, understood, or resolved, may influence the quality of dying and loss experiences.

Limitations of Research About Regret

There is still much to be learned about the concept of regret, particularly as it relates to our concerns with death, dying, or loss. First, it should be noted that the study of regret has been hampered by subjects' hesitancy to admit to the mistakes or misjudgments associated with regretful feelings and thoughts (Landman, 1993). In addition, most studies about regret have been done with people who are presumably alive and well. Relevance of the findings for the dying and bereaved populations must therefore be carefully considered.

It is also important to recognize that many studies about the content of regret have involved open-ended questions. Perhaps surprisingly, regret about death—the inevitability that it will occur and will bring with it loss and pain—is seldom mentioned by participants in such studies. Death awareness may nevertheless be present when individuals think about their life regrets: "If lives did not end, then mistakes and losses and limitations could always be repaired later" (Landman, 1993, p. 99). There would then be no need for regret.

We have described the complexity of regret—its nature, associated feelings, related concepts, varied content, and positive and negative outcomes. The experience of regret, in all its complexities, has important existential implications. Next we explore regret that is experienced when death has become salient and the effects of the regret on one's personal life journey.

REGRET RELATED TO LOSS OF SELF OR OTHER

In their comprehensive model of death anxiety, Tomer and Eliason (1996) found that there are "three direct determinants of death anxiety: past-related regret, future-related regret, and meaningfulness of death" (pp. 345–346). Tomer and Eliason also note that death anxiety may increase as death becomes more salient, as one faces one's own death or the loss of another. Our counseling work with clients supports this view.

Regret related to the end of life takes on a particular poignancy. In daily life, with no death looming, we may operate under the assumption that there will always be an opportunity to make changes, repent for our wrongs, or reconcile with those who have hurt us or whom we have hurt. When one's own death or the death of another is imminent, this assumption falls apart. The dying person begins to sense the foreshortened future, to realize that anything that needs to happen must happen now or in the very near future. Loved ones also realize that they have a limited amount of time left to interact face-to-face with the person who is dying, and thus have a limited amount of time to resolve any issues about which there is regret. When the loss of another has already occurred, the bereaved person recognizes that there is no longer the opportunity to interact with the deceased, and that unfinished business related to regret must be dealt with in other ways.

Loss of Self

Regret related to loss of self or other can take on many guises. For the person who is dying, regret can underlie the external appearances of sadness, guilt, disappointment, shame, ruminations about the past, or withdrawal. Physical pain that is unrelieved by medication and other palliative measures may also be a manifestation of unresolved regret.

Regret in a dying person may be difficult to identify. The dying person or loved ones may sense the presence of sorrow, but may not recognize or be able to articulate the underlying experience of regret. With our clients, we have found that, even if all the individuals involved recognize that regret is contributing to a dying person's emotional and physical pain, they may be hesitant to address the issue. They may understand at some level that discussion of life regret will most likely evoke anxiety and may thus be reluctant to do anything that would add to the dying person's or their own discomfort.

Furthermore, when regret is recognized and brought to the forefront, the dying person or loved ones may not know what to do with it. Platitudes such as "Don't worry about it. It doesn't matter now" or "Well, nothing can be changed. We all do the best we can" are often offered in an attempt to alleviate everyone's discomfort. Such comments, may, however, actually foreclose the dying or grieving person's opportunity to learn and grow from the experience, and to face the loss of self or another with greater peace than would otherwise be possible.

Loss of Other

Regret may wear many faces for the bereaved person as well. Grief itself is very complex, involving ever changing mixtures of sadness, anger, guilt, fear, and relief. Regret related to the loss of someone can further complicate the grieving process. Grieving persons with whom we have worked experience depression, anxiety, anger, guilt, avoidance, withdrawal, concentration problems, or somatic complaints, but they seldom connect the symptoms to experiences of regret. Again, even if regret is articulated, the bereaved may fear that looking at it too closely will be more painful than avoiding it. The grieving person may also think, "What's the use of even thinking about this? Nothing can be changed."

Other Questions

Finally, individuals experiencing regret related to loss of self or another are often struggling with questions related to life's meaning. The questions are asked whether the regret is related to one's own actions or inactions or to the behaviors of another. We have seen with our clients that with regret come questions about one's own self—about one's integrity, worth, and goodness.

What can we learn from empirical studies about death, dying, regret, and related issues? As mentioned earlier, Tomer and Eliason (1996), in research that led to a comprehensive model of death anxiety, found that the presence of past- or future-related regret was positively correlated with death anxiety. Pessin, Rosenfeld, and Breitbart (2002) concluded that "the presence of psychological distress, even to a mild to moderate level, can have a significant effect on the patient in the last weeks of life … a decrease in their capacity for pleasure, sense of meaning in their lives, and an ability to make connections with others" (p. 357). "Psychiatric symptoms can also lead to heightened distress and worry among friends and family members, possibly leading to a downward spiral as family distress further fuels patient distress" (Block, as cited in Pessin et al., 2002, p. 358). Fishman (1992) found that, with older adults, a relationship exists between death anxiety and life review, which often involves dealing with issues of regret: the greater depth to the life review, the lower the death anxiety.

Many qualitative researchers have also addressed questions related to death, dying, and regret. Hermann (2001), from her interviews with dying patients, found that dying individuals have several different types of spiritual needs, including the following: need for involvement and control, need for a positive outlook, need to experience nature, need for companionship, need for religion, and need to resolve unfinished business. The last of these needs, the need to resolve unfinished business, is related in part to regret and refers to a person's desire to do a life review, to finish life tasks, to come to terms with the present situation, and to deal with incongruent feelings. Hermann describes one interviewee's situation: she "spoke of being divorced from her first husband for years but harboring ill feelings toward him throughout her life … She recently talked with him and resolved the bitter feelings, saying that was the only way she was going to find the peace she needed before dying" (p. 71).

Sherman (2001) conducted another qualitative study, attempting to gain insight into the experience of living with and dying from AIDS. She found that patients with AIDS experience "psychosocial suffering with shattered dreams and a move toward self-acceptance, and spiritual suffering with the opportunity for renewal" (p. 7). Sherman provides quotes from study participants, including "My dreams were shattered—no one wants me in this situation. I am doomed" and "My life will never be what it was. I had a profession and I had friends, and now I have nothing." (p. 11) Other patients revealed that they experienced self-hate and self-disgust following their diagnosis. Sherman notes that many patients are able to work through these regrets and negative feelings in constructive ways: "I have a whole lifestyle I'm changing, that's evolving into something that I am proud of. I now have a life worth living" and "Your mind does playback of what you did to get the disease, but now I've learned to accept myself, and I'm more at peace" (p. 12). Finally, Sherman concludes that, for some, "the diagnosis of AIDS led to greater personal and spiritual strength ... or to a heightened sense of closeness to God" (p. 12). In still another qualitative study of feelings and thoughts of terminally ill people, Wright (2003) describes one common reaction of dying people—many terminally ill people and their caretakers not only develop a complex relationship with the ideas of death and dying, but also often move to a position of *carpe diem*, of living their lives differently, in the present, and of confronting regrets that cause distress.

We have found, however, that each client is unique. Both Wright (2003) and Feil (1985) caution against simplistic assumptions about the needs of the dying person with regard to regret. Wright notes that "for many years, normative ideas of coping have served as an illusory cure all: If we can simply help people progress to acceptance or resolution, somehow death will be more palatable—for both the dying and for us. Unfortunately, many people have embraced these notions such that any other response by the dying becomes problematic" (p. 452). Feil, in her work with older people in institutions, describes how expecting or attempting to force dying individuals to confront any aspect of reality, such as regret, may be very harmful and/or inappropriate for many individuals. Many of the older people with whom Feil has worked have ended their days at peace with feet firmly planted in the past. With these thoughts in mind, we will move to our discussion of how we might help people who are dealing with loss-related regret.

REGRET THERAPY

In the following section, we describe our own approaches for helping those facing loss of self or other. Before moving into specific ideas about such work, however, we first explore the following question: given that death and dying are universal experiences that have existed since the beginning of humankind, what role can practitioners of counseling and psychotherapy, relatively young professions, play in this drama?

Historical Perspective

Viewing death and dying from historical, sociological, and cultural perspectives is essential. As noted by Neimeyer, Prigerson, and Davies (2002):

> Grief as a human experience is both a natural and constructed event. On one hand, core features of our responses to loss reflect our evolution as biological and social beings, rooted in the disruption of attachment bonds required for our very survival. On the other hand, we respond to bereavement at symbolic as well as biological levels, imputing significance to the symptoms of separation that we experience as well as the changes in personal and collective identity that accompany the death of a member of our family or broader community. (p. 235)

For centuries, well before the advent of mental health professionals, humans used many resources for help with concerns related to death and dying. People relied upon family members, friends, other community members, medical professionals, and clergy. People also depended on religion-based rituals and ceremonies for support when dealing with death. No mental health professionals, per se, were involved; indeed, such professions did not exist until recently. An examination of cultural, social, and medical changes will help us understand how mental health professionals have come to play a role in helping people with death and dying.

Let us begin with the picture of the United States at the beginning of the twentieth century, very early in the development of the mental health profession. At that time, average life expectancy was less than 50 years. About 80% of the people in the United States who died did so at home, surrounded by family and friends, amidst familiar sights, sounds, and smells. Family members could prepare favorite foods for a dying person, bathe and clothe the person, and attempt in other ways to meet the person's very personal and individual needs. Loved ones could visit frequently. Even young children could spend time with the person who was dying. In the home, there was ample opportunity for the dying person, if so inclined, to spontaneously reflect upon one's history, to express fears, worries, or anxieties, and to share other thoughts with loved ones. In the stories told, the dying person was able to contemplate regret, as well as other feelings and thoughts, with people who were meaningful in that person's life. In the unstructured and open-ended atmosphere of the home, resolutions and reconciliations could easily and naturally flow in conversations between the dying person and loved ones, and life's meaning could be discerned. Even after death, family members or close friends were involved in bathing and dressing the dead person's body, and preparing it for a viewing, also likely to take place at home. Often, family members dug the grave or lowered the coffin into the ground (Corr, Corr, & Nabe, 2002).

By 1996, life expectancy had increased to over 76 years and about 80% of Americans who died did so in an institution of some type, such as a hospital or a long-term care facility. There are many reasons for these changes, including improved medical and health care, life-prolonging technology (located in institutional settings), increased mobility, geographic separation of family members, fewer women being available in the home to be full-time caregivers, and smaller families. Professional caregivers typically perform the basic care tasks for a dying person, such as feeding, bathing, and dressing, which were formerly completed by loved ones. Today, while family members may be present at death, the chances are also that they will not. Professionals are often the ones present (if any one is) when a death occurs. After death, professionals are the ones who prepare the body for viewing, often, ironically, presenting a body that is as life-like as possible. Professionals also coordinate and execute funeral arrangements. Although loved ones are of course involved with the professionals in making funeral plans, a primary aim during the funeral planning process is to protect the family from the distress associated with death by having professionals deal with the details (Corr et al., 2002).

One result of the changes described previously is that the role of a person in a family member's dying and death has become more of a spectator than a participating caregiver. When the dying person is removed from the home to an institutional setting that has specific hours of visitation, family members have limited time with one another. There are fewer opportunities for relaxed stories about life, feelings, dreams, and wishes, or regrets and sorrows. Indeed, in a culture that has become increasingly mobile, secular, and impersonal, there may not even be a recognition that such sharing is desirable and valuable, or that the sharing might in fact lead to growth, greater connectedness, and profound meaning for all involved (Corr et al., 2002).

Another result of the cultural and medical changes over the last century is simply that people are living longer. Longer lives bring more time to accomplish goals, more time to make mistakes or to experience broken dreams, and a longer time to live with loss and regret.

Finally, the changes have led to increased involvement of mental health professionals in helping people deal with dying and death, for many reasons. Families today do not necessarily have the internal support, geographic proximity, or history necessary for working through complicated issues about dying and death. In addition, fewer people are integrally involved with religious institutions or clergy, who might otherwise provide much of the needed support. Communities are more fragmented, and are not always able to be primary supports at times of need. Thus, mental health professionals have entered the picture.

With the unique expertise of counselors and psychologists in mind, let us examine how we as professionals have worked with clients dealing with issues of loss-related regret.

Assumptions of Work With Clients

As counselors and psychologists, we come to our work with the dying and bereaved with certain assumptions in mind. We believe that each human is born with unique potential for growth and possesses a drive toward actualization of this potential. Further, movement toward or away from actualization shapes one's personal life meaning (Frankl, 1984; Langle, 2004). We also believe that individuals have varying degrees of awareness about this journey toward self-actualization. There are differences in individuals' abilities to understand and articulate how their responses to life's obstacles might affect their perceptions of their own worth and life meaning.

Although our work with clients involves helping them to think and behave in more positive ways in their daily lives, our work is also directed toward the ultimate goal of helping them to appreciate their own worth and personal meaning through their struggles and growth. We believe, along with others, that existential anxiety can stimulate growth and change (Frankl, 1984; Langle, 2004). Personal meaning is "a complex achievement of the human spirit ... found in the individual's confrontation with the challenges of the world and one's own being" (Langle, 2004, p. 28). Frankl (cited in Langle, 2004) further discusses personal meaning:

> [E]xistential meaning is never arbitrary nor is it a construction, if it is supposed to give structure and support to one's life. Such a meaning must be based on given facts, must be hewn out of reality and cannot be changed deliberately ... We do not just attach and attribute meanings to things, but rather find them; we do not invent them, we detect them. (p. 28)

At the same time we note that each individual's path toward resolution and personal meaning will be unique (Wright, 2003; Feil, 1985).

When one experiences regret at the time of loss of self or other, regret can become the challenge that, when confronted, moves one through remorse and/or forgiveness toward realization of personal meaning.

Theories and Techniques

Our work with clients who are struggling with loss-related regret involves integration of theories and approaches from many sources. We always keep in mind the primary goal of helping clients place their own experiences within a larger context that allows for healthier perspectives and for the development of a sense of meaning and hope, even in the face of loss.

Relationship Issues. Basic to our work with such clients is the important step of establishing a positive and trusting relationship, characterized by empathy, respect, openness, warmth, unconditional positive regard, genuineness, and congruence in our interactions (see Rogers, 1951). We listen empathically; indeed, we try to listen more than talk. Sometimes simply being listened to is the primary healing experience for our clients. In addition, our work with clients involves a relationship that is collaborative, rather than hierarchical, in nature. Finally, we treat clients as individual human beings in unique contexts, not as diagnoses, illnesses, or other objects.

Our comments about the importance of establishing a productive therapeutic relationship may appear obvious to some. We have chosen to emphasize these ideas because we have found that many factors impacting our work may make this essential task difficult. As a result, we must continually call our attention back to this basic principle. First, the tendency for health care systems to *medicalize* human suffering and pain of all kinds compels us to strive to see beyond particular medical or diagnostic issues to the person beneath. Second, the structure and practice of health care delivery systems often do not allow for the time that is necessary to develop the therapeutic relationship so essential for healing to take place. In addition, we struggle with cultural practices and perspectives about people who experience emotional problems or mental illness. Such perspectives and practices often lead to negative judgment and condescension toward suffering people. There are also cultural proscriptions against suffering and pain, and for easy and quick alleviation of suffering and pain, as well as denial of the value of these experiences for many people. Finally, there are innate human tendencies to avoid pain and suffering, even when it is recognized at some level that healing through pain and suffering can strengthen an individual and enhance the person's life meaning. We keep all of these issues in mind as we try to establish a good working relationship with our clients.

Client Issues. In addition to our desire to provide a safe therapeutic relationship for all clients, we also strive to understand what is unique about each client's experience. When faced with regret at times of dying, death, and loss, each person has a unique manner of coping. Some people may adopt internal coping strategies, which are related to their beliefs about themselves and/or beliefs about the world. They may examine and revise or strengthen these beliefs to help them resolve the regret in healthy or unhealthy ways. Spiritual beliefs, as well as internal cognitive schema about self, others, and the world, are often relied upon at these times. Others use external coping strategies to help them reduce the anxiety associated with loss-related regret. Examples of external strategies include, on the one hand, religious practices, such as prayer, church attendance, journaling, talking and socializing with others, exercise, recreational activities, and, on the other hand, substance abuse, withdrawal, and aggressive or vengeful behavior.

Coping strategies for dealing with loss-related regret can be healthy or unhealthy, depending upon each individual's history and unique circumstances. The individuals who approach mental health professionals for help in dealing with loss and regret are typically using unhealthy or nonproductive strategies for coping and are also experiencing very complex emotions and thoughts. Psychologists and counselors, who have specialized training in helping people cope with both crises and normal life transitions, have thus become necessary supports for many individuals and families who are dealing with issues related to dying, death, and loss.

Developmental Issues. It is important to note that children and adolescents are not exempt from feelings of regret related to dying and/or to the loss of a loved one. Efforts to help children cope with death have been influenced by the widely held assumption that children cannot fully understand the concept of death, and that, even if they do, it would be harmful for them to be exposed to information about death (Kastenbaum & Costa, 1977). Consequently, parents and professionals alike have often felt it best to shield young children from the experience of death. Worden (2002) reminds us, however, that most significant losses occur within the context of the family unit and that it is important to consider the effect of a death on the entire family system. The impact of death and loss, and the consequent feelings, should not be ignored in children. Rather, their thoughts, feelings, and concerns need to be addressed in order for successful coping to occur. The challenge of working with children in the arena of loss-related regret is that each individual child will comprehend death differently and understand the finality of death to a varying degree. In the absence of direct experience with death, the development of a mature concept of death seems to depend to some extent on cognitive development, which typically varies systematically with age (Schroeder & Gordon, 2002). We propose, in addition, that regret experiences may be linked, at least in part, to cognitive development. For example, a very young child may feel regret, or more complex distorted thoughts such as guilt or self-blame, related to loss of a parent. The regret may, however, be closely related to the child's magical thinking and egocentric perspective. Thus, therapists who are working with children must be sensitive to the overall developmental level of their client, as well as to the cognitive comprehension of death and the understanding of its significance.

When working with children in a therapeutic setting that facilitates coping with death and dying, open and honest communication is essential. As is true for any stressful event, helping children cope by providing them with information is a process that is carried out over time, rather than a one-time intervention (Schroeder & Gordon, 2002). Furthermore, therapists need to explore familial circumstances, including psychological adjustment of the child prior to the death, the child's relationship with the ill or deceased, the functioning of the primary caregiver, the amount of stress experienced, and the available social supports, all in connection to the child's cognitive understanding of death.

Finally, we believe that therapists should be open to exploring their own ideas with regard to a child's potential for spiritual or existential growth. Two examples of young people who grew through loss and regret come to mind, one current and one historical. Mattie Stepanek died at 13 years following a lifetime with a complex type of muscular dystrophy. He lost three siblings who died of the same disease. He also watched his mother develop a mild form of muscular dystrophy.

Mattie knew his future was limited. At a very young age, he became a poet and, in his own words, an *ambassador for peace*. Although he expressed regret related to his losses and his muscular dystrophy, he also transformed these existential experiences, by communicating with the world about muscular dystrophy, life, heaven, God, gratitude, love, and hope (Stepanek, 2002).

Anne Frank also comes to mind as a young woman whose struggles with loss provided inspiration and hope for others. Facing probable loss of her own life and loved ones during the Holocaust, Anne expressed anger, sadness, and regret about her experiences and about the larger world. She was nevertheless able to transform these experiences into hope, transcending herself and providing inspiration for generations to come:

> It's really a wonder that I haven't dropped all my ideals because they seem so absurd and impossible to carry out. Yet, I keep them, because in spite of everything I still believe that people are really good at heart. I simply can't build up my hopes on a foundation consisting of confusion, misery, and death. I see the world gradually being turned into a wilderness, I hear the ever-approaching thunder, which will destroy us too, I can feel the sufferings of millions and yet, if I look up into the heavens, I think that it will all come right, that this cruelty too will end, and that peace and tranquility will return again. (Frank, 1993, pp. 263–264)

In summary, regret also occurs in children and adolescents, and should be addressed in a developmentally appropriate context. Furthermore, children and adolescents, like adults, can grow from such existential experiences.

Cultural Issues.   We also believe that it is essential to be sensitive to any cultural factors that might influence a client's experience of loss and/or regret. Issues related to particular cultures will not be addressed here. Rather, we propose that particular categories or types of cultural beliefs or practices should be considered by therapists for each individual client in order to develop an effective approach to treatment. Among the cultural factors that should be assessed are the following: religious practices and spiritual beliefs; beliefs and practices related to guilt, punishment, forgiveness, and reconciliation; beliefs in an afterlife, heaven, or hell; rituals and practices related to dying, death, and loss; and communal versus individual orientations. Thus, our work is highly individualized—the whole person of the client is always more important than any theory or technique. Our therapy develops and is paced according to client needs. Client goals and wishes are fully respected. We recognize that an approach that is helpful for one client may not be helpful for another.

Our work is also highly individualized in the sense that each client and each of us, as the therapists, is changed in unique ways through the process of counseling. When clients share their own culture and their own phenomenological experiences with us, they change by being heard and understood as unique individuals and by having their own needs recognized. The therapists change by having their own perspectives enlarged by their new understanding of the clients' cultural worlds and individual needs. We see therapy as an enactment of the I–Thou relationship, as described by Buber (1958).

Now we move to our thoughts about specific approaches to working with clients who are dealing with regret and loss of self or other, keeping in mind, again, the primacy of the therapeutic relationship.

Specific Approaches. In our work with clients who are experiencing loss-related regret, we draw upon and integrate the work of many different therapists and theorists, including Rogers (1951), Frankl (1984), Buber (1958), and Capps (1983), among others. In the following stories, we describe different ways in which we have attempted to help clients dealing with loss-related regret.

A client dealing with loss-related regret may express an awareness that there is a gap between what is real and what is ideal—between a real and ideal self, or a real and ideal other (Rogers, 1951). When the gap between real and ideal is significant, a sense of incongruence is felt and anxiety related to death may occur, along with guilt, shame, disappointment, sadness, or remorse (Tomer & Eliason, 1996). Work with such a client may involve exploration of the client's concern about the gap between real and ideal, and a discussion of possible revisions of the ideal in light of what is now real. Consider the following example:

> Cathy, the mother of a 9-year-old boy, discovered she has cancer. Cathy defines herself in large part as a mother. This definition includes the belief that a mother lives long enough to see her child at least through childhood and adolescence—this is her ideal. When she is diagnosed with cancer, Cathy is aware that this ideal may not be realized. She experiences future-related regret, anxiety, sadness, and disappointment about the possible loss of her own life and about the possibility of her son's loss of his mother. She uses psychotherapy to help her accept the reality of these possibilities and,

now, to change her feelings, thoughts, and actions related to her son. This allows Cathy to develop a positive meaning of her own life, in spite of the gap between real and ideal. By the time Cathy died, she was at peace and verbalized no regret.

Cathy's therapist was a careful listener who reflected back to Cathy her understanding of Cathy's struggles and concerns, and provided new ideas for her to consider. With such help, Cathy was able to realize her dream of being a good mother to her son, even though the particulars of her dream, or her definition of the ideal, changed. She did so by exploring and revising behaviors, thoughts, and feelings internally and in real encounters with her son and with other important people, such as her husband, extended family members, and friends. She created a paradigm shift in her life, moving from focusing on future-related regret to living more fully in a more positive reframed present.

We have often found that clients are able to gain awareness from the narrative experience of telling the stories of their lives, reviewing one's own life and relationships with others. People often discover meaning and purpose through reminiscence, life review, narrative, and metaphor with a supportive listener. With a therapist's facilitation of different perspectives of the story, a client can see one's own life story from different angles and can resolve loss-related regret by finding some meaning in the experiences in entirety. Conducting a life review in a supportive setting can move a client from despair to meaning, integrity, and peace (Butler, 1995; Erikson, 1982).

Indeed, according to Donald Capps (1983), the telling of one's life story can become a parabolic experience. Capps proposes that life stories serve as myths, metaphors, or parables that reveal many universal ideas. Many people, in his view, learn the following lessons about life in the universe from their own life stories: (a) Being human universally means living with the reality that all humans make mistakes. (b) The acknowledgment and acceptance that one is human and makes mistakes inevitably changes a person. After recognizing and facing one's mistakes, an individual is no longer the same person—the person has evolved and grown. (c) A human who confronts one's own mistakes holds a greater responsibility for living a better life in the present and for sharing one's hard-won wisdom with others, to help others evolve and grow as well. Ultimately, the individual in the present is no longer the same individual who made particular mistakes in the past. The focus shifts from past- and future-related regret to finding more positive meaning now. Jason's story is one example of a life review that is such a parabolic experience:

> Jason's 10-year-old son has a progressive life-threatening illness that was diagnosed at four years. Throughout his son's life, Jason has faced the possibility that his son will die at a relatively young age. Jason expresses both past- and future-related regret that he has not always been a perfect father and regret that he may not have his son with him much longer to live out his and his son's dreams for the future. He enters counseling with feelings of hopelessness and sadness, fearing that his life will have no meaning if he loses his son. In counseling, the therapist listens to Jason's life story, and notes many examples of how Jason has grown from the experience of parenting an ill child. For example, Jason has become involved in educating and supporting other parents whose children are newly diagnosed with the same disease, and has re-ordered personal priorities so that relationships and spiritual growth are valued more than financial success. He has also learned a great deal from interacting with his courageous son. Through the therapist's feedback, Jason is able to let go of his past- and future-related regret and despair, and to live more fully in the present. He experiences authentic remorse about some of the mistakes he made as a parent, and begins to appreciate that his painful experiences have paradoxically provided purpose and life meaning.

In constructive life reviews that help resolve regret, clients can also *write* the next chapters of their life stories, through life planning and reorganization. Jason can, for example, envision how he might continue to help other affected families, even if his own son should die. He can also commit to spending as much time as he can, now, with his son and other family members, thus imparting further meaning to his and others' lives.

What happens when it is not possible to have real encounters or interactions with important people to help one resolve issues of loss-related regret? What happens if other important people are deceased or otherwise unavailable? There is still good work that can be done through the use of other approaches. For example, we might draw on techniques arising from Gestalt theory (Perls, Hefferline, & Goodman, 1977), integrating these techniques with a client's life review. We might have a client communicate verbally, in a role-play, to the therapist who represents the unavailable person. In these role-play experiments, the client works through regret and other loss-related feelings and thoughts. The role-play, or the roles that the client and therapist play, can also be reversed to gain empathy and further insight. We might use letters written to the unavailable person, or we might even encourage therapeutic communication with a *personified feeling*, such as one's regret, sadness, or a self-critical inner voice. In such an intervention, the therapist would act as the personified feeling and the client would then confront that feeling experientially. These approaches may be helpful for one who is dying or for one who has lost a loved one. Here is Vanessa's situation:

> Vanessa's husband recently died of lung cancer, following years of heavy cigarette smoking and lack of follow-through of doctors' recommendations. Vanessa regrets a decision she made several years ago to stop nagging her husband about his health and bad habits. Although she continued to cook healthy meals and practice good health habits on her own, she stopped criticizing her husband and giving him the cold shoulder whenever he lit up a cigarette. Her past-related regret results in guilt and depression. With the help of her therapist, she role-plays scenarios with her deceased husband and uses role-reversal with herself (played by the therapist). She is eventually able to recognize her own human limitations. She is able to forgive herself and her husband, to believe that her husband would have forgiven her as well, and to grow from her painful experiences so that she feels ready to face life without her husband.

Vanessa's therapist also used *reframing* to help Vanessa see her experiences from a different perspective. Reframing is a technique that grew from the theories of sociologist Erving Goffman (1990) and involves helping a client reevaluate and perhaps revise an interpretation of a particular situation or a perspective of self. A still photo, so to speak, of a client's current interpretation of a situation, becomes a moving picture taken from many different angles. In Vanessa's case, she was helped to reframe her picture of herself as a neglectful spouse, and to see that she had been a mature adult who took care of herself, modeled healthy behavior, respected the real boundaries between her and her husband, and nurtured a positive relationship between them. In addition, returning to Capps' (1983) model of the parabolic experience, through sharing the story of her life with support from her therapist, Vanessa is able to recognize her own humanity and to grapple with the meaning of such universal experiences as love and loss. Through therapy, she has experienced greater personal meaning in her current life.

Clients who wrestle with loss-related regret are also able to use their experiences to move them to greater spirituality and connectedness with a higher power. Frankl (1984), drawing on his concentration camp experiences during the Holocaust, describes how individuals can transcend themselves and even humanity through the transformation of pain and suffering. Belinda's story portrays such a transformative experience:

> Belinda experienced many losses during her middle adult years—her father's painful death from cancer, her own loss of innocence and sense of safety when her young son was brain-damaged in a seemingly random accident, the loss of a very dear friend to breast cancer, the loss of her mother who was murdered by a mentally ill community member, and the loss of her step-father, as she knew him, from Alzheimer's. Belinda struggled in rage against her pain, and expressed anger towards God who would allow these things to happen to such good people. Complex experiences of regret lay beneath her anger. She expressed many kinds of regrets—that she did not have time to say good-bye to some of the people she had lost; that the murderer of her mother had not received adequate treatment for his mental illness, that her family's sense of safety and security had been damaged, and that her children and parents would miss getting to know each other and to spend more time with one another. Over time, Belinda began to transform her regret, pain, and anger into action in the present, including providing support to others who were dealing with family members with Alzheimer's, lobbying for responsible legislation about handguns in hopes of preventing murders similar to her mother's, and working to increase understanding of the needs of the mentally ill for adequate treatment and community support. She forgives the murderer of her mother. Her understanding of life and her faith in her God grew as a result of her own journey.

Belinda's counselor heard her client's voiced desire to find meaning in the midst of suffering. The counselor allowed Belinda to rage, cry, and grieve through her regret, then facilitated movement, helping her to consider how her experiences might be used in some positive way for herself and/or others. Belinda's story is one of self-transcendence through transformation of loss-related regret. Here is another story of a transcendent response to regret and loss:

> Michael lost a young adult daughter to suicide, which occurred in the midst of a depression triggered by her sexual assault by a boyfriend. Michael expressed regret that he had not been aware that his daughter's relationship with her boyfriend was not a healthy one, and that he had been unable to prevent her death. The therapeutic relationship provided a safe place for

Michael to explore his complex feelings about his daughter's death, as well as his sometimes confusing reactions to it. For example, in the months following his daughter's death, Michael often sensed his daughter's presence and was able to talk with her and to hear her own hopes that he and the rest of the family would be able to learn and grow from what had happened to her. From his experiences, Michael developed a strong belief that life continues in some form after death, and described feelings of hope and peace related to his contact with his daughter after her death.

The therapist explicitly supported Michael's exploration of his unique experiences, respecting his religious and cultural perspectives (which differed from her own). The respect offered by the therapist enabled Michael to come to peace about his loss, and to deepen his own spiritual life.

Finally, let us look at how Jacob, a young adolescent, deals with regret related to his own life-threatening illness.

Jacob is a 13-year-old boy whose life-threatening illness was diagnosed at birth. While factual information related to his illness has been available to him for a few years, he has just come to understand that he may die within the next decade. He expresses many future-related regrets, most of which are related to experiences he may not have. He is regretful that he may not live long enough to attend college, get married, travel, have children, and to do all the normal fun and exciting things that teenagers and young adults do. Jacob's initial response to the realization of his foreshortened future is to engage in defiant or risk-taking behavior, including refusing treatment, experimenting with alcohol, disobeying family rules about curfew, and ignoring parental advice related to his current education and activities. The therapist worked in conjunction with Jacob's Rabbi, who was helping Jason prepare for his bar mitzvah. The therapist validated the normalcy of Jacob's reactions to his illness. With the Rabbi's assistance, the therapist also helped Jacob to widen and deepen his perspective about the inevitability of suffering in life and the possibility of learning and growing from it in order to enhance life's meaning. Jacob continued to set goals for his future, but also tried to live fully in the moment and to nurture meaningful relationships with family members, friends, himself, and God.

Because the therapist was respectful of Jacob's unique situation and of his particular religious beliefs, Jacob was able to grow emotionally and spiritually beyond his regret and anger toward self-transformation. The quality of his life was enhanced in the present, though he still accepted a possibly foreshortened future.

We found that many clients struggling with loss-related regret explore spiritual issues and questions. As counselors and psychologists working with such clients, we are committed to opening ourselves to each individual's unique experience and perspective about spirituality or religion, and to setting aside our own biases and preconceptions in order to fully listen to the stories of others.

CONCLUSION

In this chapter we described how therapists can help clients grow through their experiences of regret related to loss of self or other, thus reducing anxiety and other emotional distress associated with dying, death, and loss. Such work with clients not only helps them to address concrete symptoms of sadness, anger, disappointment, shame, guilt, withdrawal, or avoidance, but also permits them to develop as humans in important ways. Working through loss-related regret often requires clients to recognize and address existential questions and issues, and leads them to discover meaning and purpose in their lives. Individuals move from self-focused pain and suffering to an expanded focus in the world beyond themselves. We described specific approaches that help the client to relate more authentically and more deeply with the self, with others, and with the Other or a higher power (see Buber, 1958). We saw that such courageous work by clients allows them to experience personal transformation, spiritual growth, and transcendence.

MAIN POINTS

1. Regret is the experience one has when realizing that life did not, or will not turn out as one had hoped.
2. Regret occurring near the end of one's own life or upon the loss of another can be accompanied by many complicated feelings and thoughts, and can contribute to death anxiety and emotional distress.
3. Working through loss-related regret often requires individuals to recognize and address existential questions and issues, and leads them to discover meaning and purpose in their lives.
4. Counselors and psychologists should be sensitive to the role that loss-related regret may play in their clients' suffering, and can use a variety of theories and techniques that can help their clients move through the regret toward greater meaning and personal transformation.
5. Common among theories and approaches used with clients who are dealing with loss-related regret are the following ideas:

- each client should be treated as an individual with specific needs and a unique story to tell;
- clients should be encouraged to recognize and accept their humanity, with the accompanying imperfection and fallibility;
- clients can be helped to resolve past- and future-related regret that adds to spiritual, emotional, and physical suffering related to loss;
- helping clients to widen their perspectives about their loss-related regret can deepen their experience of empathy for themselves and for others in their life; and
- clients can be personally transformed from their regret, suffering, and loss, allowing them to relate more fully and authentically to themselves, others, the world around them, and their other or higher power.

RECOMMENDED READINGS

Barnard, D., Tower, A., Boston, P., & Lambrinidou, Y. (2000). *Crossing over: Narratives of palliative care*. New York: Oxford University Press.

Callanan, M., & Kelley, P. (1997). *Final gifts: Understanding the special awareness, needs, and communications of the dying*. New York: Simon and Schuster.

Kuhl, D. (2002). *What dying people want: Practical wisdom for the end of life*. New York: Public Affairs.

Pearson, C., & Stubbs, M. (1999). *Parting company: Understanding the loss of a loved one, the caregiver's journal*. Emeryville, CA: Avalon Publishing Group.

Levine, S. (1997). *A year to live: How to live this year as if it were your last*. New York: Bell Tower.

Terkel, Studs. (2001). *Will the circle be unbroken? Reflections on death, rebirth, and hunger for a faith* New York: The New Press.

Walsh, F., & McGoldrick, M. (Eds.). (2004). *Living beyond loss: Death in the family* (2nd ed.). New York: W.W. Norton and Company.

REFERENCES

Buber, M. (1958). *I and thou* (2nd ed.). New York: Charles Scribner's Sons.

Butler, R. N. (1995). Foreword. In B. K. Haight & J. D. Webster (Eds.), *The art and science of reminiscing: Theory, research, methods, and applications*. Washington, DC: Taylor & Francis.

Capps, D. (1983). Parabolic events in Augustine's autobiography. *Theology Today, 40*(3), 261–272.

Corr, C., Corr, D., & Nabe, C. (2002). Death and dying, life and living (4th ed.). Florence, KY: Wadsworth Publishing.

Csikszentmihalyi, M. (1990). Flow: The psychology of optimal experience. NY: Harper & Row Publishers.

Erikson, E. (1963). *Childhood and society* (Rev. ed.). New York: Norton Publishers.

Erikson, E. (1982). *The life cycle completed*. New York, NY: Norton Publishers.

Feil, N. (1985). Resolution: The final task. *Journal of Humanistic Psychology, 25*(2), 91–105.

Fishman, S. (1992). Relationships among and older adult's life review, ego integrity, and death anxiety. *International Psychogeriatrics, 4*(2), 267–277.

Frank, A. (1993). *The diary of a young girl.* New York: Bantam Books.

Frankl, V. (1984). *Man's search for meaning: An introduction to logotherapy.* Riverside, NJ: Simon and Schuster Adult Publishing Group.

Goffman, E. (1990). Frame analysis: An essay on the organization of human experience. *Boston, MA: Northeastern University Press.*

Hermann, C. (2001). *Spiritual needs of dying patients: A qualitative study.* Oncology Nursing Forum, *28(1), 67–72.*

Kastenbaum, R. & Costa, P. T. (1977). *Psychological perspectives on death.* Annual Review of Psychology, *28, 225–249.*

Landman, J. (1993). *Regret: The persistence of the possible.* New York: Oxford University Press.

Langle, A. (2004). The search for meaning in life and the existential fundamental motivations. *International Journal of Existential Psychology and Psychotherapy, 1*(1), 28–37.

Lecci, L., Okun, M., & Karoly, P. (1994). Life regrets and current goals as predictors of psychological adjustment. *Journal of Personality and Social Psychology, 66*(4), 731–741.

Lucas, (2004). Existential regret: A crossroads of existential anxiety and existential guilt. *Journal of Humanistic Psychology, 44*(1), 58–71.

Neimeyer, R., Prigerson, H., & Davies, B. (2002). Mourning and meaning. *American Behavioral Scientist, 46*(2), 235–251.

Perls, F., Hefferline, R., & Goodman, P. (1977). Gestalt therapy: Excitement and growth in the human personality. *Gouldsboro, ME: Gestalt Journal Press.*

Pessin, H., Rosenfeld, B., & Breitbart, W. (2002). Assessing psychological distress near the end of life. *American Behavioral Scientist, 46*(3), 357–372.

Rogers, C. (1951). *Client-centered therapy.* Boston, MA: Houghton Mifflin Publishers.

Schroeder, C. S., & Gordon, B. N. (2002). Assessment and treatment of childhood problems: A clinician's guide *(2nd ed.). New York: Guilford Press.*

Sherman, D. (2001). *The perceptions and experiences of patients with AIDS: Implications regarding quality of life and palliative care.* Journal of Hospice and Palliative Nursing, *3(1), 7–16.*

Stepanek, M. (2002). *Journey through heartsongs.* New York: Hyperion Books for Children.

Stewart, A. & Vandewater, E. (1999). "If I had to do it over again…": Midlife review, midcourse corrections, and women's well-being in midlife. *Journal of Personality and Social Psychology, 76*(2), 270–284.

Tomer, A. & Eliason, G. (2000). Attitudes about life and death: Toward a comprehensive model of death anxiety. In Tomer, A. (Ed.), *Death attitudes and the older adult.* Washington, DC: Taylor and Francis.

Tomer, A., & Eliason, G. (1996). Attitudes about life and death: Toward a comprehensive model of death anxiety. *Death Studies, 20,* 343–365.

Worden, J. W. (2002). *Grief counseling and grief therapy: A handbook for the mental health practitioner* (3rd ed.). New York: Springer Publishing Company.

Wright, K. (2003). Relationships with death: The terminally ill talk about dying. *Journal of Marital and Family Therapy, 29*(4), (439–454).

14

▼▼▼▼

Separation Theory and Voice Therapy: Philosophical Underpinnings and Applications to Death Anxiety Across the Life Span

Chris Morrant
Joyce Catlett

The irony of man's condition is that the deepest need is to be free of the anxiety of death and annihilation; but it is life itself which awakens it, and so we must shrink from being fully alive.

—*Ernest Becker (1973/1997, p. 66)*

The tragedy of the human condition is that man's awareness and true self-consciousness concerning existential issues contribute to an ultimate irony: Man is both brilliant and aberrant, sensitive and savage, exquisitely caring and painfully indifferent, remarkably creative and incredibly destructive to self and others. The capacity to conceptualize and imagine has negative as well as positive consequences because it predisposes anxiety states that culminate in a defensive form of denial.

—*Robert W. Firestone (1997a, p. 240)*

We are living in a suppressive culture of denial in relation to the subject of death and dying, a defensive attitude that has a profound negative effect on our lives. As in the case of painkilling drugs and habit patterns that insulate us from feeling the anguish of the core existential issues that confront humankind, there is a price to pay for this indulgence. In a somewhat futile attempt to cut off these negative emotions, most of us are inhibited in our capacity for joyful living and, to varying degrees, have lost our desire to search for meaning in life.

The anticipation or dread of death is the greatest torment facing human beings. Much of people's destructiveness toward themselves and others can be attributed to the fact that they accommodate to the fear of death, by prematurely giving up life experiences and by conspiring with one another to create cultural imperatives and institutions that deny the fact of their personal mortality. Paradoxically, the myriad cultural patterns, racial, religious, and ethnic differences among groups of people generate opportunities for creative individuation and offer fascinating variations in the world scene. Yet at the same time, they arouse insidious hostilities that could eventually threaten life on the planet.

This chapter provides a synthesis of Robert W. Firestone's theoretical approach and focuses primarily on his ideas regarding the significant role that the fear of death plays in people's lives. The authors' purpose in writing is to stress the implications—psychological, social, and political—of the subject of death in contemporary life and to describe the myriad belief systems and maladaptive behaviors that represent defensive solutions to the problem of death.[1] We describe the dynamics involved in what must be considered the most significant cause of violence, ethnic warfare, and self-destructiveness in the world today: the compelling need of human beings to maintain powerful defenses of repression and denial when faced with the terrifying awareness of their mortality. Our other objectives are to explore the techniques of voice therapy, a cognitive/affective/behavioral methodology that can be utilized to help ameliorate the destructive consequences of these defensive mechanisms and to suggest ways to live more fully despite one's limitation in time.

DEFINITION OF DEATH ANXIETY

Firestone (1996, 1997a, 1997b) has conceptualized death anxiety as a complex phenomenon representing a blend of diverse thought processes and emotions, including: the dread of death, the horror of physical and mental deterioration, the essential feeling of aloneness, the ultimate experience of separation anxiety, sadness about the eventual loss of self, and extremes of anger and despair about a situation over which one has no control. In some ways, these death attitudes reflect core paranoia, because human beings are at the mercy of outside forces beyond their power to control, forces that threaten their very existence.

Although death anxiety includes this broader spectrum of painful emotions, Firestone's essential definition refers to the full realization that our lives are terminal, an unbearable imagination of infinite nothingness, that, when faced directly, is truly intolerable.

Death anxiety can be distinguished from the poignant feelings of sadness that emerge when we contemplate the inescapable end of our existence. We can never overcome the sadness associated with the obliteration of the self as we experience it in our everyday lives. In a sense, people must mourn the anticipated loss to retain their capacity for genuine feeling. Sadness is therefore an inescapable part of a feelingful existence.

PART 1: SEPARATION THEORY

The theoretical approach developed by Robert Firestone integrates psychoanalytic and existential systems of thought in explaining how early trauma leads to defense formation and how these defenses are reinforced as children gradually become aware of the concept of death. Thereafter, most people unconsciously accommodate to the fear of death by giving up, or seriously restricting, their lives. Through a process of self-denial and other self-destructive behaviors, they are able to maintain a sense of omnipotence, as if they can retain some power over life and death. In withdrawing feeling from personal relationships and life-affirming activity, they reduce their sense of vulnerability to pain, rejection, and potential loss (Firestone, 1985). These forms of death denial reinforce an antifeeling, antisexual existence, support the formation of a fantasy bond (an imagined connection with another person), predispose alienation from oneself and others, and lead to premature psychological and/or physical death. The formation of a fantasy bond then supersedes an authentic investment in truly loving relationships.

Separation as conceptualized in this approach is different from isolation or retreat from social affiliation or interpersonal relationships. It involves maintaining a strong identity and distinct boundaries when relating closely to another person or persons. Separation theory provides an understanding of events and experiences in early childhood that influence the way in which an individual will handle existential anxiety throughout the life span. According to Firestone, children learn to use fantasy to compensate early in life when their environment is less than ideal. Defensive reactions based on the frustration that the child experiences during the developmental years, when the brain is still maturing, limit self-actualization in later life. Parents' immaturity, ignorance, failure to effectively relate, or outright hostility toward their offspring, is compensated for by the child's developing an imaginary connection to the parent or parents. The necessity for defense is proportional to the degree of interpersonal stress to which the child is exposed, which varies considerably from one family to another.

When children experience excessive emotional deprivation, they eventually come to prefer fantasy gratification over deep feeling and associations with others. Their habitual pattern of relying on fantasy is crystallized when they learn about death. At this critical point, they tend to resolve their conflict between fantasy and reality in favor of denial rather than choosing to live fully in the real world. Clearly this is not a philosophical decision where the child meticulously weighs the pros and cons of the two choices. This conflict is resolved in the midst of turmoil and emotional upheaval that is torturous for the vulnerable child. It is a real problem for children as early as three or four years. As Ernest Becker (1973/1997) observed in *The Denial of Death*:

> There can be no clear-cut victory or straightforward solution to the existential dilemma he is in. It is his problem almost right from the beginning almost all of his life, yet he is only a child to handle it.... To grow up at all is to conceal the mass of internal scar tissue that throbs in our dreams. (pp. 28–29)

------

[1]The theoretical approach elucidated here was developed by Robert W. Firestone, PhD., during a 40-year study of people's resistance to change in psychotherapy as well as the more fundamental resistance to a fulfilling life. His investigations included clinical research into emotional disturbance in patients in psychotherapy and a longitudinal study of three generations of normal individuals, couples, and families. Over the course of the latter study, Firestone was provided with an opportunity to match internal dynamics, exposed through the participants' honest self-disclosures, with an observational study of their personal relationships and family life. This experience enabled him to extend his insight into problems in everyday living, psychopathology, and human suffering.

> Some research studies have suggested that children raised in a more nurturing, benevolent environment may be better equipped to cope with life and death, are more likely to develop a positive outlook, and tend to be less driven toward denial. (Florian & Mikulincer, 1998)

The therapeutic approach derived from separation theory emphasizes the exposure of destructive fantasy bonds (imagined connections) as externalized in personal relationships or internalized in the form of negative parental introjects. The theory has been referred to as *separation theory* because it focuses on identifying and separating from negative parental introjects (destructive thought processes or *voices*) and on moving toward individuation and autonomy. Disrupting imagined connections with parents or mates and moving toward separation and true interdependence are seen as being essential for the realization of one's destiny as a fully autonomous human being (Firestone, 1997a).

Philosophical Assumptions Underlying Separation Theory

The philosophy underlying separation theory reflects Firestone's personal view of people as being innocent rather than inherently bad or corrupt. Human beings are not innately destructive or self-destructive; they become aggressive, violent, or self-destructive only in response to emotional pain, anxiety, fear, rejection, and deprivation. Anger and aggression aroused in early relationships with parents and other family members are reinforced by the anguish and dread brought about by the child's growing awareness of their personal death.

In his work, Firestone places primary importance on the individual as a unique entity. Preserving the life and experience of each person is given priority over supporting any group or system, be it the couple, family, ethnic group, political group, nation, or religion.

Firestone emphasizes the pursuit of transcendent goals that go beyond the narrow confines of self and family, and describes the search for meaning as fundamental to living a fulfilling life. His position is similar to that of Viktor Frankl (1946/1959) who asserted that the pursuit of happiness as an end in itself is doomed to failure. Firestone contends that happiness is only attainable incidentally, as a by-product of seeking meaning in one's life, and through generosity, compassion, and concern with the well-being of others. This pursuit has a positive effect on one's mental health and leads to a truthful moral philosophy (Firestone, Firestone, & Catlett, 2003).

In this regard, Firestone suggests that we need to develop our sense of the sacred, enhance the spiritual dimensions of our experience, and explore the mysteries of existence. He stresses the importance of reaching our own conclusions and developing our own beliefs or speculations about universal questions based on our own personal experiences, rather than relying on ideas and beliefs mediated through diverse religious or secular systems. He argues that when people develop their own values and ethics from within, rather than being outer-directed, they can chart the course of their lives in a manner that is harmonious and well integrated.

Firestone notes that some people seek the sacred in their natural surroundings, others in music and the arts, and some find it in love. Indeed, if death anxiety is conceptualized as the poison, then love may well be the antidote.

Firestone sees defenses as maladaptive because they cut deeply into an individual's experience and feelings. The reality of experience and emotion is viewed as being primary. Therefore anything that fragments, denies that reality, or deprives an individual of their experience is clearly destructive. The fundamental problem is that during the social-ization process, many qualities that are uniquely human, such as the capacity for deep feeling, rationality, the ability to use abstract symbols, compassion for self and others, and the desire to search for meaning in life, are programmed out of the child, while frustration-derived aggres-sion is programmed in. To varying degrees, well-meaning parents impose a negative, self-regulating system on their children that invali-dates or fractures their experience and that conditions their thoughts and feelings to meet certain accepted standards. As they develop, chil-dren continue to impose the same conditioning on themselves in the form of a self-limiting, self-punishing thought process or voice.

The Core Conflict

There is a core conflict within each individual centering on the choice between contending with and avoiding painful existential realities. The question is whether to live with emotional pain or escape into an unreal world. Firestone proposes that we are all presented with this essential paradox and face a "no-win" situation. If we give up our customary defenses and fully live our lives, we are immediately struck with the magnitude of the potential loss we face through death. If, on the other hand, we shrink from life and fail to develop our unique potentialities, then we are plagued with regret for a life not really lived.

If we decide to defend ourselves, retreat from life, and seek gratification through fantasy in order to avoid experiencing the pain of existence, we are faced with a number of consequences. First, there is a significant loss of freedom and meaningful experience. The process of disengaging from life leads to a fundamental existential guilt resulting from the denial of a genuine life and retreating from the journey of becoming one's authentic self.

Second, anger, a normal response to frustration or anxiety, is obscured and may be internalized or projected. The former (internalization) leads to self-denigration, while the latter (projection) leads to a sense of victimization and a counter-aggressive, paranoid focus on others. Because defensive patterns spread and eventually become habitual, the mitigating circumstances have the same properties as an addiction, that is, there is a progressive debilitation in broad areas of functioning. People not only lose initiative and develop symptoms of distress, but the underlying causes of their symptoms are obscured.

Third, the defended individual lacks a basic integrity and cannot communicate honestly. For example, if people deny their genuine wants and priorities, then they deceive both themselves and others about their true intentions. If they fail to pursue the goals and experiences they claim to want, then their behavior contradicts their expressed wants. This form of internal dishonesty accounts for the prevalence of mixed messages in personal communication and in society, so devastating to each individual's sense of reality.

In contrast, a less defended life leads to an increased potential for feeling and experiencing all of our emotions. An individual who is comparatively less defended has a greater capacity to feel the joy and happiness of life and is better able to tolerate intimacy. Yet there is a heightened awareness of loss in death. People who are relatively undefended feel more integrated, have a greater ability live more fully and authentically, and tend to be more humane toward others. Thus, remaining vulnerable and undefended becomes a positive human value.

In discussing the choice of living defensively versus living with minimal defenses, Firestone poses the following dilemma: How can a person embrace life in the face of death? Why should one invest in loving relationships in a search for truth and meaning, devote oneself to humane pursuits and transcending goals of creativity, spirituality, and service to others when all will be lost in the end? Is it really better to love and lose than never to love at all? How can human beings live with existential pain and anxiety? Wouldn't it be more expedient to be concerned only with pleasure and the pursuit of happiness? Wouldn't it make more sense to put these disturbing matters out of mind, deaden oneself to the obvious facts of sickness, aging, death, the awesome reality of the unknown, and the ongoing holocaust of human brutality? Why not take the drug, cut off these unpleasantries, submit to the predicament, and put it out of mind? Why not surrender to the obvious defense mechanisms of denial, fantasy, and addiction to lead an inward, self-protective existence?

The problem is that one cannot circumvent emotional pain and suffering, repress the existential dilemma, and lead a "happy" life without losing one's real feeling and autonomy. The defensive choice dehumanizes the individual, and, as noted, there is a loss of personal identity and emotion. In addition, a person cannot be innocently defended. People's defenses hurt other people, particularly the people closest to them. Nowhere is a person's defensive posture as damaging as in response to their children. It is the primary reason why parents, unwittingly, cause harm to their offspring.

Moreover, throughout history, in spite of our scientific achievement and greater understanding, there has been a tragic progression toward defensive denial and depersonalization. As our advancing technologies outrun our rationality and our humanity, this evolution leads to anger and violence that are a threat to our very existence on the planet.

Separation Theory as Compared With Other Theoretical Approaches

Firestone's theoretical approach represents a departure from classical psychoanalytic theory and is more congenial with the theories of Rank (1936/1972), Sullivan (1953), Fairbairn (1952), Guntrip (1969), and to some extent, Kohut (1977). In his work, Firestone focuses on the polarity within the personality between self-affirming and defensive, self-attacking aspects (Firestone, 1997a). His concept of the division of the mind into the self and anti-self systems differs from Laing's (1960) description of the *divided self* (originally conceptualized by Winnicott, 1960/1965). Laing refers to the distinction between the *false self* —the mask or facade that an individual utilizes in social settings—and the *true self* —an individual's authentic feelings and real intentions, which are honest representations of self.

Firestone, as well as Becker (1973/1997), has acknowledged Rank's (1936/1972) contribution to understanding how the child deals with separation anxiety, ambivalent feelings toward parents, and the core conflict between dependency and individuation. Firestone's views are congenial with those of Rank and Becker, who asserted that an increased investment and satisfaction in life leads to a greater awareness of one's personal death and increased death anxiety. Because of this, positive experiences, progress in psychotherapy, and evolution of self often become threatening to the individual.

Research Related to the Concept of the Voice and Self-Destructive Behavior

Destructive thoughts or *voices* vary along a continuum from mild self-reproach to strong self-accusations and suicidal ideation. Self-limiting and self-destructive behaviors also exist on a continuum ranging from asceticism and self-denial, accident-proneness, substance abuse, and eventually, to direct actions that cause bodily harm (Firestone, 1997a). Preliminary clinical data indicating a relationship between internal voices and destructive behaviors suggested the research potential that might lead to an accurate estimation of an individual's suicidal intent. Subsequently, Robert Firestone and Lisa Firestone (2006) developed a scale, the *Firestone Assessment of Self-Destructive Thoughts* (FAST), to assess self-destructive behaviors and suicidal intent and tested it with 1,338 inpatients, outpatients, and normals. The results of reliability and validity studies revealed that scores on the FAST have significantly higher correlations with participants' prior suicide attempts, for the outpatient sample (N=506), than the Beck Hopelessness Scale (BHS; Beck, 1978) and the Suicide Probability Scale (SPS;Cull & Gill, 1988).

The research studies established a connection between negative thought processes (voices) and self-limiting, self-destructive behavior, and suicide. There are other important implications as well. Many of the participants in early investigations (Firestone, 1988) identified their voices as parental statements or as reflecting the attitudes they perceived directed toward them from their parents. Later, items for the FAST were obtained directly from the voice attacks reported by these participants. The use of this clinical material (participants' reported self-attacks) to develop a scale that was later found to discriminate suicide attempters from nonattempters supports the hypothesis that destructive voices are associated with self-destructive action and may well represent introjected negative or defensive parental attitudes (Firestone & Firestone, 2006).

The FAST has been translated into Swedish, Greek, Hebrew, and Urdu. In a cross-cultural study, Farooqi (2004) compared the degree of suicide potential in Pakistani and American psychiatric patients. Her findings indicated that the "FAST can be used as a valuable screening instrument for the identification of patients at risk for suicide in diverse cultural settings" (p. 19).

Preliminary findings from another study investigating the relationship between violent thoughts and violent behavior demonstrated similar results. "Of the participants [incarcerated, paroled, outpatient, and normal] identified as violent, the model [the Firestone Assessment of Violent Thoughts (FAVT)] classified 78% correctly. Seventy percent of the nonviolent participants were correctly classified" (Doucette-Gates, Firestone, & Firestone, 1999, p. 128). Violent thoughts in the form of items on the FAVT were also able to distinguish violent from nonviolent incarcerated men.

PART 2: VOICE THERAPY

"Our life is what our thoughts make it" (Marcus Aurelius, Meditations).

Firestone's life's work has been devoted to studying the problem of resistance in psychotherapy and people's fundamental resistance to a better life. In his investigations, he was struck by a seemingly paradoxical fact of human behavior: the stubbornness with which most people attempt to avoid or minimize experiences that are warm or constructive. On the basis of observations of individuals in both clinical and nonclinical populations, he hypothesized that most people reject, manipulate, or control their environments in order to avoid any personal interaction that would contradict their early conception of reality.

Resistance, the fear of a better life, is an enigma which has baffled people for centuries. Robert Burton (1621/2001), the author of *The Anatomy of Melancholy*, wrote:

> Every man [is] the greatest enemy unto himself. We study many times to undo ourselves, abusing those good things which God hath bestowed upon us, health, wealth, strength, wit, learning, art, memory to our own destruction.... We arm ourselves to our own overthrows; and use reason, art, judgment, all that should help us, as so many instruments to undo us. (p. 136)

Most people tend to cling to childhood labels which seem to be branded: the clever one, the stupid one, the beauty, plain Jane, the troublemaker, and so on. The identity formed in the family directs our lives, but it crushes our true selves and cripples our ability to love. In addition, it seems that many clients, in spite of emotional and intellectual insight achieved during psychotherapy, still hold onto familiar, negative images of themselves and are afraid to change on a deep character level (Firestone, 1988).

Historical Development of the Concept of the Voice

In 1973, Firestone and several associates formed a discussion group to systematically study their reactions to confrontation and feedback. The study was stimulated by the conundrum: Why do we react so strongly to certain types of criticism? The sardonic retort: "The truth always hurts" was unconvincing and led to ongoing discussions. It seemed that most people tended to prejudge themselves in a critical or negative manner. Therefore, any external criticism, whether mild or harsh, was capable of triggering self-critical thoughts. In the course of these discussions, participants' expressions of their thoughts and feelings clearly showed what motivates vigor, change, and what blights a personality.

From 1977 on, Firestone and his associates conducted structured investigations of this destructive thought process or *voice*, usually in a group setting. The clinical material they gathered contributed significantly to their expanding knowledge of this systematized pattern of negative thinking. Participants in the study were encouraged to verbalize their self-criticisms in the second person, as if being addressed by another person. Thus, statements such as: "I am so stupid. I'm so useless. No one would like me," would be expressed as follows: "You are so stupid. You're bloody useless! Who the hell would like you?" As they began to express themselves more emotionally while verbalizing these self-attacks, they were surprised by the grimness of their views about themselves.

These techniques elicited anger, sadness, and grief, together with self-recriminations and diatribes that shocked the other participants. The criticisms grew into angry and cruel rants against the participants, as if from an old hanging judge, soon dubbed *the voice* by those taking part. Individuals who expressed their *voice* also found recollections emerging from the mists of memory, especially from childhood, that gave them fresh perspectives on their personalities and present plights. In seminars and discussion groups conducted by Firestone and his colleagues, men and women exposed the shocking ferocity of the voice, *the enemy within*.

The voice is part of an anti-self system, like a fifth column in the mind (Firestone, 1997a). The truth of an outside criticism or negative feedback is irrelevant. It causes mental pain only if it matches the taunts and accusations of the inner voice. Firestone points out that even if a criticism is true; no one deserves a beating for it.

Voice Therapy

Firestone developed *voice therapy* from these early observations. Voice therapy is a cognitive/emotional/behavioral method of treating depression, personality disorders, and other emotional disturbances and can be applied to individual and couples therapy. In a nutshell, a client expresses their voice attacks as described earlier, and then, with the therapist, examines the statements, insights, and memories evoked. Together, they plan strategies to encourage the client to discover and express their own point of view, to contradict the criticisms and warnings of the voice, and oppose its imperatives and malignant counsel by gradually changing injurious behavior.

This collaborative effort can be distinguished from other cognitive-behavioral treatment strategies that are more directive and didactic than voice therapy methods. For example, Beck, Rush, Shaw, and Emery (1979) and Ellis and Harper (1975) suggest that therapists need to actively point out to clients the irrational and arbitrary quality of their "automatic thoughts" and beliefs.

In essence, both voice therapy and cognitive therapy help "intelligent people thinking stupid things" to think more realistically. Cognitive therapy is not concerned with a client's biography: it focuses on *how* a client thinks, upon their errors in logic. Voice therapy focuses, in addition, on *why* clients think as they do. It is emotionally enriching because it shows the links and unexpected parallels between a client's present behavior and their childhood training and experiences.

Client and therapist soon find that the voice has an intense grip and that the client's struggles to wrestle free cause great fear, mental pain, and suicidal feelings. Firestone encourages clients to try to *sweat it out*. They may ruefully recall Sigmund Freud's recipe for successful treatment, namely, "Courage, courage and still more courage."

Firestone points out that the voice derives mainly from the parents, especially the parent of the same gender, and may even take on a parent's foreign or regional accent during voice therapy. Our parents' attitudes, behaviors, and sayings become incarnate in us, that is, they haunt us and direct almost every aspect of our lives. When we defy these "parents in our heads," we feel frightened, guilty, and alone. A brief time travel may show why we clutch their hands tightly and fear to let go.

A Developmental Perspective

The Fantasy Bond—The Primary Defense. Queen Victoria's bishops prevented her from knighting Charles Darwin after he humbled us, in 1859, by implying that when the varnish is scraped away we are only animals after all, yet, blessed with self-awareness, imagination, and a knowledge of our own mortality—a mixed blessing, for we can picture our eventual deterioration, death, and decay. Psychoanalysis has helped us to understand how we cope with such horrible facts.

Sandor Ferenczi, Freud's colleague, struggled bravely with new strategies to battle resistance (Lewis & Harris, 1933). Ferenczi (1933/1955) and the Budapest School had many inspirations. One now seems surprisingly obvious, that is, the vital importance of the mother to her baby who, at first, feels physically continuous with her. Perfect mothering is impossible due to the vagaries of life and human fallibility. A mother may have insufficient *love-food*, a term that represents affection, warmth, direction, and control, all of which are necessary for the emotional nurturance of children. *Love-food* is Firestone's term for the product of sufficient love on the part of a parent as well as that parent's ability and desire to give it (Firestone, 1985).

Parents were once children too, the victims of other victims. They may have been abused and neglected, and they may suffer, as Firestone points out, from emotional deprivation which leaves the chronic, insatiable ache of emotional hunger. Some of the basic ingredients of love-food, affection and/or direction, may be meager or lacking altogether. Parents may believe they are loving but may crave love *from* the child, making them feel drained. Secondly, parents may decide to bear children less to love and enjoy, than to continue the family name and mitigate the parents' fear of death.

Imagination and the Fantasy Bond

When love-food is scanty, or the mother is mostly emotionally absent, the infant experiences "separation anxiety," a euphemism for being overcome by rage and the terror of annihilation. Then imagination, as

Healer, steps into the breach. To cope with this anxiety, the infant imagines a make-believe mother, a *fantasy*, to comfort loneliness and dread. He or she incorporates all the experiences of the mother, transforming the woman of flesh and blood into a cognitive image. The infant develops a relationship with this inner fantasy of their mother. Firestone calls this relationship the *fantasy bond* (Firestone, 1984, 1985). It is the primary and greatest defense against separation anxiety and gives a counterfeit comfort in the place of insufficient love, sensitivity, tenderness, and control.

The fantasy bond implies an inchoate withdrawal from reality because the baby has begun to parent him/herself as part of the defense against disintegration of their personality. If this defensive fantasy world becomes extreme, an individual's ability to manage the real world is compromised. This psychopathology is at the core of most mental illnesses, such as schizophrenia.

Separation Anxiety and Death Anxiety

Children may grow strong and accomplished, yet still cannot rejoice in their independence because separation anxiety increases when they learn about death. Death is separation for eternity. Everything dies, the stars die, and so will the child. As Lifton (1979) argued: "Separation is the paramount threat from the beginning of life and can give rise, very early, to the rudiments of anxiety and mourning.... Still extremely dependent upon those who nurture him, the child continues for some time to equate death with separation" (p. 68).

Firestone reminds us that we need to wed psychoanalysis and existential psychology to fully understand how we respond to the damage done by interpersonal and existential issues (Firestone, 1997a). The fantasy bond evolves and becomes strengthened to fend off death anxiety and is protected by the secondary defense—the critical internal voice (Firestone, 1985, 1988). For example, parents' positive and negative qualities continue to be incorporated. Their positive qualities are harmoniously integrated and help build the growing personality. Parents' negative qualities are not integrated, but are still deeply etched in the mind, recorded with extra emphasis in the form of a destructive thought process or voice, because negative experiences carry a higher valency than positive ones.

Parents' anger, for example, is experienced as far more dangerous than it (usually) is because a child lacks worldly experience and a sense of proportion. It is also amplified by the child's reactive anger, which is suppressed and underscores the memory. Unlike neutral memories, the recordings of abuse are replete with fear, guilt, and mental anxiety. Abuse is not always obvious. Overprotectiveness, for example, may become a mild form of manipulation through fear to enforce good behavior: "Watch out. Grab your coat or you'll catch your death."

The Voice Process—The Secondary Defense

The fantasy bond is protected by the secondary defense. The parents are idealized at the expense of the child's love for him/herself. In other words, the child develops an image of being bad, worthless, and undeserving of love. The child's efforts to parent him or herself may become addictive, for example, the use of fantasy, food, drugs, excessive masturbation, and so on. The child loses touch with their feelings, and takes on the dominant attitudes and imperatives of the family in the form of a destructive thought process or voice.

The fantasy bond and the voice process are projected onto whatever would seem to offer protection from death anxiety: a lover, a corporate body, an ideology, or religion. Such projections occur in a family, a tribe, or a nation. Firestone reminds us that no family is an ideal haven of loving encouragement and, when hostile and lovelorn, resembles a totalitarian state where the leaders (parents) are idealized or idolized.

When children idealize their parents, at the same time they project their parents' negative or destructive traits and behaviors onto the world at large, which fosters a somewhat paranoid view of other people. Conventional values are enforced by both parents, and by society, on a larger scale. Any deviation from these stated norms would tend to make a child (citizen) experience guilt or anxiety. The destructive thought process, or voice, is generalized to the greater hierarchical forms of power or authority.

The Voice Process and Guilt

The fantasy bond and the voice process make up what Firestone calls the anti-self system, a project of the mind which helps protect us from death anxiety. If any part is pruned, then death fears awaken, often disguised as emotional numbing, physical suffering, or guilt. Guilt is hatred of the self with a dread of punishment. The voice process is grafted onto the growing personality where it becomes an alien but autonomous governor which dictates our thoughts and feelings about ourselves, other people, and almost every aspect of our lives.

Voice therapy uncovers the *voice*, the language of the defensive process, which is usually tyrannical, critical, and destructive. Our parents' contribution to the voice is huge, but we are less our parents' puppets than worked by cruel inner *caricatures* of them laid down in childhood. When we defy the malignant inner voices of our puppeteers, we feel guilty and afraid. If we obey them, then we suffer from existential guilt for stunting and mutilating our potential. Our courage decides how much we live suspended between these two types of guilt.

Voice Attacks

When the voice process incorporates parental fears, anger, and contempt (or worse), it transforms them into regiments of what Firestone calls *voice attacks*. Voice attacks are well-drilled by inner repetition many times throughout a day. They are forever on parade in the landscape of the mind and emerge at any opportunity, for example, when meeting new people the inner voice would attack the self saying, "They won't like you. They'll soon realize how boring and childish you are." When starting a new job, "Pity you came, they'll find out that you are ignorant and a phony." In meeting an attractive person, "Don't humiliate yourself. She'd never be attracted to someone like you." Illness, adversity, and reversals of fortune draw a fusillade which adds great mental anxiety (Firestone, 1997a).

The Voice and Individual Defenses Against Death Anxiety

Firestone (1994) states that therapists may find it difficult to identify defenses specifically related to death anxiety, because defenses are often instituted before the client becomes aware of the anxiety on a conscious level. He notes, however, several defensive behaviors that are influenced or controlled by the voice. These include a preoccupation with pseudo-problems, which is often a displacement of the essential problem connected with death. Another defense is vanity or the narcissistic conviction that one is special and expresses itself in the belief that death happens to someone else, never to oneself. Within couples, partners often form a fantasy bond, or co-dependence, in which they maintain an illusion that they somehow can escape death by merging with the other person. Many parents try to live on through their children, achieving a sense of immortality. Parents attempt to mold their children to be like them in appearance, traits, and behavior, rather than allowing the children to fulfill their own goals, interests, and priorities. Moreover, many individuals engage in self-destructive behaviors, while not immediately life-threatening, can lead to psychological suicide, or actually shorten their lives.

The Voice, Real Love, and the Fantasy Bond

The voice degrades us and is cynical about others. An example of this is: "You're unlovable. But women (men) are a royal pain. You'd better not get too involved." We feel guilty and afraid when anything contradicts the role we played in the family or our view of ourselves (Boszormenyi-Nagy & Spark, 1984; Kerr & Bowen, 1988).

It seems like madness to sabotage love and respect, however, being loved and especially acknowledged by someone we love challenges the warped perceptions of the voice (that we are weak, unlovable incompetents protected by an omniscient inner parent). Therefore we reject love and respect for an illusion of safety and fall back on our faulty belief system (Firestone & Catlett, 1999).

Most of us have to be taught how to graciously accept a compliment, instead of shooting it down because it clashes with our negative inner convictions. When we do experience love and friendship, often our defenses swing into action before anxiety is even experienced. Firestone points out that we often minimize alarm or future rejection by generally being attracted only to those who fit our defenses and help us revive the emotional ambience of our childhood. As a result, we find ourselves reliving the role we played in our family. As a couple becomes more intimate, they regulate the warmth between them until it is bearable. If we were unloved as children, then we become suspicious of love in our lives and begin to withdraw, often ending up like those couples in a restaurant who talk only to the waiter.

Attachment theorists (Shaver & Clark, 1994) have called attention to our tendency to repeat in our adult relationships the specific pattern of attachment that we originally formed with a parent.

Firestone proposes that genuine love is a major threat to the original fantasy bond. Ironically, the imagined fusion that originally served as a compensation for the lack of love in one's early environment is disrupted by subsequent experiences of being loved in reality.

In particular, the combination of emotional closeness and sexual intimacy disturbs psychological equilibrium, triggering interpersonal pain and existential anxiety suppressed during the formative years (Firestone, Firestone, & Catlett, in press). Moreover, being close to another person in a loving relationship makes us aware that life is precious, but must eventually be surrendered. If we embrace life, then we must also face death's inevitability. In an unconscious attempt to escape the terror surrounding this existential reality, most people transform their closest relationships into a fantasy bond—an illusion of connection with their mate—that provides them with a false sense of security. The formation of this destructive tie gradually destroys the true bond that could exist between people who love one another.

Inwardness

The sexual excitement and boundless curiosity of a new love may carry the day at first, but *inwardness* gradually curbs our sense of enthusiasm and dulls the newness of the experience. Inwardness is defined as a retreat into oneself and is part of the anatomy of the voice process: energy and interest fade from concern with ourselves and others (Firestone, 1997a, 1997b). We become less aware of what we want and feel. Generally we withdraw, become less giving, and tend to bury our personal creativity, or hide our lights under a bushel.

Displacement. Death anxiety is also displaced onto life and underlies excessive worry about security, health, and money. We dull fear with defensive, self-nurturing attitudes and comfort ourselves with painkilling habits or substances.

The Voice and Vanity

Our parents' love, respect, and encouragement are easily assimilated into our personalities, fostering self-confidence and love for ourselves. However, excessive flattery and indulgence, that some parents use to cover over a lack of love or disappointment in us, swell self-approval into arrogance and vanity, which are generally disdained and may provoke anger in other people. In *The Wind in the Willows*, the vain Mr. Toad is an endearing comic turn for readers, but a cross to bear for his forest friends. As Shakespeare said: "There's nothing so becomes a man as modest stillness and humility" (*Henry V*: Act 3, Scene 1).

The Voice, Childhood, and Parenthood

Philip Larkin's (1971/1988) famous poem, "This Be The Verse," says your mum and dad: "fill you with the faults they had and add some extra, just for you" (p. 180). Most of us have regrets later about our parenthood but are good-natured, good enough parents, who would do anything for our children's welfare. However, we do adopt the attitude and defenses handed down through the generations. We all suffer as children and, unwittingly, make our children suffer as well. What angered our parents about us, angers us about our children: noise, messiness, incompetence, sexual play, and so on. We often overreact, to our sad surprise: "I swore I'd never get like Dad, but my God, guess what?"

Children are three-dimensional compliments whose love and liveliness challenge our inwardness and faded feelings. They hit our defenses like a battering ram. When peering at a child's innocent, smiling face, we feel a sunburst of love and, in its shade, the fear of its loss and a resurgence of our old feelings of isolation and dread. So we strengthen our defenses and retreat behind lectures and warnings that stifle our children's spontaneity and enthusiasm: "Settle down now, settle down or there'll soon be tears."

The Defense of a Fast or Slow Death During Life: The Enigma of Suicide

Napoleon kept a vial containing opium, belladonna, and a white hellebore on a string around his neck in case the Cossacks caught him in his retreat from Moscow (Roberts, 2001). He would have concurred with Nietzsche's (1886/1966) aphorism: "The thought of suicide is a powerful comfort, it helps one through many a dreadful night" (p. 91). The seeds of suicide are usually sown in childhood. The voice's merciless savagery is proportional to the hatred and fear suffered by the child, so one may ask of any suicide: "Who wished the [person] ... to die, disappear, or go away" (Rosenbaum & Richman, 1970, p. 1652)?

Firestone (1994, 1997b) and Heckler (1994) have noted that an increasing risk of suicide is associated with more intense, insistent, and virulent voice attacks with a deepening mental pain and dread. The voice negates hope and narrows options to a choice between endless suffering and death. As noted earlier, the *Firestone Assessment of Self Destructive Thoughts* (FAST) (Firestone & Firestone, 1996) helps to identify those at risk for suicide. It shows that as voice attacks increase, so does the risk of aggressive actions against oneself and, occasionally, others. Suicide and homicide may to some degree be related. For example, a clinical psychologist wrote: "I began to think about killing myself—and the two younger children.... I was unable to believe that I would ever feel any better.... My life was hopeless" (Rippere & Williams, 1985, p. 80).

Those assaulted by this voice are unconsoled by introspection, and the counsel of others can fall flat. As Firestone and Firestone (2002) note,

> The level of despair and hopelessness the client is experiencing makes it difficult for the clinician to fully empathize with him or her. On the one hand, the therapist may never have experienced this level of psychological pain and despair, whereas on the other hand, the client's perturbation and despair may precipitate repressed pain in a therapist who has experienced episodes of depression and despair. (p. 61)

A completed suicide is rare and relatively unpredictable, outnumbered perhaps a hundred to one by attempts at suicide. In *Man Against Himself*, Karl Menninger (1938) described a presuicidal career which, as Burton suspected, seems to be the lot of Everyman. The *career* is punctuated by what Firestone calls "microsuicides," that is, self-engineered catastrophes and assaults against the self (Firestone & Seiden, 1987).[2] These often pass as normal enough, but at best resemble a litany of gloomy virtues: progressive self-sacrifice, self-denial, self-criticism, overwork, the choice of parasitic or abusive companions, or minor forms of enslavement to exercise, television, and the computer. More obvious microsuicidal behavior includes self-neglect, ignoring medical advice, running away, and addictions including compulsive sexuality, eating disorders, and conjuring up situations that damage one's best interests.

Firestone contends that by denying ourselves pleasure and fulfillment in the relationships and activities that we most enjoy, we commit small suicides on a daily basis in an effort to accommodate the anxiety and dread surrounding our awareness of death. In attempting to exert some power over our fate, we give up broad areas of living by progressively becoming more self-denying throughout our adult years.

As unwitting authors of our own calamities, we easily explain our bad luck and may avoid dealing with our own psychological past or unfinished business. Moreover, our tendencies to become self-denying as we grow older are strongly supported by attitudes of ageism and by social mores that define age-appropriate roles and behaviors in a restrictive manner. For example, in our society, it is often considered a sign of maturity to withdraw from certain activities as one grows older. Despite society's professed beliefs in the value of staying vital and remaining youthful, social sanctions, institutions, and popular opinion support a gradual retreat from energetic activities as people grow older. This might include early retirement, limited participation in sports, a waning interest in sex, a loss of contact with old friends, and a dwindling social life.

Firestone disagrees with those who hold that we fear death because we have not fully lived (Yalom, 1980). He believes that when we invest in life and it becomes precious, then we mourn its loss. For the same reason, the paradox of successful psychotherapy is that enhanced awareness ultimately results in personal empowerment, while at the same time it increases our existential anxiety.

Firestone observes that as people adjust their behaviors and lives according to the dictates of the voice, they begin to reduce investment in energetic activities and relationships. In deadening themselves emotionally in advance, they scarcely notice the transition from living to dying. If we avoid honey and sunshine and accept a "suicidal" life of drudgery and margarine, then our journey from life to death is so muted that, apart from there being no cocoa in the coffin, we can barely tell when we have arrived.

Our poor pretensions were exemplified in H. E. Henley's poem, *Invictus*: "I am the master of my fate: I am the captain of my soul" (Gardner, 1972, p. 792). However, Sigmund Freud would maintain that we are not masters or captains, but frightened, psychologically irrational beings driven by inner forces of which we are unaware. Similarly, Firestone emphasizes that we are not harmonious and whole, but split by a civil war between our innate potential and an inner defensive apparatus that steadily and actively harms us psychologically, physically, and spiritually.

Firestone says that one cannot be innocently defended. The voice process lives and grows, fed by daily reinforcement and apparent confirmation. A young psychologist who took a serious overdose of drugs and was comatose for three days describes the voice as: "powerful— it's not a game this voice, the voice is not a game because I know what's at the extreme end of it" (Parr, 1985). The voice is the scourge of humanity, the bogeyman, and figuratively the sarcoma of the soul.

Institutional Defenses Against Death Anxiety

Firestone conceptualizes society as representing a pooling of individual defenses of all its members. Eventually, the social mores of the culture at large reflect back on the individual in a perpetual feedback loop that intensifies defensive modes of living. Much of human aggressiveness, ethnic strife, and warfare can be attributed to the fact that people collaborate with one another to create cultural imperatives, worldviews, and belief systems that are designed to deny their true existential condition.

The family is a microcosm of larger society with similar attributes of sense, goodness, lies, pieties, superstitions, and so forth, most of which support the so-called sanctity of family values pontificated about by church and state (Bowen, 1978; Kerr & Bowen, 1988). When seen through a high-power lens, the coping mechanisms of the society at large are the sum of defenses against death anxiety of individual members of society. The fantasy bond and other defenses against death anxiety are transferred onto people or *isms:* our country (patriotism), socialism, Catholicism, unionism, and so on. *Dulce et decorem est pro patria mori,* yes, we gladly die to solidify an illusion that the strength of our *ism* will save us from death (Tomer & Eliason, 1996).

Studies conducted by terror management theorists (TMT; Greenberg et al., 1990; Greenberg, Porteus, Simon, Pyszczynski, & Solomon, 1995; Greenberg, Simon, Pyszczynski, Solomon, & Chatel, 1992; Solomon, Greenberg, & Pyszczynski, 1991) tend to support Firestone's hypotheses regarding institutional defenses against death anxiety. TMT research clearly demonstrates how the fear of death contributes to people's need to bolster and defend their own worldview, including their national and/or religious immortality symbols. The heightened defensiveness, in turn, increases each person's liking for groups that validate their worldview and decreases liking for those that threaten it. Indeed, people will fight to the death to defend their customs, traditions, and religious beliefs against others who perceive and interpret reality in different terms or have different solutions to the death problem, a phenomenon that is clearly evident on the contemporary world scene (Firestone, 1996). In discussing implications of TMT research, Greenberg et al. (1990) noted that "People's beliefs about reality [and their cultural expressions of such beliefs] provide a buffer against the anxiety that results from living in a largely uncontrollable, perilous universe, where the only certainty is death" (p. 308). Similarly, religious wars and ethnic conflicts are frequent reactions, because they protect us from existential death anxiety, as expressed by Greenberg,

---

[2]Microsuicide "encompasses those behaviors, communications, attitudes, or life-styles that are self-induced and threatening, limiting, or antithetical to an individual's physical health, emotional well-being, or personal goals" (Firestone, 1988, p. 157).

et al. (1990): "Enthusiasm for such conflicts among those who actually end up doing the killing and the dying is largely fueled by the threat implied to each group's cultural anxiety-buffer by the existence of the other group" (pp. 309–310).

The promises of religion and the belief in a life after death act as another coping mechanism to reduce death anxiety. Hence, as Firestone (1996; Firestone et al., 2003) says, any attack upon these beliefs is fiercely resisted, probably because, at bottom, they do not do the job. Otherwise, we would not launch crusades against infidels and skeptics, burn their books or burn them, if torture does not win them round.

Firestone notes that whereas there are a myriad of defenses against death anxiety, these are never fully comforting because people are generally fearful of change or any alteration of habitual modes of experience. The anticipation of the ultimate change, the final cessation of consciousness as we know it, is extremely distressing for most people despite their defensive structure. Religious beliefs that feature life after death fail to completely relieve death anxiety because they represent an altered state of life that still involves a cessation of life as we know it in our present-day experience.

Summing up individual and societal defenses against the terror of death, Becker (1973/1997) wrote:

> Everything that man does in his symbolic world is an attempt to deny and overcome his grotesque fate. He literally drives himself into a blind oblivi-ousness with social games, psychological tricks, personal preoccupations so far removed from the reality of his situation that they are forms of mad-ness—agreed madness, shared madness, disguised and dignified madness, but madness all the same. (p. 27)

As Firestone (1994) points out, death is not a choice, it comes for us all. What counts is how we live and fight our resistance to the good life. He encourages us to "make each day count," as in the book of Ecclesiastes, which says, "Whatsoever thy hand findeth to do, do it with all thy might; for there is no work, nor device, nor knowledge, nor wisdom, in the grave, whither thou goest" (Ecclesiastes 9:10, King James Version).

Life-Affirming Death Awareness

Firestone (Firestone et al., 2003) suggests that although despair is endemic to the human condition, there are ways to ameliorate the anxiety and dread that emerge when one contemplates one's mortality. He believes that people can challenge the destructive thoughts or voices that urge them to give up favorite activities and loving relationships so as to avoid the painful awareness of their limitation in time. They can pursue goals that transcend the narrow focus of their own priorities and approach others with compassion and a feeling of empathy, because people everywhere face the same existential crisis. Similarly, they can share their feelings about death and dying with close friends and associates and thereby find essential meaning in their existence. With enlightenment on the subject, people could choose to embrace life and live with an awareness of death rather than deaden themselves prematurely.

Firestone et al. (2003) describe a seminar on existential issues in which a number of men and women shared their ideas and feelings about the subject of death. In the following discussion[2] they begin by identifying the negative thoughts that they had experienced during times of unusual happiness:

Kirk: What makes me feel the most about death is when I feel love for another person, or when I love my life, or when I feel really good about myself. Then I immediately have thoughts that just rip me apart, thoughts that I'm going to die or I'm going to lose the person I love. The thoughts are "You just can't stand it. You can't tolerate losing her." It's very hard to hang in there with that close feeling at that level, and I know I usually cut off my feelings at that point.

Amanda: I feel that over the years I've changed in relation to the subject of death. Three years ago, two people I knew died. I started to have the feelings I always have whenever I have any reminders of death. I had thoughts like, "This is too terrible. I cannot stand this. I hate that it's true. I just cannot stand it! This is absolutely unbearable." And then for some reason, I had the thought, "Whose reaction is this that I'm having?" It crossed my mind that maybe this wasn't even my reaction, that it was my parents' point of view, their morbid beliefs and destructive thoughts about death. Then I remembered that my parents were absolutely freaked out by the idea of death and so intolerant of the subject. I could sense it in them, and I could feel the same feelings. So then I thought, "Well, how do I really feel about death?" And I knew that I didn't feel like they did. I had never considered what I really think about it.

---

[2]This discussion includes paraphrased excerpts from Parr (1990) and from Firestone et al. (2003).

Firestone: It seems like people are split between an alliance with death or an alliance with life. A lot of voice attacks represent a drive toward death and destruction and a movement away from living, from experience. Or people can ally themselves with living and feeling and embracing life.

Amanda: I had some other thoughts, too. We get so worked up about what's going to happen after death, but whatever it is was happening before we were born, too. I imagined this long, long endless period of nonexistence with this little tiny bump in it, of life. I feel like this little time here is such an incredible gift. That's how I feel. An incredible gift. Every moment I have that feeling. I'm always aware of death, so there's always a sadness in everything that I experience. All the happiness has a poignancy to it. It actually makes it deeper and richer than when it was just "happy."

Frank: I think that you (Amanda) captured a lot of my feelings, particularly since I have had to face this issue more or less head on in the past year since I was diagnosed with cancer. There's nothing that can be done about it except live what is left. I loved your description of the long experience and the little dot, an eye-blink. Life is just an eye-blink in that perspective. And you seize the blink, or you seize the moment, which is seizing the life. But it's just a moment. It's a precious gift, as you said. And it's so momentary in the perspective of things.

Firestone: There is also a feeling of compassion and kinship with other people who are undergoing the same experiences.

Frank: We're all in the same boat; we're all facing the same fate.

Firestone: That's right, and by remaining vulnerable, we can learn to face the fear of death openly, without compensation or defenses. Our appreciation of life and the human condition would give our lives a poignant meaning in relation to its finality. Recognizing and living with existential truths would enhance the precious moments we spend with our loved ones. This awareness could serve to remind us how vital it is not to damage the feelings of others, their self-respect, special qualities and desires, and the spirit in which they approach life.

CONCLUSION

Firestone's theory and practical ideas for therapy take a clear-eyed view of life and death. His elucidation of the voice process and development of voice therapy provide us with an appropriate theory to combat the voice's destructiveness and to help us live and love more fully.

On a broader sociopolitical level, Firestone asserts that it is imperative for world leaders, (for all of us, in fact) to come to understand how the fear of death impacts individuals and their institutions. In summarizing his psychological views in relation to existential issues, Firestone (1997a) wrote:

> To find peace, we must face up to existential issues, overcome our personal upbringing, and learn to live without soothing psychological defenses. In a sense, we must mourn our own end to fully accept and value our lives. There is no way to banish painful memories and feelings from consciousness without losing our sense of humanity and feeling of compassion for others. An individual can overcome personal limitations and embrace life in the face of death anxiety. Such a person would find no need for ethnic hatred or insidious warfare. (p. 289)

ACKNOWLEDGMENTS

In the first section of this chapter—a description of the basic tenets of separation theory and research findings that support the concept of the voice—was contributed by Joyce Catlett; the second section—a discussion of voice therapy and individual and societal defenses against death anxiety—was contributed by Chris Morrant.

MAIN POINTS

1. Separation theory elucidates a significant aspect of human motivation—the compelling need to defend against the anxiety surrounding an awareness of one's personal mortality.
2. A wide variety of self-destructive behaviors as well as many religious beliefs, nationalistic attitudes, and secular worldviews function as defenses against death anxiety.
3. Recognizing how destructive thoughts influence self-destructive behaviors and support prejudicial attitudes toward people with different beliefs and worldviews from ours can assist therapists in planning effective interventions for clients at every stage in the life process.
4. The basic dilemma throughout the life span is whether to restrict ourselves and dull our experience in an attempt to escape the dread and anxiety regarding death's inevitability, or to live fully, with humility, meaningful activity, and compassion for ourselves and others in spite of our limitation in time.

REFERENCES

Beck, A. T. (1978). *Beck Hopelessness Scale*. San Antonio, TX: Psychological Corporation.

Beck, A. T., Rush, A. J., Shaw, B. F., & Emery, G. (1979). *Cognitive therapy of depression*. New York: Guilford Press.

Becker, E. (1997). *The denial of death*. New York: The Free Press. (Original work published 1973)

Boszormenyi-Nagy, I., & Spark, G. M. (1984). *Invisible loyalties: Reciprocity in intergenerational family therapy*. New York: Brunner/Mazel.

Bowen, M. (1978). *Family therapy in clinical practice*. New York: Jason Aronson.

Burton, R. (2001). *The anatomy of melancholy*. New York: New York Review of Books. (Original work published 1621)

Cull, J. G., & Gill, W. S. (1988). *Suicide probability scale (SPS) manual*. Los Angeles, CA: Western Psychological Services.

Doucette-Gates, A., Firestone, R. W., & Firestone, L. A. (1999). Assessing violent thoughts: The relationship between thought processes and violent behavior. *Psychologica Belgica, 39*, 113–134.

Ellis, A., & Harper, R. A. (1975). *A new guide to rational living*. North Hollywood, CA: Wilshire Book Co.

Farooqi, Y. (2004). Comparative study of suicide potential among Pakistani and American psychiatric patients. *Death Studies, 28*, 19–46.

Fairbairn, W. R. D. (1952). *Psychoanalytic studies of the personality*. London: Routledge & Kegan Paul.

Ferenczi, S. (1955). Confusion of tongues between adults and the child. In M. Balint (Ed.) and E. Mosbacher et al. (Trans.), *Final contributions to the problems & methods of psychoanalysis* (pp. 156–167). New York: Basic Books. (Original work published 1933)

Firestone, R. W. (1984). A concept of the primary fantasy bond: A developmental perspective. *Psychotherapy, 21*, 218–225.

Firestone, R. W. (1985). *The fantasy bond: Structure of psychological defenses*. Santa Barbara, CA: Glendon Association.

Firestone, R. W. (1988). *Voice therapy: A psychotherapeutic approach to self-destructive behavior*. Santa Barbara, CA: Glendon Association.

Firestone, R. W. (1994). Psychological defenses against death anxiety. In R. A. Neimeyer (Ed.), *Death anxiety handbook: Research, instrumentation, and application* (pp. 217–241). Washington, DC: Taylor & Francis.

Firestone, R. W. (1996). The origins of ethnic strife. *Mind and Human Interaction, 7*, 167–180.

Firestone, R. W. (1997a). *Combating destructive thought processes: Voice therapy and separation theory*. Thousand Oaks, CA: Sage Publications.

Firestone, R. W. (1997b). *Suicide and the inner voice: Risk assessment, treatment, and case management*. Thousand Oaks, CA: Sage Publications.

Firestone, R. W., & Catlett, J. (1999). *Fear of intimacy*. Washington, DC: American Psychological Association.

Firestone, R. W., & Firestone, L. (2006). *Firestone assessment of self-destructive thoughts*. Lutz, FL: Psycological Assessment Resources. (originally published by The Psycological Corporation, 1996)

Firestone, R. W., & Firestone, L. (2002). Suicide reduction and prevention. In C. Feltham (Ed.), *What's the good of counseling & psychotherapy: The benefits explained* (pp. 48–80). London: Sage Publications.

Firestone, R. W., Firestone, L., & Catlett, J. (2003). *Creating a life of meaning and compassion: The wisdom of psychotherapy.* Washington, DC: American Psychological Association.

Firestone, R. W., Firestone, L., & Catlett, J. (2006). *Sex and love in intimate relationships.* Washington, DC: American Psychological Association.

Firestone, R. W., & Seiden, R. H. (1987). Microsuicide and suicidal threats of everyday life. *Psychotherapy, 24*, 31–39.

Florian, V., & Mikulincer, M. (1998). Symbolic immortality and the management of the terror of death: The moderating role of attachment style. *Journal of Personality and Social Psychology, 74*, 725–734.

Frankl, V. E. (1959). *Man's search for meaning* (Rev. ed.). New York: Washington Square Press. (Original work published 1946)

Gardner, H. (Ed.). (1972). *The new Oxford book of English verse 1250–1950.* Oxford, UK: Oxford University Press.

Greenberg, J., Porteus, J., Simon, L., Pyszczynski, T., & Solomon, S. (1995). Evidence of a terror management function of cultural icons: The effects of mortality salience on the inappropriate use of cherished cultural symbols. *Personality and Social Psychology Bulletin, 21*, 1221–1228.

Greenberg, J., Pyszczynski, T., Solomon, S., Rosenblatt, A., Veeder, M., Kirkland, S. et al. (1990). Evidence for terror management theory: Part 2. The effects of mortality salience on reactions to those who threaten or bolster the cultural worldview. *Journal of Personality and Social Psychology, 58*, 308–318.

Greenberg, J., Simon, L., Pyszczynski, T., Solomon, S., & Chatel, D. (1992). Terror management and tolerance: Does mortality salience always intensify negative reactions to others who threaten one's worldview? *Journal of Personality and Social Psychology, 63*, 212–220.

Guntrip, H. (1969). *Schizoid phenomena object-relations and the self.* New York: International Universities Press.

Heckler, R. A. (1994). *Waking up, alive: The descent, the suicide attempt, and the return to life.* New York: Ballantine Books.

Kerr, M. E., & Bowen, M. (1988). *Family evaluation: An approach based on Bowen theory.* New York: Norton.

Kohut, H. (1977). *The restoration of the self.* New York: International Universities Press.

Laing, R. D. (1960). *The divided self.* New York: Pantheon Books.

Larkin, P. (1988). This be the verse. In P. Larkin (Ed.), *Collected poems* (p. 80). London: The Marvel Press. (Original work published 1971)

Lewis, A., & Harris, A. (Eds.). (1933). *The legacy of Sandor Ferenczi.* Hillside, NJ: The Analytic Press, Inc.

Lifton, R. J. (1979). *The broken connection: On death and the continuity of life.* New York: Simon and Schuster.

Menninger, K. A. (1938). *Man against himself.* New York: Harcourt, Brace & World.

Nietzsche, F. (1966). *Beyond good and evil* (W. Kaufmann, Trans.). New York: Vintage Books. (Original work published 1886)

Parr, G. (Producer & Director). (1985). *The inner voice in suicide* [Video]. Santa Barbara, CA: Glendon Association.

Parr, G. (Producer & Director). (1990). *Life, death, and denial* [Video]. Santa Barbara, CA: Glendon Association.

Rank, O. (1972). *Will therapy and truth and reality* (J. Taft, Trans.). New York: Knopf. (Original work published 1936)

Rippere, V., & Williams, S. (Eds.). (1985). *Wounded healers: Mental health workers' experiences of depression.* Chichester, UK: John Wiley.

Roberts, A. (2001). *Napoleon and Wellington: The battle of Waterloo and the great commanders who fought it*. London: Phoenix Press.

Rosenbaum, M., & Richman, J. (1970). Suicide: The role of hostility and death wishes from the family and significant others. *American Journal of Psychiatry, 126,* 1652–1655.

Shakespeare, W. (1998). *Henry V. The Complete Works of William Shakespeare*. New York: Bantam Books.

Shaver, P. R., & Clark, C. L. (1994). The psychodynamics of adult romantic attachment. In J. M. Masling & R. F. Bornstein (Eds.), *Empirical perspectives on object relations theory* (pp. 105–156). Washington, DC: American Psychological Association.

Solomon, S., Greenberg, J., & Pyszczynski, T. (1991). A terror management theory of social behavior: The psychological functions of self-esteem and cultural worldviews. *Advances in Experimental Social Psychology, 24,* 93–159.

Sullivan, H. S. (1953). *The interpersonal theory of psychiatry*. New York: W. W. Norton.

Tomer, A., & Eliason, G. (1996). Toward a comprehensive model of death anxiety. *Death Studies, 20,* 343–365.

Winnicott, D. W. (1965). Ego distortion in terms of true and false self. In D. W. Winnicott (Ed.), *The maturational processes and the facilitating environment: Studies in the theory of emotional development* (pp. 140–152). Madison, CT: International Universities Press. (Original work published 1960)

Yalom, I. D, (1980). *Existential psychotherapy*. New York: Basic Books.

15

Transformation of Grief Through Meaning: Meaning-Centered Counseling for Bereavement

Paul T. P. Wong
Trinity Western University

Grief is an inevitable universal experience, more commonly experienced than death. So much of life is about loss. Going through life is to endure a series of losses, which include the loss of health, roles, identity, homeland, and loved ones through betrayal or death. Grief is the normal emotional response to loss, a response all too familiar to us. This chapter focuses on bereavement grief and its transformation through meaning.

As we grow and age, we grieve the yesterdays and all that entails—the lost loves and missed opportunities, the good friends and broken relationships, the gains and the losses, the good times and the bad. We remember, therefore, we grieve. But in grieving, we relive what has been lost in time and space.

Our capacity for anticipation creates another set of challenges. For every relationship, there is separation. For every beginning, there is an end. For every embrace, there is a good-bye. We can anticipate death for ourselves and for our loved ones. We can feel the pain and void of anticipatory bereavement. Thus, we mourn for tomorrows as well as yesterdays.

The first important thing about bereavement grief is that it is importantly based on bonding: the stronger the attachment, the greater the grief. Because it is not possible to avoid all relationships and attachments, there is no escape from grief. We all have experienced bereavement grief. Children's first experience of bereavement grief may come from the death of their pets, or the death of a grandparent.

Those blessed with longevity are burdened with multiple losses as they outlive their friends and loved ones. Those who strongly cling to their love as if their life depends on it, would also suffer intensely when they lose them through death or separation. The experiences of bereavement grief vary from one individual to another, because it depends on the unique nature of the relationship, past history, as well as one's attitudes toward life and death. However, in spite of these individual differences, there are some common processes. This chapter examines the processes that contribute to good grief—the potential for personal growth and positive transformation through grief.

Grief is such an intimate and yet strange wasteland. Even though we are well acquainted with loss, we still do not know how to face it with ease and equanimity. Part of the problem is that it is difficult to separate death anxiety about one's own mortality, and worries about financial consequences from grieving the loss of a loved one. The impact of grief can be very intensive and extensive, because it touches almost every aspect of one's life.

The battle against postmortem grief is often fought on two fronts—internal and external. Internally, apart from the emotional tumult, mental disorientation, and flooded memories, the death of a loved one may also trigger an existential crisis and a spiritual quest. Therefore, religious and philosophical beliefs play a role in the grieving and recovery process.

Externally, the bereaved often have to take care of the aftermath of the death of a loved one and cope with the many demands of life. Funeral arrangements, settling the estates, taking care of the personal effects of the deceased, dealing with relatives and re-igniting past conflicts are all concomitant stressors. Another external source of stress comes from colliding cultures. Conflicting cultural prescriptions for funeral rites and mourning rituals can become a fertile ground for conflict, especially when family members involve inter-racial marriages and different religious practices. Thus, death may divide rather than unite the family.

THE NATURE OF GRIEF

Strictly speaking, grief is more than an emotional reaction to loss. It also involves a complex pattern of cognitive, existential, spiritual coping processes in reaction to the disintegration of existing structures of meaning. This loss of meaning with respect to relationships, life goals, and daily living creates an existential crisis. To the extent that death of a significant other disrupts one's continuity with the past, grief also entails existential struggles regarding the meaning of one's own identify. From this broader perspective, grief work necessarily involves the transformation of meaning structures.

Grieving Versus Mourning

Although grieving typically refers to our emotional reaction to loss, it actually involves the adaptive process of our entire being—affective, cognitive, spiritual, physical, behavioral, and social. In order to regain our equilibrium and refill the void after the loss of a loved one, the adaptive process can be elaborate, complex, and prolonged. It may last for years, even a lifetime. Grieving may involve most of the following responses:

- Yearning and pining for the deceased.
- Enduring disorganization and disintegration.
- Coping with the aftermath and changes.
- Reorganizing our lives and routines.
- Reviewing events surrounding the death.
- Working through inner conflicts.
- Seeking reconciliation.
- Sorting out confused and conflicting emotions.
- Expressing and sharing our feelings with others.
- Reaching out for help and social support.
- Finding ways to alleviate the pain.
- Transforming the pain to creative works.
- Questioning our own identify and life purpose.
- Discovering new meanings for the loss and suffering.
- Nursing and healing the wound.
- Trying out new things and new relationships.
- Re-examining one's own identity.
- Revising one's own priorities and life goals.
- Integrating the loss with the present and future.
- Attempting to move forward in spite of the wound.

Mourning on the other hand typically involves the expressing of grief, either privately or publicly, often according to cultural prescriptions. Mourning tends to be a shared communal experience. By observing religious rituals together at funerals or memorial services, the burden of grief is lightened, and the significance of the loss is recognized.

Mourning serves the adaptive function of extending comfort to each other. The outpouring of collective grief can be a powerful source of comfort to the bereaved, because it conveys the message that the deceased has not lived and died in vain and he or she matters to others. A period of mourning, which varies from culture to culture, facilitates grief work. Grief can become complicated and prolonged without the benefit of publicly acknowledged mourning. In traditional Chinese culture, mourning can go on indefinitely, when it becomes part of the ancestor worship; the offspring would burn incense, offer food, and paper money to their ancestors on various occasions each year. Such rituals provide perpetual opportunities to remember and honor the deceased.

Common Themes in Responding to Loss

In spite of individual differences, grieving responses generally fall into the following broad categories:

1. Denial and avoidance: We resort to all sorts of defense mechanisms, such as suppression or repression. We carefully avoid every reminder of our loss. We seek asylum in a bottle or a pill. We seek escape through work or love. Even when the very foundation of our lives is crumbling, we still refuse to face the reality of our severe loss. We try to convince ourselves that the pain will eventually go away. But a prolonged state of denial can only make things worse. Grief may evolve into post-traumatic stress disorders (PTSD) or some other forms of adjustment difficulties.
2. Endurance and rumination: We drown ourselves in sorrow, and make life unbearable for everyone else. We may even delight in becoming victims, because masochism helps reduce survivor's guilt. In some cases, the loss is so traumatic, so severe that the only energy left is to passively absorb the unrelenting punishment. We savor the excruciating pain and let our wounds fester unattended. We are obsessed with regrets and past failures. We become the walking dead.
3. Anger and aggression: Our inner pain becomes uncontrollable rage. We lash out at everyone or channel our anger toward those responsible for the death of our loved one. We ask for blood, for justice. Rightly or wrongly, we believe that only revenge will ease our unbearable pain. Witness the conflict in the Middle East. The escalating cycles of violence are fuelled by incessant waves of anger over individuals killed. Each funeral becomes a rally for revenge.

4. Meaninglessness and hopelessness: The loss of a loved one often creates a sense of meaninglessness and hopelessness. An untimely and unexpected death may also shatter our assumptive void. The bereaved may be troubled and crippled by a profound sense of meaninglessness and hopelessness. Depression and bad grief may set in. However, in most cases, the bereaved would struggle to make sense of what has happened and to reconstruct basic assumptions in order to accommodate the loss in building a new future.

5. Transformation and growth: The painful experience of grieving provides a unique opportunity for self-discovery and personal growth. The basic process involves some fundamental re-organization and transformation of our priorities and belief-meaning systems, but the steps may be painful and torturous, often involving some elements of the first three types of grief reactions. The process may involve a variety of strategies and practices, such as mindful meditation, spiritual pursuit, and a change of life goal.

If we remain stuck in the first four categories and are unable to function for prolonged periods of time, then we may be showing signs of pathological grief.

Normal Versus Pathological or Complicated Grief

Normal grief is supposed to be resolved within two years, whereas complicated grief may last for many years and involve clinical depression, anxiety disorder, psychological impairment, and other emotional and behavioral disturbances, similar to PTSD. Such complicated, pathological grief requires grief therapy (Rando, 1993). Apart from grieving the loss, the distress associated with bereavement can also intensify and complicate existing problems such as financial, relational, and psychological. These complications, if unattended to, can severely disrupt the grieving process.

Bereaved persons may be at increased risk for adverse health outcomes. For example, a lonely and psychologically fragile person who has depended on a caring spouse for strength may fall apart when the only support was lost through death. Similarly, aging parents who have pinned all their hopes on their son to take care of them, may be so devastated that they can no longer perform daily functions when their only son dies in a car accident. Health consequences of bereavement have long been recognized (Osterweis, 1984). Mental health providers begin to pay more attention to bereavement services to facilitate grief resolution and prevent pathological complications. Information and education regarding the grieving process, practical, spiritual, and emotional support and grief counseling can all be helpful to bereaved individuals and families.

However, we need to be careful not to pathologize grief, simply because it is protracted. More recent research has shown most do not find complete resolution; there are always some residues, especially at an anniversary or during special occasions. Rando (1988) has reported that significant temporary resurges of grief reactions may still happen for many years in normal healthy grieving. For example, the loss of a mother may be grieved by the daughter for her entire life (Edelman, 1994). But over all, there will be a decrease in the intensity and fre- quencies of waves of grief with the passage of time. Time does heal, but not completely.

Another reason for not pathologizing prolonged mourning is that continued remembrance of our deceased parents, mentors, and fallen heroes may provide a source of inspiration. Memorial Day and other types of anniversaries are examples of how to remember those who have made significant contributions to our lives. Memories have so much to offer. Our life can be enriched when it is rooted in history and tradition through the ritualistic acts of remembering and mourning. For example, remembering the Holocaust not only can help prevent it from happening again, but can also inspire the survivors to be more determined to live a full and productive life. According to Young- Eisendrath (1996), the resilient childhood survivors of the Holocaust "were able to do what most of us might think is impossible: to live with unresolved mourning. They pursued active and creative lives because they determined they would do so, in the face of constant reminders of their losses" (p. 83).

Bad Grief Versus Good Grief

The stakes of grief can be enormously high. Bad grief can lead to trauma and destruction, whereas good grief can lead to maturity and creativity. Bad grief refers to complicated or traumatic grief, which results in adjustment difficulties or clinical problems. It can become destructive at a personal or societal level. A lot has been learned about traumatic grief from Vietnam veterans. Some of them continue to show PTSD or other forms of mental disturbance because of unresolved grief over the death of comrades and innocent civilians. However, less is known about traumatic grief from the loss of a loved one in childhood. Research on motherless daughters (Edelman, 1994) has shed some light on the prolonged traumatic impact of losing a mother, if chil- dren's grief is not properly recognized and treated.

Good grief is the best possible outcome of a bad situation. Even bad grief can be transformed into good grief, but it often requires faith and meaning. For instance, after losing his wife Joy Davidman to cancer, C. S. Lewis was devastated and overwhelmed by grief and his assumptive world was shattered. He lost all senses of meaning of life. With courageous honesty, Lewis documented his personal struggle with pain, doubt, rage, and fear of personal mortality and his eventual recovery in *A Grief Observed*. At the end, he was able to rediscover faith and meaning and experience growth in his soul. Listen to his poignant conclusion: "Only torture will bring out the truth. Only under torture does he discover it himself" (1961, p. 38).

Ralph Waldo Emerson once wrote, "When it is dark enough, men see stars." The stars of hope and healing often reveal themselves only to those languishing in the dark abyss of sorrow and grief. A spiritual context is often necessary for individuals to maintain a sense of hope and coherence through the darkest hours of suffering and grieving. "Spirituality and religion provide the methods and means of translating meaning from an individual level to a universal or transcendental one" (Young-Eisendrath, 1996, p. 92).

Anticipatory Versus Bereavement Grief

Anticipatory grief occurs in anticipation of the death of a loved one or oneself. Unlike bereavement grief, anticipatory grief is not socially sanctioned. Therefore, there is some reluctance in talking about the anticipated death of a loved one or one's own eventual demise. However, research (see chapter 9) shows that a period of anticipatory grief can soften the blow of bereavement. Anticipatory grief also has the advantage of enabling one to make all the necessary preparations before death arrives. More research is needed because anticipatory grief is so common and yet so little is understood.

Multiple Losses and the Accumulation of Grief

On the one hand, prior experience in grieving may prepare one for future loss. Having attended many funerals, one may become blasé about death. Prior exposure to many deaths in war time or natural disasters may also harden our hearts and make us trivialize the loss of human lives. However, on the other hand, multiple losses and the accumulation of grief may sensitize one to any future losses. When this happens, one may experience death anxiety at the slightest hint of serious illness. It is an empirical question when habituation or sensitization will occur. In either case, it would be helpful to keep in mind that death is part of the fabric of life, and we need to learn how to relate to death in such a way that we are neither devastated by death nor immunized against its sting. This would call for a deeper understanding on the meanings of life and death.

HOW WE COPE WITH GRIEF: THE ROLE OF MEANING

How we react to loss matters more than loss itself. How we are affected by the death of a loved one depends to a large extent on the meaning we attach to it. Therefore, it is not surprising that most of the psychological models have something to say about the role of meaning in bereavement.

Contemporary Models of Grieving

Stage Models. Parkes' (1971) stages of grief includes: (a) numbness, (b) searching and pining, (c) depression, and (d) recovery. This recovery stage involves the need to revise one's assumptive world and modes of thinking. Similarly, Bowlby's (1980) attachment theory recognizes four stages of recovery from loss: (a) shock and numbness, (b) yearning and searching, (c) disorganization and despair, and (d) reorganization. The last stage entails attempts to redefine one's identity and life's meaning.

Rando's Process Model. More developments switch to process models. Rando (1988) proposed a process model. Her basic ideas are: (a) the goal of mourning is to adapt to the loss of the loved one, while maintaining a connection though memory, (b) the process involves three main phases: avoidance, confrontation, and accommodation, and (c) the grief process is not linear, but rather circular. According this model, healthy accommodation is not defined by the absence of grief but the ability to accept the reality of death and move forward. (Note that Wong's chapter in this book emphasizes death acceptance as a necessary step toward pursuing a meaningful life). Rando (1993) emphasizes two processes involved in moving forward: (a) to revise the assumptive world, and (b) to invest one's emotional energy in new life goals and ideals.

The Dual Process Model. Margaret Stroebe and Henk Schut (1998, 1999, 2001a, 2001b) have put forward a dual-process model which encompasses both loss and restoration-oriented coping. The oscillation between these two processes reflects the bereaved person's need for meaning-making in order to move forward. The restoration-orientation includes attempts to reorganize one's life and develop a new self identity.

Stroebe and Schut (2001a) recognize the importance of meaning-making, but they focus on cognitive meanings which can be empirically tested. They have argued that it is imperative that first, the term "meaning" needs to be empirically defined. The cognitions involved in the loss and restoration orientations may differ, but they all contribute to meaning-making.

The Meaning-Reconstruction Model. Neimeyer (1998, 2000) is primarily responsible for developing this influential model. Rooted in constructivism, the central process of grieving involves the use of narratives to construct the experience of loss. The model conceptualizes loss in terms of the disruption of one's narrative construction of self and one's world of meaning; there is far less emphasis on the emotional upheaval following loss. The main proposition of the model is that narratives are constructed to make sense of the loss. The model also emphasizes discourse and rhetoric provided by individuals to deal with the death. The bereaved individuals take an active part in the grieving process and in constructing new meanings for transformation and growth.

Meaning-Centered Process Model. Graduate student Sherrie Mok (1996) and I first proposed a meaning-centered model, which integrates various grieving processes in the literature around the key construct of personal meaning. The seven processes are:

1. Dealing with the pain of the loss
2. Yearning for reunion
3. Coping with diverse emotions
4. Letting go
5. Filling the void
6. Confronting one's mortality
7. Reconstructing life

Although each of the processes may require different coping skills, they can all be facilitated when they are centered on one's personal meaning such as one's identity, core values, and meaning and purpose. In this model, personal meaning functions as the hub of a wheel which provides forward movement, stability, and coordination to the seven processes of coping with grief.

This model is based on the convergence of three threads of developments. First, Frankl's logotherapy (1984) emphasizes that human beings cannot live fully unless they have a sense of purpose for their lives and an understanding of the ultimate meaning for their existence. Second, Wong (1989) has made a compelling case that both specific meaning and ultimate meaning are needed for successful aging. Finally, there is clinical and research evidence supporting the important role of meaning and purpose in the grieving process (Middleton & Raphael, 1987).

Later, Wong (2002a, 2003a) revised the model, which involves four major processes, each of which follows a different path of recovery, but they can all interact with each other. The new feature of this model is the emphasis on the transformation through meaning.

1. Mourning the loss: This involves primarily the affective process, which begins with numbness and shock, moving through the roller-coaster ride of intense emotions, and finally settling into a subdued and serene sense of sadness. This process is not linear; however, the cycles may become less frequent and less intense. Recalling and reliving the positive moments may mitigate against the feelings of loss. Often, grieving involves many emotions, such as guilt, anger, shame, regrets, hostility, and sadness. Clarifying emotions is part of the process. Sorting out and reconciling conflicting feelings contribute to recovery.

2. Accepting the loss: This is the most basic and most complex task. To accept the finality of the loss, the process occurs not just at the cognitive level, but also at the social, behavioral, existential, spiritual, and emotional levels. Cognitive acceptance involves more than an intellectual understanding that death is final; it also requires some level of cognitive resolution to reduce instances of intrusive thoughts and ruminations. Spiritual acceptance may involve establishing a spiritual connection with the deceased and experiencing an inner vision of a spiritual union. Emotional acceptance may be most difficult to achieve when the initial emotional attachment is very strong, even when there is a replacement for the attachment. One can truly let go, only when one has achieved acceptance at the emotional level.

3. Adjusting to the loss: This involves the process of making a series of mental and behavioral changes to adapt to the new dynamics within the family and in the larger social network. It also involves working through personal and interpersonal issues, such as forgiveness of self and others, resolving interpersonal conflicts, and re-establishing some new relationships.

4. Transforming the loss: This process is fundamental to recovery. It moves from struggling with the loss to incorporating it into the new reality and future plans, such as redefining one's self-identity and life goals. This process will involve reinvesting one's psychological energy, making new friends, developing new plans, and engaging in productive activities. Basically, it involves the discovery of new meanings and the reconstruction of existing meaning structures. It requires the re-authoring of one's life story. In short, it provides not only a new perspective for the loss but also for narratives of one's past and future. I consider this transformation necessary for grief resolution, restoration, and personal growth. However, it would be difficult to experience the transformation without adopting the attitude of approach acceptance or neutral acceptance as described in the Death Attitude Profile (Gesser, Wong, & Reker, 1987–1988; Wong, Reker, & Gesser, 1994).

Empirical Support for Meaning-Making. There is mounting evidence that individuals tend to engage in meaning-seeking or meaning-making after loss (Davis, Nolen-Hoeksema, & Larson, 1998; Davis, Wortman, Lehman, & Silver, 2000; Gallagher, Lovett, Hanley-Dunn, & Thompson, 1989; Hogan & Schmidt, 2002; Janoff-Bulman & Frantz, 1997; Uren & Wastell, 2002). Bereaved older individuals engage in meaning-seeking as early as two months into the grieving process (Gallagher et al., 1989). There is also clinical evidence that at the beginning of bereavement therapy, there is a need to address the meaning of the loss (Raphael, Middleton, Martinek, & Misso, 1993). Wheeler (2001) reported that most parents initiated a search for meaning after the death of their child; the great majority of parents believed that their lives since the death of the child had meaning, which came from connections with people, activities, beliefs and values, personal growth, and connections with the lost child. Research also shows that it is helpful to make finer distinctions in meaning-based processes in coping with bereavement. For example, Davis, Wortman, Lehman, and Silver (1998) found evidence for both making sense and benefit-finding in parents who lost a child. Attig (2001) differentiated between making meaning and finding meaning.

Research shows that people who can recreate a high sense of purpose in life have less negative response to bereavement, and experience greater life satisfaction (Ulmer, Range, & Smith, 1991). Several studies have also shown evidence of personal growth or transformation as a result of bereavement (Frantz, Farrell, & Trolley, 2001; Janoff-Bulman, 1989; Nolen-Hoeksema & Davis, 2002). According to Nolen-Hoeksema and Davis (2002), positive outcomes typically involve "a fundamental shifting of the life goals and purposes that significantly influences one's sense of identity" (p. 599).

MEANING-MANAGEMENT THEORY AND GRIEVING

In view of the prior review, it makes perfect sense that meaning-management theory (MMT; chap. 3 this volume) should contribute to our understanding of grieving. Originating from existential-humanistic psychology (Wong, 2005a, 2005b), MMT also encompasses constructivist, narrative perspective, cognitive, and behavioral processes. Whereas the dual-process model emphasizes cognitive meaning, meaning-reconstruction model focuses on narrative meanings. MMT recognizes the importance of both. MMT is comprehensive enough to encompass a broad spectrum of responses, ranging from attribution, existential and religious coping, spiritual quest, goal-setting, life review, and personal projects. Meaning-seeking, meaning-making, and meaning-reconstruction can all contribute to the positive resolution of grief.

Another strength of the MMT is that it capitalizes on the positive, transformative power of meaning and spirituality, which are closely related (Wong, 1998b). More research has provided compelling evidence of people's resilience in coping with loss and trauma (Bonanno, 2004; Bonanno & Kaltman, 1999; Tedeschi, Park, & Calhoun, 1998). Bonanno (2004) recognizes the important role of positive emotions in extremely aversive events. Positive psychology is paying increased attention to the role of positive affect in human flourishing (Fredrickson & Losada, 2005). MMT goes one step further by recognizing that positive emotions are closely related to finding meaning and purpose (Frankl, 1984; King, Hicks, Krull, & Del Gaiso, 2006; Wong, 1998a). MMT not only affirms the positive role of meaning in resilience, but also provides a roadmap for existential and spiritual quest in adverse situations (Wong, 2005a).

Transformation Through Meaning Management

Elsewhere (Wong's chap. 3 this volume), I have described meaning management in details. Here, I want to quote the following two paragraphs to highlight the natural connection between meaning management and grief transformation:

> Meaning management refers to managing our inner life through meaning. More specifically, it refers to the need to manage meaning-based processes, such as meaning-seeking and meaning-making, in order to understand who we are (identity), what really matters (values), where we are headed (purpose), and how to live the good life in spite of suffering and death (happiness).

Therefore, meaning management is to manage our inner life, which is the sum total of all our feelings, desires, perceptions, thoughts, our inner voices and secret yearnings, and all the ebbs and flows of our consciousness. The objective of meaning management is to manage all our fears and hopes, memories and dreams, hates and loves, regrets and celebrations, doubts and beliefs, the various meanings we attach to events and people, in such a way as to facilitate the discovery of happiness, hope, meaning, fulfillment, and equanimity in the midst of setbacks, sufferings, and deaths.

The relevance of meaning management becomes self-apparent if we recognize that successful grief resolution and transformation involve the following meaning-related processes: (a) revising one's identify, (b) re-evaluating one's values and priorities, (c) seeking new purposes and directions for one's life in terms of investing in new goals and relationships, and (d) taking adaptive actions to regain the joy and passion for living in spite of the loss. These processes are attempts to repair the shattered presumptive world (Janoff-Bulman, 1989, 1992) and meet the four basic needs of meaning (i.e., identity, values, purpose, and control) (Baumeister, 1991). Bereaved individuals can learn how to manage these processes through education, coaching, and counseling taught by someone trained in meaning-centered counseling.

MEANING-CENTERED COUNSELING (MCC) FOR BEREAVEMENT

Over the past 10 years, I have published numerous papers on MCC (e.g., Wong, 1997, 1998b, 1999, 2000, 2002b, 2006). The advantage of MCC is that it is relevant not only to grief resolution but also to a wide range of personal and family crises associated with bereavement. Different from most models of counseling, MCC offers a larger and brighter vision, predicated on the need to enlarge the small "I" to encompass family, community, humanity, environment, and God. What makes MCC unique are its double-vision of healing and trans-formation, and its two-pronged strategy of solving presenting prob-lems as well as addressing larger existential/spiritual concerns. The double vision on both the present problem and the larger responsibil-ities to others helps liberate the individual from self-absorption and self-pity. MCC shows people how to create pockets of heaven on earth in the midst of sorrows, uncertainties, and adversities. Its positive approach to psycho-education emphasizes values, concepts, and skills that can be used to live a more hopeful and fulfilling life in spite of the loss and trauma. It represents the new development of positive existential psychology and existential psychotherapy that make use of concepts and findings from positive psychology (Wong 2005a, 2005b).

I have had the privilege to present MCC workshops to diverse professional groups in different countries. Not surprisingly, professionals working with terminal patients in hospices and palliative care facilities are most receptive to MCC. The message and techniques of transforming suffering and cultivating blessings are also enthusiastically embraced by occupational therapists. They find MCC a very practical and promising approach to help restore a sense of meaning and hope in patients who are severely paralyzed or handicapped. Finally, agencies and professionals providing services and support to the bereaved are also eager to learn MCC.

Like other existential theories (Tomer & Eliason, chapter 1 this volume), MCC recognizes that there is a formless and all engulfing void in human existence. All behaviors, in one way or another, are aimed at filling that primordial and universal void. Unfortunately most of the endeavors have failed. Self-centered pursuits of pleasure, possessions, and power lead only to disillusion and misery. Paradoxically, selfless compassion and surrender to a higher purpose lead to fulfillment (Frankl, 1984; Wong, 2005a, 2005b). MCC provides a proposition for positive, abundant living in spite of the existential anxieties and adverse life circumstances. Here, I can only provide a brief outline highlighting the distinctive of MCC and show how MCC can be effectively employed to help the bereaved.

Defining Characteristics of MCC

1. It emphasizes both healing and personal transformation
2. It provides psycho-education about the important role of meaning and purpose
3. It adopts a two-pronged strategy of addressing both presenting problems and underlying existential/spiritual issues
4. It takes a holistic and collectivistic approach
5. It incorporates multicultural and spiritual perspectives as an integral part
6. It emphasizes the value of compassionate and responsible actions
7. It emphasizes the need for practical changes in daily living
8. It capitalizes on people's capacity for symbolism and narratives

These characteristics are evident in the following therapeutic goals:

1. To connect individual healing with social responsibility.
2. To provide a therapeutic environment.
3. To achieve a deeper understanding of the problem from a larger perspective.

4. To achieve a deeper understanding of one's needs, desires, wants and hopes.
5. To discover one's true identity, purpose and one's place in the world.
6. To pursue what really matters in life.
7. To develop positive attitudes, actions, and habits in daily living.
8. To grow and develop one's full potential.
9. To cultivate blessings for self and others.
10. To contribute to the betterment of humanity.
11. To transform a victim's journey into a hero's adventure.
12. To recover or regain the center of the authentic self.
13. To discover meaning and hope in boundary situations.

Intervention Strategy

1. Accept and confront the reality—the reality principle.
2. Believe that life is worth living—the faith principle.
3. Commit to responsible actions—the action principle.
4. Discover the meaning and purpose of life—the meaning principle.
5. Enjoy the results of positive changes—the reinforcement principle.

The five-part intervention strategy provides conceptual framework or roadmap for counseling and therapy. Each step entails a number of skills.

Cultivating Acceptance. Cultivating acceptance is an important step toward healing grief resolution. A variety of skills are needed to reduce or bypass a client's defense mechanisms, such as denials or exaggerations in order to avoid the need for going through the process of healing. We can use cognitive-behavioral and narrative skills to make it easier to accept the reality of the painful loss. Here are some helpful skills:

- Learn all about the situation surrounding the death.
- Learn to understand the loss through life review.
- Learn how one really feels by confronting one's own emotions.
- Learn to clarify one's feelings by talking about them.
- Talk about the past and life with the deceased.
- Know what can be changed and what cannot.
- Learn to accept that the process of healing can be long and painful.
- Accept misfortune or adversity without bitterness.
- Accept one's own mistakes and regrets.
- Accept other people's mistakes and weaknesses.
- Remember both the blessings and injuries from the deceased.
- Accept suffering for the deceased as evidence of love.
- Confess one's failures, mistakes, and regrets.
- Learn to accept the loss cognitively and emotionally.
- Learn to let go behaviorally, cognitively, and emotionally.

- Learn to live with the pain and the loss.
- Accept life in its totality.
- Accept each moment as it comes without judgment.
- Accept painful reality with equanimity.
- Learn to endure suffering with patience.
- Learn to live with unavoidable difficulties.

Cultivating Beliefs and Affirmations. Acceptance without affirmation can lead to more depression. Use encouragement, validation, and other skills to reinforce positive beliefs and self-affirmations. Explore various possibilities and opportunities that are still available for realistic achievements. Bring out client's strengths and aspirations. Be sensitive to clients' cultural background and faith traditions. For those who do not believe in God, the spiritual principles of compassion, meaning-making, and higher purpose can be good substiutes for religious beliefs.

- Believe that there is a reason or purpose for what has happened.
- Believe that there are some spiritual lessons and benefits.
- Believe that God will see me through.
- Believe that the pain will be less tomorrow.
- Believe that there is some goodness in life that is worth fighting for.
- Believe that the devastating loss may be the opportunity for a new beginning.
- Believe that I can become what I am meant to be.
- Believe that the future could be better.
- Learn to appreciate life in its worst and its best.
- Recognize that breathing is the basis for hope.
- Affirm the intrinsic value of life.
- Affirm that positive meaning can be found in any situation.
- Believe that one is not alone in troubled times.
- Practice daily affirmation.
- Practice gratitude and thankfulness.

Cultivating Commitment. MCC places priority on practice and action. To practice one lesson consistently is more beneficial to the client than learning many lessons without practicing any. Commitment to action is the key to getting started on the journey of healing and transformation.

Counselors have the responsibility to work with the client to clarify the lesson, simplify the action, and explain the relevance of the practice. They need to help clients realize that commitment to action is essential to moving forward, and to use reinforcement techniques to encourage commitment and bring about the desired changes.

- Join a support group.
- Learn and practice new skills to cope with grief.
- Practice existential coping and religious or spiritual coping.
- Practice mindful meditation or relaxation exercises.
- Practice new ways of managing one's negative emotions.
- Practice meaning-seeking and meaning-making skills.
- Practice meaning-reconstruction skills.
- Practice focusing and concentration.
- Learn to live one day at a time.
- Do some kind deeds for those who suffer.
- Develop and implement a plan of action.
- Take small steps toward one's goals.
- Keep on making improvements.
- Never give up trying.

Facilitating Discovery. Many skills can be used to help clients see life in a new way and discover things they have never noticed before. Various meaning-seeking, meaning-making, and meaning-reconstruction skills can be used to discover new meanings of old events. Reframing and perspective taking are often helpful. Meaning-reconstruction can help reveal new insights about one's life. Pay special attention to special moments of awakening. Mindful meditation is useful in discovering present moments, whereas life review is useful in making sense of the past.

- Discover the bright and dark sides of life.
- Discover the significance of mundane matters.
- Discover the hidden beauty in the midst of ugliness.
- Discover the unique beauty of each season.
- Discover joy in every step and every breath.
- Discover newness in old routines.
- Discover creativity in drudgery.
- Discover sacred moments in secular engagements.
- Learn to hear, see, and think deeply.
- Learn to pause and reflect.
- Look up to the sky beyond the horizon.
- Walk toward the sun and leave behind the shadow.
- Discover the positives of one's past through life review.
- Discover a new identity and new future through re-storying.

Enjoying the Outcomes. Some progress in healing is inevitable if one follows the previously mentioned four strategic steps. Positive feelings and outcomes reinforce positive practices.

- Enjoy the liberty and relief that come from acceptance.
- Enjoy the power of letting go.
- Enjoy the hope and consolation that come from belief.
- Enjoy the healing and transformation that come from commitment and action.
- Enjoy the blessings of discovery and moments of Eureka.

CONCLUSION

MCC provides a conceptual framework and a set of skills to facilitate healing and transformation. MCC insists on the possibility of discovering hope and meaning, no matter how bad the situation. Spirituality and religious faith play an important role in getting the bereaved to gain a glimpse of hope beyond the grave. By emphasizing the need to discover a larger vision and a higher purpose for human existence, MCC provides one of the keys to resilience.

Meaning-management is essential to this transformative process. In order to move forward, we have to somehow reconstruct our meaning-systems in order to adapt to different set of realities following bereavement. This evolution of meaning in response to loss continues so that we can maintain some sense of coherence in the midst of change and loss. We can experience positive changes, when the dead are weaved into the fabric of life, and the past is integrated with the future as the basis for self-identity.

MCC emphasizes the transcendental function of grief, which awakens one's spiritual and existential yearnings, and spurs one to rise above the painful experiences of mourning. Recovery always involves the reconstructing of painful and sorrowful experiences through the transformation of assigned meanings.

One can never go back to the past. Therefore, recovery does not mean a return to normal life before the bereavement. True recovery actually means that the bereaved person has found new meaning and purpose, which enable the person to reach a higher level of maturity.

C. S. Lewis (1961) documents the transformation from overwhelming grief and anger at God to a new understanding of God and life. Such transformation can happen to any one who is open to the spiritual reality beyond the physical realm.

There is no medicine, no magic, and no logic to expel the affliction of bereavement. The only hope is to transform it into a poem, a song, or a story that makes us feel like human beings again. That tender feeling of love and liberty makes life worth living in the wasteland of death.

Even when everything is taken away from us, and when we are dying alone, we can hear the angels singing, and feel the peace from heaven. I take great comfort in the promise of Jesus: "Blessed are those who mourn, for they will be comforted" (Matthew 5:4, The Bible, NIV).

Healing is a gift, because it can neither be purchased nor manufactured, no matter how resourceful we are. It remains shrouded in mystery, maybe because its origin is spiritual and transcendental. However, we do know that we are likely to receive this gift, when we stretch our hands heavenward in our brokenness. The blessings of grieving constitute part of positive existential psychology or mature positive psychology (Wong, 2001a), which includes such phenomena as meaning-based post-traumatic growth (Wong, 2003a) and tragic optimism (Wong, 2001b). The rigor of positive psychology research coupled with the profound concepts of existential psychotherapy can break new grounds in achieving a more hopeful understanding of grieving and healing.

I want to conclude by quoting from Ringma (2000, p. 38) who eloquently expanded on the idea of the gift of healing:

> Nouwen suggests that "finding new life through suffering and death: that is the good news." Christ's death mirrors precisely that message. Suffering may seem senseless, but it need not have the last word. New hope can spring up from the ruins of previous expectations and plans. New life can come from the greatest disappointments. But this can only come if we embrace the pain of our dashed hope and grieve our losses to the point of relinquishment. It is at that place, with nothing in our hands, that good gifts will come our way.

In the final analysis, grieving is the pain of letting go of love. Grieving is also the pain of searching for what has been lost. In the process, we discover something far more precious than we ever knew. Indeed, blessed are the broken hearted, for they will find healing and transformation. This chapter proposes that the good grief can set us free and make us grow.

MAIN POINTS

1. This chapter clarifies the nature of grief and bereavement.
2. It reviews major theories on grieving and examines the role of meaning.
3. It presents the meaning-management theory of coping with grief.
4. It introduces meaning-centered counseling (MCC) and shows how it can be applied to grief counseling.
5. Finally, it discusses the positive transformation of grief as being part of positive existential psychology, which injects the research of positive psychology into existential psychotherapy.

REFERENCES

Attig, T. (2001). Relearning the world: Making and finding meanings. In R. A. Neimeyer (Ed.), *Meaning reconstruction and the experience of loss* (pp. 33–53). Washington, DC: American Psychological Association.

Baumeister, R. F. (1991). *Meanings of life.* New York: Guilford.

Bowlby, J. (1980). *Attachment and loss: Vol. 3. Loss: Sadness and depression.* New York: Basic Books.

Bonanno, G. A. (2004). Loss, trauma, and human resilience—Have we underestimated the human capacity to thrive after extremely aversive events? *American Psychologist, 59,* 20–28.

Bonanno, G., & Kaltman, S. (1999). Toward an integrative perspective on bereavement. *Psychological Bulletin, 125,* 760–776.

Davis, C. G., Nolen-Hoeksema, S., & Larson, J. (1998). Making sense of loss and bene-fiting from the experience: Two construals of meaning. *Journal of Personality and Social Psychology, 75,* 561–574.

Davis, C. G., Wortman, C. B., Lehman, D. R., & Silver, R. C. (2000). Searching for meaning in loss: Are clinical assumptions correct? *Death Studies, 24,* 497–540.

Edelman, H. (1994). *Motherless daughters: The legacy of loss.* New York: Dell Publishing.

Frankl, V. (1984). *Man's search for meaning: An introduction to logotherapy.* Riverside, NJ: Simon and Schuster Adult Publishing Group.

Frantz, T. T., Farrell, M. M., & Trolley, B. C. (2001). Positive outcomes of losing a loved one. In R. A. Neimeyer (Ed.), *Meaning reconstruction and the experience of loss* (pp. 191–209). Washington, DC: American Psychological Association.

Fredrickson, B. L., & Losada, M. F. (2005). Positive affect and the complex dynamics of human flourishing. *Journal of the American Psychological Association, 60(7),* 678–686.

Gallagher, D., Lovett, S., Hanley-Dunn, P., & Thompson, L. W. (1989). Use of select cop-ing strategies during late-life spousal bereavement. In D. A. Lund (Ed.), *Older bereaved spouses: Research with practical applications* (pp. 111–122). New York: Hemisphere.

Gesser, G., Wong, P. T. P., & Reker, G. T. (1987–1988). Death attitudes across the life-span: The development and validation of the death attitude profile (DAP). *Omega, 18,* 113–128.

Hogan, N., & Schmidt, L. A. (2002). Testing the grief to personal growth model using structural equation modeling. *Death Studies, 26,* 615–634.

Janoff-Bulman, R. (1989). Assumptive worlds and the stress of traumatic events. *Social Cognition, 7,* 113–116.

Janoff-Bulman, R. (1992). *Shattered assumptions: Toward a new psychology of trauma.* New York: The Free Press.

Janoff-Bulman, R., & Frantz, C. M. (1997). The impact of trauma on meaning: From meaningless world to meaningful life. In M. Power & C. R. Brewin (Eds.), *The trans-formation of meaning in psychological therapies* (pp. 91–106). New York: Wiley.

King, L. A., Hicks, J. A., Krull, J. L., & Del Gaiso, A. K. (2006). Positive affect and the experience of meaning in life. *Journal of Personality and Social Psychology, 90(1),* 179–196.

Lewis, C. S. (1961). *A grief observed.* New York: Seabury Press.

Middleton, W., & Raphael, B. (1987). Bereavement: State of the art and state of the science. *Psychiatric Clinics of North America, 10(3),* 329–343.

Mok, S. (1996). *Elderly spousal bereavement: An integrative model.* Unpublished master's thesis, Trinity Western University. Langley, BC.

Neimeyer, R. A. (1998). *Lessons of loss: A guide to coping*. New York: McGraw-Hill.

Neimeyer, R. A. (2000). Searching for the meaning of meaning: Grief therapy and the process of reconstruction. *Death Studies, 24*(6), 541–558.

Nolen-Hoeksema, S., & Davis, C. G. (2002). Positive responses to loss: Perceiving benefits and growth. In C. R. Snyder & S. J. Lopez (Eds.), *Handbook of positive psychology* (pp. 598–607). Oxford, UK: Oxford University Press.

Osterweis, M. (1984). *Bereavement: Reactions, consequences, and care*. Washington, DC: National Academies Press.

Parkes, C. M. (1971). The first year of bereavement. *Psychiatry, 33*, 444–467.

Rando, T. A. (1988). *Grieving: How to go on living when someone you love dies*. Lexington, MA: Lexington Books.

Rando, T. A. (1993). *Treatment of complicated mourning*. Campaign: Research.

Raphael, B., Middleton, W., Martinek, N., & Misso, V. (1993). Counseling and therapy of the bereaved. In M. S. Stroebe, W. Stroebe, & R. O. Hansson (Eds.), *The handbook of bereavement: Theory, research and intervention* (pp. 427–453). New York: Cambridge.

Ringma, C. (2000). *Dare to journey with Henri Nouwen*. Colorado Springs, CO: Pinon Press, Reflection 128.

Stroebe, M. S., & Schut, H. (1998). Culture and grief. *Bereavement Care, 17*(1), 7–10.

Stroebe, M. S., & Schut, H. (1999). The dual process of model of coping with bereavement: Rationale and description. *Death Studies, 23*(3), 197–224.

Stroebe, M. S., & Schut, H. (2001a). Meaning making in the Dual Process Model of coping with bereavement. In R. A. Neimeyer (Ed.), *Meaning reconstruction and the experience of loss* (pp. 55–73). Washington, DC: American Psychological Association.

Stroebe, M. S., & Schut, H. (2001b). Models of coping with bereavement: A review. In M. S. Stroebe, R. O. Hansson, W. Stroebe, & H. Schut (Eds.), *Handbook of bereavement research: Consequences, coping, and care* (pp. 375–403). Washington, DC: American Psychological Association.

Tedeschi, R., Park, C., & Calhoun, L. (Eds.). (1998). *Posttraumatic growth: Positive changes in the aftermath of crisis*. Mahwah, NJ: Lawrence Erlbaum Associates.

Ulmer, A., Range, L. M., & Smith, P. C. (1991). Purpose in life: A moderator of recovery from bereavement. *Omega, 23*(4), 279–289.

Uren, T. H., & Wastell, C. A. (2002). Attachment and meaning-making in perinatal bereavement. *Death Studies, 26*, 279–308.

Wheeler, I. (2001). Parental bereavement: The crisis of meaning. *Death Studies, 25*, 51–66.

Wong, P. T. P. (1989). Personal meaning and successful aging. *Canadian Pyschology, 30*(3), 516–525.

Wong, P. T. P. (1997). Meaning-centered counseling: A cognitive-behavioral approach to logotherapy. *The International Forum for Logotherapy, 20*, 85-94.

Wong, P. T. P. (1998a). Meaning-centered counseling. In P. T. P. Wong & P. S. Fry (Eds.), *The human quest for meaning: A handbook of psychological research and clinical applications* (pp. 395–435). Mahwah, NJ: Lawrence Erlbaum Associates.

Wong, P. T. P. (1998b). Spirituality, meaning, and successful aging. In P. T. P. Wong & P. S. Fry (Eds.), *The human quest for meaning: A handbook of psychological research and clinical applications* (pp. 359–394). Mahwah, NJ: Lawrence Erlbaum Associates.

Wong, P. T. P. (1999). Towards an integrative model of meaning-centered counseling and therapy. *The International Forum for Logotherapy, 22*, 47–55.

Wong, P. T. P. (2000). Meaning in life and meaning in death in successful aging. In A. Tomer (Ed.), *Death attitudes and the older adults: Theories, concepts and applications* (pp. 23–35). Philadelphia, PA: Bruner-Routledge.

Wong, P. T. P. (2001a). *A new algebra for positive psychology*. Retrieved on November 1, 2006 from http://www.meaning.ca/articles/presidents_column/new_algebra.htm

Wong, P. T. P. (2001b). *When terror hits home: A case for tragic optimism.* Retrieved on November 1, 2006 from http://www.meaning.ca/articles/presidents_column/tragic_optimism_sept01.html

Wong, P. T. P. (2002a). *From death anxiety to death acceptance: A meaning management model.* Retrived on November 1, 2006 from http://www.meaning.ca/articles/death_acceptance.htm Accessed April 10, 2003.

Wong, P. T. P. (2002b). Logotherapy. In G. Zimmer (Ed.), *Encyclopedia of psychotherapy* (pp. 107–113). New York: Academic Press.

Wong, P. T. P. (2003a). *Pathways to posttraumatic growth.* Retrieved on November 1, 2006 from http://www.meaning.ca/articles/presidents_column/post_traumatic_growth.htm

Wong, P. T. P. (2003b). *Transformation of grief through meaning-management.* Retrieved on November 1, 2006 from http://www.meaning.ca/articles/transformation_grief_march03.htm

Wong, P. T. P. (2005a). The challenges of experimental existential psychology: Terror management or meaning management. [Review of the book *Handbook of experimental existential psychology*]. *PsycCritiques (Contemporary Psychology: APA Review of Books).* Retrived on November 1, 2006 from http://www.psycinfo.com/psyccritiques

Wong, P. T. P. (2005b). Viktor Frankl: Prophet of hope for the 21st century. In A. Batthyany & J. Levinson (Eds.), *Anthology of Viktor Frankl's logotherapy.* Phoenix, AZ: Zeig, Tucker, & Theisen Inc.

Wong, P. T. P. (2006). From logotherapy to meaning-centered counseling. *Insight,* January, BC Association of Clinical Counsellors.

Wong, P. T. P., Reker, G. T., & Gesser, G. (1994). Death Attitude Profile–Revised: A multidimensional measure of attitudes toward death. In R. A. Neimeyer (Ed.), *Death anxiety handbook: Research instrumentation and application* (pp. 121–148). Washington, DC: Taylor and Francis.

Young-Eisendrath, P. (1996). *The gifts of suffering: Finding insight, compassion and renewal.* Reading, MA: Addison-Wesley Publishing Company.

16
▼▼▼▼

Making Meaning of Infertility and Death Through the Use of Spirituality and Growth-Fostering Relationships in Counseling

Donna M. Gibson
University of South Carolina

We've learned a lot from the whole experience ... we can see the pluses, and there have been many ... maybe this is where God comes in because this experience was such good preparation for dealing with other things in our lives (Anonymous infertility research study participant).

—*Daniluk (2001, p. 444)*

In the United States, 6.1 million women have experienced some form of infertility (Centers for Disease Control [CDC], 1995). This could include both primary and secondary forms of infertility, with the distinction between the two being that primary infertility is the inability to conceive a first child after one year of regular sexual relations without the use of contraception (Cook, 1987; Meyers et al., 1995; Porter & Christopher, 1984; van Balen, Verdurmen, & Ketting, 1997) and secondary infertility is the inability to conceive after one live birth. Although the statistics are reported for women in the 15–44 age range (CDC, 1995), only a small percentage of the younger age group of women have reported fertility problems. In a study by Mosher and Pratt (1990), 10% of females aged 15–30, 14% of females aged 30–34, and 25% of females aged over the age of 35 have fertility problems. This indicates a trend of increased fertility problems with increased age in females, which is being reported more with the continuing trend among young couples toward delaying marriage and childbearing in favor of career pursuits (Eunpu, 1995; Matthews & Matthews, 1986; Stewart & Robinson, 1989).

The causes of infertility are multiple and varied, but are equally diagnosed in men and women (Robinson & Stewart, 1995; Trantham, 1996). There are several physiological factors that contribute to a diagnosis of infertility, such as inadequate frequency of intercourse, problems with sperm (e.g., too few, antibodies to sperm, impaired motility), problems with eggs (e.g., no ovaries, problems with ovulation), and blocked fallopian tubes (Meyers et al., 1995; Robinson & Stewart, 1995; Trantham, 1996). Additionally, research has indicated psychological disorders that may affect infertility. These include absent or infrequent vaginal intercourse, amenorrhea or impaired fertility secondary to eating disorders, and use of psychotropic medications that can inhibit ovulation (Robinson & Stewart, 1995).

As indicated earlier, the trend for younger couples is to delay childbearing in favor of establishing careers. However, having children versus having a career is not the most significant issue affecting infertility in individuals (Robinson & Stewart, 1995). More importantly are the psychological effects of the infertility experience. In effect, experiencing infertility creates a "crisis" for many individuals and couples (Cook, 1987; Leader, Taylor, & Daniluk, 1984; Menning, 1980; Robinson & Stewart, 1995). This chapter focuses on this crisis, its connection to theories on death attitudes and associated treatments that can be effective in both areas of study on infertility and death attitudes.

The Experience of Infertility

For those who experience infertility, a myriad of feelings, thoughts, and beliefs are encountered and are a consequence of physical, economic, social, and psychological factors (Gibson & Myers, 2000). Due to the technological advances in maternal medicine, a variety of diagnostic and treatment options are available and are being utilized by women (CDC, 2003; Meyers et al., 1995). However, the utilization of reproductive technology has a variety of physical consequences, not all of which are positive (Robinson & Stewart, 1995). The use of infertility drugs, participation in invasive infertility treatments, and procedures such as in vitro fertilization (IVF) and gamete intrafallopian transfer (GIFT) can produce several uncomfortable physical side effects. Additionally, the economic costs of treatment can become burdensome and add negatively to the infertility experience.

In 2003, over 123,000 assisted reproductive technology procedures were performed (CDC, 2001). What does an assisted reproductive technology procedure consist of? In vitro fertilization consists of the woman's ovulation and menstrual cycles being synthetically produced. Therefore, her normal, biological system is turned off via the use of medications in order for the *synthetic* cycle to take its place. One synthetic-hormone-induced menstrual cycle can cost $50,000–$12,000 (Domar, 1997; University of North Carolina Hospitals, 1998). On average, treatment options available to women can run from $7,000–$14,000. This is significant in that reproductive medicine costs for infertility may be considered *elective* by many insurance carriers and may not be either fully or partially covered (Meyers et al., 1995). Hence, many individuals and couples are forced to pay out-of-pocket for infertility services and can make the decision to finance infertility treatment or continuing infertility treatment very stressful. The pressure to seek or continue treatment can be also coming from the social constructions of parenthood.

In most societies, becoming a parent is an expected and normative role transition for adults, but the transition to a nonevent occurs when the individual is diagnosed with infertility (Korpatnick, Daniluk, & Pattinson, 1993). Societal expectations, family pressures, and relationships with others create a social construction of parenthood that negatively affects infertile persons (Atwood & Dobkin, 1992; Cook, 1987; Edelmann & Connolly, 1996; Matthews & Matthews, 1986; Reed, 1987). Beginning with early religious scriptures that have sanctioned procreation, women and men have been socialized to become parents (Atwood & Dobkin, 1992). For women, society has reinforced the thinking that their central role and goal is one of motherhood (Abbey, Andrews, & Halman, 1991). Not surprisingly, married couples experience increasing pressure to have children after their first year of marriage (Porter & Christopher, 1984). In fact, approximately 95% of newly married couples report that they expect and want to conceive children at some point in their lives. Most interestingly, feelings of self-worth and sexual identity are often confirmed when individuals actually become parents (Shepherd, 1992), and parenting can affirm the meaning and purpose of both the couple's marriage and existence as a couple (Matthews & Matthews, 1986).

In essence, the roles of mother and father have become a part of the constructed realities of men and women in our society (Matthews & Matthews, 1986), and this reality becomes integral to one's sense of identity. What happens to someone's sense of identity when their constructed role changes? Experiencing infertility can involve a major reconstruction of identity and reality for the infertile individual as well as the family and friends of the individual. This process of reconstruction can create tension in relationships with peers, and infertile individuals can experience a loss of these relationships (Mahlstedt, 1985). Additionally, infertile individuals will most likely experience the social stigma attached to infertility (Hendricks, 1985; Miall, 1986; Rhodes, 1987). A sense of isolation may occur when the infertile individual is attempting to cope with society's perception of him or her. Distorted perceptions of the individual by others as being unhappily married, career-oriented, psychologically maladjusted, selfish, unhappy, and emotionally immature can also increase this sense of isolation (Blake, 1979; Lampman & Dowling-Guyer, 1995; Miall, 1986; Peterson, 1983; Veevers, 1980). These pressures can contribute to a variety of psychological reactions for infertile individuals.

Although the social construction of parenthood is essentially life long, the psychological consequences of infertility begin only when challenges to procreation first emerge. In most cases, the most intense reactions occur during the process of diagnosis and treatment, which can occur over an extended period of time (Meyers et al., 1995). The experience with infertility treatments has been described as an *emotional roller-coaster ride* (Mahlstedt, 1985). Individuals in treatment can experience extreme vacillation in emotions, with consequent stress, anxiety, and depression. Hormonal changes related to drug therapy regimes can also contribute to these reactions (Robinson & Stewart, 1995).

Much research has focused on the psychological aspects of the *crisis* or experience of infertility (Butler & Koraleski, 1990; Cook, 1987; Leader et al., 1984). These aspects have been described as a sense of helplessness and desperation, loss of personal control, stress, or depression. Kübler-Ross' (1969) stages of death and dying have been used in describing this experience. There are many aspects of loss that the diagnosis of infertility can create in individuals, such as loss of a life goal, loss of a pregnancy experience, loss of fertility, loss of the potential for bearing children, loss of identity, loss of sexual identity, loss of a sense of personal control, loss of health, loss of confidence, and/or loss of close relationships with one's partner, friends, or family (Leader et al., 1984; Mahlstedt, 1985; Matthews & Matthews, 1986). Consequently, feelings of sadness, frustration, inferiority, loneliness, fear, surprise, moodiness, disorganization, distractibility, fatigue, helplessness, poor self-esteem, shame, betrayal, powerlessness, hostility, and/or unpredictability can result (Atwood & Dobkin, 1992; Butler & Koraleski, 1990; Daniluk, 1997; Fleming & Burry, 1987; Menning, 1980; Porter & Christopher, 1984).

Although much of the research has been conducted with individuals who are undergoing infertility treatments, research has indicated that the process of individuals who have accepted their state of childlessness is focused on the reconstruction of their identities as those who are infertile (Daniluk, 2001). Incorporating this idea into their identity can be a slow process that requires the acknowledgment of the many losses associated with being infertile and the ability to reject the socially constructed link between fertility and self-worth.

In essence, infertile individuals face challenges related to physical, economic, social, and psychological effects of their experiences. However, the psychological effects appear to be closely related to the socially constructed norms for forming identity and making meaning from one's identity. This is the relationship of the infertility experience to attitudes in regard to death.

RELATIONSHIP OF THE INFERTILITY EXPERIENCE TO DEATH ATTITUDES

As infertile individuals reconstruct their identities, the sense of loss is often encountered (Leader et al., 1984; Mahlstedt, 1985; Matthews & Matthews, 1986). Specifically, the piece of identity that was constructed around the idea of parenthood is often grieved. This is similar to attitudes regarding one's death, conceived as the loss of self (Tomer & Eliason, 2003). In the transition to childlessness, as with our attitudes toward death and dying, individuals may often strive to make meaning of these current and future experiences.

Making Meaning of Infertility and Death Experiences

The search for meaning can take several avenues addressing personal and existential meaning (Tomer & Eliason, 2003). In the case of personal meaning, the individual may attempt to derive meaning from past or future experiences. For infertile individuals, this process of making personal meaning is closely related to the social constructions of their identities. Feelings of self-worth, a sense of doing the right thing, and having a sense of purpose in one's life is strongly connected with making personal meaning (Baumeister, 1991), and individuals are reinforced on these factors through society and their interpersonal relationships. However, infertile individuals can lose their sense of self-worth and may be perceived as not doing the *right thing* by society, while being diagnosed and treated for infertility problems (Hendricks, 1985; Miall, 1986; Rhodes, 1987). Seeking diagnoses and treatment options for their infertility problems may be one avenue that individuals are trying to make personal meaning out of their experiences. For example, if the infertility problem can be diagnosed, then the individuals, whether he/she is the contributing or noncontributing partner to the problem, may feel better as a result of this knowledge. Striving to treat the issue may then reflect the individual's drive to adhere to supported socially constructed ideas of parenthood as the goal for all adults. Infertile individuals have learned this in their past and have been striving for it in their future goals.

In the case of existential meaning, those facing death or infertility experiences focus more on the direct connectedness to oneself and others (Tomer & Eliason, 2003). In essence, it is the ultimate search for the meaning of life (Wong, 1998). This type of meaning could be interpreted as more present-focused, and is often transformed by traumatic events in an individual's life. Eventually, a paradigm shift may occur, moving the individuals focus from efforts to *fix* the problem, to an acceptance of the life situation and, in turn, acceptance of self.

Both personal and existential meanings are affected in a profound way by negative experiences. Tomer and Eliason (2003) reported that feelings of regret often accompany failures when individuals make personal meaning of experiences. This could be true of infertile individuals making personal meaning and often reporting the regret of not becoming parents (Daniluk, 2001). However, negative interpretations have been described as those where individuals experience a disconnection from others and from the universe (Tomer & Eliason, 2003). When individuals experience a traumatic life event (e.g., anticipated death, infertility), core assumptions and beliefs can be threatened (Janoff-Bulman, 1989). For infertile individuals, the core assumption has been the ability to become pregnant, to carry a pregnancy full-term, have a healthy baby, and become a parent. Meaning, identity, and status are provided to individuals when they have children, which grant a traditional means of participation in the continuity of family, culture, and the human race (Meyers et al., 1995). When this does not occur, the long-held assumptions and beliefs have to be re-framed. Sometimes, becoming a parent is not made real for the individual through a biological process, so the assumption of becoming pregnant is discarded and a new belief is constructed. At this level of meaning-making, current beliefs, assumptions, and constructions about self are being dealt with by the infertile individual. Individuals resigned to their fertility status have reported questioning the purpose of marriage and meaning of *family* (Daniluk, 2001). At times, they reported feeling paralyzed in any plans for the future, which was accompanied by feelings of anger, ennui, and a sense of lethargy. Through a process of critical self-reflection, these individuals eventually began to accept their infertility status and were able to reject cultural beliefs regarding biological parenthood. However, this process can be long and painful, beginning early in the infertility experience.

Reflecting and Feeling the Experience

When comparing infertility and death, the most apparent similarity is how individuals cope with these experiences. In Kübler-Ross' (1969) work *On Death and Dying*, the first stage of the coping process is denial. This does apply to how individuals cope with death, infertility, or other traumatic events. In psychological terms, denial acts as a defense mechanism to protect individuals as they cope with the imminent event (Tomer & Eliason, 2003). Denial comes in many forms, often dependent upon the personality and coping resources of the individual dealing with the experience. For infertile individuals, denial of infertility helps to protect the social constructs they have developed and have maintained through adulthood. Denial gives individuals hope to carry out their long-held beliefs and assumptions about their lives. In addition, it allows individuals time to adjust, process, and accept their experiences.

Several other coping models have been used in explaining individuals' experiences to traumatic events. According to Lazarus and Folkman's (1984) transactional model of stress and coping, cognitive appraisals of stressful situations (e.g., perceived control) are the key determinants of coping efforts. Through the process of cognitive appraisal, situations are categorized as either challenging or stressful. These situations are then dealt with through two different coping methods: problem-focused and emotion-focused. Problem-focused coping involves efforts at managing and altering the problem that is causing distress. This type of coping can include instrumental strategies, such as direct action or information-seeking, that can help individuals gain a basis for direct action (Aldwin & Revenson, 1987). Emotion-focused coping refers to how an individual reacts emotionally to the situation. Research on the effectiveness of problem-focused and emotion-focused coping strategies has been equivocal (Baum, Fleming, & Singer, 1983; Felton & Revenson, 1984; Marrero, 1982; Mitchell, Cronkite, & Moos, 1983; Mitchell & Hodson, 1983). The problem-focused technique of control is used by both individuals experiencing infertility and those anticipating death.

Tomer and Eliason (2003) noted that most people do develop and maintain positive illusions about themselves, the world, their ability to control the environment, and their future. In regard to one's death, positive illusions may provide the individual with a structure of personal time as well as beliefs of high control. For infertile individuals, a belief in a high degree of control can be effective in helping them cope with their experiences. For example, women who perceived a loss of control during infertility treatment experienced more distress than women who did not perceive any loss of control (Litt, Tennen, Affleck, & Klock, 1992; Stanton, Tennen, Affleck, & Mendola, 1992). Women who perceived they had personal control reported greater satisfaction with treatment than those who did not perceive themselves as having a general sense of personal control over anything (Halman, Abbey, & Andrews, 1993). Therefore, seeking diagnoses, treatment, and connections with those who could help them understand the infertility experience may be part of individuals' attempts to achieve and/or maintain personal control in an effort to cope with their infertility. Personal control, used in this manner, may be a very beginning to the process of acceptance of infertility for these individuals. Yet, anxiety and/or distress will occur as individuals attempt to make existential meaning from their infertility experience.

In a review of studies of couples in infertility treatment programs, Abbey et al. (1991) found that women perceived their (couple) fertility problem as significantly more stressful than did their partners, having experienced more disruptions and stress in their personal, social, and sex lives. The rigorous medical tests and treatments that women endure can cause some of this distress, as well as the effects of social stigma on being childless when motherhood has been perceived as the central role of women's lives in society. In being denied the role of motherhood, women may perceive themselves as failures (Matthews

& Matthews, 1986). Hence, more anxiety may result from the thought of failing themselves, their partners, their family, and their society.

Anxiety for infertile individuals can be reduced through adjustment to changing social constructions and making meaning of their lives. One's identity and self-esteem is maintained and reinforced through socially constructed beliefs and constructions about infertility and death. According to Becker (1969), character and society are tools used by individuals to maintain self-esteem and are viewed as basic defenses against the terror of death. According to Greenberg, Pycszynski, and Solomon (1986), anxiety about one's death will be defended against when individuals put their faith in the cultural system in which they live and behave according to the system's values and expectations. Borrowing from these ideas, socially constructed beliefs and assumptions are often held onto by infertile individuals as they cope with their experiences in order to protect them against anxiety resulting from the process of dealing with their life situation.

As infertile individuals progress through their experiences, they may engage in processes that redefine their notions of family, femininity, and masculinity (Daniluk, 2001). Attempting to initiate closure, to accept their identities as infertile, to make sense of their infertility and treatment efforts, to acknowledge their fertility status to significant others, and to acknowledge and accept the uncontrollability of their lives, can help them make existential meaning of their experiences. However, anxiety will still be experienced as individuals reject accepted societal expectations of adults as biological parents. According to Firestone (1994), existential anxiety and awareness of mortality can be experienced as an individual refuses to conform to societal or familial standards. This can be compared to the existential meaning-making for infertile individuals in that these individuals have faced a type of mortality by acknowledging the death of a dream for their own biological children, the death of their identities as constructed through the present time, and the death of their perception of control over life events. Additionally, anxiety is produced when new beliefs, ideas, and constructions are adopted and practiced. Combating accepted societal norms in reference to becoming a mother or father is an anxiety-producing practice. Part of the experience may include dealing with insensitivity from medical professionals, family members, friends, co-workers, and strangers regarding their inability to produce a child, being viewed as selfish in their pursuit of treatment options, or in their lack of willingness to take on the parenting of a child with special needs (Daniluk, 2001).

However, the anxiety and other emotions experienced by infertile individuals can be decreased and/or alleviated when effective psychosocial treatments are offered and implemented. For example, social support is positively correlated with both physical and emotional health (Pearson, 1986; Ulione, 1996), and has been found to have positive effects on health and adjustment (e.g., Komproe, Rijken, Ros, & Winnubst, 1997; Lee, 1997; Stewart & Clarke, 1995), such as providing a buffer against stress (Dalgard, Bjork, & Tambs, 1995). Although the existence of social support as a coping resource is important, research indicates that the quality and nature of individuals' relationships is more important than their mere existence (Connor, Powers, & Bultena, 1979; Fiore, Becker, & Coppell, 1983; Liang et al., 1998). Specifically, relationships that are mutual and intimate can facilitate self-disclosure, coping strategies, emotional resiliency, and additional social support (Genero, Miller, Surrey, & Baldwin, 1992; Jordan, 1997, Lin, 1986; Miller & Stiver, 1997). For infertile individuals, these relationships may also help to alleviate the stress associated with the experience of infertility. Additionally, these relationships may be beneficial to those experiencing death anxieties.

A RELATIONAL APPROACH TO COUNSELING

In the research dedicated to examining counseling techniques for working with infertile individuals, cognitive-behavioral counseling (Myers & Wark, 1996; O'Moore, O'Moore, & Harrison, 1983), grief counseling (Daniluk, 1991; Forrest & Gilbert, 1992; Luske, 1985), and support groups (Cook, 1987; Daniluk, 1991; Forrest & Gilbert, 1992; Goodman & Rothman, 1984) have been viewed as the most utilized techniques with this population. At the same time, there is limited research demonstrating the effectiveness of counseling with infertile individuals. In a meta-analysis of infertility studies, only two studies out of thirty demonstrated cognitive-behavioral and grief counseling as effective in decreasing the negative impact of infertility (Wright, Allard, Lecours, & Sabourin, 1989). However, the existing counseling techniques did not address how relationships could be utilized in counseling to cope with infertility. For example, women often react to infertility by telling their stories to others, and this sharing through relationships with others seems to be a major resource for coping (Keystsone & Kaffko, 1992; Williams, Bischoff, & Ludes, 1992). Unfortunately, traditional psychological theories have been criticized for devaluing women's unique experiences (Enns, 1991). Many of these psychological theories are based on theories of human development that view separation and individuation as the primary developmental task that an individual must accomplish to become a healthy member of Western society (Bowen, 1978; Erickson, 1963; Mahler, Pine, & Bergman, 1975; Nelson, 1996). In addition, several feminist psychologists assert that traditional theories of human development and psychology reflect a Western view of male development and question whether the individuation process is the same for girls and women as it is for boys and men (Gilligan, 1991; Green, 1990; Jack, 1991; Kaplan, 1986; Miller, 1991; Surrey, 1991). These researchers suggest that women are basically relational beings and view a woman's development of self as occurring within the context of relationship and because of relationship. As a result, they created the Relational/Cultural Model of Development through their work at the Stone Center at Wellesley College (Jordan, Kaplan, Miller, Stiver, & Surrey, 1991).

The Relational/Cultural Model of Development

The theory group at the Stone Center proposed that women grow in, through, and toward relationships, and that connections to others is central to psychological well-being (Jordan et al., 1991; Jordan, 1995). This model of development has significant implications for understanding women's development, understanding women's experiences, and for counseling women. Women are provided with a sense of connection to others when they experience life as arising from a relational context (Miller, 1988). When this occurs, women can discover a sense of value and effectiveness in themselves. In essence, these relationships are growth-fostering and can enhance the psychological development of all individuals in mutual interactions (Miller, 1988; Miller & Stiver, 1997).

The Relational/Cultural Model has been applied successfully in counseling with individuals, couples, and groups (Bergman, 1991; Fedele & Harrington, 1990; Jordan, 1995; Miller & Stiver, 1997; Schiller, 1997). Furthermore, the Relational/Cultural Model of Development has also been used in working with clients who are dealing with various issues, such as communication difficulties, parenting, depression, anxiety, diversity, and homosexuality (Fedele & Harrington, 1990; Jordan, 1993; Miller, 1988). In couple's therapy, the focus is often on relational awareness within the couple's system in an effort to work toward a mutually empathic connection, mutual responsibility, mutual empowerment, and an elimination of power and control struggles (Bergman & Surrey, 1994). Relational approaches to group counseling are focused on providing opportunities for individuals to work through previous relational difficulties within a supporting relational context (Fedele & Harrington, 1990), which can provide a sense of safety and similarity (Schiller, 1997). Infertility has also been addressed in a group setting using the Relational/Cultural Model. The model provides a context for conceptualizing individuals' experiences of infertility, predicting difficulties in adjustment, and structuring appropriate interventions with individuals, groups, and couples to enhance the process of adjustment (Gibson & Myers, 2000). Additionally, understanding the nature of growth-fostering relationships within this model may provide a context for developing counseling techniques to help those dealing with death anxiety.

The Use of Growth-Fostering Relationships in Counseling

When considering the use of the Relational/Cultural Model as a basis for counseling infertile individuals and individuals with death anxiety, the types of relationships that are a used in the model need further examination. Surrey (1991) defined growth-fostering relationships as those that allow the individual the ability to identify with a unit larger than the single self and establish a sense of motivation to care for this new unit. It implies a sense of knowing oneself and others through a process of mutual relational interaction and continuity of mutual empathy over time. There are five positive things that have been proposed to emerge from these relationships (Miller, 1986). For each person involved in the relationship, he or she has a more accurate picture of him/herself and the other person(s), feels a greater sense of worth, feels more connected to the other person(s), and feels a greater motivation for connections with other people beyond those in the specific relationship. Basically, individuals involved in the relationship or the relational unit empowers each other.

In a research study, the use of growth-fostering relationships and their effects on infertility stress were examined (Gibson & Myers, 2002). The results indicated that an increase in reported use of growth-fostering relationships resulted in a decrease of reported infertility stress. Participants reported the use of specific types of growth-fostering relationships including, peers and different types of community groups. Of the participants, 92% reported using a female peer while 5% reported using a male peer and 3% reported no choice of gender for the peer in the growth-fostering relationship (Gibson & Myers, 2000). Of the community groups, 46% were work-related groups, 24%

were religious groups, and 16% were school-related groups. The use of religious groups as source for growth-fostering relationships for coping with infertility stress deserves some attention because of Kübler-Ross' (1969) stage of anger, possibly toward "God," for the perceived injustice of having the burden of childlessness inflicted on them (Daniluk, 2001). In a study conducted with 25 couples who exercised an active religious faith, many couples reported dissatisfaction when scriptures that cast childlessness in a negative light were used during Mother and Father's Day celebrations (Smith & Smith, 2004).

What is the role of religion and/or spirituality in counseling infertile couples with an emphasis on growth-fostering relationships? Although, religion and spirituality share commonalities, there are significant differences in meaning (Eliason, 2000). Religion can be viewed as the organized practice of worship and ritual of a certain sect or denomination of individuals. Spirituality is the phenomenological experience of relationship and the existential search for meaning. Based on these definitions, spirituality appears to be more relevant to the purpose of developing growth-fostering relationships. In addition, spirituality also incorporates the individual's unique *I and Thou* experience with God (Buber, 1970).

When spirituality is incorporated into the counseling process, it is important for both counselor and client to agree on its use in their sessions. Martin Buber (1970) refers to the spiritual relationship as the *I and Thou* experience, or the human and the Holy. In individual counseling, counselor-client relationship is vitally important in helping both infertile clients and clients coping with death anxiety to find a connection that they are seeking. By demonstrating mutual respect and openness, the counselor immediately ameliorates any power differential that the client may perceive in counseling (Gibson & Myers, 2000). Part of the mutual empathy process (mutuality) is the counselor's ability to share experiences regarding infertility and/or death with an openness to learning and being emotionally affected by the client's experiences. Through sharing of experiences and ultimately the I and Thou experience, meaning and self-awareness can be found by the client (Eliason, 2000). When clients experience the counselor's willingness to risk sharing clients' experiences, the feelings and thoughts about infertility and/or death can be validated (Gibson & Myers, 2000). Thus, clients can often regain their sense of worthiness, control, purpose, and/or meaning.

One of the main purposes of using the Relational/Cultural Model of Development in counseling is to help clients learn how to empathize with themselves and to develop a new integration of self-other experience (Jordan et al., 1991). With infertile individuals, the ingrained feelings of *deserving* to feel guilty, inadequate, or shameful, inhibit their ability to feel empathic with others (Gibson & Myers, 2000). This may be true of individuals facing death who are feeling anxious, depressed, or dissatisfied with their lives (Eliason, 2000). In counseling, the counselor is to model empathy and acknowledge clients' feelings in an effort to normalize them. When clients begin to feel heard and understood by the counselor, this facilitates more positive self exploration in an effort for self awareness and self-validation (Gibson & Myers, 2000).

Consistent with constructivist theories of psychology, a second purpose of using the Relational/Cultural model in counseling is for the counselor to help clients deconstruct "fertility" or "death" and what that means to clients (Gibson & Myers, 2000). In this process, clients may have to review relationships in their lives that represent incongruencies between the old construction and the new construction of infertility or death. Identification of feelings, thoughts, and beliefs associated with these incongruencies are integrated in this process, and the counselor responds empathically. In this process, clients begin to form a new image of themselves, relationships with others, and their relationship with God.

Overall, the use of the Relational/Cultural Model of Development in counseling offers counselors a way of connecting with their clients. It extends the opportunity to clients to learn how to empathize with themselves and others. When coping with infertility or death, meaning can be found by examining clients' constructions of these events. Through the clients' process of deconstructing old beliefs surrounding these events via a mutually empathic relationship, they may gain a better awareness of their experiences, reframe personal perceptions, create new meanings, and cope more effectively.

CONCLUSION

Infertility is complex and has been described as a crisis for individuals and couples who have experienced the physical, economic, social, and psychological effects associated with diagnosis, treatment, and acceptance of the event. In comparing this experience with death attitudes, the most striking similarity is how individuals seek to make meaning. For infertile individuals, existential meaning-making is closely linked to the social constructions of parenthood in our society. This can also be true about individual beliefs and assumptions about death. In deconstructing these socially supported beliefs and assumptions, individuals can begin to form a new identity of themselves while re-establishing feelings of self-worth.

The process of meaning-making can be painful for individuals experiencing traumatic events, such as infertility, death, or dying. In these instances, individuals may cope more effectively when they are able to tell their stories to someone who demonstrates empathy and the ability to be affected by their experiences. Using the Relational/Cultural Model in counseling these individuals, growth-fostering relationships are created and allow individuals to empathize with themselves and others. In essence, they are able to deconstruct old beliefs about infertility and death in order to create a new identity for themselves. This new identity provides the foundation to accept the experiences of infertility or death.

MAIN POINTS

1. The experience of infertility is a crisis that consists of physical, economic, social, and psychological effects on the individual and can lead to feelings of loss, anxiety, low self-esteem, and feelings of no control.
2. The process of meaning-making in infertility or death experiences can be linked to the social constructions of beliefs and assumptions of these events. This process can be emotionally painful, yet the outcome can help individuals gain a new sense of identity.
3. Similarly to coping with death and dying, individuals coping with infertility may feel angry at "God," but through the process of forming mutually empathic relationships can reform a connection to others and to God.

RECOMMENDED READINGS

Greil, L. L. (1991). *Not yet pregnant? Infertile couples in contemporary America.* Piscataway, NJ: Rutgers University Press.

Lisle, L. (1999). *Without child: Challenging the stigma of childlessness.* New York: Routledge.

May, E. T. (1997). *Barren in the promised land: Childless Americans and the pursuit of happiness.* Cambridge, MA: Harvard University Press.

Monach, J. H. (1993). *Childless: No choice: The experience of involuntary childlessness.* New York: Routledge.

Stanton, A. L., & Dunkel-Schetter, C. (Eds.). (1991). *Infertility: Perspectives from stress and coping research.* New York: Perseus Publishing.

REFERENCES

Abbey, A., Andrews, F. M., & Halman, L. J. (1991). Gender's role in responses to infertility. *Psychology of Women Quarterly, 15*, 295–316.

Aldwin, C. M., & Revenson, T. A. (1987). Does coping help? A reexamination of the relation between coping and mental health. *Journal of Personality and Social Psychology, 33*(2), 337–348.

Atwood, J. D., & Dobkin, S. (1992). Storm clouds are coming: Ways to help reconstruct the crisis of infertility. *Contemporary Family Therapy, 14*, 385–403.

Baum, A., Fleming, R., & Singer, J. E. (1983). Coping with victimization by technological disaster. *Journal of Social Issues, 39*, 117–138.

Baumeister, R. F. (1991). *Meanings of life.* New York: Guilford.

Becker, E. (1969). *Angel in armor.* New York: George Braziller.

Bergman, S. J. (1991). Men's psychological development: A relational perspective. (*Work in Progress, No. 48.*) Wellesley, MA: Stone Center Working Paper Series.

Bergman, S. J. & Surrey, J. L. (1994). *Couple's therapy: A relational approach.* Wellesley, MA: The Stone Center.

Blake, J. (1979). Is zero preferred? American attitudes toward childlessness in 1970. *Journal of Marriage and the Family, 41*, 245–257.

Bowen, M. (1978). *Family therapy in clinical practice.* New York: Jason Aronson.

Buber, M. (1970). *I and thou.* New York: Charles Scribner's Sons.

Butler, R. R., & Koraleski, S. (1990). Infertility: A crisis with no resolution. *Journal of Mental Health Counseling, 12*, 151–163.

Centers for Disease Control. (1995). Infertility. Retrieved December 16, 2004, from http://www.cdc.gov/nchs/fastats/fertile.htm

Centers for Disease Control. (2003). 2003 Assisted reproductive technology success rates: National summary and fertility clinic reports. Retrieved January 4, 2007, from http://apps.nccd.cdc.gov/art2003/nation03.as

Connor, K. A., Powers, E. A., & Bultena, G. L. (1979). Social interaction and life satisfaction: An empirical assessment of late life patterns. *Journal of Gerontology, 34*, 116–121.

Cook, E. P. (1987). Characteristics of the biopsychosocial crisis of infertility. *Journal of Counseling and Development, 65*, 465–470.

Dalgard, O. S., Bjork, S., & Tambs, K. (1995). Social support, negative life events and mental health. *British Journal of Psychiatry, 166*, 29–34.

Daniluk, J. C. (1991). Strategies for counseling infertile couples. *Journal of Counseling and Development, 69*, 317–320.

Daniluk, J. C. (1997). Gender and infertility. In S. R. Leiblum (Ed.), *Infertility: Medical, ethical, and psychological perspectives* (pp. 103–125). New York: Wiley.

Daniluk, J. C. (2001). Reconstructing their lives: A longitudinal, qualitative analysis of the transition to biological childlessness for infertile couples. *Journal of Counseling and Development, 79*, 439–449.

Domar, A. (1997). Stress and infertility in women. In S. R. Leiblum (Ed.), *Infertility: Medical, ethical, and psychological perspectives* (pp. 103–125). New York: Wiley.

Edelmann, R. J., & Connolly, K. J. (1996). Sex role and emotional functioning in infertile couples: Some further evidence. *Journal of Reproductive and Infant Psychology, 14*, 113–119.

Eliason, G. (2000). Spirituality and counseling of the older adult. In A. Tomer (Ed.), *Death attitudes and the older adult.* Washington, DC: Taylor and Francis.

Enns, C. Z. (1991). The "new" relationship models of women's identity: A review and critique for counselors. *Journal of Counseling and Development, 69*, 209–217.

Erikson, E. (1963). *Childhood and society.* New York: Norton.

Eunpu, D. L. (1995). The impact of infertility and treatment guidelines for couples therapy. *The American Journal of Family Therapy, 23,* 115–128.

Fedele, N. M., & Harrington, E. A. (1990). Women's groups: How connections heal. (*Work in Progress, No. 47*). Wellesley, MA: Stone Center Working Paper Series.

Felton, B. J., & Revenson, T. A. (1984). Coping with chronic illness: A study of illness controllability and the influence of coping strategies on psychological adjustment. *Journal of Consulting and Clinical Psychology, 52,* 343–353.

Fiore, J., Becker, J., & Coppell, D. B. (1983). Social network interactions: A buffer of stress? *American Journal of Community Psychology, 11,* 423–439.

Firestone, R. W. (1994). Psychological defenses against death anxiety. In R. A. Neimeyer (Ed.), *Death anxiety handbook* (pp. 217–241). Washington, DC: Taylor and Francis.

Fleming, J., & Burry, K. (1987). Coping with infertility. *Journal of Social Work and Human Sexuality, 6,* 37–41.

Forrest, L., & Gilbert, M. S. (1992). Infertility: An unanticipated and prolonged life crisis. *Journal of Mental Health Counseling, 14,* 42–58.

Genero, N. R., Miller, J. B., Surrey, J., & Baldwin, L. M. (1992). Measuring perceived mutuality in close relationships: Validation of the mutual psychological development questionnaire. *Journal of Family Psychology, 6,* 36–48.

Gibson, D. M., & Myers, J. E. (2000). Gender and infertility: A relational approach to counseling women. *Journal of Counseling and Development, 78,* 400–410.

Gibson, D. M., & Myers, J. E. (2002). The effect of social coping resources and growth-fostering relationships on infertility stress in women. *Journal of Mental Health Counseling, 24*(1), 68–80.

Gilligan, C. (1991). Women's psychological development: Implications for psychotherapy. *Women in Therapy, 11* (3–4), 5–31.

Goodman, K., & Rothman, B. (1984). Group work in infertility treatment. *Social Work Wwith Groups, 7,* 79–97.

Green, G. D. (1990). Is separation really so great? In L. S. Brown & M. P. P. Root (Eds.), *Diversity and complexity in feminist therapy* (pp. 87–104). New York: Harrington Park Press.

Greenbert, J., Pyszczynski, T., & Solomon, S. (1986). The causes and consequences of a need for self-esteem: A terror management theory. In R. F. Baumeister (Ed.), *Public self and private self* (pp. 189–212). New York: Springer-Verlag.

Halman, L. J., Abbey, A., & Andrews, F. M. (1993). Why are couples satisfied with infertility treatment? *Fertility and Sterility, 59,* 1046–1054.

Hendricks, M. C. (1985). Feminist therapy with women and coupes who are infertile. In L. B. Rosewater & L. E. Walker (Eds.), *Hormones and behavior* (pp. 147–158). New York: Springer.

Jack, D. C. (1991). *Silencing the self: Women and depression.* Cambridge, MA: Harvard University Press.

Janoff-Bulman, R. (1989). The benefits of illusions, the threat of disillusionment, and the limitations of inaccuracy. *Journal of Social and Clinical Psychology, 8*(2), 158–175.

Jordan, J. V. (1993). Challenges in connection. (*Work in Progress, No. 60*). Wellesley, MA: Stone Center Working Paper Series.

Jordan, J. V. (1995). A relational approach to psychotherapy. *Women and Therapy, 16,* 51–61.

Jordan, J. V. (1997). Yes: The relational model is a source of empowerment for women. In M. R. Walsh (Ed.), *Women, men, & gender: Ongoing debates* (pp. 373–379). New Haven, CT: Yale University Press.

Jordan, J. V., Kaplan, A. G., Miller, J. B., Stiver, I. P., & Surrey, J. L. (1991). *Women's growth in connection.* New York: Guilford Press.

Kaplan, A. (1986). The "self-in-relation": Implications for depression in women. *Psychotherapy, 23,* 234–242.

Keystone, M., & Kaffko, K. (1992). The braided threads: Intimacy, sequences of commitment to and disengagement from incentives. *The Canadian Journal of Human Sexuality, 1,* 47–54.

Komproe, I. H., Rijken, M., Ros, W. J. G., & Winnubst, J. A. M. (1997). Available support and received support: Different effects under stressful circumstance. *Journal of Social and Personality Relationships, 14,* 59–77.

Korpatnick, S., Daniluk, J., & Pattinson, H. A. (1993). Infertility: A nonevent transition. *Fertility and Sterility, 59,* 163–171.

Kübler-Ross, E. (1969). *On death and dying.* New York: Macmillan.

Lampman, C., & Dowling-Guyer, S. (1995). Attitudes toward voluntary and involuntary childlessness. *Basic and Applied Psychology, 17,* 213–222.

Lazarus, R. S., & Folkman, S. (1984). *Stress, appraisal, and psychology.* New York: Springer.

Leader, A., Taylor, P. J., & Daniluk, J. (1984). Infertility: Clinical and psychological aspects. *Psychiatric Annals, 14,* 461–467.

Lee, C. (1997). Social context, depression, and the transition to motherhood. *British Journal of Health and Psychology, 2,* 93–108.

Liang, B., Taylor, C., Williams, L. M., Tracy, A., Jordan, J., & Miller, J. B. (1998). The relational health indices: An exploratory study. (*Work in Progress, No. 293*). Wellesley, MA: Stone Center Working Paper Series.

Lin, N. (1986). Conceptualizing social support. In N. Lin, A. Dean, & W. Ensel (Eds.), *Social support, life events, and depression* (pp. 129–152). San Diego, CA: Academic Press.

Litt, M. D., Tennen, H., Affleck, G., & Klock, S. (1992). Coping and cognitive factors in adaptation to in vitro fertilization failure. *Journal of Behavioral Medicine, 15*(2), 171–187.

Luske, M. P. (1985). The effect of group counseling on the frequency of grief reported by infertile couples. *Journal of Obstetrics and Gynecological Neonatal Nursing, 14,* 67.

Mahler, M., Pine, F., & Bergman, A. (1975). *The psychological birth of the human infant: Symbiosis and individuation.* New York: Basis Books.

Mahlstedt, P. P. (1985). The psychological component of infertility. *Fertility and Sterility, 43,* 335–346.

Marrero, D. (1982). *Adjustment to misfortune: The process of coping with diabetes mellitus in children and their parents.* Unpublished doctoral dissertation, University of California, Irvine.

Matthews, R., & Matthews, A. M. (1986). Infertility and involuntary childlessness: The transition to nonparenthood. *Journal of Marriage and Family, 48,* 641–649.

Menning, B. E. (1980). The emotional needs of infertile couples. *Fertility and Sterility, 34,* 313–319.

Meyers, M., Diamond, R., Kezure, D., Scharf, C., Weinshel, M., & Raite, D. S. (1995). An infertility primer for family therapists: I. Medical, social, and psychological dimensions. *Family Process, 34,* 219–229.

Miall, C. E. (1986). The stigma of involuntary childlessness. *Social Problems, 33,* 258–282.

Miller, J. B. (1986). What do we mean by relationships? (*Work in Progress, No. 22*). Wellesley, MA: Stone Center Working Paper Series.

Miller, J. B. (1988). Connections, disconnections, and violations. (*Work in Progress, No. 33*). Wellesley, MA: Stone Center Working Paper Series.

Miller, J. B. (1991). The development of women's sense of self. In J. V. Jordan, A. G. Kaplan, J. B. Miller, I. P. Stiver, & J. L. Surrey (Eds.), *Women's growth in connection* (pp. 11–26). New York: Guilford Press.

Miller, J. B., & Stiver, I. P. (1997). *The healing connection.* Boston, MA: Beacon Press.

Mitchell, R. E., & Hodson, C. A. (1983). Coping with domestic violence: Social support and psychological health among battered women. *American Journal of Community Psychology, 11,* 629–654.

Mitchell, R. E., Cronkite, R. C., & Moos, R. H. (1983). Stress, coping, and depression among married couples. *Journal of Abnormal Psychology, 92,* 433–448.

Mosher, W. D., & Pratt, W. F. (1990). Fecundity and infertility in the United States, 1965–1988 (Advance Data from Vital and Health Statistics No. 192). Hyattsville, MD: National Center for Health Statistics.

Myers, L. B., & Wark, L. (1996). Psychotherapy for infertility: A cognitive-behavioral approach for couples. *Journal of Family Therapy, 24,* 920.

Nelson, M. L. (1996). Separation versus connection, the gender controversy: Implications for counseling women. *Journal of Counseling and Development, 74,* 339–344.

O'Moore, A. M., O'Moore, R. R., & Harrison, R. F. (1983). Psychosomatic aspects in idiopathic infertility: Effects of treatment with autogenic training. *Journal of Psychosomatic Research, 27,* 145.

Peterson, R. A. (1983). Attitudes toward the childless spouse. *Sex Roles, 9,* 321–331.

Pearson, T. E. (1986). The definition and measurement of social support. *Journal of Counseling and Development, 64,* 390–395.

Porter, N. L., & Christopher, F. S. (1984). Infertility: Towards an awareness of a need among family life practitioners. *Family Relations, 33,* 309–315.

Reed, K. (1987). The effect of infertility on female sexuality. *Pre- and Peri-Natal Psychology, 2,* 57–62.

Rhodes, R. (1987). Women, motherhood, and infertility: The social and historical context. *Journal of Social Work and Human Sexuality, 6,* 5–20.

Robinson, G. E., & Stewart, D. E. (1995). Infertility and new reproductive technologies. *American Psychiatric Press Review of Psychiatry, 14,* 283–306.

Schiller, L. Y. (1997). Rethinking stages of development in women's groups: Implications for practice. *Social Work with Groups, 20,* 3–19.

Shepherd, J. (1992). Stress management and infertility. *The Australian and New Zealand Journal of Obstetrics and Gynaecology, 32,* 353–356.

Smith, J. A., & Smith, A. H. (2004). Treating faith-based infertile couples using cognitive-behavioral counseling strategies: A preliminary investigation. *Counseling & Values, 49*(1), 48–63.

Stanton, A. L., Tennen, H., Affleck, G., & Mendola, R. (1992). Coping and adjustment to infertility. *Journal of Social and Clinical Psychology, 11,* 1–13.

Stewart, D. E., & Robinson, G. E. (1989). Infertility by choice or nature. *Canadian Journal of Psychiatry, 34,* 866–871.

Stewart, J. A., & Clarke, V. A. (1995). The role of social support in ameliorating reproduction. *Fertility and Sterility, 46,* 545–466.

Surrey, J. L. (1991). The "self-in-relation": A theory of women's development. In J. V. Jordan, A. G. Kaplan, J. B. Miller, I. P. Stiver, & J. L. Surrey (Eds.), *Women's growth in connection* (pp. 51–66). New York: Guilford Press.

Tomer, A., & Eliason, G. (2003). Theorien zur erklärung von einstellungen gegenüber sterben und tod [Theoretical approaches concerning death attitudes]. In Wittkowski, J. (Ed.), *Sterben, tod und trauern [Dying, death, & bereavement].*

Trantham, P. (1996). The infertile couple. *American Family Physician, 54,* 1001–1010.

Ulione, M. S. (1996). Physical and emotional health in dual-earner families. *Family and Community Health, 19,* 14–20.

University of North Carolina Hospitals. (1998). *UNC Assisted Reproductive Technologies Clinic IVF Financial Information.* Chapel Hill, NC: Author.

van Balen, F., Verdurmen, J., & Ketting, E. (1997). Choices and motivations of infertile couples. *Patient Education and Counseling, 31,* 19–37.

Veevers, J. (1980). *Childless by choice.* Toronto, Canada: Butterworth.

Williams, L., Bischoff, R., & Ludes, J. (1992). A biopsychosocial model for treating infertility. *Contemporary Family Therapy, 14,* 309–322.

Wong, P. T. P. (1998). Meaning-centered counseling. In P. T. P. Wong & P. S. Fry (Eds.), *The human quest for meaning* (pp. 395–435). Mahwah, NJ: Lawrence Erlbaum Associates.

Wright, J., Allard, M., Lecours, A., & Sabourin, S. (1989). Psychosocial distress and infertility: A review of controlled research. *International Journal of Fertility, 34,* 126–142.

17

▼▼▼▼

The Historical Advancement of Grief Counseling

Grafton T. Eliason
California University of Pennsylvania

Mark Lepore
Chatham College

Rick Myer
Duquesne University

What though the radiance which was once so bright
Be not forever taken from my sight,
Though nothing can bring back the hour
Of splendour in the grass, of glory in the flower;
Grief not, rather find,
Strength in what remains behind,
In the primal sympathy
Which having been must ever be,
In the soothing thoughts that spring
Out of Human suffering,
In the faith that looks through death
In years that bring philophic mind.

—William Wordsworth (1888–1999)

While you are not able to serve men, how can you serve spirits [of the dead]?...While you do not know life, how can you know about death?

—*Confucius (ca. 500 BCE, The Analects, 2:11.11)*

Grief is a universal experience that is both a natural emotional response to loss, as well as an expressive response learned in the context of our individual cultures. This chapter examines the evolution of grief counseling, including contemporary theories. It also suggests that aspects of Tomer and Eliason's (1996) Comprehensive Model of Death Anxiety may be helpful to clients experiencing grief and loss. A key element in assisting a client's grieving process is to address regrets and to facilitate balance of the emotional response with their belief system. When unbalanced, regrets impede a client's ability to reconcile the grief experience through their belief system and/or culture.

Prior to beginning our discussion of grief and loss models, we believe a definition for the grief experience is needed. Many authors distinguish between grief, bereavement, and mourning (e.g., Attig, 1996; Bernstein, 1997; Corr, Nabe, & Corr, 1997; Rando, 1984, 1995). In general, this group defines grief as people's responses to a loss, including psychological, behavioral, social, spiritual, and physical experiences. Bereavement is considered the state or condition caused by the loss. Mourning, on the other hand, is the attempt to cope with the loss or resolve the experience of grief. This involves both psychological processes as well as cultural belief systems. We believe grief is a process in which an individual actively readjusts to their subjective world and culture, redefining relationships, after a loss. Grief is not linear in nature with people moving from one step to another; rather grief is cyclical with people re-experiencing the loss repeatedly as they learn to relate to the world and themselves (Humphrey & Zimpfer, 1996; Rando, 1995). Therefore grief includes people's reactions and adaptations to a loss, either due to death or another circumstance. In the latter case, the loss must be perceived as permanent or irrevocable with no hope of regaining that which is gone. That is, the loss must be perceived as something that cannot be regained. Rando (1995) points out that there are two categories for loss, physical and psychosocial (or symbolic). A physical loss is the loss of something tangible, such as when a house is destroyed by fire. A psychosocial loss is less tangible, such as when an individual experiences a divorce or a lost dream (pp. 216–217).

A HISTORICAL PERSPECTIVE OF GRIEF AND LOSS COUNSELING

The process of grief has been studied using many theoretical perspectives and methods. The results of this inquiry are a variety of models, each attempting to explain what happens when people are grieving. These models are diverse and, in some cases, do not agree on the definition of grief. In spite of this variance, a method for understanding models of grief is suggested by Attig (1996) who categorizes them into three types: (a) stage or phase models, (b) medical models, and (c) task models. This approach is useful for understanding the beneficial aspects of the models as well as their drawbacks. An exhaustive discussion of grief models is beyond the scope of this chapter and not practical. Therefore the following discussion is an overview of prominent models that represent either milestones in the field or are representative of one of the three categories proposed by Attig.

Stage or Phase Models

Sigmund Freud. Freud (1917) proposed, in *Mourning and Melancholia,* an elementary model for understanding grief that focuses on the concept of attachment and can be related to depression. According to Freud, the ego and id are involved in this process. When faced with a loss, individuals must disengage their identification with the lost object and eventually withdraw energy. This process reframes multiple attachment layers (e.g., memories and symbols) on two levels: (a) the lost interpersonal relationship and (b) intrapersonal meaning of the loss, or narcissism. These two events take place simultaneously as individuals let go of the previous attachment, and begin searching for new attachments. Freud suggests that grief is a slow process of adaptation and accommodation. Although fundamental, Freud provides a foundation from which to build a framework for comprehending grief and loss combining a stage/task perspective.

Erich Lindemann. In his work with survivors of the Coconut Grove Night Club fire in 1942, Erich Lindemann (1944) looked at grief from the perspective of crisis intervention and developed a model for understanding grief and loss based on six characteristics of grief analogous to psychiatric symptoms (Attig, 1996; Rando, 1995). Among the characteristics identified by Lindemann (1944) are somatic distress, pre-occupation with thoughts of the deceased, guilt related to the deceased or the death event, hostile reactions, loss of function, and a tendency to assume traits and behaviors which belonged to the deceased. Lindemann also uses a task model adding an additional component to Freud's (1917) model by proposing three tasks that individuals must undertake in the resolution of a loss. These tasks include letting go of psychological attachments with the deceased, assimilating to an environment without the deceased, and building new relationships.

John Bowlby. John Bowlby (1980) became a pioneer of attachment theory, which can be directly applied to grief and loss. Expanding on psychoanalytic theory and incorporating concepts from attachment theory and others, Bowlby suggests that uncomplicated grief has four general phases: (a) numbing, (b) yearning and searching, (c) disorganization and despair, (d) and reorganization. He uses the belief that the foundation of individuals' relationships stems from the early attachment between individuals and their mothers or caregivers. By incorporating a unique cognitive component in his model, Bowlby suggests that cognitive biases influence personal perceptions and belief systems. This concept is based on individuals' experiences of attachment, and the later separation anxiety that children experience with maturity and the absence of their caregivers. Separation anxiety is a response to the threat of loss, and bereavement is a reaction to the loss. Subsequent losses and relationships are influenced and processed by cognitive biases formed early in life evoking similar emotions. Movement through these stages and their ultimate resolution involves individuals searching for the lost object, recognizing the permanence of the loss, and finally reorganizing the perception of the lost object along with forming relationships with new objects.

Elizabeth Kübler-Ross. By interviewing and observing over two hundred patients dealing with terminal illness, Kübler-Ross (1969) developed a five-stage model of death and dying that has become an established method for describing an individual's personal dying process. Though her model identifies stages and coping mechanisms leading to the acceptance of one's own death and loss of self, the stages can also be applied appropriately to the grief involving loss of other. The stages she identified include: (a) denial and isolation, (b) anger, (c) bargaining, (d) depression, and (e) acceptance. She believes that individuals progress through these stages at their own speed, with some having more difficulty in specific stages than others. In addition, Kübler-Ross felt that progression was not linear and that individuals may cycle through the stages more than once. However, she did believe that everyone experienced all of the stages.

Medical Models

Osterweis, Solomon, and Green.   Osterweis, Solomon, and Green (1984) use a more extreme medical perspective than Lindemann (1944) in explaining grief. These researchers suggest that a biological relationship exists between the psychological and physical well-being of individuals. Through observations, these researchers found that individuals may experience negative respiratory, cardiovascular, immune system functioning, autonomic, and endocrine system responses to the loss stressor. These findings seem plausible given the research on stress that has been demonstrated in numerous bereavement studies.

Task Models

J. William Worden.   Other theorists focus on tasks that individuals must accomplish throughout the grieving process. Unlike stage and medical models of grief, these models suggest that grief is an active process in which individuals must perform a series of tasks leading to the resolution of grief. A well known task model of grief was developed by Worden (1991/2002) who, according to Humphrey and Zimpfer (1996), integrates Lindemann's (1944) and Bowlby's (1980) ideas to form a practical model for understanding grief. Worden (2002) believes grieving is necessary as individuals adjust to life without the object that was lost, and he identifies four major tasks involved in the process: (a) accept the reality of the loss; (b) experience the pain of grief; (c) adjust to an environment in which the deceased is missing; and (d) to emotionally relocate the deceased and move on with life (Worden, 2002).

The first task according to Worden involves the acceptance of the reality of the loss. This process is a cognitive task that must be performed prior to moving to subsequent tasks. The second task Worden identifies is affective and involves experiencing the pain of grief. In this task, individuals encounter a rush of emotions that must be felt in order to grieve their loss. The emotions experienced in this task may continue to be present and emerge throughout the grief process. In this sense, the resolution of the task is ongoing as individuals work through their grief.

The third task is adjusting to the environment and involves individuals resolving issues related to physical sensations and behaviors associated with the deceased. Worden states this task is pervasive and a continuous aspect of the grief process. As individuals encounter various environmental stimuli such as locations, people, events, music, and holidays, they are reminded of the deceased. As a result, the completion of this task may be long term as individuals encounter situations that remind them of the deceased. The final task is emotional in nature and involves moving on with life. This task involves recognition that emotional energy targeted for the deceased cannot be returned and therefore, individuals cease attempting to meet their emotional needs in that manner. Worden has drawn from recent research and modified this stage maintaining that "people do not decathect from the dead but find ways to develop 'continuing bonds' with the deceased ... One must find a place for the deceased that will enable the mourner to be connected with the deceased but in a way that will not preclude him or her from going on with life" (Worden, 2002, p. 35).

Both Rando (1995) and Worden (2002) stress the need to consider mediators of the mourning process in order to understand why individuals handle the tasks of mourning in different ways. Worden identifies seven mediating variables: (a) how the person was, (b) the nature of the attachment, (c) the mode of death, (d) historical antecedents, (e) personality variables, (f) social variables, and (g) concurrent stresses. In Addition, Rando adds physiological factors.

Therese A. Rando. Rando (1984, 1993, 1995) has developed a task model of grief that broadens Worden's (1991/2002), providing a more extensive base for assessment and intervention strategies (Humphrey & Zimpfer, 1996). Rando's (1995) model is divided into three phases: avoidance, confrontation, and accommodation. Throughout these three phases it involves six tasks, which build upon one another, but can also occur simultaneously.

The "Six R" Processes of Mourning:

Avoidance

1. Recognize the loss.
   a. Acknowledge the death.
   b. Understand the death.

Confrontation.

2. React to the separation.

    a. Experience the pain.
    b. Feel, identify, accept, and give some form of expression to all the psychological reactions to the loss.
    c. Identify and mourn secondary losses

3. Recollect and reexperience the deceased and the relationship.

    a. Review and remember realistically.
    b. Revive and reexperience the feelings.

4. Relinquish the old attachments to the deceased and the old assumptive world.

Accommodation

5. Readjust to move adaptively into the new world without forgetting the old.

    a. Revive the assumptive world.
    b. Develop a new relationship with the deceased.
    c. Adopt new ways of being in the world.
    d. Form a new identity.

6. Reinvest. (Rando, 1995, pp. 223–238)

In the avoidance phase, individuals first experience shock and overwhelming emotions. As a result, they often attempt to cope with the trauma by avoiding acknowledgment of the loss. This may be unconscious or conscious disbelief, or it may become denial as the reality of the loss begins to set in. Ultimately, they must recognize the loss (Rando, 1995, pp. 224–225).

The second phase involves confrontation in which individuals must react to the separation, recollect, and relinquish attachments related to the loss. Difficult learning takes place during this phase that includes yearning and searching for the deceased loved one. The tasks in this phase involve issues related to the present and past with respect to the deceased. Rando believes individuals must react by finding appropriate methods for expressing emotions that occur because of the loss. In addition, individuals must identify and grieve secondary and symbolic losses that are related to the deceased. For example, an individual whose spouse dies will not only grieve the loss of their partner, but possibly the loss of income if the partner provided that in the relationship, help with cooking and cleaning around the home, and help parenting if they had children. Rando also indicates that individuals must come to terms with the past through recollecting and re-experiencing the deceased individual. This process involves reviewing and remembering. The final task in this phase is relinquishing, which involves letting go of the deceased and the old assumptive world. For Rando this task means that individuals must surrender their efforts of meeting needs through the deceased in order to progress to the final phase and tasks of grief (Rando, 1995, pp. 230–235).

Rando calls the final phase of grief the accommodation phase, in which individuals readjust and reinvest themselves. These two tasks involve revising and updating one's assumptive world, without forgetting the old, and reinvesting in a meaningful life experience without the lost object. Rando believes that a new, healthy, symbolic relationship with the deceased can be developed, as long as it meets two simultaneous criteria. The mourner must fully understand that the loved is in fact dead, and the mourner must be able to move forward, healthily, in their new life (Rando, 1998/1995, pp. 235–236). As individuals advance through these tasks, they separate themselves emotionally from the deceased, allowing for the possibility of those emotions to connect with new individuals (Rando 1995, pp. 230–239).

Other Grief Models

Robert A. Neimeyer. The work of Robert Neimeyer (2000a) takes an alternative view on grief and loss counseling which differs from the stage or medical models. His work is strongly influenced by George Kelly's 1955 philosophy of constructive alternativism construction which posits that humans attribute individualized meaning and perceptions (alternative construction) to their experiences (Neimeyer, Epting, & Krieger, 1984). This meaning does not need to be based in reality, but is instead an intimate construct based upon close relationships and the surrounding culture (Neimeyer, 2000b). A loss can challenge these constructs as it does not fit within the existing framework of how an individual functions in daily life (Neimeyer, 1999). This challenge can result in an identity upheaval leaving the individual without viable constructs as they were ineffective at processing the loss. Neimeyer focuses on this challenge, this upheaval, which can initiate a search for meaning to the loss, taking the form of new constructs. This type of grief counseling, aptly designated *reconstruction*, conceptualizes grieving in terms of narrative construction which aids in coping with the change that loss brings (Neimeyer, 1999). The stories that people tell themselves shape and inform their perception, essentially creating their world (Neimeyer, 1993). Neimeyer contends that narratives are an active process which can harmonize loss with new constructs, essentially reconstructing meaning. The use of narrative enables the bereaved to place the loss in the context of a larger story: his or her life. This narrative connects the past experiences with the future and in doing so makes the loss meaningful and understandable (Neimeyer, 2000a).

Though a highly individualized process, the narrative is influenced by the social and cultural forces which surround the bereaved individual. Furthermore, the new meaning needs to be shared with other individuals in order for it to be socially validated (Neimeyer, 1999). This sharing of the narrative does not imply that the new meaning can be fully articulated in words, there is a facet which is incapable of being articulated. The reconstruction of meaning is a process of trying on different roles and different conceptualizations, through which a new narrative is formed, thus enabling the individual to make sense of their new life after loss (Neimeyer, 2000a).

Paul T. P. Wong.   Paul Wong (2006, Wong & Frey,1998) introduces Meaning-Centered Counseling (MCC) and Meaning-Management Theory. This theory integrates many schools of psychotherapy, especially existential, logotherapy, and narrative therapy, as well as, spiritual wisdoms from the Eastern and Western traditions.

> MCC recognizes that a formless and all engulfing void preceded human existence. All behaviors, in one way or another, are aimed at filling that primordial and universal void. Unfortunately most of the endeavors have failed. Self-centered pursuits of pleasure, possessions, and power lead only to disillusion and misery. Paradoxically, selfless compassion and surrender to a higher purpose lead to fulfillment. (Wong, 2006, p. 3)

Though MCC addresses many different psychological issues, we have found it to be especially successful with issues of death anxiety, grief, and loss. It uses three primary meaning processes: meaning-seeking, meaning-making, and meaning-reconstruction. Meaning-reconstruction specifically focuses on individuals' cognition and transformation through the changing, or reframing, of attitudes and perceptions. For instance, one can move from a victim's mentality to a heroic viewpoint (Wong, 2006).

> For the MCC, the key construct is meaning, which is central to understanding of the impact of culture on the coping process (Wong & Wong, 2005); physical and mental health (Wong & Fry, 1998); spirituality and religion (Wong, 1998b). Related constructs include cognitive reframing, existential and spiritual coping, attribution retraining, stress appraisal, transformative

coping, life review, re-storying, self-actualization, and organizational and cultural transformation. (Wong, 2006, p. 42)

When applied to death anxiety, grief, and loss, Meaning-Centered Counseling becomes a useful and valid choice of treatment.

Alan D. Wolfelt. Alan Wolfelt advocates that grief counselors move from a strict medical model of care to a broader approach. He claims that our current models need alignment with a more spiritual, growth-oriented attitude. Grief need not be defined, diagnosed, and treated as an illness, but rather should be an acknowledgment of an event that forever changes a person's worldview. The caregiver, through careful listening and observation, learns to support mourners and help them help themselves heal (Wolfelt, 1998a, b, c, 2005).

The Companioning Model of Bereavement caregiving developed by Wolfelt shows bereavement caregivers how to help people integrate life's losses by observing them and being present with them—*companioning*. Companioning focuses on honoring the spirit rather than the intellect, learning from others as opposed to teaching them, listening with the heart rather than analyzing with the head, understanding a person's struggles as opposed to directing those struggles, and being present to another person's pain not taking away that pain. It respects the confusion and is not intent on imposing order and logic (Wolfelt, 1998a, b, c).

Utilizing this method of bereavement counseling the caregiver listens in a supportive manner to the individual's concerns and helps the survivor recognize that their emotional reactions are natural and to be expected. Survivors are assisted to organize and prioritize day-to-day recovery tasks. The individual is helped to understand and recognize the wide range of reactions to trauma, and to draw on their strengths to develop health coping mechanisms and gradually resume their prior level of functioning. Individuals are helped to grieve their losses in their own unique ways (Wolfelt, 1998a, b, c).

COMPLICATED GRIEF AND MOURNING

Complicated grief and mourning is quite common and it is important for professionals to recognize. Presenting problems and symptomology may also be a result of unresolved grief issues. Complicated grief may be identified by an extended amount of time that an individual remains in grief without being able to move through the stages of grief or to resolve the loss emotionally. It might be referred to by some as feeling "stuck," or unable to move on in life. It is most often connected to more intense symptomology ranging from change in mood, sleep patterns, or eating patterns, to adjustment disorders, depression, anxiety, substance abuse, or even post traumatic stress disorder.

Complicated grief may result from many situations, such as, an individuals prior history of mental health issues; a lack of social support for the client; a relationship with the deceased that is marked by anger, turmoil, abuse, or dependency; trauma or unanticipated death; a number of losses experienced in a short period of time; the death of a loved one over an extended period of time; the death of a child; or death that results in feelings of self-blame, guilt, or regret on behalf of the survivor. Worden (2002) and Rando (1993, 1995) have outlined aspects of complicated grief in detail. In this chapter, we look specifically at regrets associated with grief and the application of Tomer and Eliason's (1996) model.

Regrets Associated With Grief and Loss

In part grief is a culturally learned process (Irish, Lundquist, & Nelsen, 1993). Therefore, without taking into account people's belief systems that are learned in the context of their culture, models of grief are incomplete. A model for explaining death anxiety developed by Tomer and Eliason (1996) provides a template for adding this component. This component, we believe, is critical in developing therapeutic strategies for helping people resolve their grief.

Just as Kübler-Ross' model of death and dying is transferable to grief and loss, we propose that Tomer and Eliason's (1996) Comprehensive Model of Death Anxiety is also applicable to grief and loss. We suggest that grief may be viewed as a threat to closure for past events and unrealized future hopes. Death anxiety and grief can be differentiated in that death anxiety refers to individuals' fear of their own death, whereas grief is a reaction to the loss of something or someone else. This loss may be through death, a broken relationship, a life change such as relocation, diagnosis of a life changing medical condition, or other similar events.

Death and Loss Salience. Tomer and Eliason (1996) use a model that identifies four aspects of death anxiety. The first aspect involves the concept of death salience. For these authors, this idea refers to the degree to which individuals contemplate their own mortality and death. The intensity by which death salience is experienced is related to their exposure to death in their lives. For example, if individuals experience numerous losses through death, death salience may increase. The amount of emotional closeness of the relationship in conjunction with the recentness of the loss also influences the extent of death salience. We maintain that it is appropriate to substitute loss salience for death salience. The mechanism by which individuals experience grief and loss are similar to what is described previously. Salience is increased or decreased by the quantity of loss experienced as well as the quality of the loss. Quantity concerns both the number and time frame of the losses that have been experienced. For example, time mediates loss salience. Time in this instance means the amount of time that has past since the loss event. Yet, care must be taken not to assume that time automatically decreases loss salience. To do so, relies on Western cultural traditions and does not respect other possible cultural differences. Quantity also refers to the number of losses within a particular time frame. Generally, the more losses that occur the greater the loss salience. But again, cultural belief systems may influence this dynamic. Quality, on the other hand, concerns the importance of the loss. The more importance placed on the loss, the greater the loss salience. For example, losing a family member for most cultures has a greater impact on loss salience than the loss of an acquaintance.

Internal and External Belief Systems. The second aspect involves individuals' belief systems that are moderated by coping processes. These two systems include beliefs about the world, or external assumptions, and beliefs about the self, or internal assumptions. Aspects related to beliefs about the world are culturally determined and involve individuals' identification with culture, religion, politics, and education. Related issues include whether or not life is fair, the justness of the world, and personal control over the environment. Beliefs about the self include self-esteem, locus of control, and individuals' perception of virtue. These beliefs impact individuals' concept of the ideal self and the actual self. Tomer and Eliason (1996) speculate that the greater the differences between these two constructs, the more likely individuals will experience death anxiety and/or grief and loss. Both belief systems act as coping processes in reaction to changes in death salience. An example of this interaction is seen when individuals' experience the death of a loved one. If death salience increases due to this loss, then beliefs about the world and self are activated as coping mechanisms. One person might cope by questioning their own virtue, thinking they have done something to deserve this loss. In reaction, they increase religious participation in an attempt to lower death anxiety. Another person might react by questioning their ability to control events in the world. This person might cope by altering their perceived locus of control by becoming more flexible and allowing spontaneity. In a similar fashion, the experience of loss activates the same coping processes described previously to manage, in this case, loss salience.

Regret

The third aspect of this model involves regrets: past, future, and present. Tomer and Eliason (1996) define regret as the inability to resolve or fulfill basic aspirations due to death or loss. Similarly, the model uses the concept of regret to refer to the inability to resolve aspirations in the context of a relationship due to the loss of another.

Past-Related Regret.   Past-related regret takes two forms involving acts of commission and omission. The acts of commission concern feelings, behaviors, and cognitions a person regrets having felt, done, or thought in the past. For example, an individual may have argued with another person leaving unresolved issues and a broken relationship. The results are feelings of remorse, possible depression, or a lowered self-concept. An act of omission is the opposite of commission in that this type of regret involves feelings, behaviors, and cognitions a person regrets not having felt, done, or thought within the relationship. A key element in determining this type of past-related regret is a person's belief that they should have felt, done, or thought a specific thing. Because the person did not complete this action, the issue is left unresolved. Examples are not disclosing feelings such as love to another person, not spending enough time with family or friends, or wishing they had worked harder. Like in regrets of commission, a person may experience numerous psychological problems such as depression, anxiety, or lowered self-concept.

Future-Related Regret.   Future-related regrets are somewhat different for grief and loss than death anxiety. For death anxiety, these regrets concern the availability of time to achieve perceived individual goals (Tomer & Eliason, 1996). For grief and loss, on the other hand, individuals focus on relationships and the realization that no more time to cultivate this is available. These goals include feelings, behaviors, and thoughts that involve participation in meaningful events with the person who is no longer present. Shared future experiences that are no longer possible due to loss of another may include such things as children's' weddings, the birth of grandchildren, vacations, or simply spending time with the deceased loved one. Once again, the development of psychological problems may result from this type of regret.

The key for the therapist is to help the client maintain an appropriate perspective of future-regrets within their cultural belief systems. For example, the Hmong believe the souls of the dead can cause harm and sickness to the living if not sent to the spiritual world properly (Bilatout, 1993). A person from this culture could get so involved in this belief that they are not able to function at an acceptable level now. The therapist must help this person balance the influence of the future-regret with the ability to live now.

Present-Related Regret and Present Meaning.   Present-related regret and meaning are issues associated with one's current quality of life (Tomer & Eliason, 1996). Intricately involved in this regret are two inter-related concepts, the meaningfulness of life and death. Typically people explore issues concerning self-satisfaction when pondering the meaningfulness of life. They ask themselves questions such as "Am I happy with who I am as a human being," "Am I doing the things I want to do," and "Am I satisfied with who I am?" As people consider the meaningfulness of death, they weigh issues involving the impact of their lives and deaths on others, and inversely the effect others have had on their own lives. It is in the resolution of this regret that a person finds a measure of comfort and meaning in the relationship experience. The interaction of two primary concepts determines how a person resolves present-related regret. First, a person must come to terms with the impact the lost relationship has had on their life. The person must recognize how they have been shaped by the interactions with the deceased person. An example is the knowledge and experience passed on generationally from a grandparent to a grandchild. This would include cultural belief systems, traditions, general knowledge, and the human dynamic. Second, a person must reconcile the other's death experience especially as this relates to finding peace after death. If these emotions are too overwhelming either by quantity or intensity, people are not able to fully live in the present thereby lowering their current quality of life. For different cultures this may have unique meanings and therapists must guard against imposing their personal interpretation on the therapeutic process.

Cultural Aspects.   If issues of regret in the past, present, or future are unresolved or not balanced within the cultural belief system, then the ability to function at a healthy level is impaired. Each culture has its own unique belief systems that help people cope with issues throughout their lives. If working properly, then belief systems can facilitate resolution of grief and subsequent personal regrets by balancing the way people view themselves and their outlook on the world. If the coping process involving beliefs about the self and/or world are not working properly, or if unhealthy coping mechanisms are being used, then grief becomes complicated and potentially psychologically debilitating. The goal of therapy is then to restore the individual's homeostasis through personal psychological growth within the context of the client's cultural belief systems.

This model incorporates the cultural component in the way people regret, resulting from their belief systems. For example, in the Orthodox tradition of Judaism, as the person nears death, they ask for forgiveness for errors of judgment and action, as well as expresses hope for family members (Cytron, 1993). Should a family member not be able to be present at this time, then they may experience past-regret regarding the inability to be part of this ritual. This cultural dynamic is then introduced into the therapeutic process by directly integrating cultural awareness in the understanding of loss and grief. The therapist is, therefore, prompted to be cognizant of the clients' world view, respect their belief systems, and work therapeutically within the context of their world view and belief systems (Sue & Sue, 1990).

Therapeutic Application.   Therapeutic applications help to reframe clients' perception of self and outlook on the world within their cultural belief systems. The reframing process involves helping a client view their role in the world from a different angle. The result is a change of perception, or a paradigm shift, effectively bringing the client back into balance with their belief system. As this process takes place, a client addresses issues related to regrets. By helping a client to reframe perceptions, the regrets surfacing due to grief may be seen from a new perspective. This allows a client to focus on relevant concerns breaking the unhealthy cycle in which they have been caught. Resolution of the loss is, therefore, possible within the context of their culture. A client is able to accept regrets and mistakes as part of the growing and learning human experience of life (Capps, 1984, 1990; Eliason, 2000).

Techniques useful in helping a client to reframe are both supportive and confrontational. Supportive techniques are those that demonstrate empathy, rather than sympathy, and help clients to balance past and future regrets. These techniques encourage the expression of grief and assist a client as he or she moves through the process. Clichés are to be avoided. These are generally for the relief of the counselor's discomfort and can block the expression and resolution of grief. For example, "They are in a better place," disregards a client's possible belief systems, as well as their future regrets by saying, do not worry about what you will miss or not be able to say to the person who died. With respect to past regret, the cliché "You have your whole life ahead of you" asks the client to pretend the past is not important. Counselors must remember that even though the client is in a sense of disequilibrium, placating or talking down to them will only delay the experiencing of the grief. Instead, supportive techniques encourage the expression of grief emotionally and cognitively. Once verbalized, the client understands how to utilize their belief system and cultural background to bring regrets into balance.

Just because a client asks a question such as "Why did my spouse die?" "Why didn't I say that before?" "Will I ever feel the same?" or "What if I only would have been more loving?" counselors do not have to answer. Simply being patient, silently, actively listening to the client express the grief, or empathically reflecting the client's feeling, may help to facilitate resolution of regrets. Supportive techniques must bolster a client's ability to experience regrets that are often painful feelings and thoughts by helping them place these in an appropriate cultural perspective.

On the other hand, confrontational techniques invite a client to move beyond expression alone and experience the regrets in the present. These techniques are useful when a client is stuck, unable to move beyond the verbalization of regrets. We encourage the utilization of these techniques after an assessment that the client is unable to resolve their grief. An example of a confrontational technique is the "empty chair." A counselor may ask a client to look at an empty chair and talk to it as if the deceased person was sitting in the chair. The client may then be asked to reverse roles and to play the role of the deceased individual in response. In a variation of this technique, a counselor may ask the client to speak as if they were a person who might typically help to resolve grief within the culture such as a shaman, priest, or village elder. This should only be used when it is impossible to speak with the actual individual. This technique challenges a client to reframe their perspective actively experiencing their regrets. Actively experiencing regrets facilitates awareness, allowing the counselor and client to process the meaning of the regrets within the client's culture.

Another confrontational technique asks a client to experience the regret to the "nth" degree. Used properly, this technique provides a paradox for the client by asking them to exaggerate the regret. If the client is able to do so, then it demonstrates that the regret can be controlled; if the client is not able to do this, then it implies that the regret may not be as debilitating as originally experienced. Again, confrontational techniques are used to help a client who appears stuck, unable to resolve regrets within their belief system. These techniques stimulate a client's awareness by asking them to reframe perceptions or regrets and examine these from different perspectives.

A fine therapeutic line must be walked between utilization of these two general strategies. This fine line is primarily based on timing. Counselors must be observant in order to know when and how to confront a client. Counselors must also be attentive to signs when supportive techniques are more helpful for a client. Switching between the two techniques is more of an art than science. Although we cannot anticipate all situations that suggest the switch from one set of techniques to the other, we have listed several examples. These are meant as examples not as a set of hard standards. Each situation and client is unique and should be treated as such, therefore, we caution against applying these examples without question. Repetitious patterns of thoughts, behaviors, or feelings are one clue to signal the need to switch from supportive to confrontational techniques. Another sign is a client who constantly asks a counselor to answer questions. Indicators that suggest a need to switch from confrontational to supportive techniques include extreme emotional expression or inability to structure thought processes. In addition, a client who is unable to perform tasks necessary for routine day-to-day functioning may also need techniques that are supportive in nature. A critical aspect of the timing concerns understanding the cultural belief system of the client, specifically those beliefs associated with grief. Without this understanding, counselors can misinterpret the meaning of a client's feelings, thoughts, or behaviors.

Understanding the client's culture is therefore a key issue in the use of supportive and confrontational techniques. Counselors must be careful not to assume that the experiencing of regrets will match their own cultural experience of grief. For example, some cultures experience regrets in an emotionally charged manner, whereas other cultures may discourage an outward show of emotions. We encourage counselors to learn about the client's culture prior to working with them if it differs from the counselor's own culture. Two methods to learn about another culture include, asking another person from that culture or reading about the culture. Counselors may also ask the person in grief about their culture. Many times explaining cultural beliefs is therapeutic for a client and helps them to develop a new perspective resolving issues related to regrets. It can also have a positive effect by strengthening the therapeutic relationship. (The chapter on Regret Therapy looks at this subject with additional detail.)

CONCLUSION

This chapter provides a brief overview of grief theory, as well as a foundation for further research and more extensive therapeutic applications. It is our hope that through a deeper understanding of grief and loss, cultural belief systems, and practical therapeutic interventions clinicians will be better able to facilitate growth and resolution in clients experiencing loss.

ACKNOWLEDGMENTS

We would like to thank Jayna Rubin and Travis Schermer, graduates of Chatham College, for their contributions in the editing and revision of this chapter.

MAIN POINTS

1. A method for understanding models of grief is suggested by Attig (1996), who categorizes them into three types: (a) stage or phase models, (b) medical models, and (c) task models.
2. In general, theorists define grief as people's responses to a loss, including psychological, behavioral, social, spiritual, and physical experiences. Bereavement is considered the state or condition caused by the loss. Mourning, on the other hand, is the attempt to cope with the loss or resolve the experience of grief. This involves both psychological processes as well as cultural belief systems. We believe grief is a process in which an individual actively readjusts to his or her subjective world and culture, redefining relationships, after a loss. Grief is not linear in nature with people moving from one step to another, rather grief is cyclical with people re-experiencing the loss repeatedly as they learn to relate to the world and themselves (Humphrey & Zimpfer, 1996; Rando, 1995).

3. Task theorists maintain that individuals must accomplish specific tasks throughout the grieving process. Unlike stage and medical models of grief, these models suggest that grief is an active process in which individuals must perform a series of tasks leading to the resolution of grief.

4. Neimeyer (2000a) takes an alternative view on grief and loss counseling which differs from the stage or medical models. This type of grief counseling, aptly designated reconstruction, conceptualizes grieving in terms of narrative construction which aids in coping with the change that loss brings (Neimeyer, 1999).

5. Tomer and Eliason's (1996) Comprehensive Model of Death Anxiety is also applicable to grief and loss. We suggest that grief may be viewed as a threat to closure for past events and unrealized future hopes. This model also incorporates the cultural component in the way people regret, resulting from their belief systems.

RECOMMENDED READINGS

Capps, D. (1984). *Pastoral care and hermeneutics.* Philadelphia, PA: Fortress Press.

Capps, D. (1990). *Reframing: A new method in pastoral care.* Minneapolis, MN: Augsburg Fortress.

Epting, F. R., & Neimeyer, R. A. (Eds.), *Personal meanings of death* (pp. 1–8). Washington DC: Hemisphere Publishing Corporation.

Kubler-Ross, E. (1969). *On death and dying.* New York: MacMillan.

Littlewood, J. (1992). *Aspects of grief: Bereavement in adult life.* London: Tavistock/Routledge.

Lindemann, E. (1944). Symptomatology and management of acute grief. *American Journal of Psychiatry, 42,* 141–148.

Neimeyer, R. A. (2000). The language of loss: Grief therapy as a process of meaning reconstruction. In R. A. Neimeyer (Ed.), *Meaning reconstruction and the experience of loss* (pp. 261–292). Washington DC: American Psychological Association.

Rando, T. A. (1993). *Treatment of complicated mourning.* Champaign, IL: Research Press.

Rando, T. A. (1995). Grief and mourning: Accommodating to loss. In H. Wass & R. A. Neimeyer (Eds.). *In dying: Facing the fact* (3rd ed.). Washington, DC: Taylor & Francis.

Sue & Sue. (1990). *Counseling the culturally different: Theory and practice* (2nd ed.). New York: John Wiley & Sons.

Tomer, A., & Eliason, G. (1996). Toward a comprehensive model of death anxiety. *Death Studies, 20,* 343–365.

Wong, P., & Frey, P. S. (1998). *The human quest for meaning: A handbook of psychological research and clinical applications.* Mahwah, NJ: Lawrence Erlbaum Associates.

Worden, J. W. (2002). *Grief counseling and grief therapy* (3rd ed.). New York: Springer.

REFERENCES

Attig, T. (1996). *How we grieve: Relearning the world.* New York: Oxford University Press.

Bliatout, B. T. (1993). Homng death customs: Traditional and accultured. In D. P. Irish, K. F. Lundquist, & V. J. Nelsen (Eds.), *Ethnic variations in dying, death, and grief: Diversity in universality* (pp. 79–100). Washington DC: Taylor and Francis

Bernstein, J. R. (1997). *When the bough breaks*. Kansas City, KS: Andrews and McMeel.

Bowlby, J. (1980). *Attachment and loss: Vol. 3. Loss: Separation and depression*. New York: Basic Books.

Capps, D. (1984). *Pastoral care and hermeneutics*. Philadelphia, PA: Fortress Press.

Capps, D. (1990). *Reframing: A new method in pastoral care*. Minneapolis, MN: Augsburg Fortress.

Confucius. (ca. 500 BCE). *The Analects*. Retrieved January 24, 2007 from htp://classics.mit.edu/Confucius/2ndedition2.2.

Corr, C. A., Nabe, C. M., & Corr, D. M. (1997). *Death and dying life and living*. (2nd ed.). Pacific Grove, CA: Brooks/Cole.

Cytron, B. D. (1993). To honor the dead and comfort mourners: Traditions in Judaism. In D. P. Irish, K. F. Lundquist, & V. J. Nelsen (Eds.), *Ethnic variations in dying, death, and grief: Diversity in universality* (pp. 113–124). Washington, DC: Taylor and Francis.

Eliason, G. (2000). Spirituality and counseling of the older adult. In A. Tomer (Ed.). *Death attitudes and the older adult: Theories, concepts, and applications*. Philadelphia: Taylor and Francis, pp. 241–256.

Freud, S. (1917). Mourning and melancholia: *Standard edition of the complete psychological works of Sigmund Freud*, Vol. 14. London: Hogarth Press.

Humphrey, G. M., & Zimpfer, D. G. (1996). Counselling for grief and bereavement. London: Sage Publications.

Irish, D. P., Lundquist, K. F., & Nelsen, V. J. (Eds.). (1993). *Ethnic variations in dying, death, and grief: Diversity in universality*. Washington DC: Taylor and Francis.

Kubler-Ross, E. (1969). *On death and dying*. New York: MacMillan.

Littlewood, J. (1992). *Aspects of grief: Bereavement in adult life*. London: Tavistock/Routledge.

Lindemann, E. (1944). Symptomatology and management of acute grief. *American Journal of Psychiatry, 42*, 141–148.

Neimeyer, R. A. (1993). An appraisal of constructivist psychotherapies. *Journal of Consulting and Clinical Psychology, 61*, 221–234.

Neimeyer, R. A. (1999). Narrative strategies in grief therapy. *Journal of Constructivist Psychology, 12*, 65–85.

Neimeyer, R. A. (2000a). The language of loss: Grief therapy as a process of meaning reconstruction. In R. A. Neimeyer (Ed.), *Meaning reconstruction and the experience of loss* (pp. 261–292). Washington DC: American Psychological Association.

Neimeyer, R. A. (2000b). Searching for the meaning of meaning: Grief therapy and the process of reconstruction. *Death Studies, 24*, 541–558.

Neimeyer, R. A., Epting, F. R., & Krieger, S. R. (1984). Personal constructs in thanatology: An introduction and research bibliography. In F. R. Epting, & R. A. Neimeyer (Eds.), *Personal meanings of death* (pp. 1–8). Washington DC: Hemisphere Publishing Corporation.

Osterweis, W., Solomon, F., & Green, M. (Eds.). (1984). *Bereavement: Reactions, consequences, and care*. Washington, DC: National Academy Press.

Rando T. A. (1984). *Grief, dying, and death: Clinical interventions for caregivers*. Champaign, IL: Research Press Company.

Rando, T. A. (1993). *Treatment of complicated mourning*. Champaign, IL: Research Press.

Rando, T. A. (1995/1998). Grief and mourning: Accommodating to loss. In H. Wass & R. A. Neimeyer (Eds.). *In dying: Facing the fact* (3rd ed.). Washington, DC: Taylor & Francis.

Sue & Sue. (1990). *Counseling the culturally different: Theory and practice* (2nd ed.). New York: John Wiley & Sons.

Tomer, A., & Eliason, G. (1996). Toward a comprehensive model of death anxiety. *Death Studies, 20*, 343–365.

Wolfelt, A. D. (1998a, July/August). Companioning vs. treating: Beyond the medical model of bereavement caregiving: Part 1. The Forum Newsletter. Association of Death Education and Counseling.

Wolfelt, A. D. (1998b, Sept/Oct). Companioning vs. treating: Beyond the medical model of bereavement caregiving: Part 2. The Forum Newsletter. Association of Death Education and Counseling.

Wolfelt, A. D. (1998c, Nov/Dec). Companioning vs. treating: Beyond the medical model of bereavement caregiving: Part 3. The Forum Newsletter. Association of Death Education and Counseling.

Wolfelt, A. D. (2005) *Companioning the bereaved: A soulful guide for counselors & caregivers.* Fort Collins, CO: Companion Press.

Wordsworth, W. (1888/1999). *The Complete Poetic Works.* Retrieved January 24, 2007 from http://www.bartleby.com/145/ww331.html.

Wong, P. (2006). *A brief manual for meaning-centered counselling.* Langley, BC: International Network on Personal Meaning (INPM) Press, & The Meaning-Centered Counselling Institute, Inc.

Wong, P. & Frey, P. S. (1998). *The human quest for meaning: A handbook of psychological research and clinical applications.* Mahwah, NJ: Lawrence Erlbaum Associates.

Worden, J. W. (1991/2002). *Grief counseling and grief therapy.* (3rd ed.). New York: Springer.

18

▼▼▼▼

Conclusion

Adrian Tomer
Shippensburg University

Grafton T. Eliason
California University of Pennsylvania

Paul T. P. Wong
Trinity Western University

An examination of existential thinking, as formulated in both philosophical and psychological texts, reflects a variety of death attitudes. Some of these reflect a purely negative approach. For example, Sartre's view as expressed, contra Heidegger (1927/1996) in *Being and Nothingness*, is one that refused to confer death any meaning or dignity, much less to see it as an opportunity to express one's uniqueness (Heidegger). Other positions, while seeing death anxiety as an inescapable facet of one's existence (as existential anxiety), managed to express attitudes vis-à-vis death that were, at least in part, positive. Mainstream psychology, however, focused until recently almost exclusively on measuring and formulating models of death anxiety rather than death acceptance. One indication is the large number of instruments that measure death anxiety versus the relative small number of instruments that measure acceptance (Neimeyer, Moser, & Wittkowski, 2003). Another indication is the existence of elaborate models that specify mechanisms of defense or management of the "terror" associated with the awareness of one's mortality. In this volume, Hart and Goldenberg, adopting the perspective of terror management theory, present interesting empirical evidence relating attitudes toward the body with the need to defend against the terror associated with death. Still the two authors are hopeful that the right type of spirituality, one that is more than a pretty transparent defense mechanism and one that really allows us to transcend our fear of death, will be found. One goal of this volume is to emphasize the need to develop tools and approaches that reflect the entire spectrum of death attitudes and, in particular, death acceptance.

What does it mean to accept death? We may suggest tentatively several indicators of acceptance. Death may be a goal (rather than something to avoid at all cost). In a sense, this is the case of the being-towards-death (Heidegger, 1927/1996) but also the case of the person who, for one reason or another, is "tired of life," sees death as an escape, and so forth. The concept of escape acceptance (Wong, Reker, & Gesser, 1994) would fit under this rubric. A second indicator is related to the positive versus negative aspects of death. We can say that an individual tends to accept death if the positive aspects of death supersede the negative aspects. The balance between the positive and the negative suggests, indeed, several possibilities. For example, a person may accept death because they believe it is the transition to a happy after-life. This view suggests a strong acceptance based on a strong positive advantage. Another person may believe, as claimed by Epicurus, that there is nothing to fear about death because, when death is around, he or she is not. In this case, the acceptance may be based on little negativity rather than much positivity. Positivity and negativity can and should, therefore, be constructed as two distinct dimensions, rather than as two poles of a unitary dimension. Such a view may go some way toward explaining an apparently paradoxical result: Death anxiety (fear) and death acceptance do not appear to be strongly (negatively) correlated. This finding was emphasized in this volume, particularly by Wong in his chapter on Meaning-Management Theory and death acceptance, Ardelt in her chapter on wisdom and death attitudes and Tomer and Eliason in their chapter on regret and death attitudes. These results are also consistent with the original findings reported by Wong et al. (1994). Indeed, it is possible to fear death because of the negativity involved (for example pain) but also to accept it, at the same time, because of the positive aspects (for example as the way to heaven).

A third way to accept death consists of seeing death as a price that one has to pay for living. Neutral acceptance (Wong et al., 1994) is close to this concept. Moreover death awareness, as discussed in this volume, may urge us to lead a more meaningful life, motivates us to accomplish (Death as Motivator; see Cicirelli, 2001) or provides an opportunity to leave a legacy and to be recognized (Cicirelli, 2001). Indirectly therefore, death awareness and death anxiety may increase meaning. Indeed according to Wong and his Meaning-Management Theory death anxiety may be a facilitator of self-actualization and self-transcendence.

Still the questions may persist: How are positive attitudes possible? Doesn't death put an end to our attempts to make meaning by terminating our life? Doesn't it rob our life from meaning? Existential and religious thinkers have formulated a few concepts that may help us to answer this difficult question. Perhaps the more straightforward mechanism involves a religious belief in the hereafter. Such a belief indeed might not completely alleviate death anxiety since it raises also issues related to the type of experiences that are waiting for us in an after-life, including the possibility of judgment and punishment, and so forth. Indeed, the analysis of the Fear of Personal Death scale developed by Florian and Kravetz (1983; see also chap. 2, this volume) revealed a factor of death anxiety that expressed fear of punishment in the hereafter. Similarly, Rose and O'Sullivan (2002) found a positive association between the belief in an after life and the expectation of punishment and judgment. The belief in an afterlife can be either conceptualized as a defense mechanism (e.g., Yalom, 1980, p. 129) or, in a variation of the concept of the defense mechanism concept, as a positive illusion (e.g., Baumeister, 1991, p. 280). A third interpretation may see belief in a hereafter as a form of transcendence. Self-transcendence mechanisms presume that the self is capable to move beyond itself or beyond its present position. Transcendence toward an after-life may increase acceptance and diminish fear of death (when the fear of punishment is not great) but does not suffice to explain all the empirical findings. For example, a number of researchers have provided evidence for a curvilinear relationship between religiousness and fear of death (see, e.g., Wink & Scott, 2005), with some people scoring low on both religiousness and fear of death. Although these findings do not speak directly to the issue of acceptance, they suggest that death acceptance may be achieved via other mechanisms than religiousness. We are suggesting that there are at least two additional types of self-transcendence: toward the Other and toward the Cosmos. The first type is based on the recognition that there is no fundamental distinction between myself and the Other.

Several philosophers, including Heidegger, Buber and Levinas, have articulated positions consistent with this view (see also Spinelli, 2005, p. 120). The second type of transcendence is inspired more by Eastern philosophy than be existential philosophy and may be illustrated by Tornstam's work on gero-transcendence. Self-transcendence might not be, however, the only road to acceptance. In the case of the being-towards-death (Heidegger, 1927/1996) we have a movement toward oneself, rather than beyond oneself, that allows to see death as belonging to us and as presenting a possibility for an authentic, unique realization. It is not clear, however, how many people can approach this ideal goal put forward for us by Heidegger. In this volume Cicirelli raises the important question of the relationship between end-of-life decisions and the ability of individuals toward the end of their life to deepen their spirituality. We can speculate that the ability to do so exists only in individuals who have devoted energy and time throughout their life to spiritual concerns. But, to reiterate Cicirelli's comments, this issue is in need of further exploration.

Perhaps one of the best "answer to death" is the "oblique" answer mentioned by Yalom (1980, p. 482). This answer emphasizes the meanings at hand, the leap into commitment. One version of the oblique answer is the emphasis on present time as a repository of meanings, as proposed by Frankl (1955/1986) and documented empirically by the studies dealing with the Socioemotional Selectivity Theory (Carstensen 1991, Lang & Carstensen, 2002). We could perhaps call this type of answer "transcendence toward meanings." Those are meanings that one can find in life (rather than "*the* meaning of life"); meanings, which, while threatened by death, are reaffirmed by the individual as being the true locus of eternity.

The perspective of transcendence toward meaning was further elaborated by Wong in his chapter dealing with Meaning Management Theory (MMT) and death acceptance. As opposed to TMT (Terror Management Theory) that deals with the defense against "the terror," the MMT focuses on death acceptance and describes processes of meaning-seeking, constructing, and reconstructing. From the MMT perspective, identification with one's culture is a meaning-making mechanism, rather than a purely defensive mechanism, as in TMT.

The chapters in this volume illustrate in different ways the effort to construct or reconstruct meanings threatened by the approach of death, by the loss of the other, or by other losses. In this context an interesting distinction is made by Orbach who, following Baumeister (1991), distinguishes in his treatment between low-level and high-level meanings. Suffering results in a loss of low-order meanings and it may, perhaps, be alleviated by finding a higher-order meaning (spiritual growth). In this interpretation, the person who suffers transcends their suffering by becoming, in a sense, more spiritual, by finding, or constructing a higher-order meaning. It would, of course, be both foolish and naïve to construct a Pollyanish view according to which the higher meanings are up for grabs. Baumeister in his discussion of the myth of higher meaning (1991, pp. 58–74) is right to point out the unrealistic expectations people have sometimes about the meaning of life, and primarily the expectation that everything, in a person's life should have a special human meaning. Randomness, caprice, accident, all tend to be discarded and reinterpreted in the light of this myth. Correspondingly, according to Baumeister, we tend to "impose meanings on death" (p. 286) as, for example, in the cultivation of ideas of sacrifice and martyrdom or in the devotion to one's children as a continuation of life. Baumeister's comments alert us to the difficulty of achieving "ultimate meaning" and, perhaps, to the necessity of accepting elements of meaninglessness into our life. In this sense, the tasks of meaning-seeking and meaning-constructing are never finished or accomplished. More specifically, it is arguable that only self-transcendence, as a movement beyond oneself, is the key toward full death acceptance. Meaning-making and meaning-finding, as well as the possibility of an authentic transcendence and its concrete manifestations, were the main topics of this volume. A theory such as the Meaning-Management Theory (Wong, this volume) is a psychological model that deals with the important issue of specifying mechanisms that may allow individuals to accept death by infusing meaning into their life. The emphasis in this volume on meaning-making is consistent with the idea of emphasizing positive subjective experience, as well as the strengths of character related to it, such as hope and spirituality (Peterson & Seligman, 2004; Seligman & Csikszentmihalyi, 2000). Empirical results documenting the value of maintaining a sense of optimism and a sense of hope for dealing with life threatening events (e.g., Taylor, Kemeny, Reed, Bower, & Gruenwald, 2000), or for achieving life satisfaction (Park, Peterson, & Seligman, 2004), are promising as to their applicability to the issues discussed in this volume. We hope that the emphasis on meaning and spirituality, and more specifically, theoretical frameworks, such as the Meaning-Management Theory that unites an existential-humanistic approach with a positive psychology approach, will stimulate theoretical and empirical research dealing with the impact of meaning and spirituality on living and dying well.

REFERENCES

Baumeister, R. F. (1991). *Meanings of life*. New York: Guilford.

Carstensen, L. L. (1991). Selectivity theory: Social activity in life-span context. *Annual Review of Gerontology and Geriatrics, 11*, 195–217.

Cicirelli, V. G. (2001). Personal meanings of death in older adults and young adults in relation to their fear of death. *Death Studies, 25*, 663–683.

Florian,V., & Kravetz, S. (1983). Fear of personal death: attribution, structure, and relation to religious belief. *Journal of Personality and Social Psychology, 44*, 600–607.

Frankl, V. E. (1986). *The doctor and the soul: From psychotherapy to logotherapy*. New York: Vintage Books. (Original work published 1955)

Heidegger, M. (1927/1996). *Being and Time*. (J. Stammbaugh, Trans.) Albany NY: State University of New York Press. (original work published 1927)

Lang, F. R., & Carstensen, L.L. (2002). Time counts: Future time perspective, goals and social relationships. *Psychology and Aging, 17*, 125–139.

Neimeyer, R. A., Moser, R. P., & Wittkowski, J. (2003). Assessing attitudes toward dying and death: Psychometric considerations. *Omega, 47*(1), 45–76.

Park, N., Peterson, C., & Seligman, M. E. P. (2004). Strengths of character and well-being. *Journal of Social and Clinical Psychology, 23*, 603–619.

Peterson, C., & Seligman, M. E. P. (2004). *Character strengths and virtues: A classification and handbook*. New York: Oxford University Press/Washington DC: American Psychological Association

Rose, B. M., & O'Sullivan, M. J. (2002). Afterlife beliefs and death anxiety: An exploration of the relationship between afterlife expectations and fear of death in an undergraduate population. *Omega, 45*(3), 229–243.

Seligman, M. E. P., & Csikszentmihalyi, M. (2000). Positive psychology: An introduction. *American Psychologist, 55*, 5–14.

Spinelli, E. (2005). *The interpreted world: An introduction to phenomenological psychology*. London: Sage

Taylor, S. E., Kemeny, M. E., Reed, G. M., Bower, J. E., & Gruenwald, T. L. (2000). Psychological resources, positive illusions, and health. *American Psychologist, 1*, 99–109.

Wink, P., & Scott, J. (2005). Does religiousness buffer against the fear of death and dying in late adulthood? Findings from a longitudinal study. *Journal of Gerontology, 60B*, P207–P214.

Wong, P. T., Reker, G. T., & Gesser, G. (1994). Death Attitude Profile–Revised. In R. A. Neimeyer (Ed.), *Death anxiety handbook* (pp. 121–148). New York: Taylor & Francis.

Yalom, I. D. (1980). *Existential psychotherapy*, New York: Basic Books.

Author Index

Subject Index

A

Absurdity of the world, 15–16, 282–283
Acceptance, death
  end-of-life period and, 130–131
  HIV/AIDS and, 188
  meaning-management theory and,
    77–78, 440–441
  meanings of, 66–67
  in older adults, 151–154
  self-actualization and, 81–83
Accountability and responsibility,
  meaning as, 285–286
Actions and regret, 161, 320–321
Activism, empathic, 236, 239–240
Activist mothering, 239
Adam and Eve, 101
Advance directives, 120–122
Affective dimension to wisdom, 140
Agape and Eros, 25–26
Age and end-of-life decisions, 128–129
Aging adults. *See* Older adults
Anatomy of Melancholy, The, 354
Anger and aggression, 378
Angst and fear, 13–14
Anticipated outcome of goal pursuit, 55
Anticipatory grief
  versus anticipatory mourning, 210–211
  benefits of, 211–213
  bereavement and, 211–213
  versus bereavement grief, 381
  of caregivers, 213, 214
  coping with, 215–219
  defined, 209–210
  and the dying of a loved one, 214–219
  implications for counseling, 227–228
  meaning and religion and, 226
  regrets and, 215, 227
  social support and, 227
  study
    methods, 219–221
    quantitative data, 223–225
  results, 221–225

Anticipatory regret, 320–321
Anxiety
  attachment, 48–49
  death
    defined, 346–347
    empirical studies, 165–170
    institutional defenses
      against, 365–367
    management of, 50–54
    meanings of, 67–68
    microsuicide and, 29–30
    ontological anxiety and, 22–24
    regret and, 163–170
    self-actualization and, 81–83
    socioeconomic status and, 143, 147
    Terror Management
      Theory of, 30–31, 50, 79–80
    Tomer-Eliason model of, 32–33,
      163–170, 427–428
    voice and, 360–361
  near death experiences and, 81
  separation, 357–359
  sex and, 96–97
Appraisal of threats/demands in
  goal pursuit, 55
Assisted suicide, 119–120, 126
Attachment style, 48–49, 420
Attacks, voice, 360
Attitudinal value in life, 75
Authenticity, meaning as, 283–284, 290–291

B

Bad grief, 380–381
Battle for God, The, 107
Becker, Ernest, 24–26, 92
  terror management theory and, 93–95
Being and Nothingness, 16, 439
Being and Time, 8, 13, 17
Bereavement, maternal.
    See also Children
  anticipatory grief and, 211–213
  culture and, 253–254